VOLUME 1

THE COLLECTED WORKS OF ARTHUR SELDON

The Virtues of Capitalism

THE COLLECTED WORKS OF ARTHUR SELDON

VOLUME 1 The Virtues of Capitalism

VOLUME 2 The State Is Rolling Back

VOLUME 3 Everyman's Dictionary of Economics

VOLUME 4 Introducing Market Forces into "Public" Services

VOLUME 5 Government Failure and Over-Government

VOLUME 6 The Welfare State: Pensions, Health, and Education

VOLUME 7 The IEA, the LSE, and the Influence of Ideas (includes an index to the series)

Arthur Seldon

VOLUME 1

THE COLLECTED WORKS OF ARTHUR SELDON

The Virtues of Capitalism

ARTHUR SELDON

Edited and with Introductions
by Colin Robinson

LIBERTY FUND, Indianapolis

This book is published by Liberty Fund, Inc., a foundation established to encourage study of the ideal of a society of free and responsible individuals.

The cuneiform inscription that serves as our logo and as the design motif for our endpapers is the earliest-known written appearance of the word "freedom" (*amagi*), or "liberty." It is taken from a clay document written about 2300 B.C. in the Sumerian city-state of Lagash.

Printed in the United States of America

06 05 04 C 5 4 3 2 1
06 05 04 P 5 4 3 2 1

Library of Congress Cataloging-in-Publication Data

Seldon, Arthur.
The Virtues of Capitalism / Arthur Seldon;
edited and with introductions by Colin Robinson.
p. cm.—(Collected Works of Arthur Seldon; v. 1)
Includes bibliographical references and index.
ISBN 0-86597-542-6 (alk. paper)—ISBN 0-86597-550-7 (pbk.: alk. paper)
1. Capitalism. 2. Capitalism—Social aspects. 3. Socialism.
I. Title

HB 501 .S545 2004
330.12'2—dc22 2004040830

LIBERTY FUND, INC.
8335 Allison Pointe Trail, Suite 300
Indianapolis, Indiana 46250-1684

CONTENTS

GENERAL INTRODUCTION TO THE COLLECTED WORKS OF ARTHUR SELDON

Arthur Seldon is one of the principal classical liberal figures of the last hundred years. He was born in 1916, in the middle of the First World War. Thus, at eighty-eight years old, he has lived not only through the massive technological changes of the twentieth and early twenty-first centuries but also through the momentous political and economic events of that time—the Great Depression, the Second World War, and the ascendancy of Keynesian and interventionist economics. In the second half of the twentieth century, he was one of the most powerful exponents of classical liberalism, helping to stimulate its revival both through his own writings and through the publications of the London Institute of Economic Affairs, of which he was editorial director for more than thirty years, from 1957 to 1988. In 1983 he was made Commander of the Order of the British Empire (CBE); he became the first Honorary Fellow of the Mont Pelerin Society in 1997; and he was granted an honorary degree of doctor en ciencias sociales by La Universidad Francisco Marroquín in Guatemala in 1998 and an honorary degree of doctor of science by the University of Buckingham in 1999. Most recently, in 2001, he was made Fellow of the London School of Economics.

Early Days

His life is a story of achievement by a person with steadfast principles who refuses to deviate from them, whatever the prevailing orthodoxy.[1] Seldon was raised in the working-class East End of London by his adoptive parents after his own parents died when he was only two. After his adoptive father also died, when Arthur was eleven, not long before the 1930s depression, his mother had to struggle to make a living on her own: self-help was then still

1. A brief biographical note by his wife, Marjorie, appears after this introduction.

the order of the day rather than reliance on the state. At the age of eleven, he went to the local "grammar" school, an institution that in those days was considered the backbone of the British educational system and which produced many of the leading figures in British economic and political life. He there met one of the first people to influence his career—an economic history master who explained to him the contrasting ideas of mercantilism and classical liberalism and who stimulated his interest in economic ideas.

In 1934 Seldon enrolled in the London School of Economics (LSE) after winning a state scholarship, for which competition was fierce. Although founded by socialists Sidney and Beatrice Webb, the London School of Economics was by then a place where many contrasting ideas—classical liberalism as well as socialism—flourished. It was the academic home of F. A. Hayek, who had just recently arrived from Austria, and of the British classical liberal economists Lionel Robbins (later Lord Robbins) and Arnold Plant. After graduating from the LSE in 1937 with first-class honors, Seldon became a research assistant to Arnold Plant before he was called to serve in the wartime army, spending periods in both Africa and Italy.

After the war, Arthur was tutor to Plant's part-time students, became an LSE staff examiner, and worked as an economic adviser to the brewing industry. His interest in pensions—which is reflected in his later writings—began to emerge when he was a member of a Liberal Party Committee on the Aged in 1947–48. As part of his work for the committee he was in contact with Sir William Beveridge, who had in 1942 written a report on the social services that was very influential in the formation of the state pension system in Britain after World War Two.

The Institute of Economic Affairs

The principal turning point of Arthur's professional life came in 1956, when he was approached to join the Institute of Economic Affairs (IEA), then being reorganized after its formation in 1955. In 1957 he began his career at the IEA, first as part-time editorial adviser and later as full-time editorial director. He worked there for many years with Ralph Harris (later Lord Harris) to form one of the most fruitful partnerships in classical liberal history.

Harris and Seldon were pioneering intellectual entrepreneurs. As general director and editorial director, respectively, of the IEA they started in the 1950s and the 1960s with the most modest resources and in the most unpropitious of circumstances. But Seldon's intellectual rigor, Harris's ability to spread their message, and their sheer perseverance ensured that, in the end, their influence was felt worldwide. In personalities and talents they complemented each other. In Milton Friedman's words, "Ralph was a brilliant voice of the Institute; Arthur an unrelenting enforcer of intellectual standards in the Institute's books and the celebrated Hobart Papers he created."[2]

Harris and Seldon were advocating market solutions, and more generally the freedom of individuals to make decisions for themselves, in a country where many believed that centralized government "planning" had won the Second World War and could be equally successful in peacetime. Long after the war, in the 1950s and the 1960s, the state still dominated life in Britain. The symptoms of the planning mentality that prevailed at that time were almost everywhere: the existence of government plans and policies for all major sectors of the economy, culminating in the "National Plan" of the mid-1960s; the presence of a large nationalized sector; special privileges for labor unions; the persistence of wartime shortages because of an unwillingness to allow prices to clear markets; the inability of citizens to spend their money as they wished, to take significant sums abroad, and, because of "incomes policies," to have the incomes their employers wished to pay them. The government attempted to suppress the price mechanism wherever it thought it could do so, despite the shortages thereby created. Opinion leaders had no interest in market solutions.

Author famine was another problem for the fledgling IEA. To establish its reputation, it needed to publish clear yet intellectually rigorous papers, preferably by authors with their own independent reputations. Few established authors were willing to write for an unknown institute whose directors evidently had ideas far outside the mainstream economic and social wisdom of the day, and many potential authors feared that writing for such an organization would damage their credibility among their peers. More and more authors came forward in the course of time, but in the early days Harris and Seldon had to write many of the papers themselves or, occasionally, in conjunction with others. In 1957, for example, the year in which Arthur Seldon joined the institute, he wrote one of its first papers, *Pensions in a Free Society*. Subsequently, he returned many times, in his own writings and those he commissioned from others, to the reform of pensions and other aspects of the "welfare state" and to ways in which the state could be rolled back.

2. Milton Friedman, "The IEA's Influence in Our Times," in *A Conversation with Harris and Seldon*, IEA, Occasional Paper 116, 2001, p. 70.

Changing the Climate of Opinion

Initially, academic economists, social scientists, journalists, and the bulk of intellectuals (in Hayek's sense)[3] were not only unwilling to be IEA authors but were also most unreceptive to market ideas that, in the 1950s, the 1960s, and the early 1970s, were regarded as passé. The economics profession in particular was resistant to change, having become bound up in macroeconomics as practiced by the followers of Keynes and in various forms of planning: there was little interest in microeconomics and price systems. Harris and Seldon went about the formidable task of changing this antimarket climate by patient explanation of the virtues of the price mechanism—both as a matter of principle and in case studies of particular markets—and of the benefits of consumer choice. But they had to be entrepreneurial in devising new ways of reaching the intellectuals, on whom they necessarily had to depend to spread their message. Neither economists nor other social commentators would be convinced by mere advocacy. Hard evidence and clear-cut argument were required.

Seldon's key role in this venture of reaching and convincing a substantial number of the intellectuals was to formulate a publishing program for the institute, to recruit authors, to edit their work, and to ensure that they were not constrained by inhibitions about what might be "politically possible."[4] In so doing, Seldon in effect invented a new form of publication. It was fairly brief (normally 10,000 to 15,000 words), was based firmly on economic principles, and avoided unexplained technical jargon. Each publication formed part of a series (for example, Hobart Papers or Occasional Papers) to indicate that it was not a solitary venture but part of a more general view of the world of which any one publication was but an example.

3. Hayek defines intellectuals as "second-hand dealers in ideas" rather than original thinkers or scholars. He includes among intellectuals journalists, teachers, ministers, lecturers, publicists, radio commentators, writers of fiction, cartoonists, and artists, as well as professional men and technicians who become carriers of new ideas outside their own fields. See F. A. Hayek, *The Intellectuals and Socialism,* first published in the *University of Chicago Law Review* in 1949 and reprinted by the Institute for Humane Studies (IHS) in 1990. His definition of intellectuals is on pages 6 and 7 of the IHS reprint.

4. For an explanation of how Harris and Seldon worked and of their respective roles, see the Liberty Fund video of a conversation with the two men, conducted by Stephen Erickson and produced in 1999 as part of its Intellectual Portraits series. A transcript of the video, accompanied by eight commentaries by distinguished scholars, was published in *A Conversation with Harris and Seldon.*

The IEA's publishing program, now more than forty-five years old, has attracted as authors some of the world's most eminent economists and other social scientists, including a number of Nobel Prize winners. Seldon was always quick to embrace and publicize new fields of research before their significance was widely recognized. For example, in the days when fiscal fine-tuning was still in vogue in Britain, Seldon foresaw the importance of the work of Milton Friedman on monetary policy. The IEA brought Friedman to London to give a lecture, which proved very influential with governments.[5] He also realized the radical implications of public choice theory for the balance between state and voluntary activity and in 1978 organized a conference on the subject that was attended by, among others, James Buchanan.[6] It was Seldon, in conjunction with Harris, who imported the public choice ideas of Buchanan, Tullock, and their followers into Britain.

Seldon spent a great deal of time working on the manuscripts that he received from authors, using his editorial skill to transform the drafts from turgid academic papers into intelligible and highly readable publications that could be instantly recognizable as IEA series contributions. Seldon drew into IEA publications, as authors or commentators, critics of the market or people who were skeptical of its virtues. Critics would also be asked to referee IEA publications: hearing and understanding critical views before publication are often the best ways of sharpening an author's analysis. Thus, the IEA's network of contacts stretched well beyond its "natural" supporters.

The Influence of Seldon and the Institute

The influence of the IEA's publications was eventually more directly observable than is generally the case with the work of "think tanks." By the early 1980s the incoming Thatcher administration had seized on the institute's ideas about smaller government and the widespread use of markets, putting privatization of the nationalized corporations, labor union reform, abolition of exchange control, and other IEA ideas not just onto the political agenda but into practice. Civil servants were given reading lists of IEA papers by Mrs. (now Lady) Thatcher and by Lord (previously Sir Keith) Joseph, one of her intellectual mentors. Hence, the proposals of IEA authors, as edited by Seldon, became reality, albeit often not quite in the form that either Seldon

5. The First Wincott Memorial Lecture, 1970. Subsequently published by the IEA as *The Counter-revolution in Monetary Theory,* Occasional Paper 33, 1970.

6. Published by the IEA as *The Economics of Politics,* Readings 18, 1978.

or the authors intended, because they were filtered through the political process and were hence subject to government failure.

Moreover, the radical change in the climate of ideas that Harris and Seldon helped implement was not confined to the Conservative governments of the 1980s and the early 1990s. The Labour Party was left high and dry: it became unelectable, as Seldon had foreseen in 1980, when he said, "Labour as we know it will never rule again."[7] To restore its electoral fortunes, the party had to be gradually and painfully transformed from "Old Labour" into "New Labour," which accepted the bulk of the Thatcher reforms—namely, the benefits of consumer choice and the virtues of competition.

Similarly, the ideas of Harris and Seldon and the IEA, as well as the subsequent liberalizing program of the Thatcher administrations, were influential outside Britain, having an important international demonstration effect. Governments around the world came to acknowledge the benefits of market solutions and to apply them, as did the major international institutions in their dealings with developing countries. The most obvious symbol of this liberalizing trend is the privatization movement, which began in Britain, spread to many other developed countries, and has now extended to much of the developing world.[8] As a result of the changed agenda, most politicians and civil servants in the developed world, and most officials in the international institutions, now proclaim the virtues of markets, even if their conversion is as yet incomplete.[9] According to Milton Friedman, "The IEA's influence has not been confined to the United Kingdom. Its publications and the able group of scholars who became associated with it contributed greatly to the change in the intellectual climate of opinion around the world."[10]

Another important by-product of the IEA's influence was the establishment in other countries, including the United States, of numerous think tanks that promote the cause of economic liberalism and form an integ-

7. "Socialism Has No Future," letter to the *Times,* 6 August 1980. See also Arthur Seldon, *Corrigible Capitalism, Incorrigible Socialism,* this volume, pp. 35–36.

8. A useful review of the progress of privatization is an annual survey by the Organisation for Economic Co-operation and Development, which analyzes privatization programs around the world. The survey is published as "Recent Privatisation Trends" in the annual June issue of the OECD's *Financial Market Trends.*

9. David Henderson, *The Changing Fortunes of Economic Liberalism: Yesterday, Today and Tomorrow,* IEA, Occasional Paper 105, 2d ed., 2001.

10. *A Conversation with Harris and Seldon,* p. 71.

ral part of the international movement for continuing economic reform. There are now more than one hundred such organizations in seventy-six countries.[11]

Arthur Seldon's Written Work

Despite the amount of time that Arthur Seldon spent on editing the work of others—he edited about 350 papers during his time at the IEA—he has a large output of published work, consisting of twenty-eight books and monographs and about 230 articles. The highlights of this output are gathered in the seven volumes of these Collected Works. Jointly authored works have been omitted, with one exception—the *Dictionary of Economics,* written with Fred Pennance, the second edition of which was very much Seldon's work and which forms volume 3 of the Collected Works. A full bibliography of Seldon's publications, including the jointly produced papers, is in volume 7. A contents list for each of the seven volumes of the Collected Works is found at the end of this volume.

Arthur Seldon began publishing when he was only twenty-one. The earliest paper included in this collection (in volume 2) is from 1937, from the *Clare Market Review,* the LSE students' journal, and is a review of W. H. Hutt's *Economists and the Public* written when Seldon was twenty-one.[12] Seldon's subsequent publications, as can be seen from the bibliography in volume 7, range from books to short newspaper articles. In addition, he composed a large number of prefaces and introductions to IEA papers, and a collection of some of his prefaces (*The Making of the Institute*) is included in volume 7.

Viewed as a whole, Seldon's published work is a major contribution to classical liberal thought, covering to date no less than sixty-five years, from his first paper in 1937 to his most recent in 2002. Seldon's oeuvre covers a wide range of subjects as well. His early interest in pensions and reform of the "welfare state" has already been mentioned. Those subjects have been recurring themes in his work, and so two volumes of this collection are de-

11. Richard Cockett, *Thinking the Unthinkable: Think-Tanks and the Economic Counter-revolution, 1931–1983,* HarperCollins, 1994, discusses the development of some of these institutes.

12. "The State v. the Market: Socialism v. Capitalism," in *The State Is Rolling Back,* Economic and Literary Books, 1994, pp. 3–9 (reprinted in volume 2 of these Collected Works).

voted to them: Volume 4 includes his papers on charging for "public" services and the contribution that vouchers can make, and volume 6 deals with pensions, health, education, and other aspects of the welfare state.

The problem of over-government has also been a concern for Seldon from the beginning. For him, public choice theory shone a light on the reasons why government tends to encroach on voluntary activity and why government action cannot reasonably be assumed to be the work of wise and disinterested servants of the public good. The collection of his short articles, written over many years, entitled *The State Is Rolling Back* and published here as volume 2, shows how his arguments for rolling back government developed while still retaining the same core of economic principles. Similarly, volume 5 includes some of Seldon's most powerful pieces on government failure and how citizens should and will try to escape from big government.

Volume 7 includes papers on the IEA, on the London School of Economics, and on the influence of ideas. Of the two remaining volumes: volume 1, *Capitalism,* is dealt with at more length below in the introduction to volume 1, and volume 3 is in a slightly different mold from the rest and includes the previously mentioned *Dictionary of Economics.*

Each volume of The Collected Works of Arthur Seldon begins with an introduction that draws attention to the principal features of the included works and fits them into the context of Seldon's works as a whole. Within each volume, the works appear in the order in which they were published. The volumes are individually indexed, and volume 7 includes an index for the collection as a whole.

Seldon's great gift, seen in his writings, was his ability to absorb the literature of economics, synthesize it in his own mind, and then distill it in his publications into a form that could be understood by a wide audience, not just by technically trained economists. From the beginning he detected the fallacies of socialism and appreciated the benefits of capitalism. Despite the changing fashions of economics, he expounded these truths relentlessly.

Colin Robinson
January 2003

BIOGRAPHICAL NOTE

Arthur Seldon was born in 1916 in the East End of London. When the shadow of the Spanish 'flu darkened the world in 1918, both his parents died leaving five children under eleven. Arthur was adopted by a childless cobbler and his wife, which he describes as the first of his lucky chances in his life. Another was meeting Antony Fisher and Ralph Harris and continuing his life's work at the Institute of Economic Affairs.

He is surprised when anyone calls his childhood among the poor streets of London "deprived," because, he says, he had the most important asset, the devoted love of adoptive parents. Harder times than helping with selling repaired boots at a Saturday morning market in the Whitechapel Road outside the Watney, Combe Reid Brewery were to come.

When he was eleven his adoptive father, the family bread-winner, died and the widow's financial assets became the £100 from a Friendly Society. She consulted neighbours, the usual source of advice before the advent of "counsellors," and began to make a meagre living from selling lisle stockings at 1s. 11¾d. from the front room at their home in Oxford Street, E.1, later destroyed by bombs.

Some years later she married, "for Arthur's sake," an elderly tailor with a workshop of five people who was relatively prosperous—until the 1931 Depression, when the payment from the retail shops for making a jacket was reduced by a third from fifteen shillings to ten shillings and sixpence.

At eleven Arthur passed from the Dempsey Street Elementary (state) School to Raine's Foundation (grammar) School in Arbour Square off the Commercial Road. There he was influenced by the sixth form economic history master who taught him about the state regulation of economic life in the

Reprinted with permission from Marjorie Seldon, *Letters on a Birthday: The Unfinished Agenda of Arthur Seldon*, Highland Press for Economic and Literary Books, 1996 (printed for private circulation).

Middle Ages mercantilist system and the contrasting philosophy of classical liberalism. When his pupil in 1934 won a rare State Scholarship, he advised him to take it at the London School of Economics. There an economist lately arrived from Austria, Professor F. A. Hayek, was teaching economic liberalism, then in the ascendant under Professor Lionel Robbins, against the influence of the famous and influential economist Keynes at Cambridge.

Arthur's undergraduate days at the LSE led to an enduring belief in the supremacy of markets over government in delivering prosperity and diminishing poverty among the ordinary people. Price-less goods and services, those supplied "free" by government but paid for by taxes, would do neither. From Hayek, Robbins, and his tutor Professor Arnold Plant he learned about famous liberal economists in other countries, such as Mises of Vienna, Knight of Chicago, and Wicksell of Sweden. But he was not influenced by Sidney and Beatrice Webb who had founded the London School of Economics in 1895. After their visit to Russia in 1935, the Webbs argued that communism was a new civilisation that would supply the needs of the common people.

A First Class Honours degree in 1937 earned Arthur the post of Research Assistant to Plant until he was called up to Army service in Africa and Italy. There he noticed and wrote to Plant about the waste and inefficiency of large-scale distribution of food and clothing without prices.

Demobbed, he sought out Beveridge when studying pensions for a Liberal Party Committee on the Aged in 1947–8. He later wrote papers for the IEA warning that the National Insurance Fund would be misused by government short of revenue from taxes and in time the taxpayer would have to pay the state pensions.

This was one of his occasional "predictions" about economic developments (below). Beveridge, author of the famous 1942 Report on the social services and a former Liberal MP, had recommended that the post-war state pension should not be paid in full until the Fund had been built up over 20 years.

During the following years Arthur tutored Plant's part-time students in the Commerce Degree Bureau, was appointed an LSE staff examiner, and worked as economic adviser in the policy-forming central council of the brewing industry headed by the war-time famous Air Force Marshal Lord Tedder, Deputy to Eisenhower in the invasion of Europe. Arthur recalls that Lord Tedder was sceptical of the tied house system in the restrictive licensing after 1870.

In 1956 he was approached by the Liberal Lord Grantchester, who had been given his name by Plant, about whether he would join the new Institute of Economic Affairs to run its academic work and build a reputation divorced from Party politics.

In January, 1957, the Institute, begun in 1955, was reorganised with Ralph Harris as General Director and Arthur as part-time Editorial Adviser and working on several projects until he could join full-time. He wrote its first Paper on pensions in 1957.

The Harris-Seldon Institute, which became known as the IEA, opened on a slender financial string with an office in a basement in Hobart Place, S.W.1. Proselytising was not the aim, which was rather to deliver authoritative and well-digested economics for the general reader and opinion formers.

The history of the Institute, its operation and influence, is documented in Richard Cockett's *Thinking the Unthinkable.* The title well describes Arthur's commissioning of young, unknown authors to write on neglected problems requiring new solutions. *The Price of Blood,* for example, had a surprising origin. Arthur's rare absence from IEA work, in 1964, was caused by an operation on a duodenal ulcer (a procedure now obsolete). A haemorrhage after the operation required an urgent blood transfusion. Through a nearly fatal oversight, blood of Arthur's unusual group was not available in the small hospital in central London or in neighbouring large hospitals. After a hurried search, the required blood was finally found just in time many miles away. A bus-driver in Edgware was a donor of the required blood-type.

Eventual recovery found the patient turning his mind to finding an economist to write on new ways to increase the supply of blood.

It was one of Arthur's axioms that his authors should not dilute strong economic arguments by fretting about what might be "politically possible." If an author had been working on an important subject that had been neglected he was invited to write for the Institute even if he did not entirely share the IEA interest in finding new market solutions. Douglas (later Lord) Houghton, a member of Wilson's Cabinet in 1964 who retired in 1967, wrote a Paper, *Paying for the Social Services,* on how tax revenue would not be enough to keep up the welfare state benefits so that people would have to pay as consumers. And other IEA Papers by authors of varied political sympathies enabled the Trustees of the Institute to fend off assaults against its charitable status.

Arthur's writings contained occasional predictions. In 1979 after Mrs. Thatcher's victory he told a sympathetic journalist "Labour as we have known it will not rule again." In 1981 in an IEA Paper he wrote that Russian communism would not survive the century and that China would go capitalist and asked a Chinese economist then in the USA to discuss how the process might take place. Recently he has been writing that the rejection of onerous taxation, and its corollary the increasing cash economy, was being under-estimated by governments everywhere. It would lead to falling revenues, destabilising government expenditure and forcing it to withdraw from subsidising welfare as people use their "underground" cash to buy better services than government can provide.

The IEA's work was publicised and reinforced by Arthur's periodic articles in *The Daily* and *The Sunday Telegraph, The Times,* and other newspapers and magazines. Some were reprinted in his 1994 book, *The State Is Rolling Back.*

He is now working on *Democracy* (Blackwell, 1997).

M.S.
2 July 1996

INTRODUCTION TO VOLUME 1

The principal work in this first volume of The Collected Works of Arthur Seldon is what many people consider to be his finest piece—*Capitalism.* It is, as Seldon's preface[1] makes clear, not a defense but a celebration of capitalism, a wide-ranging book that embodies many of the ideas he developed over a long period. In 1991 *Capitalism* won the Antony Fisher Award from the Atlas Economic Research Foundation.

Corrigible Capitalism, Incorrigible Socialism

Capitalism is preceded by a shorter paper, published by the IEA ten years earlier, "Corrigible Capitalism, Incorrigible Socialism," which is an important precursor, setting out in concise form much of the analysis later elaborated in *Capitalism.* "Corrigible Capitalism" grew out of a paper written for the New Zealand Employers' Federation, entitled *A Credo for Private Enterprise* and presented to a February 1980 conference in Auckland. Seldon's dedication of the IEA version of the paper, "To Capitalists in All Economic Systems and to Socialists in All Parties and All Continents," is significant, echoing Hayek's dedication of *The Road to Serfdom* to "socialists of all parties."[2]

As the title of the paper suggests, capitalism is, like all human institutions, a system with faults. Its critics are blinkered because they concentrate on capitalism's apparent deficiencies, failing to understand the corrigibility of capitalism. Capitalism is redeemable: its faults are capable of being corrected, and indeed the capitalist system is "adaptive" in the sense that it contains automatic corrective mechanisms. It enforces its own disciplines

1. See p. 55.
2. F. A. Hayek, *The Road to Serfdom,* University of Chicago Press, 1944.

on the growth of private power and other problems that markets may produce. Socialism, however, is incorrigible. It is an irredeemable system, the idea of which is sustained only by the romantic notions of self-styled idealists and which contains within itself no means of correction; when translated into the real world, it leads inevitably to loss of freedom for citizens and increasingly oppressive government. As Seldon explains it, "Private enterprise has produced the wealth of the world; yet it has suffered more calumny and obloquy than any other system. Its alternative, state economy, has retarded the production of wealth; yet it has been lauded and deified" (13).

On the thesis of the remediable defects of private enterprise, as compared with the impossibility of taming Leviathan, Seldon builds the rest of this brief text, which concludes that government should confine itself to the supply of genuine "public goods,"[3] withdrawing from many of the activities on which it has embarked during the years of collectivism.

Seldon begins by confronting the supposed defects of capitalism (18–25). First, there is the claim that capitalism produces inequality, or as Seldon more accurately describes it, differences in incomes. He points out that such differences are the consequence not of capitalism but of the unequal distribution of talents, and he favors market-based means of helping to reduce such differences. A tendency to monopoly is the second "defect." Seldon argues that capitalism contains its own remedy for monopoly—the entry of competitors into markets where monopoly profits are being earned. Temporary monopolies under capitalism are much less damaging than monopolies created by the state, which cannot readily be undermined by market forces and are consequently extremely hard to remove. Third, capitalism is alleged to promote worker alienation. Critics argue for various forms of "in-

3. A pure "public good," to an economist, is one the consumption of which is "nonrivalrous" and "nonexcludable." Nonrivalrous consumption means that consumption by one person does not reduce consumption by any other. If, for example, there were so much fresh air that it was essentially in infinite supply, I could consume it without diminishing the consumption of anyone else. The good would then have no scarcity value and its price would be zero. Nonexcludability means that it is impossible to stop an individual from consuming a good. If people cannot be excluded from consumption no price can be charged. Markets work because suppliers are providing goods that are scarce and have prices attached. If no price can be charged, potential producers cannot appropriate any benefits from supplying the good and so have no incentive to do so. The argument then is that the state should step in to provide public goods, financing their supply from general taxation and remedying this failure of the market. In practice, there are very few pure public goods. Quasi-public goods can sometimes be provided by voluntary groups that raise the funds from their members.

dustrial democracy" with workers, or more often their unions, involved in management decisions. Seldon argues that the premise that capitalism is undemocratic is false: consumers are the "ultimate controllers" of the firm because only by satisfying them can any company prosper. Private enterprise allows employees to own shares in their companies if they choose to do so, an option not open to employees of state-owned firms.

"Externalities" are a favorite of critics of capitalism: they are the fourth of the defects examined by Seldon.[4] But why, he asks, are they attributed to capitalism? Take environmental pollution as an example: "Collectivist smoke pollutes social democratic Sweden and Austria, or communist Poland and Bulgaria, as much as market smoke pollutes Britain, Canada and Australia" (24). Externalities, such as environmental pollution, Seldon says, are a problem that arises mainly where property rights are not well defined. Unlike socialism, capitalist systems can define these rights, embodying them where necessary in legislation. Seldon then contrasts the remediable defects of capitalism with the "incurable defects" of state enterprise (27–36). He considers not only authoritarian collectivism but also "milder forms" of state initiative, such as "social democracy, which is paternalist in spirit and benign in execution" (27).

The first defect of state planning is ignorance. In markets, private suppliers discover the preferences of consumers and meet them, "not from benevolence" (as Adam Smith put it)[5] but because they expect to make profits from doing so. There is no parallel mechanism in a state system. "Without markets, state economy is blind" (30).

Then there is the second defect, the inefficiency of state action, which results from the state's inability to identify and satisfy the preferences of con-

4. "Externalities" are cases where there is a divergence between private costs (those incurred by the person taking the action) and "social costs" (the costs to society of an action—which incidentally are extremely difficult to identify, let alone measure). They can be negative external costs, which are supposedly not taken into account in markets because suppliers consider only their private costs, not the wider effects of their actions on society; or positive external benefits that spill over to the benefit of society. In the case of "public goods" (see note 4, above), all the benefits are externalities. Environmental pollution is often regarded these days as the worst example of the failure of capitalism to take into account external costs. Producers are said to act without regard for the effects on the environment of what they do: for example, they are said to use the environment as a low-cost sink for their waste products because they are not charged for its use.

5. Adam Smith, *An Inquiry into the Nature and Causes of the Wealth of Nations*, 1776, Book 1, chapter 2, Everyman's Library edition, 1991, p. 13.

sumers: "in state economy the consumer takes what the machine produces" (31). So shortages or surpluses, compared with what consumers want, are the norm.

Social conflict is the third defect of state initiative. Wherever goods or services are supplied by the state, social conflict is likely to arise because minority wishes are bound to be overridden. To the extent that supply by the state is unnecessary (that is, where the goods in question are not true public goods), the potential for social tension and social conflict is greater than it would have been in a market regime.

Fourth, a state economy "lives by monopoly and abhors competition" (33). It cannot permit private effort for fear that it would show government provision to be inferior. Because the state denies itself the discovery mechanism of the market, it cannot match the market outcome.

Fifth, coercion, like monopoly, is inherent in government action. The more economic activity is under state control, the greater the degree to which citizens are coerced.

Corruption is the sixth defect of state action. Where markets are not permitted to operate, the activity in question tends to go underground into black or gray markets and the heavy taxes that have to be levied to finance state activity are widely evaded or avoided.[6] So state economy corrupts "the politician as the creator of favours, the official as the dispenser of contracts . . . the citizen who depends for his livelihood on government contracts, and the citizen as taxpayer" (34).

The seventh, final, defect of state action is secrecy. As an example Seldon points to the concealment of information in the Soviet Union (still in existence when he wrote), particularly under Stalin. It is here that he makes one of his most penetrating and accurate predictions—that, with the British Labour Party dividing into socialist and social democratic components, it would never rule again. As he put it more precisely in a letter to *The Times* (of London) a month after the publication of *Corrigible Capitalism,* "Labour as we know it will never rule again."[7]

To sum up, "Corrigible Capitalism, Incorrigible Socialism" argues that whatever the faults of markets, government failure is always and everywhere

6. Avoidance is legal; evasion is illegal. Seldon coined the term "tax avoision" to indicate the difficulty of maintaining the distinction. See Arthur Seldon, "Avoision: The Moral Blurring of a Legal Distinction without an Economic Difference," in *Tax Avoision,* IEA, Readings 22, 1979 (reprinted in volume 5 of these Collected Works).

7. Seldon, "Socialism Has No Future."

the more serious problem because the faults of state economy are incurable. Government should confine its activities to laying down a general framework of law for private enterprise rather than detailed rules, and to the supply of public goods that genuinely have to be financed from general taxation. The resulting withdrawal of government from much of what it does would, as Seldon says, leave "a large field for the expansion of private enterprise" (45).

Capitalism

Readers of "Corrigible Capitalism, Incorrigible Socialism" will, of course, find similarities between it and *Capitalism;* both works are founded on the same bedrock of principles. In *Capitalism,* however, Seldon refines the argument and presents much more evidence to convince the critics. He sets out a compelling synthesis of the arguments for classical liberalism that is of special interest because at the time he wrote the book, between October 1988 and October 1989, he had been considering those arguments, and those of the critics, for more than fifty years. During those years his ideas had been complemented and augmented by the insights of "Austrian" scholars such as F. A. Hayek and of the public choice school led by James Buchanan and Gordon Tullock. Furthermore, because he was writing ten years after the publication of "Corrigible Capitalism," some of the predictions he had made in the earlier paper were beginning to come true. Writing in 1988–89, at the time of *glasnost* and *perestroika* in the (then) Soviet Union, the beginnings of the collapse of the seventy-year communist experiment—which he had predicted in 1980—were just discernible. In *Capitalism,* he makes the further prediction that the "political life of socialism" is likely to end "in the 1990s" (83).

Seldon lays out the central theme of *Capitalism* in his preface: "Political democracy is not enough. The market is a better guarantee of personal freedom." For capitalism to "yield its best results . . . the political process must be confined to the minimal duties of the state" (58). He recalls that during his time at the IEA, he saw some of the best minds embrace the "false faith" of socialism, dismissing the intellectual inheritance of liberalism as "outdated superstition" (57).

Why then, asks Seldon, is anticapitalist feeling so strong? He identifies a deep-rooted tendency to contrast capitalism as it is, with its failings exposed (and often exaggerated), with an idealistic vision of a socialist society as it might be, but never has been nor ever could be. This idealized version of socialism, which superficially appears more attractive than capitalism, was (and to a large extent still is) embedded in the educational system in Britain and other countries with "mixed" economies. In his partly autobiographical chapter 2, Seldon recalls his own indoctrination against capitalism at school and within his own peer group, until in his final years at school he had the good fortune to be taught by a history master who explained the essence of liberal capitalism and who influenced him more than his economics master, who, like many at the time, was imbued with Fabian socialist principles. Seldon therefore went on to the LSE with more of a feeling for the benefits of capitalism than most of his fellow students would have had. That feeling was powerfully reinforced by what he saw of planning during the Second World War and, even more, by the long years in which the British establishment tried to cling to planning in peacetime until, in the 1980s and the 1990s, the classical liberal ideas championed by the IEA came to the forefront of the political agenda.

In chapter 3, Seldon discusses the supposed inevitability of socialism and analyzes the arguments used by socialists to support the "inevitability" view and the change in intellectual climate in the 1980s, which induced some socialists to modify their opinions. "Socialism is being abandoned by politicians of the Left not only because it has failed as an economic method," he notes, "but because it has been seen to have failed by the people" (130). The demonstration effect of successful capitalist economies has combined with the obvious failure of socialist economies to make capitalism, not socialism, "inevitable throughout the world" (131).

Chapter 4 considers socialism in practice, as found particularly in the (then) Soviet Union. Seldon argues that "Soviet communism is a political interlude" (140). Capitalism had appeared in Russia in the thirty years before the revolution of 1917 and was again, temporarily, tolerated by the authorities in the 1920s under Lenin's New Economic Policy. Russia will have to adopt capitalism for the third time, in the 1990s, says Seldon, because it failed during the communist period to resolve one of the principal internal contradictions of the communist form of organization—that the communist controllers require political centralization, whereas economic decentralization is required to satisfy the "expectations of the masses" (151). He also argues that China will have to go capitalist in the 1990s if the demands of the masses are to be met and living standards are to rise, and predicts that privatization will become a worldwide movement. The new capitalism, says Seldon, will be given different labels by politicians who want to conceal their embarrassment at having wasted a century in experiments with various forms of socialism.

Capitalism as a form of democracy is the theme of chapter 5. Political democracy works by head-counting, overriding the views of minorities, as Seldon points out. He takes essentially the same view as Lionel Robbins: that the market is akin to a continuous referendum on the products and services on offer, and so is an instrument of democracy.

Political democracy cannot deal effectively with the views of minorities, but the market can deal with the problems that arise through its own operation (such as the low weight it places on the demands of those with small incomes), for instance by reverse income taxes and vouchers. Both socialism and capitalism must limit access because resources are limited. But it is a myth that socialism promotes equality of access to services. Instead of limiting access on the basis of financial resources, socialism imposes constraints based on political, social, occupational, and economic factors that make it very hard to correct the inequalities it produces. Under such a regime, it is the articulate middle classes who do best. The power of "exit" (escape via the market from the use of goods and services the consumer does not want) is, as always, greater than the power of "voice" (the right to participate in political action). Capitalism is compatible with political democracy, although the two do not always go together. The centralized planning of state socialism, however, is incompatible with political democracy. Politics should be the servant of people in the market: government should provide the few goods and services that are genuinely "public" but otherwise should let markets develop spontaneously to satisfy people's demands.

Chapter 6 argues that the price system is the essence of capitalism: "pricing is the device for deciding where resources are to be used according to individual preferences" (196). Attempts to combine market pricing with public ownership are bound to fail, says Seldon, quoting Hayek to support his point that socialist managers cannot know what costs and prices would emerge in a competitive market. "Political pricing" is the likely outcome of centralization.

In chapters 7 and 8 Seldon turns to "Intellectual Reinforcement for Capitalism"—ten recent developments in economic thinking that strengthen the case for capitalism: (1) the rejection of the Marxist (immiseration) interpretation of economic history; (2) the renewed emphasis by economic historians on the importance of property rights in promoting economic growth; (3) the switch of economists away from studying the aggregates of macro-economics toward the microeconomic study of the market process; (4) the growth of the public choice school in economics, which stresses the imperfections of government action; (5) the analysis of government regulation, mainly by American economists, which shows that regulation, far from being in the public interest, often leads to the regulators being "captured" by the regulated industries; (6) the realization that a large part of the goods and services supplied by government is not genuine "public goods"; (7) an awareness that the case for government intervention on "externality" grounds is often exploited for political ends; (8) the better understanding of the role of money in the economy, which should lead to a reduced role for politicians in macroeconomic control; (9) the invasion by economists of areas of academic research (such as the family, marriage, and crime) previously the preserve of political scientists, sociologists, and others; and (10) the reaction against the "fiction" of the social welfare function—the aggregation of individual preferences to indicate a supposedly representative choice that could be imposed by central planners.

Seldon devotes chapter 9 to discussing the criticisms of capitalism. He discusses, among other things, the "contradictions of capitalism" argument of the Marxists; the democratic socialist critique, which makes the mistake of comparing imperfect markets with perfect (and therefore unrealizable) political processes; and the criticisms from political conservatives in Britain who have doubts about the market.

Chapter 10 sketches a "vision of capitalism,"[8] which, according to Seldon, is one that operates "with a political process that enables it to work through a free market—a political process confined to the minimum of unavoidably collective functions" (288). Government should, as Adam Smith wrote, do only what cannot be done in the market. But, as Seldon says, capitalism has never had such a government, even in the United States. Seldon's aim would be to "make democratic politics the servant of market forces" (292). To make explicit his vision of capitalism, one must first assess how the freedom of exchange that characterized nineteenth-century capitalism would have developed if the state had not stopped it.

This "galloping horse" theme—that services now "public" were developing well in the nineteenth century before the state intervened—is the sub-

8. Although Hayek implicitly pointed to the lack of vision among liberals when he wrote, "Liberals also should have a Utopia." Seldon uses that quotation, which is from *The Intellectuals and Socialism,* as an introduction to chapter 10.

ject of chapter 11,[9] which contemplates the prospect of government withdrawal from many of its existing activities, including welfare services. He produces evidence to show that in Britain spontaneous developments in education, health, housing, and pensions were hindered, and in some cases destroyed, by the intervention of government. There were galloping horses in all these services before the state intervened—"the state jumped on all of them and slowed them all down" (337).

In chapter 12 Seldon addresses the charge that capitalism lacks a moral base. The service of self is universal, says Seldon; the relevant question is whether self-service serves or harms others. His answer is unequivocal: "The virtue of capitalism is that it divorces purpose from result: it does not require good men or women. The vice of socialism is that men and women who may start with good intentions, but who are skilled in acquiring coercive power, can use it to do harm" (344).

Moreover, capitalism is corrigible: "The market discovers and ejects its bad people sooner than politics" (345). Seldon also discusses related arguments. First, the "cultural" critique that seeks state subsidies for the arts: he points out the advantages of the private patronage that once existed and the danger of providing subsidies on the basis of supposed external benefits (which could be claimed by many other activities). Second, there is the argument for state finance for the press on the grounds that a market in journalism does not work well. Third, there is the religious critique: British clerics, says Seldon, have become rent-seekers who "capitalize on their spiritual authority to urge compassion for the poor at no cost to themselves" (361).

In chapter 13, "The Verdict," Seldon summarizes his views on why he believes that capitalism is superior to other known systems of economic organization. He sees essentially three reasons for the superiority of capitalism: (1) it is the most effective means of organizing human cooperation in production the world has known; (2) it is the only economic order that combines high productivity with individual liberty; and (3) it is more conducive to peace, because international associations through markets produce a vested interest in peace.

9. The late Edwin G. West, who in 1965 wrote a radical critique of the state's role in education for the IEA (*Education and the State*), pointed out that in the nineteenth century the education system in Britain was expanding and producing good results before the state intervened, so it was as if the state had "jumped into the saddle of a horse that was already galloping." The quotation is at the beginning of chapter 11 of *Capitalism*. The theme is one to which Arthur Seldon returned, with the aid of fellow authors including Edwin West, in *Re-privatising*

In chapter 14, the final chapter, Seldon views the future of capitalism with qualified optimism. He bases this view on four trends: first, the waning of Marxism; second, a decline in "obstructive interests" and the rent-seeking that occurs because people often put their interests as producers before those as consumers; third, the emergence of individuals who have been effective in espousing capitalism; and fourth, a number of "conspiring circumstances," such as the emergence and expansion of "underground economies" as people escape from government or, perhaps most important, the now-obvious failures of socialism.

Colin Robinson
January 2003

Welfare: After the Lost Century, IEA, Readings 45, 1996. Seldon's contributions to this volume are reprinted in volume 6 of these Collected Works.

PART I

Corrigible Capitalism, Incorrigible Socialism

A New Approach to an Age-Old Debate: An Essay on the Relative Perfectibility of Competitive Private Enterprise and Monopolistic Government Production

To Capitalists in All Economic Systems
and to Socialists in All Parties and All Continents

PREFACE

As part of the Institute's educational purpose in explaining the light economic analysis can shed on public policy, the *Occasional Papers* were created to bring outstanding essays and lectures to wider audiences than those to which they were originally addressed.

Occasional Paper 57 is a version revised for a British audience of "A Credo for Private Enterprise" written for the NZ Employers' Federation and presented in outline to its February 1980 Conference in Auckland. Mr. Seldon seized the opportunity to deploy the case for a liberal economic order with a vigour that must have surprised its faint friends among the business community, as it will confound its captious critics in academia. There can be few economists who will not gain new insights from this refined restatement of the relative merits of state and private enterprise. Yet in its appeal to intelligent laymen without special knowledge of technical jargon it will bear comparison with the classic statements of the 19th century economic essayists.

I envy any reader who comes to this sample of Arthur Seldon's writing for the first time. As Editorial Director of the IEA from the start, he has done most of his best teaching by stealth. Having chosen the topics and authors of some 300 *Papers* and books, he has performed a rare service for both authors and readers in clarifying the writing while strengthening the rigour of the analysis. The impact of the IEA's work is a lasting tribute to his unique ability to improve the writing of others.

But where the casual reader of other IEA *Papers* may be unaware of the invisible editorial hand in the author's glove, this *Occasional Paper* is pure Seldon. It reveals his special combination of talents in deploying the essential analysis, developing the argument most cogently with well-chosen examples from history or contemporary experience, and again and again finding *les mots justes* to stimulate the palate of even the most jaded reader. The one possible drawback is that the clarity of the exposition, which carries the reader along with such ease, may conceal the subtlety and sophistication of the underlying analysis. The unfortunate reader of modern journals of economics will find that many economists wrap up empty propositions in pretentious, even incomprehensible, technical jargon which Keynes used to mock as "Cherokee." In contrast, Arthur Seldon has a rare mastery of English prose that is not only a pleasure to read, but invests with renewed significance the classical conception of the free society that was for a time in danger of being dulled by familiarity.

In the end, what comes through this *Paper* most vividly is the enduring strength of the central analysis of the market economy as a social arrangement that harnesses the strivings of free men to achieve unprecedented standards of living, leisure, work, charity—in short, individual fulfilment—that are beyond the reach of state economy, however well-intentioned its original proponents and its initial phases. Mr. Seldon has been stung by the long one-sided intellectual assault on private enterprise into writing a powerful yet scholarly polemic in its defence. The argument ranges widely and is inevitably highly condensed. Although it is impossible to pick a single passage that summarises the whole, one that goes to the heart of the case for the market is on page 39:

> The only way to find new social stratagems that work is . . . by experimentation. That is the way of private enterprise, the scientific method, the bedrock of Western civilisation that proceeds by cautious steps to teach from experience. The alternative is the holistic solution of nationalised industry or totalitarian state economy that pretends to knowledge it lacks and then excludes reform that would demonstrate its error. Private enterprise is imperfect but redeemable. State economy promises the earth, and ends in coercion to conceal its incurable failure.

Arthur Seldon wrote this *Paper* in his personal capacity without committing his colleagues or others associated with the IEA. But I have no hesitation in commending it enthusiastically to fellow economists, journalists, business men and politicians as a timely stimulus to reconsideration of fundamental values that are more widely shared than may appear from the habit of superficial pleading by rival party zealots.

Lord Harris of High Cross
July 1980

CHAPTER 1

Mobilising Humanity for Progress

The Awakening

Private enterprise has been on the defensive too long. It has taken 50 years or more of assault and battery by the intellectuals of the world.

Not surprisingly, it has become apologetic, inhibited and debilitated. Its practitioners too often attempt to explain their profits away instead of explaining how they are earned. People in industry are too ready to accept criticism of private enterprise without showing that in competitive conditions it produces the profits of success by imposing the losses of failure. And they often under-state the strength of the intellectual case *for* private initiative in a framework of law.

The repute of private enterprise in the parliaments of the Western world, in their academies, and in their press and broadcasting is epitomised by the long-prevailing contrast in the attitudes to the philosopher/economist Hayek and the populist/economist Galbraith. For many years the teachings of Hayek, with a long ancestry going back to the most civilised thinkers of the Western world, were ignored or derided. In sharp contrast the writings of Galbraith, based on ephemeral wartime experience, were lauded, popularised, widely broadcast in the English-speaking world. Yet the works of Hayek will live as part of the lasting literature of liberalism, and the writings of Galbraith have begun to lose influence and will not survive their author.

This imbalance in attention to the works of scholars would not have been decisively damaging if it were confined to the ivory castles. But for a time it was so generally incorporated into public attitudes that it made private enterprise difficult to work in the form in which it could most effectively contribute to the well-being of the Western world. For some years there has been a reversal of the trend. For 10–15 years in North America and Europe former critics of "capitalism" have been recognising its strengths as long experience of totalitarian economies in Eastern Europe, Asia and Africa and of oppres-

It will be evident from the text—and the dedication—that "Socialism" is used to refer to an economic system, not to the doctrine of a political party.

sive state intervention in the deceptively described "mixed" economies of Western Europe has repeatedly failed to produce the results their advocates foretold. State economy in both totalitarian and mixed economy is now seen to produce impoverishment, sacrifice liberty and endanger peace. It suppresses voluntary co-operative group activity. It replaces the rule of law by the rule of men. It destroys spontaneity and erects centralised, contrived authority. It is inefficient, rigid, inhumane and irreversible except by revolution. It treats mankind as a collection of human factors of production to be moulded to serve the "national" interest as decided by a handful of men who rise to the top in the struggle for power. It paradoxically claims to aim at maximum happiness for individuals whose circumstances, requirements and preferences it studiously ignores, not least in the welfare states of the West.

After a century of denigration, scholars are increasingly dismayed by the performance of the state direction they induced politicians to foist on the people. And some are disconcerted at their repeated condemnation and destruction of the capitalism whose faults are gradually being removed to yield rising standards *without* sacrificing personal liberty.

Principles of Economic Organisation

The supreme task humanity has faced down the centuries has been to discover and mobilise the abilities, talents and genius of individuals in the creation of civilised society. The *rationale* and vindication of decentralised initiative independent of the state, described popularly as "private enterprise," historically as "capitalism," technically as "the market economy," is that it has proved more effective, with better results in living standards, than any other system from the benign mixed economy of social democracy to the rigorous centralised planning of communism.

The "mixed economy" has had strong attraction as the name for the attempt to combine the *best* of both state and market economy. In practice, as experience in the Western world since the war indicates, it commonly combines the *worst* of both worlds—the rigidity, susceptibility to sectional pressure, obstruction to change of state economy, with the rigidity, unfulfilled expectations and monopoly of market economy distorted by price and income controls, high taxation and arbitrary subsidy. The mixed economy would be the desired objective if it combined state economy in public goods that yield collective benefits (defence, law and order, local roads, public health, some scientific research etc.) with market economy in the mass of economic activity that yields personal benefits (from food and clothing to education and medical care). But in practice "the mixed economy" has been used to enable the state to regulate, control, direct and run industry in ways that have distorted private initiative and prevented its prodigious productivity.

The task is not simply the technical/managerial mobilisation of men, as in the armed forces. If it were, the autocracies would have survived and the market economies would have withered. Coercion would have sufficed to dragoon men into work. The task of a free society is the more subtle one of inducing men to contribute their skills, talents and genius to the common pool by incentives varying with contribution. In trying to secure co-operation by coercion, centralised societies down the centuries to our day in all the continents of the world have suppressed individual decision but reached only modest living standards. By working through individual decision—based on aspiration, emulation, concern for family, friends, "good causes" of all kinds—the market economy has preserved individual liberty and reached unprecedented living standards.

The private enterprise economy has shown that the more scope it creates for individual initiative, the higher living standards can be raised. Except to intellectuals who reject evidence that conflicts with their conjectures, the last half-century provides telling contrasts in living standards and human liberty between countries or regions that are otherwise culturally similar or comparable. If the obvious contrast between present-day America and Russia is inconclusive because their cultures are divergent, the contrast between Russia as it has developed since 1917 and Russia as history elsewhere indicates it would have developed, as the emerging "capitalism" of the late 19th century continued into the inter-war era of liberal international trade, technological advance and political freedom, can hardly be dismissed. There can be little doubt that the gap between Russian and American living standards would by now be far narrower. Russia might now be leading the world in liberal culture as well as capitalist economy. But the easier contrast—because it has taken place post-war—between West and East Germany, South and North Korea, Taiwan and mainland China, Hong Kong and Shanghai, Singapore and Sri Lanka, Japan and India, Rhodesia and Tanzania, Kenya and Uganda cannot be explained away by the premature critics of capitalism or the starry-eyed advocates of socialism.

The Wide Gap between Promise and Performance

The intellectual predicament of academics who hope against hope that all will yet turn out well with state economy is significantly demonstrated by a

British economist who remains the most sophisticated critic of capitalism and advocate of socialism. Lady (Barbara) Wootton has lately been driven back by her respect for intellectual economic reasoning—at least in her academic writings—to reply[1] that, because collectivism had not so far in history been found to be compatible with human freedom, it did not follow that it would never be. What was once the confident assertion that socialism would produce results—liberty, justice, etc., etc.—has been turned on its head as a defence that there is no proof that it cannot produce what it has never yet produced: instead of "glad confident morning" (Robert Browning, "The Lost Leader"), a tortuous double negative.

The defenders of the centralised state now try to save their theories by defending or condemning the record of Russia: either it has had only 60 years and requires more time, or it has not faithfully applied the principles of collectivist economy. Logically, the "give-it-time" school will claim more time for Soviet communism until the end of time. The "Soviet-Russia-is-not-truly-Socialist" school will never recognise as collectivist any state economy that fails to work as the conjectural textbooks of hypothetical collectivism proclaim. To both schools no evidence of the failure of collectivism in practice, even at high cost in living standards and human dignity, will ever be accepted as reason for questioning collectivist theory. Socialism is thus exonerated from fault by denying it has ever existed.

Living Standards Vary with Economic Liberty

Even in the community of Western countries, where private initiative independent of the state is more or less common, productivity and living standards broadly vary with the extent of the independence. Relative productivity in the four largest economies is broadly:

USA	5
Germany	4
France	3
Britain	2

Living standards in the USA are thus 2½ those in Britain, in Germany twice and in France 1½ times. The fundamental reason is that the process of discovering and mobilising human capacities by private enterprise has been

1. Barbara Wootton, "Can we still be Democratic Socialists?," *New Statesman*, 4 August 1978.

constricted or obstructed by the state, by corporate monopoly or by trade unions more in Britain than in France, more in France than in Germany and more in Germany than in the USA.

Apart from the two methods of incentive and coercion used in the West and the East, there is a third method of mobilising human talents: disinterestedness or "love." It strongly attracts the critics of both private enterprise and of collectivist coercion as the solution that could dispense with "selfish" incentives and brute force. Yet even if their criticisms of both incentives and direction were valid, their method provides no adequate alternative in the 1980s. A free economy based on private initiative is powered by self-knowledge, not "selfishness." It does not exclude compassion for the "under-privileged." Its productivity creates opportunity for making compassion *more* feasible and *more* generous than in state economy. A free economy creates no hindrance to disinterested effort organised for the benefit of people or causes: from the old or sick, who cannot help themselves, to art galleries, opera or other artistic activities that consumers will not finance in the market. Many British schools and hospitals were built out of the profits of industry in the heyday of 19th-century capitalism. The market does not inhibit giving; man may do what he likes with his earnings. And he is more likely to give if he earns more than if he earns less. He earns more—and pays lower taxes—in a market than in a state economy. There is more selfless, voluntary giving in capitalism than in socialism.

Selflessness Cannot (Yet) Replace Incentive or Coercion

If love were sufficient to motivate mankind, it would create a state of bliss—with selflessness and superabundance—that could dispense with both privately-motivated individual initiative and state-enforced central direction. That day may dawn. Christian teaching to love thy neighbour may hasten it. The high productivity of private enterprise may in time create the material conditions for it. The micro-processor may bring it a century nearer. The deadly serious Marxist/Leninist conception of the second or higher phase of communism, in which there is production "from each according to his ability" and distribution "to each according to his need," is always a conceivable possibility. J. M. Keynes, in more fanciful mood, looked forward to the day when scarcity was abolished and men could dwell on more elevating activities than earning a living.

All this may come to pass. No-one can say when. (In a letter to me as a 1930s student at the LSE, John Strachey said it might take 75 years.) But it is day-dreaming or, even worse, distraction to advocate policies based on the supposition that it has come to pass and is now with us. Absolute poverty persists in Asia and Africa. The report of the independent commission numbering among its members the paternalist Conservative Edward Heath and the paternalist Social Democrat Willy Brandt, *North-South,* said, self-evidently as though it were a new imperative: "The world must aim to abolish hunger . . . ."[2] Disease weakens the developing countries. Stark contrasts between the capitalist West and the pre-capitalist East strain international harmony. In the developed West, followed by the developing Third World, improving supply of goods and services creates new expectations of rising standards. Yet although private enterprise has raised incomes spectacularly in the two centuries since the Industrial Revolution, we cannot assume that scarcity will be abolished in the foreseeable future. Even the microprocessor, if it heralds the end of physical labour, will create opportunities for leisure that will produce a new crop of expectations, so that economy, efficiency and sensitivity to consumer preference will remain essential to satisfy them. John Strachey would not have seen superabundance in Russia at the end of his 75 years in AD 2010.

Until therefore love—selflessness in everyday life—takes over as the prime mover of human effort, which may be in several centuries, the two alternatives left to mankind will remain the incentives of the market and the coercion of the state-planned society. The Western world, with some hesitation, has declared for the market. Even the communist countries are trying to restore the market as the means of feeding information to the central planners, although as an instrument to be suppressed when it weakens their political power. In Russia, where the industrial population had relatively short experience of private enterprise, it has been less difficult to suppress private initiative, though it has to be tolerated, not least in agriculture and housing, more than the planners would wish; and the régime has tried to use "autonomous" plant managers responding to market forces in industry. But increasing coercion will be required to suppress the trend to initiative stimulated by knowledge of the West, and it is hardly likely to survive the century. Forty years later in China, where the individualist trading tradition is stronger and markets are a Chinese cultural inheritance, the régime is less self-conscious (or guilt-ridden) about the use of "capitalist" devices, and the return to official recognition of markets is easier. For this reason alone China is likely to emerge economically stronger than Russia in the coming decades.

2. Brandt Commission Report, *North-South,* Pan Books, 1980.

The replacement of the centralists by the "liberals" was foreseeable. At a conference in Europe in May 1979, three Chinese economists, members of the Chinese Academy of Social Sciences, though speaking as private individuals, described the "major mistake" of Chinese socialist construction that it had ignored the market mechanism. Although we shall see ritual genuflection to the ideas of central planning, we may also expect a gradual re-development of private institutions in the scope allowed to market forces to shape the development of the Chinese economy.

Tolerant Markets; Intolerant Statism

The strength of the private enterprise economy is that it can tolerate pockets of non-market economy. In the shape of voluntary co-operatives or communes, individuals may freely "drop out" and live lives of money-less barter. And as long as they can latch on to the information on costs provided by the surrounding market economy, they may be able to continue with tolerable living standards for some time. They create no threat to the market economy in which they subsist. Private enterprise can operate without obstructing or suppressing non-conformists of all kinds. On the contrary, it is continuously nourished by the unorthodox, the adventurous and the dissident. Even those who reject "capitalism" are themselves practising private enterprise in establishing unconventional life-styles to express their rejection of what they consider hedonism. A private enterprise economy is the only one in which they can practise their forms of private enterprise unharassed by the régime.

But centralised coercive planning does not tolerate independent pockets of market economy because, if uncontrolled, markets would spread and by their productivity largely displace the state. Markets in the communist economies of Eastern Europe are permitted when the system is weakened by economic arthritis or liable to seizure because of over-centralisation. But they are restricted or suppressed when they grow to undermine the ability of the central planners to operate with brittle economic institutions that cannot tolerate non-conformity for fear of being revealed as inferior.

The Elusive Alternative: Three Flaws of Statism

The critics of private enterprise have for decades taught that its faults are inevitable, and that the only remedy is to abolish the system root and branch and replace it by centralised control. Their claims have gone largely unchallenged because they offered promises of a new order that never came into being and so could not be examined. Even when some forms of central planning were applied, as in nationalisation of fuel and power, education and medical care, or a wide range of local government services, failure was invariably condoned on the ground, again impossible to disprove, that nationalisation or municipalisation had not been sufficiently stringent, wide-ranging or long-lived; more power, more restrictions, more exclusion of competition or more taxpayers' money would bring the long-promised benefits.

This defence has three decisive flaws. First, the advocates of state control in its varying forms could claim experimentation to test their claims. And a market economy could permit experimentation without endangering the main market structure. But the advocates of state economy shunned local or temporary experiments. They demanded (i) national (ii) monopoly (iii) for all time. It was *assumed* that state monopoly would succeed; but in practice it has to be "irreversible," whatever the consequences. That in itself should have been a sobering shock to the many men of intellect and integrity who hoped for much from the beneficent power of the state. It was a negation of the scientific method. It not only seemed to claim knowledge of the consequences; it demanded they be overlooked if they proved undesirable. Who now admits that nationalisation of fuel or transport, medical care or education, or anything else, has failed?—or can ever fail? If for no other reason, state economy—comprehensive and permanent—would have to be rejected *whatever the disadvantages and abuses of private enterprise.*

Second, state control claimed that to give it the best prospects of showing its advantages, all other methods and techniques would have to be excluded. Nationalisation of coal would require the suppression of private enterprise in coal; of transport, suppression, or at least severe control by licensing, of private transport; state control of education would require discouragement or at least hobbling of private enterprise in education; state medical care required the expulsion of private medicine. The logic of this reasoning is undeniable. Coal nationalisation would work best if its planning and investment decisions and labour deployment were not liable to disruption by unforeseen supplies from private mines at home or imported coal. And a tax on substitutes would help to avoid loss of markets to oil consumers like power stations or domestic households. But if the exclusion of the new knowledge that would come from private enterprise was a necessary condition for the success of state control, then the whole of the Western tradition and its reverence for scholarship would cry out for the condemnation of the state, whatever its claims. The suppression of knowledge is too high a price to pay for the unproved benefits of state monopoly.

Third, to pass from the supposed or real defects of private enterprise to the tall claims for state control was to leap a million miles in logic. This is the supreme intellectual sleight-of-hand of the 20th century. The *non-sequitur,* "Private enterprise bad, state economy therefore good," has bemused politicians, mesmerised business men, misled students, confused academics. It has wrought a revolution in public policy in the Western world, in both hemispheres, based on nothing more than the intellectual blunder of comparing the present, scarred by its known faults, with a romanticised future, free of its unknown faults.

The Choice

There is no convincing reason to suppose that even more coercive centralised state control, even more rigidly exclusive state monopolies, even more strictly enforced regulation of private industry, even more pretentious fixing of wages, salaries, profits, dividends, prices or rates of change in them, or any other powers exercised by a relative handful of politicians, state planners or bureaucrats will have any more success in discovering and motivating human abilities in the future that it has had in the past. The only certainty is that they will require even more loss of liberty, with no certainty of more productivity, equality or humanity.

A century is a long time for the increasing restrictions of state economy to have shown what they can do. State control has invariably burdened the Western countries with a slower rate of progress than they would otherwise have achieved because it has required more bureaucracy, higher taxes, more restrictions on the individual impulse to advance than a more open society would have required for the minimal functions of government.

Private enterprise has produced the wealth of the world; yet it has suffered more calumny and obloquy than any other system. Its alternative, state economy, has retarded the production of wealth; yet it has been lauded and deified.

Such has been the *trahison des clercs* who concentrated on the defects of private enterprise without seeing its benefits. They found more intellectual satisfaction in aggrandising a non-existing system whose economic claims no-one could challenge because no-one had experienced its defects.

Experience has now taught better. The claims of collectivism in theory are unproven. Its faults in practice are plain for all to see. And they are incurable. The faults of private enterprise are curable. The way ahead lies not in entrenching systems of state economy with unsubstantiated benefits and obvious blemishes, but in removing the defects from a system of private enterprise with proven blessings and remediable imperfections.

CHAPTER 2

Market Success: Curable Defects

For two hundred years the evolving system of private enterprise in the Western world has been accompanied by continuous appraisal and criticism as it changed agrarian poverty into industrial wealth. The critics varied from the sympathetic classical economists to the hostile Fabians and Marxists. The criticisms ranged from the "market failure" that still fills the textbooks of economists of all schools to the poverty and "immiseration" for which the Marxists blamed early industrialisation and which still fill the history books of schools and colleges.

It is a remarkable feature of intellectual history that the parallel study of "government failure" began, or rather has been revived, only in the last 25 years. The classical economists of the early and middle 19th century were alive to the limitations of government. Their proposals for government economic policy reflected their scepticism about the ability of politicians to remove the defects and improve the outcomes of private economic activity. Their study of the shortcomings, abuses and corruptions of the mercantilist guild system—a medieval form of state-supervised corporativism—made them doubt the claim that power would be exerted in the public interest even if it were in the right hands. So they advocated the replacement of mercantilist regulation by free markets.

Early Industrialism and Poverty

These lessons of experience, and the analytical insights of the English and Scottish economic philosophers from David Hume and Adam Smith to David Ricardo and John Stuart Mill, were forgotten and blurred after the middle of the 19th century. Economists, political theorists, philosophers and other thinkers, and public men unconsciously absorbed and applied their thinking. Yet when they observed the hardship and disturbance that accompanied rapid change from man-power to machine-power, from farm to mill and factory, from rural spaciousness to urban crowding, they illogically blamed the developing private enterprise system and market capitalism rather than the high rate of technical and economic change. They were led, or misled, by their generous instincts, compassion for suffering, or (as were Disraeli and Gladstone) by their instincts to acquire power by responding to the votes of the newly-enfranchised town electorates, to take a more charitable and romantic view of the capabilities and intentions of men in politics and government. Hence the stream of doctrines in the last 100 years on extending the functions and rôle of government, widely divergent in form but basically common in their unfounded assumptions about the intentions and capacity of politicians to serve the public good.

These doctrines underlay the thinking of Marx and Engels in the Communist Manifesto of 1849; of the Fabians from the 1880s; of the municipal Conservatives who, like the Fabians, proposed wide extensions in the power of local government, some desirable, like public health, others questionable, like education. These doctrines influenced the Labour Party advocacy of nationalisation or state regulation in the inter-war years, approved by the Liberal Party and enacted by the Conservatives in coal, transport, agriculture and elsewhere. The implicit trust in the politician was reflected in *The General Theory* of J. M. Keynes in 1936, and his followers to this day, that government could maintain full employment by managing demand in budget deficit financing. Not least, the faith in the beneficent state was asserted in the all-party sponsorship through Beveridge, Bevan and Butler of the post-war welfare state to supply comprehensive education and medical care without charge (that is, paid for by taxes), subsidised housing (ditto), and unemployment, sickness and retirement income financed by "national insurance" (a political euphemism for a poll tax).

A New/Old Realism: The Economics of Politics

The unrealism about the nature of man, the working of parliamentary democracy, the ballot box and other "representative" political institutions, the motivations and results of bureaucracy that underlay all these apparently diverse, even conflicting, proposals for the enlargement of government has been newly examined in the restoration of the classical realism in the new/old study of "public choice" or the "economics of politics." It began in the USA and has spread to Europe and other Continents. It has restored the scepticism both about the capacity of men in government to discover the "public interest" by political machinery and about their private interest in serving it even if they could discover it. These studies have created a new scrutiny of "government failure" with far-reaching implications for public attitudes to government policy.

The wheel has turned full circle. The classical teaching was that government had irremediable faults and was a necessary evil that should be confined to the unavoidable supply of "public goods." It is now being refined in modern dress. The century of faith in beneficent government—that it could be used to remedy the deficiencies of economic and social change and repair the damage of "market failure"—is being seen as a long but passing interval in the developing view that *government, or over-government, is itself the cause of economic degeneration.* The freedom and material well-being of mankind lie in preventing government from suppressing the spontaneous urge of people to come together as buyers and sellers. These are the informal relationships that have come to be formalised as private enterprise in a framework of law governing the operation of competitive markets in which the buying and selling take place. And, to discipline government and its urge to extend its power over people in the name of justice, compassion or equality, the economics of politics is producing a new structure of sophisticated proposals, from economic restraints on the power to tax to constitutional limitations on the power to print money.

The essential difference is that "market failure" is remediable but "government failure" is irremediable. Private enterprise, the market economy, capitalism, have faults: and often in the past two centuries they have been severe. The critics have often accurately identified and documented the faults, but without good reason they thought them irremovable and thereby reached their conclusion that the system itself should be abandoned. In so doing they would also have sacrificed its unprecedented power to expand production. They not only threw the baby out with the bath water; to vary the metaphor, they threw it from the bath into the fire.

The experience of history and the logic of analysis combine to demonstrate this conclusion. Capitalism is corrigible: state economy is incorrigible. The *rationale* of private enterprise is that its defects are less difficult to remove than are those of state economy in all its forms, from state ownership and control through "mixed" economy to social democracy. The reason is clear. *State power,* once it is entrenched, *is more difficult to discipline than private power.*

Remediable Imperfections

The four main defects of private enterprise that have appeared in the last two centuries are wide differences in income, monopoly, the gulf between employers and employees, and the divergence between the private and social ("external") effects of private trading in the market.

(i) Differences in Incomes

Differences in incomes are the outcome of the market in persuading people to exchange with, and so enrich, one another. Given the tardy development of selflessness—the readiness to serve others without reward—difference in payment is more humane than direction of labour backed by coercion in a centrally planned economy, and less arbitrary than the differences in privileges or power used to induce effort and reward talent in a mixed or state economy.

"Inequality" is the question-begging description of differences in payment or reward applied by the critics of a free economy. The use of the otherwise neutral term "inequality" is intended to imply that differences are undesirable. Yet the alternatives to differences in payment for services of different value are either the abolition of the freedom to exchange services or the determination of pay and incomes by political authority in "incomes policies" rather than by the consumer in the market. And, so far, all "incomes policies," except for short periods in especially favourable circumstances, have done little more than to postpone long-delayed adjustments and build up damaging distortions in the distribution of labour and the structure of industry.

Insofar as human differences of any kind are considered objectionable, private enterprise is imperfect. But it did not create the differences in talents that require differences in payment. And, insofar as the differences in income are considered too wide to be morally acceptable, the lowest can be raised by taxing the higher incomes and redistributing the proceeds *outside* the market. The private enterprise system has long developed redistributive taxes on income and wealth for this purpose, of which the latest, and perhaps potentially most effective, would be a reverse income tax to "top up" low incomes with unearmarked purchasing power and vouchers to supply purchasing power earmarked for specified services such as education, health, housing, etc.

A reverse income tax, as its name indicates, is the reverse of an income tax.

In contrast to a tax on incomes *above* stated amounts for people in varying circumstances, a reverse income tax is a tax in reverse, that is, a payment from government to people with incomes *below* stated amounts. In time it could increasingly replace cash benefits tied to specified conditions such as sickness and unemployment. Vouchers embody earmarked purchasing power for education, medical care (insurance), housing (rents or purchase) or other services to which it is judged everyone should have access in minimum amounts and qualities. These two measures would make it possible in stages to remove welfare bureaucracies that hobble many Western democracies by their high taxation, misuse of manpower, absence of accountability and resistance to change. A reverse income tax would enable tax-producing private enterprise to replace tax-consuming government production. And education vouchers would raise the quality of schooling and reduce its costs by empowering parents to remove their children from schools that (as in the UK, the USA, Australia and elsewhere) failed to teach the basic skills required for working and earning. In time they would make all schools efficient because those that were not responsive to parents and the requirements of industry would lose their incomes. Reverse taxes and vouchers could create market disciplines for welfare as well as for industrial production and rid the Western democracies of the dead weight of over-government.

A reverse income tax has been tested in the USA (New Jersey), education vouchers have been tested in the USA (Alum Rock), are being introduced into Spain, are to be tested in Britain and are being investigated in Australia.

There is a dilemma, again not the outcome of private exchange in the market. Maximising redistribution beyond a stage conflicts with maximising total incomes. Despite doubts about measuring the disincentive effect of taxes on income or wealth, leisure (i.e. not working) is preferred to effort if the reward is reduced below the value of the leisure. The choice is then between further redistribution by taxes to reduce differences, and higher but more unequal incomes. If, by taxing higher incomes less, incomes for all are raised because of the rise in general productivity, the lower-income ("poor") people may prefer more "inequality" if their incomes would be lower with more equality. In a free society they would be able to influence the choice of policy: and it is hardly likely that most would prefer lower income to less "inequality." Yet the sociologists of poverty like the late Professor R. M. Titmuss and the surviving Peter Townsend, who have had much influence around the world, argued that poverty was harder to bear as it was shared less when the incomes of some of the former "poor" rose. It is conceivable that the relatively affluent intellectual may see philosophic advantages in equal poverty (for others) over unequal affluence. But the implausible notion that the poor prefer poverty to inequality could be tested by asking them. That is not what the sociologists proposed. Public policy has been based on the opinions of intellectuals unchecked by the opinions of the people who have suffered from their teaching.

The emancipation of the market

Here again the market system scores over the state economy. The market system would tend to redistribute benefits in purchasing power (generalised in cash or earmarked by voucher) that facilitates access to the market. And in time it would emancipate people with lower incomes from their relative poverty by creating access as paying consumers to education, medicine, housing and other family requirements as well as to everyday purchases. The state economy tends to redistribute in kind: services organised by politicians and administered by officials in which the beneficiary is a passive recipient, if not a supplicant, rather than an active consumer learning discrimination and judgement by the regular exercise of choice. The bargaining power of the recipient of benefits in kind is clearly inferior to that of the customer spending benefits in cash (or voucher). Recipients cannot escape; consumers can withdraw their purchasing power. Benefits in kind are supplied by a state monopoly, even if distributed by local government agents. Benefits in cash (or voucher) can be used to buy from a wide variety of competing suppliers, government and private. The classical advantages of choice between competing suppliers over monopoly could apply to the Western welfare state as well as to the everyday consumer goods supplied in the private enterprise market.

Not least, the private enterprise system scores in its superior ability to correct undesirable differences. In the market, access to goods and services is determined by possession of purchasing power. In the state economy, access is determined by possession of cultural power—accent, personality, temperament, character and cultural influence (in persuading officials and government-employed teachers, doctors, etc.), family or social connections, occupational pull, political links. *It is easier to lessen differences in purchasing power than differences in cultural power.* Differences in incomes can be remedied by redistributing purchasing power. Differences in cultural influence on state education, medical care, housing and so on cannot be remedied by "redistributing" or equalising cultural or other power. How do you "equalise" accent, personality, temperament, character, cultural origins, family or social connections, occupational pull or political links? That is the central question the egalitarians have never asked, still less answered. It is their Achilles' Heel.

(ii) Monopoly

Monopolies may arise in private enterprise where there are economies in large-scale technique, management, marketing, financing or risk-covering. Here again means have been developed of disciplining monopoly. It is prevented by maintaining open doors to competitors with new ideas and methods or dissolved by anti-trust laws. Keeping doors open, by refraining from protecting existing producers, requires an act of omission by government, and is less risky than dissolving monopoly, which requires an act of commission. The lesson of experience, that government is rarely competent, even in redistributing money, is amply illustrated in legislation on anti-trust or restrictive practices. Government is applying a very inexact science with very imprecise tools. In practice it tends to prevent or restrict too much or too little, too soon or too late. And, once it is engaged, it cannot easily withdraw at the right time either because vested interests develop expectations that demand long-drawn-out de-control, or because the bureaucracy is always reluctant to relinquish authority. It may be that a little temporary monopoly is worth a lot of lasting, burgeoning, irreversible government control or regulation.

This is a minor fault contrasted with the potential abuse of monopoly created and operated by the state, in trade unions as well as in industry. For the first time, the Western world is being shown by recent developments in Britain the anguished "withdrawal symptoms" of disengaging from state activity of almost any kind, which will have to be expected in welfare services as well as in postal services, fuel, transport and steel and in a wide range of local services. The lesson for the West is that, except for unavoidable public goods, it is better not to allow government to control industry or supply services in the first place, but to leave them to private enterprise in the market.

Whatever the difficulties of cleansing private enterprise of monopoly, they are trifling contrasted with the task of removing the power of the state over the economic lives of the people once it has been allowed to gain control. The state can, possibly, purge private monopoly; it will not readily purge itself, especially where it is opposed by bureaucracies and trade unions of "public servants." It requires determined public insistence: that is why change in state economy is more disturbing and convulsive than in market economy.

The irreversibility of state economy is perhaps its most fateful weakness and its strongest condemnation.

(iii) Alienation

The "alienation" of the worker under capitalism was a major theme of the Marxist critique. Its present-day version is the claim for "industrial democracy."

Private enterprise in principle presents no obstacles to "employee involvement" or the other variants that critics of private enterprise think would remove the gulf between employer and employed. But there is no case for giving the employees of each enterprise authority over the firm (or other unit) that others have created or run as entrepreneurs, still less for giving it to their trade union spokesmen.

Employees in general are not debarred from acquiring direct entrepreneurial or indirect equity interests in industry. They can do so by starting new firms, at first on a small scale, or buying ordinary shares with voting rights in existing businesses, small or large. And throughout the economic history of Western countries, in the Northern and Southern hemispheres, they have done both. Many large firms have grown from small—very small—entrepreneurial beginnings. And employees have acquired equity interests in industry, some by direct purchase, a few by special offers of shares in their employer's firm, more by buying unit trust units and life assurance policies, most by membership of pension funds. It is true that the sense of participating or influential ownership is most vivid where ordinary shares have been bought, yielding regular dividends and the right to attend and interrogate the Directors at Annual General Meetings. Such direct equity holdings have been growing; they are more common in the USA than in other Western industrial countries, where they could be encouraged by better marketing and other means.

But there is no argument for giving ownership and control to people who, on an arbitrary date, happen to be employed by a firm. In private enterprise the ultimate owners of a firm are the people who have risked their savings in ordinary shares. In a competitive economy private ownership is in a sense held in trust for the general public who are the ultimate controllers in their capacity as consumers. If a firm satisfies consumers in the market it prospers, and its "equity" owners may be enriched. If it fails to satisfy its consumers, possibly through no deficiency in management but wholly because of changes in market supply or demand such as an invention it could not have foreseen, the firm fails and its equity owners may own nothing.

The sacrosanctity of state monopoly

Only in monopoly can there be a secure holding of property. The critics of private enterprise rightly want monopoly removed but, illogically, not in the government sector. Yet it is only state monopoly that is secure against both criticism and anti-trust law. The critics of private enterprise who argue for state monopoly do not generally argue for direct participation of the employees in its ownership or control. The assertion, now repeated as though it were a new truth, is that "public" (i.e., state) ownership would be more responsible because it would, through its political controllers, be more "accountable" to the people. Here is yet one more essay in unreality. The reality, evidenced by recent examples in economies as diverse as the "mixed economy" of Britain and the "liberal" communism of Yugoslavia, is that state enterprises are operated in the interests of the people who control them. And if those who happen to be employees are given control they are operated in the interests of its current workers, not of the community at large, which is the proclaimed objective of "public" ownership wherever it is installed, in capitalist, mixed or communist economies. The "alienation" of employee from employer of which Marx complained is not as deep as the alienation of the general consumer from the syndicalist "owners" of state enterprises who expect to be kept in employment out of taxes when they fail to produce what he (and she) wants and will pay for in the market.

The best prospects for employee involvement in industry, and for ending the alienation between employee and employer, is for employees to become owning employers. There is nothing in private enterprise to prevent firms from being owned by the employees who hire the managers and the capital required for their enterprises. Firms can be owned not only by absentee share-holders who leave the salaried managers to control them, but also by active managers, technicians, floor-cleaners or tea-ladies. In private enterprise this is how very small firms—workshops, car servicing garages, shops, hairdressing and many others—are owned, run and operated. But not in a state economy, which allows employees to become employers only on sufferance, with no prospect of growing from small to big at all. Marx envisaged the day when the worker would take over from the capitalists and "the expropriators would be expropriated." State economy does not emancipate the alienated; it suppresses them. Private enterprise can accommodate worker-managed co-operatives or other forms of industrial organisation that are competitive and survive by efficiency. As elsewhere, state economy does not cure the ills of private enterprise; it conceals the symptoms.

(iv) Externalities

Private enterprise does not invariably take into account the "external" effects of private contracts. It thus creates noise, smell, congestion and other damage to third parties whom it does not compensate.

This allegedly callous disregard of "social costs" has been made one more major criticism of private enterprise. As with other criticisms, the means of removing the defect were not examined too closely. And the premature conclusion was soon reached that the solution was to intervene in, or to suppress, the market. Environmental pollution became one more condemnation of private enterprise.

The weakness of the criticism was not long in being demonstrated. The obvious solution lay in legal requirements to "internalise" the external costs. Motor-cars, for example, can be fitted with exhaust suppressors, warning lights and seat belts; hotels with fireproof doors, hydrants and fire-escapes; factory chimneys with smoke filters; and so on. There is no technical or political difficulty about enacting legal "internalisation." The question is, indeed, whether the prevention of "externalities" is proceeding too far, so that it raises costs and puts motor-cars, hotel rooms and factory products beyond the pockets of many, especially the relatively poor, who can no longer pay for them.

No doubt the control of social costs in private enterprise has to be further refined. And no doubt it will be if the economy is competitive. But state economy offers no automatic solution. There is no reason to suppose that the central planners of a state-controlled economy are more competent to detect a divergence between private and social costs, or more anxious to close it. Since they are even further removed from the day-to-day lives of the people, and are *less* answerable to them, they are *less* capable of detecting the divergence, and *less* anxious to close it than are private enterprisers.

Collectivist smoke pollutes social democratic Sweden and Austria, or communist Poland and Bulgaria, as much as market smoke pollutes Britain, Canada and Australia. The difference is that it is easier to remedy abuses in a market economy where government is more under the influence of people at the grassroots than in a state economy where influence is cornered by people at the top. The people in a free enterprise society, armed with a free press, freedom of speech and access to information, are more able to require government to monitor and discipline the sources of pollution than are the people in a state economy. State enterprises are only nominally "accountable" to the people through their "representatives"; since the people have no free press, no freedom of speech and no access to information they cannot make their voices heard. And if their voices are ignored they cannot escape from the state—either to the market or to other countries.

Environmental pollution and other externalities are a problem of the application of science to industry where the legal/property rights to require compensation for damage are not (yet) clearly defined. Once defined, these rights are easier to enforce in a free enterprise than in a closed state society. They are gradually being refined and embodied in legislation, such as the prohibition of smoking coal to maintain clear air in residential areas, traffic and parking regulation to reduce congestion. Better still, they are disciplined by charges to discourage pollution or congestion (as in Singapore), and so on.

Emulation and Self-Interest: The Motive Force of Enterprise

Private enterprise does not require man to be envious and avaricious. It is based, in direct contrast, on emulation. Individuals must be free to pursue their goals, so long as they do not collide with others, because only they know their circumstances, requirements, hopes, anxieties, those of their family and their immediate community, and the causes they wish to serve—from local hospitals and schools to churches, old people's homes, centres for dyslexic children, the blind and the deaf. Individuals must be free to emulate others, otherwise there is stagnation, as there was for centuries in the Middle Ages before private enterprise was fertilised by industrial invention and discovery. In this twin sense—self-knowledge and emulation—self-interest is a necessary ingredient of progress from poverty to sufficiency, from subsistence to affluence, from working life to leisure.

Thomas Hobbes, the English philosopher (1588–1679), proclaimed that, to serve self-interest, men would have to live together to forge rules in which individual self-interests were harmonised to serve one another. So each man abandons a little of anarchy in freedom from common rules to form a larger whole in which the bulk of his freedom, which might otherwise be insecure, is made more secure. But he must sacrifice only the amount of independent action required to make his private life more secure, not to enable the state to order the life he should lead. So the private enterprise system requires law the better to trade, not to permit government to order it what goods to make or where to sell them. Friedrich Hayek, the most considerable philosopher of our times, put it simply: we require rules of the road so that we do not get in one another's way, not to tell us where to go. The critics of private enterprise offer a political super-being who will tell us how to live, when to trade, where to go. No such being, or collection of economic planners or well-intentioned politicians, is equipped for the task. Not Sir Ian Gilmour, nor Mr. David Steel, nor even Mr. Anthony Wedgwood Benn, nor any other paternalist, autocrat or romancer.

CHAPTER 3

Government Failure: Incurable Defects

A rationale of private enterprise is based both on its proven achievements and on the defects of state economy. Since the critics of private enterprise insist on judging it by its performance in the past, the alternative they offer cannot be accepted on their word of how it will perform in the future.

The alternative to private initiative is state initiative, varying from the milder forms described as social democracy, which is paternalist in spirit and benign in execution, to the wilder forms described as collectivism, which is authoritarian in spirit and totalitarian in execution.

Until recently Sweden was the exemplar of social democracy most quoted in evidence of the achievements of mixed economy. Austria has more recently been favoured by Mr. Denis Healey, the last British Labour Chancellor of the Exchequer. Britain, the founder of the post-war welfare state, to a degree copied elsewhere in the West, has lost favour as the exemplar, even among the British philosophers of social democracy. Its most characteristic form, the National Health Service, is still advertised as the ideal, in aspiration if not in performance. But it is copied nowhere in the West except in Italy since January 1980, where it exists mainly on paper, and is likely to remain there, not least because the Italians, well versed in the arts of tax avoidance and evasion, will not accept higher taxes to pay for a service that would not respond to their individual preferences or payments.

The root-and-branch critics of private enterprise have in recent years become more reluctant to name the communist countries of Eastern Europe as their preferred alternative, although the newly emerging China, especially in its latest "liberal" phase, is honourably mentioned. They are now more likely to indict Russian and other communist economies as caricatures of "true socialism" and to condemn them as "state capitalism."

Yet the critics of private enterprise in the Western world have been so self-confident, and their claims for their alternatives, whether social democracy or state collectivism, so insistent that they cannot escape examination and testing in the light of logical reasoning or historical evidence, or both.

The Large Claims for State Economy on Paper

The claims for the alternatives to private enterprise have been that, by abolishing private property ownership or control, and transferring them to the state, representing and accountable to the people, the alternatives would also abolish poverty, insecurity, inequality, selfishness, acquisitiveness, exploitation, alienation, social divisiveness, class, oppression, even crime and war. Above all, state economy in its varying forms was to be a more moral order. It would establish fellowship, fraternity, unselfishness, co-operativeness.

The intellectual assault on private initiative and the intellectual claims for state initiative have been largely conducted by British writers about British conditions, but the general principles apply more or less all over the world. A 20th-century Marxist historian, E. P. Thompson, wrote of the early English factory system:

> its new disciplines . . . contributed to the transparency of the process of exploitation and to the social and cultural cohesion of the exploited.[1]

William Morris, the 19th-century advocate of romantic socialism, said it was:

> a rich condition of society in which there should be neither rich nor poor, neither master nor master's man, neither idle nor over-worked, neither brain-sick brainworkers nor heart-sick handworkers . . . all men would be living in equality of condition, would manage their affairs unwastefully, and with the full consciousness that harm to one would mean harm to all. . . .[2]

Yet state initiative in the real world bears little resemblance to the vision held out by its philosophers. It was, ironically, this vision that inspired the formation of political parties to bring it into reality in every country in the world wherever private enterprise capitalism maintained freedom for political dissent. There is no parallel freedom in countries with state economy for political parties to create a vision of political liberty based on personal property, private initiative and independent enterprise.

1. *The Making of the English Working Class,* Pelican Edn., Penguin Books, 1968.
2. *How I Became a Socialist,* Pelican, Penguin Books, 1962 Edn.

The Defects of State Economy in Practice

The reality contrasts sharply with the vision. In practice state initiative suffers from more stubborn because organic defects than private initiative. The very centralised power that enables them to emerge and permits them to continue will resist attempts to remove them because it could not exist without them. The main incurable defects are ignorance, inefficiency, social conflict, monopoly, coercion, corruption and secrecy.

(i) Ignorance

State "planning" is based on the premise that it is possible for the central "planners" to discover and satisfy public preferences better than competing private suppliers responding to consumers in free markets. For simple, static agrarian societies such a system seems plausible. For complex industrial societies with rapid technological innovation and changing individual preferences, habits and requirements, it is pretentious. Even if the political controllers were supreme philosopher-kings and officials were selfless public benefactors, the machinery for transmitting the mass of moving information from millions of consumers to central planners, and for re-transmitting it to managers of plants, firms, stores and distribution centres is non-existent. Some years ago the Polish economist Oskar Lange claimed that state economy could use speed-of-light computers to make possible the swift adaptation of production to consumer preferences. No doubt today he would call micro-processors in aid. That is to confuse technical possibilities with political probabilities. The prospect that politicians, officials and managers would not only be able but also anxious to apply the daily changing preferences to daily production schedules is fanciful. The market incentives to respect public preferences and the penalties for ignoring them are missing.

The logical probability is that consumers would be confronted with what the productive process could produce. And that is the political reality. The notorious weakness of all state initiative—from Russian communism to the British National Health Service—is that it tries to vindicate itself by reaching measurable targets of *quantity* at the expense of immeasurable *quality.* The familiar criticism of private initiative is that it pays too much attention to individual idiosyncracy. The opposite and more valid charge is that state initiative pays too little attention to personal preference. In real life the choice is not between too much attention by private enterprise and optimum attention by state economy but between too much and too little attention. There is little doubt which the people—whether the Russian shopper or the British hospital patient—would prefer. But state planners at best strive to reach visible quantifiable targets because their efficiency is judged by them. They cannot be judged by invisible, unquantifiable indicators of quality—choice, convenience, timing, respect for individual idiosyncracy; yet these are the ultimate criteria of success of an economic system and its use of scarce resources.

Without markets, state economy is blind. Little wonder that the economists of Hungary, Poland, Yugoslavia and Russia are still intermittently trying to build market indicators, signals, incentives and disciplines into their politically-controlled economies. They are all doomed to failure because their use of market disciplines is ultimately decided by the political power.

In the early years of the debate between economists on the use of markets by state economy to allocate resources and satisfy consumer preferences, Hayek described the theoretical constructions of the collectivist economists as "playing at competition." Recent writings by economists in communist countries designed to refine market signals rest on the romantic hope that the sole purpose is to devise the machinery for transmitting information to be operated by selfless controllers and operators. It makes the same error as the advocates of love as an economic engine; they contend not only that mankind should be selfless but also that the state of selflessness has arrived. Central planners are not (yet) selfless servants of the people; nor is it likely they ever will be.

(ii) Inefficiency

The incapacity of state economy to discover and apply information on public preferences makes it inherently inefficient. In collectivist economies—and in state industries producing public and private goods in Western mixed economies—commodities and services are often produced in excess or short of requirements. They are too soon or too late, in the wrong places, in the wrong shapes, sizes, colours or combinations. Even if living standards are measured in quantities of output per head, they are throughout the world lower in countries with state planning than in countries with private initiative. It follows that they would be higher if state economy were replaced by private enterprise, and *vice-versa.* British living standards, which have become stagnant, would fall to those of Spain if more of the economy were transferred to the state. Russian living standards would rise nearer to those of the USA if state initiative were relaxed and private enterprise resumed where it was suppressed in 1917—except for the controlled tolerance of markets in the New Economic Policy of 1920–29, although it would take two or three decades to liberate individual aspirations and re-invigorate the processes of voluntary exchange and consumer-oriented production.

The contrast between living standards is sharpened immeasurably when the invisible and intangible elements of choice and convenience are added and weighed in the balance. The contrast is not only that Russian or Polish families still commonly share bathrooms and British or American families increasingly have sole use. The even more telling contrast is that the bathroom is where the British (except the one in three in government housing) and American families want it, but the Russian or Polish bathroom is where the apparatchiks put it. The decisive contrast is that in state economy the consumer takes what the machine produces; in private enterprise the machine produces what the consumer wants. No amount of qualification for poverty, monopoly, advertising, gullibility or irresponsibility in the economies based on private enterprise destroys the ultimate contrast.

(iii) Social Conflict

State initiative, even in its relatively benign form based on representative democratic institutions, creates social conflict. The governments of most Western economies—from the USA and even Switzerland to Holland and Belgium and certainly Austria and Sweden—have extended their province from public goods to essentially personal services. The supply of public goods is necessarily undertaken by (or through) government and financed by taxation because they create joint benefits (such as protection from external soldiery or internal burglary) from which individuals who refuse to bear a share of the cost cannot be excluded. The decisions on how much of such goods to produce, and on what kinds, are necessarily made by majority or other kind of voting in elected assemblies. Minorities, small groups and individuals must be over-ridden, and civilised co-operative living is made possible by their agreement to accept the decisions of majorities. In countries without proportional representation, majorities of representatives can be elected by minorities of electors, a defect of the electoral machinery that the minority or even the majority may have to tolerate.

But such electoral over-riding of minorities (or majorities), small groups and individuals is unavoidable only in public goods. It is unnecessarily self-imposed in all other goods and services that could be supplied by competing private producers in the market, which does not over-ride but caters for them—at a price. And these marketable goods and services are a very large part of government supply (and taxation and expenditure). An estimate for Britain I attempted in 1977 put the proportion of government expenditure that is unnecessarily raised in taxes and repaid in cash benefits or marketable goods and services at two-thirds. The proportion for other Western countries may be less, but it would still be considerable.

To this extent social tension and incipient conflict are created even in benign social democracies. If essentially personal goods that people could obtain in the market from private suppliers, with attention to minority interests and personal preferences, are provided by "public" authorities with little effective influence by the individuals compelled to pay for them by taxation, majorities (or minorities or even small côteries controlling the electoral machine) are, even if unintentionally and unknowingly, tyrannical. If the main structure of education, medical care, housing, pensions and many smaller personal or family services is decided by national political élites or activists, and payment is enforced by taxation, the only way in which minorities can escape is by migration. Escape by emigration is now experienced by countries with large welfare bureaucracies. Escape by internal movement between states is spreading in the USA; it will spread between local councils in Britain. The normal processes of political debate and persuasion that transform minorities into majorities are not available if minorities are based on religious, regional, sectarian, occupational or other unchangeable characteristics. A Catholic whose children are educated at schools controlled by Protestants does not renounce his church. He moves to a Catholic-dominated area (where Protestants may have similar cause for complaint), forfeits his taxes and pays fees at a private school, or is reduced to protest, resistance, tax avoision[3] or outright rebellion. Such civil discord and strife are the result of the unnecessary coercion of minorities in the production of private goods by the state in the socialist or the mixed economy.

The only way to avoid this incipient social conflict is to supply personal

3. The mixture of (legal) tax avoidance and (illegal) tax evasion created by the confusion in the taxpayer's mind between the legal and the moral, in which what is legal is no longer accepted as necessarily moral, nor what is illegal as necessarily immoral. The resulting "black economy" is a growing element in all countries with high taxation to finance non-public goods—capitalist, social democratic, socialist, communist or mixed. (*Tax Avoision,* IEA Readings No. 22, IEA, 1979.)

services in such a way that individuals, small groups or minorities can pay for what they want and reject what they do not want. The only way is that of private enterprise in a market with choice of competing suppliers.

(iv) Monopoly

State economy lives by monopoly and abhors competition. Since it claims to know what the people want or is good for them, it cannot permit private effort to do better. And that is as true of wholly centralised communism as of mixed economy in which the state supplies private as well as public goods. That is why state initiative, which denies itself the discovery mechanism of the market, is inferior to private enterprise, which thrives on it.

(v) Coercion

Coercion is the essential instrument of government in a state economy. It is used benignly in social democracies with mixed economies, and with increasing severity the more economic activity is controlled by the state. In the fully-fledged state economy all private supply is forbidden except where it is authorised or tolerated. The more it is forbidden, the more coercion there is of people who would prefer something different from what is supplied by the state.

State economy maximises coercion by supplying personal as well as public goods. A private enterprise system minimises coercion if the state limits itself to the supply of public goods.

(vi) Corruption

Despite the coercion of government, markets are irrepressible because they express the elemental urge of ordinary people to come together as buyers and sellers.

Where markets are officially forbidden, and all supplies must be sold through state agencies, black (or "grey") markets grow up in private exchanges which the state cannot detect through its police and sanctions. Where markets—with honest even though illegal exchange—cannot develop, because activity is under the direct control of government, officials sell unofficial permissions, permits, licences, authorities or exemptions. This has long been true in India and parts of Africa. It is spreading in Europe. And the taxes to pay for the wide range of government activities or services are widely avoided (legally) or evaded (illegally) until the two are merged as tax avoision.

The less economic activity takes place in open markets, the more corruption spreads. It appears as "gifts" where markets or market prices in private enterprise are suppressed by law as in resale price maintenance. The more markets are suppressed in government activities or services, the more corruption grows. There can be little doubt that corruption has spread in Britain as local government has extended its activities to private services, not least in contracts for housing and council building.

State economy maximises corruption of the politician as the creator of favours, the official as the dispenser of contracts, orders and other valuable trading or production rights, the citizen who depends for his livelihood on government contracts, and the citizen as taxpayer. The corruption has attacked the once-admired social democratic Sweden, whose population, says the Social Democrat economist Professor Gunnar Myrdal, has become "a nation of cheats."[4]

(vii) Secrecy

Not the least defect of government economy is that it is secretive. This is clearly not an easily removable fault. Secrecy is an instrument of government of a state economy which compels its critics and victims to overthrow the incumbents by force as the only way to reform it.

A characteristic contrast between a private enterprise society and a state economy is between publicity and secrecy, information and no information, or significant information and manipulated information.

It was for long an unsophisticated but nonetheless common criticism of capitalism, in the Stalin years when even less was known about Russia than recently, that capitalism was flawed by unemployment or inflation, both supposedly absent in Russia. The truth, long explained by liberal economists such as Wilhelm Röpke, was that unemployment had not been "abolished" but disguised by the coercive direction of labour and inflation by the simple suppression of statistics. Röpke demonstrated that the pre-war "trade cycle" of oscillations of booms and slumps could be identified even from the meagre information and questionable reports that escaped from Russia.

Soviet Russia concealed a symptom of economic dislocation even more

4. "Dags für ett bättre skattesystem," *Ekonomisk Debatt,* No. 7, 1978, p. 500.

damaging to human values than unemployment or inflation. Whatever the upheaval in the private enterprise world in 1929–32 (caused, Milton Friedman has shown, by monetary contraction rather than, as the critics argued, by the inherent contradictions of capitalism), it did not suffer mass starvations or death caused by a total collapse of agriculture. Hardship yes, famine no.

In 1929, after Lenin's New Economic Policy, Stalin moreover ordered the collectivisation of farming by eliminating the private farmers. In 1933 this enforced change in agricultural ownership produced famine. But it was concealed even from sympathetic observers who visited Russia to appraise the new society. Sidney Webb, a Cabinet Minister in the Labour Governments of 1924 and 1929–31, and Beatrice Webb, an experienced social observer, visited Russia in 1932 and wrote *Soviet Russia: A New Civilisation?,* published in 1935. For the Second Edition in 1937 they dropped the question mark: they no longer doubted that they had found a new civilisation. It is impossible to believe a private enterprise society, such as Canada, Holland or Australia, even if it had suffered a famine, could have concealed it from such sophisticated investigators. Many years later, Professor Alec Nove of the University of Glasgow recorded that "well over 10 million people had 'demographically' disappeared between 1929 and 1939."[5] Some starved, others were executed, some were deported. The crimes of private enterprise are an open book. There is no record of such mass inhumanity.

The critics of private enterprise, on the other hand, have not only wrongly attributed the Great Depression to "capitalism," a ceaselessly repeated but no less unsupported assertion. They are now using the talk of world recession to repeat, with no more ground than before, that the solution is to replace capitalism by socialism. This time the restiveness with the continued vitality of private enterprise and its capacity to provide living standards unknown ever in any socialist economy has led former social democrats in the British Labour Party to advocate the more extreme form of state planning known as "socialism."

The danger of social democracy has always been that, when it showed incontrovertible evidence of failure, as it has now done in Britain, some of its advocates would claim the reason was inadequate state control. State control failed because it was too mild. Again there is no evidence or argument; there is still no more than unsupported assertion. But now it seems that the British

5. Alec Nove, *An Economic History of the USSR,* Penguin Books, 1969.

Labour Party will sub-divide into its Socialist and its Social Democratic parts, so that it will never govern again. And the same may be the fate of Social Democratic or Labour Parties in other countries.

The Catalogue of "Government Failure"

Whatever the disadvantages of "market failure," the case for private enterprise is that "government failure" is more severe because its faults are inseparable from state economy and it is therefore incurable.

(i) Government has failed to master inflation and will be unable to master it as long as it is vulnerable to pressure from trade unions or industries clamouring for favours.

(ii) It has loaded the economy with swollen welfare bureaucracies that are not disciplined by market costing, so that the burden of maximising the efficiency of labour and capital is imposed on the shrinking market sector in industry and trade.

(iii) It tries to run large sections of "public enterprise" transport and fuel, education and health, as monopolies that can be controlled by a Minister and his officials without assistance from information on costs and values that only market pricing can create.

(iv) It fails to run down state activity and disentangle itself from industry when economic and social advance makes it increasingly outdated and unnecessary, not least in education, medicine, housing and pensions.

(v) It fails to create the conditions in which the private sector of industry can work efficiently.

(vi) By over-extending itself on superfluous activities, government fails to provide efficiently the public goods only it can supply.

CHAPTER 4

The Reigning Error:
State Holism *v.* Market Experimentation

The essential weakness in philosophies and political systems that dispense with the information-gathering mechanism of the market is that they pretend to powers they lack. They envisage the whole of society as a large family, or a club, a firm, political party or army, to be managed from the centre by well-meaning men supplied with information by loyal members or officials.

This error is embraced by politicians in partly or largely free societies. Recent British experience may be repeated elsewhere. The three Conservative Ministers in charge of education, medical care and housing are trying to reduce government expenditure by their departments almost solely by issuing orders not to exceed stated limits or ceilings. They are acting "holistically" like heads of large firms (or commissars of large industries) who expect their requirements to be obeyed. Like Atlas, they try to carry the world on their backs. Their orders are necessarily transmitted and enforced by officials who apply the "cuts" in expenditure in each sub-department and sub-sub-department with no knowledge of what the consumers, recipients or beneficiaries would prefer. Not only do they, naturally, tend to cut services that deprive consumers rather than jobs that deprive themselves. Far worse, they apply the cuts indiscriminately—like a scythe that cuts the heads of flowers as well as weeds. They may therefore do fearsome damage to services, such as health, on which individuals may wish to maintain or increase their expenditure even in a period of general retrenchment. Yet only individuals know their circumstances, requirements and preferences. The Minister and his officials cannot possibly know millions of individual desires and hopes. The only way to draw on all the vast structure of information is to lower taxes and let individuals make their personal "cuts" by paying for the services they want—the method of the market.

Self-delusion

The self-delusion that men at the centre can know enough about the periphery, and that they can then run the whole machine like a well-oiled turbine, misleads politicians in both wholly socialised and mixed economies into believing they can maximise public well-being, living standards and happiness. The more modest, but in the light of history more successful, conception is that government exists to provide the framework and services that will enable the populace to avoid thwarting one another. The object is rather to minimise conflict, misdirection, unhappiness. And its economic instrument is decentralised private initiative and enterprise. The declared claim of the holistic "social engineers" is that the state will do good. The implicit aim of liberal philosophers is the state that avoids doing harm. The aims, if not the means, of the new British Government, at least as stated by some of the Cabinet, are far ahead of those of most governments in Europe, North America and Australasia.

The state economy is based on the notion of the economy and society as a whole: a holistic entity. The market economy is based on the notion of the economy and society as a medley or network of independent entities that by experience learn to discover ways of serving one another in the main by using the market as buyers and sellers.

State Monolith or Market Diversity

The state economy is run by social engineers. With enough power, money and police enforcement, they hope to solve problems—poverty or inequality, unemployment or inflation.

The market economy has a government to provide services desired by all but capable of being supplied individually by none. For the rest it comprises individuals or groups that exchange goods or services. All they require is, first, laws to govern their exchanges: laws on property, companies and trade unions, contract, sale of goods, monopolies and restrictive practices; second, services to safeguard contracts, defence against disturbance from overseas or at home, environmental and preventive services in health protection, coast protection, street lighting; and, third, redistribution of purchasing power outside the market to even up wide differences in income.

Government services should largely be confined to "public goods" that only government can supply. If the market cannot supply them, they are "public goods." By and large, Western societies know, or can discover, which are public goods and which are not. Yet most have not applied the distinction, and many of their troubles—over-government, oppressive taxation, obstructive bureaucracy, weak resistance to inflation, reactionary trade unions, sluggish economic growth—arise from that failure.

The supreme virtue of private initiative in a market is that it can be built piece-meal with local and temporary experimentation, so that false steps can be retraced or reversed, and the lessons learned in new initiatives.

The contrast with the holistic method of the state economy is striking. It is best illustrated from what was hoped to be the most unsordid product of holism. In 1946 post-war Britain embarked on constructing a National Health Service. There was no knowledge of how it would work. It rested on good intentions derived from wishful thinking. Its inspiration was a schoolboy howler. Voluntary, local, piece-meal insurance, it was argued, had not worked sufficiently well to cover everyone with health insurance. Therefore, it was concluded, the solution was compulsory, national, comprehensive "insurance" for everyone.

The National Health Service is now inefficient, rigid, inhumane (the old and the mentally subnormal fare worst), authoritarian and virtually irreversible except by political earthquake. Even worse, whatever its failings in practice, it is defended emotionally in terms of its noble aim of providing everyone with medical care without payment (of what quality, or after how long a wait, is never stated). Whatever the difficulties, deficiencies and abuses in private insurance, other Western countries are refining insurance systems in which the weaknesses are openly revealed and gradually removed. The National Health Service has swept all its weaknesses under a carpet of wishful thinking, occupational vested interests that oppose change and political defensiveness which fears to lose face.

Natural scientists, although they have as technocrats often been the worst offenders in favouring state economy, should have seen through the fallacies of the social scientists who taught collectivism. The only systematic way to discover new chemical compounds in a laboratory is by experimentation. The only way to find new social stratagems that work is likewise by experimentation. That is the way of private enterprise, the scientific method, the bedrock of Western civilisation that proceeds by cautious steps to teach from experience. The alternative is the holistic solution of nationalised industry or totalitarian state economy that pretends to knowledge it lacks and then excludes reform that would demonstrate its error. Private enterprise is imperfect but redeemable. State economy promises the earth, and ends in coercion to conceal its incurable failure.

CHAPTER 5

Reversing the Tide

Some years ago, until the middle 1960s, it would have been possible to speak of the tide of collectivisation as almost irresistible. Since then, sobering experience of the Great Society in the USA, which its advocates thought would solve social problems by increasing welfare bureaucracies armed with tax money, police powers and government authority; further evidence in Britain of the ineffectiveness of government in social engineering; the results in the industrial countries of Europe of liberating human energies by reducing barriers to exchange; the prodigious success of the market oases of Asia: all these developments have gradually but fundamentally changed the attitudes of thinkers in diverse schools and of politicians in all parties to the long-repeated but never demonstrated claims for state collectivism. The move of intellectuals from the state to the market, visionary or belated, is historically remarkable. Not least there has been increasing rebellion in all social classes in almost all countries against governments that claim more taxes but fail to provide acceptable benefits in return.

Intellectual Reaction

The intellectual reaction against the state has been strongest in the USA. In Britain, the home of much that has gone wrong since the war and now of the hope that it may go right, there has been an unprecedented intellectual conversion among the leaders of the Conservative Party. But many Conservatives, some senior and influential, remain paternalists or collectivists and look nostalgically to the state to preserve a "sense of community." The senior Liberal politician has re-affirmed the classical liberal place of the market in economic policy,[1] though the official party leader remains a Beveridge-type paternalist. Not least, a former Labour Chancellor of the Exchequer has

1. Jo Grimond, *The Common Welfare,* Maurice Temple Smith, 1978.

also put a return to the market as the centre-piece of his economic policy for a new alignment of non-socialist politicians.[2]

Several more junior Labour thinkers have been vividly sensing that the ordinary people are reacting against the state. Although, not unnaturally, reaffirming their "socialist" principles, they are using a new language—or a language they had not used before their party polled a smaller percentage of votes (28 per cent) than at any time since 1931. A former Minister of Education said:

> modern democratic socialism must oppose concentrations of economic and political power whether in private or State hands. It must seek to disperse power. . . .[3]

A former Minister of Transport has said:

> What is wrong with choice and diversity? Why should enterprise and opportunity be dirty words? . . . many people see social progress as a higher net income and more money to spend on themselves.[4]

All three Party groups are, in effect, revealing the conviction that experience has at last taught them that state economy has failed and that the hope of the future lies with a large element of private enterprise despite its known defects. All three parties are thus experiencing agonising intellectual reappraisal. The post-war all-party consensus on state compassion and beneficence is increasingly contested by a classical liberal reaction against overcentralised government.

This intellectual/philosophic conversion may both reflect and confirm the public's rejection of the state, of which it has had 30 post-war years' experience. It has become disillusioned with big government, antipathetic to bureaucracy, resentful of high taxation, suspicious of monopoly whether "public" or private, in industry or among trade unions.

The Two Nations: Private Affluence, Public Squalor

All this is to be expected. It could hardly have been supposed that people accustomed to rising standards, personal service and choice in everyday personal purchases or household budgeting would have continued much longer

2. Roy Jenkins, *Home Thoughts from Abroad* (the 1979 Richard Dimbleby Lecture, first reprinted in *The Listener,* 29 November 1979), BBC Publications, December 1979.

3. Shirley Williams, "Why we lost—how to win," *Observer,* 13 May 1979.

4. William Rodgers, "A good time to learn and listen," *Guardian,* 14 May 1979.

to tolerate deteriorating standards, impersonal service and denial of choice in government-supplied monopoly transport, fuel, education, medicine, housing and a host of smaller services.

The intellectual tide has turned. Public opinion is not far behind. But the politicians lag behind both. Many seem to wait until their followers are out in front. What is now required to restore in the public mind support for the principles of competitive private enterprise sufficiently to give it the prospect of showing what it can do? There are five main requirements:

1. education—public, academic, political, industrial;
2. the removal of poverty;
3. pruning the public sector;
4. competition in the private sector;
5. new entrepreneurs.

1. Education

(a) The general public in the post-war Western world has been misled about social democracy, the welfare state, the alleged beneficence of government. It is still told by a former Labour Prime Minister that it is essential for government to supply welfare, otherwise the social fabric and family life will fail.

The two massive errors in this conventional view hardly require much emphasis. First, most people, even with middling and lower incomes, are paying in taxes, direct or indirect, more or less what they receive in social benefits. They do not therefore have to buy education, medical care (apart from public health), housing or other "social" benefits from the state.

The notion that state welfare services maintain the family is, moreover, the opposite of the truth. Family life has been weakened because the state has usurped the rôle of parents as providers. Children sense that their parents have little influence in their education, their health care, their homes, their national insurance when unemployed or sick and so on. Little wonder the bonds of the family have weakened.

Neither do transport, fuel, postal services, libraries, sports amenities, abattoirs, car-parking, home helps, employment agencies or many other goods and services have to be supplied by government, central or local. Public complaints about deteriorating standards could be shown to be based largely on a lack of consumer control because of the absence of choice between competing suppliers.

The costs of supplying services now supplied by government would often be lower in private enterprise, as they are in countries overseas. Office staff in Britain are being trained by private colleges at one-third to one-half the cost of government Further Education Colleges.

(b) Academics and teachers now in their 40s and 50s were taught 20–30 years ago by early post-war graduates who absorbed the ruling Beveridge-Bevan-Keynes consensus. They find it difficult to adapt their thinking to the adverse experience of post-war state economy, to the more recent developments among younger academics such as the "economics of politics" school who examine "government failure" as well as "market failure," or to the change in aspirations of the new generations with higher real incomes who want better services than the state aims (but fails) to supply equally out of taxes.

It seems doubtful whether most teachers or preachers in their 40s and 50s will change. They are now increasingly lagging behind events, new teaching and public sentiment and the younger generation whose world confounds their faith in the state.

(c) Many politicians of all parties, Conservative and Liberal as well as Labour, are inclined to think there is little wrong with state economy as long as *they* run it. Many Conservatives in Britain resist their Government's effort to "roll back the state." They have yet to acknowledge the massive failure of government to disentangle itself from, not least, rent control and the housing market as rising incomes make the state an increasingly embarrassing encumbrance.

(d) Industrialists accustomed or tempted to seek assistance from government naturally see the advantages but overlook the risks of gradually increasing political influence. Protected industrialists are often critical of "market forces" (that is, the men and women who are their customers). The more adventurous entrepreneurs recognise that their safety, as well as their long-term prosperity, lies in their ability to adapt themselves to changing markets. Change is uncomfortable, but political influence can be death to the independence of private enterprise. It can now rise from its knees before its detractors but must drop its crutches of political protection to regain its moral stature with public opinion. Industrial organisations could alert entrepreneurs to these dangers.

2. Removal of Poverty

The most stubborn objection to the restoration of private enterprise in services and industries now dominated by government is that some people could not pay market prices. The remedy is not "free" services but to top up low incomes so that all can pay. This task has not yet been faced or solved, even by governments that value private enterprise.

The ultimate solution lies in a form of reverse (or negative) income tax and a structure of vouchers.

3. Pruning the Public Sector

When poverty has been removed it will be easier to prune the public sector of the services that could be farmed out or returned to private enterprise. They include parts of the transport and fuel industries, much of education, medical care, all of housing, many welfare services and a wide range of local authority activities misdescribed as "public services." Where such services are supplied or controlled by government, their claim to be competently managed and sensitive to consumer preferences would be securely based only where they are not protected from competing private enterprise in a free market. Even where very large economies of scale limit enterprises to a few, possibly to two or three in small countries, general government surveillance combined with private commercially-motivated management may give better results than direct government administration of day-to-day activities. Government is better confined to *government*—laying down the framework of general law, but not detailed rules—for private enterprise; it is rarely better than private enterprise in running competitive business, especially in international markets. Even if it were as efficient as private enterprise, its Achilles' Heel is its political inability to disengage itself from involvement when technical or social change renders it superfluous. Private enterprise in a market has to change gear, accelerate, decelerate and reverse. Government is not designed for flexibility, loss-cutting, reversibility. Its engine is used too long, its gears tend to jam, its brakes fade, and it has no reverse gear.

Government should largely confine itself to "public goods"—defence, law and order, environmental protection and other activities that require finance by taxation because their benefits cannot be refused to people who refuse to pay in prices. The remainder is better left to private enterprise to finance by charging. The dividing line between public and private goods is not always sharply defined; a practical working rule-of-thumb is: tax where you must (because pricing is impracticable); charge where you can. This rule yields approximate results, a kind of rough justice. But contrasted with the deficiencies, inefficiencies, inflexibility and corruption of government in state economy it scores very high. Of that the history of the West since the Industrial Revolution, and especially since the 1939–45 war, leaves no doubt.

There is thus a large field for the expansion of private enterprise. Unless it is envisaged that the Western countries will huddle behind their home markets artificially protected by tariff walls, more of the activities of private firms will be subject to competition from imports. Expansion into formerly "public" services should be welcomed by private enterprise as new markets with a measure of natural "protection" from overseas competition. This new scope for private enterprise has been neglected because of outdated political and sociological arguments for state (or municipal) supply.

4. Competition in the Private Sector

Private enterprise entails risks—of changing consumer preferences, technical innovation, new firms, new ideas. Enterprise is vindicated only if it faces these risks and earns the rewards of success. It must therefore not expect to be protected from competition, internal or external, when market conditions change. There is no lasting safety in resisting change. The search for "security" ends in suppressing progress. Economic systems that cannot cope with uncertainty do not survive.

The best hope for private enterprise lies rather in international accord to remove the plausible reasons for complaint—selling below cost to gain temporary advantage, etc., rather than in sheltering behind tariffs that encourage sluggish reactions to change in overseas markets. There is no lasting refuge, especially by small countries, in excluding imports, except possibly to bargain for *reduction* of trade barriers. Protection of high-cost industries against imports is, in any event, a crude instrument: it may preserve jobs at the expense of shrivelling living standards. Protective devices should be used, *if at all* (and that is a strong reservation, since it cannot be assumed that government will so use them), for the very opposite from their conventional purpose—to remove rather than erect trade barriers.

5. New Entrepreneurs

In post-war Britain and other Western countries too many university graduates have gone into teaching, "public" services and social work, and not enough into private enterprise. No doubt this is in part the result of the 20th-century version of the 18th-century aversion to "trade," but intensified by the sociologists' condemnation of private enterprise, profit-making, advertising and commerce in general. Living standards can be maintained and raised only by using human and natural resources to produce goods and services wanted by the world. National self-sufficiency has retarded or destroyed economic growth and reduced living standards. The market inducement of profit and capital gains would encourage individuals to make a more than proportionate contribution to prosperity and rising living standards for all.

CHAPTER 6

Finale: Summary and Policy

1. Private enterprise is the source of economic growth and rising living standards because it works with the grain of human nature expressed through voluntary exchange in the market.

2. For over a century private enterprise has been the object of intellectual assault based on contempt for public preferences and unfounded faith in the power of government. In all Western countries the people have been misled by a small number of intellectuals who taught the erroneous contrast between the "*market* failure" of capitalism and the theoretical but nowhere realised achievement of state economy. Their power over public opinion has now been undermined in all Western countries by experience of the "*government* failure" of state economy. Experience has caught up with ideas thought wildly premature 10—even five—years ago. Economists ignored by knowing "practical men" are being heard—belatedly.

3. The lessons of this experience can now be reinforced by education of employees, men and women in public life, the bureaucracy, the press and broadcasting, not least the general public.

4. Government is necessary only for the supply of public goods, but it is a necessary evil since its authority is easily abused even by well-meaning men and asserted by increasing coercion. On the side of demand it tends to neglect or over-ride public preferences. On the side of supply it tends either to retard technological advance by creating monopoly and protecting established industries or to inflate technological possibilities beyond their economic optimum at grievous hidden costs borne by the public—as in the Anglo-French Concorde, the British National Health Service's extravagant use of resources in spectacular surgery, the Russian and American investment in space research and the expenditure of poor, developing countries on prestigious but uneconomic industry and airlines.

5. Private enterprise is a more invigorating avocation than administering others from a government office. It engages the most stimulating faculties in a battle of wits with the consumer—not to outwit but to anticipate and serve him. It can be made to appeal to young people anxious for adventure. And their sympathies can be engaged by showing that it alone produces the wealth from which to help the developing countries establish their own market economies to raise their living standards.

6. The choice for private enterprise is to be indebted to the politician, and fall under his influence, or to serve the consumer, and retain independence from eventual political subservience. Government protection tends to make private enterprise neither private nor enterprising. It would produce the corporate state by sliding into government "power-sharing" with "representatives" of industry and trade unions.

7. Private enterprise requires to encourage and facilitate labour mobility. Maintaining high employment independently of market conditions requires inflationary budget deficits and debilitating balance-of-payments deficits and retards the long-run rise in living standards.

8. The effort of government to organise society from the centre has had a long trial and has failed. It has ended by concealing and trying to escape from the reality of supply and demand—technological change and public preferences. The only policy that can satisfy the aspirations of the people of free societies is to work with the market by nurturing private enterprise.

9. Government failure is incorrigible; market failure is corrigible.

10. To strengthen private enterprise in a market economy we have to
    (a) remove poverty once for all by reverse income taxes and voucher systems as the means to eventual reduction in taxes;
    (b) replace benefits in kind by benefits in cash;
    (c) charge for "public" services and let private enterprise try to replace them at lower cost;
    (d) confine government to its unique function of providing public goods;
    (e) remove protective devices from private enterprise, especially where it serves a large internal market, such as transport, because they discourage efficiency, expansion and growth by tolerating second-rate technology, management, financing and marketing;
    (f) enable private enterprise to progress from manufacturing to services where manpower is deployed more effectively to satisfy demand at home or from overseas;

(g) encourage the opportunities for profits to indicate, in competitive conditions, where earnings are high so that more capital could be used productively;

(h) as industry is made competitive, remove legal privileges that enable trade unions to drive wage costs beyond output, reduce employment, discourage investment and retard improvements in living standards;

(i) use emigration as an index and a danger-signal that living standards have been depressed below those obtainable in culturally comparable countries;

(j) as industry adapts itself to changing technology and markets, ease labour mobility by insurance, loans for removal to new jobs and areas and by restoring a free market in housing;

(k) agree with like-minded nations to remove subsidies to exports and the remaining barriers that obstruct mutually beneficial international exchange.

A Short Reading List

Buchanan, J. M., *The Calculus of Consent* (with Gordon Tullock), University of Michigan Press, Ann Arbor, 1962.

———, *Limits of Liberty,* University of Chicago Press, Chicago, 1975.

Buchanan, J. M., *et al., The Economics of Politics,* IEA Readings No. 18, Institute of Economic Affairs, London, 1978.

Gilmour, Ian, *Inside Right,* Quartet Books, London, 1977.

Grimond, Jo., *The Common Welfare,* Maurice Temple Smith, London, 1978.

Hayek, F. A., *Collectivist Economic Planning,* Routledge & Kegan Paul, London, 1935.

———, *Law, Legislation and Liberty,* Vols. I, II, III, Routledge & Kegan Paul, London, 1972–79.

Hobsbawm, E. J., *Industry & Empire,* Weidenfeld & Nicolson, London, 1968.

Jenkins, Roy, *Home Thoughts from Abroad* (The 1979 Richard Dimbleby Lecture), BBC Publications, London, 1979.

Joseph, Sir Keith, and Sumption, Jonathan, *Equality,* John Murray, London, 1979.

Laski, Harold, *Liberty and the Modern State,* Faber, London, 1930.

Lenin, V., *State and Revolution* (British Socialist Party, 1919), Revised Edition, Central Books, London, 1972.

Marx, K., *Das Kapital* (Sonnenschein, 1887), Penguin Books, Harmondsworth, Middlesex, Vol. I, 1976, Vol. II, 1978.

Morris, William, *How I Became a Socialist,* Pelican, Penguin Books, Harmondsworth, Middlesex, 1962 Edn.

Nove, Alec, *An Economic History of the USSR,* Penguin Books, Harmondsworth, Middlesex, 1969.

Seldon, Arthur, *Charge,* Temple Smith, London, 1977.

———, *Everyman's Dictionary of Economics* (with the late F. G. Pennance), J. M. Dent, London, 2nd edition, 1976, Paperback edition, 1980.

———, *Over-ruled on Welfare* (with Lord Harris of High Cross), Hobart Paperback No. 13, Institute of Economic Affairs, 1979.

Strachey, John, *The Nature of Capitalist Crisis,* Gollancz, London, 1936.

Tawney, R. H., *Equality* (1931), Allen & Unwin, London, New Edn., 1965.

Thompson, E. P., *The Making of the English Working Class,* Pelican Edn., Penguin Books, Harmondsworth, Middlesex, 1968.

Tullock, Gordon, *The Vote Motive,* Hobart Paperback No. 9, Institute of Economic Affairs, London, 1976.

———, *Private Wants, Public Means,* Basic Books, New York, 1970.

Titmuss, R. M., *The Gift Relationship,* Allen & Unwin, London, 1970.

Webb, S. & B., *Soviet Communism: A New Civilisation,* Longman, London, 1937.

PART II

Capitalism

I dedicate this book to

Marjorie Seldon

who provided a family ambience
of selfless love and devotion
in our forty-two years of
companionship in marriage

FOREWORD

Reading Arthur Seldon's powerful book has been educational, challenging and painful. It is painful to acknowledge the truth that, however badly capitalism may sometimes function, it has produced the goods and services that the overwhelming majority have found beneficial. To maximize the benefits of the choices that capitalism creates, we must choose wisely, and some are financially and educationally advantaged in making their choices. Yet, overall, the market society is the freest system devised by man.

My own experience of the good intentions of government is that they are, to say the least, disappointing. I also have experience of the hypocrisy of people on the Left who want to liberate the workers, but one at a time, and themselves first. The Russian, and more recently the Chinese, experience shows that the end-product of their endeavours leaves us with societies in which no-one is able to challenge the mistakes of the leaders.

I have to conclude that Arthur's basic message is right. Socialism as it has thus far been practised does not work. The new Soviet man we were promised has not been born, and he is unlikely ever to appear. Arthur's challenge to those of us who had hopes of socialism is this: take advantage of capitalism and all its works. The freedoms it offers are opportunities to all of us, in all "classes" and parties, to improve upon what it provides. In the end this is the only protection for those whom the system fails, or who fail the system. Those failures, however, do not justify the political exploitation of those who seek power. The book lends objectivity to both the vices and the virtues of capitalism. It thus thrusts a dagger into the heart of socialism. The perfect society does not work.

I have long been of the opinion that neither the friends nor the foes of the market will in the last analysis have much influence over its success or failure. For, notwithstanding the intellectual argument, markets flourish wherever people forgather. The art of making a mutually agreeable exchange leads to greater satisfaction than winning arguments about the morals of society.

The book is bound to arouse criticism from those who, having liberated themselves, live on a higher moral plane than the rest of us who have to be satisfied with much simpler virtues. This is a timely and instructive book. It ought to be read especially by those on the Left who will dislike its message.

Lord Chapple of Hoxton

PREFACE

Capitalism requires not defence but celebration. Its achievement in creating high and rising living standards for the masses without sacrificing personal liberty speaks for itself. Only the deaf will not hear and the blind will not see.

Its achievement prevails over its defects. Yet its critics continue decade after decade to be preoccupied if not obsessed with its defects. Even those who acknowledge its achievement continue to urge the alternative of socialism without reason or demonstration from world experience to suppose it could equal and surpass capitalism.

Until recently the critics of capitalism, predominantly the socialist-minded, both academics and politicians, were united. Academics characteristically discover defects in order to propose solutions. Politicians deploy the defects to present themselves as leaders in implementing the solutions.

Of late the academics and the politicians have been parting company. The academics continue to emphasize the defects of capitalism and to urge the solution they call socialism, recently modified and strengthened by the capitalist instrument of the market. They proclaim as new truths about the market old truths they once rejected as falsehoods. The politicians have found that the academics' original solution of socialism was a failure. It did not work. It does not produce high and rising living standards, and it adds insult to injury by suppressing personal liberties. The socialist politicians are therefore abandoning the socialist solution, and turning to the capitalism they once rejected and suppressed.

The politicians' rejection of the socialist solution is strongest where it was applied most rigorously—where living standards lagged most obviously, and liberties were suppressed most severely—in the communist or socialist countries of Europe and Asia. Where the socialist solution was applied with least disruption of capitalism, in the United Kingdom and Europe, so that living standards lagged least and liberties survived best, politicians who had adopted and long urged the socialist solution make reluctant and qualified obeisance to the achievements of capitalism but continue to urge what they still call "socialism," but latterly accompanied by qualifying adjectives—"supply-side" socialism, "individualist" socialism etc.—that disguise past errors, with the additional claim that they will make more and better use of capitalism. The academics, who respect truth more than expediency, are more honest in their acknowledgement of the achievement of capitalism, admonish their politicians (and students) that they can no longer deride capitalism and indicate more rigorous conditions for the incorporation of its techniques into their still favoured socialism.

This book is a salute to the economic system that has displayed two centuries of steady though fluctuating development despite wars, rumours of wars, political convulsions, bloody revolutions and, most damaging, unremitting condemnation by the world's outstanding philosophers and scientists that has misled the people everywhere. It is also a celebration of its intellectual triumph over its alternative—the socialism that is fading by dilution and is being rejected by the people in every continent.

Capitalism is triumphant because it rests on the elemental urges and aspirations of the common people everywhere, from the industrial West to the ancient civilizations of the East, from the older world of Europe to the new world of North America, from recently feudal Russia to emerging Africa. Socialism is failing because it rests on three errors of the academics: that the defects of capitalism were incapable of being removed from within, that it required to be replaced *in toto* by a very different system of organizing human activity and that the only alternative was socialism.

Capitalism has triumphed finally in the late twentieth century because the teachings of socialist thinkers of various types in the United Kingdom and Europe induced the people to tolerate experiments with socialism of varying kinds until recent years. But the socialist politicians, who wax in the political processes of socialism, have everywhere failed to harness the technological advances accelerated by the Second World War to provide rising living standards; they have dissipated much of it in power-seeking adventures and the conspicuous self-aggrandizement of incalculable scientific opportunism in space research and other extravaganzas at the expense of the living standards of the people, not least the poorest.

In setting out to salute and celebrate capitalism the book has emerged with two elements in sharper focus than intended at the outset. The assessment of the central, indispensable and indestructible role of the market and the market process has had to conclude that the culprit in preventing it, so far, from realizing its potential is the political process. Even bad men are led by the market process to do good, but good men are induced by the political process to do harm. The conclusion is that the solution for the defects of capitalism is not to jettison it, which would sacrifice the irreplaceable good with the dispensable bad, and which cannot be done without coercion, but to discipline the writ of politics to the bare minimum. The object has to be not the "limited" state, based on no clear principle of the functions of government, but the minimal state, based on the principle that government shall do only what it must. And this solution also minimizes socialism.

The second element in unanticipated focus is the criticism of socialist opinion about capitalism. I set out to write on the fundamental relative economic strengths and weaknesses of capitalism but have had to reject continuing unremitting error in socialist writing by outstanding, often distinguished, academics. In his classic on *The Relation between Law and Public Opinion in England* A.V. Dicey anticipated J. M. Keynes's emphasis on the power of ideas "both when they are right and when they are wrong." The unrelenting impenitent, immodest flood of writing on the grandeur of socialist ideas over a century has, until very recently, obscured the merits of capitalism. I have been more severe than I intended on the intellectuals who condemned capitalism both when it was good and when it was bad, and influenced political and public opinion in favour of socialism when it was bad as well as when it was good (or rather unavoidable in the "public goods," a misleading term that I argue should be replaced by the morally neutral and more informative "unavoidably collective functions").

I now see the socialist mind in all parties as turning the common people away from their true inheritance of prosperity and dignity under capitalism. Able and well-meaning thinkers and writers with diverse political labels have been the misleading Moses who made empty promises, wasted 150 years and deferred the promised land. Some of the best minds of my lifetime and to this day have embraced the false faith that socialism would emancipate the people. But when they could see it did not, many persisted in teaching its errors. Throughout my life, and especially in my 30 years of sponsoring economic liberalism at the Institute of Economic Affairs, I saw the liberal intellectual inheritance dismissed as outdated superstition, liberal scholars derided as enemies of the people, "lackeys of capitalism," young liberal academics cold-shouldered by their collectivist-minded colleagues at universities and liberal writers dismissed as uncomprehending ignoramuses. I intended to follow the advice Hayek enjoined on liberals: *suaviter in modo, fortiter in re*—mild in manner, strong in argument. I had in mind the advice I gave others to assail the errors, not the perpetrators.

Yet in reflecting on the continuing power of ideas in the persistent derision of capitalism, I have been led into counter-criticism of socialist arguments that may offend their authors. It has been especially puzzling to witness the insouciance, the hubris, perhaps better expressed in colloquial English as the gall, with which the socialist solution is periodically revised, redefined and, most recently in the late 1980s, reconstructed to shed socialism and incorporate capitalism, yet newly presented as the latest form of the benevolent socialist alternative to what the American socialist academic Professor Robert Lekachman has called "depraved" capitalism.

I have therefore not withdrawn criticism of the mostly middle-class academics and writers who, for over a century since the time of Sidney and Beatrice Webb to this day, urged socialist solutions without suffering their coercions nor their forgone living standards, but who continued their comfortable lives as teachers in state-financed universities, politicians in state or local government, administrators in state institutions, writers of "fiction" that transparently condemned capitalism or beneficiaries of government grants in academia, the arts and cultural life provided in part by the poor whose living standards their teaching and administrations have repressed.

Yet some, applauded in these pages, are compensating for the wasted years of conventional socialism by advising their followers to purge their errors. I address the arguments here, more in sorrow than in anger, to the able men and women who now see the socialist fallacies, misjudgements and self-deceptions, and maintain the socialist faith with diminishing conviction. Error can be contested; faith is impregnable.

The central theme maintained here is that political democracy is not enough. The market is a better guarantee of popular freedom. People the world over, as the USSR, China and all the communist/socialist countries are discovering, do not work harder or better because they have votes but because there are goods in the shops. In the minds of the people the capitalist system has finally triumphed over socialism. Yet, if capitalism is to yield its best results, so far unrealized anywhere, the political process must be confined to the minimal duties of the state.

The central arguments are intentionally repeated in varying contexts and with varying illustrations because they are rare in, or absent from, the continuing voluminous writings of the socialist-minded under numerous doctrinal or party labels.

The occasional personal episodes are introduced to enliven and dramatize the otherwise abstract argument.

Arthur Seldon

ACKNOWLEDGEMENTS

My main debt is to Marjorie and Peter Seldon for urging me to work on the book after I withdrew from active service at the Institute of Economic Affairs in June 1988. Marjorie Seldon read the drafts, indicated improvements, supplied material for several passages and proposed literary allusions to support the argument. My more personal debt to her is recorded in the dedication.

Peter Seldon, a new entrepreneur of the reinvigorated capitalism of the 1980s, provided the Honeywell Bull word processor and the Hewlett Packard laser printer, technological masterpieces without which this book would have been even more demanding of time and endurance.

I have to thank several readers of early drafts for suggestions and criticisms who may not share and bear no responsibility for my judgements and opinions, not least my profound scepticism on the role of government. Ralph (Lord) Harris's annotations on manner and matter, echoing our 32 years' collaboration, persuaded me to amplify or clarify the argument. Professor Patrick Minford's reaction to a sample of chapters served as a timely admonition to anticipate criticism. Professor Stephen Haseler pointed to political arguments I might emphasize. Frank (Lord) Chapple suggested objections from the Left I should meet. I tested extracts on Dr. Joanna Seldon who reacted helpfully. Ronald Stevens responded shrewdly to extracts as a former teacher of the history of the physical infrastructure, and as a bonus reminded me of the minimal government of Robert Walpole. Dr. David Green reacted to, and supplied information from his scholarly researches for, chapter 11. Chris Tame read the text and checked the references; his unequalled knowledge of the literature of liberty contributed to the Descriptive Guide to Readings. My other old IEA colleagues, John Raybould and Ken Smith, helped with the detail of sources. Ruth Croxford patiently tutored me in learning to master the word processor and prevented the disaster of losing drafts I thought I had "saved." Not least I have to thank John Davey, Rene Olivieri,

Mark Allin and several others at Basil Blackwell for guiding me in preparation of the material for publication.

As I worked with no research assistance while writing the book I can attribute to no-one, but regret in advance, the remaining errors in recollection of detail that survived checking but do not impair the substance of the argument.

The book can be seen as a testament of personal philosophy, with the illustrative episodes as pages from an autobiography. In a sentence I was persuaded into economic liberalism by intellectual conviction and the evidence of events and into Liberal Party sympathy because the Conservatives were too socialist and the socialists too conservative.

AS

Godden Green, Kent

CHAPTER 1

The Stake

> If we ask what men most owe to the moral practices of those who are called capitalists the answer is: their very lives . . . most of the Western proletariat, and most of the millions of the developing world, owe their existence to opportunities that advanced countries have created for them.
>
> Communist countries such as Russia would be starving today if their populations were not kept alive by the Western world . . .
>
> F. A. Hayek, *The Fatal Conceit*

The assessment in this book of capitalism by its mechanisms and institutions, potential as well as present, derives from a lifetime of reflection which began with antipathy and has changed to wonder and gratitude.

The approach is to emphasize the fundamental features of capitalism, its strengths and weaknesses, rather than the refinements of the arguments for and against it, the stuff of the continuing and fluctuating debate and revision among its academic supporters as well as between them and its opponents, but unlikely to disturb judgement on the ultimate superiority of imperfect capitalism over imperfect socialism.

Whatever the weight of current, often ephemeral, argument from the thinkers and writers, the politicians and preachers, capitalism emerges in markets official or unofficial, legal or illegal, in socialist as well as capitalist economies, because it is the instrument which people in all societies and stages of economic development instinctively use to escape from want and enrich one another by exchange. It is the natural growth that finds a way through, under or over the pervious concrete of coercion that men with power erect to enforce their pretentious imaginings of political perfection. And the market is a capitalist instrument that requires the responsible private opportunities and rewards, the risks and penalties of individual ownership and judgement, not a socialist instrument subject to the irresponsible mercurial collective decisions of "public" men or women who control other people's resources but are ultimately impelled, like the rest of fallible mankind, to put their personal interests first.

I judge the wood rather than the trees, though I have tried to cut out dead socialist and conservative trees to envisage the liberal wood. The finer points in abstract analysis, essential to me as a student and always of stimulus, are dissected at length in the numerous books on both sides of the argument. The latest, and the best in stating the essence of the case for and against capitalism and socialism, both published in the late 1980s, are Professor Frederick Hayek's life testament in *The Fatal Conceit*[1] and Professor Raymond Plant's scholarly contribution to *Conservative Capitalism in Britain and the United States.*[2] Hayek's book is sub-titled "The Errors of Socialism." Plant's chapters, which repay study by liberals, set out as a critique of capitalism but ended with advice to socialists to adopt its techniques; the final sections in effect reveal the errors of socialists.

Yet the necessary continuing refinement of the intellectual trees has tended to obscure the comparative natures, forms and shapes of the capitalist and socialist woods, and to distract attention from their underlying strengths and weaknesses.

Throughout a working life of observation, research and the application of economic thinking to industry and government, the more I have studied the case for capitalism, the stronger it has seemed, and the more I have read the case for socialism, the weaker it has emerged. I now wonder how socialism ever seemed as formidable as it once did. It was always impressive in its promises but everywhere disappointing in its performance.

A discussion of principles is necessarily couched in generalizations, except that I have tried to illustrate them from the real world. All generalizations can be contested, as many will be here, but they can also be defended.

Capitalist Principles and Political Practice

The argument for an economic system is not absolute but relative. The world, its countries and its peoples can choose between capitalism and socialism. If they cannot, if the Marxists are right in supposing that the collapse of capitalism is (periodically or intermittently) imminent and the triumph of socialism repeatedly inevitable, there would be little purpose in writing

1. F. A. Hayek, *The Fatal Conceit*, Routledge, 1988.

2. Kenneth Hoover and Raymond Plant, *Conservative Capitalism in Britain and the United States*, Routledge, 1989.

for or against either capitalism or socialism with the intention of influencing politicians and the public to favour one or the other. To put the case for one is, in this sense, to imply the case against the other. Hayek's case against socialism is, in effect, the case for capitalism. Plant's case against capitalism is the case for socialism.

Hayek's case against socialism is the most subtle of his long intellectual life. Plant's case against capitalism is the most persuasive among socialist writings so far because it is based on a rare attempt to understand the capitalist market and to rescue economic liberalism intellectually from political authoritarianism, with which it is much confused in recent critiques of the so-called "New Right."

For decades after the war the writings of the opponents of capitalism dominated the British (but not the American) academic and literary scenes. Samuel Brittan led the professional observers with the most profound examination of the essentials of capitalism. Changing the title of the 1972 first edition of *Capitalism and the Permissive Society* to *A Restatement of Economic Liberalism* for the 1988 second edition clarified the distinction between classical philosophy and contemporary application in "politically possible" forms.[3] It should strengthen the changing mood to consider the immutable principles of political economy as well as the changing policies of practical government, the innovation begun among politicians on the Conservative side by Sir Geoffrey Howe in the early 1960s followed by Lord (then Sir Keith) Joseph and encouraged by Mrs. Margaret Thatcher in the mid-1970s, by Dr. David Owen among the Labour "defectors" in the early 1980s and by Bryan Gould, the former academic at Oxford, and Roy Hattersley among socialist-thinking Labour unrepentants later in the mid-1980s. The socialist critics of capitalism can no longer discredit it by emphasizing, however justifiably, the misdeeds of non-socialist or Conservative governments.

Capitalism has been traduced and defamed; yet the belated recent recognitions of its accomplishments are reluctant and the acknowledgements anonymous.

In recent years the critics have been more ready to examine the arguments for economic liberalism as they have seen the increasing influence of market analysis on political thinking in all schools of thought, even the Marxist, and on the policies of all political parties, even the British Labour Party. It may still suit their defence of socialism and their counter-attack on capitalism to

3. Samuel Brittan, *Capitalism and the Permissive Society*, 1972; *A Restatement of Economic Liberalism*, Macmillan, 1988.

move vicariously or tactically from examining the principles of economic liberalism, which they now treat with respect, to condemning the practice of political Conservatism, which they find more vulnerable. But the debate now increasingly joined between the academics, who are interested in the fundamentals of capitalism and socialism in order to arrive at the truth, is yielding more of value than the dispute between the political tacticians and the politically minded on their achievements and failings in government that rarely produce lasting conclusions for policy.

Capitalism: Past, Present and Future

The liberal critic of socialism confronts the destructive defence that socialism has not yet been established anywhere. Therefore, runs the implication, criticisms of alleged socialist economies, from Sweden to China, leave the case for socialism unimpaired. It remains inviolate above the vulgar debate of the day.

This defence is deceptive. Socialism as it has been is in its essentials socialism as it must be. Its defects are the consequences of its principles and its institutions.

Not so with capitalism. The system of markets, private property rights, decentralized power and individual responsibility for human behaviour is now increasingly examined for the lessons it can teach its opponents as well as its supporters, rather than cast into outer darkness to eternal damnation. But its lessons will be lost if it is judged solely by its past and not also by its possible future.

Both socialist writing in condemnation of capitalism as well as liberal writing in its defence are often historical rather than analytical. Capitalism is judged by its accomplishments or its failures in the past. It is time to assess its potential in a future of unprecedented technological change, social advance and the revolution in individual aspirations as well as expectations.

The treatment here of general principles, illustrated by personal experiences and impressions in 50 years of consuming intellectual interest in politico-economic systems, reinforced by working in capitalist industry, emphasizes the three main strengths of capitalism: its unequalled vitality in recovering from adverse conditions in war and peace, its unrivalled power, acknowledged by Marx, to produce goods and services for the sustenance and comfort of mankind, and its unique advantage for the common populace of replacing their subjection to authoritarian or paternalistic politics by the populist democracy of the market.

The study and research were conducted mainly at the London School of Economics (LSE) from 1934 to 1941 and at the Institute of Economic Affairs (IEA) from 1957 to 1988. Lessons were drawn from the socialist interregnum of experience in the army at war between 1941 and 1945, and from work in industry between 1946 and 1957, as editor of an independent journal in large-scale retailing and an economic adviser in the (misnamed) brewing industry, which in my ten years was concerned relatively more with property and investment, marketing and taxation, competition and social change, food and soft drinks, than with alcoholic beverages.

The interlude from 1941 to 1945 in North Africa and Italy provided experience of living under the opposite of capitalism, the socialism of the army, a planned economy directed from the top, necessarily because it was a "public good" (redefined here as an unavoidably collective function). The wartime civilian economy was also run on socialist lines, with rationing of essential or basic foods, clothing, fuel and other items according to "need" (one of the most dangerous euphemisms in the sociological vocabulary, a misnomer for a political decision based on questionable advice by idiosyncratic or paternalistic experts). The distribution system of wartime civilian life was arguably unavoidable in war, but became a scourge in peace. For a few months I was a minor cog in the socialist civilian machine when a group of economists from the LSE under Professor (later Sir) Arnold Plant (no relation to Raymond Plant) ran the Wartime Social Survey to inform Churchill and the War Cabinet of civilian reaction to rationing and other wartime socialist expedients.

Civilian socialism was more objectionable because less unavoidable than military socialism. The liberal Professor Lord Robbins argued in post-war lectures[4] that military socialism was regrettably tolerable in the exceptional circumstances of war. Yet its doctrinal supporters in all political parties, eager to continue and make it permanent, ignored his warnings and the high costs—in bureaucracy, untraceable inefficiency, arbitrary allocation between individuals, jobbery, bribery, corruption and encouragement of underground trading—that made it unsuitable for peace.

These defects were severe. Yet in retrospect it is possible to see that the most damaging consequence of wartime and post-war socialism was that, once installed, it could not adjust itself to the changing conditions, opportunities and public preferences of the peacetime decades. Its political

4. Lionel Robbins, *The Economic Problem in Peace and War,* Macmillan, 1947.

sponsors, its managers and its beneficiaries developed vested interests, organized to protect them, intimidated government by "rent-seeking" (nothing to do with housing rents: a term used by the new economics of politics for the privileges extracted from the political process without serving the tax-paying public) and distorted the economy away from serving the consumer who pays by taxes or prices.

War and Peace

The decisive argument against the peacetime socialism that still lingers after 40 years into the 1990s is that it was based on the wrong lesson, drawn mainly by the socialist school of sociologists and accepted by most politicians, that the production and distribution system of war had worked so well that it should be extended into the peace. This was the main source of the fallacy that generated post-war socialism in the form of nationalization and state welfare. During the war and after it, when I joined the IEA and had time to study the activities of the state in financial management, industry and welfare, it was evident that the decisive error of wartime thinking, as in the Beveridge Report on social services, and post-war policy was to draw the wrong conclusion from the wartime experience.

From the war years, I had drawn the lesson that wartime socialism would not suit the ethos or opportunities of peace. Politicians of all parties, not only in Britain, drew the opposite conclusion. Despite the forgotten warning of the essentially liberal Beveridge, but influenced by pre-war Fabian and post-war sociological thinking, activated by the prospect of electoral support and encouraged by bureaucrats who shrewdly saw increased demand for their services, they concluded and preached that the methods of war were appropriate to peace. Their state socialism, urged or accepted in all political parties and opportunistically described as "nationalization" or "public ownership," two of the most confusing euphemisms in the political vocabulary with their implication of serving public rather than private interests, continued until the late 1980s, long after its inadequacies were revealed, long after it has been outdated by scientific innovation and social advance, and long after it has been rejected by the people wherever they can escape from it. The opinion polling that has found a predilection for state services even at the expense of higher taxes is based on the economic error, which students learn to avoid in their first year, of supposing that preferences can be stated in ignorance of price and on the optical illusion that the higher taxes would be paid by other taxpayers: political "compassion" is made to seem cheap, and encourages irresponsible voting (chapter 13).

The continuation of wartime thinking into post-war policy further strengthened the growing conviction in the 1950s that decentralized private capitalism would have freed itself from the crisis economy of the war more expeditiously and more smoothly, with less friction and discord, than centralized politicized socialism, which postponed the adaptations to peace and made the eventual adjustments more disruptive and convulsive. By now, in the 1990s, we should have developed fuel, transport and other industries and education, medical care, housing, pensions and other welfare services more appropriate to the twenty-first century than the lingering nationalized industries and services that remain after 40 years despite the change in the direction of government policy since 1979.

Economic Advance Obstructed by the Political Process

A stubborn obstacle to the further advance of capitalism, little understood in contemporary debate, is the political process in which public opinion and preferences are translated only indirectly and very imperfectly into government thinking and policy.

Adjustment of the economy as a whole, and of individual industries and firms, to changing conditions of supply and demand both at home and in the outside world, not least in Europe, is everywhere hobbled for short-term party advantage unavoidable in a regime of frequent elections, arbitrary contacts between electors and representatives, the influence of bureaucratic expertise on inexperienced ministers and short parliaments punctuated by periodic by-elections which reflect and project transient events and passing moods more than long-term economic trends and underlying public philosophies, a flaw reflected in and exacerbated by opinion-polling that is especially irresponsible when it investigates preferences without supplying the prices of the alternatives between which citizens are asked to choose.

However public-spirited, patriotic and far-sighted, politicians can plausibly justify or logically rationalize the necessity to take short-term steps to stay in office and complete their work by excluding the harmful opposition. The opposition, similarly public-spirited, patriotic and far-sighted, opposes government on principle; thus, almost every announcement of a reduction in work-forces is condemned as inhuman and callous. Job protection has became a political holy grail and a by-election imperative. Every party must show environmental anxiety. Marching activists must be placated. Farmers damaged by ministerial statements, true or false, must be salvaged. Looming elections must be heralded by myopic inflations.

If this is the working of representative democracy, its machinery must be re-examined to make it more representative of the long-run interest of the people than of the short-run interests of pressure groups: the rent-seekers have been allowed continuing influence on government under capitalism to extract indirectly from unsuspecting taxpayers monies they could not persuade knowing consumers to pay directly in the market.

The Acceptable Faces of Capitalism

The weaknesses of capitalism are acceptable because they are far outweighed by its strengths. The former Conservative Prime Minister who spoke of the "unacceptable face of capitalism" implied that it had acceptable faces but rarely identified or commended them.

The faults—relative poverty, inequity, injustice, unemployment, inflation and more—that have appeared in the past will reappear, modified by experience, even in the most ideal form of capitalism in the future. They are a product of unpredictable social and technological change, fallible humans, incomplete knowledge and imperfect political institutions, and they recur in more objectionable form under socialism. They are easier to correct, if only partially, under capitalism. They are the price to pay both for the productivity and recurring opportunity that have kept populations alive and for the liberty and human dignity that make life worth living. The man or woman who says that the defects of capitalism can be abolished under socialism is misleading mankind by faith unfulfilled.

The discussion has therefore had to be about socialism as well as capitalism. The case against capitalism as we have known it has often been made by asserting strong claims for socialism. The case for capitalism is not that it is faultless but that its deficiencies are easier to correct than those of its alternatives, which in practice are all variants of socialism. The arguments against capitalism are legion. Some are valid. The defenders of capitalism weaken their case by denying them. Defending the indefensible in capitalism is not the way to vindicate its superiority over socialism.

There is no way yet discovered to rid capitalism, completely, continually and permanently, of destabilizing contractions or expansions, inflations and deflations, unemployment or overfull employment, inequality or poverty, monopolies or restrictive practices, uncovenanted beneficial or damaging social (external) costs on innocent third parties. Some defects (fluctuations) are unavoidable: some (monopolies) are mostly temporary, certainly more so than under socialism; some (inequalities) are necessary for the incentives to make it work and just because equal incomes for people in unequal circumstances ("needs") would be inequality and injustice.

The defects could in time be reduced by the removal of political barriers to gradual market adjustment. To deny or make light of the defects is to lose the argument to the socialist who easily and eloquently, by printed fact in the press or spoken "faction" in the theatre, demonstrates them from contemporary experience. The *Cathy Come Homes* of the contemporary theatre are more a reflection on the authors for misreading the causes of homelessness or other social deficiencies than on the capitalism distorted by the politically prolonged rent-restriction and other government failures of half a century. The author of *Cathy Come Home*, Jeremy Seabrook, an embattled socialist critic of capitalism, is reported by *The Sunday Times Magazine* as working on a documentary, *Cathy's Not Come Home*, for BBC TV, which often emphasizes the shortcomings of capitalism.

The more fruitful course for the defender of capitalism is to concede its defects but to explain them as the result of human and natural conditions common to mankind everywhere. Capitalism is relatively superior because socialism not only suffers from the same or similar defects—unemployment, inflation, inequality, poverty, externalities—but also compounds the offence by disguising their symptoms and suppressing their evidence. It thus makes them more difficult to mitigate or minimize. The belated *glasnost* in the autocratic socialism of the USSR began to create openness in public discussion after nearly 70 years, but the failures of democratic socialism in Western Europe were concealed by government subsidies to the inefficient or the strong-armed, by "managed" statistics and not least by the economic underground to which it drove its citizens.

These are the reasons why it is relevant and necessary to discuss socialism in a book on capitalism.

Socialism in Capitalism; Capitalism in Socialism

Concentration on the dominant characteristics rather than on the refinement in the continually updated arguments for and against capitalism, on the essentials rather than statistical illustrations of the argument (there are no charts and few figures), runs the risk of oversimplification. To talk of capitalism (and socialism) is not to overlook variations. There are elements of both in all countries of the world. The capitalist countries of the West contain elements of socialism, to some extent necessarily where the market cannot produce public goods, and the socialist countries of Eastern Europe contain elements of capitalism, unavoidably because the most repressive government is unable to suppress underground markets. Some countries, perhaps Sweden and Austria, can be argued to be capitalist and socialist about equally, so that they lend little clear evidence to support the case for either capitalism or socialism.

The distinguishing difference between essentially capitalist and essentially socialist countries is that capitalism *consciously uses* socialism where it is unavoidable or, more rarely, serviceable, and socialism *attempts but fails* to suppress capitalism. I define capitalism as the system that makes as little use of the political process (which creates socialism) as necessary and as much use of the market as possible. Conversely socialism makes as much use of the political process as it can without arousing public revolt and as little use of the market as is required to maintain tolerable productivity and minimize politically dangerous privation.

It follows that the academic, politician, writer or any other in any party who would make more use of the political process than is necessary is a socialist, in a philosophical sense. That label would have to apply to Conservatives and Democrats, Social or Liberal, who would continue education or medical care as state services controlled by collective decision in the political process when they could largely be controlled by individual decision in the market. Conversely, the opposite label—liberal (rather than capitalist, below)—would apply to people in any party who would use the market wherever possible and confine the political process to the functions that could not be performed in the market.

If this formulation seems severe, I would claim that it emerges from the familiar time-honoured classical statements of the socialized agenda of government. These are essentially the so-called public goods or rather "unavoidably collective functions," a term that removes the unfounded implications both that they are more "public" than other services and that they are morally "good." The classical lists are briefly as follows.

1. Following Adam Smith, the nineteenth-century economists developed a list comprising external defence, internal law and order, some kinds of money, tax collection, some education, relief of (some kinds of) poverty, roads, bridges, canals and harbours.

2. Keynes's formula for "the most important" items on the agenda related "to those decisions which are made by *no-one* if the state does not make them." That delineation is crystal clear. Keynes emphasized it: the business of government was not to do "a little better or a little worse" the things already being done by individuals but only those "*not done at all*" (emphasis added).[5] Ten years later he added socialized investment.[6] His followers claimed that he also meant, or should have added, much more, but he would probably have rejected much of their thinking.
3. Lionel Robbins's agenda was comparable: defence, laws to create and defend property rights and contract, security, provision against infectious diseases, some means of communication (probably roads), possibly compulsory acquisition of land for railways, canals, drainage, water supply, electricity, the telegraph and telephones.[7]

These have been thought the extensive but necessary functions of government: the regrettably essential element of socialization. Their classical authors would now no doubt wish to prune the list in the light of technical invention (chapter 7). They would not all necessarily be public goods in the 1990s because some are no longer unavoidably collective functions. Some are being de-socialized; I argue below that more could be. But, whatever the list, Western politicians must sometimes wonder whether they are justified in controlling much larger empires, comprising vast investments, spending half the national income, employing millions and determining the lives of further millions, in supplying services that are in no sense public goods that only government can provide.

Who would not be a politician with so much of other people's money to spend? If these definitions of socialist and liberal seem severe, it is because politicians are empire-builders who tenaciously cling to their power when it no longer serves the public interest, even if it once did. A century of prime ministers and ministers—Conservative, Liberal and Labour—who professed to serve the people, all the people, and no-one but the people, have

5. John Maynard Keynes, *The End of Laissez Faire*, 1926; in *Essays in Persuasion*, W. W. Norton, 1963.

6. John Maynard Keynes, *The General Theory of Employment, Interest and Money*, Macmillan, 1936.

7. Lionel Robbins, *Economic Planning and International Order*, Macmillan, 1937.

saddled them unnecessarily over much of their lives with a political process that has served politicians, bureaucrats and political importuners.

The countries of the world range from the most to the least capitalist and from the most to the least socialist. There are many variants of both. A young British socialist political scientist, Anthony Wright, has written a clear account of *Socialisms*[8] to emphasize their "sheer variety"; perhaps one of the growing band of young liberal scholars in Britain or the United States, in both the universities and the proliferating think-tanks outside the universities, will write a study of *Capitalisms* to distinguish the varying forms of market-based economies in old and new, large and small, differentiated and homogeneous countries. At least Dr. John Gray has produced a volume on the political philosophy, if not the practice, of *Liberalisms.*[9]

Yet most economies are predominantly capitalist or socialist in the relative writs of the state and the market, or more generally in philosophical spirit and attitude to the primacy of the individual. If the principles of both systems are to be understood, so that observers can judge them and the peoples of the world choose between them, simplification must be the method and oversimplification the risk.

The Upsurge of Liberal/Capitalist Intellectuals

Liberal economists, political scientists, philosophers and historians have become more assertive in recent years. The stimulus to rise to the defence of capitalism against misunderstanding and misrepresentation, to salute its achievements and to assert its potential has been intensified by the persistent socialist critics of capitalism. The very word "capitalist" was, and still is, spoken with revulsion or ejected with venom. The liberals at the LSE—Robbins, Plant, Gregory, Paish, Schwartz, Coase, Ponsonby—taught me in the hostile anti-capitalist environment of the 1930s; most have passed on but some, not least Hayek, are still alive to witness the vindication of their teaching.

Most of the growing number of market liberals associated with the IEA as authors, researchers, advisers, sympathizers or friends are happily pursuing their scholarship. I learned from them especially where, as Editorial Director, I urged some to make more of the implications of their analysis for policy and to dismiss as irrelevant the distractions of the politically impossible. Echoes of their thinking will be found in this book. Most were of my vintage,

8. Anthony Wright, *Socialisms: Theories and Practices,* Oxford University Press, 1988.
9. John Gray, *Liberalisms,* Routledge, 1989.

but it has been a unique personal reward to observe the surging stream of young academics and other acolytes of the IEA who are invading the world of economic activity with their confident assertion of the superiority of market capitalism for the solution of tasks untouched or exacerbated by socialism. Some of their ideas were assembled in a collection of 20 essays by young people in *The "New Right" Enlightenment* in 1985 heralded by Hayek.[10]

In the United States a main instrument in the sponsorship of scholarship by young liberal academics, the Institute of Humane Studies, is linked with George Mason University in Fairfax, Virginia, the present home of the original school of "public choice" or what I prefer to call the economics of politics. So far there are no corresponding British nurseries of young liberal academics, which must be a reflection on the country that bred David Hume and Adam Smith, James and John Stuart Mill, A. V. Dicey and Lord Acton, and gave a home to the Austrians Karl Popper and Friedrich Hayek who became British by choice.

The overt critics of capitalism have unintentionally inspired examination of their criticisms over 50 years. I acknowledge writers who may be surprised to find themselves on this list: from the LSE academics of the 1930s, not least Evan Durbin, and Left Book Club authors, predominantly John Strachey, who dismissed capitalism for its weaknesses, to the best of the 1980s critics who have been trying to understand its strengths, ranging from the Fabian academics, Professor Raymond Plant, Professor Julian Le Grand and Professor David Collard, to some writers in *Marxism Today*, the academics Professor Andrew Gamble and Professor Stuart Hall, and the exceptional journalists John Lloyd and Charlie Leadbeater whose work in *The Financial Times* makes them especially telling assessors of capitalism.

The Socialist Acceptance of Capitalism

In the last decade, especially after the second Labour defeat in 1983, there has been an unprecedented revolution in the readiness of socialist-minded writers to turn from denigrating the market to urging it as a necessary instrument of socialism. They have yet to acknowledge that the market cannot work if it is held on a tight leash as a closely controlled agent of the state and its *political* motivations because it requires the capitalist ambience of private property rights and its *commercial* motivations of profit for success and loss

10. A. Seldon (ed.), *The "New Right" Enlightenment*, Economic and Literary Books, 1985.

for failure. It requires taxation low enough not to distort market signals. It must be allowed room to explore and innovate, to discover and make mistakes. Politicians who want its productivity must defend it when it falters. But the political process, as Professor David Marquand says,[11] will want to dominate it, not to liberate it. That is why it will not work under socialism.

The debate between intellectuals who seek "the public interest" is now not on "Market or state?" but on "How can the market be best used?" The dispute is not only between liberals and socialists on the political institutions required for the market but, perhaps even more, between socialists like Raymond Plant who accept the market in principle and those like the Marxist Eric Hobsbawm who still reject it.

It has been a rare intellectual experience to have worked with some of the most original minds in Britain and overseas who were exercised to refine the operation of markets as the prime mover of capitalism and the institutional environment required for them to produce their best results. It has also been a rare historical experience to witness the change, unimaginable in the 1930s and unpredictable in the 1950s, 1960s or even 1970s, from the denigration of the principle of markets to their acceptance and welcome by politicians around the world, not least in the socialist countries.

The long antipathy to capitalism, despite the reappraisal since the mid-1980s, has left a legacy of stubborn misunderstanding about capitalism among socialist critics, capitalist practitioners and political defenders. The phalanx of antipathy is formidable: the socialist/Marxist criticism of capitalism is still widely taught to innocent students in British and overseas universities; academia and the literati are still the sources of hostility to capitalism; the church still predominantly sees capitalism as immoral; the bureaucracy in central and local government, even where individuals vote for market-capitalist parties, resists market-oriented reforms; trade union leaders obstruct the operation of markets even where their rank-and-file members would benefit from them and have abandoned socialism as voters; the general public is taught to see the disadvantages of capitalism but rarely its advantages.

The antipathy is expressed in the denunciation of people alleged to "know the price (or cost) of everything and the value of nothing," a characteristically clever but shallow literary taunt recently revived from Oscar Wilde's

11. David Marquand, *The Unprincipled Society,* Cape, 1988.

Lady Windermere's Fan. This is not a sophisticated reference to the complication of the external effects of exchange in which agreed prices do not reflect the benefits or harm to third parties (chapter 8). Rather, it indicates the claim to judge value without knowing the opportunity cost—the sacrifices of others, often the poor, who are denied resources in favour of people with the presumed wit to know aesthetic, artistic, literary or generally cultural value. The pretence of knowing "real" value without knowing price is arrogant and, in the end, more a defiance of cultural values and more callous about third-party strangers, and especially the meek and the humble, than the supposed claim to know price but not value.

The result is that the advance to capitalism, especially in the poorer regions and countries where it would do most good, is being retarded. A better understanding of capitalism would do more to solve the "social" problems of the world than the efforts of "caring" political or literary people who see no further than redistribution.

Capitalist and Socialist Living Standards

A rare exception to the self-denying ordinance to avoid statistics is relevant at this stage. The case against capitalism was once that it was inefficient: destabilized by booms and slumps, unnerved by inflation or unemployment, defaced by poverty and inequality. The present-day contender for the main charge is that, even if it has brought prosperity to many, capitalism is immoral. Moreover, the state could and would ensure a more equal and morally more satisfying distribution of worldly goods. But the corollary, that socialism would sacrifice productivity and living standards in driving towards its objective of equality, is rarely added. If the sacrifice were negligible, it might be a small price to pay for a more equal, more moral distribution. But if it were large, the poor might lose as well as the relatively rich. Few middle-class, relatively affluent socialists ask whether the poor would prefer more equality at a lower standard of living to inequality with a higher standard of living for all, including themselves. What would the poor prefer? It is hardly moral to deprive them of judgement. The late Professor Richard Titmuss implicitly questioned the beneficence of growing affluence that made the dwindling poverty of capitalism harder for the poor to bear because there were fewer to share it. Yet, as J. M. Keynes said, "many of the evils of society arise from a lack of material wealth."

What, then, is the order of magnitude? What is the price of equality?

What is the difference in living standards between people under capitalism and under socialism? How much help could the poor be given if the production of goods and services were enlarged? For they stand to gain more from increasing production than from redistribution.

Government statistics are invariably unreliable. They are "macro-totals" of output from many sources, most of which have to be taken on trust. I recall the Director of Medical Services of Hong Kong saying that he plucked a number out of the air to supply the earnest request from the World Health Organization for medical statistics. Government figures, especially in the socialist countries, are politicized instruments of propaganda rather than neutral scientific measures of economic activity. Their accuracy cannot be assumed. At best, they measure quantities, not qualities. There are numerous reasons for taking them with a large pinch of salt. Not least is that no-one checks them outside government. In recent years the most important reason is the growth in the "unrecorded" economy, or black market, which probably varies from 10 to 30 per cent or more in the West to even larger percentages in the communist countries.

What do the most reliable, or least unreliable, estimates suggest? The latest, published at the end of 1988,[12] are listed for (mostly) capitalist and (mostly) socialist countries, with some for more or less mixed countries. The gross domestic product (GDP) per head per year, to the nearest thousand US dollars, for mostly capitalist countries is shown in Table 1. The figures are best compared for countries of roughly similar size. The United Kingdom is far down the list. Its living standards were once higher than those of Italy, but are now no longer. Italy also has a larger underground market, possibly up to 40 per cent of the official total contrasted with 15–20 per cent in the United Kingdom, so that the real difference is larger. Italy has bounded ahead of the United Kingdom because, despite the backward agricultural *Mezzogiorno* in the south, the capitalist market in the north has developed faster since the war than in the United Kingdom, where free markets began to assert themselves only in the last decade.

An assorted selection of mainly socialist countries would show much lower figures. For communist countries they are of "net material product" (NMP), which is gross national product (GNP) less depreciation and most services, but is probably inflated to conceal the large shortfall behind capitalist countries. On this uncertain basis the figures are as follows (to nearest

12. *The World in 1989*, Economist Survey, 1988, pp. 81–7.

thousand US dollars): East Germany, 5,000; USSR, 4,000; Yugoslavia, 3,000; Poland, 2,000. Even more uncertain are the GDP figures for China (US$330) and India (US$370), which are both a tenth or less of even the communist countries of Europe.

A contrast can also be drawn with the new, though small, capitalist countries—Hong Kong, US$10,000; Singapore, US$9,000; South Korea, US$5,000 (all GDP)—up to twice as much as the communist countries of Europe.

The mixed capitalist-socialist countries, mainly Sweden (US$22,000) and Austria (US$18,000), show high figures which are attributable as much to their capitalist private property with more or less open markets as to their socialist elements of large welfare states financed by high taxes and exacting the high price of individual enervation and restricted liberties, neither of which is shown in the statistics.

Table 1. Gross domestic product per head per year (US$)

Switzerland	30,000
Japan	26,000
Norway	24,000
USA	22,000
Denmark	21,000
West Germany	21,000
Canada	21,000
France	18,000
Netherlands	17,000
Belgium	16,000
Italy	15,000
Australia	15,000
UK	15,000
Ireland	9,000
Spain	9,000

This is a very rough measure of the price in material living conditions of suppressing capitalism and enforcing socialism. It is not small. Even with these uncertain figures, living standards under capitalism seem to be around three, four or five times higher than those under socialism. The concealed loss of quality in goods and services is severe, and the loss of economic, political and cultural liberty is incalculable. These statistics are hardly required to confirm the evidence of wide differences in living standards observed by visitors to capitalist and socialist countries.

This is a heavy price—in food, clothing, housing, household amenities and comforts, education, medical care, private transport, holidays and much else—for the common people to pay for socialism. What do they receive in return? If socialist politicians or intellectuals claim it is worth paying for the higher morality of equity or equality promised by the state, the reply must be that it is not for others to say. What would the people of socialist countries say? They were not, until recently in some countries, still not in all, asked by their leaders. But they speak to outsiders.

Shortly after the Massacre of the Innocents in Tiananmen Square in June 1989, a Western journalist was asked by a young Chinese in Beijing (Peking) "Why do you in Hong Kong have so much more than us (we) here? Why do you have an air conditioner and a private bathroom?" The journalist thought the questions "unanswerable," and added others: "Why should one man walk when another rides? Why should one man toil around on a clapped-out bicycle while a party cadre lords it in a limousine?"[13]

The "beneficiaries" of socialism are not asked whether they prefer socialist equality at a third or a quarter of the unequal but universally higher standard of living of capitalism. They are not told, of course, that, in practice, incomes in a politicized society are biased in favour of the politically influential, which excludes the common people.

The Promise of Capitalism

To understand capitalism it is necessary to grasp the essentials of economic thinking, which mostly emerge from the application of common sense to the elements of human nature (as it is, and not as Marxists have hoped it would change). Although mostly simple, they are not at once obvious even to sophisticated minds, including some in political science and sociology. The functions and properties of prices can be particularly elusive. The rationing role of price is rarely self-evident. The notion that supply and demand are not fixed but "elastic," that they can, and in the real world do, change in response to movements in prices—of goods and services, labour and skills, homes and land, savings and money—is often difficult to grasp.

13. Christopher Lockwood, "Three weeks in the heart of China," *The Telegraph Weekend Magazine*, July 1989, p. 41.

Socialists often misunderstand the case for capitalism because they misunderstand the notion of price (chapter 6).

That is perhaps why the very interest in prices is dismissed as irrelevant, if not morally offensive. Market price is sometimes an imperfect indicator of value, but the political artefact of prices in socialism is often meaningless. The use of the free-market pricing system explains the relative success of capitalism and the failure of socialism.

Moreover, in recent years economists have developed new theories to explain the real world that substantially strengthen the case for capitalism rather than socialism. Some developments, like public choice, in the political process, or the economics of politics, are becoming known to the socialist critics, who are accordingly tempering their criticism of capitalism. Others, like the economics of the market process, property rights, public goods, externalities, regulation and capitalist history, still seem largely unknown (chapters 7 and 8).

The case for capitalism has not only been strengthened by the experience of socialism round the world, which is increasingly plain for all to see. It has also been immeasurably reinforced by refinements in abstract economic thinking, which have yet to reach the public, the socialist critics, the politicians, the literati, the bishops and the capitalists.

The critics of capitalism are losing the argument. The acceptance of intellectual defeat by socialists is painfully slow, understandably when it requires abandonment of errors absorbed and taught over a lifetime. It is hardly slower among many academic, political, literary and other critics of socialism reluctant to be seen following behind the leaders. But the case is stronger than appears in current debate. Liberals can put against the vision of socialism offered by socialists not the alternative of imperfect capitalism as we have known it but the opposite vision of capitalism as it could be. This is the alternative that does not appear in socialist writing; it is missing from textbooks written by socialist-inclined authors, and it is absent from popular writing in the material prepared for the press and broadcasting, and in the written and spoken word in the theatre, especially where fiction is used as a more powerful form of proselytizing and persuasion than the facts of the real world.

I approach capitalism as a much maligned system that has been prevented by the intellectuals from raising the poor faster out of poverty. We have spent years anguishing over the defects of capitalism. The dissection of capitalist imperfection by social scientists should continue, not least as the way to minimize them; total removal may be technically possible but not beyond a price. Unemployment can be entirely prevented, as is claimed in socialism, but only by the suppression of change, by industrial retrogression and stagnant living conditions. But capitalism offers the best hopes of all systems in an imperfect world because its potential can be realized more closely than the promises of socialism can be fulfilled.

What is at stake is not only survival, not only liberty. It is both. *Circumspice, si monumentum requiris.* If you want the evidence, I am tempted to advise the reader, do not read the biased books, even this one, or the biased reports of observers in the press or broadcasting; look around you.

CHAPTER 2

Indoctrination Against Capitalism

> In terms of the values held by the majority of people in the world today, a choice in favour of capitalism is more plausible in the light of the empirical evidence . . .
>
> The commonly raised issues of "mixed systems" and "third ways" generally obfuscate the empirically available options . . . every existing system is "mixed" . . . the question will be whether [it] is *primarily* organised along capitalist or socialist lines.
>
> . . . *that,* precisely, is the crucial choice . . .
>
> Peter L. Berger, *The Capitalist Revolution*

> Berger does not persuade me that the living presence of depraved capitalism is preferable to the vision of democratic socialism . . .
>
> Robert Lekachman, on the back cover of *The Capitalist Revolution*

The unrelenting barrage of argument against capitalism for a century can hardly have failed to miss many in any social class. It has been a formative cultural experience. The thinking classes, directly or indirectly, consciously or unconsciously, have influenced the outlook of most people, although the interests of many have cautioned them before translating thought into votes. Such second-hand attitudes have had more effect than reasoned reflection on the good or evil of capitalism or of its much lauded alternative socialism. Attitudes formed in youth or early childhood are not easily discarded, whatever the experience of later years. I draw on the case study I know best, which I have little doubt is not unique or rare but probably similar to those of millions of children or young people in Britain.

Early Impressions and Lifetime Opinion

People of my generation must have suffered much the same distortion of news and opinion about capitalism and socialism in their youth. In my childhood and early teenage years I was told of the evils of capitalism, never of its achievements. I was buoyed up by the promise of socialism, never warned of its evils.

Since then I have come to think of both capitalism and socialism as, in the language of the economist, the "opportunity costs"—the sacrifices, the lost worlds—of each other. The opportunity cost of capitalism is very low—the socialism it displaces. The people of capitalist Switzerland do not lose much by missing socialism. The opportunity cost of socialism is very high—the capitalism it displaces. Few Swiss have wanted to live in the USSR. But the people of East Germany have paid a high price in the 40 years of capitalism they have sacrificed for their socialism, and many of them have wanted to move to West Germany. Some gave their lives fleeing from paradise. In late 1989 some were allowed to escape because the rebellion against socialism had become too strong to suppress, with civil strife simmering below the surface.

In my lifetime the peoples of diverse cultures have shown they sense the system that serves them better. Where they have been free to move, they have moved from socialism to capitalism. Capitalism is the system to which people in the West, in the Far East and most recently in Eastern Europe have aspired where they have been free to follow their instincts, their observations of other peoples or their understanding of the world about them. Capitalism has required no Berlin Wall to prevent an exodus to socialism. That is the ultimate evidence of its standing with the common people of the world.

Liberals who advocate capitalism would accept the verdict of the people; socialists would not. Liberals envisage a world market of ideas and practice that would enable the people to choose between economic systems; socialists would not accept their verdict. (I use "liberal" in the classical European sense, and not in the British party-political illiberal distortion or in the American sense where it is virtually a euphemism for "socialist.")

Little wonder that socialism is invariably the system into which they have been misled by the emergencies of war and their momentum into the peace, or persuaded by demagoguery, or seduced by promises of economic prosperity, social security and political liberty, or coerced by despots, benevolent or autocratic. The exceptions, or apparent exceptions, democratic socialist countries like Austria and Sweden and imposed capitalist economies like Taiwan and Singapore, remain exceptions (below).

Seventy Decisive Years

In living memory contemporary capitalism, through war and peace, boom and slump, prosperity and poverty, has been contrasted unfavourably with a vision of socialism, free, equal and just. It is high time to contrast and judge socialism at its worst, as it has been in Europe and Asia, with capitalism at its best, as it could be, round the world. It is time to judge "depraved" socialism with the "vision" of capitalism.

I am a year older than scientific socialism. My life began in 1916 in the East End of London; socialism in its most elemental experiment in history began a year later, in 1917, in Russia. The human and the political spans now seem almost certain to diverge.

Human life in the West under the rising living standards of capitalism has been lengthening from the Biblical 70 years into the eighties and nineties. It has been poetic justice that the teachers of liberal market capitalism, some of whom became my friends—Ludwig von Mises, Lionel Robbins, Arnold Plant, F. A. Hayek, John Jewkes, W. H. Hutt, Frank Paish, Fritz Machlup, Gottfried Haberler, Graham Hutton—survived almost into their tenth decade. Their long lives dramatize Hayek's lesson, re-emphasized in his latest work, *The Fatal Conceit,*[1] that it was capitalism that kept people alive and made possible new generations that would otherwise not have survived under primitive, stagnant and hierarchical economic systems.

In ironic contrast, the political life of socialism that began in the USSR in 1917 looks like ending not long after its 70 years in the 1990s, and elsewhere in Asia and Africa probably sooner. It may linger in name, but its substance, its economic methods and its political techniques will be discarded because it cannot keep pace with the unprecedented rate of change and advance under capitalism. Where it lingers, socialism will lag increasingly behind capitalism in living standards, technological achievement and cultural liberty. That is the consequence of the internal contradiction of socialism (below).

The failure of socialism to provide a better life than capitalism is now clear for all to see but the purblind among the embattled ideologues of socialism. They continue their prophecies of the collapse of capitalism under its "internal contradictions." They refuse to see the lethal contradiction of socialism, amply confirmed by history—the incompatibility between the decentralization of property required for economic productivity and the centralization of power required for political control. Socialists in the West, even the well-intentioned, disinterested and high-minded, can refuse to acknowledge the socialist contradiction, but it is becoming more difficult to disguise and conceal from the populace in the socialist countries, not least

1. F. A. Hayek, *The Fatal Conceit,* Routledge, 1988.

the two archetypes of the USSR and China and their conquered colonies or satellites in Eastern Europe and Asia.

It would be a happy outcome if the Russians can accomplish the transition from socialism, "to each according to his work," to capitalism without the convulsion of a "hard landing." (They have never reached the communist mirage of "to each according to his needs" [chapter 3].) A civil war between the liberal reformers and the conservative military and civil officialdom could ironically reverse the revolt of 1917, in which the soldiery organized in Soviets joined the Soviets of peasants, often their family relatives, friends or neighbours (Soviet: the Russian for committee or council, originally the workers' councils formed against the Tsar in 1905, ultimately the machinery of the Bolshevik Revolution in 1917 and later applied to the nominally elected councils that administered the planning system and to the republics). But the truth about the crisis of the long-concealed contradiction in socialism has come late in Russia, perhaps too late for peaceful evolution. The escape from socialism is now a desperate political gamble, with the risk of communal strife and the disintegration of the Union of Socialist Soviet "Republics," unlike the original 13 American colonies a forced union of peoples in the south and on the Baltic who will use national or regional aspirations to cloak their resentment against political subjugation by communist Russians in Moscow.

The risk of civil strife and cultural disintegration has been made unavoidable by unprecedented advance under capitalism in the West and in the Far East. It has not been a spontaneous domestic decision of the Soviet politicians to restore the freedoms emerging before 1917, but a necessity induced by external evidence of domestic failure. Despite imitation of the West, the socialist standard of living has been lagging too far behind the world capitalist standard for the gap to be closed in the lifetime of most of the present-day Russian and other peoples forced into the Union. The claim of Khrushchev in 1956 that communism would overtake capitalism by the end of the century is, at last, being seen as the empty boast it always was. But the more urgently the Soviet Union has to escape from its socialist contradiction and the more centralized planning must be relaxed to raise living standards nearer those of capitalism, the nearer the end of socialism in substance approaches. The same risks of liberalization inadequate for productivity yet excessive for the political safety of the planners emerged in China in 1989. New names coined by socialists in the West to save their self-respect will not conceal the subterfuge from the common peoples, who will judge economic systems by their results in their daily lives, not least in their food, clothing and housing.

Technical marvels in telecommunications that the Soviet politicians cannot always suppress, and many more to come both inside the USSR and with the capitalist world long before the end of the century, will tell the people of socialist countries the inconvenient truth about the standard of living that is daily familiar to the inhabitants of capitalism. Whatever their past, the peoples of the communist world will expect a better life than most have tolerated so far (chapter 4). And if living standards do not rise much faster than in the past, the urge to escape will become intensified. The immigrants to socialism, the refugees from capitalism, will remain the sad handful of ideologues or spies. The common people will want to move from socialism to capitalism in growing numbers: the Russians who fled Russia to escape from the Tsarist oppressors will be followed by their grandchildren who want to escape from the communist oppressors. The difference is that the grandparents could escape; their grandchildren, so far, mostly cannot, though the imperative of keeping in the good books of the capitalist West may force the communists' hands.

Communism and Capitalism in the 1920s

Whether or not this fate of socialism, the politico-economic system as it is in practice rather than in the imagination of socialists, could be foreseen in 1917, I heard nothing of its risks and dangers in the 1920s.

When, at the age of eight, at the General Election of 1924 in which Labour won electoral power for the first time, I cheered the Labour candidate, the respected Catholic John Scurr, outside the polling booth in my Dempsey Street Elementary School in Stepney, I vaguely understood that he would save the workers from the class enemy, the Conservative spokesman for capitalism, Dr. W. J. O'Donovan, a doctor at the nearby London Hospital.

When, at the age of 11, I saw my foster-mother (my parents had died in their thirties in the Spanish 'flu in 1918) return down Oxford Street, E1, burdened with a parcel of lisle stockings in each hand, to our home at number 154, where she had started a "shop" in the front room to pay the 12 shillings weekly rent after my foster-father died in 1927, I had not yet learned, but was taught later, that inequality was the result of capitalism. And when, after a year or two, her efforts had finally exhausted the £100 life assurance brought by a kindly secretary of the Friendly Society, she sent me to ask for emergency help from the Board of Guardians (promptly supplied with eight shillings' worth of groceries in a stout brown paper bag), I had not yet learned that poverty was also the inevitable outcome of capitalism.

The indoctrination against capitalism continued throughout my formative years. In my teens, from the age of 12 in 1928, when I moved to Sir Henry Raine's (Grammar) School off Commercial Road, to 18 in 1934 at the LSE, I found the working classes around me in the East End were taught that all the ills of the world, from sickness and unemployment through exploitation and imperialism to hunger and war, were caused by capitalism. I later came to doubt, and then resent as an irresponsible assault on young minds, the heavily insinuated implication that the ills of capitalism would be ended by socialism. The most plausible excuse for the deception was that the ills of capitalism were all around them in their daily lives but socialism was the new hope dawning in the new Russia, cleansed of the Tsars, from which the parents of some had fled.

Thus were the toiling masses misled for decades by the most destructive *non sequitur* in British history, the fabrication of a handful of the leisured, mostly affluent, middle-class men and women, from politicians to scholars, who preferred to capture the machinery and financial resources of government first, to do in the welfare state the charitable works that the best of them had been doing far better voluntarily and, then, by nationalization to create the prosperity from which all would, they said, gain—equally.

Emerging capitalism in Russia, barely 30 years after it developed from around 1885, was ended by duplicity and force, and socialism was created with no idea how it would work, as Shinwell was still to find in 1946, and socialists are still claiming to know in 1990. Yet in the 1920s and 1930s, the USSR was beatified by largely middle-class academics and writers as the economic system that would rid the working classes of their sufferings under capitalism.

Some of the older socialist writers, perhaps Sir Stephen Spender, Lord Soper and others, may recall the triumphant sense of vindication, plainly evident from admirers of the USSR at the LSE in my undergraduate days, when Stalin produced his "liberal" constitution of 1935, offering "democratic" rights to all the people. Their friends, Sidney Webb (as a young student I was intrigued to see him looking spry at 77, with pointed beard, asking for a book at the desk outside the Haldane Room in the LSE on a Saturday in 1936) and Beatrice Webb, both assiduous researchers into the failings of capitalism, had failed to discover by research during their visit in 1934 that Stalin was preparing the liquidation of the small farmers to expedite the industrialization of the Russian economy.

I cannot recall a barrage of questioning from the British middle-class socialist intelligentsia at any time on why Stalin had not followed the example of Lenin in opening up the economy in his New Economic Policy of 1921 to 1928 as the more humane, even if slower, way of encouraging productivity without suppressing personal liberties and without large-scale "liquidation." (Where in capitalism has economic growth been bought at the high price of six to ten or 20 or 40 million lives?) Instead, the socialist intellectuals of the 1930s presented socialism as they claimed it was henceforward going to be—democratic, humane, prosperous. Where is there such a rogue's gallery of kindly but irresponsible intellectuals as portrayed in David Caute's *The Fellow-Travellers,*[2] with its scores of political analysts, philosophers, scientists, writers, publishers and even clerics, many of whose unholy texts I read as an undergraduate in disbelief, a band of muddled Moses who misled the masses for 40 years in the socialist intellectual wilderness to seek the economic promised land that has ended in a mirage? To this day the preoccupation of many socialists, who seem to have learned nothing, is still with political democracy, to the neglect of the democracy of the economic market which offers the masses more assured prospects of emancipation from undisciplined power (chapter 5).

Young students were strongly influenced by such wishful thinking, based on little argument and no evidence. Its plausibility came from the assertion that the crisis of capitalism in 1929–31 denoted its certain collapse (as socialists had asserted for every "crisis" since the 1840s) and that the alternative was plainly socialism. That is how socialism was portrayed in the 1930s and for 15 years in the stream of writing from the Left Book Club. Its most widely read luminary, John Strachey, later sufficiently overcome by doubts about communism to serve as Minister of Food under Attlee, foretold the ugly end of capitalism in the *Hochkapitalismus,* the final "high" phase of capitalism, of Hitler's Fascist Germany. In this euphoria, the unfortunate fate of the Russian kulaks under Stalin is still, as with other sins of socialism, related in socialist writing as a "mistake," not at all the humane socialism taught by socialists as it was meant to be by Marx and Lenin.

Some lessons have been learned. There is a tentative approach to the

2. David Caute, *The Fellow-Travellers,* Yale University Press, 1973; revised edition 1988.

use of markets, the essence of capitalism. But there is still no scholarly generous acknowledgement of the record, the achievements, the superiority of capitalism.

The Latter-day Communist Confession

It has taken almost exactly 70 years for the failures of socialism in Russia to be confessed by Russian leaders, but not sufficiently to induce them to risk their power, though no longer their lives, in the unprecedented policy of advancing to capitalism. Confession had come first from Khrushchev in the mid-1950s. Stalin had died (so it was said). It should have been safe to begin the escape from the socialist contradiction by changing policy away from the centralized polity to the decentralized economy. Russian economists—Liberman, Nemchinov, Trapeznikov and more, reviewed in two IEA studies by Margaret Miller[3]—had in the 1950s, nearly 40 years after 1917, begun to talk the long-suppressed language of markets, profits, inefficiency and waste. Stalin's immediate successor, Malenkov, might have been more adventurous. But both the "reformers" were removed before their senility, Malenkov barely after he had begun and Khrushchev after nine years in 1964. It must have been judged that the opposition from the official vested interests of socialism—the planners, the bureaucrats, the armed services, officials of all ranks, far more powerful than the unofficial vested interests, the rent-seekers, of capitalism—would be too formidable. It was too soon to risk political power to save the masses from poverty by embracing markets. No wonder the genie was soon thrust back into the bottle to prepare for 25 years of conserving socialism by Kosygin and Brezhnev.

None of the original destroyers of nascent capitalism in 1917 Russia, from Lenin to Stalin, thought that the time had come to concede that the socialist solution for the ills of capitalism had failed and would have to be abandoned. For Lenin it was too soon: socialism was only four years old and had not yet had time to show what it could do; even so it had to be replaced in 1921, temporarily of course it was announced, by the New Economic Policy. For his successor Stalin in the mid-1920s socialism was necessary for its machinery of centralized political control to force the people from agriculture into heavy industry.

3. Margaret Miller, in *Communist Economy under Change*, Institute of Economic Affairs, 1962; *The Rise of the Russian Consumer*, Institute of Economic Affairs, 1965.

The final confession that socialism had, after all, failed and would have to be abandoned, had to await a younger man born 20 years after the upheavals of 1917 and therefore safely immune from blame for their aftermath of deprivation and death. Gorbachev's relative youth has enabled him to propel policy better than Kosygin and Brezhnev, and the short-term stopgaps Andropov and Chernenko. But even he has been pushed by events: the urgency of reducing public discontent with the stagnant living standards and backward lifestyles.

This is the underlying reason, not openly confessed but plainly implied, why Russia is resuming its forced march to capitalism, with no certainty of a "soft landing" in which the people will have more consumer goods and officialdom will be placated by keeping their privileges. The resistances—cultural from the conservative intelligentsia, economic from the plant managers and officialdom, military from the armed services—will be stubborn. Understandably, to pacify the Marxist ideologues, Gorbachev attributes the inspiration of *perestroika* (reconstruction) to Lenin's market-based New Economic Policy. But the resistance of the vested interests will have to be overcome by the awakening aspirations of the young, the innate urge to freedom of the Russian and non-Russian literati and the long-suppressed desire of the long-silent non-communist Russians to resume the emerging role that Russia would have displayed after 1917 as a cultural leader of the West. The open question for the 1990s is whether the resistance will be overcome by persuasion or conflict (chapter 4).

It must be expected that the uncertainties will retard the reconstruction. For a time the communist resistance may prevail. It may replace the liberal Gorbachev by a conservative who protects the posts and powers of the political and military establishments. But that would provide no lasting solution to the socialist contradiction, because Russian production would then again flag. For the USSR there is no safety in *immobilisme:* she must go forward to capitalism, whatever it is called, or backward into stagnation. And in both she risks civil war.

The new liberal revolution will not be prevented for long by the Russians' attachment to their historical traditions emphasized by George Urban and other students of Russian history,[4] although they may delay the market-based reforms at the high price of continued stagnation. The Russian experience of capitalism from the 1880s to 1917 was short, and it did not touch the

4. George Urban (ed.), *Can the Soviet System Survive Reform?*, Pinter/Spiers, 1989.

lives of most Russians. The return to capitalism in the New Economic Policy was even shorter lived and under political surveillance, although robust. The Russians of the 1990s and their conquered peoples will find it perplexing to learn in a few short years the attitudes and ethos of the commercial society required to rescue them from the long night, the cul-de-sac, of socialism. But they will have to learn fast if they want the living standards and liberties of the West.

The Tardy British Confession

In Britain (and elsewhere) no more than a relative handful of the still numerous long-serving advocates of socialism have acknowledged that it has failed. Even where the market is no longer reviled but belatedly seen as a necessary mechanism to be incorporated, somehow, into socialism, its required capitalist institutions and commercial ethos are stubbornly resisted. And there is now a new last defence by British socialists: if the long-suspected market must reluctantly be embraced, they assert, it must be by socialists in socialist institutions, because the humane civilized values of socialism cannot be entrusted to capitalism or to markets operated by capitalists.

In Britain capitalism is still, secretly or subconsciously, rejected by most advocates of socialism, even by academics and politicians who have belatedly recognized the market. There is still an unconquerable inconsolable distaste in acknowledging that, by the evidence of history and the logic of argument, capitalism has triumphed over socialism. "The market," if only as a technique safe in socialist hands, is increasingly the subject of socialist writing in Britain: capitalism as a politico-economic system capable of good, of benefiting mankind, is still *verboten;* it is still too difficult to abandon the faith of a lifetime. A century of denigration and derision cannot lightly be replaced by acknowledgement and acclaim without risking repute for historical sense and political integrity. Yet the old pretext, that the cause of socialist failure was fortuitous mistakes or the unfortunate capture of power by tyrants, is being painfully and reluctantly abandoned. (If only Lenin had been followed by Trotsky, who understood and would have introduced markets as he advised Lenin in the New Economic Policy, rather than by Stalin, who rightly saw them as his obstacle. . . .) Better still, the 70 wasted years might have been saved for sanity if Kerensky the democrat, who came to tell LSE students (in French, translated by his son) of the Russia that might have been, had been allowed to govern in the way of the West. After 70 years in the USSR, 40 years in Britain, Europe and China, 20 or 30 years in Asia and

Africa, the failure of socialism round the world can, at last, no longer be denied or dismissed.

Socialist discussion is now in turmoil. For some five years the preoccupation of its main dialectical components in Britain, from democratic socialist to Marxist, has not been how to use the state as the unfailing agent of benevolence but how to accept the market into socialist thought with the maximum of philosophical dignity and the minimum of intellectual contrition. The persistent unresolved practical task is how to incorporate the institution of the market into socialist society. The ghost of Mises, who said in 1921 that it could not be done, cannot be exorcised. The repeated denial of Hayek has not been confounded (chapter 6). The latest revisions, retractions, recantations, confessions and conversions fill the pages of the monthly "theoretical" (that is, explanatory) journal of the Communist Party, *Marxism Today.* The formerly influential weekly, the *New Statesman,* once in the 1930s under Kingsley Martin read more avidly than the textbooks prescribed by LSE lecturers, after recognizing the dilemma during the short-lived editorship in the mid-1980s of John Lloyd, has sadly relapsed into denouncing the capitalist cloud that produces the capitalist silver linings of affluence, ownership and independence inconveniently welcomed by the working classes.

The essence of capitalism, under more acceptable names, and the necessity of the market are very slowly being acknowledged by the best of the British socialist academics of varying shades, notably the Fabian Professors Raymond Plant (Southampton University) and Julian Le Grand (Bristol), the Social Democrat Professor David Marquand (Salford), and the Marxist Professors Andrew Gamble (Sheffield) and, on some aspects, Stuart Hall (Open University), followed at a calculated distance by a handful of socialist politicians led by Bryan Gould, the New Zealander who taught law at Oxford (his book, *Socialism and Freedom,*[5] was a courageous attempt to integrate the newly necessary liberalism with the old framework of socialism). Intellectual dignity is being salvaged by the stubborn claim that capitalism cannot be left to the capitalists, nor the market to the academic market liberals.

There is some truth in the first of these assertions (chapters 10 and 13), but the second is transparently unconvincing. The liberal academics and their interpreters, who in the past 30 years, not least at the IEA, have by intensive care nursed the idea of the market and its necessary (*capitalist*) environment

5. Bryan Gould, *Socialism and Freedom,* Macmillan, 1985.

back to life as concepts worthy of attention in academia and by men of affairs, know more of their limitations, and the solutions, than the socialists who have only recently shown much interest in them. Yet the converted socialist critics now claim that the market is safe only in socialist hands, and that only socialists will know how to use it for the advantage of the common people.

The long-standing socialist approach, recently revived, is to find fault with the theory or performance of capitalism in practice and imply, without argument or evidence, that the faults will be removed by socialism in ways yet to be revealed. This is the historic *non sequitur,* the South Sea Bubble, of socialist writing from Marx in the mid-nineteenth century to Hobsbawm in the late twentieth. We are witnessing a revolution in the century-old self-confident socialist assertion that capitalism was destined to collapse. It has long been an unquestioned supposition that it would be succeeded by socialism, and an unquestioned article of faith that socialism would undo its sins and right its wrongs.

A long-held belief, even when its emptiness is revealed, is a long time a-dying. Its slow abandonment by socialists reflects the understandable human reluctance to admit error and to keep faith with the essence of the time-honoured belief in socialism—its preference for the political process over the market process as the better way to a humane society. The capacity for self-deception is easily fortified by the Micawber expectation that something may turn up: perhaps socialism somewhere will find new ways to combine political centralization with economic decentralization; perhaps capitalism somewhere will collapse because of its much-canvassed internal contradictions; perhaps capitalism will conveniently show that it cannot nurse the values of community, generosity or compassion. Perhaps a new synthesis will emerge between capitalist efficiency in production and socialist equity in distribution. The peoples of socialist countries will not wait until the hopes of the intellectuals are fulfilled.

The reluctance to yield to the argument of liberalism and the evidence of events is also reinforced by the familiar urge in socialist writing to capitalize on every capitalist cloud and minimize every capitalist silver lining. There is the even less enviable subconscious desire to reject intellectual responsibility for misleading the populace, the masses, the working classes, not least the poor, the ageing and generations of students.

The still influential, if no longer dominant, British middle-class advocates of socialism rarely evince, still less express, remorse, humility or apology for repeating and refining a century of intellectual error. Their admissions are reluctant, grudging and defensive. Capitalism and its instrument, the market, they say, as in the Labour Party's latest series of revision papers and Roy Hattersley's *Choose Freedom*,[6] may be serviceable or even essential for the production of some goods or services, but not all. It must be used with care; in particular, its external "social" effects must be weighed before the market is let loose, and only socialists will know how to weigh them. Not least, the socialist values of caring, compassion, sharing, fraternity and community must be observed, and again only socialists are equipped to observe them.

None of these claims is based on argument or evidence. They remain unsupported assertions.

Reaction against Error

Doubts about socialism, and excited discovery of the market, came earlier than predictable in young people enthused by the gospel of socialism. Many persuaded in their growing minds of the attractions of socialism seem to have kept their faith into their thirties or forties. Beyond these middle years it is increasingly painful to confess the pursuit of a mirage, the sin of teaching false promise to the young child or the innocent adult, the failure to concede intellectual error, the refusal to see the evidence of history or of immediate familiar surroundings. It is painful to acknowledge the achievements of a politico-economic system after decades of condemning its injustices, its inefficiencies and its immorality. It is disagreeable to acknowledge that the evils *under* capitalism—slumps, unemployment, inequality, poverty—were not necessarily the evils *of* capitalism. Most rarely, it is damaging to acknowledge, in simple historical logic freed from Marxist confusion of *post hoc* with *propter hoc*, that the experience of capitalism in the past was not a measure of the potentialities of capitalism in the future.

Early prejudices cannot easily be abandoned in an ambience of hostility. In my formative years, after my foster-mother had remarried in 1931 (a tailor whose occupational forerunners had been studied by Beatrice Webb in the 1890s), to ensure a secure home, and we had moved to the relatively middle-class suburb of Stroud Green, my continuing links with former Left-inclined friends at Raine's School maintained the anti-Fascist sentiments acquired from our Fabian teacher of economics. It produced the familiar

6. Labour Party, *Revision Papers*, 1989; Roy Hattersley, *Choose Freedom*, Michael Joseph, 1987.

responses from ardent youth in those politically charged days, including an anti-Fascist shirt to denote disapproval of Sir Oswald Mosley's march through the East End in 1936. Yet my fortune was to have doubts about socialism sown earlier in the two years from 1932 to 1934 in the Sixth Form by the history master, E. J. Hayward, a Liberal of the old school, whose teachings on the guild system and its replacement by industrial capitalism, with its advantages for living standards and liberties, intrigued me more than the Fabian influence of the persuasive economics master, J. M. Bence.

It was predictable that the present-day criticisms of capitalism by E. J. Hobsbawm and the still numerous Marxist academics given generous space in the so-called *New Palgrave Dictionary of Economics*[7] would concentrate on the ills of early capitalism and minimize or ignore its intellectually inconvenient achievements. It is the never-failing depressant urge of socialist criticism to obscure its achievement by its imperfections. The television documentary on the advances of the post-war years that acknowledged capitalism as the genesis rather than the welfare state has been a rarity.

Doubts about socialism were powerfully confirmed at the LSE, founded by the Webbs in 1911 to continue their Fabian work, where I went in 1934, with a state scholarship worth £78 a year, without which my stepfather indicated I would have to find a job, then easier as the slump of 1929–31 receded (another "crisis of capitalism," said the Left Book Club books). When he died in 1936, the grant was raised to £100. Perhaps I should have felt more gratitude to the state for at least this one good deed in its long history of coercion and injustice.

The unformed doubts sown at school and refined at the LSE were further confirmed by the corporatist/socialist policies in agricultural marketing, transport licensing and international trade protectionism of the Conservative or Conservative-dominated National Governments of the early 1930s. The characteristic undergraduate impulse to work for a cause, especially in a university institution where politics was the subject matter of lectures, seminars, meetings, study, essays, debate and conversation, sought a vehicle in a political grouping. The Conservatives were too socialist, so I joined the LSE Liberal Society, then comprising a dozen members contrasted with the hundreds of the intellectual Marxists and of the rugger-playing Conservatives. Michael (later Lord) Young and Huw (later Sir) Wheldon were among the activists in other parties.

7. John Eatwell, Murray Milgate and Peter Newman (eds.), *New Palgrave Dictionary of Economics*, Macmillan, 1987.

My Liberal activities had a mainly intellectual content, strongly influenced by market philosophy which resisted socialist thinking in the Conservative Party as well as the Labour Party. Early work in 1938, a year after graduating, for a committee on the distribution of property, recounted below, was followed in 1940 by a paper, "The corporate state," on the post-war dangers I thought would follow the war economy. Liberal involvement resumed soon after my return from Italy with a meeting in the House of Commons in 1946 on post-war economic policy chaired by the Party leader, Clement Davies, and attended by the Oxford economist R. F. Harrod, an early biographer of Keynes and a later Liberal parliamentary candidate. In 1947 I chaired a small committee on the aged, described in chapter 11. Living near Orpington led to activity with the Liberal Association in the mid-1950s when the number of Liberal Councillors increased as the prelude to the historic victory of Eric Lubbock in 1962.

From 1957 the IEA, a charity that had to avoid direct influence on political affairs, ended my Liberal activities. I retained private hope of a Liberal revival under Jo Grimond but abandoned it when he was followed in 1967 by David Steel, a Party manager with little interest in policy and, it seemed, almost no understanding of economic liberalism indicated by a remark in a *Marxism Today* interview about my outdated *laissez-faire.*

Despite the astringent teaching of the great Hayek and the other economic liberals of the 1930s, whose thinking could not have been foreseen by the Webbs, socialism attracted as much intellectual interest as capitalism. The lectures and writings of the Left-inclined historians Eileen Power and H. L. Beales (of Penguin fame), the early market socialists, especially Evan Durbin, a friend of Hugh Gaitskell whom he might have succeeded as Labour leader, and the offerings of the Left Book Club by Marxist or self-styled democratic socialists commanded almost as much attention as the courses required to achieve the prized degree that might lead to the work and earnings required for domestic support.

The LSE, which was to be the home of Fabian research and socialist conclusions, led me to strike two modest blows for capitalism. The Liberal Party had established in 1937 a committee of enquiry into the distribution of property (including Harcourt Johnstone, who served in Churchill's wartime Government) and had asked Plant and Robbins for advice. They introduced me, fresh from graduation at 21, to write on the effects on the distribution of property of a change from a legacy to an inheritance tax (the fee was £5, more than my weekly £3 15s as Plant's research assistant). That led the Chairman, Elliott Dodds, the widely respected Editor of the *Huddersfield Examiner* and former aide to Sir Herbert Samuel, the leader of the Samuelites when the Liberal Party divided in 1931, to suggest that I draft the Committee's Report, which they called *Ownership for All.* Their proposals in 1938 for the diffusion of private property rather than its replacement by public (socialized) property raised the flag of classical liberalism for the last time in the Liberal Party. After the war it was seduced by socialism. The Conservatives under Anthony Eden wisely stole the powerless Liberals' clothes in their advocacy of "a property-owning democracy."

The second modest blow was to influence Herman Finer (the older brother of Professor S. E. Finer), another Fabian (Professor of Public Administration), who later became better known for a defensive criticism of Hayek's *Road to Serfdom* that he mockingly entitled *Road to Reaction.*[8] Finer had written a study of *Municipal Trading*[9] for which he wanted the central economic argument in a mainly administrative study checked in manuscript. Plant suggested I might serve. As it was too late to alter the book in its generally uncritical approval of local government trading, I suggested he anticipate criticism from the economists by amplifying his Preface to recognize the advantages of competition even in local government services, then a rare notion. He inserted the argument, as though it were self-evident, that municipal trading would benefit from the "administrative jostling" of alternative methods and suppliers. The revised Preface displeased another Fabian Professor of Public Administration, William A. Robson, who roundly condemned it.

The Lessons of War Socialism

The interlude of war provided a practical lesson in socialism as it would be in real life. It amply confirmed the liberal lectures and the liberal reading so far, and it denied and defied the socialist lectures and the socialist reading. As a "public good" the army, on active service an instrument of defence, had to be run on socialist principles—autocratically. It had paternalistic pretensions to care for its soldiery, but there was little room for individual sensitivity in its central allocation of resources, based on standardized ideas of ability and need, and distributed by authoritarian rationing. It had to interpret rules mechanically to avoid confusion, although in practice they were sometimes applied under the influence of jobbery and favouritism. The

8. Herman Finer, *Road to Reaction,* Dobson, 1946.
9. Herman Finer, *Municipal Trading,* Allen & Unwin, 1941.

whole was held together essentially by the common urgency of staying alive and defeating Hitler.

The opportunity for displaying humanity by breaking the rules was rare. Efficiency required close observance and conformity, with defiance punished summarily under the rules of King's Regulations; humanity to provide for individual circumstances risked chaos. A catering corporal in North Africa was authorized by the rules to refuse extra vegetables to a private who could not stomach the offered dish, but he was permitted to make the exception by the humane supervising sergeant. The staff sergeant sent a camp bed from home after the fighting in Italy was better able, by avoiding the cramped sleeping space on marble floors, to administer the return home of casualties, and was allowed to break the rules. The brigadier who "promoted" a warrant officer to staff captain duties, to strengthen his staff after the 1942 landings in Algiers, was bending the rules in order to increase the efficiency of his command. But battles could not be fought, or the war won, by such acts of unorthodox rule-breaking individualism that ignored and defied the bible of army administration.

Such were the standardized, repressive, essentially socialist imperatives of war. But they dramatized severe lessons for the unnecessary application of socialism in peace. In 1943 or 1944 I wrote from Italy to Arnold Plant about such desirable (but in a socialist system necessarily exceptional and suppressed) individual flexibilities. He replied from his wartime work as a director of rationing (for which he was knighted) that he had used my "report" on socialism under fire in an address on the economic conduct of the fighting services (he was particularly interested in large-scale administration).

But the lesson was not learned. The war was used, mostly by sociologists and economists with socialist leanings, to urge the use of socialism in peace—in the nationalization of industry, and in the state control of national finances to prevent inflation and expand employment, not least in the welfare state. Yet the question for the peace, not answered convincingly by the socialist textbook, was whether such methods could be operated or would be tolerated elsewhere in the home economy when there was no emergency, no common enemy, no imperative standardization, no ready conformity, no implicit acceptance of centralized planning, autocratic or benevolent. But the socialist texts offered no answers because they did not put the questions.

Such a system, unavoidable in the emergency of war, was arguably the most efficient in the supreme single-purpose task of defeating the military enemy. The socialism of war was thus extended into the peace. The intellectuals taught it; the public was led to think it was desirable; therefore the politicians acquiesced in it for electoral expediency even more than from philosophic conviction; and the bureaucracy revelled in its extended powers. That is why post-war Britain embraced socialism: by the accidental advent as a European leader of a megalomaniac German-Austrian corporal, by the accumulated effect over 60 years of Fabian teaching, by the ironic advice of two influential academics, Keynes and Beveridge, who saw themselves as Liberals, and by parliamentary democracy activated more by articulate group interests than by individual unknown because unexerted preferences.

The Secular Faith in Socialism

Marriage in 1948 led to family discussions in the 1950s that further refined my thinking on capitalism and socialism. My wife's father had been extensively wounded in the First World War, in which he had lost many young Cambridge friends. After some years in which he turned to Christianity as a devout churchman to restore his hope in humankind, he changed to the faith of communism as a more direct way to the brotherhood of man. His wounds had left him unable to complete his studies of medicine at the London Hospital; after partial recovery he had taught himself ornithology at home in a Kentish village, writing to supplement his war pension as a subaltern. A. & C. Black published his books on birds and flowers and *The Daily Worker* printed his weekly articles on nature.

He could not see the brotherhood of man emerging from capitalism based, as he saw it, on the motive of self-interest, but he was strong in his hope, or faith, that it would emerge in the socialism of the USSR. We had many tightly argued and evenly drawn discussions. He had a remarkably lucid intelligence that went to the essentials of an argument. But conviction and secular faith proved strong.

He was disturbed by the invasion of Hungary in 1956. If he had not died in 1961, his life shortened by his war wounds, he might have supported Gorbachev against the old guard. He was one of the socialists from whom I learned how to temper and refine the argument for capitalism.

Early Experience of Capitalism

I saw capitalism in practice after the war in two spells of research and advisory work in retailing (two years in the late 1940s as editor of an economic/management journal) and brewing (eight years in the 1950s in an office headed by the war-famed Marshall of the Royal Air Force Lord Tedder).

The Tedder office, in Dean's Yard, near Westminster Abbey, was the meeting-place for discussion by the gentlemen-capitalists, many descended from brewer-bankers, who ran family businesses with famous names—Guinness, Bass, Whitbread, Watney, Combe, Reid, Barclay, Charrington, Allsopp, Younger, McEwan-Younger and many others—paternalistic squires as well as commercial entrepreneurs. They politely listened to (and several heeded) the strange advice from the economist who they learned had come from the LSE, the reputed left-wing home of Laski and Dalton. Some later confided it had made them suspicious of my presence among them, especially when they heard of connections with the Liberal Party, still associated with Methodism, the non-conformist conscience, temperance and the Lloyd George hint of nationalization, and therefore regarded as another source of antipathy to brewers.

The take-over bid in 1957 for one of the largest, Watney, Combe, Reid, made some see that they could not depart too far from the market. Several saved themselves by unwontedly rapid adaptation to changing market conditions. Capitalism is tolerant of the preferences of owners of resources, but before too long the market reminds them that they hold property in trust for the community. The lesson not yet learned by even the most sophisticated socialists is that the community can express its "commands" or "sovereignty," its preferences and its wishes for (most) goods and services, better through the supply-and-demand processes of the market than through the political-electoral processes of the state (chapter 5).

The Tedder office, under a formerly Liberal lawyer R. E. Haylor, who had met liberal "capitalist" economists at the Reform Club, sensed the necessity to add economic to its legal, parliamentary and literary sources of advice. The post was tantalizing: to tell the office what economic advice it required. The task that evolved, of advising or "teaching" the industry to adapt itself to the coming competition of new amenities and social habits in the post-war world, was received at first with caution and then with welcome from some brewers, but especially from Tedder.

Even men of exceptional intellect find economic reasoning difficult. Tedder conducted the staff meetings like a don at a seminar. (It seemed he was as much an academic thinker as a military leader. As Vice-Chancellor of Cambridge, his University benefited from his mind as well as from his international fame as Eisenhower's Deputy in the invasion of Europe.) When it was explained privately in his room that the brewers' tied house system, then under severe criticism by the Labour MP Geoffrey Bing for restricting the customer's choice, was the method of ensuring retail outlets which they had to use because the licensing of public houses was often very restrictive, especially from 1869 after a period of free trade since 1830, he responded, sceptically, that the explanation seemed a sophistry. The explanation stands. Only one brewer, Guinness, has survived without tied houses, but by a method, extensive and costly advertising, that is itself the indirect result of restrictive licensing. The brewing industry has moved a long way from its production of alcoholic liquors for consumption by standing working-class drinkers in sawdust-strewn public bars.

In 1989 the Monopolies and Mergers Commission recommended that the number of tied houses owned by each firm be limited to 2,000. This is the political process clumsily trying to undo its own error. The British anti-trust laws are now probably doing more harm than good by distorting the structure of industries away from the form they would take in free markets and impairing their ability to respond to changing markets. In the 1950s, before the era of take-over bids to make better use of under-used assets, brewers as gentlemen-capitalists had to be advised sensitively as by a sympathetic friend rather than a censorious critic. The advice, based in part on visits to brewers to learn their attitudes and experience, was in part put into reports to Tedder, which he used in half-yearly addresses to brewers (some seemed surprised at his knowledge of the internal workings of the industry) and partly in occasional articles in *The Financial Times, The Economist* and *The Times* which analysed trends in the industry for outsiders but were also addressed to brewers.

Several of these articles, especially when signed, raised eyebrows. One in *The Financial Times* (signed) was regarded as too revealing of pricing policies. Another in *The Economist* (unsigned) in 1950[10] argued that the brewers should relax the link between their roles as producers of beers and property-owners of licensed houses: the voluntary loosening of the "tied-house" system would then enable both sides of their business to be developed more profitably. A third, in *The Times* in 1957 (signed), argued that changing market conditions would make the tie less enforceable and that the brewers should therefore welcome the liberalization of the restrictive licensing laws, which had virtually forced their brewer forebears to become bankers in financing their tenant-shopkeepers.

The Economist article presaged the specialization into brewing and retailing that some brewers contemplated after the Monopolies and Mergers

10. "The brewers' dilemma," *The Economist,* 30 December 1950.

Commission Report in 1989. *The Times* article was also a long way ahead of its time. The liberalization of the licensing laws developed 30 years later. The savage surgery of restricting brewers to an arbitrary number of retail outlets proposed by a technocratically minded Monopolies and Mergers Commission, which may have seemed electorally appealing, was wisely abandoned. Even well-intentioned trust-busting can impair the competitive system it is designed to perfect. All regulation is politicized: some is more damaging than others.

By the late 1950s all that should have been said by an economist had been said to the agreeable country gentlemen who were having to learn the opportunities and risks of capitalism.

The Intellectual Power-house of Market Capitalism

Chance had led in mid-1956 to advice from a Liberal Party leader, Lord Grantchester, who had been given my name by Arnold Plant, of the newly forming Institute of Economic Affairs (IEA) and his anxiety that it should carry a liberal intellectual thrust. Here, to put the saga of three decades into ten lines, the intriguing partnership of complementing contrasts with Ralph Harris, a former lecturer at St. Andrews University turned front-man fund-raiser, with a former LSE researcher turned back-room academic, with similarly humble social origins that belied their championship of the hated capitalist system, by previous political attachment Conservative and Liberal, by temperament Tory and Whig, led for over 30 years to the most rewarding work that could have been wished for a life's career.

The IEA, the inspired creation essentially of Sir Antony Fisher, an innovative entrepreneur, was the first of a score of similar institutions he founded or nurtured round the world. The IEA was the intellectual flagship of a growing fleet. Historians have compared the British IEA with the Anti–Corn Law League and the Fabian Society in its influence on the intellectual debate and political thinking of the 30 years following 1957. In 1988 the partnership ended with my withdrawal from active service, although I remained as a Founder President with (then Lord) Harris, and a new era under younger men opened. I have assessed the interaction, in its first era, of IEA teachings and public policy in a 1989 paper.[11]

The historian of the Conservative Party, Lord Blake, has seen the IEA as

11. Arthur Seldon, "Economic scholarship and political interest," in *Ideas, Interests and Consequences*, Institute of Economic Affairs, 1989.

the catalyst that moved the Party from its long corporatist attachment to the economic liberalism adopted by Sir Keith (later Lord) Joseph, with Enoch Powell one of the two most considerable Conservative intellects of recent decades, who transmitted it to the redoubtable Margaret Thatcher. "The libertarian doctrines of the Institute of Economic Affairs, after years of near-exile in a kind of intellectual Siberia, had great influence on Sir Keith Joseph and Mrs. Thatcher."[12] Lord Blake's judgement awaits the assessment of other historians, perhaps in the projected history of the IEA and its works. In the meantime, a comparable political judgement emerged from Enoch Powell, a Conservative minister in the 1950s and 1960s, in a book of assessments of the influences on the governments of Mrs. Thatcher: "No account of . . . the exploration of the market mechanism . . . in the Conservative Party with widening enthusiasm from the mid-1950s on . . . would be well balanced which underestimated the effectiveness of the work of the Institute of Economic Affairs and its proselytizing influence . . . It challenged head-on the prevailing orthodoxies of natural—and therefore presumably irreversible—public monopoly and of the use of collective action—from government planning through to private cartels—as an instrument for the allocation of resources."[13]

Several market-oriented organizations followed, after 20 years, in the 1970s to reflect and strengthen the influence of the IEA, although, with the exception of the David Hume Institute in Edinburgh, their approach differed in proceeding from the "artillery" of principles to the "infantry" of proposals for political implementation. The 1990s will indicate whether dilution by the dictates of the political process has done more good by enactment of compromise practical proposals than harm by discrediting the principles of market competition under capitalism, by subjection to the often short-term expediencies of the "politically possible" which in practice can be a euphemism for electoral party advantage.

The personal cooperation of complementary opposites in the direction of the IEA reveals a main reason, perhaps the main reason, for the effectiveness of the first post-war academic power-house that questioned the economic potency of the state and thereby rehabilitated the repute of liberal capitalism.

The funds had to come initially from industry, yet private industry was not unequivocally in favour of the market process: it generally, and logically,

12. Lord Blake, *The Conservative Party from Peel to Thatcher,* Fontana, 1985.

13. In Dennis Kavanagh and Anthony Seldon (eds.), *The Thatcher Effect: A Decade of Change,* Oxford University Press, 1989, p. 84.

welcomed competition in the objects and services it bought, but understandably found it a severe task-master in those it sold. Ralph Harris combined knowledge of the case for capitalism with good-humoured wit to become the archetypal persuader of capitalists to support the study, and where academically necessary the criticism, of capitalism. It was a task that combined the arts of advocate, adviser, candid friend and salesman.

The Gilbert (Seldon) and Sullivan (Harris) combination of producer and projector respectively of the case for liberal capitalism unconsciously drew on Dickens's partnership of the solicitors Spenlow and Jorkins, in which each assured clients that unfortunate, though necessary, decisions were made by the other. The General Director explained to subscribers that the Editorial Director had to allow academics as scholars to speak their minds about industry; the Editorial Director reconciled authors to the occasional displeasure from subscribers who supplied the funds to support their independence. The first disaffected subscriber disturbed the precarious early finances of the office by withdrawing his subscription over the celebrated Hobart Paper on the case against resale price maintenance. That uncompromising stand on academic supremacy above subscriber sensitivity set the strategy. It withstood the criticism of Conservatives that the espousal by Edward Heath of the IEA argument had lost the Conservatives the 1964 General Election (subscribers in the late 1950s and early 1960s included supporters of corporatist policies). Moreover, it earned the respect of the capitalist subscriber who returned with his subscription after a short defection.

The failure of socialists to analyse and understand this complex relationship between capitalism and the capitalists, and their underlying Marxist oversimplification of "the class struggle" (as in the writings of the Italian Antonio Gramsci [chapter 3]) with the capitalists as the defenders of capitalism and the workers as its enemies, partly explains their inability to explain why workers as well as capitalists all over the world, in the East as well as the West, have been accepting or welcoming capitalism, under this or other names, in the 1980s and 1990s.

The IEA provided the opportunity to help in building what the Left describes as the original British right-wing or New Right think-tank. Its *Weltanschauung* was scepticism of the economic performance of the state. It thus focused attention on three aspects of the market as the long-neglected alternative to the state, the central theme of this book: first, the performance of capitalism in the post-war years; second, its potential performance; third, its prospective performance in the years ahead into the twenty-first century.

Socialists have been hoist with their dialectical petard. Since Friedrich

Engels they have seen almost every substantial economic downturn as the final "crisis" of capitalism. Wishful thinking led some to proclaim the end of the capitalist world after the October 1987 stock exchange downturn and yet again in the stubborn though modest inflation of 1989. They have been perplexed by the recent developments in capitalism around the world in the East as well as the West, and in communist as well as in capitalist countries, because they have absorbed the Marxist prediction of the ultimate inevitability of the capitalist collapse.

In contrast, the IEA provided the time and resources to study capitalism not only as it was from the 1950s to the early 1980s, and the reasons for its successes and failures. Even more, it created the opportunity to study capitalism as it could have been in the last three decades if its potential market processes had not been frustrated by the state and its obstructive political processes. Not least, it facilitated study of the work of many individual scholars in Britain and overseas who had analysed the working of capitalism and provided a vision of what it could be in the future. These three sources have inspired the ideas and the argument in this book.

The 30 years of producing several hundred texts of liberal or neo-liberal economists, political scientists, historians and other scholars, from the inexperienced to the world-renowned, both inspired and continually postponed the hope of turning the intellectual tables on the critics of capitalism who were so preoccupied with its failures that they could not, or would not, see its triumphs. At last 1988 provided the leisure to match the socialist tactic of contrasting imperfect capitalism as it has been with "perfect" socialism as they said it would be; the opposite contrast emphasized here is of socialism as it has been with capitalism as it could be.

Purist scholars would properly maintain that the valid comparison must be between both systems as they have been, at their worst, or as they could be, at their best. Yet since there is no lack of studies of capitalism at its worst and socialism at its best, and since the student and the television viewer have been acclimatized to the socialist approach, the effective antidote to this distortion of public understanding and education, the only way to redress the imbalance of analysis and advocacy, is the rare exercise attempted here. The unacceptable face of socialism as evidenced round the world will be contrasted with the acceptable face of capitalism as revealed by scholarly research, so that the student and the general public asked to vote, and perhaps even the socialist with an open mind and not too proud or too old to admit error, can make the choice of the more persuasive analysis.

The Socialist Acceptance of Capitalism

It no longer seems convincing to persist in the rearguard action, common even in the best socialist writing, of acknowledging the achievements of capitalism but obscuring the recognition by contorted labels that incorporate the essence of capitalism in a new form of socialism. Socialists should be candid enough to use language that no longer bemuses the public, especially the working classes who increasingly contrast the evidence of their eyes with the continuing condemnation of capitalism by their political party or trade union leaders.

The verbal contortion that capitalism is admirable but still vicious is becoming difficult to sustain in the West. There is more candour in the East. Three short visits to Hong Kong, Taiwan, Singapore and Japan in 1968, 1981 and 1988 bore witness to the visibly rising living standards in 20 short years of economic miracles and removed any lingering doubts. Despite Marx's condemnations of capitalism that still influence non-Marxist as well as Marxist scholars, his ironic acknowledgement in *The Communist Manifesto*[14] of its prodigious productive power is graphically exemplified in the newer and smaller countries of Asia, where it has not been trammelled by the conservative industrial, professional and trade union institutions and vested interests of the West.

The celebrated Marxist acknowledgement of capitalist productivity would be recognized by the common people of the capitalist world in their living standards. Capitalism, said *The Communist Manifesto,* had "accomplished wonders far exceeding Egyptian pyramids, Roman aqueducts, and Gothic cathedrals . . . during its rule of scarce one hundred years [that is, since the mid-18th century, the beginning of the Industrial Revolution], it has created more massive and more colossal productive forces than have all preceding generations put together." The people of the capitalist West and East hardly require further evidence than the goods in their shops, and more recently the plaintive mystified complaints liberated by *glasnost* in the USSR and China, that the people of the socialist world lack bathrooms and air conditioning. The well-endowed intellectuals may emphasize the freedoms of democracy, which they require for their professional trade; the people want bread and butter, shoes and shelter, with freedoms to produce more.

14. Karl Marx and Friedrich Engels, *The Communist Manifesto,* 1848; Penguin, 1967, pp. 83–5.

The ironic display of intellectual conservatism by socialist academics in the capitalist West who now lag far behind their counterparts in the communist world is becoming too difficult to disguise. The economists of Yugoslavia, Hungary, Poland (one came to the IEA some years ago to ask about the shadow or transfer pricing between departments evolved by large capitalist firms), Russia and China have had to study the market because of the urgency of rescuing their economies from continuing decline relative to the capitalist West. Recent books by three of the better British socialist academics, Plant, Marquand and Gamble, who are political scientists rather than economists, show more sophistication than most socialists, and yet there is still reluctance to acquire the instinctive understanding of the market by the liberal economists, not least its unequalled potency in creating a libertarian society that tends to create equality by demolishing monopoly and privilege, not the coercive equality enforced by the state.[15] The advantage of the liberal is to understand that the strengths of capitalism cannot be won without risking weaknesses. The socialist wants the strengths of capitalism in a new form of socialism that would emasculate the market and destroy its strengths. The socialist acceptance of the market has been intellectual, because it is indispensable, but not spiritual, because it would discipline the political process that is the machinery of socialism.

Contradictions: Capitalist and Socialist

Further acts of intellectual confusion require to be corrected. The familiar socialist doctrine that the demise of capitalism is "inevitable" must by now seem increasingly disreputable in the light of the evidence of recent decades. The notion that the contradictions of capitalism—seen in its monopoly, inequality, poverty, injustices, unemployment, inflation, booms and slumps—are unavoidable, but the disappointments of socialism—dare one list stagnation, coercion, suppression, low living standards in food, clothing, health services, housing and household amenities, restricted freedom to read, discuss, debate, differ and travel internally or overseas, jobbery and corruption, inequality, concealed unemployment, concealed inflation, concealed booms and slumps, arbitrary imprisonment, political murder—are the results of "mistakes" or the fortuitous accession to power of tyrants, has

15. Kenneth Hoover and Raymond Plant, *Conservative Capitalism in Britain and the United States,* Routledge, 1989; David Marquand, *The Unprincipled Society,* Cape, 1988; Andrew Gamble, *The Free Economy and the Strong State,* Macmillan, 1988.

had a long run. There has been too much socialism of all kinds round the world to make the "vision" of socialism plausible.

Socialists and liberals who look for truth agree at least that both systems are imperfect, defective and disappointing. It remains to contest the socialist case. The opposite of socialism is liberalism, which produces imperfect capitalism. But the worst ills of capitalism can be removed at lower cost than the ills of socialism because capitalism is more corrigible than socialism. The experience of the decades has finally demonstrated that the ills of socialism are irremovable except by the mechanisms of capitalism.

That is why capitalism deserves celebration, and why this book is a salute to the imperfect but least objectionable method of organizing production known to the world.

CHAPTER 3

The Inevitability of Capitalism

> Capitalist concentration, determined by the mode of production, produces a corresponding concentration of working human masses. This fact underlies all the revolutionary theses of Marxism [and] the conditions of the new proletarian way of life, the new communist order destined to replace the bourgeois way of life and the disorder of capitalism arising from free competition and class struggle.
>
> Antonio Gramsci, *Factory Councils and Socialist Democracy: Conquest of the State*

The destiny of capitalism, its inevitable replacement by socialism, has been a unifying refrain running through socialist writing and thinking, hoping and conspiring for more than a century from Marx to the present day. In the last few years, and increasingly during the late 1980s, doubts among Marxist-inclined socialists have been engagingly candid and venturesome. The 1919 formulation by Gramsci, a continuing Marxist favourite, states the essentials.[1] It dates back to the time when hopes were understandably running high, the second year after the replacement of capitalism by socialism in the USSR and the year of Lenin's celebrated *State and Revolution*.[2] But Marxist texts tend to be read as authoritative sources of doctrine long after events have removed them far from reality.

The Circular Reasoning of Socialism

The theory (explanation) of capitalism and its domination and exploitation of the common people was that it was founded on the technical, financial and other economies of the very large-scale industrial organization of

1. Antonio Gramsci, in David Forgacs (ed.), *A Gramsci Reader: Selected Writings 1916–35*, Lawrence & Wishart, 1988.

2. V. I. Lenin, *State and Revolution*, 1919.

production. The sequence of reasoning to the inevitable downfall of capitalism then followed. Gramsci's sequence is common to the Marxist analysis: concentration of production creates concentrations of workers and their proletarian lives; their resistance to, and rejection of, the harsh conditions of capitalist life foment rebellion; capitalist exploitation is sooner or later inevitably replaced initially by socialism, the first or lower stage, and then by communism, the second or higher stage, with its final abolition of want and the rewards of superabundance.

The two-stage advance from capitalism, dating back to Marx's *Critique of the Gotha Programme,*[3] with its vision of the final abolition of scarcity, is superficially paralleled by Keynes's sanguine prospect of the coming of superabundance 100 years from when he wrote in 1930 that would end the search for sufficiency and permit concentration on the ultimate purposes of life. Both were writing as seers, evocative in their visions, but irrelevant in the common round and the daily task of earning a living, and harmful in distracting attention from the inescapable economic task of satisfying demands outrunning supplies that will confront both capitalism and socialism until the end of time. The 100 years after 1930 are rapidly approaching in 2030: there will be increasing wealth under capitalism, but scarcity of goods and services undreamt of by Keynes in 1930. Socialism has abandoned the hope of increasing wealth, still less of abolishing scarcity.

Economists have the unpopular role of insisting that there is a demand side as well as a supply side to the equation of scarcity and abundance. Lenin was a better economist than Marx; he understood the two requirements of communism. The analysis of his *State and Revolution* seems to be forgotten by Marxists. It explained that communism required not only the abolition of scarcity but also a change in human nature. But this is its fatal flaw. Communism requires not only unprecedented expansion in the output of suppliers but a new attitude of relative indifference from "demanders" (consumers). However much supplies of goods and services are expanded, "scarcity" (in the sense of inadequacy for all possible purposes, not absolute want) will persist because demand will grow with supply. Word processors make the task of composing books such as this technically easier than the former methods of writing, dictating or typing, but the demand for them will for that very reason grow; word processors will become more common, but they will remain "scarce." And the degree of their scarcity will be indicated by their price. Like the original ball-point pen, they will become

3. Karl Marx, *Critique of the Gotha Programme*, 1857.

cheaper in the next five and ten years, but as long as they command a price they will remain "scarce." And as long as word processors—and everything else—remain scarce they will command, and produce, a market price that makes their production profitable.

The visions of Marx and Keynes embodied a decisive difference in the economic systems they favoured. Despite his criticism of free-market capitalism, Keynes did not embrace socialism, and he would certainly not have followed his "sour and silly" acolytes into Marxism. Keynes's capitalism, as he envisaged it improved by his reforms, would generate productive forces that shrank elemental scarcities in the substances that sustain life; Marx's socialism has shown no such comparable powers of production. Capitalism has abolished famines in countries where it is allowed to activate and reward human effort. The remaining famines of the globe plague socialist countries of the Third World, not the commercial societies of the Far East.

The Marxist sequence from socialism to communism reveals a damaging error: the circular reasoning in socialist economic thinking. The celebrated formula in the *Critique of the Gotha Programme* is falsified by history and contemporary experience but remains a seductive text in socialist writing. The original German is rarely quoted:

> *Jeder nach seinen Fähigkeiten,*
> *jedem nach seinen Bedürfnissen.*

The English is preferred:

> From each according to his abilities,
> to each according to his needs.

Fähigkeiten are identifiable capacities or talents because they command a market price, but *Bedürfnisse* are the elusive "needs" that have plagued the social sciences and government policy for decades. This formula is repeated by Marxists as the outcome of a practical political policy that will lift mankind to an unprecedented life of ease, contentment and harmony. The simple solution is that by replacing capitalism with socialism, it will replace scarcity by abundance.

This, the second ("higher") phase of socialism, called communism, is the fantasy offered the labouring masses by "scientific" socialism. The first ("lower") phase was based on a feasible formula:

> From each according to his ability,
> to each according to his work.

The socialist difficulty is that the method of organizing production in the first phase, by centralized direction and planning, neither encouraged each to contribute according to his capacity nor rewarded him (or her) according to his contribution. On the contrary it was capitalism that evolved methods in the labour market of inducing effort according to ability and paying according to output. They were imperfect, but they worked. Their effectiveness, contrasted with the ineffective methods of prescribing tasks and rewards by central authority, are evidenced in the wide gaps between the standards of living of capitalist and socialist countries.

The leap from technically conceivable but inefficient socialism, with its now acknowledged inability to generate production and allocate scarce resources, as conceded by Alec Nove in 1983,[4] closely followed by Gorbachev in 1985, to Utopian communism, with its miraculous abolition or annihilation of scarcity, shirked the four tasks of economic systems everywhere. First, they must develop techniques of valuing scarce resources; second, they must evolve incentives to concentrate on the most productive methods; third, they must devise the means of assembling and distributing information on relative efficiency in alternative employments; fourth, they must create principles of allocating the output to the most urgent or highly valued uses. Yet these are precisely the methods and devices developed by the market. They remain imperfect, although they are continually refined, but socialism has failed to develop comparable techniques and has no other way ahead but to accept the capitalist methods of the market. For the final irony of socialism is that it promised the people superabundance and condemned them to privation.

This is the Achilles' heel mystery of the socialist/communist vision that no Marxist has since solved. How is scarcity abolished? It requires supply to exceed demand over the whole economy. And that requires, as Lenin sensed, unprecedented productive power on the supply side and a change in human nature on the demand side. But these were no more than assertions, statements of the obvious. Socialist communism does not produce these miracles; yet it would require miracles to produce the plenty and selflessness that Marx called communism. Either production must overwhelm requirements, or desire for output must shrivel below productive capacity. There is no sign of either miracle in the socialist countries. Production flags and the people want more than the system produces.

4. Alec Nove, *The Economics of Feasible Socialism,* Allen & Unwin, 1983.

The next socialist step would be to demonstrate the economic machinery that creates superabundance and the psychological revolution that produces altruistic indifference. This economic machinery remains a mirage. Human nature has inconveniently come between socialist visionaries and the realization of their socialism. They have earned the taunt "If you cannot change society, change the people," inspired by Bertolt Brecht's proposal after the 1953 Berlin uprising that, if the Government of East Germany had lost confidence in the people, it should elect a new people. In 1989, East Germans began to leave for West Germany because Soviet *glasnost* made it impolitic to hold them by coercion. East Germany will keep its people only by producing the relative plenty of West Germany; and that will require the relentless replacement of socialism by capitalism. If the East Germans want to live better they must go capitalist whether they remain in East Germany or move to West Germany.

Socialism has so far demonstrated neither the production miracle nor the psychological transformation. And it indicates no insights into the required economic revolution or the human metamorphosis. Selflessness can be a motive for "public" service, but it is hardly a dominant characteristic of political people. It is necessary for Marxist socialism to envisage that scarcity will be abolished and human nature be transformed, by means unknown, to present the world of communism in which the mechanisms of capitalism that measure the value of scarce resources in alternative uses will be unnecessary because there will be plenty for all. Nove's courageous attempt[5] to salvage feasible socialism based on markets by jettisoning Utopian communism based on metaphysical conjecture may have been studied by the economists advising Gorbachev. But the further stage of providing "socialist" markets with the necessary capitalist institutions of private property to create the required incentives will be the most difficult, because it will require no less than the abandonment once and for all of the state ownership of resources obligatory in the socialist vision. That cathartic revolution back to capitalism would endanger the socialist establishment. It could conceivably be a peaceful "soft landing," with a settlement acceptable to liberals who welcome reform and conservatives who fear it, if it appeared less traumatic than a revolution of violence in which all might lose. But it would be the end of socialism.

5. Ibid.

Marxist Doubts about Marxism

Doubts about the long-prophesied self-destructive trends in the structure of production under capitalism have been sobering Marxist and socialist writing for some years. After a confident 4,000-word re-assertion of "Marxist economics," together with the familiar "analysis" of contradictions and crisis, in the misleadingly entitled *New Palgrave Dictionary of Economics* (which uses Palgrave's name but does not reproduce the spirit of his approach), Andrew Glyn, the socialist academic at Oxford, ends with engaging uncertainty:

> Whether the microchip, decentralization of production, Japan-style industrial relations, more freedom for market forces and so forth provide a "new way" out for capitalism in the 1990s is currently under intense discussion.[6]

"Intense discussion" is a euphemism for agonizing re-appraisal. But there is no hint here of the desperate search by Gorbachev, and others in Eastern Europe and China, for ways of using market forces as a new way out for socialism. Since Marxist writing has until recently shown little capacity to anticipate the trends in capitalist industrial production, but has repeated its uncompromising prediction of the destiny and doom of capitalism, Glyn's concluding laudation of Marxist economics is at least a *non sequitur,* at worst chutzpah (cool nerve, gall). After conceding that "the days of Stalinist orthodoxy and dogmatic repetition of the texts are gone," the denouement proceeds: "Marxist economics is again making a forceful and imaginative contribution to the analysis of contemporary society," a brave attempt to demonstrate the triumph of conviction over evidence.[7]

This admission of error in Marxist economics but stubborn assertion of its continuing importance and influence, possibly written in 1986 before the more recent events in the USSR, could not have foreseen the further concession by British Marxist writers in 1988 that all was not well with the Marxist repetition of the perennial demise of capitalism. Wiser Marxist/communist observers then unexpectedly raced ahead with the volte-face that, after all,

6. Andrew Glyn, "Marxist economics," in John Eatwell, Murray Milgate and Peter Newman (eds.), *New Palgrave Dictionary of Economics,* Macmillan, 1987, vol. 3, p. 394.

7. Ibid.

the industrial structure of capitalism, which had long been supposed before and since Gramsci to contain the seeds of collapse, was changing radically, and Marxists/socialists would be wise to heed its changing development, unfortunately not foreseen by Marx and his followers. Late in his day Marx was led to deny he was a Marxist.

This further ideological retreat came from the intellectuals who evidently advise the British Communist Party. Like Khrushchev's disguised confession of Stalinist tyranny in 1956, the latest skilful Marxist confession of dialectical failure will take time to be understood by the socialist rank and file and to penetrate socialist writing. It was, moreover, deployed as a criticism of the intellectuals of the British "conservative" Labour Party, which the communist critics said had failed to observe and analyse the implications of the changing industrial scene. Its reasoning bears on the debate about whether it will be capitalism or socialism/communism that will collapse.

The question, to adapt Gramsci's language, is whether it is the destiny of socialism to replace the bourgeois way of life of capitalism. If not, it may be the destiny of capitalism to replace the proletarian way of life of socialism. That is now much more likely.

The Communist Party draft statement[8] was published in the September 1988 issue of *Marxism Today,* self-described as "the theoretical and discussion journal of the Party." The editorial introduction was revealing: "The Left has been in retreat for a decade. It has lost out badly in its contest with Thatcherism. Even more seriously, it has failed to address the new world of the 1980s. Too often it has seemed more interested in the past than in the future." The new discussion document, commissioned by the Party from eight writers, including the Editor of *Marxism Today,* Martin Jacques, who has taken the lead in rethinking the Marxist analysis of capitalism, Beatrix Campbell, and Charlie Leadbeater of *The Financial Times,* was presented as a preliminary to redrafting the Communist Party programme of 1977,[9] pointedly claimed as "a pioneering document in the reconstruction of the Left."

The purpose in preparing the Communist Party document was "the need to confront the radically-changed world in which we now live" which "requires us to rethink the Left's policies and perspectives." The document begged some questions. It continued the confusing use of the political label

8. Martin Jacques et al., "Facing up to the future," *Marxism Today,* September 1988.

9. *The British Road to Socialism,* 1977.

"Thatcherism," the current *bête noire* of the Left, to describe the economic philosophy of liberalism developed for decades by scholars with no necessary party allegiance. The "new world" of industrial change did not begin in the 1980s (below). And the rethinking on the political Left is belated, perhaps because until 1987 it thought it could win political power, aided by "the working human masses," without discarding the once politically profitable scapegoat of capitalist exploitation, injustice and poverty. But the document will prove to mark a historic revision and rejection by younger Marxists of conventional Marxist thinking on the structure of capitalist industry and its false, and falsified, prediction of the collapse of capitalism.

The impact of this report, entitled "Facing up to the future," is significant for the study of the thinking on the Left in Europe, where the fundamental re-appraisal of capitalism is being led by the Marxist intelligentsia followed at some cautious distance by the politically expedient revisionism of the Labour Party. "Facing up to the future" was revised and amplified as "Manifesto for new times," published with the June 1989 *Marxism Today*, introduced on 27 October 1989 with eloquence and wit by Professor Hall to a well-attended weekend conference of probably over 1,000 at the Institute of Education of the University of London, and discussed by an impressive politically catholic international panel chaired by Martin Jacques and comprising Beatrix Campbell of the British Communist Party, Bryan Gould of the British Labour Right, Giorgio Napolitano of the Italian Communist Party, Karsten Voigt of the West German Social Democratic Party, and a spokesman for the Green Party. Ken Livingstone of the British Labour Left was billed but could not attend. The essence of the argument on the changing nature of capitalism and the necessity for rethinking on the Left was put with more intellectual purity in "Facing up to the future," which is examined here.

Although peppered with the Marxist language of "hegemony," "legitimacy," "struggle" and, of course, "crisis," the analysis was clearly argued and remarkably undoctrinaire. It would seem that Gorbachev has induced *glasnost* (openness) among British as well as Soviet socialist or communist writers. Its description of the trends in industry read as much like the capitalist *Financial Times* as the socialist/communist *Marxism Today.* (Both "socialist" and "communist" have to be used since, despite the official Marxist distinction between them, they are often used interchangeably.)

"Western industrial societies," ran the new thinking, "are being fundamentally reshaped. New technology is transforming the way people work and what they produce. Cultural and social life is becoming more diverse. Most women have a dual social role, in employment and in domestic work. Old industrial areas are in decline and new sunrise corridors are growing."[10] This reconsideration of capitalist industry was made to seem a recent discovery. But none of it is new to the student of capitalism; its early forms appeared in the 1930s. It is hardly new to the capitalists who have been adapting themselves for decades to the new structure of industry. Nor is it new to millions of "the working human masses" who in the 40 years since the war have moved from declining to growing industries, except where they have been prevented by trade union restrictions or discouraged by politicized housing and rent controls, building restrictions and regional subsidies.

It is the critics of capitalism, from Marxist to social democrat, as well as the corporatist-minded capitalists and trade union leaders, who have sought to slow down the transition from old to new techniques, firms, industries and regions by importuning government to provide privileges of varying kinds (the political process of rent-seeking analysed in the economics of politics), who have prevented capitalism from working, and thus denied its benefits to Gramsci's "working human masses." Since its earliest years capitalism was geared to produce goods and services for the "working masses" whose wants and tastes were despised by their supposed cultural betters. The task now is to devise disciplines on politicians that will prevent them forming unholy corporatist alliances with vested interests against the common people. The required solutions in the role and functions of government will not come from socialist intellectuals and politicians, who still look to the political process, but from the liberal intellectuals and politicians who would strengthen the flexible market process against the distortions imposed by the political process.

That is the reply to revisionist academics of the Left, from Bryan Gould to David Marquand, who look to the "democratic" political process to dominate the market process (chapter 5). Since the war the powerful democracy of the market, imperfect but reinforceable by redistribution of purchasing power, would have done more for "the working human masses" than the culturally precarious, socially vulnerable and politically manipulated "democracy" of politics has done, not least in education, medical care, housing and pensions (chapter 11) as well as in local and national government services generally.

10. Jacques et al., "Facing up to the future," p. 2.

From Fordism to the Domestic System

The old industrial order, said the communist report, was based on large-scale factories, typified by the car-making Ford works, which employed large numbers of generally semiskilled workers engaged in routine tasks producing standardized goods. The workers were also the consumers of a new flow of cheapening labour-saving and amenity-creating goods that produced "a social revolution in leisure and consumption." This sophisticated view of late twentieth-century capitalism was commendably reproduced in *Marxism Today* for the enlightenment of socialist/communist readers long taught to think of capitalism as it was in the middle or late nineteenth century. The new technology, said the report, would display flexibility, a wider range of industrial enterprises, attention to individual consumer preferences and a larger output of personal services. Production units would be small and medium scale as well as large scale, with a wide range of forms of ownership from one-man bands through cooperatives to large firms owned by the employees or consumers. "Fordism," or "Fordist" concentration, was no longer the necessary "mode of capitalist production."

Even the welfare state did not escape. The revisionist document declared unpalatable truths, belatedly but with candour in a Marxist journal, to an embattled left-wing audience. The welfare state form of unnecessary socialism (below), still hailed as the greatest achievement of the post-war consensus, had brought "poor quality, lack of choice, and paternalism."[11] When this criticism of state pensions, council housing, the National Health Service and state education came from the New Right, as in the growing stream of papers generated by the IEA from the late 1950s, it was repelled as outdated *laissez-faire*, callous and suggesting reforms that were "politically impossible."

The recognition by the communist intellectuals of decades of doctrinal error was not a triumph but a torpedo of Marxist economics. It was a root-and-branch rejection of the Marxist prediction of the inevitability of capitalist collapse. Despite Gramsci and the long school of Marxist analysts, there will be, it is at last accepted, no "corresponding concentration of working human masses." Gramsci's "capitalist concentration" will no longer underlie "all the revolutionary theses of Marxism." It will no longer underlie "the conditions of the new proletarian way of life." The new communist order will therefore no longer be "destined to replace the bourgeois way of life."

11. Ibid.

It will no longer replace "the disorder of capitalism arising from free competition and class struggle." Capitalism, after all, will continue. It will take new forms, more varied and flexible than foreseen by Marx, but it will not be replaced by Nove's feasible market-allocating socialism nor by the Marxists' continuing mirage of superabundant communism.

This recantation of Marxist dogma, like some others, came from the Marxist rather than from the "democratic" Labour wing of socialist thinking. It was outlined in a new statement of rethinking by intellectuals for the Communist Party, and discussed at length, as other recantations or results of rethinking have been, in the avowedly Marxist *Marxism Today* rather than in the more severely doctrinaire Marxist *New Left Review*, the not generally Marxist *New Statesman* or the avowedly non-Marxist Labour Party organ *New Socialist*. The recantation was engaging and creditable, but not as candid as it might have been. It was presented as new Marxist thinking emerging from insight into events in the development of capitalism; in truth it was a confession of error in persevering with erroneous thinking that had been long outdated by the adaptation of capitalism to the accelerated advance in technology analysed by liberal market economists for decades.

The new capitalism that is absorbing the technical marvels of the age will decentralize industry in much economic activity from the Fordist factory to the home, equipped with the latest computerized technology in a new "domestic system." It is elephantine socialism that will continue with Fordist industry in the USSR and East Europe long after it is outdated and discontinued in the capitalist West.

Capitalist Flexibility, Socialist Stagnation

Yet the manner of the recantation deserves some censure for misrepresenting history. The gradual change from mass large-scale to middle-scale and small-scale production dates from the interwar years. The early signs were evident in the 1930s, or the 1920s. For decades they were largely overlooked or ignored by the archetypal socialist critics, misled and bemused by their unquestioned belief in the eventual collapse of capitalism. If the critics had examined these trends in the structure of capitalist industry much earlier and more closely they would have come to understand the superior ability of capitalism, despite its combines and cartels created by capitalists with the connivance or encouragement until recent years of Conservative and Labour Governments, to embrace technical advance to the benefit of the living standards of the "working human masses."

Moreover, they might have been induced to acknowledge that capitalism had adapted itself to the computer, the microchip, mechanical automatism and the other marvels of information technology, the new methods of financing industry, the more open markets of Europe, the new methods of discovering consumer wants, the advantages of team over mass production and much else much earlier and more smoothly than the socialism of the USSR in the countries of the Comecon, still weighed down in the 1990s by its massive socialist Fordism. It was precisely the open markets of capitalist Western Europe in contrast with the politically dominated bilateral trading of communist Eastern Europe and the consumer sovereignty of capitalism in contrast with the consumer subjection of socialism that enabled the West to race ahead of the producer conservatism and producer conservationism of Eastern Europe in the post-war years.

Nor is the capacity of the USSR to engage in space research and discovery evidence of its industrial or technological achievement. A politically controlled economy, driven by the anxiety of the politicians to demonstrate superiority in industry or technology that will impress or awe or warn other countries, can invest disproportionately vast resources in projects remote from the market where the common people, living with indifferent food, dowdy clothing and cramped housing, would express very different preferences. The politicians can emerge with technically advanced but economically foolish products—vast flying machines, elaborate sea-going transport, complex underwater submersibles that serve as political advertising for the planners at the expense of the comforts of the people.

The market, where competition is imperfect, may stop short of the optimum size of product; the state is tempted to go far beyond it. Here, as elsewhere, the choice may be between too large and too small. The market is preferable because it is easier to correct by competition from new suppliers with better or cheaper products than the state run by planners who have to serve a small band of uncontrollable politicians.

In politicized socialist systems production is dominated by political decisions for political purposes. That markets driven by competition between suppliers to meet consumer preferences may emerge with products that fall short of the technically possible is a familiar complaint of the technical mind in the natural sciences, which rarely understands the primacy of the economic over the technical optimum because the technical mind ignores the cost in alternatives sacrificed. The decisive political question is whether the resources of the earth are to be used as the people wish or as the politicians, elected or self-selected, dictate. The ultimate test of technical achievement is its price—the necessary measure of the alternative uses of labour, capital, land and other resources. Soviet space achievement has been reached at the high price of depriving the common people of capitalist standards not only in the daily staples of food, clothing and shelter, but also in medical care, education, transport and much else that the people of capitalism accept and expect as commonplace. The central role of the pricing mechanism and the reason for the superiority of capitalism over socialism are still misunderstood even in the latest revisionist thinking of socialist intellectuals and Labour politicians.

Not least, the error of the socialist critique continues, until this day, to mislead "the working human masses" who, though in diminishing numbers, follow the faith of the intellectuals in the coming collapse of capitalism. And it continues to mislead students in British universities and polytechnics whose generous impulses to rescue the poor are exploited in the propagation of a political order that would deepen their dependence and perpetuate their poverty.

The belief in the eventual collapse of capitalism because of its supposed internal contradictions, or its demise because it fails to satisfy the populace in the undeveloped countries, or its overthrow by revolution has bitten deeply into the socialist psyche and will not easily be dislodged or discarded. It will be many years before it is abandoned by socialists in capitalist countries, because capitalism will always display defects for them to denounce as well as achievements they will ignore or depreciate. Sombre clouds will always be found to obscure the silver linings.

The irony is that the doctrinal belief in the collapse of capitalism will linger longer in Britain, Europe and elsewhere in the capitalist world than in Hungary, Poland, Czechoslovakia, Yugoslavia and elsewhere in the socialist world because their economists and politicians will have the more compelling and more urgent reason—economic reconstruction by capitalist markets to raise living standards—for abandoning socialist practices, whatever political expediency dictates that they claim are the continuing socialist objectives or values.

The Literati against the People

The opportunity for the common peoples of capitalist as well as socialist countries to hear the case for capitalism has suffered because the socialist interpreters of day-to-day events have retained a lingering hope that after all, despite the evidence to the contrary, the outlook for a politico-economic system based on a philosophy of humanism and compassion must be bright.

It is difficult not to sympathize with them. Many grew up and were taught the benefits of socialism during or after the war. Army education material was plentiful and persuasive on "the inauguration of the millenium," as the Head of the Cabinet Economic Secretariat described it in early 1946 when I was sent to him for a job. (He emerged later as a Social Democrat.) I went into capitalist employment instead. The tempting hustings invitation that won the 1945 General Election for the Labour Party might have read "Turn left for the Elysian fields"; it misled millions of trusting electors into voting for industrial and welfare socialism from which they cannot easily escape when it becomes outdated, as most of it soon became in the post-war years. It is still possible, the socialist-inclined hope, against the evidence, that socialism can work in peace to ensure "fair shares" (a characteristic question begger, like "reasonable" working conditions and "adequate" pay) and maintain the sense of community.

Their dilemma is partly demographic. They lived in years when incomes were generally much lower than in the 1990s, with memories of the Great Depression of 1929–31, household means tests, barefoot children and miners' silicosis. It is unlikely that the present-day children of the then poor, with higher living standards, who own their homes rather than pay rent for council houses or high-rise flats, will share the interwar memories of the ageing literati, their perennial hopes for socialism or their congenital contempt for capitalism. But the culpability of British writers remains for using their literary gifts to spread unfounded faith in socialism by overstating its prospects and continuing the distrust of capitalism by understating its achievements.

The writers of fiction have used it as propaganda against the capitalism they do not understand. Although democratic government is not necessarily representative of the people's opinions, politicians heed them when they seem to support their inclinations. One of the main inclinations of politicians is to extend their influence over the economy and much else, to leave their mark on society and to ensure a place in history. Their main arguments are those that writers before and after Charles Dickens have used as the themes of their novels and other fiction—the suffering caused by poverty. The balance of argument in public understanding of the relative merits and defects of capitalism and socialism has for a century and more been pushed in favour of socialism because of the influence on opinion of the playwrights, novelists, poets and journalists who in general benefit from the liberties and opportunities created by capitalism.

The John Mortimers, Dennis Potters, Margaret Drabbles, Peter Flannerys, Harold Pinters and many more on the socialist Left have no counterpart on the capitalist Right because they still outnumber the Kingsley Amises and others who have turned from socialism but are less inclined to proselytize for capitalism. Economic understanding on the literary Left is surprisingly shallow, surprisingly because its writers might occasionally take the precaution to check their reasoning with their confrères, the socialist economists who might add sophistication to their earnest but unenlightening writings. Like what George Watson called the Victorian "sages"—Carlyle, Ruskin, Arnold[12]—the post-war socialist critics evince a distaste for the industrialism, commercialism and system of economic liberty that have rescued from poverty the masses they affect to champion.

The literary Left deal in symptoms rather than causes, but their influence on public and even political opinion is disproportionate to the validity of their reasoning because they dramatize (literally and figuratively) the defects of capitalism and largely ignore its strengths. By implication, or explicit assertion, they argue for socialism by ignoring its weaknesses and failures. They do so because they are, rightly it could be argued, more distressed by the visible immediate evidence of poverty, insecurity, inequality and inequity than by the invisible underlying long-term evidence of their replacement by growing and widening affluence.

Ironically, even affluence does not persuade them of the beneficence of capitalism. J. K. Galbraith, the economist better known among the general public for his wit than among economists for his economics, found more to condemn in public squalor than to praise in private affluence. And the sociologist Richard Titmuss waywardly argued that poverty was easier to bear when it was more widespread. Yet good intentions have once again had bad consequences: compassion for the poor has produced policies that prolonged their poverty; the appeal of equality has created the advocacy of coercive socialism that has confirmed inequality; the demand for liberty has produced advocacy of politicized art and culture that destroy it.

The literary hostility to capitalism varies from the dialectical to the emotional. Professor Ludwig von Mises, a leader of the Austrian school of market economists and a confident combative critic of socialism who, only four

12. George Watson, *The English Ideology: The Language of Victorian Politics*, Allen Lane, 1973.

years after the 1917 Revolution, taught socialists about the defects of socialism that some have come to acknowledge long after years of contemptuous dismissal, wrote of *The Anti-capitalistic Mentality* in 1956.[13] Professor Hayek went to the historical—or anthropological—root of the hostility to capitalism: the reluctance, when emerging from small-scale face-to-face contacts in early communities, to adopt the impersonal indirect relationships required for the assembly of information about the wants of millions of unknown consumers and the facilities of unknown producers that make possible the unique productivity of markets.[14]

The modern version of the anti-capitalistic hostility is the confusion between the wish to display generous impulses—care for the unfortunate, concern for the poor—and the self-evident impulse to use personal talents that produce income and wealth. The spectacle of the rejection of commerce by the commercially successful—not least, the suppliers of art and culture in its varying forms who respond to the very market forces that they find offensive—is ironic but revealing in its demonstration of the unreasoned preference for socialism over capitalism, the support for socialism despite its failure and the opposition to capitalism despite its success.

"Britain's most prolific and commercially successful comic dramatist," as Sheridan Morley described Alan Ayckbourn, who said "I'm not even totally fashionably anti-Thatcher," declared himself "concerned" about "a certain commercial heartlessness and loss of spiritual values that I now see all around me."[15] Morley spoke of "an age when playwrights and novelists are somehow expected to express sternly anti-Thatcherite views" and exempted Ayckbourn as "very much his own man." Yet the instinctive if unconscious technique of the anti-capitalist literati is transparent. They have, intentionally or otherwise, blurred public understanding, misled public opinion and distorted public preference between capitalism and socialism by their search for the dark cloud behind every silver lining. Capitalism produces wealth, but it is not shared fairly. The market increases the rate of economic growth, but the poor are always with us. Individuals are encouraged to do well, but they ignore the less fortunate. Industry changes from loss to profit, but ravages the environment. The socialist literati are the one-eyed accountants who see the liabilities but not the assets in every capitalist balance sheet, and

13. Ludgwig von Mises, *The Anti-capitalistic Mentality,* Van Nostrand, 1956.

14. F. A. Hayek, *The Fatal Conceit,* Routledge, 1988.

15. Alan Ayckbourn, in "A cold eye on the Thatcher scene," a profile by Sheridan Morley, *Sunday Telegraph,* 20 November 1988.

the assets but not the liabilities in every socialist balance sheet, the incurable depressants who will not rejoice at the full half of the bottle but mourn the empty half, the cultural conservatives who cannot tolerate the withdrawal symptoms of recognizing that they have lived a life of intellectual error.

The Press versus the People

The bias against understanding capitalism is no less marked in some constituents of the Fourth Estate—the press and now broadcasting. In general, and with honourable exceptions, it has failed to enlighten its readers, listeners and viewers on what is at stake, often obscured by the reporting of daily events and weekly developments, in the great debate between capitalism and socialism. The day-to-day events are too often reported without political interpretation or historical depth. Current events are dramatized in graphic prose but without explanation of causes or a perspective of history.

The USSR is embarking on capitalist techniques that could convulse its body politic. China is opening itself to the outside world, tortuously but inevitably. The capitalist countries seem to be doing very well in expanding production and raising the living standards of their masses. Labour governments in Spain, New Zealand and France are introducing market techniques. There are unrelenting contrasts between capitalist Japan and socialist India, the free people of West Germany and the unfree people of East Germany, the prosperity of capitalist Hong Kong and Taiwan and the backwardness of communist China.

Yet many of the reports fail to relate the passing events to the underlying trends. They omit to explain that socialism is dying all round the world, despite political life support, and that capitalism is being reborn, despite decades of suppression. The main reason is that the daily changes they have to report are creating a world the reporters were taught to revile. The capitalism they see emerging belies the socialism to which they gave their youthful sympathy. Their allegiance was often undoctrinaire, they were not always of the Left, but some or many are increasingly living in a world of institutions or values they were taught was dead or dying.

There are praiseworthy studies, some by journalists on the spot, of developments in socialist countries that are evolving (or no longer violently suppressing) capitalist institutions.[16] But books on passing events based on a

16. Philip Short, *The Dragon and the Bear,* Hodder & Stoughton, 1982; Michael Binyon, *Life in Russia,* Hamish Hamilton, 1983; Hedrick Smith, *The Russians,* Ballantine, 1976.

spell of duty date quickly. The most recent events in a fast-changing world are found only in the press and broadcasting. A historian has said that as sources of contemporary perceptions, sequence and fact, the press can often provide material unavailable elsewhere and is one of the major under-used sources for the historian. Since it is the only or main source on contemporary history, its influence is incalculable.

In preparing for this book, to learn how a world changing from socialism to capitalism was seen by its closest observers, I took the four main daily serious, heavy British newspapers for six months from May to October 1988. The interpretations and opinions in the editorial, staff and contributed columns were revealing. Where they recognized the dominant trend away from socialism to capitalism the editors, writers and contributors seemed to think that it was socialists, in the USSR as well as in Britain, who had discovered new truths. That these were old truths, long suppressed or minimized by socialist teaching, seemed less worthy of attention than the recognition by socialists that they were truths after all.

The Sunday Times, which editorially recognized the politico-economic trend most clearly, carried a column by the former Labour MP Brian Walden, who had long understood them, and produced editorial leaders that emphasized the advantages of developing capitalism rather than lamenting its disadvantages. But it evidently felt that writers who had been wrong in the past would interpret them best for the future, and so columns by Martin Jacques, of *Marxism Today,* and Professor Ben Pimlott, the socialist political scientist, confidently explained why the world was changing to capitalism and how the parties still espousing socialism could best save the silver lining of compassion and community from its capitalist cloud of autocratic centralism and environmental degradation.

Of the four daily newspapers, *The Guardian,* treasured in my youth as the guardian of liberalism, dwelt the most obsessively on the weaknesses or abuses, real, imagined or exaggerated, of Thatcherism as the exponent of liberalism, and was grudging and churlish in its recognition of the benefits of both. It did not clearly distinguish between the political achievements of a government in adopting market-oriented policies and the analytical achievements of the economic liberalism that created the market, assailing whichever of the two—the market or Thatcherism—seemed the more vulnerable on the subject in hand. *The Guardian* seemed to cater for the disaffected and the disgruntled, the conservative-minded socialist who could not see the new directions in economic thinking or political policies in the last decade, the eternal perennial student indulging the luxury of protest "agin the government" and rejection of the established order, and the aesthete pained by the new attention to the cost of "public" services before assessing their benefits. *The Guardian* was taking the easy way of living on the remnants of readers, still sizeable in number but increasingly fractious in argument, who remain too infected with distaste for capitalism, whatever it does for the working classes, or too old to see the world changing before their eyes from the imaginations of their youth.

The Daily Telegraph, with exceptions among its contributors, had changed from the generous editing of Maurice Green, Colin Welch and W. E. Deedes in the 20 years from 1965 to 1985 when it gave a fair wind to some very unconservative writing from outsiders. It allowed me 65 leader page articles on arguments for reform that are now commonplace if not (yet) embodied in legislation. Sadly, under a new Editor, it has reverted to Tory complacency, concerned with the politically expedient (camouflaged as the "politically possible") rather than the politically desirable, with the oppressive implication that most of what a Conservative Government does is probably best.

The Independent offered the advantage of diversity with its risk of confusion, in which the editorial leaders controverted, or were controverted by, staff writing. Its editorial judgements were usually superior to the prejudices of its writers, especially in education, health services, other welfare subjects, and particularly the column on political trends by Peter Kellner, formerly of the *New Statesman*, and a socialist who has recognized the weaknesses in the socialist case and the necessity for the market but unaccountably persisted in the faith that socialists suspicious of the market would provide better market-based government than New Right Conservatives inspired by market liberalism.

The reader's confidence in the general direction of the newspaper was occasionally weakened by uncertainty whether the editors regarded the staff as stimulating irritants or licensed jesters. On some days the leaders seemed to indicate that the Editor could not have had a high opinion of the judgement or common sense of his writers. On the central issue of the trend to capitalism from socialism in Britain and abroad the newspaper often appeared as all things to all men. Even worse, it sometimes risked being dismissed as "impartial between right and wrong."

The Times came best out of this choice in a free market for newspapers. Its leaders were (are) the best informed on the underlying philosophical implications of day-to-day policy. Its articles are more varied, but even its critics of capitalism know the case they have to answer. It also reminded me of more and better examples of economic policy for attention in this book.

The general anti-capitalist bias in broadcasting against capitalism, not so much its politico-economic system as against its supposed values—selfishness, materialism, commercialism, priority for the rich against the poor, the go-getter against the ordinary man, private affluence against public squalor, neglect of the old, the poor, the halt, the lame and the blind, the barbaric neglect by the Conservative Government of the arts, the callous sacrifice of the environment—will be denied by its BBC and ITV managements. But the prejudices of its producers and interviewers, again with clear exceptions, cannot be concealed.

In a sense they are predictable. The ills of capitalism make more dramatic programmes than its successes. It is easier to find witnesses, from pensioners through farmers to university vice-chancellors, who lose from the immediate and direct effects on personal income of government liberalization than witnesses who will gain ultimately if indirectly from the prospective price or incentive effects in galvanizing industry into higher efficiency and increased output.

The Spread of Capitalism

Now that the inevitable collapse of capitalism because of its structural contradictions is no longer a tenet of socialist teaching, it is hardly likely that anti-capitalist opinion, prejudice or mentality, maintained sincerely or cynically, will alone cause its collapse. Socialism has demonstrated its failure and capitalism its achievements to all the peoples of the world. The uncritical popularity of socialism for the past century rested largely on the contrast between capitalism as it was experienced, with all its faults (whether arising from capitalism or imposed on it by the political process was rarely examined by socialists) and socialism as it was portrayed with all its imagined virtues.

In a world of uncertainty no politico-economic system is inevitable for all time. But if inevitability refers to the foreseeable future, in the light of current trends and their probable course, there are strong grounds for the argument that the collapse of capitalism is not inevitable, that socialism is less inevitable than capitalism and that socialist true believers as well as the philosophically uncommitted general public now have to contemplate, absorb and digest the probability that capitalism will continue in added strength and spread throughout the world.

It is the inevitability of capitalism in more countries that is the relevant theme of our lives, our day and our times. Technical change now undreamed of may again, some time in the twenty-first century, make large-scale industry economic and even better managed by government than by the market. The socialist-inclined mind may yet generate new arguments for suppressing the consumer in the market and aggrandizing the politician in government. The alleged inability of the market to safeguard the sense of community, or the environment, or the perpetuation of the world seems to be a likely successor to the discredited arguments of boom and slump, inflation and unemployment, inequality and poverty. But after the experience of the post-war years, or the whole of the last century, it will be more difficult to sell socialism to the masses now that they know it carries coercion rather than compassion, penury in a world of capitalist prosperity and yet one more unfounded promise to do better against the evidence of capitalist performance.

The Adam Smith, Fabian and Hayek Tides

An elder statesman of the new liberalism, the Nobel Laureate Professor Milton Friedman, writing with his conjugal collaborator Rose Friedman, has said that "a major change in social and economic *policy* is preceded by a shift in the climate of intellectual *opinion,* itself generated, at least in part, by contemporaneous social, political and economic circumstances" (emphasis in the original).[17] The shift in opinion, say the Friedmans, is a tide which recedes after an advance, ebbs after the flow (Shakespeare's "tide in the affairs of men," *Julius Caesar*). At first the advance of liberal (European sense) academic opinion has little effect on policy. After a lag, perhaps decades, the shift may spread to the public, whose pressure on government changes policy. But as the tide in the resulting events reaches its flood, the intellectual tide ebbs because the intellectual promises tend to be Utopian: they disappoint expectations. The cycle of advance and retreat of liberal opinion repeats itself, as in the change from nineteenth-century *laissez-faire* economic liberalism (the Adam Smith tide) to the early twentieth-century welfare state (the Fabian tide) to the present late twentieth-century free-market economic liberalism (the Hayek tide).

This argument is used to caution the Friedmans' fellow liberals; there is reason, they say, for confidence, but not for complacency. The length of the previous tides suggests that the present (late 1980s, early 1990s) flow in liberal opinion is half-way through its course and that Hayekian policy is in its early stages. The flood in opinion may have been reached; in policy, it is yet

17. Milton Friedman and Rose Friedman, "The tide in the affairs of men," in *Thinking about America: The United States in the 1990s,* Hoover Institution, 1989.

to come. But in the human span of time and space, political freedom has been exceptional: "tyranny, servitude, and misery" have been the typical lot of mankind. In the language of this book, socialism in varying forms has been typical, and capitalism exceptional, in human history.

The Friedmans drew on an English poet to dramatize their politico-economic hypothesis by a vivid metaphor to counsel caution against complacency: history indicated that the liberal counter-revolution to destroy socialist tyranny had not been won for all time. Liberals owe the Friedmans a debt of gratitude for the intellectual reinforcement with which they have strengthened the liberal cause. Their beneficial externalities are incalculable, and the market has no way of measuring it, although liberals can show their gratitude voluntarily. Their counsel is timely. A touch of complacency would be understandable among politicians who felt they had prevailed against the false socialist policies of 40 years.

Yet historians like Lord Blake have spoken of the most fundamental change in the direction of British government policy for a century. Those whom the Left call political Thatcherites may be forgiven a sense of triumph over their political foes, the Labour Party and its state controls, nationalization, bureaucracy and high taxation, and the general flavour of regulation, suppression and coercion that continues despite its nominal acceptance of the market. Liberal academics may properly applaud the achievements of the Thatcher Conservatives in the restoration, principled or pragmatic, of market capitalism in its tenth year so far, not least in the de-socialization (privatization) that few had anticipated.

The removal of the outdated, unnecessary and oppressive post-war socialism enacted by all British political parties has barely begun but, whatever their administrative successes or failings, the new liberal Conservatives have demonstrated, above all, that socialist institutions were not as deep-seated, nor socialist mores as ingrained, as had been feared, nor as socialists had secretly hoped. Socialism is not inevitable, neither technically, as Marx taught, nor politically, as Mrs. Thatcher has demonstrated.

Liberals may have even more deep-rooted cause for optimism. For economic liberalism to prevail, it required the political triumph, over several General Elections, of a party that seemed to heed their advice. Whether, as Keynes might now have said, it was the victory of the liberal over the socialist idea, or, as Marx would have insisted, it was the vested interest of a new class, the people who have risen out of their humble social origins, or, as John Stuart Mill might have suggested, the accident of "conspiring circumstance," Britain has been ruled, for the first time in the twentieth century, perhaps for the first time in the century since Gladstone's last Liberal Government of 1892–4, by a Prime Minister seized with the dangers of socialism and a government sufficiently free from the distractions of war or slump to reshape society into a liberal, even libertarian, mould.

History will tell how far the new liberal Conservatives have led market forces in restoring capitalism, how far market forces have eased the political path by creating conditions of supply and demand that made economic liberalization electorally rewarding. So far industrial policy has led market forces; welfare policy has lagged behind them.

Whether or not the new Conservatives win a fourth term, their Labour opponents of the 1970 vintage will clearly not govern Britain again in the foreseeable future. Their proclaimed policies have changed; their deeds in office remain obscure. The Labour Party of the 1980s and 1990s may declaim the battle-cries of socialism but are absorbing the institutions and the lessons of capitalism. It may be a happy consequence of the demise of socialism that capitalism is now safer in the hands of British politicians than ever before, not only because some prefer it philosophically, but perhaps mainly because it is politically more "possible," imperative and profitable in winning votes.

It is difficult to believe that people in the West and the East who are able to influence the conditions under which they live will knowingly repeat the errors of the past. It is no less difficult to suppose that the shortcomings of the guild system, mercantilism, syndicalism, corporatism, municipalism and nationalization will provide easy votes for politicians of any party. Socialism is being abandoned by politicians of the Left not only because it has failed as an economic method but because it has been seen to have failed by the people. They will not lightly vote for a system that failed in the century from the 1880s to the 1980s. Yet the political process, in which decisions are made in substantial ignorance and therefore irresponsibly, may produce a new lease of life for a political system that will ironically frustrate the underlying economic aspirations of the voters.

The improving literacy brought by capitalism is extending its life. And literacy is being reinforced by the acceleration in improved communications that the capitalist countries have absorbed better than the socialist countries. When the size of the radio receiver has shrunk from feet to inches it will no longer be possible to hide from the inhabitants of socialist countries the fourfold or fivefold higher living standards in the capitalist world. It is not Gorbachev who is driving the Russians to *perestroika* (reconstruction) but the *glasnost* (openness) of the West that is goading the Russians to drive him.

Embourgeoisement in the communist as well as the capitalist countries behaves not like Shakespeare's flowing and ebbing tide but like a rising curve, with undulations, but steadily moving upward. It has done so since the Industrial Revolution and there is no visible reason to suppose that it will stop in its tracks or turn downward. It accounts for the large operational markets, called by a wide range of names from underground to black, some outlawed, some tolerated, that appear the more the official white markets are repressed and that make the socialist systems tolerable until white markets openly replace black, as they will more rapidly in the 1990s.

For the first time in their history the peoples of many countries have had experience, or have heard, of markets and the freedoms and higher living standards they can bring. Once the people of the 1990s have them, they are not as likely as their grandfathers or fathers, who did not have them, to abandon them in return for promises that the state will do better. It is the very demonstration effect of the existence of successful capitalist America, and West Germany, and Japan, and Singapore and Hong Kong, of the enactment of capitalism in "Labour" New Zealand, Australia and Spain, and of the belated recognition by socialists of the failure of the state in Portugal, Finland, Austria, the Argentine and even Nicaragua that is making capitalism inevitable throughout the world.

CHAPTER 4

The Return and Advance to Capitalism

> Services such as education, health, electricity, telecommunications, transport and water . . . can be provided privately at competitive standards and prices . . .
>
> Gabriel Roth, *The Private Provision of Public Services in Developing Countries*

> . . . economic hardship . . . would force the Kremlin to move further and faster towards a market economy.
>
> Vladimir Bukovsky, *Can the Soviet System Survive Reform?*

> The strength of Hong Kong's capitalist system is a better guarantee of its survival than the 1984 Sino-British Declaration [on maintaining the free market for 50 years after the withdrawal in 1997].
>
> Zhou Nan, Deputy Foreign Minister of China, *The Times,* 6 March 1989

For more than a century socialism has been the inspiriting revolutionary creed that raised the hopes of mankind, and capitalism the dispiriting defensive regime that protected the wealth of the rich. Historians of the twentieth century will record that an intellectual climacteric in the eighth and ninth decades reversed the roles. Capitalism became the saviour of the masses, and socialism was seen, at last, as the instrument of the politically powerful. Socialism was discarded (in all but name) as conservative, reactionary, immobile; capitalism was hailed as liberating, progressive, revolutionary.

Professor Peter Berger's *The Capitalist Revolution*[1] in 1987 was an assertive confident title that could mark the end of the era of apologia by the liberal intelligentsia. More of them have moved cautiously from tempered to unhesi-

1. Peter Berger, *The Capitalist Revolution,* Gower, 1987.

tating espousal of capitalism. The titles of their writings in the 1950s and 1960s and even in the 1970s were defensive, cautious or querulous. They were preceded in 1943 by Joseph Schumpeter's *Capitalism, Socialism and Democracy*,[2] a pessimistic book by an avowed supporter of liberal capitalism who yet lacked the vision to see its future because, like many intellectuals, he was overconcerned with the anxieties of intellectuals; he did not anticipate the degeneration of socialism and the resurgence of popular capitalism among the masses. He earned the rebuke of Professor Arnold Heertje of the University of Amsterdam: "There has been more room for dynamic entrepreneurial activity than Schumpeter foresaw. . . ."[3] Two years after Schumpeter, Hayek's implied assertion in 1944 of the superiority of capitalism followed from his prescient analysis of the consequences of socialism in *The Road to Serfdom*.[4] *Capitalism AND Freedom* (capitals added; the two were significantly linked) asserted the unapologetic Milton and Rose Friedman in 1962.[5] But Irving Kristol and Daniel Bell gave only tepid support in *Capitalism Today* in 1970 and Kristol only *Two Cheers for Capitalism* in 1978.[6] As late as 1979 Ernest van den Haag edited seven essays enquiring into *Capitalism: Sources of Hostility* and the stout-hearted American Ben Rogge asked *Can Capitalism Survive?*[7] There was rare confidence, even among sympathetic or embattled intellectuals, in capitalism. They lacked the instinctive sense of the common man.

Other scholars who declared their confidence in the future of capitalism by labelling their writings with explicit titles risked, and received, ridicule from the then optimistic advocates of socialism. Hayek, Robbins, Jewkes, Friedman, Stigler and other adherents of the Mont Pelerin Society espoused capitalism in their academic texts under sometimes technical titles. But only a few showed the flag. Graham Hutton's unequivocal *All Capitalists Now* in 1960, a confident verbal riposte to Sir William Harcourt's "We are all socialists now" in 1895, was an early assertion of the general tone of IEA papers, of which over 350 had appeared by the mid-1980s.[8]

2. Joseph Schumpeter, *Capitalism, Socialism and Democracy*, Allen & Unwin, 1942.

3. Arnold Heertje (ed.), *Schumpeter's Vision after 40 Years*, Praeger, 1981, p. x.

4. F. A. Hayek, *The Road to Serfdom*, Routledge, 1944.

5. Milton Friedman and Rose Friedman, *Capitalism and Freedom*, University of Chicago Press, 1962.

6. Irving Kristol and Daniel Bell (eds.), "Capitalism today," *Encounter*, 1970; Irving Kristol, *Two Cheers for Capitalism*, Basic Books, 1978.

7. Ernest van den Haag (ed.), *Capitalism: Sources of Hostility*, Epoch Books, 1979; Ben Rogge, *Can Capitalism Survive?*, Liberty Press, 1979.

8. Graham Hutton, *All Capitalists Now*, Institute of Economic Affairs, 1960.

The intellectual prospect in the 1990s is of an increasing flow, or flood, of books showing where and how the century of socialism will be replaced by an age of capitalism, returning or newly emerging in varying forms and at varying paces, in all the continents of the world.

Words must not conceal deeds. The emotional appeal of socialism is still strong enough for politicians to ride to power on a platform of socialism but with the intention of introducing capitalism as the only way to escape from their economic weaknesses and provide the standards of living their peoples expect. But the seductions of the socialist label may fade sooner than historians have expected. In Britain, which led, or misled, the world with its socialist teachings, from Marxist to Fabian, it has required no more than ten years of a capitalist government to acquaint the people with the new language of popular capitalism—markets, competition, profits, shares and many more concepts and ideas long ignored or anathematized by the intellectuals of socialism.

Historians of linguistics will have a rare case history in the changing language of the 1980s. Geoffrey Sampson, Professor of Linguistics at Leeds University, wrote *An End to Allegiance* in 1984 to provide a guide to the new thinking of "The most important political movement today . . . formed by the new liberals . . . [which] heralds the most significant break in the continuity of political evolution for more than 100 years."[9] And historians of politics may award their accolades to the ministers, under the Prime Minister, who taught the British the new language of economic liberalism—Howe, Joseph, Lawson, Tebbit, Ridley, Young and more. Since I have condemned some newspapers, I must applaud the individual editors or journalists who, without necessary approval, opened the way to a more worthy assessment of capitalism: the doyen of the editor-scholars Samuel Brittan, Peter Jay, son of a socialist minister Douglas Jay and son-in-law of a Labour Prime Minister, William (later Lord) Rees-Mogg, the Conservative who changed from a sceptic to an admirer of the new liberals, Bernard Levin, a rare literary convert from early socialism, Andrew Alexander, a brilliant writer unappreciated by the Conservatives, Russell Lewis, a thoughtful journalist who used his economics training, and others in provincial newspapers, not least Bernard Dineen of *The Yorkshire Post,* one of the earliest to understand the new liberalism.

9. Geoffrey Sampson, *An End to Allegiance: Individual Freedom and the New Politics,* Temple Smith, 1984, p. 10.

Capitalism round the Continents

Capitalism may return earliest in the countries with a Western culture from which it was excluded by a political process which, with disputable electoral support, nationalized industry and socialized welfare. It may have emerged earlier in war-ravaged Germany or newer developing countries where, as Professor Mancur Olson has argued, there were fewer established interests of corporate industry, professional associations or trade unions to resist innovation.[10]

South America may appear unexpectedly as a theatre for developments in capitalism. The teachings of Hernando de Soto of Peru[11] on the remarkable success of underground capitalist markets for goods and services in replacing the inefficiency and corruption of the official politicized, socialized economy is spreading throughout the continent despite the superficial seductions of liberation theology and the derision by the Left of the Chicago economists who emerged in Chile as ministers under General Pinochet. The attractions of free markets for the farmers and traders of the new republics of Africa may rapidly increase when, as Professor Lord Bauer and Professor Basil Yamey indicated many years ago, the promises of their socialist leaders show no signs of fulfilment.

The underlying strength and independent vitality of capitalism may yet be demonstrated nowhere better than by its gradual, tortured but irresistible return to Russia and its colonies and to China despite the trauma of Tiananmen Square.

The USSR was the world's first "scientific" socialist society; it was to show the way to emancipate mankind by abolishing scarcity, struggle and strife under communism. If capitalism can return to the two most populous socialist societies despite the political, military and bureaucratic vested interests that will resist it after decades of consolidation, it can be expected to return elsewhere in the world with less resistance and more popular welcome. This is the importance of analysing the reasons why the USSR and China are trying to find ways out of their socialist structures and to thaw out and liberate their potential productive powers by introducing capitalist techniques,

10. Mancur Olson, *The Rise and Decline of Nations: Economic Growth, Stagflation and Social Rigidities,* Yale University Press, 1982.

11. Hernando de Soto, *The Other Path: The Invisible Revolution in the Third World,* Harper & Row, 1989.

whatever else they are called for political acceptability. The resistances that will obstruct or slow down the underlying changes from socialism to capitalism seem formidable; the time required to neutralize them seems incalculable. But if, as seems probable and unavoidable, capitalism returns to Russia and its colonies after 70 or 80 years of Soviet socialism, and advances in China after 40 years of Maoist repression, it can be expected to return, or to emerge and develop, in other countries and continents with less disruption and dislocation, and less risk of civil upheaval or civil war.

The necessity of capitalism will be understood even better in China than in the USSR. The centuries-old traditions of trading, the mechanisms of merchanting and the cohesion of the family in China have been suspended for only 40 years. Capitalism is returning after a short interlude. Capitalist organization and investment will be demanded in the Third World of Asia, Africa and South America the more socialist experimentation under military or civilian dictatorship has depressed living standards below those of the countries of the West.

If capitalism is welcomed in the Third World continents where its early beginnings were prematurely repressed by varieties of socialism in the former British territories of Africa, it will return in stronger form to the industrialized countries with Western cultures, Australia and New Zealand, Canada and South Africa, in some of which it was partly and temporarily displaced by varieties of Labour, Liberal and Conservative Party social democracy. Capitalist organization will be applied to the socialized (nationalized) industries and welfare services of otherwise capitalist countries in Europe and America. De-socialization (privatization) will become more urgent as the contrast with the rapid progress of their newer market-based vigorously competitive industries demonstrates that socialized heavy industry and state welfare in the West will lag behind capitalist-inspired innovation and investment.

Everywhere the historically unprecedented advance of "the little economic miracles" of Asia will be regarded as exemplars. The socialist criticisms of their politics fall on deaf ears in the bustling colourful streets of Hong Kong, Taipei and Singapore. The sensitive criticism of restricted liberties voiced in the West will be heard sooner in the capitalist miracles of Asia than in the socialist autocracies of Africa because markets work better with political as well as economic freedom. In the Labour-socialist countries of the former British Dominions, Australia and New Zealand, capitalism is forcing itself by economic necessity on politicians who fear the loss of their power to non-socialist rivals who are uninhibited by socialist dogma in acknowledging the power of markets to raise living standards.

The resistance to returning or newly emerging capitalism in the West and the East comes not from the people, who want higher living standards, but from socialist-inclined politicians under varying party labels who know that markets will offer them less scope for power. The leaders of the economic miracles in Asia are primarily interested in economic efficiency to justify their power; economic penury would endanger it. The freer their markets the less their political authority. Yet they continue to free their markets. (The leader of one suggested an extended version of an IEA Paper[12] for use in his schools.) Communist China, despite lapses, will tolerate capitalist Hong Kong after 1997 not only for its links with world capitalism but also as a demonstration of how to embrace the capitalism it requires to raise living standards and retain its influence in world affairs. It risks emulation inside mainland China, which would dissolve communist political power, but the risks of external eclipse are the less acceptable.

The Return of Russian Capitalism

The return of capitalism to the USSR, both to the Russian region and the non-Russian dependencies, has been accelerated in the 1980s not by Russian choice but by the demonstration of unremittingly capitalist superiority, by the political compulsion of capitalist contrast.

After a struggling but promising youth of some 30 years from the 1890s to 1917, maturing capitalism was destroyed by law, military power and violent suppression. Yet it did not disappear. It made a tolerated temporary reappearance in Lenin's expedient pragmatic New Economic Policy (NEP) in the 1920s. Even during Stalin's 30-year reign of terror from 1929 to 1953, capitalism survived underground in varying forms and degrees. In the 1950s it surfaced in tentative academic discussion of the desirability or necessity of markets, pricing and profit. And in the 1980s it returned with official political sponsorship, under doctrinally discreet names, and with the implied blessing of Lenin. The Soviet socialist cul-de-sac has been abandoned at last.

Too little is made known in socialist writings of the stirrings of capitalism in the 1920s. Until Gorbachev the Russians were not disposed to acknowl-

12. Arthur Seldon, *Corrigible Capitalism, Incorrigible Socialism*, Institute of Economic Affairs, 1980.

edge the dormant unofficial capitalist aspirations of the people to advance themselves and their families, except where they broke out in the illegal underground. Adam Smith's urge of every man "to better his condition" may vary in intensity in different cultures, but it resides near the surface under socialism as well as under capitalism, and in Russia (and China) as well as Europe and America. It was suppressed from 1917 to 1921 but was restored to avoid chaos until suppressed by Stalin in 1928.

The rarely remarked significance of this eight-year interlude of politically tolerated capitalism in a sea of socialism is that Russian traders emerged in the early 1920s despite the uncertainty and the risk that their tolerance might be short-lived. They could not have known how long they would be permitted or welcomed—whether for two years or 20. Some must have thought that the absurdities of state socialism would be so evident that it would soon be abandoned for ever. In the event some, especially the larger and more adventurous who could be accused of illegal trading, were imprisoned or executed within the eight years. By 1929 the "new bourgeoisie" had been liquidated. Although it was discredited by the politicized bureaucracy in the subsequent period of Stalinist forced industrialization, the historical evidence of potential Russian capitalist vitality must now in the 1990s be studied by the Gorbachev economists to see what can be learned in re-awakening the dormant urge to individual initiative without which the Gorbachev reforms will founder. It will now not be so easy to suppress the 1980s New Economic Policy.[13]

The short-lived restoration of Russian capitalism under communist tutelage is not only a historically significant testament to the irrepressible urge to capitalist initiative that Gorbachev may have to rehabilitate as a neglected Russian achievement. He may have to rekindle it as a Russian example of the 1920s for emulation in the 1990s. The "NEP men" could be restored in Russian folklore as evidence of the latent Russian ability to hold its place with the West. Innovative entrepreneurship is just as much a part of the Russian character and culture, in a country of literary, musical and artistic achievement, as its apparent supine capitulation to Tsarist or Marxist autocracy. A people, even a peasantry, with innate cultural potential does not lightly submit to political primitives except by the brutality and coercion of the mental hospital and the labour camp.

The capitalism that Gorbachev is having to accept must be re-created at

13. Alan M. Ball, *Russia's Last Capitalists,* University of California Press, 1987. "Last" means in historical sequence, not prospective probability.

the circumference of society; it cannot be imposed by the centre. It must come from the people at the bottom, not from the politicians at the top. The market must be given its head if it is to produce the results that the Gorbachev "liberal party" wants, whatever the opposition of the military-industrial "conservative" coalition. But there is no other way. That is the lesson the Russians may find hardest to learn. The market has defects—it "creates" losses and unemployment for the slothful and the slouch—but its unique strengths cannot be earned without its penalties: they are a small price to pay for its unique rich rewards. The penalties may have to be endured for five years if the Russians are to rejoin the Europeans in prosperity and liberty.

The Russian NEP in the 1920s and in the 1990s teaches a further lesson for Britain and the West in the 1990s. The market will not produce its best results if it is "permitted" under political tutelage and bureaucratic sufferance. It must be accepted as an institution with its risks and defects sanctioned by public understanding and approval. Without it, economic life is at the mercy of myopia in political systems that permit short-sighted producer interests to prevail over ultimate long-term consumer interests.

The market is not safe with politicians in any party. It requires popular approbation and blessing. The new British Conservatives who ruled in the 1980s understood it better than the old Conservatives of the 1950s and 1960s; if the old Conservatives return to influence, the power for good of the market will become precarious. It is a long-term institution; its decisions—in contracts, investments, property rights—require time to mature. It cannot be subjected to the changing fortunes of individual politicians. It cannot work under a political sword of Damocles that threatens its existence every few years if it does not serve short-term *political* purposes—notably re-election. It may have no more certain outlook under the Labour Party and its intellectuals who have belatedly embraced it on sufferance than it had under the NEP when Lenin was followed by Stalin.

Capitalism by *Perestroika*

The daily developments in Gorbachev's *perestroika,* the reconstruction of the Soviet economy by relaxation of controls and thawing out the frozen socialist system, will vary according to the urgency of market reforms and the resistance to them. But the internal contradiction of Soviet communism—the imperative to abandon socialism or to fall further behind the West, the disagreeable and dangerous political decision to embrace capitalism or retreat as a world power—will have to be resolved in the 1990s. Capitalism will have to be accepted, perhaps under a politically innocuous name, even at the high price of the risk of civil discord and bloody civil war if *glasnost* is to bring its economic rewards by new thinking, "new" ideas (copied from the capitalist West) and a new readiness to take responsibility, initiatives and risks.

Soviet communism is a political interlude. The 30-year first phase of Russian capitalism before 1917, never entirely suppressed, will have to return to resume its development. From the 1990s onwards it will have to proceed at an accelerated rate to make up for the 70 wasted years of socialism. The reason for this urgency is the very rapidity of the development of capitalism in the outside world. Russian communism did not come in 1917 as a dawning recognition and understanding of its superiority over capitalism. There was no demand, registered in the ballot boxes of representative democracy, for the expulsion of the capitalist exploiters and their replacement by a benevolent regime of humane socialists maturing into a withering away of the socialist state by self-abnegating communists as foretold by Marx. Socialist communism came out of the war. It was an escape to peace, not a vote for a new social order. Most Russians were peasants still living with the remnants of Tsarist feudalism. In 1917 they did not compare themselves with the working classes under the capitalism of Europe or America, and wonder what was standing in the way of similar living standards for them and their children, as the young Chinese did in 1989 after Tiananmen Square. In 1929 the Russians were told that capitalism had, once more, finally collapsed into world economic depression, slump, unemployment, bankruptcies, suicides from seventeenth-floor Wall Street stock exchanges and premature death. Half a century later, in the 1980s and 1990s, their grandchildren have been promised that their living standards would reach and exceed those of the capitalist West. But they can now learn more easily that the working classes of capitalism have standards of living "beyond the dreams of avarice." Samuel Johnson was writing of the proceeds of the sale of a brewery, but the Russians would now regard with awe the riches of the common man under capitalism. They must now, at long last, be told by *Pravda* (*Truth*) what can no longer be concealed.

The contrast will be more difficult than ever to obscure by criticisms of the capitalism that now has to be emulated. On the contrary, the new element in the day-to-day explanation of the advantages of economic reconstruction by brazen politicians, academics and public relations spokesmen is that the Gorbachev campaign may have to emphasize rather than minimize the gap between Russian and world living standards in order to encourage the Russians to see how much they stand to gain from the free-market reforms. A fourfold gap (in *The Sunday Times* Norman Macrae, lately retired as anonymous Deputy Editor from *The Economist* and rejuvenated as a named columnist, put it at sevenfold) is the strongest inducement to hope for belated emancipation from the charade of socialism. The Gorbachev liberals clearly require the skills of capitalist advertising in a Soviet Saatchi and Saatchi or J. Walter Thompson. They will learn nothing, but damage their cause, from the chidings of the Russian Galbraiths, the leading articles of Russian *Guardians* or the vain effort of Russian Hattersleys to reconcile the market with socialism. Delaying the day of well-stocked shops will hasten the days of social unrest.

Capitalist food is better in quality, more varied and plentiful; capitalist clothes are of higher quality, more fashionable and better tailored; capitalist housing is more spacious, with more privacy, better equipped in kitchens and bathrooms, more comfortable and designed to individual preferences; capitalist amenities and entertainments are more plentiful, with cars, telephones, television, washing machines, dishwashers, refrigerators, freezers, lawn-mowers, sprinklers and much else available to almost all. Capitalist private education and medicine are of higher quality. Capitalist mortality rates are lower and expectations of life are longer. The term "doctor" does not mean the same as in the United States; there are more but most are inferior. The USSR has hidden the often poor quality of many products and services by statistics of quantity. The accidents in industry and transport are not accidents in the official statistics; they are still understated or concealed.

For how many more years will the Russians fear to ask why they should not enjoy the bounties of capitalism? How soon will they insist on knowing the secret that provides them, and the failure of socialism that denies them? Are the Russians so sunk in subjection to authority that they will suffer personal privation for ever?

These are the questions that are relevant to the judgement of whether the USSR can resist the encroachments of capitalism much longer. The underground markets are large and continually expanding. The evidence is incontrovertible from the testimony of emigrants, dissidents, journalists and academics.[14] The most severe penalties will not suppress them, especially

14. Michael Binyon, *Life in Russia*, Hamish Hamilton, 1983; Hedrick Smith, *The Russians*, Ballantine, 1976; Mervyn Matthews, *Privilege in the Soviet Union*, Allen & Unwin, 1978; Trevor Buck and John Cole, *Modern Soviet Economic Performance*, Blackwell, 1987.

after the promulgation of *perestroika.* The Russians will have to discard the socialist doctrine that teaches the supremacy of politics over the market and learn that government must in the end accept the verdict of the people expressed more emphatically and more effectively in the market than in the ballot box.

The Russian Past versus the Capitalist Future

Doubts about the acceptance of capitalism, in substance if not in name, and certainties that the Russian character will obstruct the replacement of socialism continue from distinguished observers of the Russian scene. It seems difficult to accept that the Russia of the past will have to yield to the Russia of the future. The latest persuasive versions of the doubts and the certainties appeared in a collection of penetrating "colloquies" (interviews) with Russians and other observers of Russia conducted and analysed by the noted Polish historian George Urban.[15]

The apprehensions are that the Russian character has accommodated itself to a communist or socialist civilization and will be resistant to individualistic capitalism. If they are well-founded, capitalism has little prospect of acceptance in Russia. If not, and the Russians and their subject peoples want higher living standards and personal liberties, capitalism will return even to the supposedly inhospitable cultural environment of the USSR.

The obstacles to the resumption or development of capitalism in the seemingly hostile cultural climate of the USSR are argued to be insurmountable. After seven decades of socialist communism, no-one younger than 70 has lived under any other system, and few under 80 or 85 can recall life before the Bolshevik Revolution—the ten days that shook the world.

The argument is persuasive. For two millennia since the birth of Christ, most people have lived under despotisms of barons, warlords, religious fanatics, autocrats, dictators and other absolutist rulers. Today two in three people round the world still live lives of oppression. Few have known representative government. Moreover, fewer still have known free markets. Even in Europe both political democracy and free markets were destroyed, for a time in our lives, by two dictatorships. Both appealed to the narrow invocation of nation and race—German National Socialism (a technically correct description of Hitler's Nazism) and Italian Fascism (a less correct name for

15. George Urban (ed.), *Can the Soviet System Survive Reform?*, Pinter/Spiers, 1989.

a mixture of socialism and corporatism). The difference is that Marxism made the much wider appeal to liberation from oppression, to social justice, equality and solidarity of the masses. Urban tellingly maintains that the appeal of Marxism is made "in the name of an impassioned though ill-defined Utopia which draws its vocabulary from science but has penumbral [half-shadowed, part-eclipsed] associations with religion."[16] Intellectuals were attracted to Marxist socialism because, unlike insipid parliamentary democracy, it promised to humble plutocrats and capitalists.

The question is whether the Soviet economy is so bankrupt that the common people will demand radical transformation or be content with a lowly but risk-free egalitarianism. If they are comfortable with authoritarian regimentation, perhaps the Western notion of self-determination should reconcile Europe and America to respect and accept the Russians' choice, although events in 1989–90 suggest that their subject peoples in the Baltic states and in Georgia and other southern republics will be less tolerant.

History, runs the argument, does not decisively indicate that totalitarian systems can be reformed from within. Russia and China may seek a solution—an escape from socialism to capitalism—but they have not found it. Half-measures—economic decentralization of varying kinds—in the Soviet satellites have so far proved destabilizing and unsettling. There are clearly stubborn obstacles to evolutionary reform. The dilemma of Gorbachev's reconstruction is that, although it must be presented as strengthening rather than abandoning socialism, it requires that the working people, who are supposed to provide Marx's "dictatorship of the proletariat," are slowly vanishing; they are becoming the new bourgeoisie that socialism was designed to destroy. *Embourgeoisement* is undermining socialism in socialist as well as capitalist countries.

This growing flood of aspiration, even in the "scientific" socialism of Russia, reveals the ultimate contradiction of socialism everywhere: that the common people for which it was ostensibly created will reject it because the higher living standards they were promised, which they now see vividly in the capitalist West, cannot be produced by socialism. They require not only bourgeois values, culture and lifestyle; they necessitate the institutions of commercial society and popular industrial capitalism of the West—which the socialist-minded intelligentsia of the West still blindly deride.

Yet peoples disciplined and marshalled for 70 years by an oppressive and

16. Ibid., p. ix.

impoverished socialism, which tried to run the USSR as a nineteenth-century empire in the twentieth century, will not accept it in the approach to the twenty-first century. They may have tolerated it so far because their forebears were inured to authoritarian Tsarist rule, although less severe than communism because moderated by inefficiency, corruption, widespread bribery of bureaucrats and trade in the unofficial underground. Gorbachev's reconstruction now requires Russians to learn unaccustomed habits of work disciplined by the consumer in the market, with accounting systems that reflect real economic costs rather than politicized artefacts. But the alternative is even more uncomfortable. The Russians and the Baltic and other non-Russian peoples they have colonized will otherwise have to be content with nineteenth-century living conditions in the twenty-first century. If they want twenty-first century lifestyles they will have to prepare for them in the last decade of the twentieth century.

All the peoples collected (and collectivized) in the Soviet Union are consumers as well as producers. Only a market society enables individuals to assert their interests as consumers over their interests as producers. For this supreme purpose, without which the economy seizes up, socialism has been as much a failure as mercantilism, syndicalism or corporativism.

Moreover, a market society shifts power from men to women. A transfer from the political process, where men have prevailed, and still do in Russia, to the market process moves decisions from mainly male-dominated representative assemblies to mainly female-oriented retail shops: shopping becomes more important than voting. Soviet socialism had to draft women into industry to sustain production, under the guise of an early form of "women's liberation." They will want the higher living standards that are at last within their grasp. Mikhail Gorbachev is not the only Russian with a fashion-conscious or worldly-wise Raisa as a wife, or daughter, or niece, or daughter-in-law or grand-daughter. In the 1990s Russian and non-Russian women will become the dominant pressure group demanding more and better food, more fashionable clothing, more living space, household amenities and family comforts, not least refrigerators and washing machines, motor cars and much else they learn about from *glasnost.* And that means they will demand capitalism—not the capitalism run by men dominating the debating chambers of political assemblies but the market-dominated capitalism that produces the goods—in the shops.

There is no other ultimate solution for the Russians except work for the market. There is no escape in cheap foreign labour in a subdued empire. On the contrary, yet one more socialist contradiction will be resolved: national or cultural declarations of independence by the Russian colonies in the south and the Baltic seaboard will free them also from the economic control of planning from Moscow.

It is unrealistic, and unhistorical, to suppose that the new generation of Russians will much longer put their history of Tsarist subjugation, or the sufferings of their grandparents, before their aspirations, for themselves and their children, to live as well as the young people of the West in the 1990s. Nor are they likely to be deterred by politicized history texts. It is implausible to suppose that they will put Marxist doctrine on the evils of capitalism, based on outdated early nineteenth-century industrialism, before the opportunities of a new age of unprecedented technological invention and innovation. The name capitalism will not deter them even if it is still anathematized by their parents.

The Russian dissident Vladimir Bukovsky, the Italian Euro-communist Giorgio Napolitano and the former Yugoslav minister (under Tito) Milovan Djilas indicated in their discussions with Urban that change away from Soviet socialism was unavoidable. Urban had suggested that "the single-party dictatorship [would] become more diversified and marginally more popular as it [became] more deeply entrenched in Russian values and the Russian past."[17] The acceptance of the system as a "participatory" but not liberal state, socialist in form as much as nationalist in content, would increase. Communism would then reach its final stage of development as a feckless Russian form of corporativism. The notion of saving the state for the political hierarchy and the bureaucracy by changing it into a vast national talking-shop of participating citizens, urged in Britain, could thus be transplanted to the USSR.

The idea has the political attractions but the public limitations of its cousin, the participatory state nursed by anxious because interested political people of all parties. George Orwell called it the system in which some were more equal than others. I argue in chapter 5 that it is an illusory, inequitable artefact. In the USSR Bukovsky saw more in current events than supposed cultural links with the past. Gorbachev and his supporters have indicated that a conflict has developed between "social relations" and "productive forces," Marxist jargon for the conflict between the ruling classes and the Gorbachev economic reforms which would destroy their privileges. But unless the liberalizing reforms are made, Soviet society will continue to deteriorate. If the reconstruction is shirked, the result will in any event be social disaffection, turmoil and possibly revolution. In short, it is too late for

17. Ibid., p. xix.

the Soviet economy to turn back. Upheaval is the risk whether reconstruction is pursued or not. If it is, living standards will rise but the *nomenklatura* may rebel. If it is not, they will stagnate and the people will rebel. The Russian masses have nothing to lose but their potential gains.

Socialist and Real Private Property

The Russian impasse teaches a lesson about the nature of property ownership that socialism has obscured. The century-old Fabian argument that the abuses of private property can be avoided by replacing it with "public ownership" is now being turned on its head. In the Russians' attempt to escape from the inefficiencies of "public" ownership they are discovering that it destroys the efficiency of private ownership because it destroys the reality of ownership.

Private ownership can be abused by monopoly, but it creates incentives to conservation and good husbandry, not least in the natural resources of the environment. A private owner in capitalism takes care of his property precisely because it is identifiable with—exclusive to—him. If he takes care of it, he benefits proportionately, as does his family and the good causes he wishes to support, because he may donate it, lend it, hire it or bequeath it. But if he owns it in common with many others as public property, he gains in miniscule amount if he takes care of it and loses in miniscule amount if he does not. That is the key to the debate on private and "public" property: private caring is effective because it brings rewards or penalties; "caring" for public property is ineffective, rare or non-existent.

Private property works because it creates direct incentives, effective ownership and disposable property rights. Public property does not work because it creates miniscule incentives, ineffective nominal ownership and no disposable property rights. The private ownership of capitalism is a powerful inducement to protect, conserve, improve and expand private property. The "public" (or "common," or "social," or "communal," or "collective") ownership of socialism, whether the socialism of Russia or the socialism of the National Health Service, British Rail or public libraries in Britain, destroys the incentives to protect or improve property. No public owner can care for a Russian or a British state hospital. Private property is a potent working institution. Public ownership is a myth, a socialist euphemism for political power cornered by handfuls of irresponsible non-ownerships.

Hayek has restored the term "several," that is, separate rather than joint, used by the nineteenth-century English jurist and anthropologist Sir Henry Maine, as more precise than "private," and credited the Greeks as the first to see that it was inseparable from individual freedom: the makers of the constitution of ancient Crete supposed that "liberty is a state's highest good and for this reason alone make property belong specifically to those who acquire it. . . ."[18]

The unpalatable truths on the necessity of private or several property and the emptiness of public property are at last emerging in Russia. The Gorbachev reforms must replace meaningless public ownership by effective private property rights if the Russians are to begin to become caring property owners. They will then use their property efficiently and thus both expand private production and raise national living standards. This is how it is done in the capitalist West. There is no other way in which it will be done in hitherto socialist Eastern Europe, unless by the coercion to which socialism has ultimately to descend or the fanciful change in human nature to which the reformer retreats when the institutions he proposes will not work: the "change the people" syndrome.

The Marxist notion of public property is of state ownership, use and management. The Gorbachev reformers have understood that some property rights at least have to be made private. Revolutionary notions, beginning with private share ownership, could by degrees lead to doubts about the principle and the necessity of state ownership and therefore of socialism.

The contortions will become apparent. Bukovsky pointed to the parable of the cow. To encourage good husbandry in agriculture, peasant farmers are being encouraged to "rent a cow." Two purposes are intended: first, the farmer is induced to increase his (and her) efficiency by selling her milk on the open market for the highest ruling price; second, the honour of socialism is saved because the cow remains owned by the state. But the shift from public to private ownership has not gone far enough: the farmer will not produce as much as he could unless he can sell not only the cow's milk but also the cow, perhaps for a better milker, or hire her to his good neighbour, or bequeath her to his son. Being a "cow-tenant" is evidently not enough. Capitalism has by experience learned to refine the incentives (and the laws) of cow-ownership and concluded that it must be private. Socialism stubbornly sticks to dogma which prescribes public ownership. ". . . In accordance with the economic theory and political economy of socialism . . . there is not going to be private property here," said Evald Figurnov of the Central Committee in March 1987.[19]

18. F. A. Hayek, *The Fatal Conceit*, Routledge, 1988, p. 30.

19. Evald Figurnov, quoted in Urban, *Can the Soviet System Survive Reform?*, p. 239.

Here is the difference between capitalism and socialism. Capitalism learns by experience; socialism is chained to dogma. It will take time for the Russians to accept private property, but until they do they will not generate the output that remains unproduced in the USSR. The choice is Marxist doctrine for the socialist purist or higher living standards for the people: ". . . even [the] 'radical' innovation of renting has failed to induce enthusiasm among the farmers for better production," observed Bukovsky, almost in refutation of Figurnov.[20]

Capitalism has also refined the specialization of land ownership and land-farming. The tenant does not have to find the funds to buy the land; he can specialize as a farmer. But even 50-year leases of land will not suffice: it cannot be sold or bequeathed. That is why capitalist property ownership provides for freeholds or the virtual equivalent of 999-year leases as well as short leases that can be sold in a market. The British 50-millionth part owner of a British Rail engine or state school or "public" library cannot sell his 50-millionth part. But he will be able to sell his shares in privatized water. The power to sell is the essence of private property.

The Russians will have to suffer for the long neglect of the arts of commercial society. Bukovsky said that no-one in the USSR knows how a market economy operated. It would take a long time to understand and apply, by laborious trial and error, the unfamiliar and once spurned ideas of cost-effectiveness, profitability, quality control and the like. That is why *perestroika* has not shown early results in higher output. These are precisely the skills taught by the market in capitalism, not in socialism. Gorbachev's economist, Abel Aganbegyan, had pointed to the paralysis: ". . . the managers are afraid of independence . . . They continue to ask permission to do this or that even though they no longer need permission."[21] Little wonder that the shops remain half-empty after the early years of *perestroika*. But the longer they remain only half-full, the more the reforms will have to be pushed and the more the risks of offending the vested interests must be taken. In the end the political expropriators of the masses, the military-industrial *apparatchiki*, will have to be subdued, disciplined and expropriated. Marx's resounding prediction on the expropriation of the expropriators will have come full circle. But the expropriators will have been the moguls of Marxism.

20. Ibid., p. 240.
21. Abel Aganbegyan, in ibid., p. 241.

Capitalist Truths Survive Suppression

These capitalist truths have long been known to the Italian Euro-communists. Giorgio Napolitano, a long-serving leader of the Italian Communist Party, understood the necessity for reform in Russia better than some Russians. The labour force, he said, has been accustomed to "secure jobs, poor productivity, minimal quality control, low discipline and non-legal perquisites." Moreover, "the Soviet policy of egalitarianism" had prevented "the economy from offering proper [that is, market] rewards to the highly skilled."[22]

Most significantly for the historical doubt whether inherited Russian culture can and will reject the unique rewards of capitalism in the decades ahead, the Italian Euro-communist leader, who has seen the flaw in communism, saw growing pressure for change. And the Gorbachev liberals are having to recognize it. There is no longer talk of a struggle to the end between socialism and capitalism. No more is heard of Khrushchev's "We will bury you."

The imperatives to accept capitalism are international as well as internal. Russia faces new risks and dangers unknown to Stalin. They require global cooperation with capitalism. Gorbachev has been emphasizing the new conditions of world existence—nuclear power, Third World indebtedness, famine—which have moved the world far from the interwar years. In such a world Russia would have little influence if its economy continued to deteriorate as a nineteenth-century relic. The objections of the Russian "conservatives" who fear for their jobs will have to be overruled. Socialism cannot keep pace with capitalism. The choice is capitalism (perhaps called something like "people's socialism") or contumely.

The Italian Euro-communists saw these developments in the 1960s. The Russians under the old guard ignored them. They cannot now remain oblivious of, or indifferent to, world developments. It cannot be much longer before the unpalatable truths about socialism re-asserted by communists outside the USSR penetrate into the USSR, or to the Marxists who still teach them in British and other Western universities, and repeat them in their journals, or to the clerics in Britain and the United States who innocently repeat them in the bland language of the Bible.

The truths are multiplying. The nationalization of all the means of

22. Giorgio Napolitano, in ibid., p. 277.

production is "unnecessary and undesirable" said Napolitano. "[We] used to believe that once the working class had seized power and the means of production had been . . . put in the hands of the state, the class struggle would end and social conflicts would disappear . . . that analysis was false. Antagonisms continue in the U.S.S.R. and Eastern Europe. . . ."[23] Yet the precepts of a century of Marxist teaching persist tenaciously in Britain and other Western countries.

When Lionel Robbins in the 1930s refuted these simplistic Marxist notions of the class struggle,[24] the socialists at the LSE took little notice. If they had, the myth of socialist harmony in the USSR—taught for half a century in hundreds of books and thousands of articles—might not have taken root.

Yet poetic justice is being done after the long 50 years since 1939. The Marxist myth, which camouflaged socialist excesses and inhumanity in the USSR, is being abandoned at last: ". . . the changes [Gorbachev] is now setting in motion will be very difficult to stop."[25] Although Gorbachev calls Lenin in aid to support his "New Economic Policy" of reconstruction begun in 1985, he is preparing the way for a dismissal of the Marxist tablets: "Just as not all propositions of Marx and Engels could be dogmatically extrapolated to the . . . beginning of the century, so the postulates of the 1950s and 1960s are of no use in assessing the world today. A new reading is needed of the theoretical legacy of our predecessors in the name of man's social emancipation."[26] In short, Gorbachev is having to say that we in the USSR who see the urgency of economic reform towards the market will not *say* that we are abandoning socialism but we shall have to *practise* capitalism; we may go on revering the names of Marx and Engels, Khrushchev and Kosygin, but we shall have to discard their precepts.

Gorbachev's book is a historic statement. It is difficult to envisage its production by any of the long line of his predecessors. If Lenin had lived, perhaps if Trotsky had not been banished or other leaders not liquidated, Russia might have understood the changing world and rejoined the human race sooner. Gorbachev addresses his book to "the citizens of the world about things that . . . concern us all . . . they, like me, worry about the future of our planet . . . We must tackle problems in a spirit of co-operation rather

23. Giorgio Napolitano, in ibid., p. 286.

24. Lionel Robbins, *The Economic Basis of Class Conflict*, Macmillan, 1939.

25. Giorgio Napolitano, in Urban, *Can the Soviet System Survive Reform?*, p. 287.

26. Mikhail Gorbachev, *Perestroika: New Thinking for Our Country and the World*, Collins, London, 1987.

than animosity . . . we need normal international relations for our internal progress."[27]

The prosperity and future of the USSR rest on the outside capitalist world more than the world rests on the USSR. Despite the confident bravado of Gennady Gerasimov and other spokesmen, the popularity of Gorbachev in West Germany, Poland and in Europe reflects anxiety about the reserve Russian power to make war. We do not have to suppose that Gorbachev intends the good of the capitalist countries; we do not have to ascribe higher motives to politicians in socialist countries than to those in capitalist countries. Adam Smith's dictum suffices here as elsewhere: the self-interest of the butcher and the baker ensures that they have to serve the rest of us with good meat and bread. The self-interest of Russia will have to lead her to serve the capitalist countries with agreements that they want as much as she does. We may doubt whether she can remain socialist if she wants to keep pace with us, but she will soon discover that herself.

Russian history or folk-memory does not seem to have much chance of standing in the way of the new leaders of Russia and their belated recognition that Marxist teaching and economic precepts will have to be jettisoned to satisfy the hunger, especially among the young, for Western cakes in place of Soviet bread.

Russia will have to adopt capitalism for the third time—the first between 1885 and 1917, the second between 1921 and 1929—because it has failed to find the solution to the socialist contradiction between the political centralization demanded by the privileges of the controllers and the economic decentralization demanded by the expectations of the masses.

Milovan Djilas, the Yugoslav second in command dismissed by Tito, has doubted whether the Russians could ignore the human urge to the civilized living of the twenty-first century. In 1946 he had ventured the prophecy that Yugoslavia would catch up with the United Kingdom in production per head in 10 years. In 1961 Khrushchev more modestly foretold that the USSR would overtake the United States in 20 years, an appointment with destiny that arrived and passed without the miracle in 1981. In 1988, 30 years after the Khrushchev forecast, Djilas had learned from experience: "The crisis of communism . . . is world wide."[28] Both his reasons—the flight from centralized power and the conflict between economic planning and human nature—make the future of socialism in the USSR precarious.

27. Ibid., pp. 9, 11.

28. Urban, *Can the Soviet System Survive Reform?*, p. 300.

The politicians of every other communist country, from Yugoslavia to China, are trying to devise solutions within a socialist framework to preserve their power. All will fail until they understand and resign themselves to the truth that it is socialism itself and its "public" property that stand in the way.

The economist has to say that the outcome depends on the price, the alternative in living standards and liberty lost if the Russians continue to indulge their supposedly deep-rooted national characteristics of subservience to paternalism and regimentation. The market—both inside and outside the USSR—will encroach on the polity and make the decision sooner than may seem possible to the Russians and their leaders. In 1917, 1929 and 1956 they could hope to ignore the outside world without too much sacrifice of comparative daily standards of living. Near the end of the twentieth century the price of continuing as a nineteenth-century relic is now too high for many, especially the young. With every year that passes they will increase in numbers and form the majority. But before that stage, it will become apparent that, as long as they persist in socialist subjugation to authority and collectivist economic organization, twentieth- and twenty-first-century living standards will be deferred. Even before that stage, worse may come: their place as a world power will fade.

The Chinese Trauma, Tiananmen, 1989

The delicate task of avoiding a hard landing in the approach to capitalism is faced in all the major communist/socialist countries. It is an unavoidable dilemma in allowing economic liberalism at precisely the rate required to avoid premature loss of political power by the commissars at the centre. If it is allowed too slowly and late, productivity will flag; if it is allowed too rapidly and early, political power is risked. The dilemma erupted into a crisis in the Massacre of the Innocents in Tiananmen Square, Beijing.

Yet the final outcome will be broadly as in the USSR: the demands of the masses for higher productivity will be too strong to avoid the risk of political defeat at the centre. The conservatives may have won the round in 1989 to suppress the incipient urge to freedom, but the liberals will have to win the contest in the 1990s. The uprising was expressed tactically as a demand of the students, joined by "the people," for political freedoms, but it was essentially a demand for the freedom of the market to yield the lives they knew their kinsmen and countrymen were living in Hong Kong and the other capitalist economies of Asia and the West.

China will therefore have to resume in the 1990s the cautious steps to collaboration with external Western enterprises and galvanize internal economic activity if living standards are to rise. If not, the latent yearning for economic emancipation will reappear with quickening urgency until it is satisfied. Political liberties—the conventional freedoms of the press and assembly—may be easier to grant, but they are the means to satisfy the elemental desire for higher living standards that require economic liberation.

It may be that China will abandon socialism, again perhaps under politically innocuous labels, before Russia. Three years before Gorbachev, in 1982, the IEA asked the Chinese economist Professor Steven Cheung, then at the University of Washington and later at the University of Hong Kong, to analyse the prospects of China "going capitalist." His findings left no doubt: he argued that mainland China would develop a system of private property rights approaching those of capitalist Hong Kong and Japan.[29]

De-socialization in Asia, Africa, South America

Whichever of the two main communist powers is the first to abandon socialism, the return or advance to capitalism of socialized industries in the mainly non-socialist continents of Asia, Africa and South America will not provoke proportionate dislocation.

De-socialization is a largely British invention. Again the gods have done poetic justice. Britain began the rush down the socialist cul-de-sac in the late nineteenth century; it is seemly that, a sad century later, she should show the way back, and that British authors should explain the developments.

The return has barely begun. Although de-socialization has for decades been advocated by liberal economists, privatization was not anticipated in the form that it has taken. The political motive may have been partly revenue to facilitate tax reduction, but the effect has been unprecedented dispersal of ownership from public to private among managers and manual workers no longer antipathic to capitalism but quickly learning its advantages.

The economic arguments and early developments in Britain are recounted by Cento Veljanovski.[30] Two of the pioneers who worked together in government and financing institutions to devise the British privatization *perestroika,* especially in the second Thatcher Government of 1983–7, John

29. Steven Cheung, *Will China Go Capitalist?,* Institute of Economic Affairs, 1982, 1986.
30. Cento Veljanovski, *Selling the State,* Weidenfeld & Nicolson, 1987.

Redwood, the former Oxford economist who moved to the House of Commons, and Oliver Letwin, have analysed causes and consequences.[31]

Letwin reviewed developments in the main countries where formerly state-owned undertakings were de-socialized by selling property rights to the public. By 1987, in eight short years, privatization in the United Kingdom, France, West Germany, Japan, the United States, Canada, New Zealand and Jamaica had attracted 25 million investors and given a million employees a stake in their firms as worker-capitalists. Privatization has created political support for further de-socialization. The British Labour Party has weighed the electoral effects and abandoned its historic intention to nationalize the means of production, distribution and exchange.

Letwin saw public offers of shares spreading to state- or local-government-owned public utilities (another misleading socialist description of local monopolies) and the railway and coal industries. In Europe the privatization movement could spread to Austria (thus depriving the social democrats of their exemplar), Portugal and Spain (both also social democrat in political flavour), and Turkey. In the Far East, Singapore, Malaysia and the Philippines, followed by Sri Lanka and even "socialist" India seem likely to join the de-socialization movement. Australia and New Zealand, again both run by Labour politicians, will not be far behind. And Japan, says Letwin, "may well dwarf the rest of the world."

More competition will in time be incorporated into the reconstructions from socialist to capitalist ownership. The benefits of privatization are not nullified if they remain monopolies. Of two evils, public monopoly is more objectionable than private monopoly, which is still subject to external commercial discipline because it raises capital in the competitive market. And technical change will undermine it sooner if it is private without the protection of government. If the Cable & Wireless subsidiary Mercury is not allowed to provide a better household telephone service than British Telecom in the near future, a third service will be demanded by industry and the public and emerge sooner than when telephones were run by the socialized Post Office.

In time perhaps half the population of the world could become private owners of industry. Africa, said Letwin, may lag in share purchase (although de-socialization could take other forms), but other Caribbean countries could copy Jamaica. In South America, Mexico and Brazil could follow Chile

31. John Redwood, *Popular Capitalism*, Routledge, 1988; Oliver Letwin, *Privatizing the World*, Cassell, 1988.

in privatizing on a large scale. Not least, some of the provinces of Canada, though not the federal government so far, were setting about privatization "with gusto."

The methods of de-socializing government-owned industry will, as hitherto in capitalism, be evolved to suit the conditions of peoples with varying preferences in the varying political and other institutions of different countries. New forms of capital markets will be developed. The methods extend with experience. Madsen Pirie of the Adam Smith Institute reviewed 21 methods of privatizing government industry and services—from selling shares to the public or to the employees through ending monopolies by competition to a new private power to replace government by private services.[32] Like Letwin and Redwood, he saw scope for considerable extension in Britain, other industrialized countries and the developing countries.

East and West; North and South

More British studies of de-socialization will be written in the coming years, some by former socialists or by socialists searching for new ways of saving the good name of socialism by unburdening it of the industries and services it does not run well or should not run at all: transport, especially the railways; fuel, not least coal mining; welfare, certainly most of education and medical care, undoubtedly housing and as soon as possible pensions and insurance against sickness and unemployment; not least, most local government services, especially the extravaganzas and the exotica that are neither public goods nor demanded by the public.

Studies of de-socialization are emerging from American and Australian authors. The Pacific Research Institute, a Californian "Institute of Economic Affairs," published a study of varying forms of de-socialization of government services from transport and water to skating rinks and fire protection.[33] An Australian study edited by Michael James, comprising 12 papers and commentaries at a seminar of the Centre for Independent Studies, is entitled *Restraining Leviathan*.[34] A collection of 15 essays on *Privatization and Competition* appeared in 1989 from the IEA with studies of telecommunications, the postal services, electricity, coal, the railways and other

32. Madsen Pirie, *Privatization: Theory, Practice and Choice*, Wildwood House, 1988.

33. Randel Fitzgerald, *When Government Goes Private*, Pacific Research Institute, Universe Books, 1988.

34. Michael James (ed.), *Restraining Leviathan*, Centre for Independent Studies, 1987.

industries.[35] Early IEA studies from the late 1950s, long before the politicians thought of privatization, argued for de-socialization of the four main components of the welfare state (chapter 10) and other services and industries.

These are historic developments round the world that few academic observers ten or 20 years ago would have said were likely or "politically possible." The title of this chapter may have seemed sanguine to many readers at first sight. So was Gabriel Roth's study for the World Bank when he told me he was embarking on it in 1985.[36] If the developing countries can provide public services privately, without government supervision or political distortion, in response to market forces and despite relatively low incomes, as in nineteenth-century Britain, there are fewer obstacles to prevent the developed countries from replacing political control by the democracy of the market in the higher incomes of the twentieth and twenty-first centuries.

A Worldwide Movement from a Mirage to a Miracle

Capitalism, in forms varying with cultures and values, could raise the living standards of people everywhere, in degrees varying with the disposition to learn and apply its principles—work directed to satisfy one another as consumers, saving to build capital, the primacy of liberty over equality, acquiring experience in judging the risk of new ventures, low taxes, minimal government. And capitalism has raised living standards wherever it has been adopted in every continent. The most difficult requirement is to discipline the political process, so that the democracy of the market enables the peoples of the world to be left in peace from the short-termism of electoral manoeuvring and political mismanagement of the economy to the daily business of producing what they best can, and living by exchanging it with one another, individually and internationally, to their mutual advantage.

We could now, after the traumas and tyrannies of the century of socialism since the 1880s, enter a prolonged period, perhaps a metaphorical "century," of liberal capitalism in which the common people would prevail over the false prophets who promised them plenty and liberation but substituted penury and coercion.

The new capitalism may be given varying labels by politicians to conceal their embarrassment for wasting the past century by their numerous socialisms from benign social democracy through state-sponsored labour-

35. C. Veljanovski (ed.), *Privatisation and Competition,* Institute of Economic Affairs, 1989.
36. Gabriel Roth, *The Private Provision of Public Services,* World Bank, 1987

capital corporatism to savage communism. And it will take varying forms and proceed at varying paces in different countries according to social progress and technical advance. But it will embrace the essentials of the principles taught by the classical English and Scottish economic philosophers—a minimal state put into its relatively small place by a public ethos that demands disciplines on temporary elected majorities, private property wherever possible, open markets for competing suppliers to dissolve monopoly, rewards for achievements without obsession about inequality but with assurance of resources sufficient for tolerable living by people who cannot compete in the market.

The chief remaining uncertainty is the power of the political obstructions. Marx emphasized the power of interests to determine "social relations," but drew the wrong conclusion for policy to "expropriate" the interests by aggrandizing the state. Keynes emphasized the supremacy of ideas over interests, but taught the wrong ideas. Capitalism in the decades ahead will be obstructed both by the political use of the wrong ideas and by the political tolerance of vested interests that support them. The many of socialist mind in politics, academia, the literati and the various churches in every continent from Europe, North America and Australasia to Asia, South America and Africa will resist the emergence of capitalism because they cannot shake off the influence of the socialist century of intellectual error. And more in all walks of life, who may think themselves opposed to socialism, will unwittingly reinforce the socialist mind because the free market of capitalism will disturb their industrial, professional or labour expectations developed under the restrictions and privileges of the century of socialism.

The defence and assertion of the common people, especially the poorest in every continent, lie in demonstrating the errors of socialism and the strengths of capitalism, so that countervailing ideas and interests emerge to combine in defeating the century of false hopes and failed practice. That is the purpose of this book.

CHAPTER **5**

Political and Market Democracy

> . . . the activity of politics is both a precondition and a necessary characteristic of genuinely socialist societies . . .
>
> Bernard Crick, *In Defence of Politics*

> . . . the old politics is dying. It is possible, just possible, that . . . the new politics . . . will be a politics for people.
>
> Shirley Williams, *Politics Is for People*

> [In] the notion of politics as mutual education . . . [p]olitics ceases to be . . . reserved . . . to politicians. All citizens are politicians.
>
> David Marquand, *The Unprincipled Society*

> It is critically important that we . . . shed once and for all the romantically idiotic notion that as long as processes are democratic all is fair game . . . democracy has over-reached its limits . . . [in] the excessive political exploitation we exercise against each other . . . nearly all end as net losers.
>
> J. M. Buchanan, "The Legal Order in a Free Economy" in *Thinking about America*

Capitalism is superior to socialism because, by minimizing the writ of politics and maximizing the writ of the market, it creates a more effective form of democracy for enabling all the people, the common people as well as the political people, to decide their lives.

The criticism of political democracy and representative government is not that they are essentially undesirable in principle but that, first, as they have developed so far they are defective in making the people sovereign, and, second, that even if effective they are applied where they are unnecessary.

They have to be employed where they are the only available methods of producing goods and services that people want but that cannot be produced in any other way. But they are a necessary instrument with defects, not an absolute blessing. Their characteristic working method of making decisions by majorities, or counting heads, and ignoring many heads merely because they are less numerous, is a childish and uncivilized way of deciding the use of resources when there is a working method of making decisions in active use in capitalist countries that provides for all heads, including those of minorities and even of independent or idiosyncratic individuals.

The alternative method that counts, or could count, all heads, is the market. Its drawback is that instead of counting heads it counts pennies. The defect of counting heads in the political process is that many are *necessarily* ignored; the defect of counting money in the market process is that some people with too little money *may* be ignored unless they are given more money. The central question is whether it is easier for the political process to include all the heads or for the market process to endow all the people with money. Neither is ideal, but the market process can approach the ideal nearer than the political process. In so far as capitalism makes more use of the market and socialism more use of politics, capitalism is superior to socialism.

The two processes differ in the ease of access to the services they produce. Both systems of access are defective in so far as access is influenced or determined by differences in means. Access to the services produced by the political process has been claimed to be equal. It was the essential socialist argument that the political (socialist) system would produce equality of access; the argument was also applied to the services, such as education and medical care, produced by the political process under capitalism.

Experience of all socialized politicized services, from food in the USSR to health in Britain, is that access is not equal but is determined by a range of influences—political, occupational, economic, social and others—that can be described collectively as "cultural." Access to services produced by the capitalist market process is also unequal, and is based on differences in income and wealth and is thus "financial." The question in the choice between capitalism based on the market and socialism based on politically elected government is whether it is easier to mitigate or remove financial differences or cultural differences. I contend that the capitalist market system is superior to the socialist political system because financial differences can be more easily corrected than cultural differences.

Democracy and the Market

Although Professor Buchanan was writing about the United States, his stricture on the exaggerated and unfounded faith in the political system of democracy, common in much British writing on political institutions, and exemplified in the extracts from the three varied types of British socialist at the beginning of this chapter, applies no less to Britain. Mrs. Williams's faith that "participation" can discipline big government so that it is rendered benevolent government that rules "for the people" is dangerous: by misunderstanding the daily real-life working of representative government as it has developed it sets the seal of approval on big government. In practice big government, called representative political democracy, has not served all the people but those who have inherited or acquired the political or cultural skills that enable some to derive more equal benefits than others. Democratic politics as envisaged by Abraham Lincoln has not materialized under the big government favoured by the socialist approach.

The language of liberty, freedom and democracy has been captured for socialist politics and the political process. Hayek speaks of "Our Poisoned Language" and singles out "the weasel word 'social,'" derived from "society" (and easily elongated into "social-ism") as especially vulnerable.[1] "Society" is commonly used to imply a gentler and more benevolent form of authority than the sometimes oppressive, coercive and corrupt authority of duly elected "democratic" government. Many more of the terms used in political science are misleading or mischievous.

Democracy is commonly understood to refer to the paraphernalia of political elections, with their components of canvassing and voting, elections and electioneering, leading to the formation of idealized representative assemblies objectively passing laws in the public interest. When every man has a vote, runs the teaching of political democracy, he has an equal say in the choice of his representatives, and thereby in the conduct of the government that rules the country in which he lives; he has exerted freedom and liberty, and—whether he approves the outcome or not—can regard it as democratically producing laws, regulations and controls of economic, social and cultural as well as political life in the interest of the people or "the public interest."

1. F. A. Hayek, *The Fatal Conceit,* Routledge, 1988, p. 114.

This is not how representative government works in the real world. Lionel Robbins saw through the simplistic pretence 50 years ago. And that is why the purpose must not be that proposed by Professor Marquand—of subjecting the market to politics. We must consider how far the aim is the opposite: to make the political process the servant instead of the master of the people in the market process. Government may have to create the legal framework, although some rules, as Professor Robert Sugden argues (below), emerge better spontaneously by private agreement. But even where government must "lead," it should "follow" the people, and it cannot do that faithfully because the political machinery does not indicate the vast range of diverse individual preferences. The weakness of the legal framework created by government in the political process is that the machinery of elections and pressures is the same flawed instrument for creating the framework as it is for conducting the economic activities within it.

Capitalism is, or can be made, more democratic than socialism. It has not always been democratic, and there are small capitalist countries, such as several in the Far East, that are not as democratic as the larger capitalist countries in the West. The fundamental questions, not all resolved in the literature, are whether capitalism becomes more democratic as it matures, whether there is a choice between capitalism and democracy, what the people rather than politicians would prefer, whether capitalism can work without democracy, whether its results are better with more than with less democracy and what developments around the world reveal as the evidence in practice.

The sociologist Professor Peter Berger of Boston University, a former bourgeois socialist, has related why he was converted to support for capitalism by his study of the empirical evidence on the working of capitalism and socialism in the East and the West.[2] The conclusion from his study is that, whatever its other virtues or vices, capitalism is compatible with democracy. Capitalism can evidently work with varying degrees of political democracy at different cultural stages and in different countries, but political democracy conflicts with the centralized planning of state socialism. The communist countries that wish to introduce a multi-party democratic system, essential to evoke a better productive response, are now discovering and revealing to the world that centralized political control is incompatible with

2. Peter Berger, *The Capitalist Revolution,* Gower, 1987.

decentralized economic initiative. The managers who no longer have to ask for permission, but who are habituated to wait for orders from above, go on asking for permission.

Socialism as the world has known it has nowhere been democratic, and there is no way to make it so. The supposed exceptions, mainly Sweden and Austria, are not exceptions. There is no escape from this conclusion. Socialism by state control of the economy is incompatible with political democracy, because it would give individual citizens the power to require the economy to be run in non-socialist and anti-socialist ways which undermined or removed the power of the state planners.

Neither is there escape by redefining socialism in forms that include the free market, with all its risks and disadvantages. There has been much redefining in the last ten years since it has become apparent that the socialism we have known in the real world since the end of the war has failed. The new definitions reveal anxiety to abandon the conception of socialism as an economic system run by the political process through the state and its organs. The Marxist sociologist who has displayed most awareness of the inadequacy of state socialism, Professor Stuart Hall, has ironically, in view of their reputation for moderation, blamed the Fabians for tying socialism to the chariot of the state and eloquently affirmed, in a disquisition on the recent Marxist notion of "New Times" at a *Marxism Today* weekend rally, that the Left had sadly to abandon its hopes of state socialism.[3]

The Fabian or democratic socialist urge is now, and has been for some ten years, to return to what is claimed an early tradition of socialism in small-scale local voluntary communal effort by the people to better their condition. A courageous early essay by Evan Luard argued that state socialism had "failed to increase equality . . . to abolish alienation . . . to provide any genuine sense of control for the worker over his own destiny or for the citizen over the decisions which affect him" (the last is the crucial failure, especially of socialist government because it was, and is, big government).[4] Luard concluded logically: ". . . some of its tenets may require to be radically reappraised." The solution offered was a new socialism based, insubstantially, on small-scale "grass-root" communities in a "wider socialist world." An earlier book by R. N. Berki reviewed the diverse forms of socialism from Marxist,

3. Stuart Hall, *Marxism Today* weekend, Institute of Education, University of London, 27 October 1989.

4. Evan Luard, *Socialism without the State,* Macmillan, 1979, p. 9.

which he seemed to favour, to libertarian.[5] A more recent exposition by Anthony Wright contends that the Marxist tradition of a single socialism must be "unlearned" and salvation found in a series of "submerged, neglected, and minority socialist traditions."[6] He called on George Orwell's satires for the argument that "democratic socialism should be embraced . . . and authoritarian socialism attacked." Professor Bernard Crick has struggled manfully to save Orwell for socialism, but has not resolved the dilemma that the more socialist the system, the more precarious the democracy.[7] Orwell saw that the traditional (that is, I would emphasize, capitalist) decencies were more common among the ordinary people than among intellectuals. He did not wish to live "in a world in which everything could be manipulated, *even for the public good*."[8] But manipulation for "the public good" is the essence of socialism. Even the newly enlightened Goulds and Hattersleys believe that government knows better than individuals. The essence of capitalism, as it could be even more than as it has been, is that it allows individuals to take the risks of living their lives as they see best. The spirit of Orwell is with the liberties of the market, not with the tutelage of politics.

There is still no recognition in revisionist socialist writing that without the market, created by private property and creating consumer choice between competing suppliers, democratic freedoms are unsecured. The latest efforts to save socialism persist in the central fallacy that any system emerging from the political process of democracy is sufficient to ensure popular sovereignty over government or economic life.

The National Debate for the Elites

The essential strength of the case for capitalism is that the democracy of the market offers the masses more than the democracy of politics. The insufficiency and inequality of "pennies" can be corrected. The inequality in cultural power cannot. Political democracy has therefore been distorted in favour of the politically influential, skilled and adroit; its nominally representative assemblies reflect the influence of the organized at the expense of the unorganized; it has built a hierarchy of power; it is therefore inequitable

5. R. N. Berki, *Socialism*, J. M. Dent, 1975.
6. Anthony Wright, *Socialisms*, Oxford University Press, 1986, p. ix.
7. Bernard Crick, *George Orwell: A Life*, Secker & Warburg, 1980; Penguin, 1982, p. 17.
8. Ibid., p. 19.

and arbitrary. The doubt is whether the defects of the political process can be removed by the political process.

This indictment of the political process that underlies socialism has rarely been understood by the critics of capitalism. Since the re-assertion of capitalism in the past decade in the political form it has taken under Mrs. Thatcher's Governments, socialist writings have condemned them (and her) as authoritarian, insensitive and materialistic, but have largely ignored their achievements in the emancipation from the state that they have attempted in their short ten years so far.

The extract quoted from Marquand at the beginning of this chapter indicates the conclusion of *The Unprincipled Society,*[9] a widely praised book by the former Labour, later Social Democrat, political scientist, now Professor of Contemporary History and Politics at Salford University and an active Social and Liberal Democrat. The book rejects both socialism and capitalism, the state and the market, in favour of a third principle designed to avoid the shortcomings of both. Professor Marquand's analysis is elegant and seductively persuasive. It reveals why former socialists find it difficult to understand capitalism and its market, and why they are slow to accept them as the best, or the least imperfect, of the alternative politico-economic systems. But as envisaged by Lenin in 1919 and satirized by Brecht after the 1953 convulsion in East Germany, the Marquand solution repeats the injunction "change the people." It is one more escape from reality.

The Marquand "third way" is to replace the commands of state socialism and the exchanges of the capitalist market with "persuasion, discussion, indoctrination, conversion," in short, "precept," a term borrowed from the American political scientist Professor Charles Lindblom.[10] The contrast is put eloquently:

> They are the relationships, not of masters to servants or buyers to sellers, but of pupils to teachers or teachers to pupils.
>
> If a society operating by the command mode would be rather like a regiment, and in the exchange mode like a bazaar, a society operating by the preceptoral mode would be more like a classroom, a debating chamber . . .[11]

9. David Marquand, *The Unprincipled Society,* Cape, 1988.
10. Ibid., p. 229.
11. Ibid.

The notion of the affairs of society being conducted like a debating chamber comes naturally to middle-class academics who use words effectively in spoken politics and written journalism. The approach is a clue to the century-old middle-class advocacy of socialism and its use of the political process in representative assemblies. He quotes in support a London University PhD thesis which describes politics as "'a civilised and civilising' process, through which free men and women assume the burdens of social choice and decision, instead of handing them over to a charismatic leader or an impersonal social process."[12]

Liberals (of the European philosophical, not the British political, kind) must welcome Marquand's recognition that preceptoral relationships are not morally superior to the others and can be abused by tyrants. He seems to approve of Gladstone's Midlothian campaign during the 1876 General Election to persuade the electorate of the Bulgarian atrocities against the Turks, but not of Mao Tse Tung's Cultural Revolution of 1966–9. Even less would he approve of Adolf Hitler's Nuremburg or of Benito Mussolini's Palazzo Venezia "precepts." The difficulty about a preceptoral society is that tyrants are more likely to rise to the top, often with resort to violence and torture, than in a capitalist market society where, as in Switzerland, the names of heads of governments are barely known.

Again there is the now increasingly familiar refuge in the new-found emphasis on community, or communitarianism, which, on examination, emerges as little more than dependence on the political process. But there is aspiration without solution: the task, it is argued, is how to empower men and women to realize themselves not merely as consumers but also as producers and as citizens. The Marquand solution is "yeoman democracy" in which yeomen democrats exercise "active citizenship and reject passive subjecthood"[13]—but so far it evidently lacks machinery. The poet Roy Campbell would have asked: "Where's the ruddy horse?" Market liberalism abolishes the abuses of the socialist state by narrowing the scope of political power; "yeoman democracy," it seems, would widen and generalize political power, but only to political people. The contrast is revealed: market liberalism would draw in the frontiers of politics; "yeoman democracy" would extend them. "Yeoman democracy" avoids the language but embraces the machinery of socialism—the political process.

12. Ibid., p. 232.
13. Ibid., p. 237.

Preceptoral politics is yet one more middle-class vision to confuse the working masses. Thatcherite liberal economics has harnessed the prime mover, the motive power of the market, Campbell's "ruddy horse." "Public power" was the original inspiration of socialism: the notion that men or women with political power acquired through the open hustings of electioning or the closed closets of conspiracy would use it for the common good. The capitalist market depends on no such fabrication of good intentions or wishful thinking. It does not depend on the equal exertion of equal political skills. It does not entrust the people to the political process. It does not suppose that, whatever the good intentions of democratic socialists, "politics is [necessarily] for people." It puts power—effective purchasing power—directly into the hands of the common man and woman for them to use where they wish, or to deny where they decide. There is no such power for them in the political process. That is why the market is more essentially democratic than government, capitalism more than socialism. That is why the market in capitalism could be made even more democratic than politics under socialism in the future.

Liberals who understand the market process, and its immeasurable superiority over the political process, cannot follow Marquand's misapprehension that the market excludes preceptoral relationships. He says that "Men and women do not only command and obey, and exchange one good for another. They also teach and learn, persuade and are persuaded."[14] But the glory of the market system is that it opens all three alternatives of regiments, talking shops and bazaars. It is for men and women to decide which affairs and how much of them they wish to decide by command, which and how much by exchange and which and how much by persuasion. Some (mainly the public goods, like defence or pure research, that cannot be arranged by individual exchange because they create inseparable benefits) must be decided by command, some affairs like charitable voluntary work and giving are influenced by moral attitudes and can be facilitated by persuasion; but most human relationships in a modern economy are arranged by buying and selling in the market because that is how men and women want to live with one another, not least because no other method produces the living standards made possible by liberty with advancing technology. The market sublimates the energies of people as they are, good, bad or indifferent; all other systems coerce, cajole or distort them, with disastrous results.

14. Ibid., p. 230.

Unequal Cultural Power: Equalizable Financial Power

The case for the capitalist market system is thus that it allows men and women to minimize the role of command, to maximize the scope for exchange and to indulge in persuasion where they prefer. There is good reason: the mass of ordinary people do not wish to engage in preceptoral political argument, or sense that they cannot hold their own against political people richly endowed with political skills in public affairs. That is why the vast mass of people do better in the market. The distinction is clear. The ordinary man's penny counts as much as the cultured man's, or the socially well-connected man's or the politically skilled man's. He may not have as many pennies. But it is easier to make up for unnecessary differences in the number of pennies (some differences are necessary as incentives—as socialist systems have long recognized) than it is to remove the arbitrary and chance differences in the cultural power that prevail in preceptoral society.

That is the essential difference between the state and the market, between socialism and capitalism. Self-conscious socialists have difficulty in grasping the distinction, perhaps because most of them are instinctively or congenitally political people adept at the theory or practice of government socialism. I recall the Labour politician Ian Mikardo, in debate with the later "defector" and Conservative Minister Reg Prentice, arguing at a Labour Party meeting in Orpington in the early 1970s that the "active" people (he meant, and may have said, Labour loyalists) who attended meetings or other political activities should have more influence on policy than those who went home at night to watch television. This is the attitude induced by active participation in the political process: it regards unpolitical people as inferior, unworthy and unequal.

That would be the fate of most yeomen in a yeoman democracy. Capitalism makes no such distinction, because the market is colour-blind, accent-deaf and indifferent to social origins. The common criticism of capitalism, that the single-minded pursuit of profit excludes wider considerations, is basically its moral strength as well as a possible source of weakness (in its externalities) because it also excludes political partiality, racial prejudice and not least cultural influence. The penny of the plasterer counts as much as the penny of the plutocrat in the private shop, and certainly his credit card does in the impersonal cash dispenser of the capitalist bank. Individual suppliers may be influenced by accent or race, but the market puts a high price on such indulgent discrimination: loss of customers, reduced sales, vanishing profits and ultimately bankruptcy. The plasterer's vote counts equally with the plutocrat's in counting numbers at infrequent elections, but less, usually hardly at all, in the activist lobbying and the rest of the paraphernalia of politics between elections.

This is the trump card of the individual in the capitalist market that he cannot exercise in socialist public services: any who sense discrimination can escape by exit to other suppliers. The power of escape from unacceptable suppliers or purchasers in capitalism has no parallel in socialism, which offers only the precarious power of "voice," the right to "participate," that is inherently unequal and that usually favours and strengthens the already strong and influential, usually the articulate middle class well endowed with cultural power.

Moreover, voice is generally ineffective without the power to exit. A parent who cannot escape from a state school, or a patient who cannot escape from a National Health Service (NHS) hospital, or a tenant who cannot escape from a local government home is heeded less readily than one who can take his money to pay rent, school fees and health insurance premiums elsewhere. (These concepts were initially developed by Hirschmann,[15] although he would not necessarily agree with the applications here.)

The distinction between the relative powers of political voice and market exit may be penetrating the socialist mind, perhaps unconsciously. Professor Crick warned his friends "In socialist societies . . . people may not like what they are given and must be free to challenge by public debate (or by turning their backs on it all) both values and policies."[16] Voice and exit both appear here as defences of the people against presumably "their" government, but the emphasis is still on the familiar political voice, with the market exit ("turning their backs") as a bracketed afterthought. The less articulate will not hold their own with the politically practised in public debate; their power to make the politicians, the officials, the planners and the controllers sit up and take notice lies essentially in "turning their backs." But to do so effectively they must have the reserve power to switch their money from "what they are given" to what they prefer: they must have a market.

Without a market the less literate parent (probably a product of a state school) is lost. An example is probably typical of many thousands. "My daughter," wrote a mother from Liverpool to Friends of the Education Voucher Experiment (FEVER), "did not like her primary school [ages 5 to 11] because of the fights and bad language. So I took her to a school in the next town and said we lived there. But after a year the social worker found out and

15. Albert O. Hirschmann, *Exit, Voice and Loyalty,* Harvard University Press, 1970.
16. Bernard Crick, *In Defence of Politics,* Penguin, 1982, p. 215.

told the education authority. They moved her back to the school where she was unhappy. The Headmaster of the new school wanted to keep her as she had improved her work and her attendance was so good, but she had to go back."[17] This child is not the only victim of the political process from which she could not escape, and of the socialist mind that still urges it where it is unnecessary after decades of failure to save uninfluential domestic people, like this working-class mother, from being degraded, in Orwell's language, as less equal than influential political people.

Political People and Domestic People

The political process is worlds apart from the market process. It is the arena of *specialists*—in the arts of persuasion, organization, infiltration, debate, lobbying, manipulating meetings, moving resolutions at conferences or hard bargaining behind closed doors. The market is the world of *generalists*—ordinary men and women who do their work by day and go home at night.

Let the advocates of the political process contemplate the kind of people who escape from it, because they feel they are overtaxed and underserviced, to the underground, where they can live better by their elemental skills in buying and selling, and supplying what the consumer will pay for. Here they can earn a living with no cultural authority, no social connections, no membership of professional associations or trade unions, no political influence. They have been driven by politics to live as unpolitical people.

> . . . the rejection of government takes the main form of tax evasion in the underground economy, which should raise a silent cheer from classical liberals since it is in principle as much resistance to unacceptable political coercion as the French resistance to the Nazi occupation . . .
>
> . . . the underground . . . is even more fundamentally a return to the free market of individuals with commercial talents who have to compensate for the lack of political skills required to extract favours from government.
>
> Those who cannot "join" government by "voice" are "beating" it by "exit."[18]

17. Quoted in Ruth Garwood Scott, Marjorie Seldon and Linda Whetstone, *The Education Voucher System,* National Council for Education Standards, 1977, p. 17.

18. Arthur Seldon, "Public choice and the choices of the public," in C. K. Rowley (ed.), *Democracy and the Public Choice,* Blackwell, 1987, p. 131.

That people with inferior cultural power are elbowed out of the state economy by those with superior cultural power is a hypothesis that could have been formulated long ago with commonsense assumptions on human nature and everyday experience. The escape from the politicized state should have been foreseen by the political scientists like Crick and other socialists: it foreshadowed the developing disillusionment with the state economy and its most compassionate component, the welfare state.

But these early consequences were largely ignored by the socialist mind or given passing reference. An early insight into them came from Professor Brian Abel-Smith, the best of the trio of socialist sociologists who exerted most influence on the post-war consensus on the welfare state (perhaps because he had some grounding in economics, unlike the other two, Professor Richard Titmuss and Professor Peter Townsend). But he drew the wrong conclusion for policy. Abel-Smith protested in the 1960s that the middle classes were doing best out of the welfare services. His inference, that the working classes should be given higher standards (including smoked salmon in NHS hospitals), opened the prospect of interminably higher standards financed with eternally higher taxes. This error made no allowance for the rising incomes that could enable eventually (almost) all to pay for what they wanted in the market, but with the added advantage of widening choice from competing suppliers, especially for the working classes.

In 1981 Shirley Williams referred to "the extraordinary ability of the middle classes to get most out of public services by a combination of know-how, self-confidence, persistence and articulacy."[19] Since then detailed research has confirmed the extent of the failure of the post-war state, especially the welfare state, to perform its intention of providing equal access to all.

Among the most up to date is the study by Le Grand and Goodin of the middle-class efforts not only in Britain but also in the United States and Australia to derive more than their "fair" share of benefit from the welfare state.[20] Their title—*Not Only the Poor*—might suggest that the welfare state was intended only, or primarily, for the poor; it was sold politically as a social advance for all classes which, moreover, would then integrate them by social cohesion and enable all to share in the benevolent welfare of the state. But their analysis justifies their two main conclusions: that the "non-poor," and especially the middle classes, have benefited from welfare services designed

19. Shirley Williams, *Politics Is for People*, Penguin, 1981, p. 36.
20. Julian Le Grand and Robert Goodin, *Not Only the Poor*, Allen & Unwin, 1987.

for the poor, and moreover that they have resisted recent attempts to withdraw their gains.

What is surprising is that these findings are surprising the academics of the Left. The appropriate sentiments are perhaps disappointment and dismay: one more application of the doctrine that public expenditure would ensure the public interest has failed. But the surprise derives from the unrealistic supposition that, by an alchemy yet to be discovered, politicians are transformed from fallible humans into disinterested saints, or that people in any walk of life will desist from using their abilities to obtain the best bargains from their fellows, not least from the open-ended resources of the state, so that both parties are bargaining over other people's money. Professor Buchanan's adjective "romantic" may seem charitable for the notion that anything produced by democracy was beneficient, and his adjective "idiotic" will ring harsh. But it is time to question the judgement, the good sense or the knowledge of history of those, essentially on the Left but also on the Right, who persist in the grand delusion of our age that the political process has finally realized the vision of Abraham Lincoln: government of the people, by the people, for the people.

There is no way to ensure social justice for the culturally weaker by bureaucratic ordinance. The solution is to enable the underprivileged in the state economy to escape from the unacceptable. The solution was, and remains, emancipation by purchasing power. The treatment for unavoidable inequity in the state is not to attempt to equalize voice, which is unequalizable, but to facilitate escape by exit, which can be evened up by redistribution of purchasing power. The solution adopted by British governments of the 1980s for education and perhaps medical care is "opting out" by schools and hospitals, but opting out by producers retains the political process of bargaining between state institutions and the state. It will postpone the better solution of opting out by individual consumers in a market. Opting out is an advance as a principle, but in the practice of politics, where a new idea cannot easily be abandoned even if it works badly because it generates vested interests, the apparently or immediately better may be the enemy of the practical and ultimately best. In a market, buttressed by purchasing power, all the people could have the best; in the political process they are given half measures.

The choice is between two imperfect approaches—the political process and the market process, between politics and markets, between the political and the commercial ethic—rather than two imperfect systems, since both are necessary. But the mix can differ widely between the minimum use of government combined with the maximum use of the market, which I define as capitalism, and the maximum use of government combined with the minimum use of the market, which I define as socialism.

Politics and politicians, government and bureaucracy play too large a part in our daily, personal lives. I would judge that they loom three or four times too much because public goods are only a third or a quarter of public (government-supplied) services. The triumph of capitalism is that it minimizes, or could minimize, their power but socialism maximizes them.

Government of the Busy, by the Bossy, for the Bully

The democracy of politics is less effective for the common people than the democracy of the market. The political way to democracy has been overestimated, and the market way underestimated.

The supposition that the democracy of politics is satisfied by representative government elected by the people to execute its wishes has been revealed as unfounded. The familiar case for democratic politics is put by Mrs. Williams: ". . . most men and women who join political parties or who embark upon a political career do so with the intention of bettering the lives of their fellow human beings." But "to bring about improvements, politicians must acquire power. The temptation of politics is to seek power for itself and for the status it confers. . . ." And again: "Practical politics is about ruling classes, bureaucrats, parties, lobbies, interests and advancement."[21]

Socialist politicians have urged the political way to democracy; non-socialist politicians unfortunately have an occupational interest in advancing the political method but presumably a doctrinal objection to it. The Thatcher Governments set out to push back the influence of the state and therefore of politics. In the 1980s they pursued policies like de-socialization (privatization) that reduced the political influence but others (higher total taxes) that enlarged it. The judgement of history is yet to be made. The outcome turns not on what well-intentioned politicians intend to do, but on what the machinery and the electoral rewards of representative politics induce them to do.

The question resolves itself into three sub-questions that follow Abraham Lincoln's three-part vision of democratic government. Is it "of" (elected by) the people? Is it "by" (conducted by) the people? Is it run "for" the people?

21. Williams, *Politics Is for People*, pp. 204, 209.

So far, no government in the world has fully realized Lincoln's vision. Most governments are undemocratic: they do not represent (are not elected "of") all the people, they are not run "by" all the people and they are usually not run solely "for" all the people.

It is the implication of socialist doctrine, even the latest revisions, that so-called democratic governments that are elected by the political process are necessarily "of," "by" or "for" the people. In practice they can be, and usually are, distorted by pressures from interests that develop within the political process itself. This is true of the "public" sectors in capitalist systems as well as of socialist systems. But it is more true the more government controls economic activity. It is therefore more true of socialist than of capitalist countries.

An even more fundamental conclusion follows. For the resources of a country to be used as the people wish, political democracy is not enough. The *frisson* of excitement among academic, political, journalistic, broadcasting and other observers of the stirrings of "democracy" in Hungary and other communist countries betrays the long error in the West that political democracy is sufficient to create rule by the people. The Crick, Marquand and Williams error is shared by many democrats. The truth, which post-war experience has graphically demonstrated and the (still too little studied) economics of politics (chapter 7) has clarified, is that for democracy to become a reality in the daily lives of the people, the democracy of politics must produce the democracy of the market.

The relationship between the two is intriguing. It may seem obvious that political democracy is required to vote in a liberal market economy. But it is not true that all the rules required for a regime of free markets necessarily require to be enacted by government: Professor Robert Sugden has argued persuasively that individuals will spontaneously evolve many rules that enable them to live harmoniously together without action by government.[22] Yet if government must enact some rules and provide some services (the so-called public goods [chapter 8]) that individuals cannot generate spontaneously, it has a dangerous tendency to exceed these necessary functions. If the communist countries restore full political democracy, with multi-party elections and so forth, the use of resources will be influenced by the politicians of several parties instead of one, but still not by the people. They will create a politicized market by the political process. A real "people's democracy,"

22. Robert Sugden, *Economics of Rights: Co-operation and Welfare*, Blackwell, 1986.

unlike the fraud of the communist versions, requires free markets with the minimum of political influence. Even with restricted political democracy, free markets could create the indispensable liberties required for the democratic control of resources by the people. Without free markets, political democracy creates political control of resources. If Lincoln returned he would see government not of the whole people but of the activists busy in the political business, not by the people but by the bossy managers who are skilled in running government, not for all the people but for the groups organized to influence, blackmail or bully government.

Political "Democracy" in Practice

This is a truth that was known to the classical liberal economists. In 1861 John Stuart Mill wrote: "the very principle of constitutional government requires it to be assumed, that political power will be abused to promote the purposes of the holder; . . . such is the natural tendency . . . to guard against which is the especial use of free institutions."[23] Mill was quoted by Professor Buchanan, regarded as a Founding Father of the modern study economics of politics (in academic writing "public choice"), in a lecture at the IEA in 1978.[24] In the 1930s, when I was looking for a philosophy to replace socialism, Lionel Robbins put the essence in a few simple words (I quote from memory): "A man with £50 in his pocket has more freedom than with a vote on a committee."

Lincoln's vision has not yet become reality because there are imperfections or obstacles in the way of all three parts of the political process before government can be "of," "by" and "for" the people, the whole people and nothing but the people. These are the findings of the economics of politics, to be analysed at length in a forthcoming publication.[25]

First, government cannot be "of" the people as long as there are difficulties in devising methods of election that indicate the most accurate pattern of electors' wishes. All known methods, even the apparently purest forms of proportional representation, are imperfect. The latest demonstration is the voting machinery established for decisions on opting out of the British

23. John Stuart Mill, *Representative Government,* Dent, 1861.

24. J. M. Buchanan, in *The Economics of Politics,* Institute of Economic Affairs, 1978, p. 18.

25. Charles Rowley, Arthur Seldon and Gordon Tullock, *Primer on Public Choice,* Blackwell, forthcoming.

structure of state schools (chapter 10); a majority of the parents who voted "Yes" for one school and "No" for another spoke for a minority of parents, since almost half did not vote at all. A majority of parents will thus have to accept a decision for which they did not vote. In a free market for schools it is inconceivable that the non-voting parents would not have "voted" with their money if they had been able to opt in or out as individuals armed with the required purchasing power. Moreover, unsurprising to students of the economics of politics, there has been political activity to intimidate parents, school governors and teachers who favour opting out by others who favour state schools. This is the reality of political democracy in practice in contrast with the dream of democracy of the romantics, or of the political people who can work the political process to their advantage. The Minister has had to issue guidelines to prevent opponents of opting out from misleading supporters. Students of politics will be familiar with these predictable electoral stratagems—lobbying, canvassing, pressurizing and so forth—of putting the intimate family decision on schools into the political process with the familiar advantage to the political people.

Second, government cannot be "by" the people at all, but must be indirectly by the members of assemblies whom they elect to represent them. The control by the sovereign people of their spokesmen is very tenuous. In the market all the people make decisions themselves individually and enforce them by paying or moving elsewhere. There are no representatives to misrepresent them.

Third, government cannot be "for" the people as long as the representatives they elect have motives other than serving their voters' interests. That they may have is incontrovertible, not least in the prospects of preferment by serving party leaders interested as much in achieving or continuing power in the short run of three-, four- or five-year governments as in serving the sovereign people in the long run. Professor Tullock wrote of "log-rolling" in Britain,[26] a form of horse-trading between Members of Parliament in which they exchange support for each other's measures, perhaps designed to do sectional good but in total likely to do national harm. A well-known former Cabinet Minister protested that no such improper practice was known in the British House of Commons. A then less well-known MP promptly, but unconsciously, provided examples.

26. Gordon Tullock, *The Vote Motive*, Institute of Economic Affairs, 1976.

Political and Market Decisions

The political process differs fundamentally from the market process in ways that make it less democratic. This is a fundamental reason for the superiority of capitalism over socialism.

Governments that attempt to dispense with the information-gathering function of the market, and its coordinating links with the millions of citizens and their individual decisions, must resort to the collective decision-making of representative assemblies, varying from the 15 members of English parish councils through the 100 of the Israeli Knesset and the 600 of the British Parliament to the 2,000 of the USSR Supreme Soviet.

There are five main differences between markets as the vehicles of individual decisions and governments as the vehicles of collective decisions. They explain the very different results of capitalism that makes the minimum use of government decision-making (which no existing capitalist government, except perhaps Switzerland, now does) and socialism that makes the maximum use (which most socialist governments try to do).

I here draw on the literature of public choice, not least the last two IEA Hobart Papers I edited in 1987–8, written by an American political scientist and a British political scientist whose political science is stronger for being informed by the economics of politics.[27]

First, in the market people make decisions as individuals; in government they make them collectively with many others. In capitalist markets they do not have to wait for others to agree; in the political process (in socialism or the socialist sectors of capitalism) they have to persuade enough others to form majorities, to organize "movements," to march with banners or create deputations to intimidate politicians. This is the source of the innate discrimination of the political process between the activist political people who are adept in these activities and the quiet domestic people who lack the temperament, character, social skills or robust health required for the life political. The retention of British education and medicine in the political process explains the Conservative anxiety to galvanize "active citizens" to offset the activists of the Left on school Boards of Governors or NHS committees. To achieve equality of treatment by the state in socialism, and in the socialist

27. William Mitchell, "Government as it is," IEA Hobart Paper, Institute of Economic Affairs, 1988; Norman Barry, "The invisible hand in economics and politics," IEA Hobart Paper, Institute of Economic Affairs, 1988.

sectors of capitalism, every man and woman must be a politician. That is a bizarre requirement for a society of free men and women.

Second, since individuals in markets decide for themselves or for small private units like families or voluntary associations, all know one another. In the political process collective decisions are made for thousands or millions who are generally and necessarily strangers. They must remain mostly herded into group categories—householders, rail passengers, parents, patients, pensioners. Differences between individuals in personal circumstances, requirements, preferences must be ignored. The state provides table d'hôte for groups; the market provides à la carte to individual taste. The administrative herding indispensable in the state must produce equal treatment of unequal people or unequal treatment of equal people. That is not what the socialist mind has confessed.

Third, individuals in markets make decisions directly, in face-to-face or otherwise personal exchange with other individuals. In government decisions are made indirectly by delegation to representatives. In the long chain of instruction or command from voter to representative to minister to bureaucrat and back, there is considerable room for misunderstanding of preferences, misinterpretation of circumstances, misrepresentation of wishes, ambiguity of instructions and misdirection of effort. The First World War "Enemy advancing on the west flank, send reinforcements" is often corrupted into tragic forms in the socialist state: "Enemy dancing on wet plank, send three-and-fourpence."

Fourth, in markets people generally spend their own money; governments spend other people's money, always, and in much larger quantities. There are no safeguards in representative bodies that reproduce the intimate personal knowledge in the market of the conditions or requirements of each man or woman; no comparable anxiety to make the most of every penny, franc or florin; no consciousness of the personal consequences of error, carelessness or foolishness; no corresponding sense of responsibility in spending, saving, investing or wasting money.

There are no democratic safeguards for political irresponsibility because the "other people" whose money is being spent cannot closely approve the reasons, check the calculations or trace individual losses. The politician can divide and conquer. The extraordinary subsidy of £18 million paid to British egg farmers in 1989 for the losses arising from the extraordinary alertness of a junior minister on the risk of salmonella may have been justified, but no taxpayer who involuntarily "contributed" £10 or £100 could judge the wisdom of yet one more subvention to the farmers (or landowners), who could have been expected to finance the risks.

Fifthly, in the market individuals who suffer from poor service can generally escape to other suppliers, and the very knowledge that they can escape prevents poor service being widespread or prolonged. In government services, individuals are generally tied. They may have to wait for a new government, or buy from other countries (which government can prevent by import restrictions) or move their purchasing power overseas (which government can prevent by exchange controls).

Fallacies in the Resort to Government

Although the classical liberals were aware of the *naïveté* of regarding government as invariably a neutral benevolent institution, political thinking for a century has been dominated by the view, or hope, that it could be used to cure the ills of mankind. It underlies the unceasing flow of proposals from politicians, compassionate people, rent-seeking clerics, scientists, artists, pacifists, friends of the earth and many others for government action to right wrongs, repair injustices, succour the lame, humble the mighty, produce "funding" for all manner of desirable purposes, abolish poverty, strengthen industry, "protect" jobs, ensure minimum standards, cure unemployment, master inflation and generally create the good life for all.

The resort to government is the characteristic instinct of the socialist mind that until recently had infected politicians of all parties in the West and undermined the development of voluntary institutions which had been spreading under capitalism. (The researches of Professor E. G. West on education and Dr. David Green on medicine are incontrovertible [see chapter 11].)

The instinct had six main sources: first, the notion that if the market failed, the only alternative was the state; second, the superstition that collective action would secure better use of resources than individual action; third, the myth that public control was more responsible than private; fourth, the *non sequitur* that, since government was obviously necessary in external defence and internal safety, it could also properly supply many other services; fifth, the wishful thinking that, since government has the resources to create good works, able people should join it to ensure that it did—as in Mrs. Williams's affirmation about "most men and women"; sixth, the self-delusion that government is the arena of professionally inclined people who would rather provide a service to others than work for profit for themselves. Dr. Anthony King, Professor of Government at Essex University, recently warned the Government that it would lose the support of professionally minded people, from generals to university professors, who cared not for personal gain but wished to live a life of service.[28] This is not an untypical misunderstanding of the market process and its pricing function from a political scientist. Professor King has claimed that unpriced opinion polls in 1986 presaged "a nasty shock" for Mrs. Thatcher at the 1987 General Election.[29]

All six notions are debatable. First, if there is market failure, government is not necessarily superior because there is also government failure. The flaws of untried government were not given much thought by the Fabians; Beveridge and Keynes should have known better. The sequence "Capitalism bad, socialism good" is the most persistent but most damaging *non sequitur* in political science.

Government failure, moreover, is more objectionable than market failure because it is more difficult to ameliorate or eradicate. Both are flawed; that is agreed by scholars on both sides of the argument. The central difference is that the market failure of capitalism is mostly corrigible, but the government failure of socialism is generally incorrigible. The main reason is that capitalist government does not have such a large stake in the political process as socialist government.[30]

Second, the notion that "society as a whole" can control "its productive resources"[31] is common in socialist writing but is patently unrealistic. The machinery of social control has never been devised. There is no conceivable way in which the British citizen can control the controllers of "his" state railway or NHS, except so indirectly that it is in effect inoperative.

Third, the notion of public control is vacuous. Day-to-day control may have to be delegated to officials in government and to company directors in the market, but the difference between the tenuous power to escape from inefficient or corrupt officials and the ease of escape from inefficient or corrupt company directors is so wide in degree as to constitute a difference of principle. The term "public" is designed to convey the impression of effective control over public assets through the trusteeship of politicians. This is the

28. Anthony King, *Sunday Telegraph*, February 1989.

29. Anthony King, *The World in 1987*, Economist Intelligence Unit, 1986.

30. Arthur Seldon, *Corrigible Capitalism, Incorrigible Socialism*, Institute of Economic Affairs, 1980.

31. Gareth Stedman Jones, *Marxism Today*, June 1985.

objection to de-socialization (privatization) that has infected non-socialists: the former Conservative Prime Minister, Harold Macmillan, spoke of "Selling the family silver." But the employees who bought shares in the National Freight Corporation (NFC) had a much more vivid sense of ownership, not least because they could sell their NFC private shares, than the nominal political owners have in their public ownership of the NHS. This is the reply to the radio interviewer who asked innocently, "Why do we want to buy shares in the water industry that we already own?" "We" do not *effectively* own nationalized industry; we own private industry *effectively.*

Fourth, government is unavoidably the supplier of public goods. It does not follow that it should also supply other goods, as it now does in Britain. It certainly does not follow that it should exercise a monopoly. Yet it generally fears to prove itself in competition with private suppliers. Even after the de-socialization of industry most welfare services, which are not public goods but intensely private and personal, remain controlled by the state in the 1990s.

Fifth, that people in government can do good is also undeniable. The question is rather the opportunity cost: whether they would do more good outside government. Mrs. Williams's public-spirited people are not saints. They enter politics because it is a profession in which they hope to do well for themselves; others, the people in general, may benefit, but incidentally. If there is a clash of interest, the people cannot depend on the politician putting himself second. The wealth of talent in politics is a loss to private industry, although not all politicians would be worth their parliamentary pay in the market.

Sixth, the public official is also not transformed from a selfish mortal into a public benefactor. He or she is often among the best-educated, most talented and most cultured people in the country. It is certain that far too many are engaged in the immeasurable tasks of government administration instead of in the measurable, because competitive, functions of private industry. Again, it is the advantage of capitalism that it can operate with a much smaller bureaucracy than socialism.

Man as Consumer and as Producer

The democracy of the market is based on the sovereignty of the consumer. Here there is another confusion. Observers of the political scene speak of parliament informing itself of the opinions of consumer as well as producer organizations. The consumer is not a different man from the producer. Apart from the young and the old, we are all both. The task is to devise institutions that subordinate our interests as producers to our own interests as consumers. Only capitalism can make the consumer in us sovereign, and has in varying degree done so in history, because the competition of the market can prevent us from myopically asserting our interests as producers by protecting established but outdated industries, occupations and jobs. "Job creation" and "job protection" are retrogressive impoverishing policies that can be sustained only by the political process. They embody socialist thinking and require state coercion.

All other politico-economic systems have subjected man's consumer interest to his producer interest. Feudalism saw the rule of the land-owning lord of the manor. Mercantilism was run by producer guilds. Syndicalism envisaged rule by worker-producers. Corporatism sought to combine employers and employees as producers. Municipal socialism ran public utilities as work creators. State socialism ran national industries as job protectors. The British post-war consensus was democratic corporatism. Yugoslav worker management is syndicalism writ large. The welfare state has put jobs before services. M. Jacques Delors's promise of "social partners" is the socialist/syndicalist notion of the British trade unions' "industrial democracy."

All these alternatives to the market were and remain myopic expressions of the anxiety to secure the producer interests of owners, employers, traders, merchants or employees. They were and remain protectionist conspiracies or "rackets" that obstructed change to safeguard established producer expectations. Where they prevailed in the Middle Ages, and in some countries in modern times, they brought stagnation and eventual decay. In time the economy slowed down and seized up. The market is the only mechanism that has evolved to induce man to look to his long-term interests. He does not consume in order to produce. He produces in order to consume.

The market is uncomfortable. It gives innovators a free rein. It makes people move from habitual surroundings and familiar faces. But it produces the high living standards that producers ultimately want more than their immediate jobs. That is the economic reason for the superiority of capitalism. But in practice politicians have not always allowed it to produce its best results. In Britain the Liberal Party did so for a few decades in the nineteenth century. The Labour Party in its early years in office had some remaining liberals like Philip Snowden, but was generally the protectionist arm of the reactionary and retrogressive trade unions. The Conservatives in general have had an indifferent record. In the 1930s they sponsored producer protection when they abandoned free trade in 1932, introduced transport licensing, agricultural marketing boards and other "anti-capitalist" restrictionist policies.

Capitalism has not been safe with British politicians until the new Conservatives, non-conformist libertarian Whigs were added to the remaining High Tories in Mrs. Thatcher's Governments. It has been a strenuous effort to rid the British economy of a century of overgovernment, mercantilism, protectionism and over-regulation, and to restore the free markets in which the primary consumer interest in every man can prevail over his myopic producer interest. In ten years it has turned the tide in the affairs of men, but it will require at least ten more to liberate and liberalize the British economy.

The task is not easy because we all see our producer interest more vividly than our consumer interest. The rewards we can reap by prevailing on government to yield to our request or importunities or demands for "help" are larger than the immediate losses we suffer as consumers. When farmers, coal miners, teachers, nurses, railwaymen, university professors, polytechnic teachers or government officials ask for and obtain larger subsidies, higher pay, shorter hours, longer holidays or better conditions than they are worth because it is politically expedient to keep them quiet, they gain as producers but lose as consumers in higher taxes or higher prices. But their gain is immediate, apparent and sizeable; their loss is distant, obscure and minuscule.

The results are damaging to democracy. Since the cost of pressurizing government yields a much larger return in producer gains than it imposes in consumer losses, we tend to organize as producers rather than as consumers. But in the end we all lose far more as consumers than we gain as producers: old industries, firms and occupations are kept alive, government is aggrandized, taxes are inflated, the articulate are incited to organize, the citizen is impelled to take to the streets to gain a hearing, parliament is bypassed.

In the end the political democracy that is supposed to create impartial representation in national affairs is undermined in two ways. First, parliament is bypassed: it is replaced by the rule of influence, preferment and the politics of sectional producer power. Democratic politicians who have capitulated to organized producer interests have provoked a weakening of political democracy and undermined their authority. Second, the inflation of the political market in which the unorganized are elbowed out by the organized has driven economic activity underground. The British black market is much larger than the official estimate of 7.5 per cent of the national product, probably nearer 20 per cent, not least because it takes no account, because it cannot take account, of barter, which requires no money payment at all but the extent of which is incalculable. Official statistics, here as elsewhere, may therefore be severely misleading on the official as well as on the black economy.

The ultimate requirement is a public philosophy that teaches it is immoral to use democracy for sectional advantage by extracting favours at the (apparent) expense of others but ultimately of ourselves. It may be the most fundamental achievement of the new Conservatives under Mrs. Thatcher to have begun that process of public re-education, although the immorality of political pressure to suborn the elected representatives of the people has yet to reach the professional teachers of morality.

But the "technical" means that government must use to master the pressure groups is to restore the free market of capitalism. Here the difficulty is that the market may work slowly, so that it takes longer to show its benefits than the four years or so of political power—hence the paralysis of governments that judge it politically safe to enact desirable but unpopular measures only in the first one or two years of a five-year term.

The American "public choice" economists emphasize in a growing literature the necessity and scope for constitutional reform to limit the economic powers of government.[32] Without a written constitution, Britain may have to devise other solutions, not least longer parliaments. But means must be found to prevent "short-termism" in politics from frustrating the public interest by disrupting the market as the only instrument of long-term consumer sovereignty for the common people.

That is why the Marquand formula puts the cart before the horse. If market forces are made the servants of democratic politics they are prone to be suppressed or distorted by politicians to frustrate the public interest. Democratic politics needs to be reformed and disciplined by inalienable citizen rights, but it will always be tempted to distort the market. Mrs. Williams's "new" politics remains politics, and politics is for political people. Professor Crick's politics may be necessary for socialism but it can be kept in its place in capitalism.

The purpose of politics, apart from supplying the small sector of public goods, is to make the best use of the market by letting it develop spontaneously to serve the public interest. Politics is the servant of the people in the market.

32. Two of the most recent are Richard Mackenzie (ed.), *Constitutional Economics*, Lexington Books, D. C. Heath, 1984, a collection of 14 essays, and J. M. Buchanan, *Explorations into Constitutional Economics*, ed. Robert D. Tollison and Victor J. Vanberg, Texas A&M University Press, 1989, a collection of 31 essays.

CHAPTER 6

The Capitalist Open Secret

. . . decentralised control over resources through several [private] property leads to the generation of more information than . . . under central direction . . .

F. A. Hayek, *The Fatal Conceit*

A market economy . . . "aggregates" private information . . . prices . . . [provide] signals for the allocation of resources [and] from the informed to the uninformed. Hayek . . . is right in arguing that these considerations cast a baleful eye on comprehensive planning at "the centre."

But an alternative to planning might be the conscious creation of a much better market economy than that provided by a capitalist society. This was the claim of market socialists like Lange and Lerner.

Frank Hahn, in Robert Skidelsky (ed.), *Thatcherism*

"Take what you want," said God, "and pay for it."

Spanish proverb

Put a price on everything, and know the truth.

Anon.

The essential instrument that has enabled capitalism to reach standards of living that are multiples of socialism, and to combine them with liberty unknown in socialism, is the pricing system of the market. There are other differences between the two systems, not least in the structures of property rights, but this is the main distinguishing mechanism, which is closely linked with the others. It cannot be used in the centralized form of state socialism because it decentralizes the power to make decisions to individual buyers and sellers in markets far removed from the control of the political planners at the centre. Neither can it be used in the decentralized form of "market socialism" that socialist economists have been trying to devise for half a century since Evan Durbin, H. D. Dickinson, Abba Lerner and others in my years at the London School of Economics. Their efforts in "playing at competition" were rejected by Hayek and other liberal economists.[1] But the notion of using markets in socialism has been periodically resuscitated in the tenacious attempt to show that the values of socialism can be combined with the productivity of capitalism.

The Perennial Search for the Socialist Market

Since economists and politicians in both communist and capitalist countries[2] have renewed in the 1980s the search for means to absorb decentralized markets into socialism, there is little purpose in traversing the well-trodden ground and contesting the continuing faith of socialist political scientists like Ernest Mandel of Brussels University or historians like Professor Hobsbawm that centralized state socialism will one day, sooner or later, create higher living standards than capitalism.

What is surprising is that a sophisticated economist of the eminence of Professor Frank Hahn of Cambridge (President of the Royal Economic Society) confidently repeated in 1988 the unfounded hope of the 1930s that one day, sooner or later, market socialism will create a better market economy than capitalism—and presumably realize Khrushchev's boast that socialism would finally demonstrate its material productive superiority over the capitalist market. The formula is much the same as that of the 1930s. "Let the means of production be owned collectively but instruct managers etc. to act as they are supposed to act in the text-book . . . ," says Professor Hahn; ". . . the centre can attempt inter-temporal co-ordination by guiding the expectations of managers. That is . . . what was fairly successfully done in France through 'indicative planning' and what still seems to be happening . . . in Japan."[3] The 50-year argument on both sides has intermittently been restated without the socialist side coming anywhere near a solution.

The socialist market economy was, as Professor Hahn accurately says,

1. F. A. Hayek (ed.), *Collectivist Economic Planning,* Routledge, 1935, including Mises's original demonstration in 1921 of the impossibility of socialist calculation.

2. Alec Nove, *The Economics of Feasible Socialism,* Allen & Unwin, 1983; Bryan Gould, *Socialism and Freedom,* Macmillan, 1985; Roy Hattersley, *Choose Freedom,* Michael Joseph, 1987, particularly ch. 8, "There must be markets."

3. Frank Hahn, "On market economics," in Robert Skidelsky (ed.), *Thatcherism,* Chatto & Windus, 1988.

"the *claim* of market socialists" (added emphasis). It was never demonstrated as a feasible system, not even in Professor Nove's earnest effort in his long book. And it has nowhere come to pass in practice.

The socialist countries in Eastern Europe that at last see the urgency of markets are only now grappling with the task of grafting them onto a socialist system of state ownership of resources and political direction of their use. But they will fail unless they satisfy the imperative that a price mechanism requires private property to create and calibrate the incentives to innovate, invest, anticipate demand, adjust supply and take the risks in all these decisions, with rewards for success but penalties for failure. The dilemma is that socialism is founded on public property, which does not reproduce the required incentives, rewards and penalties.

If "indicative planning" once worked in France it has long been abandoned for de-socialization and free markets. Whether it now works in Japan is contestable. Japanese government "direction" is often ignored by highly competitive technology-driven industry that is responsive ("directed") by severely discriminating Japanese consumers in the market. Information from central planners in government is to private industry with commercial incentives to use it where it chimes with their markets, overseas as well as domestic, not to the managers of collectively owned state plants with political incentives to exploit it or personal incentives to misuse it. State planning would, of course, conflict with the private market socialism urged by Professor Hahn. And the notion, nursed by the Left, that Japanese prosperity is based on anything like state direction or guidance has been contested and scouted by a British economist, Professor G. C. Allen, who knew Japan from the inside, and by Japanese economists.[4]

Professor Hahn perseveres: ". . . on some important matters information at the centre is better than that available to any one agent."[5] But to use it does not require the massive transformation of private into public property rights. Some information is a public good that requires government dissemination because it would not be generated in the market, but much, probably most, does not. Private firms generate most of the information they require, and only they know what information is desirable and worth paying for. The market provides a mass of information on prices, stocks, yields on invest-

4. G. C. Allen, *How Japan Competes,* Institute of Economic Affairs, 1978; *Japan's Economic Policy,* Macmillan, 1980; Yutaka Kosai and Toshitaro Ogino, *The Contemporary Japanese Economy,* Methuen, 1984.

5. Ibid., p. 114.

ments, the range of risks, future prices and much else. Government information is often defective or irrelevant, essentially the macro-statistics of totals and averages, but industrial decisions are generally based on the micro-statistics of small "marginal" changes in prices when output is expanded or reduced. Government statistics are often erroneous or outdated. Not least, they are not produced by neutral sources but are sometimes, or often, politically motivated. Premature publication can influence by-elections.

Real (Private) and Unreal (Public) Property

Socialists have persistently avoided acceptance of the truth that public property destroys the essence of property. By diffusing nominal but ineffective public ownership it changes real ownership into paper ownership. Changing private identifiable property into public unidentifiable property is to destroy the incentives to protect, conserve, improve and render it productive by using it profitably in making goods and services for which consumers will pay.

"Whether it is possible in this way [combining collective ownership with instructions to non-owning salaried managers] to have one's cake and eat it," concluded Professor Hahn, "is too large a question to tackle now [presumably in his text]."[6] But he referred to no full explanation elsewhere. Until socialist economists have tackled the task of resolving the dilemma that public property is irresponsible and unaccountable property, and convincingly demonstrated the feasibility of socialist markets with non-owning managers conscientiously acting like the textbooks that analyse the reactions of owning managers, they will continue to confuse the debate by making no more than "claims." The East European economists who have tried for many years to devise markets without the incentives of real ownership have done their best, but are still floundering with paper schemes that do not give the results of capitalist markets based on private property.

Without this information, the attempt to increase agricultural production in the USSR will fail. The Gorbachev liberals have suggested a property rights solution: the long-term leasing of land to sharpen the incentive to efficient farming. The dignity of socialism is thereby saved because the state remains the owner. But long-term leasing would weaken the control over land use by party officials. The economist Professor Nikolai Shmelyov has

6. Ibid.

insisted that "compulsory deliveries" from farms to the state at its fixed prices must be abolished and replaced by leases that can be bequeathed. "No-one will believe in leasing until people can leave the lease to their heirs."[7] Nor will they be content with rent-a-cow. This is the reintroduction of private property, the ultimate ideological blasphemy. It is being resisted by the conservatives (their putative leader, Yegor Ligachev, was virtually Minister of Agriculture) because they rightly see that they would lose political control of agricultural production, a fear they disguise by appeals to the still influential but fading doctrine of socialist ownership.

The example shows five basic truths: first, ownership is the key to productivity; second, the Russian sense of family has not been obliterated by 70 years of collective ownership; third, the instinct to own, especially land, is common to people everywhere; fourth, the Gorbachev liberals can expect a large reserve of political support if they eventually promote private ownership; fifth, the view (chapter 4) that the Russians will continue to submit to authoritarian paternalism into the twenty-first century looks very precarious. In 1875 Marx admonished the workers of the world to unite because they had nothing to lose but their chains. They might now be advised that socialism has nothing to offer them but the denial of the property rights they would acquire under capitalism.

The Long Socialist March to the Market

The capitalist secret of market pricing has divided socialists for half a century. Evan Durbin led the market socialists at the LSE, and was the most engaging of Hayek's critics, and the most persuasive, because he understood markets. Of all the academically esteemed I listened to in the lecture rooms, Durbin came second only to Arnold Plant as the most cogent lecturer. Of the left-inclined academics at the LSE in the 1930s—the economists Hugh Dalton and Nicholas Kaldor, the public administrators W. A. Robson and Herman Finer, the historians Eileen Power and H. L. Beales—Durbin was one of the few who could have influenced me as a bridge between the economic liberals then led by Lionel Robbins and the democratic socialists. He both understood markets and stoutly rebutted the Marxists—Harold Laski and his confrères in the Left Book Club.[8] Herman Finer, who was later dismayed by Hayek's *The Road to Serfdom* in 1944 and wrote an anguished ri-

7. Nikolai Shmelyov, *The Times,* 20 February 1989.
8. Evan Durbin, *The Politics of Democratic Socialism,* Routledge, 1940.

poste, was less effective because he was a public administrator rather than an economist.

Socialist divisions on the market appeared early. The academics who joined with G. D. H. Cole in rejecting market economics and market socialism were hoping to revolutionize the distribution of power by combining public ownership with participation of workers in industrial decision-making. Both parts of this political confection are now seen, even on the Left, as defective and delusive. Public ownership is not accountable. Worker "participation" (without ownership), as in Yugoslavia, is (logically) myopic: it puts current earnings before investment for a future in which they will *not* "participate."

Yet "those who agreed with Durbin and Gaitskell," affectionately wrote Durbin's daughter, Professor Elizabeth Durbin, of her father and his close friend, "rejected both the Webbian vision of administrative control [of industry] and the guild socialist faith in workers' control. They shared the market economists' belief in the freedom of choice and economic efficiency afforded by the market pricing system."[9] This is what, though they remained socialists, they had accepted from Mises and Hayek, Robbins and Plant. There was intellectual excitement in witnessing the debates between the two market schools—both thought markets necessary but within different political institutions: the liberals said they had to be the capitalist institution of private ownership; the socialists claimed it could be public ownership. In the light of events since the 1930s there can be no doubt which group has been vindicated.

It is intriguing to reflect on the possible course of events in Britain if Durbin, later a Labour Member of Parliament, had not died early (at 42) and tragically in 1948 in an effort to save children in difficulty in the sea off Cornwall, and if Gaitskell, then Leader of the Labour Opposition, had not died early at the age of 57 in 1963. Durbin had been working on his next book, *The Economics of Democratic Socialism,* which would certainly have continued his thinking on the use of markets in socialism and analysed Hayek's assault on the notion that socialism could be democratic.[10]

If Gaitskell had won the 1964 General Election instead of Harold Wilson, and, with Durbin as his Chancellor of the Exchequer, had introduced pricing into the British socialized (public) services, the sad era of corporatism in the 1960s, which Wilson engineered by seducing capitalist industrialists into

9. Elizabeth Durbin, *New Jerusalems: The Economics of Democratic Socialism,* Routledge, 1985, p. xii.

10. F. A. Hayek, *The Road to Serfdom,* Routledge, 1944.

alliance with the trade unions, would not have debilitated the British economy. British Labour might then have anticipated the David Owen secession of 1981 and made the British democratic Left, like the German Social Democratic Party for a short span in 1966–7, the champion of the market. The Thatcher era might then have been anticipated; the market-inclined wings of the Conservative and Labour Parties might have overwhelmed their corporatist interests of capital and labour and fused to govern Britain for 40 years to echo the Whigs in the eighteenth century. Or British government might have alternated between two market-inclined Whig-Conservative and Radical political parties.

Public Property and the Market

Error on the nature of the market pricing system persists. It is still necessary, it seems, to explain and illustrate both the several functions of the pricing mechanism, especially in promoting and distributing production, and its too little understood strengths in economic, political and social life.

The feasibility of pricing and markets in the decentralized system of "socialist markets" has been made highly topical by the Gorbachev reforms and the new freedom of manoeuvre it seems to have given in the more Westernized Hungary, Poland and Yugoslavia, and in time perhaps elsewhere in the communist world, where the reformers can, at last, anxiously examine and nervously try market structures.

The question is, as always: can socialism with public ownership use the markets that so far have worked only in private property capitalism? In 1982 Hayek (aged 82) sent the IEA a short script entitled enigmatically "Two pages of fiction: the impossibility of socialist calculation." I knew about the "impossibility," but why two pages? He said that he was tired of continuing misrepresentation by socialists of the use of markets in socialism. He was "particularly indignant about the repeated silly talk of Lange to have refuted Mises." Would we take his text as a short paper? I had edited several of his IEA papers, including the long *Denationalisation of Money* which had required anglicization (he said he wished he had called it "demonopolisation of money" since it was an argument against monopoly *per se,* state or private), and I was familiar with the Germanic flavour of his English prose when he was away from England. The text was too short for a Paper and he agreed it go into the newly established IEA journal, *Economic Affairs.*[11]

11. F. A. Hayek, "Two pages of fiction: the impossibility of socialist calculation," *Economic Affairs,* April 1982.

Throughout his life Hayek had seemed to follow the advice he gave liberals to be mild in manner but strong in argument even when under savage assault. The argument in the short script was strong, but the manner was not mild. He counter-attacked several distinguished economists. His charge was against "the endless repetition of the claim that Oskar Lange in 1936 [had] refuted the contention of Mises in 1921 that 'economic calculation is impossible in a socialist society.'" The secret of the "two pages" was that Lange had argued on pages 59–61 of his paper[12] that calculation was possible under socialism. Hayek's dissection of 3,000 words occupied nine pages. He examined Lange's two pages almost line by line.

In Hayek's final chapter in *Collectivist Economic Planning*[13] he had drawn on David Hume's writings on the nature of property[14] as interpreted by Arnold Plant, then working on a book on property which was unfortunately not completed. Hume had seen private property emerging as the best way to conserve it when it was scarce. Hayek argued that markets were not feasible under socialism because, *inter alia*, the plant managers who were to be instructed, as Professor Hahn has now repeated, "to act [on pricing] as . . . in the text-book" did not own the plants. They would therefore not necessarily interpret their instructions to ensure the efficient use of public property if it conflicted with their private interests. There is ample evidence of this conflict in the worker management of Yugoslavia, as shown in the writings of Dr. Ljubo Sirc, the Yugoslav economist, who fled after his imprisonment under Tito but maintained a close study of his country.[15]

Hayek had also drawn on my teacher and colleague, Ronald Fowler, who was unfortunately lost to academia by being drawn into the wartime civil service. Hayek said that Fowler had argued[16] that interest and depreciation on fixed plant in public utilities could be determined only *after* the price obtainable for their product (transport, fuel, etc.) was known. Fixed costs can be ignored in the short run when setting prices of products, but sooner or later, when capital is replaced, no costs are fixed, all are "marginal" and prices have to reflect or cover all costs. Hayek concluded "To make a monopolist charge the price that would rule under competition" (as Professor

12. Oskar Lange, in B. E. Lippincott (ed.), *On the Economic Theory of Socialism,* University of Minnesota Press, 1938.

13. Hayek, *Collectivist Economic Planning.*

14. David Hume, *Enquiry Concerning the Principles of Morals,* 1740.

15. *Yugoslav Economy under Self-management,* Macmillan, 1979; *Economic Devolution in Eastern Europe,* Longman/Institute of Economic Affairs, 1969; and other writings.

16. Ronald Fowler, *The Depreciation of Capital,* P. S. King, 1934.

Hahn in effect suggested in 1988), "or at a price equal to the necessary cost, is impossible, because the competitive or necessary cost cannot be known until there is competition."[17] In short, to argue for socialist pricing, as the market socialists have done from Lange to Hahn, is circular reasoning.

That was the refutation of the market socialists in 1935. In 1982 Hayek returned to the intellectual fray. He criticized a raft of well-known names. First came Lange, the Polish communist economist who had later asserted that all the information required by a socialist system could be assembled by speed-of-light computers. He was assailed for his "most extraordinary 'solution'" in 1935, which asserted that a socialist economy could have the information on the preferences of individuals and the resources as was available in a market economy, and it could therefore calculate prices. "The administrators of the socialist economy," Lange had said, "will have exactly the same knowledge . . . as the capitalist entrepreneurs."[18] It was a "brazen assertion," replied Hayek, for which he had offered "no evidence or justification," to suppose that the data *presumed* by economists to exist were indeed *known* to a planning agency.[19] If Lange had offered "no evidence or justification" in 1935, neither, it seems, has Professor Hahn in 1988.

Second, Robert Heilbroner (a combative Marxist analyst and critic of capitalism, idiosyncratically chosen by the editors to write the entry on capitalism in the misleadingly entitled *New Palgrave Dictionary of Economics*[20]), was condemned by Hayek for making "the even more fantastic assertion" that a central planning board "would receive exactly the same information from a socialist economic system as did the entrepreneurs under the market system."[21] This, observed Hayek, was "a blatant untruth, an assertion so absurd that it is difficult to understand how an intelligent person could ever honestly make it."[22] The error was to suppose that the information *required*, but dispersed among millions of people, would be *known* to the planning authorities without showing how, or from whom, they would obtain it. Capitalism supplies the mechanism for assembling it—the market. Socialism does not.

17. Hayek, *Collectivist Economic Planning.*

18. Lange, quoted in Hayek, "Two pages of fiction," p. 136.

19. Hayek, "Two pages of fiction," p. 136.

20. John Eatwell, Murray Milgate and Peter Newman (eds.), *New Palgrave Dictionary of Economics,* Macmillan, 1987.

21. Robert Heilbroner, *Between Capitalism and Socialism,* Vintage, 1980, p. 88, cited in Hayek, "Two pages of fiction," p. 137.

22. Hayek, "Two pages of fiction," p. 137.

Third, the fellow-Austrian whose faith in capitalism had waned, the august Joseph Schumpeter, had been "seduced . . . like many mathematical economists . . . to believe that the relevant facts [about demands and supplies] which the theorist must *assume* to exist are *known* to any one mind" (emphasis added).[23] And he had made a "most startling assertion" about "economic rationality" in a planned system in which the *technical* possibilities were known: that was "sheer nonsense," because what had to be known was their *values* depending on their relative scarcities, which were not known without a market (emphasis added). Schumpeter had offered "equivocation, but no real explanation."

The economists, not all avowedly socialist, who had asserted, or assumed, that the information required for intelligent, "rational" allocation of scarce resources, and generated by the capitalist market, would also be available to a socialist planning authority, were charged by Hayek of "negligence and carelessness with which words have been used throughout this whole, long, discussion" on economic calculation for 50 years since the mid-1930s. It was "a comic fiction," and "the crowning foolery of the whole farce," to assert that the planning authority could enable plant managers to do their job by fixing uniform prices. "What prices *ought* to be can never be determined without competitive markets" (emphasis added throughout).[24]

This "fiction" and "foolery" have not always been avoided despite attempts in some communist countries to introduce elements of capitalist calculation. And the reason is "the contradictions of socialism." The attempts to restore markets have been under the sufferance and control of the political authorities, whose power is lessened by every extension of the market. That is now the dilemma of Russian *perestroika,* and the Hungarian and Polish urge to reconstruct the socialist system without the property rights of capitalism. It is also the dilemma of the British Labour Party which has come to accept the necessity of markets but clearly intends them to be subject to close political surveillance and is fundamentally reluctant to acknowledge the superiority of private over "public," that is, socialized property. The absence of free-market pricing, with its defects of inequality as well as strengths of efficiency, remains the missing link in the latest revisions of the British market socialists.

The solution is technically clear: to motivate the plant managers by introducing private property rights. That is what would have to be done in

23. Ibid., p. 139.

24. Ibid., p. 141.

Yugoslavia, Hungary, Poland and even East Germany and the USSR, but it would end their socialism.

Private Property and Market Information

And so to today. The necessity for the information required for the rational use of scarce resources and the impossibility of assembling it unless there is a structure of spontaneous decentralized markets resting on private property was restated by Hayek yet again in 1988:

> Order and control extending beyond the immediate purview of a central authority [can] be attained by central direction only if . . . local managers who [can] gauge visible and potential resources [are] *also* currently informed of their *constantly changing* relative importance [that is, their *competitive prices*], and could then communicate full and accurate details . . . to a central planning authority *in time* for it to tell them what to do in the light of all the *other,* different, concrete information it had received from other regional or local managers—who in turn found themselves in similar difficulties in obtaining and delivering any such information.[25] (Emphasis added, except *also* in line 3.)

That is a reasonably clear, but formidable, statement of the administrative task of planning without *capitalist* markets. It is reinforced by the further political difficulty in the way of *socialist* markets. Even if the information from plant managers were based on freely competitive markets, it could not be assumed to be authentic. We must suppose that it would be manipulated for political reasons to exaggerate success and disguise failure in achieving plans. This distortion has been true, not least, of East European statistics of plant production. The claims for burgeoning output are made misleading or meaningless by representing *quantity* and pushing *quality* into second place.

The statistics assembled and disseminated even by a Russian or Hungarian IBM or Honeywell Bull or Amstrad computer would be late, contrived, ambiguous and politicized. Even if it could perform the required millions of equations daily, or hourly, it would not reproduce the information generated by capitalist markets.

As the final irony in the political unreality of benevolent socialist planning, it is implausible to suppose the national Gosplan would transmit in-

25. F. A. Hayek, *The Fatal Conceit,* Routledge, 1988, p. 86.

formation that threatened to undermine its power. Capitalist market information is often very imperfect, but it is mostly beyond the reach of politicians. Information that has to be filtered through political machinery runs an additional gauntlet. The national planners are not solely interested in transmitting information on consumer preferences. They have an interest in enlarging the production of some goods or services (perhaps armaments or space research) beyond, or restricting other goods and services (like dishwashers which use steel) below, the extent indicated by consumer statistics. Or they falsify price information to clear surplus stocks or to discourage the demand for goods underproduced by inefficient or corrupt plant managers. Such political risks are rarely, after 50 years, discussed by the market socialists.

Socialist plant managers will, of course, justify their tampering with consumer statistics by appeal to their superior knowledge of the "real" national interest. As Professor Hahn put it, ". . . on some important matters information at the centre is better than that available to any one agent."[26] It also lends itself to concealment or distortion by political misuse. Socialist academics who have absorbed something of Austrian economics on the market still mostly overlook the economics of politics.

The socialist contradiction between centralized political power and decentralized economic decision reappears. The more the people are liberated as consumers to buy the goods and services they want, not least to provide stronger incentives to work efficiently and raise earnings, the more they will expect civic rights to read the books, newspapers and magazines they prefer, and the more they will demand political rights as citizens to form groups or parties to reflect their opinions. If they can choose consumer goods in the market, why should they not choose political policies in the ballot box? And how are they to choose between candidates if they are not to discuss their policies, the pros and cons, the costs and the consequences? The dilemma of the socialist planners—the contradiction of socialism in the late twentieth century—is that the more increased national production is required to be generated by decentralized markets, the more liberties will be demanded in all other spheres of human behaviour. But the more they are granted the more the political authority of the planners is undermined. That dilemma intensified in the late 1980s, almost came to a head in China and will further intensify in the 1990s.

26. Hahn, "On market economics," p. 114.

The ensuing alternation of policies—economic liberalization to stimulate production and political centralization to preserve power—may persist with some stability for some years. But sooner or later it will go too far in one extreme or the other. Both will provoke discord and unrest. If economic liberalization goes too far, it will produce excessive political, civic and cultural liberalization. If authoritarianism goes too far, it will provoke protest and defiance. In the mid-nineteenth century Marx envisaged the expropriation by the proletariat of their bourgeois exploiters. In the late twentieth century the socialist exploiters of the world look like being expropriated by the newly embourgeoised workers.

Socialist markets conducted by neutral selfless benevolent politicians and bureaucrats remain a mirage. Socialist and liberal scholars could use their talents more profitably to envisage and devise the fullest scope for market institutions that will make the common people sovereign by preventing them from being exploited by politicians of all parties.

The Desirable Purposes of Pricing

Market pricing is the characteristic machinery of capitalism, and it has further deep-seated inherent advantages that remain ignored. It could be employed much more widely if it were not repressed by governments in capitalist countries which have abolished or manipulated prices in the goods and services it provides in the public sector. Political pricing or nil pricing is characteristic of socialism, but it is ignored in the underground of their black markets.

Market pricing is imperfect, but so is political pricing. The difference is that the causes and solutions are usually very different. The main imperfections of market pricing cause market failure. The imperfections of political pricing cause government failure. But the advantages of pricing over other methods of allocating resources are more fundamental than is commonly understood. Above all, political pricing can do more damage than market pricing.

Prices have two main functions. The obvious function is to provide forms of income through the market as a result of bargains on wages, salaries, fees, charges, rents, royalties, stipends and so on. In this form prices are used in socialism as well as capitalism, but in capitalism they are characteristically decided by agreements between buyers and sellers and in socialism by political decisions.

The other function is less obvious but more vital: pricing is the device for deciding where resources are to be used according to individual preferences.

Generally the higher the price of the product, the more resources are allocated to a use in a firm, an occupation or an industry. Socialism has no comparable device: resources are allocated by the planners who, since socialist market pricing is impracticable, have no other instrument for discovering individual preferences, which can be, mostly are and generally must be ignored. Whatever use the planners make of prices, they are not so much to discover the people's preferences as to conceal the politicians' mistakes. Even where they are used to discourage demand for particularly scarce goods or to encourage demand for goods produced in excessive quantities, the decisions are political, usually to disguise inefficiency in central planning.

The income function of price is obvious. The information-rationing incentive-signalling function of price is more abstract and more elusive. Moreover, the information conveyed by prices, or changes in prices, may be unwelcome or disagreeable. The rationing, or changes in availability of goods and services, that they induce may be adverse or harmful to their producers. The signals they represent may require or induce movement from producing some goods and services to very different goods and services, from comfortable jobs to uncertain new jobs, from familiar to unfamiliar housing and surroundings.

This is the source of much antipathy to free markets. It accounts for the resentment against competition, which reveals the firms or industries that fail to adapt themselves most expeditiously to price changes. And it explains the political opposition to the capitalist system which creates the environment for free markets, flexible pricing and economic liberalism generally.

Political parties of the Left hope to exploit the unavoidable discomforts of social and technical change by blaming their political Conservative opponents. Their opponents have not learned to reply that change must take place under all economic systems, and that the choice is not between change and no change but between the gradual change of a market economy and the arbitrary unpredictable change of a politicized system in which it is timed to suit political calculation. If the pricing of capitalism is not used, the alternative is the political machinery of socialism which orders people to produce more, produce less, change their jobs, move homes and generally runs their lives.

The harmful effects of confusing income effects and price effects are mostly the consequences of government policies. Politicians must be sensitive to the short-run effects on themselves as well as the long-run effects on the people. The income effects of many policies on education, medical care, housing, pensions, unemployment and sickness insurance, and widows', unmarried mothers' and other social (cash) benefits are mostly immediate and apparent, and the accompanying electoral byproduct is sometimes rewarding, especially in the approach to by-elections or General Elections. The price effects are mostly distant and indistinct.

Yet the price effects may do more harm than the income effects do good. It is a basic law of economics and general human conduct that the higher the price available, the larger the supply. The higher the social benefit, the larger the number of claimants. The newspapers may seem cynical when they make play with the number of young women who bear children without benefit of marriage in order to claim the benefit of a subsidized council house or flat. Perhaps some married couples bear children in order to claim child (cash) benefits or tax allowances. The state cannot separate the unintended price effects on the number of claimants from the intended income effects in helping those with low incomes or exceptional requirements. But the harm remains. And the political process is such that, to quote a former Chancellor of the Exchequer, "Once you give a social benefit, you cannot take it away." The inability of government to change its policies with changing circumstances is a standing defect of the political process that the socialist mind (in all parties) rarely adds into the calculus of good and bad in weighing socialism against capitalism.

This is a disadvantage of proposals for government redistribution of income to correct the differences that unavoidably emerge from the market. Money supplied "free" by government increases the number of people who can make themselves eligible by working less than they otherwise would, by not working at all or by acquiring dependants. The American writer Charles Murray has documented the evidence of the harmful, debilitating and disruptive effects on supposed beneficiaries, the poor, of the 30 years' measures to help them since the 1950s.[27] This stubborn truth was known to the classical liberals like Alexis de Tocqueville. Cash grants alone will affect the incentive to earn, and the best that can be done is to combine the minimum disincentive with the maximum income assistance. A pilot study in New Jersey in the early 1970s found that the optimum figure was to subtract 50 or 75 per cent of benefit from each unit of earnings.

This dilemma is an unavoidable consequence of human nature, and has to be solved in socialism as well as capitalism. It may have to be accepted that no system can cure it until human nature is changed. It will therefore remain for many decades. Lenin saw that communism would require a new kind of

27. Charles Murray, *Losing Ground: American Social Policy 1950–1980*, Basic Books, 1984; *In Pursuit of Happiness and Good Government*, Simon & Schuster, 1988.

human being. But he shrewdly made selfless unworldly man a feasible being by abolishing scarcity, so that if one man ate without working there would not be less for others who worked. Since scarcity will not be abolished by capitalism, because human demands grow with production, and certainly not by socialism, which restrains production and makes scarcity more pressing, mankind must accept a disagreeable compromise.

The failure to understand, and the failure to explain, are exemplified in the radio or television interviewing of employees, from nurses to teachers, miners to railwaymen, who want higher pay. The emphasis by the interviewers is invariably on the income effect in helping the needy, rarely on the price effect of increasing unemployment. If their rate of pay is "too low" for what is considered acceptable living, but their supply is sufficient, it should be supplemented by government from taxes. To raise their pay by higher wages or salaries would increase the supply of their labour and require government rationing of jobs, which would let in the familiar instruments of the political process—lobbying, pressurizing and their patent arbitrary injustices to the inarticulate and the poorest. The difference is that the rates of pay are more likely to be appropriate in competitive private industry, because excessive pay in state monopolies can more easily be passed on by government to the unsuspecting taxpayer than it can by firms to the complaining consumer. Suspicion of, and prejudice against, private commercial pricing has thus been built up. It often seems harsh, but it is more humane than the political alternative.

Moreover, people want the long-run advantages of markets and pricing in raising production, creating choice between competing suppliers and stimulating innovation, all of which serve them in their capacity as consumers. The dilemma is that they are naturally more conscious of their short-term interests as producers with concern about the incomes they earn from work than on the eventual effect on unemployment, including their own prospects of employment. This is the internal human conflict that all economic systems have to resolve, socialist as well as capitalist. Capitalism has resolved it, or could resolve it, better than any other system known in British or world history.

Rationing by Price or by Politics

There are eight main advantages of rationing by price over political rationing: it is neutral, informative, cautionary, pacific, humane, non-authoritarian, the essential missing link between supply and demand, and in any event indestructible. Pricing is imperfect, but the imperfections are outweighed by the advantages. Political rationing, the method of socialism, is not always dissected candidly by socialist academics as the alternative they offer. Yet its defects, abuses and excesses are apparent from the history of socialism. The new form of politicized market offered by market socialists would not avoid the politicization of economic life that markets are designed to remove or minimize. And it lacks the qualities of market, private property pricing of capitalism.

First, price is neutral: it emerges spontaneously where people who want to sell meet others who want to buy. Price expresses the terms on which they voluntarily exchange. Unless both sides do better, they do not exchange. If there are several buyers or sellers, each seller is protected by all other buyers from accepting too low a price, and each buyer by all other sellers from paying too high a price. Together the buyers and sellers form a market.

Second, price is informative. If a seller wants to know what his article or skill is worth, so that he does not sell too cheaply, the market will tell him. If there are not several buyers and sellers he can have it valued to indicate the price he is likely to have to pay or can expect to receive. The market is the most neutral instrument for revealing value.

Third, price is cautionary. The buyer will think twice before buying. If there is no price, because he is paying indirectly through government by taxes, he will not think twice, but ask for more services than he "needs." Ralph Harris expressed the principle graphically with humour: "If it's free, put me down for two." The humour is moderated when it is recalled that nil pricing, or rather indirect pricing disguised as taxes, can induce waste, callous disregard for friends and neighbours and in the end a war of all against all in which we impoverish one another. The obvious example is the "free" NHS, in which we are all tempted to take the time of overworked doctors, ask for more pills than we require, stay in hospital longer and use equipment carelessly. "Free" services induce irresponsible mutual impoverishment. By destroying information, they generate a society which discounts caring, concern and compassion. Only the market tells the truth that there is not, and cannot be, enough of every medical aid to avoid all pain or save all life. No politician will say that. But by revealing the truth, pricing induces caring for scarce supplies. Politics incites profligacy.

Much the same is true of prices artificially depressed, even if the reason seems well intentioned. If the price of hiring house-room is subsidized by rent restriction so that low-income families can pay the depressed rents, they will occupy more space than they require or remain in it after their children have moved. They thus prevent new families with young children from moving into homes with more space. The better way is to supplement their low income to enable them to pay the market rent. The supplements can also be varied with income. And they can be reduced in time when income rises more easily than artificially low rents can be varied because they create vested interests and are politically difficult to raise, as the British experience demonstrates.

Yet the existence of prices even below the full market rate creates a symbol and a reminder of value that is too lightly discarded, especially in the political process. It is evidence of human decision, choice and sacrifice. As long as prices (fees), although often low, remained in British state secondary education (mainly grammar schools), parents broadly accepted that those who paid them, whether the more wealthy or the more self-denying, were making a decision and sacrificing other purchases. When the remaining fees were abolished in the wartime coalition/consensus 1944 Education Act, much trumpeted as the final "freeing" of schools from the thrall of payment, it was overlooked that pupils would have to be selected by some other criterion, which emerged in the political process as local government judgement of ability (or potential ability). The consequence, unforeseen by the politicians, was a new form of envy of parents whose children were more favoured, producing discord between friends and neighbours, generally rare before market selection by pricing had been replaced by governmental selection by local politicians.

The consequence of replacing the market, even in its attenuated form of low nominal fee pricing, by political regulation and political rationing was a further unforeseen effect. The selective grammar schools were virtually replaced by supposedly all-ability, supposedly more socially integrating comprehensive schools, which, not long after, ironically emerged as socially divisive, since they were mostly attended by pupils of differing income groups in the surrounding neighbourhoods. The children of the inner-city slums do not generally attend the better state schools of the suburbs. The state blundered yet again: its "comprehensive" schools separated the social classes.

Again, the political device of free supply was the wrong solution for deficient demand arising from low income. The better solution was not to destroy the price barrier, and the indispensable information it carried, but to retain the fees and enable more parents to pay them. The central method is the school voucher proposed by liberal economists, propagated by the Friends of the Education Voucher (FEVER) and much later adapted by socialist academics and educationalists in *Market Socialism* and *Samizdat*.

Such reinforcement of individual parent purchasing power would have accelerated the financial thrust behind the demand for schools responsive to family hopes, and in particular for the grammar-type schools. The supply-side response, by expansion or replication of the best private or state fee-charging schools, would have appeared in ways far beyond the imagination of the political minds that have dominated British schooling.

Fourth, pricing is pacific. By indicating where scarce resources are best used, pricing also indicates which uses must be excluded. This is Professor W. H. Hutt's "impersonal" decision of the market, made up of the interplay between all buyers and all sellers. The alternative is for people in political democracies to argue and debate, to organize political parties and control government in order to enforce the wishes of majorities on minorities—or, even worse in multi-party systems, the wishes of minorities on majorities. In Fascist or socialist totalitarian systems they fight and kill one another. Pricing is the peaceful way of resolving argument and conflict.

Fifth, pricing is humane. No-one in a market has to say "no" to an offer of goods or services: as a buyer he reduces his offered price; as a seller he raises his asking price. The buyer then decides whether he accepts the price or not. In the private market, the would-be buyer of a house withdraws his bid; the would-be seller raises his price. In government employment, the political difficulty of pruning the over-inflated bureaucracy by dismissals or early retirement, which is arbitrary and loses men or women of experience, can be avoided by reducing the pay of surplus grades of officials until each official decides to withdraw in the light of personal circumstances. Some will withdraw on the first reduction in pay; others will accept lower pay until the third or fourth reduction. Each individual makes his own decision. The government does not dismiss anyone.

Sixth, pricing is non-authoritarian. The alternative to allocation by price is political allocation by authority. This is the method in both East Germany and the British NHS, where the money that family doctors may spend on medicines, sums no doubt less than people would be prepared to spend as individuals by insurance in the market, is limited by political decision, which is not far removed from electoral timing.

Seventh, pricing is a teacher. It enables us to compare values, it enjoins care in using resources, it encourages economy in managing money and it stimulates long-term thinking in household budgeting. It necessitates care and reflection before making decisions after which it is too late.

Eighth, and not least, pricing is the missing link between buyer and seller.

For years thought was confused by the sociologists who spoke of price as a barrier to be destroyed. They thus also destroyed the unique information on relative values that it generates. Without prices that reflect individual preferences, circumstances, conditions, requirements and even idiosyncrasies, human behaviour lacks a map and a compass. Socialism is the system in which the impertinent blind who claim to know lead the innocent blind who are prevented from learning.

The Three Errors

Economists hostile to the market economy of capitalism have been so interested in the technical imperfections of pricing—in monopoly, monopsony (a single buyer facing competing sellers) and so on—that they have become obsessed with its differences from "perfect" markets (which exist only in textbooks for teaching purposes) and overlooked its primary purposes and its fundamental strengths. They have veritably made dunces of themselves by three errors of judgement.

First, the Cambridge economists in the 1930s led by Joan Robinson (and accompanied by the American E. H. Chamberlin) embarked on a clinical dissection of market imperfections (mainly by geometrical drawings), which was technically true but of little or no application to the real world, and promptly lost sight of the unique uses of the market. Most, if not all, human institutions are imperfect, but the world would be lost without them. They are treasured and used in human activities because their advantages exceed their disadvantages, and because their balance of advantage is larger than that of alternative institutions.

Second, critics treated the market as a static structure and did not understand its dynamic role as a continuing process. This is the essence of Hayek's emphasis on the market as a device for alighting on new and better methods of production, cost-reducing devices and so on—its role as a "discovery procedure." The writings of the economists who work in the Austrian tradition of markets as registers of subjective valuations, from the veteran Professor Ludwig Lachmann, through the (originally British) Professor Israel Kirzner and Professor Murray Rothbard to the younger men like Roger Garrison, Gerald O'Driscoll, Mario Rizzo and others at George Mason University (and its associated Institute of Humane Studies) and elsewhere in the United States, are still too little known to British economists and economic journalists who were caught in the fashion of Keynesian macro-economics and are unable to unlearn error. Some Austrian writings are briefly indicated in the Descriptive Guide to Readings. The essence of Austrian thinking is clearly presented by Alexander Shand and by Wolfgang Grassl and Barry Smith.[28]

Third, until recent years, critics have overlooked the weaknesses of the politicized alternatives. Pricing is an imperfect method of allocating resources and is deficient as a method of distributing incomes. But the world has nothing better. The conventional socialist approach was to remove pricing; it now again, after a 50-year interval, wishes to use it in socialism, but it still has no idea how. There is no better way than studying it to remove its imperfections. The capitalist secret is open to the world. Only Bourbons, simpletons and the suicidal think they can live without it.

28. Alexander Shand, *The Capitalist Alternative,* Wheatsheaf, 1984; Wolfgang Grassl and Barry Smith (eds.), *Austrian Economics,* Croom Helm, 1986.

CHAPTER 7

Intellectual Reinforcement for Capitalism

> Human affairs could not be made ultimately predictable by any centralised coercion, but the proliferant germination of ideas in millions of brains could be killed by it.
>
> G. L. S. Shackle, in Alexander Shand, *The Capitalist Alternative*

> Strict standards are enforced on the contents of a business prospectus; it is a pity the same standards of veracity cannot be enforced on some politicians . . .
>
> John Jewkes, *A Return to Free Market Economics?*

> I consider both the complex theory of welfare economics—the economic analysis of market failures—and the blend of hope and cynicism which passes for political wisdom to have been infertile and obfuscatory.
>
> George Stigler, *The Citizen and the State*

There is now more understanding about the market by scholars and politicians, although continuing obfuscation from the literati. Yet the academic critics of capitalism have rarely absorbed the developments in economic analysis in recent years that reinforce the empirical evidence of its superiority.

The new developments in economic thinking and interpretation of the real world, collectively described as the "new economics," have formed the essence of the writings mobilized by the IEA. They originated mostly in the United States, which is not surprising since American economists outnumber those of any other country or continent. British economists have also been innovative in the new economics, and there have been some outstanding British contributors in several of the developments: in monetary economics by Professor Patrick Minford, in the economics of politics by Professor Sir Alan Peacock, Professor Charles Rowley, Professor Jack Wiseman and Professor Norman Barry, and by promising younger economists like Professor Martin Ricketts, in the economics of standards in safety by Professor Michael Jones-Lee and by others.

France has provided active acolytes in *les nouveaux économistes;* their most systematic chronicler, the clear-thinking former journalist turned economist Henri Lepage, who saw the light in the late 1970s, has produced interpretations of the new economics that have won well-earned acclaim.[1] There have also been original contributors in Switzerland, notably Professor Peter Bernholz and Professor Bruno Frey, Austria (Professor Friedrich Schneider and Professor Erich Streissler), the Federal Republic of Germany, Scandinavia and other countries.

Not all the exponents of what I see as the ten main developments in the new economics would agree with my conclusion that its general effect is to strengthen the case for capitalism. Although they are more inclined to see the strength of the market and the defects of the political process, some still cling to the hope that government will work better if run by the right people, which in practice means socialists rather than liberals or conservatives.

The new economics is mainly a rediscovery, refinement and restatement, in modern language and application to the contemporary world, of British, or Anglo-Scottish, classical economic thinking and policy. All knowledge is derived from previous knowledge; if the advance is substantial in insight or application it is permissible to describe the new knowledge as different from the old, and therefore new.

The main elements can be arranged in ten groups:

1. the new interpretation of capitalist history;
2. the new analysis of property rights;
3. the new emphasis on the market as a process;
4. the economics of politics (public choice);
5. the critical examination of government regulation;
6. the sceptical view of public goods;
7. the nature and effect of externalities;
8. the monetary control of fluctuations;
9. the economics of self-investment in human capital;
10. the limited and the minimal state.

1. Henri Lepage, *Demain le Capitalisme,* Open Court, 1981, and others.

The New Interpretation of Capitalist History

There have been two intellectual developments in the study of history that reinforce the case for capitalism. One is the counter-revolution in the economic analysis of history which rejects the materialist interpretation of Marx. The other is the new emphasis placed on the role of private property rights.

The first has restored and reinforced the classical interpretation of capitalism as the source of increased productivity and rising living standards. For long decades, British economists and economic historians, notably G. R. Porter, T. B. Macaulay, famed for his Whig interpretation of history, John Stuart Mill (with some lapses), J. E. Cairnes, Alfred Marshall and Herbert Butterfield, found that the Industrial Revolution, the dawn of capitalism, had led to improvements in the condition of the mass of the British people from their almost unchanging or only very gradually changing standard of life for centuries until the late 1700s. Early Marxist or other forms of socialist writing—by Engels and Marx from the 1840s reinforced from about the 1880s by Arnold Toynbee, the three essentially socialist man-and-wife teams of historians, the Hammonds, the Webbs and the Coles, and more recently the Marxists Professor Eric Hobsbawm and E. P. Thompson—have taught the opposite: that living conditions deteriorated, in some periods more than others, that capitalism had produced immiseration. Socialism, it was strongly argued or firmly implied, offered the only hope of improvement.

The classical view was self-evident common sense. The capitalist Industrial Revolution drew people in from the primitive dwellings of the countryside to the more substantial homes of the towns. It replaced coarse apparel by woven clothes. It replaced the endless hours of cottage working by legislation on factory hours. It also brought the task of providing drainage and public order for large congregated numbers and other new conditions of urban living. But to attribute these new evils to capitalism is as plausible as blaming every human advance for its incidental disadvantages, unforeseen but temporary until new measures can be organized to remove them.

The Marxist critique is presented as scientific and sophisticated. Its jargon camouflages its essential *naïveté*. Were the technical discoveries in steam power and traction, the manufacture of textiles, printing and other industries to be foresworn because they brought new problems to solve? Would the guild system—or trade unions—have embraced them for their advantages or resisted them for their disturbance to established interests? Would government and bureaucracy have correctly assessed the balance of advantage of beneficial innovation and costly new tasks? Would a socialist society have introduced technological invention at a rate to suit the unexpressed interests of the uninfluential people at large in as rapid a change as possible? Or, would it rather have timed them more slowly to suit the vocal interests of the established producers, planners and bureaucrats?

The Marxist critique has suffered from historicism—the historical method of assessing economic systems and judging them as causes followed by consequences, the familiar fallacy of *post hoc, ergo propter hoc.* It argued that capitalism was accompanied by drawbacks; therefore it caused them. The Marxist critique then went on to the other common fallacy of the *non sequitur:* because capitalism caused problems (not proven) it should therefore be replaced by socialism in various forms from the dictatorship of the proletariat to gas and water municipalization. But the socialists were guessing: they had no reason to suppose that socialism would be an advance.

They have continued to condemn capitalism and have urged socialism for 200 years or more, and many are still condemning capitalism and urging socialism without putting the two pertinent questions asked and answered by the liberal economists and historians. First, would the eventual rise in living standards have taken place without capitalism? The answer is that it would not have done under the medieval guilds or under state socialism. Second, would the tasks of organizing urban living have been foreseen, avoided or accomplished better under socialism? The answer is that its record, wherever in the world it has been introduced, indicates no reasons to suppose that it would have been more prescient, prompt or proficient.

It could not have been long before the unbelievable Marxist/socialist interpretation of history was in turn repulsed by the restoration of the classical interpretation of capitalism. The original counter-revolutionaries of the 1920s, the historians John Clapham, Dorothy George, Dorothy Marshall and later Ivy Pinchbeck, were followed by W. H. Hutt on the factory system and trade unionism, T. S. Ashton on aspects of industrialism and more systematically by the Australian economist and historian R. M. Hartwell, who challenged the essence of the Marxist interpretation. Hayek and Hutt were joined in the 1950s by the French political scientist Bertrand de Jouvenel and the American L. M. Hacker (previously Marxist-minded) in reasserting the classical Clapham approach. The Marxist immiseration doctrine was rejected: the Marxist proletariat were not early or mid-nineteenth-century working people pauperized by early capitalism; many were the new population that would not have been born at all, or would not have survived, but for the new capitalism that created unimagined livelihoods by the new machinery of its technical revolution. Falling death rates following improved sanitation kept some alive who would have died earlier, but the Industrial Revolution produced the new tools that created the new occupations that gradually raised the living standards that sustained life for more people for more years.

The Marxists have made much of the fall in general incomes in some periods. It was hardly likely that the new conditions of industry and work would proceed uninterruptedly. (The notion that socialism proceeds smoothly upwards without fluctuations is a myth, bolstered by the suppression of statistics.) But the Marxists were disposed to see (almost) every downturn as terminal; they would understandably not want to see the upturn beyond the next crisis of capitalism at whatever stage they happened to be, from the first crisis observed by Engels in 1844 to the last crisis of October 1987 (or the autumn of 1989, and no doubt more, real or imagined, to come in the 1990s). There is a lot of theorizing about social relations, conflicts and hegemony, but in the real world of the everyday life of the people socialism is a vaguely desirable system to which many still aspire though few understand, but a system that is being replaced by capitalism everywhere, from Europe to the Far East.

The repute of capitalism has nevertheless suffered from the continuing influence of Marxist history. It is still taught widely in the Western world. It is still fallacious. It still fails to ask what the world would have been like without capitalism. And it cannot now explain why the world aspires to capitalism, especially where it has experienced socialism.

The New Interpretation of Property Rights

The second development in the reinterpretation of history is the emphasis on the evolution of private property rights. Hayek has restored the term "several" property (separate, as distinct from joint or common).[2]

A crucial difference between capitalism and socialism is in the role of property. Capitalism in principle maximizes the scope for private property; socialism maximizes the scope for public or nominally common property. In capitalism ownership is direct by the individual or group; in socialism it is indirect through the state or other representative body. In capitalism

2. F. A. Hayek, *The Fatal Conceit,* Routledge, 1988.

property rights—to hold, sell, hire, lend, bequeath or give—tend to be maximized; in socialism they tend to be attenuated—the citizen may have some rights of use but ownership resides with the state, a kind of superior landlord. In capitalism the owners of property are typically named, identifiable and responsible; in socialism the nominal owners, the people, are typically anonymous and unidentifiable and the effective owners, the planners, are in practice not responsible to the nominal owners and therefore irresponsible.

Since capitalist systems contain some socialism, and socialist systems some capitalism, these differences may be of degree rather than absolute principle: in capitalism some private property is owned jointly in groups—commercial companies, cooperatives or voluntary associations; in socialism some property is personal and private. But the differences of degree are wide enough to be analysed as differences of principle. And capitalism is passing through a period in which the large commercial groups that dominated the ownership of property (the Fordism of the Marxist critics) are yielding to smaller units in which more ownership will be personal and identifiable.

The central advantage of capitalism over socialism in the husbandry of property is that the real owners in capitalism take care of their property; the nominal owners in socialism cannot because they do not know what they own. What belongs nominally to everyone on paper belongs in effect to no-one in practice. Coalfields, railways, schools and hospitals that are owned "by the people" are in real life owned by phantoms. No nominal owner can sell, hire, lend, bequeath or give them to family, friends or good causes. Public ownership is a myth and a mirage. It is the false promise and the Achilles' heel of socialism. The effort required to "care" for the 50-millionth individual share of a hospital or school owned by 50 million people, even if identifiable, would far outweigh the benefit; so it is not made, even if it could be. The task is deputed to public servants answerable to politicians who in turn are in socialist mythology answerable to the people. In this long line of communication the citizen is often in effect disenfranchised. The wonder is that the myth of public ownership continues to be propagated by men and women who aspire to political leadership. In commercial advertising it would be denounced by socialists as a fraud on the people.

The task of husbandry and conservation recurs in the joint ownership of private property in private companies or associations (housing and others), but the difference is decisive. An individual owner can sell individual property rights: he exercises control by the power to exit because there is a market; in the political process he has to settle for the ineffectual exercise of voice in the control of mass ownership of common or joint property.

It is evidence of the power of repeated political propaganda that many ordinary people continue to believe in the reality of public ownership, and it is a reflection on non-socialist politicians that they have not destroyed the myth. The uncharitable but realistic explanation must be that, at least until 1979, politicians in all parties had aspired to the control of government-owned nationalized or municipalized property that they knew was in no effective sense public.

This well-established truth of classical liberalism is a decisive component in the historical counter-reaction to the Marxist critique of capitalism. Two American historians, Professor Douglass North and Robert Thomas, have explained the transition from the stagnant feudal and guild systems to progressive economic growth in Europe, first in Holland and then in England, by the transition from common property, then typically in land, to personal property.[3] The method was essentially the enclosure of common land into plots for the exclusive use of individual owners.

This is the precise opposite of the continuing socialist teaching, even in the latest revisions of Labour Party policies, that progress lies in passing from private to public ownership. Now that *glasnost* has induced the Russians to release even unfavourable information, we are not surprised to learn that the productivity of private plots in the USSR is 10 to 20 times that of socialized land. Tolstoy the landowner and Lenin the land-coveter, like their opposite numbers in eighteenth-century France and twentieth-century South America, wanted land taken from the rich and given to "the people." If it had been parcelled out into personal plots it would have been worked more efficiently. But by "the people" the socialists meant that the land should be owned in common, not in the reality of everyday life by the people as individuals. The effective owners who control its use form an amorphous mass of unidentifiable politicians and bureaucrats who cannot easily be brought to book for their stewardship. And, supreme irony, even if they are identified they defend themselves with financial and other resources belonging to their victims.

Individual ownership has been anathematized by socialist teaching. Socialists did not, and still do not, understand that it is private ownership that produces results. So it could be also in the private ownership of the deserts, the sea beds and air space when means are devised to enclose and appropriate "plots" to individual owners who will find it profitable to invest in

3. Douglass North and Robert Thomas, *The Rise of the Western World*, Cambridge University Press, 1973.

making them productive.[4] Until then their use will be decided by governments driven by political aims, which may be put before the best use with maximum efficiency for the benefit of the common man.

It was the development and refinement of the law of private property rights that explains the replacement of medieval stagnation by modern progress. North and Thomas[5] presented a reinterpretation of British and European history that makes most history textbooks out of date.

Serfdom, unpaid labour on land of the lord of the manor, was the payment for his (public good) services of defence and security, justice and courts. The custom in serfdom of exchanging labour services for public goods was cheaper than contract because it lowered the information costs and transaction costs that would have been entailed in periodic revision of the labour payment for the lord's services. Payment by taxes was impracticable because cash was not used widely. Payment in kind was inconvenient because markets were not yet developed to ease the measurement of the value of labour. But in time markets developed: the growth in population brought new land into cultivation; specialization and therefore exchange increased; money and credit came into growing use; more and more serfs became land-owning peasant farmers as they were encouraged to bid for private plots on which to grow products of which the surplus available after family subsistence could be sold at a profit in markets.

The role of the law on property was probably more important in stimulating economic growth than the technical advances of the Industrial Revolution. Population increased and techniques (in agriculture) advanced in the eleventh century but they brought little economic growth because land was still owned communally, with little incentive for individuals to invest and expand production. But in the eighteenth century the further increases in population and technical advance were accompanied by economic growth because there was by then enough private ownership of land to make private investment profitable. The peasant owner had developing property rights: since exclusive personal ownership told him the costs and benefits of investment, he found that his decisions would benefit (or harm) him and his family. The individual farmer could advance on his own without waiting in a political process for agreement by a committee, or a majority, and without incurring the transaction costs of organizing agreement (and what might be called the associated discussion, persuasion, negotiation and consensus

4. D. R. Denman and Jack Wiseman, *Markets under the Sea?*, Institute of Economic Affairs, 1984.

5. North and Thomas, *The Rise of the Western World.*

costs in time, energy and money). When one farmer forged ahead, the information costs of learning about the effects of new methods were lowered for all the others. Productivity and living standards improved all round. Private property made for growing public prosperity in the real sense that it was shared by the people, not controlled by politicians and bureaucrats.

That was the capitalist secret: markets and their prices told farmers the vital information on earnings, costs and profits required to make decisions on what to grow, how much to grow, at what prices to sell and how much to reinvest. In contrast, the now century-old socialist claims for the rewards of public ownership and the venality—the selfishness, greed, exploitation, alienation—of private ownership have been a confection of wishful thinking, an escape from the real world, as tragically confirmed by experience in every country that has tried socialism from the USSR through China to Africa.

Two more conclusions, both disagreeable for socialism but hopeful for the common people, must also be drawn. The history of Europe demonstrates that inequality is necessary to reveal progress by different people and reward those who take the risks of the unknown by exerting effort and initiative to discover new ways of solving known tasks or new tasks to solve, but it is also essential to stimulate emulation, from which all eventually gain. If equality is enforced by socialist law, or encouraged by conservative custom, it slows down or suppresses progress. The peoples of Europe would have remained poorer longer.

Moreover, since the power to persuade and organize others in collective organizations is itself unequal, the ability of people to advance as individuals in the market without waiting for others is in the end more egalitarian than the socialist method of waiting in the political process for agreement, universal or by majorities, in debating chambers. The evolutionary spontaneous freedom under capitalism for individuals to act *without* collective restraint is necessary for some to forge ahead and show the others the way. In the end, as the others follow, more can share in the advance. Inequality in action is the way to equality in result.

The market, in short, is a surer way to an egalitarian ambience, in which all can feel they have achieved as much as others by their own efforts, than is the enforcement of equality by the state. The equality of socialism is deceptive: in the real world (but rarely in socialist textbooks) deep-seated inequality is grounded in wide differences in personal political and cultural power, generally wider and deeper-seated than the differences in income or wealth in capitalism. The eventual equality-creating mechanism of the market under capitalism is based on liberty to compete and emulate, and is more enduring than the equality enforced by the political process under socialism. Equality is the indirect outcome—unintended but more secure—of the liberating market process; if equality is the direct goal of policy, it creates impulses and pressures for it to be pursued at the expense of other purposes, and among them intangible liberty is the politically more likely sacrifice. The equality of socialism ends by being forced on the people by coercion; the irony is that the political people are more equal than the common people. That is reality; the rest is self-deception or wishful thinking.

The evidence is around us. The capitalist United States has achieved more equality, indirectly and less systematically but more surely, than the USSR. In Britain the market takes longer to achieve equality because it is impeded by hierarchical resistances to, and cultural distaste for, competition, so that able young people from the working classes still take longer to penetrate the higher-paid professions than in the United States. British workers from the north are not always readily welcomed in the middle-class suburbs of the south; professional parents resist the competition in "their" state schools of working-class children who could be enabled by vouchers to escape ("exit") from sink state schools in working-class areas.

How far it is the legal refinement of property rights rather than technological advance that explains economic growth and progress remains debatable. The conclusion of North and Thomas[6] that the crucial condition of progress was law rather than technology seems persuasive. The new avenues for economic activity created by invention and innovation, both in the original Industrial Revolution of the late eighteenth century and in the even more rapid contemporary Information Revolution of the late twentieth century, provided then and provide now the scope for new forms of property rights in manufacturing in industry and personal services.

Yet the economic advance made possible and stimulated by open markets has been impeded by laws, on copyright and patents and other political creations, that prevent the market from performing its wealth-creating function. This was the conclusion of Professor Sir Arnold Plant, whose lectures developed the teaching of David Hume (that private property was necessitated by scarcity) and strengthened the view that private ownership was essential for its conservation and optimum use, not only directly for the owner but also indirectly for the community, for whom the private owner acted as unofficial trustee much more effectively than the political trustee in the pub-

6. Ibid.

lic ownership of socialism. The private owner in the competitive market is penalized if he uses his property inefficiently; the public owner in the political process conceals his inefficiency and sails on to the next episode of inefficiency. The collectivized farmers of socialist countries, who will have to be given private plots in order to increase the production of staple foods, will both increase their private incomes and enlarge the supply of food for the population as a whole. But the idolatry of public ownership is the economic obstacle to production in socialist countries and to the avoidance of starvation in the African socialist states. No less, it is the persistent political obstacle to further de-socialization of property in Britain and other capitalist countries in Europe and other continents. That is the dilemma, that public property creates private destitution: the contradiction that socialists persist in ignoring, even in the Britain of the 1990s.

Capitalism forged ahead in the eighteenth century under the impetus of the technological revolution, but it was retarded by the slow refinement in the nineteenth century of the property rights required to give it maximum scope. The early inventions of the 1760s and later created enterprises that were financed partly or largely by private loans from family, friends and neighbours. The company laws that created joint-stock firms with limited liability to encourage strangers to lend and invest came 90 years later in the 1850s.

The enclosures of fifteenth-century England were the forerunners of the return in the twentieth century from common ownership socialism to private ownership capitalism in the denationalization or privatization of the 1980s. The belated transfer from the nominal ownership of public property in nationalized airways, gas, water and other corporations to the real ownership of private property in the shares of airways or gas companies has fastened academic attention on—and public interest in—the nature of property rights. The transfer from unreal to real ownership of the coal mines and the railways is impeded by party political calculation of electoral timing, but can hardly be far behind. The even more belated release from state and political control of schools and hospitals may require new forms of property ownership.

These are the new tasks for economists, historians and lawyers. But the fundamental obstacle is political. In capitalism as it has been allowed to degenerate, desirable reforms have to be piloted through the political process. The reforms required to enable capitalism to yield the best results of which it is capable will not be enacted unless they suit the politicians and their bureaucratic entourage. We must discard once and for all the superstition that, although we have to look to the self-interest of Adam Smith's baker to supply us with edible bread, we can depend on the selflessness of the politician to provide good policies. Politicians are bakers in politics. The significant difference is that we are not tied to bakers for four or five years as we are to politicians. We can desert unacceptable bakers every day. It is less easy to escape from the large semi-monopoly suppliers of heavy Fordist industry with projects that last for years or more, not least in the nationalized undertakings. They are being undermined by technical invention and replaced by smaller units providing escapes to competitors. Again, the political process provides no better protection for the consumer in "regulation" that is captured by the regulated or in watchdog bureaucracies that are pawns of the political process.

As we are tied to politicians for years on end, we must create new safeguards against their waywardness. Politicians will produce good policies if their interests are also served, or at least if they are not seriously disserved. There need be no conflict, but the aim must be to go further and ensure harmony between the politician's interest and the public interest. That requires an arsenal of incentives and inducements, disciplines and penalties to ensure that in serving themselves politicians serve the people. Politicians have disserved capitalism by overtaxing, overinflating, oversubsidizing, overcentralizing . . . and many other acts of commission and omission. They have had a long run of preventing open markets from abolishing want.

The package of incentives and disciplines is not yet in place. A transfer from all unnecessarily public property to private property where possible is a first essential. The underlying obstacles to the required measures are that it is taking a very long time for anti-capitalist scholars to understand why private is superior to public in property rights and that politicians and bureaucrats will resist the lessons of post-war experience. That is the province of the economics of politics, government, democracy and bureaucracy, or public choice, as it is described by its Scottish-American founders (below).

The Market as a Process

The third reinforcement for capitalism is the refinement in economic thinking on the idea of a market. For decades the notion that human beings should be subjected to the market was anathematized, especially by politicians who, even if unconsciously, were presenting themselves as the more desirable alternative. Market forces are still regarded, even in the serious press and by the literati, as an elemental power beyond human sympathy or control. The politicians, especially the socialist inclined in all parties who thought that government existed to promote worthy causes, presented themselves and were regarded as more human, more compassionate, more accessible and more civilized.

The sobering truth is almost the opposite. Markets comprise men and women who meet to exchange objects or services they want for others they offer in return. That in practice markets are imperfect has obscured the more fundamental truth that they are the best-known way of enabling individuals to meet for mutual benefit. The socialist criticism has been obsessed with the imperfections of the market to the exclusion of its unique properties. In return socialism offers aspirations without performance. World practice and experience in all the continents show no better, less imperfect, mechanism than capitalism as it has been, still less as it could be with free markets unimpeded by the political process.

The incalculable loss—the opportunity cost—of half a century of Keynesian macro-economics has been the neglected refinements in the micro-economic study of the market that would otherwise have been made. New ways would have been devised to deal with its imperfections—the public goods it has been thought it cannot supply, and the monopoly, externalities and unnecessary differences in incomes that it has not so far avoided.

It is intriguing to envisage the world without Keynes. The economists who were, or still are, inspired by his teaching—Professor James Tobin and Professor Paul Samuelson in the United States, Professor Hahn in Cambridge and many others—seem to imply the worst of unemployment and perhaps general social breakdown. Yet the countries that ignored Keynes, not least Germany and Japan and for many years the United States, have prospered with negligible unemployment. So should Britain have prospered as the slump of 1929–31 receded in the later 1930s if she had developed a liberal market system instead of the post-war Conservative-Labour corporatist state.

Now, after 50 years, micro-economics is again being applied intensively in the newly systematic study of the market process in the United States and Britain. The German economists who inspired the economic miracle—Walter Eucken, Ludwig Erhard, Alfred Müller-Armack and others—rejected (or ignored) Keynesian macro-economics. The macro-economists whose advice on incomes policies, growth targets and reflation (often a euphemism for inflation) was heeded in Britain and the United States by governments of all parties in the 1960s and 1970s have not only left a legacy of stagnation or inflation, or the ironic combination of both in stagflation. They have also weakened political democracy by weakening free markets and strengthening state controls—which meant weakening capitalism and strengthening socialism. It was not until their influence as economic advisers was replaced from the 1970s by that of economists who may have deployed macro-economic models but who instinctively understood their dangers unless applied in the light of their micro-economic foundations, that state controls were replaced by markets and stagnation by expansion.

Fundamentally, the error of macro-economic models still used in government planning is that they reflect totals or averages of production or consumption, saving or investment, but that individual decisions are mainly influenced by small marginal changes in these quantities. Macro-models that ignore their micro-foundations say nothing of significance about individual reactions to marginal changes in price. Macro-economic totals of car production conceal differences between firms; totals of bread or beer consumption conceal differences between age groups. The return from state controls to free markets could push macro-economic studies and applications back to the minimal activities of government and expand the micro-economic study of individuals.

The revival of the refinements of micro-economics would reduce the influence, and discipline the over-use, of macro-economics. Hayek emphasized the essential function of the market as not merely the rational allocation of existing resources but the discovery process of generating new ways to improve and develop them. The British political scientist Professor Norman Barry has contrasted the older end-state objectives of centralized government—if benevolent in high employment or low inflation, if authoritarian in space research or military strength—with the newer studies of human behaviour as a process of decentralized interaction between individuals as buyers and sellers which produces a better harmonization of human activity.[7] He concluded, as a political scientist judging economic mechanisms:

> Too many economists have been guilty of gleefully demonstrating how existing market structures depart from a hypothetical optimum. Political scientists too often imagine that the only way to avoid dictatorship is to let politics operate more or less unrestrained irrespective of the damage it can do to the efficiency properties of the market. . . .
>
> . . . the economic world becomes the plaything initially of . . . the headily unrealistic abstract theorist and then the defenceless target of unconstrained political authority.[8]

7. Norman Barry, *The Invisible Hand in Economics and Politics,* Institute of Economic Affairs, 1988, p. 83.

8. Ibid.

The unreality of supposing that government and its essentially macro-economic instruments can produce the best results from human and natural resources, and the necessity of making the micro-economic view of the world prevail, were put graphically by Professor G. L. S. Shackle in depicting the micro-economic jigsaw puzzle of supply and demand, decisions and expectations, as able to change "as swiftly, as completely, and on as slight a provocation as the loose, ephemeral mosaic of the kaleidoscope. A twist of the hand, a piece of 'news,' can shatter one picture and replace it with a different one."[9]

It is unrealistic to suppose that the political processes and public property rights of socialism can make as much use as capitalism of the micro-market. The revival of micro-economics is a further intellectual reinforcement of capitalism in the world ahead.

The Economics of Politics (Public Choice)

The economics of the market has been studied for at least 200 years. Little wonder that its imperfections fill the textbooks and are reflected in the journalism of writers who grew up in the post-war heyday of Keynesianism. No less predictable is the disposition of politicians, occupationally anxious to enlarge their empire, to find reasons for throwing out the baby of the market with its bath water of imperfections. "Market failure" is the irresponsible device on the banner of academic socialism, which is not examined in the same meticulous detail to discover government failure. Yet the record and history of government failure would fill a thousand Domesday Books. The pervasive repeated destructive inability of government to represent the people, keep its promises, correct its defects, discipline its bureaucracy, cut out waste, respect individual differences among citizens, avoid monopoly, provide choice and purge corruption, especially in local government and in much else, receives less attention in conventional political science or the press.

The failure of government is the main conclusion from the barely 30 years of study of the micro-economic analysis of the motivations and reactions of individuals in politics—in government, democracy, taxation, bureaucracy, electoral systems and other components of the political process. Although the subject of the analysis is *politics,* the treatment is *economic.* The

9. G. L. S. Shackle, in Alexander Shand, *The Capitalist Alternative,* 1984.

American political scientist Professor William Mitchell has said his confrères in political science have not been very quick to see its importance because the method of thinking about individuals in politics is unfamiliar and the conclusions unpalatable. Students of government do not characteristically weigh the costs and benefits of alternative policies. Since "no-one in politics knows the value of anything," the political allocation of scarce resources is likely to be less efficient than in the market where everyone has to know prices in order to make intelligent because informed decisions.[10]

The essence of the new study was put succinctly by the Swedish economist Professor Ingemar Stahl when he presented Professor Buchanan to the King and Queen of Sweden as the Nobel Laureate in Economic Sciences in 1986.[11]

Individuals in households and firms exchange property rights by a pricing system in markets, which thus coordinate billions of transactions spontaneously. Individuals may act with the *motive* of self-interest but the *consequence* is usually to serve the general interest because transactions will not normally be made unless they benefit both, or all parties. Neither does self-interest connote selfishness: people act from self-interest because it is the only interest they know and are equipped to judge. They do not profess to know the interest of others better than others do themselves. This is the profession of politicians. The assumption that they invariably do know the interests of others has rendered conventional political science not only irrelevant but also misleading in the study of present-day politics. The study of public choice (Stahl described it as "the new political economy") had expanded the scope of economics in three ways.

First, it had applied micro-economics to the political process and its associated government administration and interest organizations. Individuals who act from the motive of self-interest as members of households or firms are also members of the political system. "It is hard to believe," as Stahl put it, "that [they] drop the self-interest and turn into economic eunuchs devoting themselves completely to social engineering in the service of the general interest." Public choice was making it possible to deduce the macro-economic behaviour of political and administrative organizations from the micro-economic interests of their individual members.

Second, public choice indicated that voters in the middle of the range of

10. William Mitchell, *Government As It Is,* Institute of Economic Affairs, 1988, pp. 16–17.

11. Ingemar Stahl, *Nobel Priset,* Prize citation: "for his development of the contractual and constitutional bases for the theory of economic and political decision-making"; quoted from pp. 35–6.

interests (the median voters) will strengthen their influence as parties of the Left and the Right try to win their support to form a majority. Attempts to correct market failure by government can thus produce "government failure." Budget deficits are politically tempting because the economic benefits of government expenditure go to the contemporary citizens, who have votes, and therefore to the politicians of the time, but the cost is borne by voters of the future who cannot vote against the deficits of today. Politicians who are profligate and live on loans today may not be in public life to receive the wrath of voters tomorrow. Little wonder governments often bequeath large debts to their successors. Producer groups with clear gains although fewer votes will also be favoured at the expense of consumer groups with more votes but less incentive to organize because their individual gains are minuscule.

Third, following the Swedish economist Knut Wicksell (1851–1926), Buchanan's public choice had developed the "contractarian" view of the state to explain its decisions on government expenditure and taxation. In a private contract between two individuals agreement was unanimous: both gained and neither lost. The idea of a unanimous social contract in which all gained led to the economic theory (explanation) of the state in which the optimum rule for government expenditure and taxation was determined by the costs of unanimous decisions in which all gained weighed against the losses suffered by individuals. The outcome would depend on the constitution and the rules establishing the right balance between the government coercion required for protection against danger and the risk that the coercive powers of the state would be exploited by the interest groups.

The writings on public choice have grown faster in the last 30 years than perhaps those on other developments in economic thinking. Much of it has grown from the seminal work of Buchanan and Tullock,[12] in which Buchanan analysed politics as a process of exchange (above) and Tullock analysed "public choosers" (voters, politicians, bureaucrats) as primarily self-interested individuals.[13]

These developments and later refinements in public choice have superseded much of conventional political science and its unrealistic approach to the potential beneficence of government. It will never be the same again after its invasion by economics, and the replacement of undefined generalized

12. J. M. Buchanan and Gordon Tullock, *The Calculus of Consent, Logical Foundations of a Constitutional Democracy,* University of Michigan Press, 1962.

13. C. K. Rowley (ed.), *Democracy and Public Choice,* Blackwell, 1987.

"needs" and "priorities" by the calculated or estimated (or guessed) costs and benefits of specific policies as the criteria of political decisions and the judgement of politicians.

Scholars of all the social sciences will assess public choice by its revolutionary insights. Politicians will be sobered by its demonstration that they are not a race apart but are like other men and women. With historic exceptions, especially when they rise to a national emergency, they are no worse but nor are they better—more able, kinder, more moral, less corruptible—than other men and women. Students of political science, philosophy and sociology will want to add public choice texts to the reading lists of outdated middle-aged and older teachers.[14]

The most important twin insights of public choice, its most fundamental contributions to the formation of policy, are first the focus on the power of dominantly producer interest groups to frustrate the potential ability of free economic institutions to serve the general interest, which in effect is the interest of producers themselves as consumers, and second the inherent tendency of myopic government to yield to the organized at the expense of the unorganized, and thus to put the short-run present before the long-run future.

The first, the extraction from politicians in government of the rewards denied by discriminating consumers in competitive markets, is described as rent-seeking in the literature.[15] There seems no official public choice term for the second, the debilitating myopia created by political self-interest, but a main element is described as "log-rolling," the mutual aid between politicians who support one another's self-interested projects without regard for the eventual damaging effects on the citizenry of all their projects as a whole. Other elements have been described, significantly, if sometimes cynically, as "pensioneering," the "vote motive" (the title of Tullock's IEA Paper,[16] and the political analogue of the market profit motive), collusion, jobbery and worse. "Politicians," said Professor Mitchell, "live by stratagem and tactics.

14. A good start would be the essays by Richard Musgrave, Mark Blang, Hilder and William Baumol, Herbert Giersch and others in honour of a leading British public choice economist Professor Sir Alan Peacock (David Greenaway and G. K. Shaw [eds.], *Public Choice, Public Finance and Public Policy,* Blackwell, 1985) and the writings of Professor Jack Wiseman and Professor Martin Ricketts.

15. J. M. Buchanan, R. D. Tollison and Gordon Tullock (eds.), *Towards a Theory of the Rent-Seeking Society,* Texas A&M University Press, 1980.

16. Gordon Tullock, *The Vote Motive,* Institute of Economic Affairs, 1976.

Although their world is a monopoly, it hardly brings a quiet life . . . they must 'wheel and deal,' conceal, dissemble, lie, exaggerate and bluster. . . . They conduct the weighty affairs of state . . . without a supportive ethical setting for efficient trading."[17]

Ironically the danger could be less under socialism than under capitalism. A government of socialists that dispensed with the votes of political democracy, as some in Europe, Asia, Africa and South America do, could ignore the importunities of the interest groups and put the long-run interest of the people, as they saw it, first. But they would require to be benevolent, informed and long-sighted: rare qualities in combination. And the interest of the people as seen by the socialist controllers would not necessarily be the interest of the people as they saw it themselves.

Capitalism has been developed and is seen to be superior precisely because, except in national emergency when a Lloyd George or a Churchill puts national survival before party expediency, or in the absence of emergency when a Mr. Gladstone or a Mrs. Thatcher can impose conviction, principle or a vision of society on pragmatic (meaning calculating or cynical) ministers, men and women in government remain as human, fallible, imperfectly informed, near-sighted and self-regarding as men and women elsewhere. A century of increasing overgovernment under socialism has created the illusion of political supermen, served by bureaucrats who disguise themselves as "your obedient servants." William Shakespeare used Cassius to tell the Romans not to bend the knee to the tyrant Caesar. He might now tell the people: "Men at some time are masters of their fates: The fault . . . is not in our stars, But in ourselves, that we are underlings." Socialism risks generating Caesars. Much more than capitalism it requires planners, controllers and administrators with fearsome powers. Under capitalism the ordinary common people who do the work of the world do not depend on extraordinary people to "lead" them; capitalism runs best when a handful of reasonably able people do the relatively little that government has to do and discreetly withdraw to live their own lives. Switzerland remains the exemplar.

The transition required for capitalism to emerge from a long term of socialism may necessitate an active, even assertive, government and its forbidding risks. The charge of assertiveness against the three Thatcher Governments may reflect in part the effort required to re-establish the spirit as well

17. Mitchell, *Government As It Is,* pp. 17–18.

as the institutions of market liberalism. Yet the ultimate culprits are the governments of all parties that instituted socialist control where it was not necessary. The policy of centralization to re-create decentralization has obvious dangers; ambitious politicians with no convictions will be tempted to prolong it. Conservatives have been hardly less guilty than socialists. The obvious solution now is to limit the power of all politicians to the essential minimum. Public choice indicates constitutional disciplines on politicians to inhibit their natural proclivities. Further solutions outside the political process, considered in the final chapters, may be required.

The teachings of public choice are an intellectual reinforcement of the case for capitalism because the market minimizes the power of men and women in the political process.

The Seductions of Government Regulation

Where socialists have had to accept that private industry in the market could be superior to public enterprise controlled by government, they have insisted that government must nevertheless regulate it to safeguard the public interest. The review of socialist thinking in 1989 as reflected in the review of its principles and proposals by the Labour Party, said to be the echo, 30 years late, of the German Social Democratic acceptance of the social market economy in 1959, indicated over a hundred new regulatory authorities with political powers.

Like some of its academics, Britain's socialist politicians have belatedly heard of the market but not yet of the economics of politics. The market process was difficult to accept after decades of condemning its defects; the Labour-Socialist solution is to take it under political (democratic) control. Yet the defects of the political process will be impossible to absorb because it is the essence of socialism. Politics can civilize the market. Politics can hardly civilize politics. Political democracy as we have known it so far has not made itself representative of all the people.

The dilemma is insoluble. Yet it cannot be concealed for long. Socialist politicians concerned for electoral power can disguise it for a time. Socialist academics faithful to their science in the pursuit of elusive truth will not conceal it at all.

The new economics of Professor George Stigler, the 1982 Nobel Laureate, Professor Gary Becker, Professor Sam Peltzman and others, mainly in the United States, strongly suggests that, because of the working of the political processes, regulation invariably ends by favouring the regulated industries.

The regulated capture the regulators. The latest hope of the socialist mind, in all parties, that government and politics would find the solution has failed.

Road charges in the United States were found to be half as much again as in countries without road transport regulation like Belgium. Short-distance urban transport passengers were subsidizing long-distance passengers—as discovered more recently in Britain. The unregulated market in the newer capitalist countries produced "jitneys" (large taxis), which gave passengers more flexibility in arranging routes, but, because they were suppressed in regulated transport systems, travellers resorted to private cars and intensified road congestion. Regulation in medicines has slowed down the production of new medicines because the political regulatory authority, not least in the United States, is understandably too cautious: it will be blamed for the publicized tragedies caused by the unforeseen side-effects but not for the unknown lives that could have been saved by the suppressed medicines. Political overcaution in standards that are too high, so that political popularity is bought at the cost of the citizen, is one more defect largely ignored in political science. The use of compulsory car seat-belts has unknowingly shifted casualties from passengers to pedestrians. Government is praised for saving passengers but not condemned for killing pedestrians. Continued protection for "public utilities"—telephones, electricity, broadcasting, the post—repeated the dismal occupational disease of the political process by subsidizing producers at the expense of consumers and aggravated the offence by repressing innovation. For how many more years would British households have had to accept the stale joke about the complete choice of telephone colours provided that they chose black? The simple answer is as long as government prevented competition with the socialized telephone system.

The notion of conventional politics that the function of government was essentially to rescue the citizen from market failure is a long time a'dying. The history of government regulation vividly demonstrates the inability of the political process to cure a failure of the market process. The charge that standards in the market are too low is sometimes justified, but the reason is mostly that the market is prevented from being as competitive as it could be in generating more information from more suppliers, so that consumers have the wider choices that will enable them to avoid the lower standards by escaping to the higher standards. It is usually government that suppresses the competition by erecting vast monopolies. Obvious examples are fuel and transport, education and medicine.

The new economics of regulation has produced evidence of the undiscovered damage of even well-intentioned government. Ironically, the better the intention, the more the damage, because of the temptation to set standards too high and the anxiety to avoid the criticism that they are too low. Market standards that are too low do not last long and are corrected when consumers can escape from offending suppliers. But the political process generates strong incentives of overcaution to garner votes at the expense of eventual choice, comfort, access and lives. Of these, restricted access is the least detectable: standards that are too high raise costs, and prices that are made unnecessarily high exclude the poor more than the relatively rich. The cause of these consequences of government regulation is unavoidable: the costs and burdens of standards that are too high are more difficult to detect than in the self-correcting mechanism of the competitive market. The externalities of socialism can do more damage than the externalities of capitalism.

The central conclusion is that the much-emphasized argument for regulation by politicians makes the decisive error of socialism that it will be conducted by a new race of men and women. Some exceptional individuals have appeared in British history—perhaps Pitt the Younger, Gladstone and Churchill. There is now much argument whether Mrs. Thatcher is such a one. If history judges her as exceptional, she is aided by only a handful of others, but surrounded by mostly unexceptional conventional politicians for whom politics is their chosen profession and power their essential goal, who too often sound like barristers with briefs in which they had no heart. Yet even if the exceptional appear more frequently and more dependably on the political scene, the argument remains for capitalism to confine the powers of everyone in politics to the tasks that only government can perform.

The first five of the ten developments in economic thinking that strengthen the case for capitalism have been reviewed in this chapter. The second five are examined in chapter 8.

CHAPTER 8

More Intellectual Reinforcement for Capitalism

> Capitalism is based on self-interest and self-esteem; it holds integrity and trustworthiness as cardinal virtues and makes them pay in the marketplace, thus demanding that men survive by . . . virtues, not . . . vices.
>
> Alan Greenspan, in Ayn Rand, *Capitalism: The Unknown Ideal*

> We are radicals for capitalism . . . we advocate capitalism because it is the only system geared to the life of a rational being.
>
> Ayn Rand, *Capitalism: The Unknown Ideal*

> . . . the impressive economic and the still more impressive cultural achievements of the capitalist order . . . could lift poverty from the shoulders of mankind.
>
> Joseph Schumpeter, *Capitalism, Socialism and Democracy*

This chapter covers the second five of the developments in economics that strengthen the argument for capitalism.

Shrinking Public Goods (Unavoidably Collective Functions)

An apparently safe argument for the socialist is that socialism is indispensable for the public goods that cannot be produced in the market. Joint financing by taxation and production by (or for) government is therefore apparently indispensable.

"Public goods" is a defective description. It suggests, perhaps unintentionally, that they are produced by government necessarily for the "good" of the "public." To analyse them dispassionately, an ethically more neutral description is preferable. Until a better term is discovered, I shall occasionally use "unavoidably collective functions" to emphasize that they are necessarily collective, but not necessarily "good" as distinct from public "bads," produced by government.

That some goods and services are unavoidably functions of collectives like government is not an intellectual argument for the superiority of socialism as a principle. Collective production is necessary for a small part of economic activity—perhaps 15 per cent in Britain (see below)—but it remains as defective in principle as it is objectionable in application. Collective provision is not chosen (for public goods) because it is preferred to the market. Heart surgery is not preferred to a healthy heart but to a non-functioning heart. Government has to supply public goods not because it is better than the market but because the market cannot supply them at all. But in supplying public goods government still subjects the citizen to all the "bads" of the political process.

Socialism in modern defence and other public goods proper is unfortunately unavoidable, although the debate on the nature and extent of public goods is long and continuous. The public sector as distended by most governments in Europe and generally in the capitalist West does not stop at public goods. Socialism in fuel and transport, education and medicine, housing and pensions, most local government and other (mostly) private but "socialized" goods is not a technical necessity; it is mostly a political convenience based on fallacious socialist reasoning. It is mostly unnecessary, undesirable and avoidable. But imperialist politics has invaded and captured them and will not easily release them without explicit demonstration of public displeasure, even though government production—"nationalization" in its varied disguises—is demonstrably superfluous and increasingly inferior to the market.

Socialized public goods not only suffer from all the defects of socialized activity, but they suffer more. Escape and exit are possible from socialized non-public goods like education and medicine; escape and exit are not possible from public goods proper like defence or law and order, except by the extreme resort to emigration. The thwarting of citizen preferences in public goods proper—the forced payment in taxes for services not preferred by large minorities, the unaccountability, the political horse-trading, the social friction (as between unilateral and multilateral disarmers) and other discords, the differential influence of the organized political people and the unorganized domestic people, the bureaucratic, professional and trade union obstructions to experimentation in better methods of supply by competitive private suppliers—all these and the other defects of socialism are intensified and maximized in unavoidably public goods.

Public goods proper are distinguished from public goods "improper"—the so-called public sector services that have no business in the political process—by two characteristics: they cannot be financed by market pricing (charges of varying kinds) because individuals who do not want them cannot be excluded, and individuals who use them without paying do not reduce the supply available for others who do. The technical jargon is "non-excludable" and "non-rival." The archetypal public good, external defence, unavoidably protects all citizens, including those who evade taxes, and is therefore non-excludable. Broadcast services which can be received by all without reducing the supply to any are non-rival but can be made excludable by meters and scrambling devices so that free-riders do not exploit payers; and the broadcasts do not require tax financing because they can be based on private payment.

A distinction which affects policy is between exclusion that is physically impracticable, as in external defence, and exclusion that is practicable but financially uneconomic because the cost of collecting "entrance" fees exceeds the revenue, as for national parks; although charging is technically feasible, it is uneconomic, and it is therefore sense to make entrance "free" to all. This is another source of confusion caused by the political convenience of describing as "free" the services paid for indirectly by taxpayers—but not by tax-evaders.

The distinction between public goods proper and public sector services is clear. Public sector services are public goods improper where they are excludable and rival. Most British public services are *not* public goods proper and do *not* have to be supplied by government.

Some years ago, in an effort to gauge the extent of unavoidably governmental activity, I reached the rough estimate that only a third of the empire of government in 1976 comprised public goods proper.[1] Since the public sector has continued to expand, though less since 1979, the proportion is now probably nearer a quarter. The remaining two-thirds or three-quarters are public goods improper. The new prospects of world nuclear and non-nuclear disarmament, made likely by the belated Soviet recognition in 1989 that socialist production will lag behind capitalist production and requires not only markets but a massive shift of resources from armaments to

1. Arthur Seldon, *Charge*, Temple Smith, 1977; reprinted 1978.

consumer goods, could substantially reduce these proportions. It may also occur to the communist countries under their new "liberal" leaders in the 1990s that the output of consumer goods could be vastly expanded if transferred from socialized to market production. The danger is that the Soviet military might see an expansion of the market economy as a way to reduction in the armed forces.

Whatever the essential nature of public goods proper, about which economists and political scientists will continue to differ (the seminal thinker Anthony de Jasay has recently questioned the conventional approach [below]), a technically pragmatic device or rule of thumb for distinguishing them from public goods improper would be to apply charging. If they could be financed by charging, they are not public goods proper, because they would then be shown to have separable benefits for which users could be charged or from which free-riders could be excluded. If they cannot be financed by charging, or if the revenue would be exceeded by the costs of collection, they are public goods proper.

Whether charging would, in political practice, be used in this clinical fashion is questionable: government would be tempted to use charging to suit its short-term aims, perhaps to raise revenue from a virtual monopoly, as has been argued with nationalized gas and electricity. But the distinction remains in principle: if politicians were saints, or could be disciplined by a senatorial House of Lords or by constitutionally entrenched clauses to act righteously, charging could be a powerful instrument to settle the question in some cases. It might also perhaps dispense with the unfruitful or self-indulgent theorizing on what were and what were not public goods by academics spoiled by tax financing.

By this charging test, there is a long list of British public services that are not public goods—from railways and air transport through coal, electricity and gas to most schools and hospitals, and from public libraries to job centres. Many, like education, have been defended as the way to deal with poverty, but even when poverty gradually receded from the British scene they were continued—and enlarged—in the public sector by the momentum of party politics and by the rent-seeking vested interests that found they could extract more from political negotiation with ministers or civil servants than from the consumer in the market (chapter 11). The larger part of the public sector is a political artefact, not an economic necessity or a public preference. Its persistence can be explained only by the economic analysis of politics.

In deference to the public choice academics, I should have said that the fraud of public service is explained only by the study of public choice, but I have argued that the term was unfortunate. Public choice is the study of the behaviour of "public choosers" in the political process (its clumsy original name was "non-market decision-making"), but its essential findings are that the political process is a vast engine for the frustration rather than the satisfaction of the choices of the public. The term "economics of politics" avoids the implied approval of the political process as it has developed.

The euphemism "public" is itself a political misnomer for politicized services run by bureaucracy. It conceals the large element of public goods improper in the unnecessary socialism that distorts the British and other capitalist economies. The term "service" is another political euphemism for a range of goods and supplies which vary from the acceptable, such as the police in some but not all services like advice on burglary protection and convoying valuable loads by road, to the unacceptable, like "sink" schools, shabby hospitals and slum housing. Particularly in league with the misleading "public," the question-begging "service" suggests a benevolence that is belied by the common everyday experience of rail travellers, householders, parents, patients, council house tenants, pensioners and many more who cannot escape easily, or at all if they are poor.

Nor are public goods proper fixed for all time. Technical advance can transform some into private goods that can be financed by pricing in the market, with all or most of the advantages of consumer sovereignty. Lighthouses were once considered public goods because all ships benefited, whether they paid or not, by reducing the risk of collision. But there was also a private benefit of avoiding the risk of being sunk by rocks or other natural obstructions; to this extent ships should pay part of the cost of the service. A device such as "scrambling," which confined the use of lighthouses to ships that paid and excluded those that stole a free ride at the expense of others, might make for better use of resources and efficiency in general, since free-riders, by not paying for the equipment, labour and other resources required to provide the service of safety for them, are making journeys at less than the full costs.[2]

Nor is broadcasting necessarily a public good. In the economic shorthand, it is non-rival but not non-excludable. Sir Sydney Caine, the liberal economist who had been Vice-Chairman of the Independent Television

2. R. H. Coase, "The lighthouse in economics," *Journal of Law and Economics,* October 1974; A. T. Peacock, "The limitations of public goods theory," in *Economic Analysis of Government,* Martin Robertson, 1979.

Authority (ITA), argued many years ago that meters could enable listeners or viewers to pay for the programmes they preferred,[3] and charging for programmes was in principle commended by the Peacock Committee on Broadcasting in 1987.

Two developments put the extent and importance of public goods into question: first, technical innovation at a rate unknown since the Industrial Revolution; second, the very supersession round the world of socialism by capitalism. Public goods have loomed large in the budgets of both capitalist and socialist governments for more than half a century because the largest item has been expenditure on what politicians call "defence" but is in practice preparation for possible war or for aggression. The belated realization by the communist world in the 1980s that it will not catch up with the capitalist world, by internal productivity or imperialist adventure, is now likely, for the first time since 1917, except during the Second World War, to lessen tensions between the two worlds and enable both to beat their massive arsenals of nuclear and conventional swords into civilian ploughshares, schools and hospitals, boots and shoes, homes, motor cars, television receivers and toys. The announcement by Gorbachev to the newly "elected" (but mainly selected) Congress of People's Deputies in May 1989 that Soviet expenditure on armaments had been no less than four times the amount long announced to the world (which could still be a political understatement) was also a confession of political duplicity unequalled in the capitalist world. The vast resources of labour and equipment would have brought much comfort to Russia's ill-housed millions. But now the Russian anxiety to increase the production of consumer goods might lead to disarmament that could bring a very large transfer from public goods to private goods. Government spending on armaments by the leading countries could fall sharply; total "public" expenditure in the capitalist West could fall from 40–50 per cent of national income in Europe to 20–35 per cent or less as it is confined to public goods proper. The load of socialism could be lifted from the lives of the common people everywhere.

The advance in technology, the inability of government to raise enough taxes for services to dispense with long waiting (from medical care and the law to the processing of driving licences and passports) or congestion (from large classes in schools to hospital wards shared reluctantly by older and poorer men and women patients), the recognition by the employees of the

3. Sydney Caine, *Paying for TV?*, Institute of Economic Affairs, 1968.

public sector that, as Anthony Crosland said of local government, "the party is over,"[4] the new taste of formerly propertyless workers for a real "share" in industry, the very acceptance by parties of the Left that capitalism has come to stay . . . all these and other developments unforeseen ten years ago look likely to reduce further the weight of public goods in many or most countries of the world. The very revulsion against the excesses of the state—its gluttony, its *immobilisme* and its pretence of sainthood—will stimulate inventors, innovators and entrepreneurs to discover new ways to reduce its writ.

Services that once seemed indisputably public goods are, moreover, being performed increasingly by private suppliers, more in North America than in Europe, with Britain a latecomer. (The evidence for the Third World has been compiled by Gabriel Roth.)[5] The law concerned with the settlement of disputes can partly or largely be replaced by private arbitration. The police may have to go on ensuring public order but will probably lose some or much of their protection of persons and property to private agencies. Security at Heathrow and other airports is largely provided by capitalist companies. Prisons can be run by private firms. Taxes may have to be levied by government but could be collected by private companies. Fire services are not necessarily public: in Denmark and some towns in the United States they are sometimes supplied by private firms.

Academics and other observers are examining public goods more closely. Two Belgian academics, the economist Professor Boudewijn Bouckaert and the lawyer Frank van Dun,[6] have analysed their nature and extent with unaccustomed scepticism; they doubt whether public goods are as unequivocal or as unavoidable as is still commonly supposed. The Hungarian writer Anthony de Jasay, who lives in France, author of the penetrating dissection of *The State*,[7] has followed with another sceptical analysis of the public goods problem.[8] He argues strongly that the very effort of government to provide public goods without charge to all and sundry breeds the parasitic free-

4. Anthony Crosland's legacy is reviewed in David Lipsey and Dick Leonard (eds.), *The Socialist Agenda*, Cape, 1981.

5. Gabriel Roth, *The Private Provision of Public Services*, Oxford University Press, 1987.

6. Boudewijn Bouckaert, General Meeting of the Mont Pelerin Society, St. Vincent, Italy, 8 September 1986; Frank van Dun, *Economic Affairs*, July–September 1984.

7. Anthony de Jasay, *The State*, Oxford University Press, 1985.

8. Anthony de Jasay, "A study of the public goods problem," in *Social Contract, Free Ride*, Clarendon, 1989.

riding that it intends to suppress—one more example of the clumsy perversity of the state. He takes further the argument that many public goods are still supplied by government when they could be produced by "spontaneous group cooperation." The conclusion that, since free-riding would be difficult to exclude, there would be a drift from voluntary to compulsory solutions, seems to indicate a tendency that would meet the powerful opposite forces tending to reduce the ambit of public goods in a world that renounced nuclear armaments.

So much for public goods proper (wholly, largely or partly). The days of public goods improper are more certainly numbered. The two large bastions of the public sector, the public services of education and medicine, which provide increasingly personal separable benefits, will be eroded by rising incomes or tax evasion if government continues to prevent escape and exit by enforcing taxes for sink schools or inhospitable hospitals regarded as unacceptable. All or most fuel supply can be provided by private firms. There is no good reason for transport to be owned by the state and run by government officials. The personal services of job centres for employees of all kinds and agencies for office staff, nurses and domestic assistances can be—and are being—performed more sensitively by private agencies. Universities and other suppliers of higher learning will derive more income from their customers—students, industry or overseas institutions. More cost-covering charging for libraries, museums, art galleries, opera, ballet and beach facilities, and new charging for refuse collection and other local government services would remove them from the misnomer of public goods and move them from local government to local firms. Water supply for private homes and sewage disposal can be better provided by private companies, not least because they are more likely to introduce the metering that induces economy.

Not least, the efficient supply of public goods proper has been damaged by the inefficient supply of public goods improper long after they were made superfluous by technical and social advance. It would not be surprising if government were slow to ensure the supply of possibly new public goods, like protection against air or water pollution, coastal preservation and the conservation of ancient buildings or animal species. If it had pruned back the public goods improper over the decades, it would have better anticipated its new tasks. The political inability to change the composition of the public goods sector with changing conditions is yet one more form of government failure uncomprehended by the socialist mind.

The Political Exploitation of Externalities

The social cost imposed on innocent third parties by private exchange in the market is an allied, and apparently easy, argument for advocates of government action to correct market failure. Public goods are intended to provide joint benefits to all whether they pay or not; other goods exert unintentional external effects—benefit or damage—on third parties.

In principle the argument seems incontrovertible. Factories belch smoke. Motorways create noise. Road traffic burning diesel oil or leaded petrol exudes noxious smells or poisonous fumes. The discharge of industrial waste destroys fish. The list seems endless. "The world," says the usually sober *Sunday Times,* "is dying."[9] Let government, runs the familiar response, protect the environment by prohibiting such "externalities" or, at least, ensure compensation for harm.

The argument is not self-evident. There are at least eight difficulties. First, almost every human activity has unintended external effects; if they were all prohibited, or examined and approved by bureaucrats, the cost would exceed the benefit. Like the identification of public goods, the policing of all externalities is an economic, not a technical, task. Some externalities have to be tolerated, in socialist as well as capitalist economies. Their prevention is no more an absolute than any other human activity.

Second, some probable or possible externalities are known ahead of time and allowed for in human calculation. People do not move to houses near the likely sites of sewage farms; the market puts their prices lower to compensate them for the risk or inconvenience. Political paternalism, here as elsewhere, is superfluous; it would destroy the price signals of the market.

Third, externalities can be beneficial as well as harmful: if people who lose are to be compensated, others who gain should be surcharged; if the state taxes a factory owner for his smoke, it should compensate the local housewives for the cost of laundering their sheets. But if all the gains and losses, compensations and surcharges were assembled, the cost of compensating and/or penalizing everyone could again exceed the good done on balance to all. Pursuing externalities to their ultimate conclusion would create an impoverished bedlam, a Valhalla for bureaucrats, a cornucopia for accountants, but not much for the rest of us.

9. *Sunday Times,* February 1989.

Fourth, the theoretical solutions for harmful or beneficial externalities create an "open sesame" to the political process and all its works; we can imagine what it would make of the task of assessing millions of externality taxes and subsidies.

Fifth, an ounce of the environment is worth sacrificing for a ton of new medicine that will cure cancer. The environment cannot be saved at all costs. No-one behaves as though it should be. We despoil a village green to make a cricket pitch; humans live on non-humans (chicken, cows, sheep, fish), and non-humans live on lesser creatures. Yet the environment is safer with private property rights in the market than subject to politicized decisions by government.

Sixth, some degradation can be discouraged by the use of the market itself. A lower tax on unleaded petrol would discourage the use of leaded petrol. Professor Wilfred Beckerman, who has not invariably favoured the market, argued strongly in the 1970s, supported by the scientist Lord Zuckerman, for charges or taxes rather than government prohibitions.[10] Beckerman's analysis and proposals were amplified in an IEA Paper in 1975 and echoed in a report commissioned by the Department of the Environment in 1989.[11]

Seventh, the fundamental condition that predisposes the environment or other property to spoliation is that it is owned in common, and not appropriated by a private owner who would protect and conserve it. Before the politicians of the world draw electoral capital from preparing international cooperation on protection of the environment, which would be vulnerable to questionable political influences, let them extend private property rights wherever possible to create effective inducements to the conservation of the environment. Until they have done that, the politicians may be thought intent on empire-building.

Finally, government is itself the source of the most far-reaching externalities and the most incorrigible, because the politician or bureaucrat at fault is more difficult to discover and less likely to be penalized (or rewarded) than

10. Wilfred Beckerman and Lord Zuckerman, Minority Report, Royal Commission on Environmental Pollution, HMSO, London, 1972; Beckerman's argument was amplified by economic analysis in *Paying for Pollution,* Institute of Economic Affairs, 1975, and further refined in the second edition, 1990.

11. D. Pearce, A. Markandya and E. Barbier, *Sustainable Development,* London Environmental Economics Centre, 1989.

its citizens. Its policies would not necessarily be dictated by faithful thought for the public interest but be influenced by political, industrial and vested interests, precisely those anxious about the natural environment who would pay too high a price in other people's taxes.

Two examples illustrate the error. The universities yield incalculable externalities in stimulating respect for spiritual values, enjoyment of cultural life and so on. Therefore, it is argued by the culturally inclined, they should be subsidized by government. Many scholars, vice-chancellors and socialists of all sorts have charged the 1980s governments with philistine barbarism for making the universities dependent on private financing. The argument seems indisputable in principle but founders in practice. How extensive are the cultural externalities? How large are the state subsidies required? Who pays (their opportunity costs)? Who decides? Are the relatively poor yet again to subsidize the potentially rich? It is not very helpful to make large claims for government funds without a more or less precise notion of how much is required. It is a high-minded task difficult to fulfil at the expense of others who have to pay but have no say. It is one more irresponsible indulgence encouraged by the political process.

All these are political decisions if they are not decided in the market. The suppliers of academic culture are well equipped to justify endless subsidies. Together with the innumerable other suppliers of undeniable externalities, they could justify subsidies absorbing more than the national income. The market certainly generates externalities, but that does not make the political process the better judge of their extent. The subsidization of the universities and their separation from the market and its (imperfect) cost indicators have produced grotesque expansion in subjects far removed from everyday requirements. The Thatcher Governments have been right to shift the balance of financing away from public to private.

The political process can do harm through the best-intentioned of scholars. The Committee on Higher Education under Professor (later Lord) Robbins recommended in 1964 that no less than 10 per cent of university costs should be financed from student fees. Soon after when he came to the IEA I asked whether all members of his committee had suggested 10 per cent, whether some had preferred lower and others higher figures, and whether it would not have been more enlightening if the report had indicated the range. He replied that it had been desirable to arrive at an agreed figure; it was true some had preferred lower figures, but the higher figures had been as high as 40 per cent. This was an exercise in political tactics. The publication of the range would have inspired a much more valuable public discussion of the pros and cons of politicized university financing than the bland agreed average. The market reveals the vital differences in individual judgement; politics aims at agreement on the meaningless impersonal compromise consensus.

The second example of the excesses of the political process in framing policy on externalities is the series of accidents on British Railways in early 1989. The natural human response of the Secretary of State for Transport was to assure Parliament that "everything possible" would be done to discover the causes and prevent their recurrence. This is good politics but profligate economics. In a world of scarcity no "desirable" object—safety or life itself—can be pursued "at all costs." All objects must stop short at the stage when additional resources add equal utility in all uses, so that the community cannot benefit by switching resources from some uses to others (the economists' law of equi-marginal utility). The market enables us to measure the utility that we think will be added by labour, equipment and land in alternative uses. But in politics the decisions are likely to be short-sighted, self-interested guesswork, especially near by-elections.

Cost–benefit studies, as Professor Michael Jones-Lee emphasizes, can shed some light, although Professor George Peters showed long ago in a frequently reprinted paper that they are often precarious and pretentious.[12] The main objection is that they hand politicians yet another "scientific" instrument to wield to their advantage. Unlike the market, politics is the arena where self-interest does not generally tend to public advantage.

The most extensive, but least discussed, externalities of government are the indirect or incidental but widespread political, fiscal, bureaucratic, labour market, trade union and professional, familial, financial and international repercussions of the welfare state. It consumes much higher taxation than would otherwise be required. The taxes impose costs on the national exchequer and generate tax avoidance and evasion, and since taxes, although legal, are no longer regarded as necessarily moral, they have stimulated the new twilight of law-breaking in what I have called "tax avoision," the mixture of avoidance and evasion when the resentment of taxes levied for unapproved purposes, such as subsidies for non-poor council tenants, pass im-

12. George Peters, *Cost–Benefit Analysis and Public Expenditure,* Institute of Economic Affairs, 1966.

perceptibly into tax evasion "justified" as rejection of the impositions of irresponsible politicians.[13]

The welfare state also distorts the machinery of government. It inflates the cost of the bureaucracy, and expands its power to run monopolies that decide the choices and obscure the quality of government services. It increases the strike threat of public sector professionals and trade unionists. In replacing the individual decisions of the market by the majority/minority decisions of the political process it foments social conflict between the political people and the domestic people (chapter 13).

The welfare state is rarely debited with its opportunity costs—not least, the expansion that would have developed in the voluntary insurance and other spontaneous forms of self-help among the common people as incomes rose (chapter 11).

Although it seems ironic to emphasize the evil that emerges from services created to do good, the welfare state has created large scope for work evasion, responsibility evasion, concealment of culpability for error and waste, redistribution of income from the poor to the affluent, favouritism, jobbery, corruption and theft. It is little wonder that the middle classes, as politicians who run the services, professionals who fill secure posts and well-connected consumers who receive the most responsive attention, benefit more than the working classes.

The wonder remains that, after 40 years, socialist academics continue to see the vision of the welfare state as it was conceived in the 1940s, rather than the reality of the externalities that emerged in the everyday world of the 1980s. Still less do they envisage the welfare services that could develop in the 1990s and 2000s under the stimulus of the market forces that produced the unprecedented wealth, range and quality of personal and household consumer goods that the common people have received from capitalism as it has been, and even more as it could have been.

The Importance of Money

Capitalism has been derided for its apparently incurable instability in the roughly ten-year trade cycles that for half a century from the 1880s to the 1930s alternated between boom and slump, bringing unemployment,

13. Arthur Seldon, in *Tax Avoision: The Economic, Legal and Moral Interrelationships between Legal Tax Avoidance and Illegal Evasion*, Institute of Economic Affairs, 1979.

hardship and poverty to the common people. Capitalism went through its darkest days in the 1930s, both materially from the Great Depression of 1929–33 and intellectually from the academic/political savaging by the wide range of critics from democratic Fabian to assertive Marxists who taught the dictatorship of the proletariat, an outlook epitomized by Stephen Spender in 1932.[14] For liberals in the 1930s who had a cautious good word to say for the free society, derision was their common lot. "Market" and "capitalism" were rarely uttered with approbation, even in academia.

The new economics of money, inflation and unemployment has restored the repute of capitalism and its continuing efforts to find ways of reducing the fluctuations. There is still dispute; there is doubt about some formulations of the monetary explanation of instability, there are aspirations to forge syntheses between classical and Keynesian economics, and there is still a lingering longing for a new mixture of fiscal and monetary devices that will enable government of able upright long-sighted politicians to rid economic life of disturbing fluctuations.

But the old confidence of the critics has evaporated. The non-socialists who hoped that Keynesian control of government expenditure would discipline booms and slumps, avoid inflation and unemployment and save liberal capitalism have had to entertain doubts. The more socialistically inclined who saw Keynes as validating a democratic socialist system run by government that would combine market production with socialist distribution have had to make doctrinal concessions. Four developments in economic thinking, two familiar, two less so, have had to be absorbed.

The Friedman analysis of the essentially monetary causation of fluctuations has provided rules for government in the control of the supply of money. Economists debate the time lag and the arithmetic link between the supply of money and the subsequent rise in prices. The ample evidence lies in the socialist countries that know there is no more essential way to stop the inflation than by ending the flood of money. The Minford emphasis on "rational expectations" in the light of the efficient use of available information, developed from the American John Muth, indicated that anticipated changes in the supply of money had smaller effects on output and larger effects on prices than unanticipated changes. Government could therefore become impotent in economic management to master inflation or create high employment. Ordinary people in the market prevailed over

14. Stephen Spender, *Forward from Liberalism*, Gollancz, 1932.

ministers, experts and bureaucrats in the political process: market information was the key to anticipating and reducing the fluctuations. The hopes that government would be the vehicle of effective stabilization policy were dimmed.

The two less well-known developments are from the school of public choice and from the Austrian school of market process. The economics of politics was applied to monetary policy by Professor J. M. Buchanan and Professor Richard Wagner, who maintained that the Keynesian analysis of the use of budgetary policy to flatten the fluctuations was not only economically flawed but also politically unrealistic. Government might deploy budget deficits to inflate the economy and increase employment which would attract electoral popularity, but it was not likely to impose budget surpluses to deflate the economy and reduce overfull employment which would earn electoral unpopularity. The Lawson budget surpluses of the late 1980s are too short-lived to judge their effects on electoral sentiment. The impression created by the conventional price-less opinion polls, that the surpluses are making the public ready to continue paying high taxes in favour of higher public expenditure, has been the source of continuing confusion in political policy. The opinion polls are literally price-less and misleading because respondents are not told how much more in taxes they will pay for how much more in benefits (chapter 10). After six or seven years of budget surpluses the public will realize that it is paying far more in taxes than is required for state services and will expect tax reductions. It will not thank governments of Left or Right that deny them. The net long-term effect of alternating budget deficits and surpluses would be a gradually rising trend of inflation unrelieved by countervailing disinflation.

The fourth development was the most revolutionary. Since Adam Smith it had been supposed that the provision of money was a primary public good to be supplied by government. Hayek developed, or unknowingly rediscovered, a long-standing doubt whether, in the absence of a restraint like the gold standard which deprived national governments of the power to inflate unilaterally, politicians could be left to resist the temptation to debase the coinage (and paperage) and inflate themselves out of increasing unemployment. Arguing essentially from the micro-economic law that an increase in the supply of a commodity reduces its price, he proposed in the mid-1970s that money should be taken out of the monopoly of the state and be put into the competitive market of suppliers who would have an incentive to prevent inflation that the state lacked: they would resist the temptation to inflate the supply of their money because its value would fall and their customers would use the private money of their competitors; they would have courted and suffered bankruptcy.

In 1975 Hayek sent the IEA the draft of what was published as "The Denationalization of Money" in 1976.[15] Competition in currency had been suggested earlier (without Hayek's knowledge) by an American economist and there was a long-standing advocacy of private money in "free banking." But the idea of what would now be called privatizing money was not likely to be absorbed quickly by practical central bankers, state or private, who would lose business, or by politicians, who would lose their electoral trump card. When I put the idea to a former Governor of the Bank of England, he responded indulgently "That would be for the day after tomorrow." But we have long learned that what practical men preoccupied with the tasks of today and tomorrow judge as "politically impossible" can rapidly become politically urgent when their long-serving stratagems are seen by the electorate to have failed. Lord Callaghan was an exceptional man of courage in 1976 to have told his trade union allies in public that the old (Keynesian) superstition—that government could inflate its way out of depression—was an illusion. He may have resorted to candour to relieve pressure from the aggressive trade unions, but he took the risk of general public unpopularity and may have suffered loss of support at the 1979 General Election. More recently, in 1989, the then Chancellor of the Exchequer, Nigel Lawson, proposed competition between national currencies in place of a uniform single currency for the European Economic Community, and argued it persuasively in a Treasury document.[16] This reform for competition between state currencies would reduce the risk of national inflations, though it would be vulnerable to agreement between national politicians on international inflation. Only private money would prevent inflation.

Whether by annually balanced budgets or other constitutional means or by external disciplines like a twentieth-century version of the gold standard the proclivity of hard-pressed politicians to inflate—hoping for early expansion in output while they remain in office and delayed rise in prices after the election if they return to opposition—will otherwise not be suppressed. The search for stability in economic activity no longer looks to all-wise politicians in government as the saviour but to profit-seeking and loss-avoiding

15. F. A. Hayek, *The Denationalisation of Money,* Institute of Economic Affairs, 1976.

16. *An Evolutionary Approach to Economic and Monetary Union,* HM Treasury, November 1989.

bankers in the market. It is one more reinforcement of the case for capitalism against socialism.

New Activities for the Economic Microscope

A powerful contribution to the counter-revolution against the political process is the imperialist "invasion" by market analysis of human behaviour long thought to be the province of political science, sociology and other studies that had invariably concluded with proposals for solutions through the state: the family, the household, marriage, fertility, diplomacy, war, conscription, altruism and philanthropy, tax evasion, crime and many others.

The general conclusion from this re-examination of human activity, from wholesome to venal, sacred to profane, is that it is better understood when analysed as personal reactions to the individual incentives and penalties analysed by micro-economics, than as broad and vague sociological or psychological trends or movements. This development in economics is mainly American, originated largely by Professor Gary Becker of Chicago and brought to Britain by one of his students, Dr. Ivy Papps of Durham University.[17]

The family is best understood as a firm, a unit of production of income and children, within which there is no monetary market but which avoids the transaction costs of repeated renegotiation of exchanges of services: a long-term contract of marriage is costly in money and time to break by divorce, but it insures against the sudden loss by divorce of the specialized contribution of the partners. The family, like other units of economic activity, cannot be analysed wholly in financial terms, since as the dominant Cambridge economist Alfred Marshall taught, exchanges are based on the net balance between monetary and non-monetary advantages; but government economic policy can do grievous harm if it ignores individual reactions in the family and the household.

Other activities that have revealed new truths when examined as markets are discussed by Professor Tullock and by Professor McKenzie[18] in a book translated into German, Japanese and Spanish.

17. Ivy Papps, *For love or money,* IEA Hobart Paper, Institute of Economic Affairs, 1980.

18. Gordon Tullock and Richard McKenzie, *The New World of Economics: Explorations into the Human Experience,* Irwin, 1975.

The Social Welfare Fiction

The tenth development in economic thinking that reinforces capitalism for its market mechanism rather than socialism for its political process is the defeat of the socialist "maximum" state by two streams in liberal thinking in favour of the "limited" state or the "minimal" state.

The maximum or unlimited state is in full retreat. The notion that public services were inherently better than private services, public expenditure than private expenditure, and public enterprise than private enterprise lingers among politicians but is rapidly being abandoned by almost everyone else, including the public that once believed it.

The notion that individuals could make rational decisions collectively, and that there was a device for discovering what they had decided collectively, once had an august intellectual origin. Professor Kenneth Arrow, the Nobel Laureate, devised a "social welfare function" to assimilate all individual choices, perhaps with the assistance of Lange's phantom speed-of-light computer, and thus indicate the "representative" choice of all. Perhaps a system of voting might assemble a collective "message" to the legislature. A "social choice" would convey the highest common factor of preferences.

Yet the ultimate outcome of this attempt to put all preferences into one was ironically the Arrow Impossibility Theorem, which acknowledged that there was "no social choice mechanism" that can perform the task.

Several economists have attempted to rescue the effort, but it remains a dangerous cul-de-sac that tempts economists into thinking of ways to make the function come to life by force. A distinguished American economist said that, after all, individual preferences were not so important compared with the communal decision. Professor Amartya Sen of Oxford, reviewing "the vast literature" on social choice, comprising many articles and books by numerous economists and political scientists over more than 20 years, claimed: "As a methodological discipline, social choice theory has contributed a great deal to clarifying problems that had been obscure earlier . . . [it] has undoubtedly been a creative tradition . . . that can be used to analyse economic, social and political problems involving group aggregation." But he ended disarmingly: "Perhaps the successes have been rather mixed. . . ."[19]

This is a facile claim and a damaging admission by a senior economist who teaches and influences young students. Economists are taught to think

19. Amartya Sen, in John Eatwell, Murray Milgate and Peter Newman (eds.), *New Palgrave Dictionary of Economics,* Macmillan, 1987, vol. 4, p. 389.

of weighing the benefits of scarce resources against their costs. How much is "a great deal" (of clarification)? Who has benefited? By how much?

There is a danger that academics will choose subjects—such as the very scope of "group aggregation"—that have more interest for themselves than potential good for the community. Oxford University and its colleges are fortunate to live partly on (private) endowments, but increasingly the salaries and other costs of its academics are paid for by taxpayers, many not rich and some poor. What sort of a return—how large compared with what it might have been elsewhere—has the taxpayer had for his "investment" in the "vast" researches into "social choice"? At least the market would have compared yields with other investments. The (private) University of Buckingham has to pay more attention to the benefits and opportunity costs of its carefully husbanded revenues. Would the academics who must have spent many thousands of man-hours on "social choice" have done so if they had been financed by people who asked more questions about how the money was used?

The notion of "social choice," which meant what it said—the attempt to devise a method for unifying all individual choices into one choice—yields little or nothing of value contrasted with the analysis of the economics of politics in public choice, which sheds new light on the working of government in the real world. Not least, unlike the fanciful visions of political science, the economics of politics demonstrates that politicians cannot and do not precisely execute public choices—that even if it were possible to assimilate all choices into one by the social welfare function, it would not necessarily be enacted in the public interest.

The liberal reaction has been to question the efficacy of government and to limit it in the limited state or to minimize it in the minimal state. In essence the difference between the two liberal approaches lies in a varied view on the extent of public goods. The case for limited government has been put persuasively by the Oxford philosopher John Gray.[20] The trend to centralization must be reversed, government must "relinquish a paternal role" and power must be returned to "civil society." He quoted Professor Michael Oakeshott for the view that government must not "galvanize" its subjects but act as "the umpire . . . to administer the rules of the game. . . ." Yet, though government should be limited, Gray argued that it should go beyond Oakeshott; it had "an important positive agenda," which included first the classical pub-

20. John Gray, *Limited Government: A Positive Agenda*, Institute of Economic Affairs, 1989.

lic goods, second, and more unexpectedly, the protection of "all who wish to acquire a decent modicum of wealth and responsibility in their health, education and provision for old age," and third, and an intriguing new item, the responsibility "to facilitate the transmission of valuable cultural traditions across the generations."

The other liberal approach to the case for minimal government emerges from the work of several followers of Mises and other Austrian economists, mainly Professor Murray Rothbard, and from the "anarcho-capitalist" writings of Professor David Friedman. Both in effect mount a root-and-branch assault on the notion of maximalist or unlimited government based on variants of social choice.

The difficulty with limited government that liberals have yet to resolve is that its functions must be exercised through the imperfect political process that distorts and manipulates individual preferences. Who makes the rules that politicians are to enforce in the public interest if not the politicians themselves? *Quis custodiet ipsos custodes?* Limited government implicitly supposes that government will perform faithfully the main functions allotted to it even though it is judged incompetent in performing other functions. The notion of limited government lacks the indispensable instinctive scepticism of government taught by the classical liberal economists that led them to want government confined to its unavoidable *minimal* functions of public goods rather than to the indeterminate limited functions that could be decided by government itself. If government cannot be expected to perform acceptably the services it can leave to the market, it cannot be expected to devise neutrally the rules that decide the services it must perform itself.

Means have not yet been devised to discipline the politicians. The new constitutional economics has grown in the very attempt to clarify the requirements and discern the essentials of the solution. The liberal advocates of minimal government reflect the anxiety that government should be confined to the indispensable functions that cannot be performed in any other way. To give political man more powers and functions is to leave the potential for abuse that no democratic government anywhere in the world has scrupulously rejected or resisted.

The new trend of thinking in limiting or minimizing the power of government is the tenth development in economics that reinforces the case for capitalism against socialism.

CHAPTER 9

The Criticisms of Capitalism

> . . . "contradiction of capitalism" describe[s] virtually any malfunction or . . . objectionable feature of the capitalist system . . .
>
> . . . in Marx's theory of historical materialism one of the central tenets is that there can be a contradiction between a society's economic organization and its capacity to develop its productive potential.
>
> Andrew Glyn, "Contradictions of capitalism," *New Palgrave Dictionary of Economics*

> While capitalism may secure equal negative freedom for all . . . it cannot secure an equal or even fair distribution of . . . those goods which are necessary for such freedoms to be exercised.
>
> Professor Raymond Plant, *Conservative Capitalism*

> There are bad private restaurants.
>
> A Conservative Cabinet Minister, early 1980s

Capitalism has been the target of criticism for more than a century from all quarters, over a wide range of temper—scholarly and civilized, self-conscious and querulous, savage and assertive. The criticisms are divided here into five groups; the first come from the authoritarian Marxist socialists, the second from the democratic socialists like the original *étatist* Fabians, the third from the new Fabian market socialists, the fourth from the anti-socialist Social Market Democrats, the fifth from the new, politically Whiggish rather than High Tory, Conservatives who see that the market has a strong case but are beset by doubts.

The Marxist critique is historically the most tenacious but the least enlightening because it is impervious to argument or evidence. It has periodically been refined to jettison its least convincing elements, but is basically the same as formulated by Marx and Engels in the mid-nineteenth century.

The second assault is the general running criticism of capitalism over a century since the Fabians were established in the 1880s to argue that the inefficient or unjust market should be replaced by the more efficient or more just state in the central government and its organs in local government.

The third group is the new Fabian market socialist, intellectually more sophisticated because newly based on an effort to understand the case for pricing and competition in the market. Its origins lie in the 1930s, as related in chapter 6, but interest in it was suspended after the Second World War in the Fabian-Keynesian-Beveridge consensus on the use of the state to replace the market in industry, welfare and government direction or regulation of the economy. Its revival in recent years followed the rehabilitation of the classical liberal philosophy of the market, especially by the IEA, which promoted its presentation in modern dress by several hundred economists, political scientists and historians. In the last ten years it has become evident under the Thatcher Governments that the market can be restored where socialists had confidently predicted that it had disappeared for ever. In the last five years Gorbachev has in effect, though not candidly, finally accepted that the markets developed by the pre-Revolutionary capitalists and the Leninist capitalists of 1922–8 would, after all, have to be re-created and further developed. And if the USSR has finally accepted capitalism, its satellites and satraps could hardly remain far behind.

The fourth group is that of the non-socialist or anti-socialist academics and politicians who have advocated the social market in the Social Democratic Party and its think-tank the Social Democratic Foundation.

The fifth group of criticism, with doubts and anxieties about the market, is possibly doing the most harm to capitalism because it comes from political Conservatives supposedly favourable to capitalism.

The Perennial Marxist Prophecy of Collapse

A central argument in the intellectual assault on capitalism from socialist (especially Marxist) critics is that it suffers from incurable contradictions that will in the end precipitate its final disintegration and collapse. Marxist teaching is, it seems, hastening an inevitable development.

"The contradictions of capitalism" are a favoured and recurrent theme in the numerous periodicals of socialist writing and in the varied forms of socialist teaching. It continues decade after decade despite the historical record of the advance of capitalism, most recently in the very countries of Eastern Europe and the Far East where it was violently displaced by Marxist socialism.

The Marxist interpretation of history is an act of faith immune to reason; it is endlessly repeated despite living evidence that it fails to explain history. A recent version is dutifully repeated in *The New Palgrave Dictionary of Economics* as though the world had stood still since the first volume of *Das Kapital* in 1867. There can be a contradiction, explains Andrew Glyn in "contradictions in capitalism" for students (the supposed typical reader), between economic organization and its capacity to develop productive potential. Such a contradiction between ownership or control ("the relations of production" in Marxist jargon) and productive potential ("the forces of production") requires a transformation of the economic system "through some mechanism or other." (The vagueness suggests either scholarly reticence or dialectical bewilderment.) When the rigidities of feudalism impeded economic expansion it had to give way to production for the market.[1]

If this is what Marx meant, Marxism is common sense. Unfortunately Marx then leapt a million miles in logic: since capitalism could not proceed "beyond a certain stage," it would be superseded by socialism. This is the celebrated "contradiction" discovered by Marx. But its explanation was buried treasure not so far unearthed. Marxist socialists have been vainly hunting for it ever since. Their failure to find it leaves them undaunted.

The world has not changed as Marx thought; his simple error of projecting into the undefined future of the twentieth century what he saw in the passing events of the mid-nineteenth century leaves Marxists undismayed. They have only now discovered (chapter 3) that the structure of industry has developed differently, from large-scale Fordism to smaller-scale "post-Fordist" units under the influence of rapid technological change, which Marx could not have foreseen (not least the information technology such as in the awesome word processor on which I am "writing" these pages).

But Marxism remains the tablets of stone, and it is impossible finally to disprove it. It will go on being taught as long as the state finances its teaching in universities, and beyond, because it is holy secular scripture that does not require the proof of evidence. The virtual rejection of Marxism by the practising political Marxists of Russia and China and the theoretical Eurocommunists of Italy and other countries is explained away. The remaining

1. Andrew Glyn, in John Eatwell, Murray Milgate and Peter Newman (eds.), *The New Palgrave Dictionary of Economics*, Macmillan, 1987, vol. 1, p. 638.

Marxists in British and other universities, who appear undaunted in *The New Palgrave Dictionary* and elsewhere, have convinced themselves that capitalism is not only inefficient and unjust but also immoral; it must therefore collapse sometime. One day they may emerge as prophets vindicated. It is another of the imponderable externalities that live on because "You never know." The communist state may yet come to pass in the twenty-first or twenty-second or twenty-third century, when supply outruns demand, scarcity is abolished, humans turn into saints, and the millennium has finally arrived.

In the meantime the peoples of the gradually improving capitalist countries, now joined by the peoples of the stagnant declining socialist countries who have abandoned hope in socialism (the latest seem to be the Khmer Rouge in their Thailand refuge), will continue with the task of making the most of their lives under the very imperfect but historically more promising system of capitalism.

The Democratic Socialist Anxieties

The reservations and doubts of non-Marxist democratic socialists represented in the Fabian tradition who still wish to replace the market by the state are distinct from the intellectually more substantial approach of those who would newly welcome the market: the market socialists who refer to themselves as Fabians (although they differ root and branch from the historical anti-market Fabians), and the social market academics and politicians in the Social Democratic Party. Both have not only gone far, although some not far enough, to understand the market; they have also accepted it to the extent of wishing to incorporate it into their thinking and into the institutions they are devising for what the new market Fabians still call socialism and the Social Democrats, who have rejected socialism, call the social market or social democracy.

The old and new Fabians face ironic predicaments, and their political links are confusing. The old anti-market Fabians remain with the traditional condemnations of capitalism; the new market Fabians are conceiving a new kind of socialism with the tools of capitalism. In reaching out to the devices of capitalism the new market Fabians may not wish to desert the anti-market Fabians who have yet to understand that the socialism for which they have yearned cannot be constructed by the tools they have hitherto employed—nationalization or public regulation through the political process. Politically the old and the new Fabians now seem to cohabit precariously in the Labour

Party, which the new Fabians represent as potentially better at using the market than their Conservative opponents. The old Fabians derided the market until the 1987 General Election and continue to resist the acceptance of the market as Labour policy. Morally the Labour politicians who have finally had to accept the market must downgrade the capitalist institutions they are having to advocate and upgrade the socialist values they claim to safeguard. In the process they must appear holier than thou: their intellectuals must preserve the trust of their followers by condemning the liberal market intellectuals whose writings they once belittled, and their politicians must question the competence of the political Conservatives in using the market they now accept.

The long-standing criticisms of anti-market Fabians and democratic (non-Marxist) socialists were and remain four: first, capitalism is unstable—it fluctuates between extremes of high inflation and high unemployment, and sometimes combines both; second, it is inefficient because of monopoly; third, it is unjust because the market produces wide inequality in incomes and wealth; fourth, it degrades the environment because the market cannot take account of the external effects of private bargains in commercial trading.

The liberal reply does not deny that capitalism has weaknesses. The capitalist market sometimes displays faults in all four categories. But the choice of mankind, in Eastern as well as Western Europe, in Europe as well as Asia, and in all continents is not between imperfect capitalism and perfect socialism. It is between imperfect capitalism and one or other variety of imperfect socialism, from conventional state socialism to the newer forms of market or supply-side socialism, all of which are more imperfect than imperfect capitalism because they make unnecessary use of the state.

All four criticisms of capitalism are defective (below), but there are also general rebuttals in principle.

The general liberal reply to the Fabian-socialist criticisms of capitalism is threefold. First, capitalism shares some faults with socialism which socialists ignore, but capitalism is self-correcting to a far higher degree than socialism, not least because it discusses its unemployment and inflation and its other faults openly and endlessly, in marked contrast with the secretiveness of socialist societies. Official statistics can be manipulated by government under capitalism, but there is far more scope for suppression, and therefore less likelihood of self-correction, under socialism because there are many more official statistics.

Second, some faults of capitalism which are special to it are a price worth paying for its massive advantages, not least in living standards and liberty, over socialism. Its main fault is that it is often slower in adapting itself to changing conditions because decisions are decentralized in contrast with the centralized decisions of socialism, but the advantage in favour of socialism requires the generous assumption that the centralized decisions are better informed, which is doubtful, and politically disinterested, which is questionable.

Third, the capitalist process is very different from the socialist process. Capitalism is organic: it grows by trial and error. Socialism is a political construction: it is more likely to change by political convulsion. This advantage is the obverse of the difference in the rate of change: capitalism may change more slowly, but it changes by small *market* adjustments "at the margin"; socialism is more likely to change in large discontinuous chunks by convulsive *political* decisions, such as the change of control of whole industries in Britain or the destruction of villages in Romania.

The four faults of instability, inefficiency, injustice and insensitivity are common to socialism as well as capitalism. First, the extremes of fluctuations in unemployment and inflation disfigure socialist economies probably even more than capitalist economies. The difficulty in judging comparative capitalist and socialist unemployment and inflation is twofold: political and economic.

Since they have long claimed to conquer unemployment and inflation, socialist systems have stronger political reasons for concealing the full extent of both. No observer can believe that the socialist countries have abolished unemployment or inflation, and both can easily be concealed—unemployment by putting everyone to some kind of "work," whether it adds much to total real (market-valued) output and consumer living standards or not, and inflation can be concealed by fixing prices and silencing transgressors by fines, imprisonment or worse. (Capitalist countries that worship "job creation" at any price are no less guilty of risking economic decline.) The claims of the USSR or its satellites to be free of unemployment and inflation are empty. The more open satellites, such as Yugoslavia, have published statistics that may or may not be authentic.

The capitalist 12, 10 or 8 per cent unemployment in Britain of the late 1980s and early 1990s was a much more realistic estimate of labour not employed because worth less than the value of the output it would add at the margin, except for the unnecessary unemployment caused by restrictive practices in industry and the ill-advised decisions of government on minimum wage legislation, neither of which is the product of capitalism. Around

5–10 per cent is also probably near the proportion of the labour force changing jobs that is required in an economic system moving from old to new demands and technologies in European and world markets.

The second—economic—reason for doubting socialist statistics is more damaging because it is less easily identifiable for some years. When inflation is disguised or suppressed its full extent is difficult to measure. Soviet prices are a mishmash of significant and meaningless indicators of the underlying realities of supply and demand, surpluses or shortages, that free-market prices measure, even if imperfectly, in capitalism. Official statistics of unemployment are no more indicators of the productive use of labour than the 99 per cent turn-out of Soviet electors before the new elections of March 1989 were indicators of their approval of communism. They are certainly less accurate measures than the official (if still imperfect) statistics of capitalist countries reported to the Organization of Economic Cooperation and Development (OECD). In the absence of true measures, and allowing for the confusions of centralized planning, the low standard of living and the vast bureaucracy, the real extent of productive employment in the USSR is probably no more than around 40 per cent of the labour force, and the extent of real unemployment or misemployment or mock employment is therefore about 60 per cent. The 40 per cent of productive employment could then be increased by the productive employment in the very large underground economy—perhaps 15 per cent—leaving the real employment rate at 55 per cent and the real unemployment rate at 45 per cent. The almost 50 per cent unemployment would help to explain and would reflect the low Soviet living standards. If the emerging pre-Revolutionary capitalism or the Lenin NEP capitalism had not been suppressed, Russian living standards might now be not far short of those of the rest of Europe.

The comparable unemployment rates for the milder or semi-socialist economies are also probably higher than their published statistics, although more for the economic reason of "make-work" and other policies that waste labour than for the political reason of wilful suppression or falsification of statistics.

Capitalism suffers from unemployment essentially for two main reasons. First, it allows market forces to reveal the changes in supply and demand, technical progress and social advance, that require people to change their jobs, firms and industries, and often their homes, towns and regions. That is the most fundamental reason for the underlying shifts in employment, and why, in the average UK unemployment figure of 10 per cent, some towns may show 4 per cent and others 20 per cent until people are retrained or move. In some places it may rise to 40, 60 or 80 per cent if workers are discouraged from moving by council housing subsidies, or induced to remain by government social benefits. Second, the political systems in all capitalist countries, some like Switzerland less than others like the United Kingdom until recently, prevent the market from signalling shortages and surplus labour in occupations or regions, or allow producer organizations of firms, professions and trade unions to delay movement of labour from lower-value to higher-value occupations.

Capitalism shows its unemployment, but socialism suppresses it even more. In the most vicious years of Soviet communism, it not only cooked the books but butchered the bookkeepers.

The second charge against capitalism, of inefficiency because of monopoly and restrictive practices, is also partly true but is also partly untrue because much, if not most, monopoly would not persist without government support. A high degree of monopoly is unavoidable, at least for a time, possibly for some years, exceptionally for decades, where large firms can produce at lower costs than small firms. But it is more easily corrected in capitalism than in socialism. Capitalism has developed a structure of anti-monopoly "trust-busting" laws, although, as some economists like Professor Yamey have argued, it may on balance do less good in disciplining monopoly than harm in weakening the internal organic reaction of firms to changes in markets. "Liberal economists . . . are wary of state interventions in the working of particular markets, however well-intentioned. . . ."[2] Obsessive "fussing" about the imperfections of markets—like the hypochondriac who reacts to every change of body temperature—has produced cures that may be worse than the disease. It is a practice that suits politicians who wish to be seen actively taking action and bureaucrats whose empire is thus enlarged. (The proposal to reduce the number of "tied houses" owned by brewers is a typical technocratic reaction from "trust-busters"; the market solution would be to relax the licensing laws so that the compunction to own them would be reduced.)

But socialism enthrones monopoly as an instrument of government. It is called by other names—"public ownership" has been the favourite until the recent and equally question-begging "social ownership"—but it replaces what could have been a choice of several or many private competing suppliers by one dominant public or social supplier. Its power to exploit the citizen

2. B. S. Yamey, "The new anti-trust economics," in *The Unfinished Agenda,* Institute of Economic Affairs, 1986, p. 77.

has been concealed by describing it as public or social, and by the socialist claim to make it accountable to the citizen by enabling him to participate in its control through the indirect manipulable easily evaded signals of the ballot box or by the latest refuge of the socialist mind (in all parties), "active citizenship"—a recipe for all the ills of the political process. The virtue of the market is that the consumer can compare alternative goods and services and test them by trial. The vain public service political substitutes for the real power of the common man and woman to try alternative suppliers and reject the unsatisfactory are being recognized by some socialist academics.[3] Yet the well-worn notions of accountability and participation, raised to new heights of political prominence by Professor Marquand[4] and others, are still not abandoned by the British socialists who claim to be revising Labour Party policies.

There is also some truth in the third charge of injustice. Incomes and wealth under capitalism differ over a wide span from rich to poor. The lives of the people in the East End of London between the wars was meagre. Higher incomes trickled down to them very slowly and they gradually moved to better homes (below), but the extremes of wealth could be disturbing and offensive. The question is whether the cause was capitalism, and if it was, whether it cannot be treated to avoid unnecessarily large differences.

In a capitalist system as it could be, people would move from occupations where earnings were low to occupations where they were high. If they could move, people would not prefer low to high incomes. The higher incomes would pass down the income scale as soon as people moved, and incomes would become less unequal in two ways: wages and salaries in the jobs and regions they left would tend to rise, and those in the jobs and regions they joined would tend to fall until the movement had removed the wider differences. The trickle-down effect would certainly have been faster in freer labour markets than it was with restrictive trade unions, council house subsidies which people cannot take with them when they move (the present-day form of the eighteenth-century Settlement Acts that discouraged movement), regional aid to declining industries and other political measures that have hobbled capitalism. Far from being the cause of undesirable or unjust differences, the market, if it is allowed to work, is the most powerful instrument for equalizing incomes the world has known. The failure of the socialist mind to see this power of the market is puzzling. The reason is probably

3. Julian Le Grand and Saul Estrin (eds.), *Market Socialism*, Clarendon, 1989.
4. David Marquand, *The Unprincipled Society*, Cape, 1988.

a psychological resistance to painful truth. The important questions are: What stops it from working and people from moving?

Not capitalism. Some capitalists in some industries and for some time may want to keep their workers, but the overwhelming long-term underlying interest of the capitalist class is in a mobile labour force that adapts itself to changing techniques, changing equipment and the changing locations where factories, shipyards, coal mines and offices have to be established to keep their costs down and their prices low so that they can win new customers.

The socialist criticism that the market produces unequal incomes is true; it gives higher rewards to people with exceptional abilities in order to attract them to industries where they are scarce. But sooner or later the very movement creates equality by lessening inequalities. Industries are not created for the short run. They are built, factories are erected, money is invested and workers are trained for the long run. Capitalists and investors think not of single years but of decades, and the enterprises that they have built can last centuries. The famous names are legion, and have won fame round the world: from Wedgwood and Spode in china, Barclays and Hoare in banking, Jaeger and Burberry in clothes, Wisden and Lilleywhite in sports, Cadbury and Terry in chocolates, to Whitbread and Guinness in beer, and many more.

It is politicians in the political process, the centre-piece of socialism, who think of single years, or of three or four at the most, not because they are necessarily myopic but because it is the nature of their craft and their profession to require them to tailor their "products"—their policies—to give them the best chance of regaining office and power within the five years of a parliament in Britain. In other countries their term is even shorter: four years in the United States, and three in Australia and elsewhere. Mrs. Thatcher was exceptional when she spoke in 1979 of ten years required for her reforms (they will take much longer). The "short-termism" charged against capitalist investment is another piece of ideological myopia. It is, on the contrary, the so far uneradicated flaw of politics everywhere, including the unnecessary socialist sectors in capitalism. Socialism makes more room for politics than does capitalism. Academics who would elevate politics over the market are putting the people at the mercy of the short term and denying them the security and stability of the long term.

The removal of the mainly political obstacles to the working of the market in capitalism would hasten the rate at which incomes and wealth trickled down from the richer to the poorer. But the performance of capitalism in removing unjustifiable differences must be judged relative to the rate at which incomes and wealth trickled down in the political processes that would dominate a socialist society. The human qualities required to succeed in the political process—the powers to persuade, organize, intrigue and dominate other men and women—are more rare and certainly more difficult to learn than the inherited or acquired abilities of every man and woman to make and exchange goods and services. Politics is the happy hunting ground of the elites; commerce is the world of the common domestic people. Trickling down from the political people to the non-political people is a less certain process than trickling down, and sideways, between non-political commercial people who live by working and by buying and selling one another's products.

The rate of trickle-down in socialism is determined by the people in political power, who would suffer if they lost their control of the rate of trickle-down to growing unrest and popular demand. This is the delicate task of the leaders in the USSR and China who see the necessity for decentralizing economic initiative to boost production. If power is allowed to trickle down too slowly the people become impatient. The result may be the restrained persuasion of a Gorbachev or the guns of a Deng Xiaoping. The "descent" (or rather economic ascent) of the state to the market will have to come in both, but it could be a bumpy ride with a hard landing of civil strife or civil war near the end.

The potential equalizing power of the capitalist market is a more hopeful avenue of thought and action in removing dispensable differences in incomes or wealth than the short-term specifics devised to repair the damage done by the political process. The methods range widely from topping up low incomes, as in reverse (or negative) income tax, which varies inversely with income, to supplying capital bounties, as proposed (for students) by Professor Peacock and Professor Wiseman,[5] or the "poll grant" more recently suggested by Professor Le Grand for people with little or no savings.[6] These proposals, made by liberal and socialist (or market socialist) academics, could be effective ways of reducing the wide differences in income or wealth, and they could conceivably be applied at various stages as well as at the beginning of active life (below). Government has been too slow in adopting such devices.

Yet in the long run they may best be viewed as locking the stable door after the horse has bolted. The primary purpose is to make room for the power of capitalism as it could be to create an egalitarian society based on the natural

5. A. T. Peacock and Jack Wiseman, unpublished paper, University of York, late 1960s.
6. Le Grand and Estrin (eds.), *Market Socialism*, pp. 210–11.

or acquired ability of individuals to enrich one another. That would be a more secure foundation for Marx's "From each according to his labour, to each according to his worth" than the enforced, unnatural and unsustainable equality of socialism.

Inequality in the short run is the result of different kinds of causes in capitalism and socialism, but they are easier to modify in capitalism. In the capitalist market access to goods and services is influenced or determined by differences in income or wealth; in socialism (and no less in socialized industries and services like education and medicine under capitalism) access is influenced or determined by differences in economic, political or social connections, links, influence, personal character or temperament. The essential contrast is between financial power in the commercial markets of capitalism and cultural power (which includes political) in the political worlds of socialism (and the socialized services of capitalism).

The essential strength of capitalism and the weakness of socialism in treating inequality and poverty is that it is easier to correct for undesirable differences in financial power than for differences in cultural power. Differences in money means can be reduced by money payments, at a possible cost in disincentives. Differences in culture are much more difficult to remove, if at all; they require changes in accent, temperament and character, removal of social, occupational and political influence and ultimately the dissolution of family links. Socialism does not remove or neutralize them. The contrary evidence is that socialism exacerbates them—from the *dachas* and privilege shops of Russia to the nepotism and corruption of British local government. The articulate, adroit and literate "political" people extract more than the inarticulate, maladroit and illiterate "domestic" people from the schools, hospitals, transport and other socialized services of Britain. The cultural differences of socialism are relatively incorrigible; the financial differences of capitalism are relatively corrigible.

A difficulty common to both systems is that the labour of some people may not be worth enough to keep them and their families in civilized living. Again there is conflict between the desirable income effect of aid and the unavoidable price effect. Supplying money to people with little or none has to confront the effect of weakening the will to earn it by work. Some people will work for its intrinsic interest, or for its companionship, or for its self-respect; others will not. The human failing of relaxing effort when income is supplied without effort varies widely. This is the embarrassing dilemma in helping the "poor" that the nineteenth century faced but the twentieth century has shirked.

The classical economists sought a solution in the distinction between the deserving and the undeserving poor: the undeserving who had not tried to help themselves were to be treated less well—to be less eligible—than those who had. A century later, in our relatively affluent age, that doctrine strikes us as unnecessarily harsh and inhumane. But the politicians with votes to garner who run the twentieth-century welfare state have tended to make no distinction at all. All were to be treated alike: the "undeserving" who *would not* help themselves as though they were the "deserving" who *could not* help themselves. The insensitivity of equal treatment for unequal people degrades the deserving poor, and makes it difficult to give them more than the undeserving. In recent years the deserving have rebelled against "scroungers" and forced the vote-seeking politicians to be more courageous and honest. People who receive income without earning are to be required by law to show they have tried to earn. Such means to match assistance to resources are aids to both self-respect and justice to others who try to help themselves.

The solution will have to be a compromise between maximizing help and minimizing disincentives. This is not a fault of capitalism but of human nature. On the contrary, the richer and growing capitalist countries can be more tolerant of the scroungers than the poorer and stagnant countries because their fourfold larger national wealth enables them to absorb more easily the effects of "free income" on weakening incentives and flagging production.

There is, not least, some truth in the charge that capitalism is insensitive to the external effects of private bargains in the market. The externalities of noise, air pollution and environmental degradation are becoming more evident in all countries, capitalist and socialist. The effect on regional depopulation of responding to market change in supply and demand is also common to both systems. Cultural continuity can be put at risk. Wales was partly depopulated in the interwar years by the declining coal and steel industries. The Welsh choirs sang less joyously. When I visited the Rhondda Valley in 1937, in a very small three-wheeler Morgan car owned by a brother, I must have been thought rich, the street corners of Llanbradach were occupied by groups of the unemployed; the only men who seemed to be in work were the staff of the Labour Exchange (now job centres). The legacy of the slump of 1929–32 and the new sources of electric power, working through the market, were causing the young people to find work in England. The culture of Wales was being drained. The culprit was not capitalism but social and technical change.

The socialist alternative cannot contract out of a changing world. It makes adaptation to it more arbitrary. The political process has now replaced or complemented the market in changing the industrial structure. In 1989 Wales had an energetic Conservative Minister who extracted more in regional aid than other regions from the Treasury and the taxpayer. With 6 per cent of the population Wales has been drawing some 20 per cent of funds to regenerate its industry. Scotland has similarly been subsidized by political exertion and influence on government.

These are the choices; both are imperfect second bests. The Welsh and the Scots can depend either on the market or on politicians to provide their incomes. Neither source is certain or secure for all time. The market is a hard taskmaster; the Welsh (and others) must either change their products or move their homes. The Scots have lost many of their engineers, accountants and actuaries. The politician may seem easier to influence, but not for ever: he may be gone in a few years and have changed from a benefactor with other people's money to a defeated legislator rejoining the queue as a political supplicant for votes. The people of Wales, Scotland, England and everywhere else must decide which is the more secure: to work for the consumer who wants their products and will pay for them, or to importune the politician who wants their votes and will sooner or later lose the power to "pay" for them with subsidies, regional aid or the other *douceurs* and bribes of the political process.

Here as elsewhere it is fruitless to compare the imperfect market with a perfect political process. The market reflects underlying changes in supply and demand among the citizens. The political process reflects a wide range of influences from short-term objectives in vote winning by power-seeking politicians to long-term objectives in reforming society by conviction politicians, but who must also indulge in "short-termism" to regain power at the succeeding General Election if they are to continue their work.

The ultimate choice is between the commercial society of the market which pays ordinary people for creating satisfactions for other ordinary (but permanent) people, or the political society of government which "pays" politically endowed people for persuading a relative handful of (temporary) politically skilled people in government to distribute bounties.

The Market Socialist Synthesis

Two schools of academic and political thinking generally critical of capitalism but anxious to use the market have entered the intellectual debate: the new market Fabians who now claim the market for socialism, and the advocates of the social market who offer a new combination of the capitalist market for its efficiency and social (collective) controls to ensure that it serves social purposes. The latest version of their thinking appeared in mid-1989.

The new market Fabians amplified their articles in the special issue of *The New Statesman* in March 1987 into a book of essays[7] by Professor Le Grand of the University of Bristol (economist), Dr. Saul Estrin of the LSE (economist), Professor Plant (political scientist), Professor Peter Abell of the University of Surrey (sociologist), David Miller of Oxford (political scientist) and David Winter of Bristol (economist). Professor Robert Skidelsky, political scientist at the University of Warwick, author of the biography of Keynes and adviser to the Social Democratic Party, wrote the first paper, entitled "The social market economy," for the Social Market Foundation, the think-tank of the Social Democratic Party.

The new Fabians hoped to decouple markets from capitalism and to end a century of socialist teaching by coupling markets with socialism to serve socialist aims. To perform this intellectual and practical task, they intended "to start the radical reorientation of socialist thinking required by a proper understanding of market socialism."[8] This is engaging candour proper in scholars. After teaching and practising false doctrine for over a century, socialism is turning a new leaf, and these six young or middle-aged scholars were to be its handmaidens.

Their efforts are not the first attempt of socialists to embrace the market. The discussions of the best of them in the 1930s, Evan Durbin and Hugh Gaitskell, and the continuing running debate between other market socialists such as Oskar Lange and Alec Nove with Hayek and other liberals into the 1980s were recounted in chapter 5.

To people interested only or mainly in new ideas, this long anti-market cul-de-sac in socialist thinking may be unimportant history. What matters in political economy is the new idea. Off with the old (and wrong), and on with the new (and hopefully right this time). But to observers who have spent a lifetime interested in the interaction between ideas and the events of the real world, searching to replace wrong ideas with better ideas, and studying the power of ideas, even if wrong, to influence the policies of the politicians and therefore the lives of the common people, the uninhibited acceptance of the market by Fabian socialist academics who rejected it until the 1980s is almost apocalyptic. As they are influencing the Labour Party's shift, at least on paper, from the state to the market, even belatedly

7. Le Grand and Estrin (eds.), *Market Socialism.*
8. Ibid., p. 1.

after the pragmatic *realpolitik* of the Soviet leader Gorbachev, the new prospect is of a British parliamentary system in which power alternates between two market-oriented parties. Whether this is also the probable reality is more doubtful.

The history of the long love-hate relationship between socialism and the market is obscure. In the early IEA journal *Economic Age* Ray Fletcher, the well-informed former socialist writer, leader writer in the left-wing *Tribune* and MP, said that hostility to the market was not a necessary part of socialist doctrine. Perhaps the expulsion of the market was temporary, although [it lasted] for nearly 60 years between Lenin's NEP which outlived him until 1928 and Gorbachev's reconstruction (*perestroika*) in 1985. In the early 1970s two former Labour Cabinet Ministers who came to talk at the IEA were asked at what stage in the history of socialist thinking it had discarded the market. One asked the other to reply. He did not know either. But Lenin used markets to save socialism, and if he had lived after 1924 there is no knowing how long they would have lasted. Trotsky said in 1924 that the market would be found essential for socialism. The truth seems to be, as the incisive Marxist sociologist Professor Stuart Hall of the Open University has accused the early Fabians, that it was the middle-class intellectuals Sidney and Beatrice Webb, George Bernard Shaw and H. G. Wells who had tied socialism to the chariot wheels of the state and banished the market from British socialist thinking for a century. Perhaps Professor Plant, Professor Le Grand and their confrères will help to undo the harm of their forebears.

The new Fabians in *Market Socialism* provide the most refined and sophisticated thinking on methods to harness the market in creating a socialist society that they claim could be "simultaneously egalitarian, non-exploitative, efficient, and free. . . ."[9] They do not entirely agree among themselves. They sing the praises of the market and repeat much the same virtues as liberals have described over the years. Their arguments seem to be directed pointedly at socialists to mend the errors of the decades and abandon simplistic criticisms of the market, rather than at liberals whom their forebears had condemned for advocating the market. But for the remaining defects of the market—its externalities, the monopolies arising from economies of large-scale production (an outdated theme discarded by the Marxist recognition of the passing of Fordism), the imbalance of information between producers and consumers—they look to a redefini-

9. Ibid., p. 24.

tion of property rights in various forms of worker management or self-management, although, in the end, to the state rather than to the market.

Their familiar criticisms of capitalism are based on capitalism as it has been, at its worst, not as it could be, at its best. The new kind of socialism they present, and urge on the Labour Party, is based first on conjecture or hypothetical construction and second on isolated examples in Yugoslavia and other countries, including, surprisingly, the United States, the high noon of capitalism.

If it is permissible for political analysts concerned to uncover error and discover truth to argue for a socialism that does not exist, may prove impracticable and would be opposed by the trade union vested interests that finance the politicians and offend the literati urged to adopt it (David Edgar and Anthony Barnett among many others in numerous writings), it is impermissible to condemn capitalism for its past errors without considering whether they are inevitable or removable. This is the conventional, and by now discredited, contrast of socialism as it could be, with its warts (or cancers) removed by unspecified surgery, with capitalism as it has been, with its full complement of imperfections and failures.

"Full-blooded capitalism is unattractive because it exploits labour through its monopoly of employment and . . . consumers through monopolizing goods markets."[10] This is hardly a description of capitalism as it is becoming, with large-scale Fordist monopolies yielding to medium-sized or small-scale post-Fordist enterprise that can be exploited by large-scale monopolies of trade unions. Nor can capitalist firms exploit consumers in competitive markets. If the solution of worker management is efficient because it satisfies workers as employees as well as owners, it will emerge in largely capitalist countries, as it has done in France, Italy and Spain. Yet the market socialists have correctly identified the solution in the United States, the mightiest capitalist country in the world: the private ownership of equity (risk-bearing) shares as the way to avoid the myopic concentration on current pay and consequent neglect of investment for the future that is a common failing of Yugoslav and other worker-managed cooperatives in public ownership.

The development in the United States would also indicate the failing of another cul-de-sac of Left thinking—the worker management of so-called industrial democracy, which the socialist President of the European

10. Ibid., p. 23.

Commission, M. Jacques Delors, has been urging on Europe. Here as elsewhere the solution is capitalist ownership, with its indispensable and fortifying structure of incentives, rather than the socialist method of voting (and lobbying, and rule by majority, and the rest) that will best reconcile productivity with individuality in ownership. If self-management is efficient because it satisfies workers as consumers as well as employees, and more efficient than the division of labour between workers paid by wages or salaries and risk-bearing owners paid by dividends (when there are profits), it will emerge and spread in capitalism more securely because it satisfies consumers of its goods and services in the market more than it satisfies politicians for the power it gives them in the political process.

There is a surprising error in the market socialist analysis that suggests difficulty in escaping from established socialist thinking. The new Fabians urge "a society where power is more evenly distributed between . . . the interests of owners of capital, of workers, and of consumers . . . with none taking automatic priority."[11] This is an echo of the Marxist division of society into "classes." The simplistic Marxist world of the early capitalist decades has changed into a world in which capitalists are ambivalent about capitalism, workers are becoming capitalists and both are consumers. The significant division is not between groups or classes of different individuals but between the interests of producers and consumers *in the same human being.*

The ultimate division that has to be reconciled is that between man as producer (capitalist or worker, or increasingly both when workers own capital) and *himself* as consumer. And there can be no doubt which must come first. Men do not consume in order to produce—create jobs; they produce in order to enjoy—consume—the food, clothing, shelter, comforts, amenities and luxuries they want to make life tolerable, enjoyable and civilized. A man does not write a book because he is given a word processor; he secures a word processor because he wants to write the book. The task is to devise institutions, or to allow institutions to emerge, that firmly put the interests of the individual as *consumer* above his interests as *producer.* Consumer dominance is the essential for the good society; the continuing socialist hope that the state can capture the market and use it to reconcile consumer, producer and evidently other interests is the continuing Achilles' heel of market socialism.

If this precedence of consumption over production is not arranged, or if

11. Ibid.

it is not allowed to emerge, the individual will be severely tempted into the short-sighted and self-destructive course of putting them the other way round. He will erect barriers to protect his job and/or his investment in "his" industry or occupation. That is what socialism enables, and complaisant government in capitalism permits, landowners and farmers, coal miners and railway workers, doctors and lawyers, teachers and dockers and many other groups to do that see their interests as producers before their interests as consumers. If the anxiety about continuity, custom and tradition emphasized by socialists and High Tories allows that elemental anarchy of producer dominance to continue, society will resist improvement and change, the economy will seize up and slow down, society will stagnate, living standards will fall and the life of man, as envisaged in *The Leviathan* of Thomas Hobbes, will become, if not "solitary," certainly "poor, nasty, brutish and short."

The glory of capitalism is that, more than any other system known to history, it uses the only mechanism that can put man's interest as consumer above his interest as producer. Where capitalism performs this achievement imperfectly, as it often does, it holds the potential to perform it better. The obstacle, so far, remains the political process. All other systems that the world has known—feudalism, mercantilism, syndicalism (to which worker management could degenerate), corporatism, municipal socialism, state socialism—whatever their claims, tend to put producer before consumer interests. The market has been imperfect, but many of its omissions and excesses have not been inherent; they have been the consequences of government failure to allow it to give its best results. The market is often a hard taskmaster, but without it, or if it is regulated to suit the myopic politicians or the leisurely pace of complacent traditionalists, it is the common people, especially the poorest, who suffer. The well-off in industry, academia, the arts or in politics may prefer modulated change; the poor are raised by the power and pace of the market.

The socialist denial of personal property in equity risk-bearing shares, not only in the firm that employs him but also in other enterprises in the economy, would remove the personal incentives and inducements that make the spreading capitalist private property market both productive and the safeguard of liberty. If new forms of ownership are more effective in producing this combination, they will emerge under capitalism; if the political process forces them into being, they become political instruments of untested ideology, and their effectiveness is problematic.

The failure of worker management in Yugoslavia is difficult to reconcile with the new arguments of the market socialists. The failure is attested by the well-informed papers of the Centre for Research into Communist Economies directed by the Yugoslav economist Dr. Ljubo Sirc, formerly of Glasgow University.

The most refined socialist thinking on property and property rights has been coming from Raymond Plant, who has emerged as the leading and most stimulating academic in the market socialist school. Two strands of argument emerge from his latest writings. First, he recognizes more than others on the Left that the long socialist opposition to the market is fruitless, but he argues that the "negative" or "basic" civil and political liberties of capitalism are insufficient without the "positive" or "social" rights to the resources that make them effective—income, health, social security and education.[12] Second, he acknowledges that the conventional communal values of socialism—community, fraternity, social justice, economic equality—have been gradually but relentlessly replaced by the individualistic values of personal family advancement and private initiatives in all kinds of ways as the solidarity of the organizations linked with working life—the factory, mine, or shipyard, the trade union, the neighbourhood, the mining village—are themselves replaced by the smaller industrial units, the small-scale personal services, the self-employment, part-time employment, temporary employment and the computer-linked domestic units generated by the unprecedented post-war technological revolution unforeseen by Marx but amply accommodated by capitalism.

He suggests that market socialism is "the most serious intellectual attempt" to "come to terms" with this revolution. It differs from the neo-liberal approach to markets (as in this book) because it does not accept the existing structure of property rights, with its very unequal distribution of income and wealth, as final. Neo-liberals argue for the prevailing inequality of resources either because they have been justly acquired, and enforced government redistribution would therefore be unjust, or because the existing owners are the most likely to make the best use of them for all. A new argument that strengthens the neo-liberal approach has been added by Professor Israel Kirzner: that since new products and resources are additions to the existing stocks created by the discovery of alert entrepreneurial individuals, the moral rule of "finders-keepers" can be applied to the justice of distribution

12. Raymond Plant, "The market: needs, rights and morality," *New Statesman,* 6 March 1987; Kenneth Hoover and Raymond Plant, *Conservative Capitalism in Britain and the United States,* Routledge, 1989, and other writings.

in capitalism.[13] In contrast, market socialists reply first that it is difficult or impossible to justify the widely unequal distribution of resources, and second that resources are unlikely to trickle down to reach people with less or little. Professor Plant suggests that the movements in earnings and household income in recent years show that the trickle-down mechanism is not working as defenders of the free market hope. . . .[14]

Liberals (or neo-liberals) have pondered these possible weaknesses of capitalism and debated them with socialists over many decades. The solutions to both tasks require compromises because of the two unavoidable obstacles that have so far defied solution. First, the persistent deferment of superabundance leaves human nature requiring incentives; second, political institutions are defective instruments for translating the will of the people into their everyday lives. Marx, Engels and Lenin were wishful thinking, fantasizing and premature about the abolition of scarcity. The Marxist vision of superabundance still distracts attention from improving the world in which the tasks are difficult to solve precisely because of the persistence of scarcity. Mises, Hayek, Friedman, Stigler, Alchian, Coase, Robbins and the liberal school have been aware of the imperfections of the market, and Buchanan, Tullock, Peacock, Bernholz, Frey and the school of public choice have been realistic about the imperfections of politics. That is why the market liberals and the economists of politics have been more productive of possible solutions.

In my student days the socialists argued, in an early version of Raymond Plant's distinction between basic and social rights, that political freedom was insufficient without economic (or social) security. Professor Harold Laski had a telling phrase about the poor who were free to enter the Ritz. Political freedoms, they said, were useless without economic or social security that only government could provide. Their doubts mounted when they saw Hitler destroy political liberties, although they did not then understand, as some market socialists do now, that political liberties require the economic liberties—to publish, meet and discuss—that only the market can create. Yet the Laski metaphor was the basis of the case for the welfare state. There is little doubt that the socialist state can ensure equality of access to welfare more expeditiously than the capitalist market. But the false contrast conceals dangers. Socialism as we have known it does not work as socialists have long claimed that it would. Capitalism could have developed better

13. Israel M. Kirzner, *Discovery, Capitalism, and Distributive Justice*, Blackwell, 1989.

14. Hoover and Plant, *Conservative Capitalism*, pp. 263–8.

access to welfare by the poor if it had not been obstructed by the political process. Four dangers are overlooked by the market socialists.

First, socialism does not bring more justice in access to resources; it replaces financial obstacles by cultural obstacles. Undesirable financial obstacles, as argued above, can be remedied more easily than cultural obstacles. This ironic incurable socialist prejudice against the uninfluential is rarely discussed in the socialist literature.

Second, resources can trickle down more slowly but more securely under capitalism than under socialism, and they raise living standards higher than in socialism. The refugees from Tsarist Russia who came to the East End of London after the Russo-Japanese War of 1905 started in starkest poverty, survived the First World War and the slump of 1929–33, and by hard work and individual effort began to move to the inner suburbs of Hackney in the 1920s and the outer suburbs of Highgate, Hampstead, Finchley and beyond in the 1950s. If the trickle-down process is accelerated by the state, and equality in access to resources is pursued directly by government, the danger is that it justifies and generates increasing coercion to approach its objective. The equalization of the market is usually slower than the state could be, but it is realized without the suppression of individual liberties. The economic or social security urged by socialists in the 1930s has not, even where attained to a degree, secured the basic political freedoms that were Laski's objective, but often lost them in the process of increasing the powers of the state. From politically democratic Sweden to the politically authoritarian USSR, security has required a shift of choice and power from individuals to government. Nor has political democracy in Sweden ensured liberty in the intimate elements of everyday living in education, medicine, pensions or other forms of social security.

Third, market socialism, although it would make more use of the market than state socialism, would make less use of it than imperfect capitalism as it had been, and still less than capitalism as it could be: it would therefore have a much larger element of public property, which means politically-controlled government property. But public property loses much of the effectiveness of private property because it denies the owner of public property the decisive rights—of use, hiring, leasing, sale or other disposal—that make private property the powerful incentive to its efficient use. As the Soviet planners are discovering, leasing state property is not enough. A man wants to pass property he has improved to his family.

Fourth, liberals have long known the advantages of diminishing the inequalities in the ownership of property. ("Inequality" is another pejorative word exploited by the Left. It implies injustice. But it turns logic on its head. Equality between people with unequal talents or requirements is injustice. Professor Bauer suggests "difference" as the more accurate term.) My first introduction to politics was in 1938 by my teachers, Professor Arnold Plant and Professor Lionel Robbins, in the Liberal Party Committee on Ownership for All. It dealt with inheritance, monopoly, patents and other avoidable causes of undesirable differences in ownership of property. Its Chairman, Elliott Dodds, who edited *The Huddersfield Examiner,* liked to quote the Yorkshire saying that muck was good only when spread. The Liberals urged the Rignano (an Italian economist) proposal for the taxation of legacies inherited rather than estates bequeathed to heirs to encourage the spread of ownership. In this and other ways it anticipated by half a century Jeremy Waldron, Professor of Law at the University of California at Berkeley, whose extensive study[15] approvingly quotes the nineteenth-century philosopher, Hegel: "everyone must have property." He concludes: "Just as right-based argument for free speech [on the ground that it is ethically desirable for all] establishes a duty to see to it that everyone can speak freely," so the argument for private property based on the notion of general rights, that if private property is desirable it is also desirable for all, likewise ethically "establishes a duty to see to it that everyone becomes a property owner." Moreover, he adds, "It is in effect an argument against inequality and in favour of what has been called 'a property-owning democracy.'"[16]

This is a legalistic confusion of reason from a student of the American egalitarian Professor Ronald Dworkin. The right to free speech is not comparable with the right to property. Free speech is easy to enact; it is a public good that is non-rival: more for some people does not reduce the supply for others. The right to private property is very much a private good: more for some usually means less for others (although it may mean more both for the owner and for others by reducing prices if it induces higher productivity). It is therefore a very different task to "see to it"—another coercive power for the state—that all are made owners. Redistributing it by coercive law may impair incentives and reduce the total amount of property. Moreover, free speech is a legal right that may remain fallow but cannot be exchanged; private property can be consumed by being sold or exchanged for immediate income. Individuals would differ widely in their preferences between present and future income, and for human reasons: a person in poor health,

15. Jeremy Waldron, *The Right to Private Property,* Oxford University Press, 1988.
16. Ibid., p. 4.

or with a husband or wife or child in poor health, might prefer current income to make their lives comfortable while they survive. If they, and many others, dispose of their property, they would require periodic topping up at the beginning of the laps in the race of life. Professor Le Grand's interesting proposal for "poll grants" would provide a start in life for people without other means. If they were distributed in ten-year or five-year laps, the rate of disposal or exchange of the poll grants for current income would accelerate. This is the price effect of state income distribution that could disrupt the project and require restrictions on the right to disposal, rather like the time restriction on the resale of council houses by former tenants.

Four methods of dispersing private ownership are proposed by Raymond Plant in which "the state, rather than the market, has a central role to play":[17] individual dispersal by private shares in the employing firm or similar means, state leasing of capital to worker-owned cooperatives, a negative capital tax (like the negative income tax varying inversely with earnings) and, in welfare services, devices such as vouchers for schools and child care. If they were practicable, they might equalize capital ownership more quickly than the capitalist market, although still expose the individual to the vagaries of political chance. Apart from the other doubts, the question is whether they would be operated in the real world in the way that the scholar envisages. The study of the economics of politics suggests otherwise.

If workers acquire equity shares in the employing firm on the same scale as shares bought by shareholders, the workers become "capitalists." If the reform is called "socialism" the term must be redefined: when workers acquire as many shares as shareholders, if not before, the system has become capitalist. If the workers have a surplus of income after personal and household expenditure, they will want to buy shares in other firms and industries. At what stage does socialism become capitalism? State capital, which is taxpayers' money, would presumably have to be leased to workers at a subsidized rate of interest, which opens the proposal to the familiar abuses of the political process. A negative (reverse) capital tax would face the difficulties of disincentives through their price effects. The liberal proposal for education vouchers, long opposed by anti-market socialists but now accepted by market socialists, envisaged their eventual replacement by tax reductions precisely in order to avoid comparable political distortions.

The strength of Raymond Plant's advocacy is that he has abandoned the

17. Raymond Plant, *The Times*, 10 April 1989.

weak socialist arguments, such as their necessity to create solidarity by fostering the socialist values of community spirit or common culture, and concentrated on the supposed superior power of socialism over capitalism in achieving the values of individuality, personal liberties and private property. But these are capitalist values and institutions (chapter 12).

The Social Market Solution

The market is a living organism of millions of people with myriads of constantly changing judgements, likes and dislikes, preferences, wants, "needs" and decisions. It reflects their mistakes, misjudgements and indecisions. It is not always quick or accurate in compensating for its errors, but if it is over-regulated to avoid these errors, it will not produce its best results.

This is the Achilles' heel of the state. Even where it means well, it characteristically overshoots its objectives. Political regulation does not aim at the optimum degree of regulation but at the politically most possible or politically most expedient. It would therefore end in over-regulation, as it is now doing in financial transactions, and tends to do everywhere else. The state is driven by political expediency to aim at standards that are too high, which raise costs unnecessarily, make industry inflexible and put services beyond the reach of people with the lowest incomes.

This is the ultimate choice between political systems. The market may sometimes aim too low; the state usually aims too high. The market may regulate or restrain too little, the state too much. There are costs and risks in both undershooting and overshooting. But since the state is less likely to correct its overshooting than the market its undershooting, because the state is less controlled by the market, except in the very long run, than the market by the state, the advantage again lies with the risks of capitalism rather than with the risks of socialism.

The market must be accepted for its strengths at the cost of its imperfections. It is the world's unique generator of wealth without the sacrifice of liberty. It must be accepted as the centre-piece, the prime mover, the motor of a free and prosperous society, reflecting individual wants and the popular will, not as an instrument to be used by a dozen or a score or a few hundred men and women with temporary political power, "drest," said Shakespeare, "in a little brief authority" (*Measure for Measure*). As usual, he understood human nature better than the builders of systems based on the power politics of supposedly saintly politicians.

The failure of the state to correct market failure, but to overcorrect for it because of political expediency (or to undercorrect because of vested interest pressure) is the weakness of many attempts to delimit the ideal functions of government, even in as sophisticated a study as Professor Joseph Stiglitz's *The Economic Role of the State.*[18]

The market cannot be cleansed of its imperfections to the last detail by socialist systems introduced without examining their defects. It must be accepted despite its faults, although many or most are remediable. It is not to be seen, as it still is by market socialists, as a tiger for socialist politicians to catch by the tail in the vain hope that politics will tame and improve it.

The main difference between the market socialists and the social market advocates is illustrated in the very different spirit of the approach to the market by Professor Robert Skidelsky.[19] "The most hopeful political development of recent years is revival of belief in the market system." The market is seen by Professor Skidelsky, the biographer of J. M. Keynes, as in this book, as a political as well as an economic institution, and not perfect but increasingly perfectible: ". . . we turn to the market as a first resort and [to] the government as a last resort, not the other way round." The market is described as "social" because it is the instrument of general benefit, of "social" good: ". . . our first instinct is to use the market, not to override it."

This approach is very different in essence from that in *Market Socialism.*[20] It marks a complete break from the prejudice on the conventional British Left that the market was the engine of monopoly capitalism and had to be captured and disciplined by the well-intentioned, appropriately equipped and saintly staffed state if it was to do any good. But if the market is forced into the life of politics and deployed, in the everyday world of *Realpolitik,* by political decision, with its devices, stratagems, machinations, compromises and corruptions, it will be destroyed. The market socialists now examine it clinically for imperfections and offer ingenious proposals for reforms but, to retain their links with the socialist tradition, they make it the instrument of the political process. The social market advocates, in contrast, want to sustain the market order, if necessary by government, although, unlike the market socialists, they acutely recognize the risks of government failure.

Perfect, benevolent, selfless, far-sighted and incorruptible government may be able to do anything. The danger is that government in the real world

18. Joseph Stiglitz, *The Economic Role of the State,* Blackwell, 1989.

19. Robert Skidelsky, *The Social Market Economy,* The Social Market Foundation, 1989, p. 4.

20. Le Grand and Estrin (eds.), *Market Socialism.*

is imperfect in whatever it may wish to do, even with the best intentions, to protect the market. The unanswered question remains whether it is better to risk the often self-correcting excesses of the market than the less controllable excesses of government. This is the decisive issue discussed in the final chapters.

Political Conservative Doubts

Capitalism and socialism differ in their intellectual, political, financial and emotional support. Socialists (of varying kinds) believe in socialism (of varying kinds); they are generally unapologetic; they are industrious writers, lecturers, persuaders, activists, organizers and conference-goers, movers of motions and dealers in doctrines. Conservatives have generally lacked belief in capitalism, understanding of capitalism and commitment to capitalism. They have long been divided in championing capitalism. They remain divided in the Thatcher Governments, where, to revive seventeenth-century labels in a twentieth-century context, the radical liberal "Whigs" who have rallied to the Thatcher leadership have achieved what may be a temporary supremacy over the conservative paternalistic "Tories" who have risen to office and power by the appeal of the "Whigs" to the prospering working-class vote but who resent their ascendancy.

The "Tories" retain the ironic post-war attitude of the Conservative that state socialism is objectionable unless administered by Conservatives. In the perspective of post-war British history until 1979 the Conservatives have undermined liberal egalitarian class-indifferent capitalism as much as the socialist-oriented Labour Party, and possibly more, by persuading the essentially non-socialist British to accept socialism in the bland forms of public ownership, nationalization, the welfare state and extensive local government for a wide range of services that are in no sense "unavoidably collective functions" ripe for socialist organization.

The Conservative unease and hesitancy about espousing capitalism are encapsulated in the doubt of an intellectually inclined, morally sensitive, liberal "Whig" about de-socializing in the mid-1980s services run by the state. The anxiety was whether it could be argued that services supplied privately by competing firms were generally or necessarily superior: "There are bad private restaurants": the market did not always provide the best possible.

The case for capitalism and its markets over socialism and its political decision-making is not that private services are generally or invariably better than government services. Economic systems are not to be judged by snapshots: they are moving pictures or "kaleidoscopes." There are no doubt, at some times and in some places, "bad" private restaurants; the question is how long they last. There are also expensive private garages, untidy private grocery stores, uncomfortable private hotels and public houses, unpunctual private car-hire firms, undependable private bus and coach services, unhappy private homes for old people, overdisciplined private schools, overbearing private landlords and overcharging private banks.

All this is not a condemnation of capitalism. There are also expensive nationalized hotels, poorly run local authority homes for old people, unpunctual public buses and coaches, unhappy state schools and authoritarian NHS hospitals—and all that is a condemnation of socialism.

The difference, simply but fundamentally, is that capitalism usually offers an escape from its inferior suppliers and socialism does not. Where the escape under capitalism has not been as easy or as general as it could be, it can usually be made easier and more general by removing obstacles erected by government. In socialism it cannot, because escapes would disrupt the system. If there were no bad socialized hotels, old people's homes, transport, housing, schools and the rest, government could have demonstrated their superiority by promoting competing private services and facilitating a choice by remitting taxes topped up by grants to permit verdicts by the consumer. But socialist politicians and academics have not until the twelfth hour been conspicuous in devising ways to welcome the judgement of the market.

Capitalism has markets which offer, or could offer, alternatives and escapes—exits—to other suppliers. Moreover, their very existence prevents "bad restaurants" from lasting long. Capitalism does not even require existing alternative restaurants; the possibility that they will enter the market is usually sufficient to sober and discipline the providers of bad restaurants. But the British restaurants of the war years, essentially socialized institutions supposedly designed to serve the public with good food, were often dispensers of indifferent food indifferently served precisely because they were all the same and the public could not escape to better.

Socialism, until the late 1980s, claimed that alternatives were not necessary because it would ensure high standards—not least in schools—from which no-one would wish to escape. That illusion has had to be abandoned. And a renowned Conservative leader has said the aim was to make the NHS so good that no-one would wish to "go private." That illusion will also have to be abandoned. Yet the further illusion remains in the market socialism devised by the Fabian academics and accepted by the Labour politicians that the state run by socialist government, advised by socialist economists and served by socialist-inclined bureaucrats (though often Conservative voters), knows where the market (with its exits) should be tolerated and where it should be suppressed. That is the conceit that divides socialists, including High Tories who are socialists in action if not in name, from liberals.

The Triumph of Socialist Faith over Dialectic

The criticisms of capitalism will continue whatever the arguments and evidence that question them.

The latest occasion for the renewal of the Marxist contradictions argument was the financial downturn of October 1987, described as yet another capitalist crisis. The good sense that had newly appeared in the mid-1980s in some socialist journals, notably *Marxism Today* and the *New Statesman*, and that had produced sobering reflections on the third General Election reversal for the Labour Party and the necessity for unpalatable re-appraisal of conventional state socialism in Britain and its former attraction to the working class, gave way to a new wave of euphoria on the eventual demise of capitalism after all. There appeared renewed faith in the validity of the Marxist critique or the eventual triumph of socialist values despite defeat in the argument on institutions, not least the necessity of the market.

Only exceptionally, if ever, did socialist academics, even the most influential like Professors E. J. Hobsbawm of Birkbeck College or John Saville of Hull University, or the most intelligent like Andrew Gamble of Sheffield University or Stuart Hall of the Open University, or the most clear-sighted and courageous intellectual writers like Martin Jacques of *Marxism Today* and John Lloyd of the *New Statesman* and the *Financial Times*, pause to reflect that capitalism had survived despite the history of capitalist crises since the first joyful warning by Friedrich Engels that the financial crisis of the 1840s signalled the end of capitalism. There has been little systematic discussion of the elements in capitalism that had enabled it to surmount its subjection to defective human nature, precarious political institutions, human and natural disaster, wars and slumps, Hitler, Mussolini and Stalin and other afflictions.

The historic recuperative strength of capitalism lies in seven pillars: the human ability to recover after adversity that it liberates, the family it fortifies by refraining from paternalism, the private property it strengthens by law, the ferment of new thought and ideas it promotes by political liberty, the encouragement of scientific discovery it creates by the prospect of individual gain, the generosity in giving it promotes by low taxation and the ethical teaching that a man's worth shall be judged by his contribution to wealth as valued by his fellows in the market rather than by his political/cultural influence. This is the glory of capitalism we should celebrate.

They are not only the historic strengths of capitalism so far, despite political invasion and socialist assault. They are even more the massive potential for the future when the people, increasingly in Eastern Europe as well as in the West, understand more fully the sources of their well-being and the false gods they have been misled to worship.

There cannot have been a more ironic opposite parallel to the historic and potential inner strengths of capitalism than the failure of socialism over the decades to transform the gifts of nature and human talents, not least in the USSR, into tolerable living standards and a harmonious civil society. The essential argument for capitalism is absent from the literature that debates the relative merits of contending politico-economic systems. The contestants characteristically analyse the strengths of the system they prefer and the weaknesses of the system they reject; they tend to minimize the strengths of the system they reject and the weaknesses of the system they prefer. Social scientists are not only academics, analysts and students of society; they are also citizens, taxpayers, voters and often partisans. It is therefore difficult to identify an economist, a political scientist or a philosopher who has not formed a preference between capitalism and socialism, whose personal sympathies are not engaged, or who is immune from the sense of engagement in an intense debate, perhaps the most momentous of our day, a war of ideas that is shaping the fate of mankind in the prospect of living lives of prosperity or poverty, freedom or coercion, peace or war.

The combination of objective analysis and subjective preference, of methodology and ideology, of scholarship and partisanship in the world's best, or at least best-known, social scientists (with many absentees, including some of the best) is evident from the enormous 4-million-word *New Palgrave Dictionary of Economics* published at the end of 1987 to follow the world-renowned *Palgrave Dictionary of Political Economy* that was in use for almost half a century after its appearance in the 1890s. Many (not all) of the world's most authoritative scholars duly appear as contributors, but they are mostly adherents of one of the two dominant schools of thought. There are some strict neutrals, but also others who hold themselves aloof from the momentous debate, who claim, in the renowned phrase, to be impartial between right and wrong, philosophical eunuchs who withhold their judgement, who pass by on the other side, who would have earned the censure of Arnold Plant as "prigs who say they are impartial."

The original *Dictionary of Political Economy,* the late nineteenth-century name for the social science now called economics, was edited by Inglis Palgrave, then editor of *The Economist* and a brother of Francis Palgrave who compiled the equally long-lived *Golden Treasury of English Verse.* It was revised by Henry Higgs in the 1920s and renamed *Dictionary of Economics.* The 1987 successor was edited by three economists, John Eatwell of Cambridge, Murray Milgate of Harvard and Peter Newman of Johns Hopkins University. Its importance is that it will be regarded as the authentic successor to *Palgrave* although its contents will not be read systematically by subject but will be consulted fragmentarily on isolated topics, mostly by students and other unsophisticated users who will take it as gospel. Its relevance for the argument here is that it illustrates the sympathies, leanings, tendencies or biases of economists and other social scientists who influence political and public opinion as well as intellectual thinking. The tendency of a politician is at least indicated by his party label; the tendencies of academics, as of editors and journalists, are less apparent and their influence is therefore the stronger for good or ill.

The entries on capitalism and socialism illustrate the approach of influential economists to their subject. The 6,000-word entry on capitalism was written by a hostile critic, Robert L. Heilbroner of the New School for Social Research in New York, a centre of socialist-inclined study and teaching. This may have been an interesting idea of the editors, who declared their purpose to be "vigorous" rather than "bland" writing to stimulate the student. Rather surprisingly, the 9,500-word entry on socialism was written not by a critic of socialism, or perhaps a sceptic, but by the sympathetic Professor Nove of Glasgow University. Both Heilbroner and Nove judged capitalism by its known shortcomings and socialism by its unrealized promises, in short by their known or potential weaknesses and not by their capacity to remove them, itself a central characteristic of the capitalist system.

The dominant weight of this approach has been to create the impression that capitalism and socialism can be judged (this is the methodology part of the argument) and should be judged (the ideological part) by their strengths and defects, their virtues and vices, their advantages and disadvantages as suggested by reasoning (theory) or demonstrated by historical events (empirical evidence).

The theme of the argument in this book is very different. Theory is essential as a possible explanation of the sequence of cause and result, and empirical evidence is (according to different schools) valuable or essential in establishing a theory or possible explanation as probable (but not certain). Yet the fundamental criterion by which a judgement can be made between capitalism and socialism is not whether reason suggests or history indicates that one is, or has been, superior to the other, but whether their defects are the more easily removable so that their future potential can be gauged.

Weaknesses, defects, shortcomings and excesses will develop with time under both capitalism and socialism. Either they will have been anticipated as a price worth paying for the advantages of the system or they are openly unexpected. Capitalism in the West, and more recently in the Far East, and socialism of varying kinds in a wide range of countries from the USSR through Yugoslavia to China and Cuba, Sweden and Austria have exhibited drawbacks, either anticipated by theory or unrevealed by history. The classical economists of the late eighteenth and early nineteenth centuries who portrayed and foreshadowed the capitalist system of the West as based on decentralized markets responding to consumers did not anticipate the fluctuations of booms and slumps in the pre-war decades. The Marxists and Leninists did not anticipate the privations and coercions that continue in Eastern Europe 70 years after the Russian Revolution. The Maoists did not anticipate the Cultural Revolution or Tiananmen Square. The essential test of the two systems is how well they learn to remove whatever defects emerge, anticipated or unanticipated. The essential difference is that capitalism is largely self-correcting but socialism is not.

Capitalism embraces the self-correcting mechanisms of open discussion in free society to identify error and open competition in free markets to apply the corrections. Socialism in the USSR and its satellites, even East Germany, is only now timidly allowing free society in political democracy. The essential of free markets based on private property is more problematic: when they threaten the power of the political planners and their vested interests they will be obstructed or opposed.

Whether the corrections can be applied without civil commotion or civil war in the 1990s is the unresolved question of socialist doctrine. China seemed to withdraw from civilized society in June 1989. But if socialism in Eastern Europe is to keep pace with capitalism it will have to use free markets, and sooner or later free markets will create demands for free society. That would end the socialist system.

On this crucial test of self-correction, capitalism is the clear victor. When I put this view in an IEA paper in 1980,[21] I did not have in mind, but may have been echoing, the concept of democracy advanced by the philosopher

21. Arthur Seldon, *Corrigible Capitalism, Incorrigible Socialism,* Institute of Economic Affairs, 1980.

Sir Karl Popper.[22] He repeated it 43 years later[23] because, he said, it had been forgotten or misunderstood. Popper argued that the essential difference between democracy and dictatorship is not that democracy is good and dictatorship evil, but that the rule of law in democracy enables the people to rid themselves of bad government but dictatorship deprives the people of that power. The Popper case for democracy is that it can rid itself of evil: it is corrigible.

In this sense the argument for democracy over dictatorship is the argument for capitalism over socialism. The real or supposed defects of capitalism—alternation of inflation and unemployment, simultaneous unemployment and inflation, extremes of wealth and poverty, monopoly and "cut-throat" competition, overcentralization, oppressive bureaucracy, poor schooling, insensitive medical care, slum housing and much else—are not endemic: they are largely the results of overgovernment or mis-government. They can be removed. The real defects of socialism—suppressed unemployment and inflation, widespread privation and injustice, overweening authority, suppression of freedom in economic activity, political rights and cultural life, ingrained nepotism and jobbery and much else—are endemic. They are parts of the system; without them socialism is unworkable.

In the end that is the case for imperfect but perfectible capitalism and the reply to its critics.

22. Karl Popper, *The Open Society and Its Enemies,* Routledge, 1945.

23. Karl Popper, "Popper on democracy: the open society and its enemies," *The Economist,* 23 April 1988.

CHAPTER **10**

The "Vision" of Capitalism

> Berger [in *The Capitalist Revolution*] does not persuade me that the living presence of depraved capitalism is preferable to the vision of democratic socialism. . . .
>
> Robert Lekachman (commendation on the cover of Berger)

> Liberals also should have a Utopia. . . .
>
> F. A. Hayek

In many of the writings on capitalism and socialism the authors, like Professor Lekachman but in more restrained language, have condemned depraved capitalism against their vision of socialism. The more temperate authors of *Market Socialism,* for example, find fault with the capitalist free market and in contrast offer "a blueprint for a society that could be simultaneously egalitarian, non-exploitative, efficient, and free—that is, . . . a socialist society."

No author of writings on capitalism or socialism has judged depraved socialism against a vision of capitalism. Yet the task is easier.

The Socialist and Capitalist "Visions"

Socialists can offer no more than an unknown vision. They are necessarily driven to visions by the unwelcome reality of depraved socialism as we have known it—from the bland incompetence or obsessive inhibitions of the European social democracies to the violence of communism, which it was hoped was passing but re-emerged in Georgia and Peking in June 1989. If the reality of socialism were presentable, they would present it. But their exemplars are defective visions of socialism, and they have been retreating from the claims made for it until the 1980s when they began to acknowledge its defects.

If not literally depraved, the socialism we have known in varying forms has been deficient in the advantages confidently claimed for it for 200 years—whether the liberty, fraternity and equality of the French Revolution or the peace, bread and land of the Leninist Russian and Maoist Chinese Revolutions. Who remembers that the Bolsheviks promised land for the peasants? Instead it was forcibly collectivized, and to survive they have farmed precarious tiny private plots on sufferance. Only 70 years after 1917 has the necessity for private ownership to ensure productivity been recognized in projected 50-year leases, and they will fail unless they extend property rights to sale and family bequest.

The communist countries are no longer presented as late twentieth-century versions of the Webbs' irresponsible vision in 1935 of "a new civilisation" in the USSR of Stalin. It is no longer plausible to claim that they carry the seeds of liberty or prosperity.

Even in the two most presentable exemplars of democratic socialism, Sweden and Austria, there are blemishes of political privilege and personal inhibitions which are too easily brushed aside in the relief of finding at least two small European countries that can be claimed to show that, after all, both political democracy and serviceable living standards have been achieved under socialism. The cost of socialism in Sweden is the spiritual enervation of state-provided social security by the new totalitarians.[1] The cost of socialism in Austria is corporatist collusion between politicians, industrialists and trade union leaders. Neither displays the socialism long promised by socialists. In so far as economic socialism in Sweden and Austria permits political democracy, it is the arena of pressure groups that maintains the fabric of *étatism,* the source of their power. And in so far as socialism in both produces relatively high living standards, it is because they are small boats in a sea of capitalism which provides them with priced benchmarks or "lighthouses" in the world's international markets that prevent economic shipwreck. They depend on the trading ambience of the outside capitalist world. If the Euro-communists like Giorgio Napolitano see the geographically vast but economically blind (and blundering) communist USSR as a parasite on the international markets of the capitalist world, dependent on their competitive costs and prices for information on the real trading value of their products and exports, the little social democracies or democratic socialisms of Sweden and Austria are even more shaped by world

1. Roland Huntford, *The New Totalitarians,* Allen Lane, 1971; *Trouble in Eden: A Comparison of the British and Swedish Economies,* Praeger, 1980.

capitalism, and even further removed from the vision of socialism that is still the intellectual lifebelt of the socialist mind: independent, strong and free, still hopefully taught in the West by academics to students and more cynically by politicians to voters.

The vision of socialism harboured by socialists like Lekachman in the United States and Marxists like Hobsbawm in Britain has been destroyed by argument they have not rebutted and evidence they continue to deny. They may be admired for a faith that sustains them despite "the slings and arrows of outrageous fortune" that have destroyed their hopes. Yet they must accept the criticism that academics of their kind continue to mislead students and politicians who in turn mislead the people by a pretence that would be condemned as immoral, not least by British clerics who echo them, if it were practised by capitalists in the business of selling commercial goods or services.

The vision of socialism, at its best with the maximum of merits and the minimum of defects, therefore necessarily remains in the imagination of the socialists who must conjure it out of the artificial assumptions of selfless human nature and the mirage of unlimited production. At least here, since Marx, they have shown understanding of the two parts of the market, demand and supply. But the vision of socialism not only remains a vision after a century or more of proselytizing; it is never likely to become reality until it resolves the unending circular reasoning in which it is entrapped: that human nature will not become selfless until scarcity is replaced by superabundance, but superabundance will not replace scarcity until human nature becomes selfless. That is the tragic flaw of both Marxist socialism and democratic socialism that neither can escape because, without the market free of political domination that both reject, they cannot reproduce the productivity that removes the economic limitations of scarcity and thereby creates the universal human indifference to its distribution. The socialists who live or have lived under socialism in practice at its most scientific in the USSR and China and in Eastern Europe, who are reluctantly abandoning socialism for capitalism, have learned these truths better than the socialists in the West who persist in their visions with periodic renewals, revisions and new beginnings.

There is no such obstacle with the vision of capitalism. We know how capitalism was developing in Europe, North America and Australasia in the nineteenth century before the doctrines of socialism led government to replace the emerging market in many or most economic activities, not least the welfare services of education and medicine, with a political process that almost destroyed it. We can see how the early forms of capitalism could have been refined by now if the domain of politics had been confined to the "unavoidably collective functions" of government. The exemplars of capitalism as it could have developed if it had not been distorted and misshapen by the politicians of the nineteenth and twentieth centuries are most discernible in America and even more in Switzerland.

The critics of capitalism have persisted in the device of contrasting imperfect capitalism as it is, or has been, with a vision of socialism as it has not so far been, and could not be in the foreseeable future. This is a strong dialectical strategy for both academics and politicians because it cannot be rejected by logic: the Marxist doctrine of the inevitability of capitalist decline may yet be vindicated in the unforeseeable centuries. Until then, while capitalism continues, as they still claim, to stagger from crisis to crisis, the teachers of a socialism to be can devise graphic case studies of market failure. And the expectant practitioners of a further revised, updated and modernized socialism that has never been, as in yet one more effort by the politician-thinker Giles Radice,[2] deploy no lack of example of supposed capitalist failure—from the old staples of inflation or unemployment, monopoly or inefficiency, inequality or poverty, to the newer charges of neglect of the arts, environmental degradation and the destruction of heritage—to contrast with the promise of a new, untried and therefore indestructible socialism after the next General Election.

Yet it is an evasion of historical evidence and of sophisticated reasoning to expect the peoples of the world to act as if a remote possibility is an early probability if only they will add their cross against the right candidate in the ballot box. With still few exceptions, the visionaries of socialism will accept no evidence and no reasoning that doubts their vision. From the theoretical impossibility of rational calculation in a socialist economy demonstrated by Mises in the early 1920s to the rejection of socialism by the communist world in the late 1980s, 65 years of reasoning and evidence against socialism are spurned to maintain the beatific vision. Repeated reversal is met by redefinition or review, with new proposals for state action to cure market shortcomings that the new socialism would exacerbate because the state would enfeeble or emasculate whatever markets it licensed.

This is the act of faith that sustains the intellectual effort long performed by the critics of capitalism to show its contrasts with the alternative of faultless socialism. The familiar *non sequitur,* "capitalism as we have known it, bad; socialism as it could be, good" (or at least better), still permeates most

2. Giles Radice, *Labour's Path to Power: The New Revisionism,* Macmillan, 1989.

socialist writing. The contrast is illogical and unhistorical. It has been admissible for scholars, politicians or observers offended by the abuses or excesses of capitalism to envisage an alternative. It is inadmissible for them to create new socialisms to evade the failure of the old. They are still at fault in failing to analyse capitalist crisis—whether the abuses or excesses were organic and inseparable from the nature of capitalism, or superimposed upon it by political distortion. They invariably maintain that the evils of capitalism are endemic, although they have failed to establish the unavoidable connection, and few on the Left now accept the Marxist argument, less science than assertion, of the inevitability of capitalist collapse. While the British political instrument of socialism, the Labour Party, finally in June 1989, although belatedly after three electoral defeats, accepted the inevitability of the market, the vision of socialism is tenaciously retained by many who cannot accept spiritual as well as intellectual defeat. With honourable exceptions, they will continue to ignore the persistent evidence of failure of socialist practice and sustain their long-held faith in the vision.

Socialist Mirage and Feasible Capitalism

To retain its intellectual credibility and political loyalties, socialism has endured several periods and phases of revisionism over the decades. We witnessed the latest in the late 1980s. Socialism was again redefined and revised. The most fundamental academic attempt was made by Professor Nove[3] to persuade the remaining Marxist believers who thought that socialism could spurn the market that it could survive only with the market. The latest is the more sophisticated attempt to refashion a socialism based on the notion of citizenship, notably by Professor Plant.[4] Both remain strongly dependent on the political process, with little systematic discussion so far of the public choice analysis which indicates that it would emasculate rather than liberate the market.

The alternative to the socialist vision is not a capitalist vision but a reality. It rests on three supports: first, the developments in capitalist history; second, the logic that the peoples everywhere with the liberty to decide would have retained the best of capitalism and abandoned the worst; third, the present-day evidence of capitalist practice.

Hayek has argued that liberals might have been wise to envisage a liberal

3. Alec Nove, *The Economics of Feasible Socialism,* Allen & Unwin, 1983.

4. Raymond Plant, *Citizenship, Rights and Socialism,* Fabian Tract, 1988, and subsequent writings.

Utopia. (The reflection reappears in *The Fatal Conceit.*)[5] Liberals might have been sustained by a vision of the liberal Utopia in their dark days since the last war, and for the many earlier decades when socialism in all but name was espoused by politicians in all parties, Conservative and Liberal as well as Labour. In my student days the socialist argument seemed to carry all before it. And the war itself was quoted as confirmation of the socialist claims of efficiency, equity and humanity in a planned society. But the vision of capitalism has substance without resort to the unsupported and improbable imagination of the socialist flight from reality—the assumption, often implicit in liberal writing as well as explicit in socialist writing, that capitalism as it has been distorted by the political process so far is the only capitalism that could have developed.

It is easy to point to the short 30 or 50 years in the middle of the nineteenth century, perhaps from the 1830s to the 1880s, as the exceptional and fleeting phase of economic liberalism. There is ample debate among historians on the relevance or adequacy or appropriateness of political measures—individual laws, regulations, *ad hoc* decisions. But there are few if any efforts to depict the capitalism that could have developed if political decisions had been designed to strengthen the system in order to preserve its potential advantages for the people rather than to weaken it by serving the immediate purpose of government, or the interests of politicians or the bureaucracy, or sectional pressure groups. A rare exception is by the historian Dr. Stephen Davies of Manchester Polytechnic in a forthcoming work.

This approach raises delicate questions on the nature of democracy, its time horizons, the optimum length of parliaments and the degree to which government serves general rather than sectional interests.

Yet it cannot be supposed that all the political acts that have affected the development of the capitalist system over 200 years have been wise, long-sighted, politically disinterested and designed to maintain and strengthen it. Lord North was hardly as statesmanlike, or as shrewd, as benevolent, as far-sighted, as self-sacrificing or as wise as William Pitt, Castlereagh as Robert Peel, Disraeli as Gladstone, Lloyd George as Asquith, Neville Chamberlain as Winston Churchill ("I have always been a liberal," he said in his last years), Harold Wilson as Alec Douglas-Home, Edward Heath as Margaret Thatcher. Still more, to suppose that they were is to assume that they operated with a political system that enabled them to display and apply these virtues. Yet, whatever their qualities, they had immediate problems of home and overseas

5. F. A. Hayek, *The Fatal Conceit*, Routledge, 1988.

affairs to distract them, differences with colleagues to settle, short-term electoral popularity to weigh. . . .

No politician and no government in the last 200 years has been able, even if that had been the intention, to put as the main purpose of politics the long-term maintenance and strengthening of the economic system of markets that we—increasingly former socialist critics as well as consistent liberal supporters—can now see would have yielded the best long-term results.

Are we to suppose that capitalism was nurtured by government for two centuries? Do politicians always take the required long-term view? Do they always sacrifice their short-term political prospects? Are they always faithful to their promises of serving the public interest? Do they put themselves last after all others? Do they dissolve their empires, and withdraw to their homes and innocent pursuits when they can see that they are doing harm?

The nearest exemplar anticipated and initiated the Industrial and Agrarian Revolutions of the eighteenth century. Sir Robert Walpole entered parliament as a Whig in 1700 at the age of 24. He was the archetype of the early eighteenth-century "Old Whigs" whom Hayek saw as the exemplars for statesmanship and political philosophy. In most of the 40 years of Whig government Walpole dominated English political life as Chancellor of the Exchequer and First Lord of the Treasury from 1721 to 1742. He was an authentic liberal whose practice in government anticipated Adam Smith's teaching. He encouraged overseas commerce (although forced by the Tories to abandon a free trade Bill in 1733), improved the customs and excise by introducing bonded warehouses and reduced the National Debt. Above all the private enclosures of neglected common land of his years were the quintessential market-creating reforms that went far to create the beauties of the English landscape; the private turnpike (toll) roads built the basic road structures that, with three-yearly macadam resurfacing, have largely survived the giant vehicles 250 years later; the private canals deflated transport costs. Not least, Walpole did not aggrandize government by employing men of talent or multiplying legislation in over-active parliaments. But, apart from Gladstone, he was the last of his kind to practise minimal government. His successors, with lucid intervals in periods of emergency, have put politics first.

Certainly no socialist scholar would support such an unhistorical interpretation of history that supposed politicians to be selfless servants of the citizenry. The writings of the critics of capitalism, from Marxist to democratic socialist, are replete with criticism of socialist political leaders. There is no leader of the communist USSR who would be exonerated from blame for the belatedly acknowledged failures of Russian socialism. From Lenin through Stalin to Kosygin and Brezhnev they were charged with "mistakes," a convenient all-embracing euphemism for the gamut of evil from moderate repression to bloody violence. And now even Mikhail Gorbachev, the most civilized and humane of Russian communist leaders, is charged with the "mistake" of proceeding too fast with the introduction of markets and risking the stability of Russian society and premature revolt. He has yet to be judged by socialist critics. But socialist criticism would add to the rogues' gallery of East European communist leaders almost every other name, with perhaps the exception of the politically short-lived Czech, Alexander Dubček, and the executed Hungarian, Imry Nagy.

Nor do Western leaders escape criticism. No British Labour Party leader has been free of socialist censure, from the "treachery" of Ramsay Macdonald through the alleged duplicity of Harold Wilson to the timidity of James Callaghan which lost the 1979 General Election. The faults of the exception, Clement Attlee, were obscured by his introduction of the consensus welfare state. Hugh Gaitskell might have proved the best of British Labour Prime Ministers, not least because he was an economist who, with his close friend, Evan Durbin, understood the market, but even he would have had to work against the instincts of Aneurin Bevan and other *étatist* socialists and, even more obstructive, within a political process—democratic representative government—that has so far prevented politicians from putting the public interest before personal, party or vested interests.

Conservative and Liberal leaders, simplistically dismissed by Marxist socialists as defenders of capitalism, if not quite forming Marx's supposed executive committee for managing the affairs of the governing capitalist class, have weakened capitalism for over a century. Of the Liberals, Gladstone was the least damaging; Asquith, Churchill, perhaps his friend Archibald Sinclair and Jo Grimond, Asquith's grandson-in-law, might have followed him. But David Steel did not understand the market. And Conservative leaders, apart from Churchill and until Margaret Thatcher, because they did not wear the metaphorical beard and cloth cap of the revolutionary, were not seen as opponents of free enterprise and so were allowed to undermine liberal capitalism by aggrandizing the state in the post-war nationalization of industry and welfare.

The Political Frustration of Liberal Capitalism

If communism has been thwarted by autocratic politicians and social democracy distorted by cynical politicians, capitalism has no less been obstructed by politicians in all political parties whose possibly good intentions took second place to the unavoidable pressures of the political process. That proposition must be yielded by socialist scholars who believe that the truth about both systems will emerge only from a comparison of both as they have been and of both as they could be on realistic assumptions about human nature and the working of political institutions.

Capitalism incorporates a device, the market, which enables it to respond to public preferences in the use of resources. But the political process under which it has to work, the representative democracy of parliamentary government, has been increasingly distorted as government has been inflated, not least by the obstacles and imperfections in its procedures of elections, by its gentlemanly horse-trading of measures for mutual support in the voting lobbies (log-rolling) and by its susceptibility to sectional pressures. Representative government in all democracies has so far on balance thwarted, suppressed or weakened the market. It has undermined the instrument that could have done more for the common man than the nominal political freedoms of voting, which in practice masks his preferences.

That is why the capitalist system has so far failed to realize its full potential in creating a market that reacts to the sovereignty of the people. Its development has been shaped by government to suit pressing political purposes rather than the elemental long-term interests of the public. The political interests in the formation and conduct of government have not been designed to enable government to make the best of the capitalist system. The comparison with socialism is flawed unless it is made with a capitalism that operates with a political process that enables it to work through a free market—a political process confined to the minimum of unavoidably collective functions.

The political requirement is government that allows and enables the market to express public preferences. Capitalism has never had such government. Even in the United States, the supposedly most capitalist system in the world after Switzerland, the market has been misused, hamstrung and thwarted. Its government has never been wholly of the people, faithfully by the people, unreservedly for the people. It has never had a government that overtly set out to undermine the capitalist system, but neither, except for a decade or two around the 1890s when it attempted "trust-busting," has it had a government that set out to make the most of the capitalist system. The Democrats in general did harm and the Republicans not much good. The long rule of Franklin Roosevelt was almost a disaster for capitalism, the years of Eisenhower were neutral, the interrupted presidency of Nixon a mixed blessing, and the two terms of Reagan a well-intentioned disappointment. In Europe capitalism in every country—France, for most of the time West

Germany, Italy, Spain, Portugal, The Netherlands, Belgium, Sweden, Norway and Denmark—with the sole exception of Switzerland, has had to operate under social democratic or conservative governments run by politicians whose overt purpose was to dilute or destroy the market. Little wonder it did not perform as well as it could. The miracle is that it has survived and lived on triumphantly despite the politicians' understandable indifference, negligence or hostility. For the market is the ultimate enemy of the politician. Khrushchev said to Western capitalism "We will bury you." Although driven underground, Russian capitalism has survived, despite decades of repression and murder, to bury him.

The political requirement of capitalism, government that liberates the market, is the relationship between government and the market that the critics of capitalism misunderstand. For socialists the political process of government is the essential and effective instrument of popular sovereignty, to which it is accountable and in which the people can democratically and decisively participate. They now concede error and accept the market as desirable or unavoidable. But it is to remain the instrument of politics. This sequence puts the cart before the horse. Professor Marquand has said the aim is to make market forces the servants of democratic politics. The requirement of popular sovereignty, Abraham Lincoln's "government for the people," is precisely the opposite: to make the political process serve the sovereignty of the people, which is nowhere better exerted than in the market.

We have yet to discover the way to make the political process as responsive and accountable to the people as the market can be. Both are imperfect. In the 200 years of capitalism so far, neither has been as effective as can be envisaged. Both have been improved: the political process by extension of the franchise, the reduction of corruption and in other ways; the market process by the mastery of monopoly, the treatment of external effects and the correction of dispensable differences in incomes. But economists have been better at critical examination and identifying the imperfections of the market process than political scientists have been at critical examination and identifying the imperfections of the political process.

The American political scientist Professor William Mitchell has argued strongly in recent years that political scientists have been slow to learn the lessons of the still new economics of politics.[6] They have more to learn from economists on the working of political institutions than economists from

6. William Mitchell, *Government As It Is*, Institute of Economic Affairs, 1988.

them. Economists have been conscious of what is now called market failure since the very discovery of the potency of the market by Adam Smith. Political scientists have been systematically dissecting political failure for only some 30 years, and it was economists who drew their attention to it, and economic analysis that is providing the most penetrating insights. There are no more severe critics of the market than the liberal economists who best see its strengths and its potential. More has been done by them to remove the imperfections of the market than by political scientists to remove the imperfections of the political process. The difference between market and political imperviousness to reform and correction is a fundamental reason why the political process has to be disciplined and minimized if capitalism is to give its best results—if the vision of capitalism (below) is to be realized.

The inequality of capitalism is a fundamental socialist criticism. But the difference in access to goods and services is apparent both in the capitalist market and in the socialist political system. Access in the market is influenced or determined by differences in income and wealth, and in the state by differences in influence, persuasiveness and connections. Inequality in the market derives from flows and stocks of financial power, and in the state (not least in the most socialist country of the USSR) from deep-lying family, social, occupational and other sources of cultural power. But it is the political process that prevents capitalism from removing dispensable differences in anything except the short run, and it is the political process that provides the vast scope for the exercise of the cultural power that perpetuates the undesirable inequalities of socialism.

Four differences between capitalism and socialism are usually overlooked or minimized by socialists.

First, in correcting avoidable differences in financial power government can redistribute incomes with least harm to the market and with the most easily removable structures of bureaucracy, vested interests and taxation. It has not done so anywhere yet. Redistribution is feasible and widely practised in all capitalist countries, even the most capitalist such as the United States and Switzerland. In contrast, it is fanciful to propose the redistribution of political/cultural power arising from family, social origins, personal connections, occupational links and political ties. Little wonder it is rarely practised in socialist countries, from the USSR to Sweden and Austria, or in the socialist sectors of capitalist countries like Britain. And the stratagems to which socialists endowed with cultural power resort to maintain a semblance of equality are risible. The Secretary of State for Health who claimed that he had been treated in a general ward of a National Health Service hospital equally with the *hoi polloi* hardly expected the world to believe he had to wait his turn.

Second, it is easier to escape from unacceptable suppliers in the market, who are generally many, than from the state, which is one. In the activities where suppliers under capitalism in Britain and Europe are few, the reason is generally the activity of government in creating monopoly in fuel and transport, water and postal services, manufacturing and distribution, education and medicine, as much as the market in allowing economies of (large) scale to create oligopoly (a small number of suppliers) in power and not much else. Moreover, the monopolies created by government are permanent or long lasting; the oligopolies of the market are generally temporary or short-lived. Governments can long administer artificial respiration to its monopolies by privileges at the expense of the people: the tariff was often the mother of the trust (cartel) in the United States. The Marxist response that the trust was the mother of the tariff has an echo in the modern public choice analysis of rent-seeking, but the solutions are complete contrasts: the liberal public choice scholars look to constitutional or market disciplines to lessen the power of government; the Marxists continue the old mistake of looking to the emergence of political saints and seers to rule with ever more governmental power over the economy.

Third, people who cannot compete in the political process, because they lack the required political skills and usually have the least cultural power, can escape from the market to the underground economy, where the black market is more democratic because it is less hierarchical. Its participants compete in commercial skills which do not require the rare, arbitrarily acquired and unequally distributed political skills deployed in government by politicians, bureaucrats and their advisers. The political process has created the black free markets to which it has driven instinctively law-abiding citizens by its clumsy conceit that it can diminish the human instinct to exchange, truck and barter.

Fourth, the capitalist system does not require active citizenship: it allows individuals the liberty to choose between the two main forms of human activity. The most endlessly discussed, and most extravagant of space in the press and of time in broadcasting, is politics: its meetings, conferences, party caucuses and personalities. The least discussed are the non-political activities that many more people enjoy far more: domestic interests, artistic pursuits, charitable works, fraternizing with friends or doing nothing at all—

all ways of using leisure time that mystify the political people and mislead them into seeing non-political people as irresponsible, uncooperative or unpatriotic.

Shirley Williams's title for her book, *Politics Is for People,* reveals what political people like to think.[7] They naturally see themselves as doing good. Some of them do. That is not the question. The delicate charge to put to political people is whether they would put the good of the people before their personal good. Some might, but they would probably soon be out of politics, where, they would add, they could do at least some good. (That would be an error; most could do more good, or less harm, in the commercial market.) Mrs. Williams's title would have more accurately been *Politics Is for Political People.* These untypical unrepresentative activists choose politics for their profession or life's work rather than the law, accountancy, writing, teaching or merely making mundane goods and services, as more exciting or rewarding. Many are good at it, and build personally satisfying careers. It does not follow that we should be wise to entrust our families or our fortunes to their care. Even good people do harm in politics. The market does not require people to be good: it takes people as they are and induces them to do good by using their capabilities to provide what others want.

Socialist critics of the capitalist system in Britain have, until recently, been mostly blind to the virtues of the market. They are now beginning to see that the market is more indifferent than the political process to personal origins of social class, region, race or colour or to idiosyncrasies of character or temperament. The common people can be enabled to assert their wishes more strongly in the market than in politics, even of the most democratic kind. That is why, revolutionary though it may sound, the aim should be to make democratic politics the servant of market forces.

To suppose otherwise is unrealistic. Ideally, in the vision of capitalism as it could be the political process must preside over the smallest possible part of economic life, the public goods, which may be no more than a fifth or less of total national economic activity. (A Swedish economist has calculated 7–12 per cent.) The main item is defence; in Britain it takes some 8 per cent of the national income. If the USSR is at last, after 70 years, allowed by its military conservatives to reduce its armaments, the public goods sector could fall to some 10 per cent in all countries round the world. Capitalism could cope with the remaining 90 per cent in free markets without the influence of

7. Shirley Williams, *Politics Is for People,* Penguin, 1981.

politics. If the market became the servant of the state, run by politicians, bureaucrats and their advisers—Professor Marquand's democratic politics—in which the infrequent four-yearly voice of the people would be subdued by daily political tactics, vested interest pressures and other harmful politicking, government would soon politicize the production of food, clothing and shelter as it has politicized the state supply of education, medical care, council housing and pensions.

The Vision of Limited Government

Capitalism as it has been shaped by politics since the late nineteenth century, and as it now is in the early 1990s, is very different from the capitalism that could have developed. Capitalism with politics reduced to its essentials would have produced more wealth with less poverty and more liberty with fewer restrictions.

This conclusion remains true however democratic the political system. Representative government as we have known it since the franchise was widened to include all adults has borne out the promise but not produced the performance of its founders. Lincoln spoke of the three forms of popular sovereignty "of," "by" and "for" the people. First, government has so far nowhere been created "of" all the people: no voting system yet devised records a recognizable microcosm of the public will. Second, elected assemblies are clearly not conducted "by" the people. Abraham Lincoln must have envisaged a much smaller government that could be run "by the people." The everyday affairs of government that take half our earnings are run by elected ministers and selected officials who are not directly answerable to the people; they are accountable to a representative assembly, from the British House of Commons to the newly elected USSR Congress of People's Deputies, which is a very imperfect reflection of the general will. (Even less representative will be the Supreme Soviet, composed of selected deputies.) Third, representative government is not run "for" all the people; it responds more to backstairs "talks" with promises of financial support and to street "demos" with moral pressures of threats of violence than to the *demos* of the ballot box. Little wonder that pressure groups have tended to outmanoeuvre or, finally, to bypass elected assemblies.

However representative an elected assembly it is still operated by procedures that remove it from democratic control. The new democracy of the USSR will be an empty promise of government by all the common people of the USSR unless it can ensure the economic reforms of ending central planning controlled by Gosplan and creating markets serving paying customers. The semblance of Western parliamentary government in the newly "democratic" communist/socialist states has been superficially discussed in the British press. Of 2,250 USSR deputies elected by secret ballot, the reformers who favour market reconstruction are estimated to number from 300 to 450. We may then see a party of radicals or "liberals" who support Gorbachev faced by some 1,500 "conservatives," party officials, state plant managers, state farm directors and others who understandably prefer the status quo of state monopolies. The "democratic" government of Poland concocted in August 1989 was based on a producer interest (Solidarity), a farming interest (the Peasant Party) and a conventional social democratic group (the Democrats). There will be no effective government of, by or for the Polish people without free markets.

Students of British political history may conjure hopes of a Gladstone-Disraeli duel, perhaps even with Russian governments alternating between rule by "liberal" and "conservative" parties. Even if this transformation in Russian politics appears as the next Five Year Plan, it will not produce the people's will unless they can express it every day in the marketplace. The obstruction will be not only by the "Conservative Party" in the Congress representing or influenced by politicos, militarists, plant managers, commissars, bureaucrats and petty officials. It will also come from the Russian version of the imperfections in the political systems of the West. Until Russian capitalism becomes a reality in pervasive markets, we can anticipate the familiar round of electoral pacts, probably secret, log-rolling in the Russian parliament and rent-seeking by the vested interests of the military, the plant managers, the culture lobby, millions of minor officials, millions of farmers and the familiar parade of producers who know how to organize and pressurize. The articulate and the opinionated—some with famous names like Boris Yeltsin and other radicals—will have a voice as the new parliamentarians. But the common populace will still lack exits from the monopoly state undertakings the new "democratic" politicians will cherish until competition dominates the Russian economy. Political democracy is not enough.

Is it to be supposed that government in Britain or Europe or North America has been governing precisely as the people wished? Has it supplied the services they wanted? Is government no larger than is required to supply the public goods that only government can supply? Does it withdraw in peace from the inflated powers it takes in war? Is the bureaucracy no larger than is required? Are taxes no higher than necessary for the unavoidably collective functions of government?

Does democratic government test its efficiency by systematic experimentation in competing forms of management? Does it return taxes to dissatisfied customers? Does it adjust its distribution of cash benefits with changing individual circumstances of incomes and family requirements? Does it put compassion for the poor before concession to the powerful? Does it put the long-term interests of the people as consumers before their short-term interests as producers?

Does it alter the legally created powers of private associations in the professions and trade unions and the other Burkian autonomous institutions when market conditions change? Does it always and resolutely resist the pressures of sectional interests?

Does government limit itself to "leadership," replacing individual by collective political judgement, only where it is desirable? Or does it invade the province of the individual and the family where it is not? Is democracy in Britain (or elsewhere in the West) government of the people, by the people, for the people? Is the political process the best machinery for subjecting the politicians to the people, the ostensible servants to the supposed masters? Are its civil servants responsible agents or in practice irresponsible officials?

When then should we expect government and its appurtenances to be different in the socialist countries newly emancipated by political democracy but governed of the busy, by the bossy, for the bully?

A review of recent history provides few comforting answers. Let it be asked how much government power there would now be if Britain were a newly discovered country devising the ideal form of government. What services would be supplied by government, and which would the people insist it left to them?

What would it be doing in the archetypal public good defence? Would it be spending as much as it has been, or less? We cannot tell, because democratic politics in the polling booth provides no way of discovering public opinion on separate acts of government. Decision-making by elected government seems the only feasible way for defence, a public good. But has government experimented with other methods of discovering separate decisions? The answer is "no." And if we ask why it has not, the answer must be democratic politics: the weak control by the voters, bureaucratic obstruction and the conspiracy of silence among the freemasonry of politicians that this at least is a province of government free from the tiresome politics of public influence.

But must defence products be manufactured by government in ordnance factories? Hardly, because it is possible to obtain quotations from several

British (and overseas) firms to discover the best terms for the taxpayer. Then why have they not been used until recently? The answer must again be democratic politics, which has kept government not only in defence but in much else much larger than it could be.

The question of how much government a liberal capitalist society can tolerate without being damaged by party politics has been raised by Dr. John Gray, the Oxford philosopher.[8] All liberals maintain that the writ of government in capitalist countries has grown too far. How, and how far, to reduce it is the question. Dr. Gray argues persuasively for "limited" rather than "minimal" government—the alternatives that form the main difference between liberals.

The concept of limited government explained by a long line of liberal philosophers from Thomas Hobbes to Michael Oakeshott envisages government as limited to "protector of the peace and guardian of civil society." Except for three "positive" functions, Dr. Gray argues that government must withdraw from participation in economic life and confine itself to devising the rules under which individuals can conduct their affairs in security and peace. The three are to liberate the poor from dependence and emancipate them as independent members of civil society and to enable them to acquire the means to exercise choice to "exercise responsibility in the control of their health, education and provision for old age" and to "facilitate the transmission of valuable cultural traditions across the generations."[9]

This agenda goes far towards the limitation of government to the provision of the unavoidably collective functions (public goods), although it goes beyond the role of "limited government . . . as umpire and peace-keeper."[10] Liberals who favour either Dr. Gray's limited government or the minimal government argued below agree on much that will shock established political thinking in all British political parties. Not least, the de-socialization of the welfare state and its substantial transfer to the market will shock most politicians, all bureaucrats, all sociologists (with a handful of exceptions), most economists (with growing exceptions), most conventional political scientists, almost all education, health, housing and pension correspondents of the newspapers and broadcasting and all officials and most members of the so-called public sector trade unions. Yet none of the four main components of the welfare state—education, medical, housing, pensions—had to

8. John Gray, *Limited Government: A Positive Agenda*, Institute of Economic Affairs, 1989.
9. Ibid., pp. 15–16.
10. Ibid., p. 16.

be transferred wholly to the state. It is not the public interest but the vested interests that keep them there (chapter 11). But the difference on the limited versus the minimal state remains.

Classical liberal thought tried to identify the desirable and indispensable functions of the state by reference to a principle—the formula of Adam Smith, confirmed by Keynes before he thought that he had discovered a flaw in classical economics, and reaffirmed by Lionel Robbins and liberal economists generally—that the state should do only what individuals could not do for themselves, which meant in the market the familiar range of unavoidably collective functions. Dr. Gray asserts persuasively that the functions of government cannot be predetermined because they are necessarily determined by "time, place, and historical circumstance."[11] He defines the minimal state as that which is confined to the protection of "negative rights,"[12] and limited government as that which ensures "positive rights."[13] This view echoes the approach of Professor Plant, who emphasizes positive rights, such as the satisfaction of basic needs, which Dr. Gray sees as a development rather than a violation of the classical principle of Adam Smith: "not . . . distortions or perversions of an earlier . . . theory of negative rights, but inevitable developments of a discourse of rights whose contents are incorrigibly indeterminate."[14]

Such severely limited government prevailed for several decades in the nineteenth century, but Dr. Gray claims that a century or more of government interventionism has built up "needs and expectations which must be addressed." This duty "will commit government to activities that go well beyond the provision of the public goods of national defence and law and order" to "supplying families and communities with the means" to affirm and renew ". . . their distinctive values and ways of life . . . across the generations." Not least, the duty of government includes "concern for the health of the autonomous and intermediary institutions which stand between the individual and the state—trade unions, universities, professional organizations and the like."[15]

This is a formidably wide agenda for "limited" government. Five doubts suggest it is too wide to preserve the institutions of the liberal society of

11. Ibid., p. 20.
12. Ibid.
13. Ibid., p. 16.
14. Ibid., p. 21.
15. Ibid., p. 22.

capitalism based on the market where possible and the state only where it performs unavoidably collective functions.

First, it is true, of course, that the necessary residual functions are not fixed for all time but turn on "time, place and historical circumstance." The public goods that government must supply because they cannot be supplied through the market will be decided in part by changing technology. The development of scrambling devices that limit a service to the individuals prepared to pay for it, as in broadcasting, lighthouses and other technological devices, can exclude the free-riders and make it possible to change a state-provided public good into a market-supplied private good. Even some functions of the law, another of the archetypal public goods, can be supplied in the market: congestion in the courts can lead individuals involved in disputes to ask former judges of the high or lower courts, retired or wanting a change from political law, to arbitrate between them. Other reasons for supposing that the range and volume of public goods are not as extensive as is commonly supposed were indicated in chapter 8.

The content of the category of public goods that have to be supplied by government may expand or, I am inclined to think, contract with time and circumstance, but the principle that the state should supply only what the market cannot supply must remain as the guide to the functions of government of a liberal society. The scope and limits of government cannot be decided at one time for the decades and centuries ahead, but the principle can be formulated for a liberal society for all time.

It is founded in the economic reasoning that the market cannot produce goods or services to individual requirements if they cannot be reserved to the individuals who pay for them but can be enjoyed by everyone; in that event no-one will pay for them, and so the solution is for everyone who benefits from them to agree voluntarily to a compulsory form of payment called taxation. That simple principle can be understood by everyone and is accepted as the unavoidable method of paying for joint services which have no separable benefits. The principle is simple but its application is complex, debatable and troublesome, for in the ultimate sense almost every human activity produces "externalities"—benefits or detriments—to many other people. (The flowers in your front garden may please some passers-by.) But if the state were to supply every service that produced substantial external benefits, it would produce almost everything; no one has yet suggested that degree of ultimate universal socialization. And the very notion of public goods raises questions of the measurement of the benefit to people in different circumstances, and many others (chapter 9).

Second, many of the now very extensive functions that government acquired in the last century are not public goods or unavoidable collective functions, but are continued for no better reason than that the vested interests that supply them would be inconvenienced if they were transferred to the market. That is no reason for them to be included in the agenda of government (chapter 11).

Third, Dr. Gray argues that the "severely limited" government of the nineteenth century cannot be restored because government intervention has "built up needs and expectations."[16] But if the content of public goods cannot be predetermined, and must be expected to change with time, place and historical circumstance, the content of the group of services that were never wholly public goods, not least education and medicine, can certainly be expected to change. "Needs" are ambiguous and ultimately limitless; "expectations" are created by government and ultimately artificial. The taxpaying citizens of a liberal society with rising incomes will want to know why they are being taxed for services that government does not have to supply and some or many taxpayer-citizens do not want. Whilst the communist world in the 1980s was returning—or advancing—to capitalism at a fast rate, it is less convulsive for the capitalist world that has been emasculated and hobbled to shrug off its socialism. Indeed it has been shedding socialism all round the world (chapter 4). Dr. Gray's pessimism is therefore unwarranted: he rightly deplores that British government has been transformed "from a provider of public goods into an engine for the promotion of private interests. In suffering this metamorphosis, government has defaulted on its classical functions of defending the realm, keeping the peace and renewing and repairing the institutions of civil society."[17] And he proposes constitutional conventions to discipline government in limiting taxation, balancing the budget, maintaining a stable value of the currency and preserving human rights. The return—or rather advance—to a *minimal,* not merely a *limited,* state is therefore feasible.

Fourth, although government may be indispensable for some purposes, the reason is not that it is superior to the market but that the market cannot work at all. The classical principle, reaffirmed by Keynes, is that government should act not where it is better than the market but only where there is no market. In short, wherever it is used, government is so disappointing or worse—inefficient, unaccountable and corrupt—that it is best not to use it

16. Ibid.
17. Ibid., p. 30.

at all except for functions where all its faults have to be tolerated to obtain the services required.

If government is undesirable because inherently defective, the less the better. And this is true whatever it does. In short, the price of government is so high that it should be avoided wherever possible. And it can be avoided much more than socialists, and some liberals, suppose. The supply of money was once regarded as an unavoidable function of government. The mastery of inflation is still thought to be a function of government. The liberals called monetarists have devised rules to limit the power of government in the control of the supply of money. The difficulty is to know precisely how to assess the quantity of money. "Money" is anything that is generally acceptable in payment for goods or services—anything, not merely coins or paper money, but also promises to pay based on the possession of assets, present or expected, such as deposits in a bank, financial instruments based on ownership of a freehold home and so on (hence the various methods of measuring the quantity of money used by government—M1, M2, M3, M0—which are not motorways but different measurements, some confined to coins and paper, and others including deposits in financial institutions).

These latest substitutes for conventional money are less easy for government to control. In the short run they may stimulate the inflationary impulses following government failure to avoid excessive supplies of conventional money, as in the late 1980s, but in the long run they emphasize the political incompetence of government in mastering inflation and make more urgent other methods hitherto ignored or dismissed by conservative politicians or conventional bankers.

The difficulty of estimating the quantity of money has led to the obvious solution—that money be de-socialized and put into the market, i.e., the arguments put by Hayek and applied by Dowd and Selgin.[18] Hence the liberal dilemma. Dr. Gray says rightly that government is so unreliable that it cannot be expected to operate the optimum rules for the control of the supply of money to master inflation. This is the basic truth about government that socialists and paternalistic conservatives find difficult to accept. Even the technically most immaculate rule risks being misused by politicians, not because they are inherently mendacious but because the political process leads them to misuse it by providing opportunities in which misuse is politically

18. F. A. Hayek, *Denationalisation of Money,* Institute of Economic Affairs, 1976, 2nd edn. 1978; Kevin Dowd, *Private Money,* Institute of Economic Affairs, 1988; George Selgin, *The Theory of Free Banking,* Rowman & Littlefield with the Cato Institute, 1988.

profitable in garnering votes, winning time after a bad mistake or stroke of ill luck, or fomenting a short-lived boom before a General Election. All these politically profitable but nationally harmful acts are evident in British (and other) post-war history.

The proposal in 1989 of the British Chancellor of the Exchequer for competition between national currencies in the EEC as preferable to a single unified European currency is a half-way approach to competition in a free market in currencies in which users would gravitate towards the most reliable—perhaps the Deutschmark—and thus induce other governments to discipline their monetary excesses. But national currencies would remain vulnerable to political control, with its familiar internal risks of short-term electoral expediencies, intensified by the new international risk of political collusion between national governments. The essential strength of the gold standard, echoed in the post-war Bretton Woods system of fixed exchange rates, was that it took exchange rates out of party politics; but in its last years it was prostituted by national "neutralizing" of gold movements, which were designed specifically to produce expansion or contraction in money supplies to keep exchange rates constant.

These political advantages of fixed exchanges were forgotten by British economic commentators in the 1960s and 1970s who urged "floating" exchanges but overlooked their vulnerability to political manipulation. Competition between national currencies would be another "half-way" house, as in school and hospital opting-out and the community charge, that recent Conservative Governments have adopted from political advisers myopically concerned with the "politically possible" but careless of the long-run postponement of the required ultimate solutions. Yet the failure of conventional politicized expedients has belatedly enforced recognition of government failure and brought new consideration of market solutions. Here again, socialist thinking has had to yield to unorthodox capitalist rethinking.

These are the "dangerous toys" (chapter 14) that scholars unwittingly hand well-meaning, but necessarily self-seeking, politicians. The most notorious example was Keynes's argument for mopping up unemployment by deficit financing, which gave politicians a blank cheque to unbalance budgets and spend irresponsibly without raising taxes because an influential economist had said that it was the way to cure unemployment (and, they added *sotto voce,* win votes without offending the taxpayers).

But if government cannot be expected to apply the necessary rules faithfully, even for such a central humane task as the avoidance of inflation, we cannot expect it to perform any function without regard for its political effect—particularly not the provision of education, medical care, housing, pensions or other intimate personal services. That is the question on the welfare state too long unasked and unanswered. The state has a necessary but difficult role in the assurance of minimal purchasing power to individuals, where it can do less harm than in providing services that require vast outlays on buildings and equipment and vast armies of employees. Its role as provider, supplier, owner, employer, controller and regulator in education, medical care, housing, pensions and much else has been insensitive, unjust, coercive and often corrupt. Dr. Gray's government function of "support" for education and health services would be better performed in cash than in kind, which "support" could imply.

It follows that we should ask government to do as little as possible. In view of the risks that politicians will do harm in the effort to do good and the virtual certainty that they will not apply policy in the best way for the people that is not also the best way for themselves, we should observe abstinence from government even where it can do good, unless there is no other way. The tragedy is that although there often is another way—the market—government continues year after year, decade after decade, with tasks it performs both unnecessarily and badly. And it has continued so long that the possibility of other ways is far from the public mind. "How else can hospitals be provided?" typifies the state of public knowledge that obstructs reform. The prolongation of the political solution to often passing problems defers the emergence of market solutions.

This is a harsh conclusion. The strongest objection to the use of government is not only that it is often ill informed, or swayed by vocal interests, or that it cannot easily vary or end a policy that has become outdated by technical or social change. It is rather that it will take short views and be overcautious to create the impression of "caring" for the public and overlook the long-term costs of overcaution, not least because it may be out of office. *Après nous le déluge* is a shrewd maxim for party politics, but not for the public weal.

The over-regulation of the new financial institutions is a recent example: the public—personified by "Aunt Jane" as the elderly investor of modest means—is comforted, but the service of financing new projects is cribbed, cabined and confined. The Gulliver of capitalism has long been tied up by Lilliputian politicians. Compared with the best deeds of little political people, capitalism has the potential for good of the giant.

Fifth, and finally, Dr. Gray says that "Wise legislators (if we had such)" would ensure "both that the demands of the autonomous institutions did not become inordinate" but also that they were assured "a protective sphere of independence under the rule of law,"[19] thus maintaining what Edmund Burke described as "a balanced constitution." There are two difficulties here. First, the supply of "wise legislators" is rare or uncertain. That is why government has to be constrained and why many services it might supply if wise legislators were more plentiful are better supplied in the market where political wisdom is not a requirement. Dr. Gray re-asserts[20] Oakeshott's wise view (in *Rationalism in Politics*) that "the true office" of government is as "the umpire whose business is to administer the rules of the game, or the chairman who governs the debate according to known rules but does not himself participate in it." That was the view destroyed when the Fabians persuaded Liberal and Conservative as well as Labour politicians that they could use power to do good. In the past century governments have entered games and debates as participants with much more influence and power than individual players or debaters—or whole teams. They have commandeered the ball and kicked it out of the ground to suit their electioneering; they have dominated the debate and summed up with consummate bias to suit their political timing. They have not applied the rules as neutered eunuchs but have ignored, bent or changed the rules, always claiming it was for the good of the players and the debaters. Second, the autonomous institutions can degenerate into state-protected monopolies: the professional associations of doctors and lawyers, the trade unions of miners and railwaymen and the state universities headed by importunate natural and social scientists have been among the worst offenders. These are Edmund Burke's "small platoons" that were supposed to produce "a balanced constitution." That is a conservative mirage that turned into a corporatist nightmare in our day. The antics in the 1980s of the British Medical Association, the National Union of Miners and the scholars of Oxford University revealed their true character: they did not stand out for the individual against the state but used their power to aggrandize themselves. They are inordinate monopolies that can be disciplined only by the open door, the entrances and the exits, of the market which would humble and destroy their arrogance in a minimal state.

These doubts about limited government have led some liberals in recent years, both in the United States where the main writers, Professor David Friedman and Professor Murray Rothbard,[21] have been joined by Professor Robert Nozick of Harvard and in Britain where young academics have been active in the Libertarian Alliance, to return to the concept of devising and

19. Gray, *Limited Government*, pp. 22–3.

20. Ibid., p. 15.

21. David Friedman, *The Machinery of Freedom: Guide to a Radical Capitalism*, Harper &

refining the rules and the principles to govern the minimum rather than the limited functions of the state.

Liberals differ on the optimum use of the state; the liberal economists of West Germany, some organized in the *Hamburger Kreis,* who continue the tradition of Ludwig Erhard, originator of the German economic miracle, generally see a state active in the avoidance of inflation and the control of monopoly, as argued in their journal *Ordo.* Other liberals have become more sceptical of the state even in these functions. The "libertarian" liberals have been reinforced by the writings of Anthony de Jasay[22] and other thinkers in France, Belgium and elsewhere in Europe, and in the United States and Australia, whose writings have newly emphasized the extravagant claims made for the beneficence or competence of the state. They all further reinforce the intellectual case for the irreducible minimal functions of government under capitalism as it could be.

The Principle of Minimal Government

The Adam Smith principle, that government shall do only what cannot be done in the market, is universal for all time. It applies to the late twentieth century, and it will apply to the twenty-first century of our children and grandchildren, as much as it did to the late eighteenth century when it was first formulated.

It will also have to apply to the new capitalist democracies of the communist countries if they are to yield the freedoms that can combine high productivity with personal liberty without the enervation of social democracy or the violence of authoritarian socialism.

The state has shown itself the false god of all who have looked to it to right wrongs, ensure justice, remove poverty, master inflation and unemployment, raise living standards, employ science for the benefit of the common man, protect the environment, safeguard the cultural values desired by the people. It has not ensured government of the people, by the people, for the people. It has not brought liberty, equality or fraternity, peace, land or bread to the millions misled to trust it. It has disappointed the hopes of Marxists, democratic socialists, party political liberals and paternalistic conservatives.

Row, 1973; Murray Rothbard, *For a New Liberty,* Macmillan, 1973, and *Power and Market,* Sheed Andrews and McMeel, 1970.

22. Anthony de Jasay, *The State,* Blackwell, 1985.

The false god they have all followed, in the belief that men with power over others would use it for the benefit of the others at the expense of themselves, is the essence of socialism in its numerous varieties, including Fabian market socialism. The crucial decision, where there is room for both, is whether to put the state before the market or the market before the state.

We have learned by sobering experience what the state cannot do. What it must do, it does very imperfectly: the failures of government are even more damaging than the failures of voluntary exchange in the market. After a century the world is turning from the state to find salvation in allowing people to live together without it wherever possible, and despite it where it must, regrettably, be used as a necessary evil.

The economic system or cooperating arrangements that allow them to come together to exchange the surpluses of their skills in a system of voluntary exchange in which both sides gain—the economists' zero-plus game—has been called capitalism by its critics, who until recently have not understood it. A more descriptive name, without the bitterness fomented by Marx, would be the exchange economy. But we must judge it by what it has accomplished, and even more by what experience shows it could accomplish if the writ of the political process is minimized. The abuse, condemnation and obloquy should be turned into salute and celebration.

The task, now that false hopes are recognized and the errors acknowledged, is to withdraw from the state the functions it does not have to perform and to leave it with as few as possible, however imperfectly it performs them. We have to accept the state, however imperfect, where it is better than no state. We must accept capitalism, however imperfect, where it has been and could be better than socialism. That is the concept of the minimal state.

The task has hardly begun. A first step must be to see how what was emerging under the freedom of exchange of nineteenth-century capitalism would have developed further if the state had not stopped it. We can be sure that the activities, services and industries that the state and its agencies took from voluntary cooperation—in transport and fuel, manufacturing industry, education and medicine, local government and elsewhere—would have developed very differently from the uncontrollable, bureaucratic, insensitive, producer-dominated, inflexible, self-perpetuating structures that the people have come to tolerate and almost accept as inevitable.

Their inefficiency and irrelevance in an age of rapid scientific advance were at last being re-examined in the 1980s. Some are being rescued from the control of politics by de-socialization or privatization. The most difficult to rescue are those that provide intimate personal services and have long been claimed, by the socialist mind in all political parties and by those in all parties who do well out of them, to be the agents of social justice by ensuring that the poor have as much access to them as the rich.

Unfortunately the poor have believed them; they do not yet know that the clumsy mechanism of government has been unable to ensure the errand of mercy it set out to perform. To withdraw the functions annexed by government is supposed to be difficult, or "politically impossible"—the pretext of the politician down the ages who fails in his self-imposed and loudly proclaimed task of serving the people.

The services of mercy, compassion, equity and universal benevolence have been given a warm-sounding name, "welfare," that begs the question not asked by the socialist mind: whether they are what the people would have wanted for themselves if they had been allowed to decide. They are called by a name that reflects the salesmanship of politics: the welfare state suggests that the services supplied outside the state are less desirable, commendable or beneficial. Because the welfare state is organized by public servants they are supposed to do public good. Yet the beneficiaries for whom they are supplied would not be anxious to keep them, or to oppose reform, if they knew their opportunity cost—what else they could have had for their taxes. But that is not what politicians have told them. Political people could hardly have been expected to deprive themselves of the power or, they would prefer to claim, the opportunity to do good for which they entered politics.

Yet the task of showing what education, medical care, housing and pension income in retirement—the four main services of the welfare state—the ordinary people might now be enjoying is not insuperable. They have been the victims of a political-bureaucratic-philosophical confidence trick. It is not difficult to show what powers they could have exercised as paying consumers in the market for all four components instead of as importunate supplicants in the political process.

The task seems difficult because the services touch the lives of the people every day, or when they are most vulnerable, or without which civilized life would be difficult, or old age impossible, to contemplate. The state has succeeded in the supreme aim of the monopolist—making itself seem to be indispensable. The notion that education, medical care, housing and pensions could not be supplied except by the state has been unthinkingly absorbed by millions or most of the British people. That is one reason for the misleading if not mischievous findings of the price-less opinion polls (chapter 14). The reformers of the Thatcher Governments have had to tiptoe on political eggshells. In their efforts to loosen the bonds of the state they are forbidden to use the English language, with its graphic honesty.

Yet the British are not inherently dishonest. They would know what was meant if they were told in plain English that much of their intimate everyday personal and family lives has been the artificial creation of party politics and could be changed without injustice or hardship. They—especially the common people—do not have to suffer sink schools for their children; they do not have to wait months for varicose vein surgery nor years for hip replacement; they do not have to live in slum houses nor vandalized council tower blocks; they do not have to live in old age on a third of their earnings in work.

These are all the creation of the state and its agencies. And the complaints, mainly from their officials and employees, of underfunding are the familiar special pleading of vested interests: more money dispensed by the same people on the same principles would do little or nothing to change the mechanisms that produce the low standards, capricious quality and bureaucratic indifference of the welfare state. Nothing less will suffice than to change the status and power of the beneficiaries from grateful supplicants to demanding customers. That revolution in the status of the common man and woman requires no more than a change from government monopoly to competition between suppliers in the market: the transformation of the artificial socialist welfare created by government to the development of the capitalist welfare that the people were creating for themselves in the nineteenth century.

The notion that welfare depends on the state is unhistorical. It has been fostered in the flood of shallow post-war writing on all four main (and several secondary) services. The scrupulous nonconformist researches mainly sponsored by the IEA and presented not least by Professor E. G. West on education, Dr. David Green on medical care, the late Professor F. G. Pennance on housing and Dr. Charles Hanson on voluntary insurance for income in retirement leave no doubt that the working people of Britain were not Marx's Lumpenproletariat who had no thought for their wives or children, themselves or their future, but were beginning, despite their low incomes of a century or more ago, to save and insure, pay fees for schooling and organize medical clubs, buy homes and show providence and responsibility in the conduct of their family lives.[23] The evidence and the argument that spontaneous working-class welfare would have expanded much better in the market is outlined in chapter 11.

The question, not asked by the politicians or academics lost in wonder at

23. The argument is focused in Arthur Seldon, *Wither the Welfare State,* Institute of Economic Affairs, 1981.

the welfare state, is what the people, or their grandchildren, would be doing in our day. They have not asked whether the people would passively have tolerated sink schools, supplication at hospitals, life in slum housing or mean existence on puny pensions. Their incomes today, without the taxation of the welfare state, would have raised them out of the slums created by the state in council housing. Their low incomes decades ago could have been supplemented to enable them to exercise the authority and bargaining power of consumers in the competitive markets for welfare that were beginning to emerge. The stronger and wider demand for rising standards and choice in welfare would, as usual in the market, have evoked the faster response of increasing numbers of suppliers and kinds of schools, hospitals, homes and pensions-savings schemes. And the incomes of their grandchildren, where low today, could have been supplemented to raise them into the same bargaining class as those with higher earnings. That process would have created a "One Nation" on more secure foundations than the Conservatives have claimed, on nebulous grounds, since Disraeli.

The people of Britain would have been given the power to reject sink and slum welfare and escape to the higher standards and better qualities they now expect and receive in their personal and household purchases in the market. The politicians and academics, state school teachers and state-employed or state-contracted doctors evidently expect the common people to share their middle-class revulsion at the prospect of schools and hospitals being sold like baked beans or pea soup. The common people may counter with the sad wish that schools and hospitals had been "sold" at the high quality of the goods and services they pay for in the market. They might reflect that Marks and Spencer or Sainsbury, or the historic corner shop in Grantham scorned by Lord Hailsham, would have more respect for their customers than to supply state school baked beans or NHS hospital pea soup to customers who could escape elsewhere.

Other state services sense that their days as monopolies are numbered. They are beginning to join the spirit of the competitive market. British Rail has not only tried to restore the regional flavour of its local services by distinctive colouring and old adjectives with new nouns, like "Southern Section" (which still smacks of bureaucratic nationalization) for the original Southern Railway; it has also transformed its nationalized "passengers," who were given excuses for late arrivals, into commercial "customers" greeted at London termini with profuse apologies. The coming of competitive transport is again filling British country roads with private buses that stop when asked, as they did before state regulation, rather than to suit trade union timetables. These benefits could follow in education, medicine, housing and pensions when the delusion that public servants would ensure public service is replaced by the reality of exits by competition that humble the state monopolists.

This is the prospect of welfare and other personal services in the late twentieth century that is within the grasp of the people. A brief visit to its beginnings in the mid-1800s will reveal the middle-class myths about the callous self-neglect of their great-grandparents and show the shape that the welfare services would have taken in our day and will take as more escape from the state.

Chapter 11 is an excursion into the nineteenth century for the lessons it teaches for the twentieth. Early capitalism showed the capitalist education, capitalist medical care, capitalist housing and capitalist pensions that would have developed in the past decades if they had not been prevented by the state, its agencies, its controllers and its employees.

CHAPTER **11**

The Galloping Horses

> ... when the [British] government made its debut in education in 1833 ... it was as if it jumped into the saddle of a horse that was already galloping.
>
> E. G. West, *Education and the State*

> ... medical care organisations were founded by patients, doctors, and entrepreneurs in the market from about the 1830s ... Medical Aid Societies (Works Clubs) employing doctors ... Provident Dispensaries (semi-charities) ... commercial Medical Aid Companies ... Doctors' Clubs ... Public Medical Services founded by doctors ... Friendly Societies ...
>
> David Green, *Working-Class Patients and the Medical Establishment*

> ... by far the most serious impediments and distortions in the market for housing are the result of legislative, fiscal and direct intervention ...
>
> F. G. Pennance, *Housing Market Analysis and Policy*

> ... more and more people are accumulating wealth ... in savings with Friendly Societies, the Post Office Savings Bank, the Trustee Savings Bank, life assurance policies, houses—private property which offer more security than the state ...
>
> A. Seldon, *Pensions in a Free Society*

The vision of capitalism is the prospect of minimal government. It excludes the state, or its agencies, from the production of goods and services that individuals can arrange by voluntary exchange in the market. The vision thus requires the eventual withdrawal by government from most of its accumulated activities. It may periodically contemplate the addition of state functions made necessary by technical change, possibly environmental protection, or by social change, debatably preservation of cultural continuity in historic buildings. They may have to be added because they cannot be arranged in the market, even though government is not efficient, it loads costs arbitrarily, it may be corrupt, and it cannot wind up a function when technical or social change make it superfluous. But the prospect is that the vision would subtract more than it adds to the functions of government.

The most difficult to withdraw will be the welfare services because, as argued in chapter 10 and this chapter, they touch personal lives intimately every day. The removal from government of (part or all of) outdated nationalized or local services can be resolved by argument and evidence on whether they are supplied more efficiently by governmental or private agencies. There would seem to be a strong case for the removal from government of the railways and coal mines, the electricity (distribution), gas, water and sewage services, long-distance roads and most prisons, weather forecasting and mapping, refuse and fire services, libraries and museums, smallholdings and swimming pools, police (burglary protection though not public order) and car-parking, job centres and public conveniences, arbitration of disputes, registration of documents and many others.

There remains the debate between those who would move the services bodily by de-socialization (privatization), a political decision, and those who would do so by returning taxes or topping-up low incomes and charging prices that cover costs, making it an economic decision by the individual consumer on whether to pay for the government service or to opt for a private service in the new competitive market between both. Charging would create a new consumer power based on a new "constitutional" right of the citizen to a return of the taxes (direct or indirect) paid for services no longer wanted from government, national or local. This is the "right" created by the market, not legal but all the more powerful because economic and based on purchasing power. People would no longer be required by law to pay for relatively inferior state services when preferred services were available in the market. We have long forgotten, or never contemplated, how responsive, flexible and personally "tailored" services could be obtained in the market. If the state cannot match them the new power to demand "money back" could improve or end them.

Reform in the welfare services is more difficult. The scope for reasoned reflection is inhibited by human emotion and sympathy, the "care" and "compassion" of contemporary debate. The modernization of welfare production to keep pace with changing supply and demand, and its removal from government (except the elements of public good, as in pure medical or other research) have turned on human sentiment, if not hysteria. Academics bear some responsibility for this degeneration of debate; the honourable exceptions are overwhelmed by the many who emphasize the symptoms rather than the causes of suffering, and the income effects to the neglect of the price effects of proposed remedies. The "dismantling" of the welfare state, the question-begging formulation of those who prefer state welfare in principle, is the use of emotive language to suppress rather than elucidate debate. It has moved the order of intellectual battle from reason to prejudice. It has enabled national or local politicians who favour the state in principle, or who wish to protect their political preserves, to present the modernization of welfare as likely to endanger personal life. And it has enabled the vested interests which benefit from the *status quo* to stampede the citizen into recording support for inefficient and damaging state welfare services. The half-truths in the press "campaign" of the British Medical Association in 1989 opposing reform of the National Health Service have tarnished the repute of a once respected profession that has become embroiled in the political process.

The welfare services are the most sensitive politically but the most elemental in personal life. If reason can be introduced into the debate on the most difficult of the socialized services, there is some hope that it may remove or at least weaken the purely politicized and the largely emotional opposition to reform on doctrinal grounds. There would then be a prospect that policies could be based on considerations of human desirability rather than the perennial obstacle of "political impossibility."

The welfare state is discussed here not only as the most sensitive of the services that the vision of capitalism would see largely produced in the market; it is also the activity of government that does the most direct and the most lasting harm to the individual. It therefore claims attention not *after* all the others—fuel and transport, public utilities and local government—have been dealt with as the easiest politically to sell to the electorate but *before* many of them, precisely because the electorate requires tutoring in the harm the state is doing as long as it continues to politicize the main welfare services.

That tutoring is not likely to be done by politicians without persistent prompting from academics and other informed observers. The classical economists—John Stuart Mill, Nassau Senior, Alfred Marshall and more—sensed the probability that the state would not relax its grip once the people could decide for themselves. They were right. It has not. Means must be devised—by constitutional or other reform—to require it to bow out before it does much more harm.

State and Market in Welfare

The 40 years of the welfare state as it was systematized after the last war have resulted in the proliferation of hundreds of books and thousands of pamphlets and newspaper articles that discuss it as the acme of compassion, and innumerable political speeches that promise further extension to nurture the young, support the working population through sickness and unemployment and tend the elderly in retirement. It is not surprising that a generation that has known no other method of organizing or financing education and medical care or of providing housing and pensions for millions should unconsciously suppose, without reflection, that the state is not only the sole source but the best.

This is the heresy of the age. It ignores the spontaneous antecedents to the services created by government. It ignores the passing historical reasons for the origins of state education in 1870, council housing in 1915 and 1919, state pensions in 1908 and 1925 and the NHS in 1948. It ignores changing public habits and preferences. It does not ask how the spontaneous services might have developed if they had not been deposed by the state. And it denies experience in other countries with comparable cultures.

The changing public habits, changing preferences (not least as obscured by the flawed opinion polls) and experience in other countries are discussed in other chapters. In this chapter we recall the neglected origins of the state welfare services and argue that education, medical care, housing and pensions would have developed very differently, and more sensitively to individual circumstances and preferences, if they had not been propelled into the political process.

Commonplace assumptions on human nature and experience round the world indicate that, as incomes rise, people want better services, more tailored to personal and family circumstances, than the state supplies, or rather claims to supply, more or less equally for all. The supposition that the state has succeeded in discovering ways to supply its services with equal access to all is still widely believed but increasingly falsified and abandoned by academic researchers in all schools, socialist as well as liberal, although politicians in all parties, Right as well as Left, continue to assert it without reference to the by now well-attested evidence.

The failure of the political process in welfare is threefold. First, it has persisted from the early years of national insurance and welfare services in the attempt to maintain a structure of bureaucratized benefits without enquiring into the preferences of the people. Second, it has failed to execute even its own (erroneous) intentions by pretending that the benefits are equal despite mounting evidence that they are not: instead of redistributing resources from the richer to the poorer, it is still redistributing them in the opposite direction from the poorer to the richer, or from the poorer and the richer to the middle-income groups. Third, even where it has belatedly seen the urgency (or justice) of redistribution to the poorer by instituting selective in place of universal benefits, it is politically incapable of redeeming its failure because of the obstruction from the very middle-income interests it has created as directors, suppliers or consumers of the services it was supposed to have instituted for all, but especially for the poor.

The history of the origins or antecedents of the state welfare services provides the elemental charge-sheet of the failure of government in welfare. In education, medical care, housing and pensions it created mammoth monopolies of state services instead of redistributing income to enable all to wield the power of consumers over producers in the market that some people, and increasingly many, were developing as their incomes rose. Whether and how far it was possible to supplement income in 1870, or 1925, is discussed below. The first attempt in 1870 was destroyed by politicians—for reasons that uncannily echo the politicians of our day. But if difficult in 1870, it was more feasible in 1925, and certainly in 1948 instead of constructing the vast machinery that now employs three million, from national civil service bureaucrats and local officials to clerks and tea-ladies.

Now that, after 50 or 100 years, government is beginning to see its error and, especially since 1979, is trying to replace bureaucratic producer-dominated state services in kind by diversified benefits in cash, it is having to pretend that it is strengthening the state services in order to placate the middle-class professions and the working-class trade unionists who do well out of the welfare state as controllers, employees or beneficiaries. And the consumer, especially the poor, instead of coming first, will have to wait another decade or more before the tortuous reforms can be made with a minimum of occupational disturbance and political anxiety that long-belated improvements may precipitate electoral defeat by the very intended beneficiaries.

The continued delay in reform of the welfare state is the mark of failure of the political process. The markets in welfare that are now, at last, being built by benefits in generalized or earmarked cash, instead of the services in kind that almost destroyed the embryo markets developing in the nineteenth century, could have been established much earlier. The obstacle 100 or 50 years ago was not the market but the political process. The culprit today is not capitalism but socialism.

As incomes rose during the second half of the nineteenth century parents would have wished to pass from improving the family food and clothing to supplying their children with schooling, the whole family with medical care and housing, and themselves with income in old age. To suppose otherwise is to forget history.

Capitalist Education

Education would have been among the earliest candidates for household budgeting after the staples of everyday life.

This is not the impression conveyed by the historians or the social novelists. Yet the assumption of parental concern for children is historically valid. It is precisely what working-class parents were showing increasingly in the nineteenth century long before the state began what is uncritically called "the national system of education." (Like "public," "social" and other political euphemisms, "national" conveys the unfounded implication of benevolence.)

From the earliest years of the nineteenth century, and earlier, parents had begun to send their children to school. Their incomes were low; they required help, and received it from the church, charitable and other sources. School fees, even only a few pence a week in the early years, might still require some sacrifice of the staples of food and clothing, but it was made. Parents, themselves largely unread and illiterate, were increasingly anxious that their children should learn the elements of reading, writing and arithmetic.

Historians had drawn their evidence from official mid-century reports on the still large numbers who attended no school, and the social novelists had drawn for their fiction on the worst schools. It seems that then, as now, the failures, even if exceptional, excited more interest and sold more books than the successes. The normal was boring; the exceptional evoked philanthropic sympathy, literary imagination or political anger.

The libel on the British working-class family was raw material also for the politicians and political novelists who later exploited it in Fabian and general socialist writings. The evidence of inadequacy in schooling was plain for all to see; the solution could be offered with no risk of challenge, and with no discernible cost to anyone. Socialism has always thrived on hypothetical and apparently costless cures for painful symptoms. Private schools had failed to educate all the children; therefore government would have to fill the gaps. Thus—by a *non sequitur* that would not persuade a sixth-former—were literary and political reputations made on the backs of the workers.

When Professor West, the economist/historian come to judgement, revealed the questionable reasoning in the politicians' argument and the contrary evidence from the 1860 Newcastle Commission and other sources overlooked or dismissed by the conventional historians,[1] their reaction was to discredit it. The reasoning was questionable; the evidence could not be right: it conflicted with Dickens. It would destroy their illusions, perhaps their reputations.

But the evidence has remained unchallenged. And Professor West's further work in Britain and Canada has made him a leading world authority on the economics and the economic history of education. It was the orthodox historians who were discredited, and the social novelists who have been revealed as writing good fiction but bad history susceptible to misuse for political purposes.

The alleged neglect of education in the early and middle decades of the nineteenth century has been an influential element in the socialist discrediting and condemnation of capitalism. For some years after 1965 school textbooks repeated the canard about the nineteenth century, and politicians continue to repeat it about the twentieth. Markets, said Roy Hattersley, who aspires to rule the common people, have to be accepted by the Left, but not for education and other welfare services.[2]

The error is patent. The market, runs the *non sequitur,* must not supply education for anyone if some cannot pay for it. Their payment by taxes, originally indirect as well as later direct, is rarely discussed. That is a confusion between nationalizing supply and fortifying demand. If demand is inadequate because some incomes are low, the logical solution is to top them up so that all parents can pay, not to create a state monopoly supply for everyone without much choice, little influence and less prospect of escape. Food and clothing are more elemental than education. That is not an argument for state monopolies. Topping up low incomes risks disproportionate impairment of incentives to earn, but the defects of monopoly supply are even more difficult to remove.

The government of 1870 (headed by Gladstone) was not wise to begin the long monopoly of education. But he and Disraeli were then jockeying for

1. E. G. West, *Education and the State,* Institute of Economic Affairs, 1965, 2nd edn. 1970.
2. Roy Hattersley, *Choose Freedom,* Michael Joseph, 1987.

electoral support from the newly enfranchised voters. Perhaps it was difficult to top up incomes in the 1870s; the workers might have spent it on beer or worse, as middle-class reformers have invariably asserted. As usual the political process gave the workers advantages as organized producers in the Trade Union Act of 1871, but ignored their interests as unorganized consumers—the occupational disease of politics. (Gladstone suffered poetic justice when Disraeli trumped his 1871 Act by the 1875 Trade Union Act.) But governments since then, Conservative, Liberal and Labour, have been even more myopic and shallow in not counting the cost for future generations of continuing the state monopoly.

The evidence on fee-paid schooling supplied by voluntary teachers long before the 1870 Act is still forgotten. Returning from a holiday in the Scottish Highlands my wife and I, with a shared interest in early British schooling, saw the epitaph on a headstone reproduced in a Dunkeld hotel which gave evidence of a private school run by one Eppie Brown in the 1770s for which poor Highland parents paid a few pence a week:

> Imagine a woman o' three score and ten
> She fends off the worst o' poverty's shock
> By skuiling [schooling] bairns o' hardworking folk
> For weekly, as Monday comes round,
> There's tuppence sent with them for auld Eppie Brown.

Twopence a week was a large sacrifice in the 1770s.

In England the economist James Mill, father of John Stuart Mill, observed in 1813, 57 years before the 1870 Act, that ". . . around London . . . there is hardly a village that has not something of a school; and not many children of either sex who are not taught more or less reading and writing. . . ." How were the schools financed? Mill added: in "families in which . . . not an article of sustenance but potatoes had been used; . . . for every child the hard-earned sum was provided to send them to school."[3] In 1835 further testimony of the spontaneous spread of schooling came from the Whig statesman, Henry Brougham, born in 1776, the year of the *Wealth of Nations,* and no doubt reared in its teaching, who lived through the heyday of British economic liberalism to 1868. Brougham was prominent in the debates on the historic Reform Bill of 1832, which developed the political process of voting and elections, but he also sensed its potential danger for the liberty-creating

3. James Mill, *Edinburgh Review,* February 1813.

market process and the new schools it was producing: "We have such a number of schools . . . furnished from the parents themselves from their own earnings and by the contributions of well-disposed individuals . . . *it behoves us to take the greatest care how we interfere with a system which prospers so well*" (emphasis added).[4] His warning was ignored in 1870, when there were still more parent-financed private schools. Unfortunately the occupational disease of politicians is to succumb to the inducements of the political process to "interfere" by putting themselves at the head of "prospering systems" in order to win credit for their wisdom and public spirit but often to end by obstructing them. Professor West accused the politicians of jumping onto "a galloping horse." They also risked bringing it down. From 1870, as indirect taxes rose in the succeeding century, fewer parents could pay for the private schools they had been creating, and fewer parents came to see schooling as a service that involved them since it was being supplied by well-meaning politicians (who wanted their votes) and incorruptible bureaucrats (who gained from new posts).

The evidence is still overlooked by the socialist mind (in all parties) that sees the state as the indispensable sponsor of education because parents will not pay for it in the 1990s. Readers of the Brontë sisters for insights into life in the mid-nineteenth century miss the clues. In 1841 Charlotte wrote to her aunt, Elizabeth Branwell, "My friends . . . say schools in England are so numerous, competition so great, that without . . . six months [experience of teaching] in some school on the Continent . . . we shall have a hard struggle and may fail in the end." She thanked her aunt for her offer of a loan of £100 to open the school. With the experience gained in Brussels, she hoped Emily and Anne Brontë might join the school: ". . . you always like to use your money to the best advantage; you are not fond of making shabby purchases; when you do confer a favour, it is often done in style." She assured Miss Branwell the money would be "well employed . . . thereby ensuring a more speedy repayment both of interest and principal."[5] It would be unrealistic to suppose public servants spend with such responsibility other people's money that they do not have to repay. The derided "Victorian values" taught responsibility, economy and integrity often absent from socialized activity even under capitalism.

The number of children at pre-1870 private schools more than doubled from around 500,000 in 1818, soon after James Mill's evidence, to more than

4. Henry Brougham, *Edinburgh Review,* April 1835.
5. Muriel Spark, *The Brontë Letters,* Macmillan, 1966, pp. 93–4.

1,250,000 in 1834, a year before Brougham's report. By 1851 two out of three were receiving daily instruction from the age of four to six until the age of ten.

This is the evidence found by Professor West from the Newcastle Commission of 1861 and other sources. Professor Mark Blaug has concluded that by 1850 school attendance and literacy in England, in mainly parent-financed schools, exceeded that in the world as a whole, including the Third World, in 1950, a century later.[6]

The subtle difference in the effect on social relations between parents, sometimes in the same street, of schools in the market and schools provided in the political process is vividly illustrated by the final abolition of school fees for secondary state schools in the widely acclaimed Butler Education Act of 1944, another landmark in the complete control of schooling by the state, except for the small enclave of private schools maintained by independent-minded, self-sacrificing, religious, stubborn or wealthy parents. Together with the 1918 Fisher Act, which abolished fees for elementary schools, the Butler Act prevented the emerging working-class parents from competing with the middle classes for high-quality schooling.[7]

Before 1944 the fees paid by parents for places remaining in secondary (including grammar) schools after most were filled by children entering by examination were known to all parents and occasioned little or no apparent envy. Parents of children able to pass the examination at that age may have admired the sacrifice of the not always wealthy parents to give their children, possibly late starters, the best chance in life they could buy. Those who could not, or would not, pay the low fees (£2.50 a term at Raine's School in my day around 1930, when local annual earnings were about £150 a year) aroused no public outcry at the advertisements inviting parents to apply for the fee-paying places.

After 1944 the grammar schools provided in the political process without fees were wholly filled by children who could pass the new examination (the ill-favoured 11-plus); the remainder (about four in five) were put into secondary modern or technical schools. They were thus seen by parents whose children had "failed the 11-plus" to be segregated by a political decision based on judgement of the ability or potential of children at the early age of 11 years; some, as parents saw it, had lost their "ticket for life." And parents who

6. Blaug, "Education in classical political economy," in *Essays on Adam Smith*, eds. A. Skinner and T. Wilson, Oxford University Press, 1975.

7. Marjorie Seldon, "School grants a bar to consumer sovereignty," *Economic Affairs*, April–May 1987.

before 1944 would have paid for grammar school education after 11 were given little or no opportunity by the Butler Act to move them out of the secondary modern (or the few technical) schools, except by paying the much larger fees of private schools. After 1944 middle-class parents elbowed working-class children out of the grammar schools by political/cultural jockeying for influence with parent-governors and coaching their children for free places in the grammar school, which became a bargain when the alternative was public school fees.

It took a long time for the middle-class socialist mind to see this disagreeable consequence of "free" state education. The political falsehood of "free" education—or anything else—has often misled the innocent citizen. Working-class parents would have changed their supposed approval of state education if they had understood that they were paying for it, by indirect if not direct taxation and in rates (hidden in rents). In education, as elsewhere, they would have done better in the market than in the political process. Here, as elsewhere, the prime essential is to restore the reality (and information) of price in place of the fiction of "free." The opinion polls continue the omission and the fiction: little wonder that they find support for "free" welfare services.

The growing parental resentment in working-class families against the *inequality* of the egalitarian state system, based substantially on envy of middle-class parents for exercising a choice they could not share, was fomented by the vote conscious in all parties, and led the Labour Party to introduce comprehensive schools for all children in the mid-1960s. Except in several middle-class local governments, as in Kent and Buckinghamshire, which deployed delaying tactics, or in Enfield, where resourceful parents obstructed comprehensivation, the eventual result was the closure by Conservative as well as Labour Ministers of the grammar schools in almost all working-class areas. That offence against the common people by the politicians and the bureaucrats must be one of the most reprehensible if not callous in post-war British history. Little wonder the Bishop of Peterborough reprimanded Shirley Williams for closing his grammar school (chapter 12).

The state had aimed at equality. In the resulting administrative effort at standardization, it had, as usual, overlooked the family. It ended by fomenting discord and friction that produced yet one more growing war of all against all. It unnecessarily and myopically introduced more politics into private lives. As elsewhere it had the opposite effect to its intentions: instead of helping the low-paid parents, it harmed them by closing the grammar schools to their eventually rising incomes. Little wonder that, as incomes rose, more working-class parents turned to private schools in the market for the salvation of their children. And praise is due to the academics on the Left who, in effect, began in the late 1980s to look for ways to restore the market with schemes for replacing free state schools by schools charging fees paid with the aid of earmarked grants, which some earlier campaigners organized in the pressure group Friends of the Education Voucher (FEVER) had advocated since the mid-1970s supported by the eminent liberal economists who had advocated education vouchers for decades.

How much further would parent-influenced unpoliticized schooling have spread if it had not been discouraged and repressed by the state? How many more parents today, with much higher incomes than their great-grandparents earned in 1870, especially if raised by lower indirect and direct taxes, would willingly be paying for the schools of their choice? We shall never know. The historians do not ask. The socialist mind shrinks from the question and is blind to the prospect. But the number must be many times the 7 per cent of children at such parent-financed schools in the early 1990s. With earmarked school grants or vouchers virtually every working-class child could have the advantages of responsive schooling that treats parents as customers who pay because they have the power to withdraw from bad schools as much as from bad restaurants.

Can only the state supply schooling for all? The socialist mind (in all parties) says "yes." Could the 93 per cent never have attended schools of their parents' choice? They imply "no." Can schools be run efficiently if their pupils are liable to be moved about at their parents' whims? No, say the local government officials and teachers' spokesmen. The socialist mind has been giving much the same answers for a century. They are all wrong.

Schools for all children could have been supplied without the state building, owning, staffing and running them. Virtually all children could by now be attending schools of their parents' choice. And they would have to be run efficiently if their parents could change at a term's notice (or less).

The evidence is plain from the 2,500 schools of precisely this kind with around 750,000 children. Individual parents can compare schools because several are accessible in the area they can cover by bus or car (which most own or can share). The fee-paying schools offer high standards essentially because they compete for parents: they know parents will move their children if standards fall. No parent is tied. He does not have to explain why he wishes to move. Nor does he depend on the majority decisions of other parents. There is no subjection to the political process of election to Boards of Governors, with the more articulated salaried exercising more influence than the usually reticent or overawed wage-paid. The competitive market with unrestricted exits makes the *individual* parent sovereign.

That is the vision of capitalist education.

There were bad private schools in the Victorian era, and the social novelists exploited them profitably in their fiction. But, as argued in chapter 9, cases of bad specimens are not evidence against capitalism (nor cases of good state schools evidence for socialism). Bad schools would not have lasted long as purchasing power rose or was supplied by government to supplement low incomes. They would have lasted no longer than bad private restaurants. The private schools were spreading in a system that opened exits from bad suppliers; the state schools were created in a system that closed exits. A Director of Education in the Home Counties said in the early 1980s to the Chairman of FEVER: "We know which are the bad schools; but we have to fill them." That is the ultimate condemnation of the "system of national education" begun by the political process, not by the will of the people, in 1870. The people were not asked. Nor are they asked in the 1990s.

A century after 1870 the parents who paid for schooling directly through fees (instead of indirectly through taxes) had been reduced to one in 15 and British schooling was enmeshed in the political process. The 1989 reform that provided a qualified exit—opting out by collective decisions of Boards of Governors, even then subject to the politicized approval of a politician, the Secretary of State—keeps the state schools in the political process. It does not supply exits by independent decisions of individual parents from schools whose Boards of Governors have decided against opting out. The majority decisions are taken by Boards of Governors and parents' ballots which override individual wishes. There is no good reason except political timidity and administrative convenience to give the power to opt out of the state system to the school rather than to the parent, the supplier rather than the consumer. Opting out of the state system by schools is a political solution; the market solution would create opting out by individual parents.

In the 1990s, 120 years after 1870, some 93 in each 100 parents are still prevented or inhibited from giving their children the schooling of their choice. That is the inhumanity of the political process. The 93 are still socially segregated from the seven who make the sacrifice and pay in the market. That is the frustration of Disraeli's One Nation by the Conservative/Labour political process, which has created Two Nations. It is too late for the politicians to force the seven into the state system. The only way to One Nation is to enable the 93 to join them.

Capitalist Medicine

The spontaneous development of health services by the friendly societies, medical institutes, industrial insurance and other mechanisms of the nineteenth-century market—capitalist medicine—was hindered and finally almost destroyed by politicians, bureaucrats and producers in successive stages culminating in the 1948 National Health Service—"socialist medicine."

The embryo medical market a century and more ago was developing consumer sovereignty; the NHS replaced it by producer dominance under the guise of political paternalism and professional benevolence. The evolving buyers' market, in which the consumers employed the doctors who danced to their tune, was followed by the state-enforced sellers' market, in which the consumers became supplicants in the doctors' surgery. This sorry tale, in essentials disguised by political claims to create equality, justice and compassion, is the economic history of British medicine. Over the century socialist thinking has prevailed over liberal teaching on the consequences, in all human behaviour, of state coercion, concentration of power, monopoly and producer myopia.

British health services will not improve radically until the sellers' market of the NHS yields to a buyers' market. NHS waiting and queuing, by patients for doctors, will have to be reversed. Doctors will have to wait for patients. The difference is that the long waiting of patients in the NHS—often weeks for consultations, months for some surgery and years for so-called non-urgent surgery that causes mental anxiety and often physical deterioration—will be replaced by short marginal occasional waiting by doctors, because the market is more efficient in coordinating the time of individual patients and individual doctors than are the centralized procedures of the state in marshalling large groups of patients and doctors.

The sobering truth is that the assumption on which the NHS is based—that the time of doctors is invariably worth more to the community than the time of patients—is unfounded. It may be true of some outstanding doctors; it is certainly not true of all patients. The time of the highly trained average doctor may be less valuable than that of the humble joiner, electrician or plumber whose waiting disrupts a shipyard team working on a tanker for export.

The market would not categorize as patients the millions of people with varying ailments, aches, symptoms, temperaments and psyches. Only a vast impersonal political artefact like the NHS finds it essential to classify them in order to avoid administrative elephantiasis. British Rail is belatedly describing its passengers as "customers." Medical care would improve if it was based on the disciplines of the "doctor-customer relationship," but that would require individual payment.

The NHS was politically sold to the electorate with the promise that everyone would have the best medical care that science could produce. This echo of the second or higher Marxist phase "to each according to his needs" was a deception for which democracy, the doctors and the people are still suffering. It has degraded political democracy into a political auction, misled the doctors into thinking that government could isolate health care from the fundamental human condition of scarcity, and callously aroused unfulfillable expectations of universal medical care without limit of cost in doctors' time, hospital equipment, nurses' sympathy, ambulance facilities and innumerable other scarce resources that civilized society must husband scrupulously or lose in a scramble for survival.

Yet these principles of care and economy in the use of resources were being respected by the working men of England and being incorporated into their early efforts to build medical services for themselves and their families. The spontaneous arrangements made by them with doctors in medical institutes, clubs and other organizations would not have misled the people, the doctors or the politicians into unrealizable expectations. The capitalist idea faced reality and produced solutions to maximize the good that could be extracted from scarce resources. The socialist idea in the NHS unthinkingly begged all the questions that face humanity by applying the *naïveté* of the central Marxist fallacy on the relations between human nature and scarce resources. And when the first government for 40 years to face the truth made an effort in 1989 to introduce the economic truths of life into medicine, it was met by angered politicians who feared the loss of their electoral ace card, frustrated doctors who heard for the first time that they too, like the rest of us, would have to watch their housekeeping, and disappointed patients who would have to find that, after all the politicians' promises, medical services do not fall like manna.

The saga of a century of working-class self-help from the 1850s to 1948, denigrated and depreciated by historians, was newly told by David Green.[8] Even Macaulay's ranks of Tuscany could scarcely forbear to cheer, although

8. David Green, *Working-Class Patients and the Medical Establishment*, Temple Smith/Gower, 1985.

as a Whig he would not approve of the Johnnies-come-lately. *New Society*, the socialist-inclined journal of sociologists and social workers, acknowledged that Dr. Green had presented "a fascinating analysis of the workings of medicine under the friendly societies." "Market competition," it accepted, "served the needs [it meant wants] of the people well . . . friendly society members and medical practitioners proved to be quite evenly balanced, sharing real mutual interests. . . ."[9] (Even-balancing is not enough: the consumer must prevail over the producer.) The Left-inclined *Political Quarterly* called Dr. Green's researches "a unique study . . . of the relationship between producers and consumers . . . in the 100 years up to the NHS. . . ."[10]

In that event, it is pertinent to ask why the history of working-class self-help, responsibility and providence has been neglected. The public debate in 1989 on TV between the Minister and the spokesman for the five unions on the pay of ambulance staff pales into insignificance contrasted with the origins of the monopoly state system confronted by monopoly trade unions of which the outcome must be arbitrary and precarious because conducted in the political process. The socialist mind in all parties, including the Liberal Party of Beveridge, too lightly accepted the historically flawed argument that the costs of the spontaneous organizations were high, that they did not cover families and that the whole system was a patchwork quilt of untidy design. The clear solution, concluded the socialist mind, was a unified, uniform, centralized, standardized and comprehensive system of (on paper) equalized medical services.

Dr. Green's findings on the advance in voluntary health service organization and financing were much the same as Professor West's in education: the state jumped on a galloping horse. It slowed the steed down. The socialists, through their ubiquitous activists, from Sidney and Beatrice Webb before the First World War to Richard Titmuss after the Second World War, aided the take-over through the political process of advice to government. The producers, through the British Medical Association (BMA), abetted the take-over through the political process of pressure on government. In the end the dominance of government and the producer over the working-class consumer was almost final. The day was saved by the market in the 1950s, which kept alive the remnants of the spontaneous organizations until they could regroup and resume their politically interrupted service under the

9. *New Society*, quoted in the 1988 Progress Report of the IEA Health Unit.

10. *Political Quarterly*, quoted in the 1988 Progress Report of the IEA Health Unit.

influence of rising incomes and general *embourgeoisement* after the Second World War.

Like Professor West's *Education and the State,* Dr. Green's *Working-Class Patients and the Medical Establishment* reads like an exciting search in historical detection of long-neglected evidence. Two medical institutes, "stumbled across" in 1937, says Dr. Green, by Political and Economic Planning (PEP), later the Policy Studies Institute, a well-intended interwar think-tank that propagated in the 1930s the current socialist errors, provided comprehensive medical services which PEP had the wit to commend as "the model of any national system of medical services."[11] It was reflecting early thinking that produced the NHS, with the familiar romantic notion of the political process as the source of disinterested expertise and finance. The Great Western Railway Medical Fund Society of Swindon, established in 1847, a century before the NHS, had by 1944 employed 14 full-time doctors and consultants, visiting consultants, three full-time dentists and ran a 42-bed hospital with a large Out-patients' Department caring for over 40,000 members and their families, half the population of Swindon. The Llanelli and District Medical Service had 18,000 subscribers in 1937 to its comprehensive "model of any national system of medical services."

Swindon and Llanelli were not unique. Samuel Smiles would have approved of the self-help of the common railwaymen and miners. But when the national system of the NHS was established in 1948 it almost destroyed the Great Western Railway Medical Fund Society and the Llanelli and District Medical Service and all the other testaments to the innate urge to self-help of the British working people.

That they were not untypical of all the spontaneous organizations in medicine is indicated by two national figures that dramatize the libel on the working classes. The number of medical institutes rose from two in 1870 to 32 in 1883 with 139,000 members to 85 in 1910 with 329,000 members. Then came compulsory insurance for sickness cash grants in 1911. It played havoc with self-help. Despite increasing numbers of potential members, the number of medical institutes fell from 88 in 1912 with 312,000 members to 49 in 1947 with 166,000 members. Then came the NHS in 1948. It seemed to sound the death-knell for self-help through voluntary medical insurance. All the medical institutes had closed by 1949.

The warning of Brougham on schools was vindicated in medicine. ". . . it

11. Green, *Working-Class Patients.*

behoves us to take the greatest care how we interfere with a system which prospers so well."[12] The market was doing its work in medicine as in education. But the political process has propulsions other than those of putting the individual in command of his destiny. Of the 12 million coerced into state insurance by the 1911 Act, 9 million had been covered by the voluntary schemes, 6.6 million in registered societies and 2.5 in unregistered societies. Membership had been growing at accelerating rates for a third of a century. The 2.8 million of 1877 had risen by 90,000 to 3.6 million in 1877, then by 120,000 a year to 4.8 million in 1897 and again by 140,000 a year to 6.6 million by 1910. At the same rate of acceleration, a million more would have been covered by the 1914 war. All this was destroyed, not by the will of the people, but by the political process. The familiar pretexts of more rapid state action, widespread poverty and the untidy patchwork quilt concealed less worthy motives of party political advantage, bureaucratic empire-building and capitulation to organized interests.

Yet the market, despite suppression by government, recovered by the forces of supply and demand. After the Second World War voluntary health insurance through the remnants of the friendly societies recovered and resumed their methods of payment for medicine in the market. The gradual growth in demand came from heads of families with rising incomes and from employers who wanted prompter and better medical attention for salaried and wage-paid employees whom they were anxious not to lose when it suited the NHS—which said, in effect, "Don't call us, we'll call you."

The NHS illustrates the consequences of taking a service from the market and putting it into the political process. The medical politicians who ran the BMA showed their hand at every stage. Whether they faithfully represented the doctors is, here as in other political processes, conjectural. The familiar assertion of the spirit of service over the receipt of money was always unconvincing. A doctor in 1910 anticipated, realistically, that compulsory insurance strengthened the prospect of higher incomes: in the *British Medical Journal* he said, when the (Liberal) Government's proposal was published, "We now resume our place . . . as sellers ready to give our service to the buyer" which he rightly saw as "not the poverty-stricken wage earner, but the solvent State Insurance Company."[13] The power of the individual working man has been shifted from the market, where he employed his doctor, to the

12. Brougham, *Edinburgh Review.*
13. *British Medical Journal,* 12 November 1910, p. 1556.

state, where the politicians employed his doctor. That has been representative government in practice, so far; it replaced direct influence made effective by purchasing power in the market by indirect influence based on the ineffectual vote in the political process. Politicians do not know where the patient's shoe pinches.

Henceforward he would not be able to withdraw his money and exit as an individual if dissatisfied, but have to exercise his voice with millions of others in voting at General Elections on Sunday trading, aid for single parents, multilateral versus unilateral nuclear disarmament, expenditure on remand homes, Northern Ireland, sanctions on South Africa and many other policies. The surrogate opportunity to indicate his opinion on national policy, but even then not his preference on personal service, which is what the market enables him to do, is the opinion polls that tell him nothing about costs and alternatives so that he is like a man shopping blindfolded without knowledge of prices (chapter 14).

It was easy to see that doctors would come to favour the state as the means to discipline the tiresome workers who knew the service they wanted and would not pay doctors who did not supply it. Doctors might continue to vote Conservative or Liberal but they had become socialist in their technocratic thinking and their autocratic attitude to their patients. Among the best-known was Dr. A. J. Cronin for his novel *The Citadel,* which put his opinions into a character's mouth. He had been angered at the initial reluctance of the "unintelligent" committee of the Tredegar Medical Aid Association in the 1920s to take his advice on research into miners' diseases. The Secretary helped him to persuade the committee eventually, but he resented the loss of time required in arguing his case.

Cronin's reaction is common in the middle-class professions, medical and other, peopled by technocratic specialists who despise the "ignorant" working-man amateur. But the medical amateur miner wanted to be convinced: it was his money; he knew where the shoe pinched, which Cronin did not; the miner wanted to weigh up costs and benefits; only he could count the (opportunity) cost of the alternatives he and his family had to forgo. The market process in which the scores of Tredegar and Llanelli and Great Western Railway Societies enabled the miner, the railwayman, the steelworker, the weaver, the tailor and the cobbler to decide their lives was almost destroyed. The political process into which the socialist mind propelled them by compulsory insurance and taxation was not a substitute for the consumer sovereignty of the market but its destroyer.

The role of the doctors' political leaders in medical policy has not been glorious. Discussions over two years (1968–70) on a BMA committee of ten doctors and two patients (the other was later a Chancellor of the Exchequer) disillusioned me about the public spirit of the organized doctors. But as the BMA operated in the political process, I should not have expected better. Then, as in 1989, the BMA was opposed to government policy. In 1968 it was Labour, in 1989 Conservative. In 1967 17,000 family doctors had signed resignation notices following unacceptable terms from the government. The committee was established under the courageous Welsh family doctor, Ivor Jones, to consider alternative ways of financing health services. It recommended the replacement of political tax financing by individual payment through private insurance for a wide range of services except the public goods of pure research, infectious and contagious diseases and others. But in the two years to 1970 of the committee's many meetings and researchers, the BMA had negotiated acceptable terms. The future of the NHS, the unsuitability of tax financing for personal medical services, the nineteenth-century history of the BMA as a combination against the patient and the future of medicine were passed over. The doctors' politicians had achieved their immediate object of what the trade unions would call "more pay." The committee's detailed reasoned documented report,[14] which had surveyed health financing in every major country, was pigeon-holed and ignored. A recent Minister for Health urged its solutions on his Conservative friends,[15] but although the proposed government reforms of 1989 would make a dent in the doctors' producer monopoly, the influence of the BMA was still apparent. Medicine in the market would have put the consumer unequivocally first by clearing the obstructions for the resumption of the consumer sovereignty pioneered by Dr. Green's "working-class patient."

The NHS is not the envy of the world, as its uncritical supporters claimed. Only Italy copied it systematically in 1981, and it came to grief in two or three years. New Zealand's gradually developing state structure suffers much the same distortions as the NHS. The British attempt at socialized medicine has been a cul-de-sac that, like state education, threatened working-class subjection, from which the increasingly affluent workers are escaping only by the rising living standards provided by capitalism.

Nor is the NHS popular or cheap, as a Conservative consultant, later a government minister, had claimed. The opinion polls that periodically re-

14. *Health Services Financing,* British Medical Association, 1970.

15. Ray Whitney, *National Health Crisis: A Modern Solution,* Shepheard-Walwyn, 1988.

turn 80 per cent in favour are not based on knowledge of costs. And the low administrative costs of 6 per cent are for a streamlined utility service that would not survive in competition except by being offered "free" and by omitting items, such as political overheads, industrial documentation, waste of time and much else that raise the 6 per cent much higher as calculated by a former high official of the BMA who left because he rejected its principles.[16]

By the 1990s, when the British could be savouring consumer sovereignty in medicine, their politicians are still having to make concessions to producer dominance. That is the reality of the political process.

Capitalist Housing

Few academics, of the Left as well as the Right, would now claim that the political process has provided the British with the homes they prefer. Whether they wish to own or to hire (rent) their homes, many or most have not been able to live as they wish for over 70 years. They have been prevented by two plausible but in the event destructive political decisions. In 1915 (two years before the Russian Revolution) the wartime government restricted home rents with the plausible intention of keeping housing costs down and discouraging inflationary wage demands, which would have complicated the financing of the war. In 1919 the government required local authorities to build houses to let at subsidized rents for the further plausible reason that the rent restrictions had reduced to a trickle the spontaneous growth in home ownership and discouraged private investment in building homes for renting.

The result by the 1970s was to put more than six million working-class families into council housing or tower blocks that they would not have chosen for themselves. The political artefact mounted to one-third of the total housing stock. That was a source of pride to doctrinaire Labour and unreflecting Conservative politicians. Their legacy comprises the physical deterioration of council homes, streets and districts, the tower blocks that made millions of working men accept a window-box in place of a garden and their wives the risk of a mugger as well as a burglar, not least the denial of the opportunity of owning a home to build a nest-egg of savings for their old age. It also includes yet one more example of the government failure that

16. Frances Pigott, "The hidden costs," in Arthur Seldon (ed.), *The Litmus Papers: A National Health Disservice,* Centre for Policy Studies, 1980, p. 72.

can neither acknowledge error nor redeem it expeditiously. Although Mrs. Thatcher's Governments had by the early 1990s sold over a million council homes to their tenants, the political process in housing has grown barnacles of vested interests and intellectual *immobilisme* that will continue the council housing myth of benevolence well into the twenty-first century.

The market would have reacted promptly to a change in social conditions; it would have pulled down the council houses of the 1950s, 1960s, 1970s and 1980s, and replaced them with homes that the increasing numbers of affluent workers wanted. The political process will consign millions of the working classes to council homes for perhaps a hundred years after 1915.

The socialist vision, at its best in intention, was Aneurin Bevan's mixed council estates for middle-class and working-class tenants to encourage social integration. It made the characteristic socialist mistake of ignoring the *embourgeoisement* of capitalism. The workers were becoming middle class faster than the politicians could see, and their children with two cars, two television receivers and two holidays a year would not tolerate the slums built by the state. They did not require paternalistic politicians to tell them where and how to live. They would have been better served by the capitalist vision of a free market in which they could buy or rent the homes they preferred.

Little attention is paid by observers to the galloping horse in housing. It did not suit the argument of the socialist mind that looks to government for solutions. Professor D. V. Donnison, an influential social scientist in the 1960s, argued that the market in housing had been inoperative for so long that the prospects for its re-creation were remote.[17] Yet the market had been emerging for over a century. The stock of private-built, low-cost homes (including shops with flats) rose from 3.9 million in 1875 to 6.4 million in 1910.[18] Few academic studies have asked how much further the number would have grown if the state had supplied housing grants (or the vouchers examined by the Urban Institute in the United States) instead of cheap housing that made the tenants the submissive importunates of council officials from whom only one in six have so far escaped. Neither did any government until the 1980s have the wit to make the housing subsidies portable, as originally proposed by Professor Pennance in 1968;[19] at least it would have removed the disincentive to labour mobility from the litany of the evil consequences of council housing.

17. D. V. Donnison, *The Government of Housing*, 1967.
18. *Abstract of British Historical Statistics:* homes under £20 annual value.
19. F. G. Pennance, *Choice in Housing*, Institute of Economic Affairs, 1968.

The shabby housing of the working poor was a common complaint of the official reports and unofficial novels of the nineteenth century. But in the context of the social improvements brought by economic liberalism it was less significant in pointing to developments and solutions than the early evidence that rising incomes would provoke a supply-side response by capitalist investment in housing. Because the market is sometimes slow, the political mind looked to quick solutions in its new search for votes as the franchise was extended to all men at age 21 and women at 30 in 1918, to women at 21 in 1928 and to all voters at 18 in 1969.

But the evidence was accumulating for some who feared the power of the state over man. In 1871, a year after Forster's Education Act, the Royal Commission on Friendly and Benefit Building Societies was surprised to be told that 13,000 Birmingham working men owned their homes, and were buying them out of average wages of some £1.50 a week. In 1884 the Royal Commission on Housing learned that the Leeds Permanent Benefit Building Society had enabled 7,000 working men to buy their homes.[20] It cannot be supposed that Birmingham and Leeds were the only industrial towns in which home ownership was spreading. Some of the Commissioners were sceptical and surprised. But the market did not publicize itself as did government. And the social historians did not dig deep for the evidence of self-help in housing; the surmise must be that they did not expect to find it.

Nor did self-help in housing develop only in the towns. Observers who looked for the evidence found it. The politicians, bureaucrats and writers of fiction did not look and did not find. It may be thought that Samuel Smiles, the once-reviled author of *Self-Help* (1859), would overemphasize the evidence of self-help in housing. In a later book *Thrift,* published in 1875, another of his writings mocked in recent times, he wrote: "There are exceptional towns and villages in Lancashire where large sums have been saved by the operatives for buying or building comfortable cottage dwellings. Last year (1874) Padiham saved £15,000 . . . though its population is only about 8,000. The Burnley Building Society . . . has 6,600 investors who saved £160,000 or an average of £24 . . . principally mill operatives, miners, mechanics, engineers, carpenters, stonemasons, and labourers. They include women, both married and unmarried." Smiles's informant added ". . . great numbers of the working classes have purchased houses in which to live [and]

20. David Rubinstein, *Victorian Homes,* David & Charles, 1974, pp. 215ff.

as a means of investment. . . ."[21] Little of these early beginnings of home ownership appear in the textbooks.

If Smiles was pleased with his evidence, Thomas Wright found evidence of wider *embourgeoisement.* In *Our New Masters,* the name given the working men newly enfranchised in the 1867 Act, he wrote percipiently of the new capitalists: "The aim of the great majority of the . . . working classes—the cleverest, most energetic, and persevering men—is to raise themselves out of those classes. Numbers of them succeed, become in a greater or lesser degree capitalists, or get into positions in which their interests are identified with those of capital rather than those of labour." Their savings were expanding in various ways relevant to the fourth galloping horse of pensions (below): "Still larger numbers—a considerable section of the working classes— . . . become rich men [with] money in banks, and shares in co-operative and building societies. . . ." A further comment has an echo in the increasing share ownership of the 1980s: "they are as watchful against and strongly opposed to anything that is alleged will tend to interfere with 'the sacredness of private property' or lessen dividends, as are any of the great capitalists."[22]

There is another echo in the recent discussion of the values of community versus commercialism supposedly found by misleading opinion polling. The pertinent comment at this stage is that the pace of *embourgeoisement,* the spread of markets, the speed of the galloping horses would have been faster if government had helped the emerging workers to independence instead of tying them to the chariot of the state.

Certainly in housing the proportion of people owning their homes would by now have risen from 60 per cent to the 75 per cent of Australasia. And the market would have enabled most of the remainder to have found the homes to rent that they preferred. The dreary council houses and the Soviet-like tower blocks would have been unknown.

Seventy-five years after 1915, and nearly 70 years after 1922, five million British families are still living in council homes that they would not have chosen and cannot adapt to their liking, millions more are paying rents much higher than they would have had to pay in the open market and many towns are disfigured by council tower blocks that house crime. Such is the

21. Samuel Smiles *Thrift,* John Murray, 1875, quoted in Rubinstein, *Victorian Homes.*
22. Thomas Wright, *Our New Masters,* 1873, quoted in Rubinstein, *Victorian Homes.*

incompetence, the impertinence and the lack of humility of the political process that creates socialism.

Capitalist Pensions

The private pensions horse would have galloped more strongly if the state had helped the spontaneous saving institutions instead of making its coercive take-over bid by establishing the political fraud of national insurance. It began well in 1908 with the Liberal pensions of 50 p a week for people of 70 years with little or no other income. But in 1925 the Conservative Government of Baldwin succumbed to the political temptation to spread its wings, acquire a new device for winning the affection and the votes of the electorate and create a new source of government revenue.

The original intellectual impetus again came from the ubiquitous Webbs, who had long urged state pensions. The politicians ignored the inconvenient warning of the liberal economist, Alfred Marshall, to the 1893 Royal Commission on the Aged Poor: "universal pensions . . . do not contain . . . the seeds of their own disappearance. I am afraid that, if started, they would tend to become perpetual." But the political process induces even the most upright of politicians to take the short view. The Royal Commission did not devise a pension that would "disappear" with poverty among the aged. The state pension, nominally based on a national insurance invested fund but in truth largely financed by current taxes, is now, 80 years after 1908 and approaching 70 years after 1925, paid to nearly 10 million pensioners among whom poverty is vanishing. The state pensioners of the 1990s and early twenty-first century will be comparatively affluent. But the machinery of politics moves like a tanker. It pays the politicians to continue presenting "the pensioners" as poor and pathetic. That is the humanity and compassion of the political process.

State pensions have not only become perpetual, but they have been self-expanding, a discouragement to labour mobility, a confidence trick on the pensioner (they are not guaranteed by insurance), a further corruption of representative government and a vast and still growing liability on the national exchequer. The system rests on the irony that it grows as national and personal incomes grow. The notion that, as the nation becomes richer, it can afford higher state pensions is a confusion of thought in welfare state politics. As the national income rises, so do personal incomes. The state is then supposed to distribute higher pensions as the people who retire require less. The increasing result is that the state pension is paid to the increasingly affluent. This tragic charade came home in 1968 in Canberra when I was preparing a report for the Cabinet Committee on Welfare, which was becoming alive to it. Pensioners were drawing the pension at one post office counter and paying it into a bank account at another. It was clearly not going only for immediate spending on food or other essentials by people in need but carrying coals to Newcastle.

Perhaps the state pack of cards can be blown down better by ridicule than by argument. The illusion persists in conventional political science that the best-laid plans will be accepted by government with gratitude and alacrity. When asked by the then Chairman of the Liberal Party in 1947, Philip Fothergill, to chair a small committee on policy for the aged (with Dame Barbara Shenfield and Lord Amulree, son of a Labour peer), I asked advice from Lord Beveridge, a Liberal leader whom I had met in the 1930s when he was the Director of the LSE. He had learned his mistake too late. His famous report of 1942 had recommended wide extensions to the welfare services. Now, only a few years later, he was working on a book warning against the political danger to the friendly society and other spontaneous organizations.[23] Later, in 1961, when several early IEA stalwarts dined with him at the Reform Club, he complained about the erosion of the state pension by inflation. But by 1957 and 1960, when I returned to pensions in IEA Papers, the dangers had become formidable.

Again the galloping horse had been ignored. Like Professor West in education, Dr. Green in medical care and Professor Pennance in housing, Dr. Charles Hanson had begun to document the neglected spontaneous self-help in saving for old age and argue for ways to strengthen rather than weaken it. In *The Long Debate on Poverty* he wrote a survey, entitled appropriately "Welfare before the welfare state," of the pension saving in the spontaneous organizations.[24] He condemned several works by academics for understating the growth of voluntary insurance. Even Lord Beveridge had been misled in writing *Voluntary Action:* he had overlooked the unregistered Death and Burial Societies and other voluntary organizations with some 1.64 million members and thus underestimated the growth of voluntary insurance. The membership of the registered societies, which are well documented, had risen from 4.2 million in 1891 to 6.2 million in 1909. The

23. Lord Beveridge, *Voluntary Action: A Report on Methods of Social Advance,* Allen & Unwin, 1948; followed by *The Evidence for Voluntary Action,* Allen & Unwin, 1949.

24. Charles Hanson, "Welfare before the welfare state," in *The Long Debate on Poverty,* Institute of Economic Affairs, 1972.

population census for 1891 had shown 7.1 million men over age 24 in England, Wales and Scotland. If the membership of the unregistered societies is included, Dr. Hanson seems justified in concluding that the proportion of men not voluntarily insured against sickness, and thus to some extent against old age, was "a small minority."

The British were vindicated. They were not feckless nor callous. They had cared for their families. If the state had not taken part of their earnings, first by indirect and then by direct taxes to pay for compulsory benefits, they would have done more. And they were caring more as their income rose. Research for examination of the Crossman proposals for "National Superannuation" in 1956 (another political euphemism for compulsory social benefits) revealed that the ordinary people had amassed several billions of savings in National Savings, building society shares, industrial and provident societies, friendly societies, industrial assurance, life assurance, homes, household goods and other property.

The private horse quickened its pace with the expansion of occupational pension schemes in the 1950s and 1960s. The first scheme had come in 1931. By 1936 membership had risen to 1.8 million, and by 1951 to 3.9 million in private industry. By the 1970s the total membership in funded schemes in industry and local government was around 12 million, increasingly of wage-paid as well as salaried employees.

This movement emerged in the market. The capitalist employers were falling over themselves to attract staff by adding pensions as deferred pay to current pay. Predictably the critics fastened on the defects: not all wage-earners, especially women and short-term workers, were covered (true, but improving); mobility was impeded (true, but remediable); the insurance companies were controlling the investment of the funds in industry (would a state monopoly have been preferable?); not least, the occupational pensions created the Two Nations in old age (true, but the culprit was government for enforcing saving for retirement through social insurance). Again, the market effect was overlooked: private pensions made the workers independent of the political process and its questionable devices. Professor Titmuss complained that employees were at the mercy of "a vast commercial system"; the reply was that they were much better off with a system that offered escape to alternative schemes than at the mercy of a vast political system that offered none.

The story of the pensions horse is essentially that of the education, medical and housing horses. The education horse started much earlier than the others; the medical, housing and pension horses developed more slowly; but the state jumped on all of them and slowed them all down.

It may seem more difficult to rescue welfare from the political process than other goods and services that government has captured and will not release because the elector seems superficially fearful of letting go of nurse for fear of something worse; yet it is also easier for the more fundamental reason that all four components were developed before the welfare state almost suppressed them. Their roots lie in the British character: its innate independence, its pride in self-help and its sense of responsibility for the family. All have been weakened by the state, which usurped the role of parents, cut the bonds of sympathy between parents and children and incited all to look for succour and sustenance to officialdom. Far from the market being too long absent to be restored, it is not far below the surface. To change the metaphor, all that is required is for politicians to let the horses gallop again.

Decades after the 1908 and 1925 pensions the people who could be saving for early or late retirement in numerous ways are still having to contribute as taxpayers to a non-existent national insurance fund for a basic pension paid increasingly to the rich. The irony of the political process is that even where it sets out to do good it ends by doing harm. Compared with the racehorses of capitalist welfare, state welfare was characterized by David Low's trade union carthorse.

Conclusion

The charge against the political process for impeding the development of private, voluntary, capitalist welfare is not only that education, medicine, housing and pensions would have developed more efficiently and responsively to changing wants and circumstances in the market than under the state. It is not only that they should therefore be transferred without further political prevarication from the state to the market. It is essentially that there is ample evidence from history that they would by now have expanded in the market if they had not been suppressed by the state.

The welfare services have, in the event, developed not in response to the people's wishes but as a result of political calculation and bureaucratic suasion. Both influences were rationalized and reinforced by intellectual error on the power and beneficence of the state. The clinical academic debate on the merits and defects of the welfare state before it was established was whether the state would perform better than the market had done, not the more relevant how much better the market could have done. After it was established, the debate was whether the state had performed better than the market had done, not the more relevant how much better the market would have done. Whatever the outcome of this debate, the welfare state as it has developed was not the reaction of private welfare institutions to individual wants or circumstances but of government to political judgement of the electorally desirable and the expedient.

Once the welfare state began a century ago, it spread by the internal volition of its suppliers, not by the external approval or demand of its beneficiaries. State initiative, government direction, nil-pricing, tax financing and public (bureaucratic) administration were the chosen instruments. It is easy to see why. Poverty, stark inequality, widespread hardship and general unmet "needs" were documented by the social investigators. The poor could not be expected to raise themselves by their own bootstraps. Primitive schools, inaccessible medical care, shabby housing and little income in old age would have to be replaced and provided from outside by government. Families could not help much. Charity was insufficient—and degrading. Clearly succour had to come from outside agencies with far more resources.

It is easy to see why politicians (of all parties) and administrators (of all state services) applauded the thinking of the political and literary observers of the social scene who saw the solution only in the state. Political science has trustingly discussed the intentions of opposing politicians and their sea-green incorruptible bureaucrats as concerned dominantly with the public good rather than with the new source of political patronage and power, or high office and honours in the burgeoning welfare state. The relatively few who had doubts were largely ignored. The voluntary organizations, the friendly societies and commercial industrial insurance companies established of the people, by the people and for the people were damned with faint praise, condemned as wasteful and costly, and finally almost destroyed.

What do politicians, bureaucrats and academics learn from history? A century after the 1880s, the Fabian and other socialist minds in all parties who have profoundly influenced the course of the welfare state are beginning to concede that the hope of their predecessors has not been fulfilled, that they had not foreseen the insensitivity of the state and its agencies—the arrogance, inflexibility, bureaucracy, waste and corruption. If, like Nassau Senior, John Stuart Mill, Alfred Marshall and others they had looked ahead to the advances of the twentieth century, what would they have urged for education in 1870, for housing in 1919, for pensions in 1925 and for medicine in 1948? What is the responsibility of well-meaning men and women in politics and academia, in the sciences and the arts, as teachers and preachers who have peddled error and made others suffer?

The use of the state was the main error. And its provision of services in kind was the secondary error. The question is what else could have been done? The obvious alternative was to provide purchasing power in cash, general or earmarked, rather than services in kind. It seems unrealistic to have argued for purchasing power instead of the trade board schools in 1870. This doubt has been voiced by the scrupulous historian of economic thought, Professor T. W. Hutchison. It clearly carries weight. Cash might not have been handled responsibly by parents with low incomes short of other staples. The consumer, as present-day critics of the family urge, is not the parent but the child, who at the age of five or six could hardly be expected to handle money.

Yet history controverts even well-founded later speculation. The notion of supplying "tickets"—earmarked purchasing power designated as school fees for parents with large families—was considered by the Liberal W. E. Forster, Gladstone's Minister. It was written into the 1870 Bill, but Professor West claims that, apart from the Manchester School Board which used it for private schools, the experiment was ended by a political campaign led by the Conservative Joseph Chamberlain because it used a means test that, he said, as the socialist mind has said in our day, humiliated poor families.[25]

This is the argument perennially used by the socialist mind in all parties to obstruct policies of compassion to give more to the poorer than to the richer. The post-war consensus favoured universalist policies—the Left because they made for a larger state, the Right because it lost sight of its principles and settled for electoral expediency.

Perhaps Joseph Chamberlain in the 1870s could not be expected to foresee the humiliation in developing the welfare state of poor (and non-poor) families who lack the political skills required to obtain access to state services. Yet if the experiment in earmarked purchasing power failed in 1870 for short-sighted political reasons, money was given by the state on a means test to people aged 70 in 1908; they were not degraded by a means test, or by being given bags of groceries. Money was also later given by the social insurance system to the unemployed in 1911 and to the sick in 1925.

Clearly, even before the opening of the twentieth century, the British were not the incurable feckless irresponsible incompetents of the paternalistic

25. E. G. West, in *Education: A Framework for Choice*, Institute of Economic Affairs, 1967, 2nd edn. 1970.

imagination. There were many bad cases, but too often in British history the passing bad cases have been used to create permanent bad institutions. That is the charge against the founders, administrators and continuing supporters of the welfare state.

The politicians and their bureaucracies are also generally poor historians. The proved ability of the British to handle money was the legacy of the very market institutions in education, medicine and housing that the welfare state almost destroyed. The British had been providing cash benefits for themselves in sickness, unemployment and old age long before the state made its take-over bid for their voluntary institutions created of working men, by working men, for working men. They were elbowed out by politicians and bureaucrats who took their money, called taxes, to buy their assets, indulged in the strong-arm tactics of driving them out of the market by charging less than cost (the euphemism of free) and continually threatened them with extinction.

The circular reasoning in the long advocacy of state welfare should have been apparent. The working classes could not be left to make responsible choices. The state had to make the choices for them and their families. In the (political) process, the working-class faculties of judgement and discrimination were almost destroyed. Therefore, even when in the succeeding decades they became more competent by practice to judge private purchases in the market, they remained incompetent to judge the services supplied by the state. *Quod erat demonstrandum.*

There can be no remaining doubt that the bulk of the state services in kind could gradually have been replaced by cash, certainly from the 1920s. The welfare state created after the Second World War at the end of the 1940s could then have been avoided by refinement of methods to top up the lower incomes. All the people, including even the physically disabled and except only the mentally sick, could then have taken their place as consumers shopping for education, medicine, housing and pensions together with the increasing majority whose earnings required no topping up. That is the capitalist vision of welfare in the market.

The remaining doubts are secondary. The debilitating effect on character of unearned income from the state, the secondary poverty risk that it would be misspent and the uncertainty whether many parents can be entrusted with the interests of children have some truth. But the circular reasoning continues. It is easily refuted. Money is superior to services because it is only by human experience that error can be learned and avoided. And even if not all learn to avoid error, there is no reason to subject those who do to the same paternalism. If some parents cannot choose for their children it was the welfare state that usurped their roles and weakened the bonds of family by warning parents that they could do little for their children, and teaching their children that their parents were impotent spectators in their education, in their home conditions and when they were ill.

The vision of capitalist welfare is obstructed only by the political process. When the people can choose in the market process, with realistic calculation of individual costs and benefits (and not the shadow world of priceless opinion polls in which taxes are paid by other people), they will choose private rather than state education, private doctors and hospitals rather than the NHS, buying or renting homes of their choice rather than paying even subsidized rents in council tenantry and private, flexible and transferable rather than standardized and politicized state pensions.

The capitalist vision of liberty in prosperity has been denied by over-use of the political process.

CHAPTER 12

The Values of Capitalism

> The co-ordination of human activities by a system of impersonal rules within which spontaneous relations are conducive to mutual benefit, a conception at least as subtle as prescribing each action by a central planning authority, . . . is perhaps not less in harmony with the requirements of a spiritually sound society.
>
> Lionel Robbins, *Economic Planning and International Order*

> . . . you do not get rid of false values simply by substituting state ownership for private enterprise.
>
> J. B. Priestley, *Out of the People*

> . . . men are in general more honest in their private than in their public capacity.
>
> David Hume, "Of the independency of parliament," in *Essays Moral, Political and Literary*

> There are few ways in which a man can be more innocently employed than in getting money.
>
> Samuel Johnson, Boswell, *Life of Johnson*

> The values of the ordinary public are beyond the control of government. . . . They are shaped by experience, not theory, and mutate slowly in response to real change, not to government exhortations.
>
> Ivor Crewe, in Dennis Kavanagh and Anthony Seldon (eds.), *The Thatcher Effect*

Capitalism has stood condemned for its reprehensible morals. Even where its productivity is acknowledged, it is charged with exacting an unacceptably high price—the obsession with self.

The values of socialism are presented as self-evidently superior: the essence of selflessness—sharing, compassion, community and other plainly estimable traits of the human character. Yet in socialism as we have known it—from the totalitarian socialism of the USSR to the democratic socialism of the British nationalized industries, welfare services and local government—these qualities are not always conspicuous. Their precarious existence is too obvious to deny wherever state power, the political process in electing government and the ethos of politics dominate economic life and exchange between individuals. Their absence from the communist countries hardly requires emphasis. It is more disagreeable but no less pertinent to insist that the recent history of the British socialized coal and transport industries, state education and medicine, and municipal governments reveals abuses and excesses that socialists would not accept as characteristic of the socialism they have portrayed or envisaged.

Socialist values have been exceptional, even rare, in the socialized sectors of the British economy and society. The daily behaviour of coal miners or railwaymen, teachers or doctors (except in emergency), local councillors or their officials is not generally on a higher moral plane that makes them shine as paragons of virtue in contrast with their spouses or children, relatives or friends who work in private industry or commercial society. Nor does the ethical standard in the artistic and cultural worlds reveal itself as self-evidently superior to that of citizens working in manufacturing or trading business whose taxes support them.

Socialist and Capitalist Morals

Yet socialists continue stubbornly to claim their values as the distinctive characteristics of socialism. For decades the people have been told that the public services are morally elevated above private services, that people in government work selflessly for the general good but people in the market work selfishly for their personal good. The words of the well-worn but strange device on the socialist banner—that socialist production would be "for use, not for profit"—is an effective political slogan; it has won the support of millions of voters in the polling booth. Yet it is not the daily experience of the same people as the consumers of public service in state monopolies.

Neither socialist doctrine nor socialist practice demonstrates these tall claims to superior virtue. Human nature—a mixture of good and bad, of selfishness (not necessarily bad in its effects on others) and selflessness (not always good)—remains much the same everywhere under all economic systems, socialism as well as capitalism. What differs is the opportunities for the baser and the nobler instincts of humankind.

The service of self is universal, not because men and women are consciously selfish but because they can serve only the purposes they know, and in practice that means the interests of those nearest to them—themselves and their families. Other interests are increasingly remote: those of neighbours, friends, the community, the local hospital, school or old people's home, the town, the country.

The error is to confuse purpose with result, motive with consequence. The man or woman who intends good will do harm under perverse inducements; intentions to do good may produce harm even under benign inducements.

The decisive difference lies in the man-made institutions and their impulsions that decide whether the service of self also serves or harms others. That is the essential difference between political and commercial society, and between socialism and capitalism.

Self-proclamation of benevolent purpose is no guide to consequences. No politician has declared harm, but many have perpetrated it. Businessmen do not declare intentions to do good, but in competitive capitalism are bankrupted sooner or later if they do not. With the best of intentions the clerics of England have done harm in recent years by decrying the emergence of opportunities for men in the market to make money. Yet the men who have made money by producing objects or creating services for which others voluntarily pay have done good even if their purpose was solely to make money. The inducements of capitalism compel the money-makers to do good; the inducements of socialism enable the power-holders to do harm. The virtue of capitalism is that it divorces purpose from result: it does not require good men or women. The vice of socialism is that men and women who may start with good intentions, but who are skilled in acquiring coercive power, can use it to do harm.

Capitalism has suffered long from the easy criticism that it does not always work as intended: it is not always competitive; the inefficient or dishonest are not always discovered promptly; consumers are not always well informed. The case for capitalism, despite its absence of claims to be virtuous, is not that bad men can do no harm but that when they do they are discovered and spewed out of the system more readily than under socialism. The evil of socialism, despite its profession of high moral values, is that bad men who do harm are not promptly or easily discovered, or, if they are, can maintain themselves in power by secrecy or force for decades. The capitalist rich who live by monopoly can tyrannize their fellows for a time, but they do not always enjoy their precarious wealth, and their power does not last as long as the political power of tyrants who control the state. Commercial failure is evidence that capitalism is working; political longevity in socialism is probably evidence of prolonged irresponsibility.

The allied difference is that capitalism as it has been has not always acted as it could, because capitalism has had to work with, or under, a political process that fetters it. Socialism as it has been is the best that it could be because its defects derive from the institutions of socialism. That it has suffered from the "mistakes" of bad men is a symptom of its disease that bad men can rise to the top and stay there undetected almost all their lives and die in old age, still doing harm. No capitalist lasts a lifetime harming a whole capitalist economy.

The morals of men and women in the market are generally higher than those in public life, which includes all who live on the public purse—politicians and their employees, bureaucrats and officials, and the recipients of public funds, ranging from landowners and farmers through doctors and teachers to artists and writers, impresarios and artistic directors. The market may not initially produce good men and women but it gives them short shrift if they become bad by exploiting their power. The political process attracts the good and the bad, but the bad are rewarded arbitrarily and can be self-perpetuating.

This claim is incontrovertible in the comparative sense: the market discovers and ejects its bad people sooner than politics. Capitalism is largely corrigible; socialism is relatively incorrigible.

The assertive claim of socialism to high moral values has distracted discussion away from the values of capitalism. The frequent condemnation of the British governments of the 1980s is not always clearly distinguished from criticisms of the ethics of the market. Yet socialists would not wish to defend socialist values from the record of socialist governments, whether in the USSR, Sweden or Britain.

Capitalist government which operates a market economy is less likely to betray and diverge from capitalist values than socialist government is likely to betray and diverge from socialist values. Since departure from capitalist values is discovered sooner and corrected more promptly than departure from socialist values, capitalist government is less able to conceal departure from capitalist values than socialist government is able to conceal departure from socialist values. Capitalist government is thus less able to escape criticism from the exponents of capitalist values than socialist government can escape criticism from the exponents of socialist values.

In the relatively open economies of the United Kingdom and the United

States activity in the market in the 1980s was more exposed to examination than were the more state-directed economies of the 1960s or 1970s in both. Neither could conceal the statistics of output, employment, inflation and unemployment; even where they are manipulated, the political critics are properly in full cry. Under the post-war British governments that sought salvation in state planning and industrial corporativism, economic performance reflected less the real values put on goods and services by consumers in the market than the artificial values put on official statistics by government. The official statistics of unemployment reflect the productive employment of labour only in a market economy. When government influences a large part of economic activity its statistics may reflect little more than short-term political imperatives and expediencies.

Economic performance under capitalist government is more exposed to criticism than economic performance under socialist government because the exponents of capitalist values are less committed by philosophical belief to capitalist government than are the exponents of socialist values to socialist government. This is a profound difference in the attitude of British academics that partly explains the wide imbalance in the advocacy of capitalism and socialism for a century since Marx and the Fabians.

Liberal scholars are by nature more independently individualistic than socialist scholars. They are less likely to advise non-socialist politicians than socialist scholars are to advise socialist politicians. Hayek wrote an appendix, "Why I am not a Conservative" to his major statement of liberal policy, *The Constitution of Liberty;*[1] I cannot recall a parallel dissociative statement by a comparable socialist scholar.

The liberal tends to be more independent of political adherence and entanglement. His disinclination to party allegiance may also reflect the failure of Conservative politicians, even in the 1980s, to buttress their policies with academic reinforcement, partly because some Conservative politicians and academics hold the view that government policy must be pragmatic rather than ideological, which in practice has often meant opportunistic rather than principled. Whatever its possible merits in enabling Conservative governments to tack with the wind of popular fashion, pragmatism led them to the acceptance of socialism in the post-war years. It was left to the non-political, philosophically libertarian but intellectually radical IEA to reformulate economic liberalism for almost 20 years before Lord Joseph and the conviction politics of Mrs. Thatcher revolutionized the Conservative Party

1. F. A. Hayek, "Why I am not a Conservative," in *The Constitution of Liberty*, Routledge, 1960.

in the 1970s, and 25 years before Dr. David Owen in 1981 and 30 years before Neil Kinnock more reservedly in 1989 accepted the necessity of the market.

The politico-economic argument on the claims of capitalism and socialism has moved from their institutions to their values. On institutions the victory has clearly gone to the liberals who advocate capitalism, not to the socialists who urge socialism. The liberals have learned little from socialism; it is the socialists who have learned from liberalism. In their adoption of the market they remain ambivalent about their acceptance of the capitalism it creates and requires. But the socialist claim is now that the socialist contribution to civilized society is the emphasis on socialist values—sharing, compassion, community and their derivatives.

This change in emphasis is a defensive rearguard action in philosophical political tactics. If the socialists have lost the intellectual argument on institutions, it would be charitable to suppose that they have won the argument on values. Yet the debate is lowered from the lofty heights of philosophical principle to the mundane reaches of political machinery, where the outcome turns on whether liberal or socialist politicians are the more likely to safeguard the values of sharing, compassion, community. . . .

The immediate liberal reply is that, for three reasons, these values are more secure under capitalism than under socialism. First, the capitalist institution of personal ownership of property creates the wealth required to apply the values of compassion, sharing and giving. Second, the capitalist institution of minimal and decentralized government makes the personal ambience of the citizen more influential than the impersonal administrative ambience of the politician and the bureaucrat in disposing of it. Third, compassionate sharing in communities requires the voluntary association of individuals; it is destroyed if artificially created by the coercive direction of government. Giving is more common in the capitalist United States than in the USSR. The Community Chests of the USA stand in stark contrast to the "stock-taking" theft of spare parts from the common-owned factories of Soviet communism and from the common-owned offices and kitchens of British and other socialism.

For the political probabilities of government policy the question remains whether the capitalist institutions belatedly recognized as indispensable by socialist politicians will be as safe in their hands as with liberal politicians who have intermittently understood and applied them in their political history. The least that non-political liberals must record is scepticism. It is not impossible that socialist politicians in the 1990s will nurture capitalist institutions, as Gorbachev is having to do in the USSR and his confrères in Eastern Europe. But in Britain the long heritage of anti-capitalist academic sentiment and the reality of trade union financing must strengthen doubt whether the new doctrine of market socialism will induce a socialist-inspired Labour government to put the market before the socialism.

The values kindled and buttressed by the institutions of capitalism are, moreover, no less essential to what Lionel Robbins called "a spiritually sound society" than is compassionate sharing in communities. The socialist mind continues to repeat the circular reasoning (in his socialist phase) of John Stuart Mill in emphasizing distribution, or redistribution, but overlooking its close effect on the production without which distribution was abortive. Goods and services must be produced before they are distributed. The primary economic task is to maximize production, not to optimize distribution to satisfy a notion of justice or fairness. The poor are better served by maximizing production than by equalizing distribution. Capitalism maximizes production. The equal distribution claimed (but not achieved) by socialism reduces production.

The values essential to maximize production remain offensive to the socialist mind. Production requires ethical acceptance of the primary motive of self-regard, that it is proper for a man to do his best for the interests he knows best because they are closest to him. Its economic expression in commercial life is maximizing the surplus of receipts over expenditure in markets based on individual decisions in buying and selling. Most revolutionary for the socialist mind (in all schools and parties), individual preferences, decisions and values expressed in the market must be ranked above preferences, decisions and values expressed in the political process—the life of winning power and ruling over fellow citizens by majority decisions that require minorities and individuals to be ignored and thwarted.

The morality of the commercial life is absolute and relative. It lies not only in its necessity to produce the resources required for distribution. It lies also in its superiority to the morality of its alternative, the life political. Neither is wholly good; both have faults. Commerce and politics can be misused by people with power to further their personal purposes at the expense of their fellow citizens. But the scope for abuse of power is less in commerce than in politics. The choice is between the advantages and limitations of commerce and of politics. Capitalism rests essentially on commerce, socialism on politics. That is why capitalism is preferable to socialism: not only because its advantages are more but also because its limitations are less.

The capitalist reliance on commerce is based on the market. This form of economic life, which socialism has condemned for a century, which it now accepts and which is essential for the sustenance of what are claimed as socialist values, requires the rehabilitation of concepts that socialists in some walks of life continue to deplore. The ethical rejection of commercial values remains the stumbling block to the moral acceptance of capitalism and its values.

Four continuing sources of criticism of the commercial ethics of capitalism, similar to many others, must be abandoned if socialist values are to be saved by capitalist institutions: they are based on misunderstanding of the elementary imperatives of human life or intellectual confusion in the arts, journalism, sociology and the church.

The Cultural Critique and the Values of Culture

The distaste felt by the moralistic critics of capitalism re-emerged during the assessments of capitalist values in 1989, the tenth anniversary of Mrs. Thatcher's first election as head of government in 1979. The "celebrations" were used by the critics of Conservative government as an occasion for condemnation of the capitalist system and all its works.

The criticisms were made—and reflect the socialist mind in all the critics, whatever their political allegiance or daily occupation—about a short period of ten years, a series of three governments and a named Prime Minister, but they revealed deep-rooted hostility to the values of the capitalist economic system in principle. The critics were personifying the capitalist system in a female politician.

The Thatcher Governments of the 1980s have put into vigorous public debate the role of the market as the arbiter of taste as well as everyday goods and services. A small sample from the flood of argument in the journals and the "heavy" newspapers illustrates the fundamental issue of values in capitalism and socialism.

The historian, Professor John Vincent of Bristol University, corrected the critics' historical inaccuracies by recalling the characters of earlier Prime Ministers.[2] Criticisms of philistinism, inciting greed and selfishness, and poor taste were variously levelled by cultured and literary society at Wellington, Gladstone, Balfour, Asquith and Churchill. They reflected the remoteness of the critics from the lives of the ordinary people, whom the current critics expect to pay in subsidies for their cultured tastes and literary pursuits.

2. John Vincent, "Is the Prime Minister a philistine?," *Daily Telegraph*, 4 May 1989, p. 18.

Their case was put in a temperately worded plea by the Artistic Director of the Royal Shakespeare Company, Terry Hands, for a more generous subsidy for the arts[3] which calls for more respectful analysis than the condemnations that conceal political enmity or social snobbery.

The reasoned case touched on but did not quantify the opportunity cost of the desired subsidies: ". . . increased investment in the arts would return to the Exchequer a greater sum than it removed." This is a claim that many other activities could make but not substantiate—sport, pure research, the addition of Russian to the school curriculum and many more. Increased investment would add to their eventual yield in the long run, but government could not justify it unless it yielded more than investment elsewhere, which the artistic world does not calculate. Behind its awesome array of statistics, the government's decisions, here as elsewhere, are based partly or largely on guesswork. They are nowhere nearly as responsible as the decisions in the market, where people spend their own money and suffer if they are careless. As argued in chapter 5, individuals who spend their money responsibly in the marketplace are made to "spend" their votes irresponsibly in the polling booth for policies whose effects they are not told and whose cost they cannot calculate, but which they believe will be paid by others.

"Debate on the arts," regretted Mr. Hands, "must begin with economics." An economist must insist that it must not only begin but also end with economics, because no other approach illuminates the opportunity costs to others of political decisions. Individuals are usually acutely sensitive to the sacrifices of the alternatives they forgo when deciding their purchases in the market; governments are less sensitive because their time horizon is short and they have no way of measuring what is lost and who suffers. The market provides information on costs and preferences. It is incomplete and may have to be supplemented, but it reflects the opinions and decisions of the real people who pay. The alternative, which politicians and the artists subsidized by them would prefer, is, in effect if not intention, massive ignorance, concealed by guesswork, with a spicing of political self-interest.

Governments, it is argued, should allow for "the spiritual, educative, healing aspects of the arts"; but how much? for whose benefit? at whose expense? The artistic world is not interested in the answers, but the ordinary people are intimately anxious, because the money could go to purposes they prefer, not least to the impoverished old who cannot earn.

3. Terry Hands, "Wanted: a dramatic vision to avert a cultural deficit," *Daily Telegraph*, 8 May 1989, p. 16.

The arts have always required patronage. Nations and states have usually been proud to express their economic vitality in the creative display of their civilizations. But states and governments have used other people's money, and they have either not asked their peoples or have used the very imperfect and clumsy democratic process to discover their opinions.

Medieval prelates and landed aristocrats sponsored the arts; some were autocrats, but there were escapes. Handel could move to England, where he composed the "Water Music" for George I in 1713 and the "Messiah" in 1723. The nineteenth-century middle-class industrialists sponsored the arts; some had bad taste, but there were escapes to other patrons.

The role of the industrial patron is usually understated by artistic people who, like doctors and university vice-chancellors, would prefer their money to come from the state. Bradford produced William Rothenstein, David Hockney, Richard Eurich and other artists; it is less well known that it also produced outstanding industrial patrons of the arts in the age of Victoria, especially in the second half of the nineteenth century when men of Bradford had accumulated "brass" in the heyday of textile capitalism. Several industrial capitalists established private art collections, financed exhibitions and supported local arts clubs.

The most generous was probably Samuel Cunliffe Lister, who was born in 1815, the year of the Battle of Waterloo, and lived until the advent of the brilliant Liberal Governments under Campbell-Bannerman and Asquith in 1906, which included Winston Churchill and Lloyd George. In 1898 he gave the Bradford Corporation the then large sum of £40,000 to build an art gallery in memory of his famous uncle, Edmund Cartwright, who invented the wool-combing machine in 1789. Cartwright Hall was opened in 1904 with approaching 1,000 pictures, prints and drawings, mainly the work of artists of the New English Art Club formed in 1885.

The preference of the artist is understandably for a simple single source, especially of government, to provide funds and release the performing arts from resort to "competitive begging bowls." That is what we should all like. It is the universal Utopia, desired by doctors and scientists as well as artists. "Let government raise the money," they say in effect, "and leave us experts who seek only the public weal to spend it as only we know how."

This was the mirage of Marx. Emancipate us from the real world; we would rather not have to justify ourselves to our customers in competition with all the other calls on their pennies and their attention. But that is to formulate the human dilemma, not to solve it. No wonder it was the lodestar of the benevolent Left that it is belatedly abandoning in favour of the market, the only mechanism that teaches the unwelcome but inescapable truth that there are not enough resources in the world to do everything desirable. Little wonder economics has been called "the dismal science" by the heirs of Thomas Carlyle who have misled mankind by their rejection of the real world but offered no signposts to the world of their imagination.

The central question is whether the arts are to be sponsored directly by the people in the money they pay for visiting the theatre, opera, ballet, museums, art galleries and the like, or indirectly through government. The issues here are essentially the same as elsewhere. The choice is between the commercial and the political systems of production and payment. The commercial method is described as philistine, the political as public spirited and civilized. For the people the difference is between payment as consumers by individual decisions, or as taxpayers by political collective decision. As consumers they spend their own money; as taxpayers their money is spent for them by others.

The same risks apply as elsewhere. As consumers, people may be uninformed, take short views, be overimpressed by advertising, lose the spiritual elevation of a world of art unknown to them. Government may ideally take a longer view, keep alive the artistic works of the past from Shakespearean drama through the operas of Mozart and Rossini to the paintings of Constable, Manet and Chagall. But there are dangers.

As elsewhere, both the market process and the political process carry risks. If the producers, or reproducers, of art look to government for money rather than, or as well as, to the consumer, they will be sensitive to political authority. Politicians are not chosen as patrons of the arts but as defenders of the realm. Their tastes, or the tastes of their advisers, may be far removed from those of the taxpayers whose money they are dispensing. Not least, here as elsewhere, the middle classes with developed tastes stand to gain more from government patronage than the working classes whose taxes largely finance it.

The case for the arts is the familiar argument that activities with clear external benefits to the community as a whole justify collective finance through government. That principle—or value—does not seem to be in dispute. The latest estimate is that of the culture industry's earnings of £4 billion a year, £1.5 billion derived from overseas visitors who come to see Shakespeare in Stratford, opera at the Covent Garden and Glyndebourne, the theatre in London and much else.[4] This impressive sum provides no certain

4. John Myerscough, *The Economic Importance of the Arts in Britain,* Policy Studies Institute, 1988.

basis for a subsidy. Externalities are universal. Other industries earn US dollars, German Deutschmarks, French francs, Swiss francs . . . by their invisible exports of services—insurance, banking, shipping, brokerage and so forth. They do not claim subsidies. The visitors to Stratford, Glyndebourne, London, Edinburgh and elsewhere benefit the transport services, the shops and the hotels. If every activity that created external benefits for other individuals or industries were subsidized, there would be no end to demands on the public purse.

Even if the principle of subsidy could not be dismissed, what is very much in dispute is the competence of government to decide its extent, control its use, vary it with circumstance or finally liquidate it when outdated. The optimum amount of collective finance would be decided politically; there would be no assessment of the optimum opportunity cost in finance lost to roads, extra pensions for old people who cannot earn, the mentally ill without family, kidney machines or coastal protection. The likelihood is that politicians would take the short view between General Elections rather than the long view of decades. Experience in the past century creates no confidence that government would combine competence with disinterest.

The choice is between the risks of commerce and the risks of politics. The central risk of commerce is that consumers will aim too low and spend too little on the arts: they will tend to be philistines. The opposite risk of politics is that politicians will yield to the persuasive importunities of artistic enthusiasts and forget the silent sentiments of the untutored unorganized philistines: politicians will tend to be opportunists, pretend to artistic judgement and act as dispensers of other people's nectar. They will spend too much.

The subconscious reason for the anxiety of politicians to enter politics and to acquire power is that it gives them access to vast amounts of money that they would otherwise have no prospect of commanding. That is the aspect of "politics" overlooked by the academics who instinctively urge more power for government to improve on the free choice of consumers in the market. Politicians will understandably rationalize the process as the intention to do good. We should not be deceived.

The decisive risk of putting the arts into the political process is that it reduces the revenue likely to reach them through consumers in the market and by private subvention from industry. The artistic world is most persuasive when it speaks of public finance as supplementing private revenue. There are two errors. The two sources are not necessarily complementary; they may be competitive. State finance has made the arts (and the universities) indolent in raising supporting finance from private industry and the consumer. It is evidently easier to importune politicians, especially those with artistic leanings or reluctant to seem philistine, than to ask for support from industry or the consumer at the booking-office or pay-desk. Government takes less pains to justify its cultural subsidies to its uncultured taxpayers than company directors to shareholders. Politicians are less accountable or responsible than capitalists.

Political subsidy, here as elsewhere, weakens the instinct to win, to survive unaided. The convenience of political subvention has also distracted the arts from the task of selling its wares to the consumer. Little wonder he buys artistic wares less than the producers would like. The art world puts itself spiritually above the marketplace, yet art is sold in competition with other purchases made by the public. If it were sold as effectively as groceries it would be more profitable. The absence of effective marketing of the arts to the public that does not know of them has resulted in less frequent visits to theatres and galleries and lower prices than active salesmanship could have generated. Better marketing would have increased the demand for the arts from the increasingly affluent public, enabled prices to be raised and reduced the dependence on government.

Political subvention has had the opposite effect of encouraging overelaborate productions which have inflated costs. Yet subsidized prices in the stalls benefit the middle classes more than the subsidized prices in the galleries benefit the working classes. And the soccer patron may demand countervailing middle-class subsidies to provide seating and other comforts to reduce the risks of partisan friction. The external benefits in police time, ambulances diverted from road accidents, nurses from tending children are incalculable.

The market for art in all its forms would have been larger if its appreciation had been taught in the state schools. The state elementary school I attended until age 12 told me nothing about the visual arts or classical music. The private schools were more likely to teach the arts. By 12 my wife had learned of the great British dramatists, heard weekly readings from the classical novelists and poets, listened to classical music and opera and visited exhibitions of the great painters. The school fees were £20 a term, remitted to less than £10 because her father was a disabled soldier (and excused entirely for refugee pupils from Germany). British children would have learned more in schools responsive to the expectations of parents, who by now would have known more of the arts in the fee-paid schools that all could have attended, if the state had created a structure of choice in place of the teacher-dominated schools of state paternalism.

The British are inherently no more philistine than the Germans or the Italians who throng the opera or the Dutch and Italian families who gladly pay at the entrance to their numerous museums and art galleries. Shakespeare's plays were written for and loved by the common people of the late sixteenth century. If the British of the twentieth century have grown with little appreciation of the nuances of the English language, the philistines are those who neglected the tasks of nurturing and responding to the potential welcome for the best of English literature and light opera, Italian and French grand opera, German porcelain, Russian ballet, Austrian *lieder* and much more that would have been marketed effectively to the common people if the arts had not become divorced from popular taste by overdependence on the state.

The theatre is ideally the world of artistic excellence. Whether a theatre subsidized by the people should offend its moral sentiments is hardly irrelevant. The Royal Shakespeare Company presented in October 1989 a play that implied parallels between the concentration camps and Mrs. Thatcher's Britain. The parallels were offensive to many who paid for the Shakespeare Company. The amoral technical performance, including the direction by Terry Hands, was highly praised. The debatable ethics of state subsidy remain.

The Journalists' Critique and the Values of Journalism

The desire to escape from the market is ubiquitous. Most of us think that we are experts in our jobs; we know what is good and what is bad, and we know better than our customers who are amateurs. This self-delusion seems to be true of journalists as well as of artists, doctors, lawyers and others who can more plausibly claim the authority of experts.

Journalists have often rebelled against the central value of capitalism both that the customer knows best and that he is best placed to learn from mistakes in buying the second-best. They have been among the most persistent critics of capitalism in general. In their industry or profession they have rebelled against the commercialism that requires the press to pay by making a profit. Some British "heavy" newspapers (and periodicals) have long been, and some still are, subsidized by men of wealth, one of the more beneficent indulgences of the rich that provide cheap newspapers for the general reader. The defence of capitalism in the press runs deeper.

The emergence of newspapers that offer entertainment as much as, or more than, news and interpretation to the newly affluent working classes has offended some journalists and provoked criticism of low standards and poor taste in British popular newspapers with large circulations. And the offence is exacerbated by the concentrated control with which a handful of newspaper owners have crowded out small newspapers.

In a free society resting on free markets in capital, paper, printing machinery, journalists, printers, newspaper wholesalers and retail newsagents, new competitors would emerge sooner or later to outbid the incumbents by producing better or cheaper newspapers. If the incumbents are not protected or subsidized by the state, the new competitors will wake up the backward incumbents or drive them out, and the public will benefit.

There is no monopoly in publishing. As in the Industrial Revolution, the latest technology has swamped the present-day mercantilists in the printing trade unions; it has improved newspapers, made them better value and enabled entrepreneurial local newspapers to thrive. The aim should therefore be to remove the remaining obstacles to the free markets in the production and distribution of the press from national newspapers to small circulation specialist journals for bee-keepers and anglers.

This liberal policy, with its encouragement to progress without weakening the independence and freedom of journalism, is not enough for some journalists. They want faster, more direct solutions. An elder statesman among them, Geoffrey Goodman, who served a 1970s Prime Minister as head of a Counter-inflationary Publicity Unit, was appointed to the Royal Commission on the Press which reported in 1977. Logically for a journalist of his Labour-socialist sympathies, Mr. Goodman wrote a Minority Report with a trade union leader that recommended state finance for the press, the familiar solution of socialist-minded critics of the free market.

In the late 1980s, still dissatisfied with low standards, Mr. Goodman emerged as editor of a journal designed to "look at the Press, applaud its excellence and hold its black spots up to criticism."[5] This purpose is not only unexceptionable: it is a natural safeguard against low standards and for the protection of the consumer that a free market makes possible. There have long been similar independent assessors of goods and services in other industries, although, like *Which?* and *Where?,* they mostly came after the independent scrutinies of goods and services in the home of competitive capitalism, the United States, and they cater mainly for middle-class rather

5. Geoffrey Goodman, "Taking the long view," *The Times,* 10 May 1989, p. 34.

than working-class shoppers. I have yet to hear of *Which?*'s and *Where?*'s in the home of socialism, the USSR. Like other well-meaning middle-class efforts to guide the public, not least the Open University, they fortify the already literate.

Like some other journalists, Mr. Goodman did not see the relevance of the market—and its values—for his enterprise. The concentration of ownership had led to increasing polarization between the minority high-quality national Press and the "majority tabloid mass circulation newspapers . . . which offered only entertainment and trivia . . . with profound social and political implications." The new quarterly *British Journalism Review*, which would go beyond newspapers to television, advertising and public relations, would form the vehicle for "people who care about journalism and journalistic values." These would be reflected in articles that propagated "a humane journalism, a journalism of disclosure and information that places truth and democracy above the demands of the market."

In plain language they would be the values of journalists rather than of the masses. For, although the tabloids are owned by rich men, they are rich because the unrich masses buy their newspapers. Since the masses have a wide choice in a free market between the heavies and the tabloids, they are not entirely under the influence of journalists or proprietors who would like to produce the newspapers they think the masses ought to read.

But the masses can be influenced by introducing material reflecting journalists' values—like Mr. Goodman's "truth and democracy." The values of journalists, at best, would be those of the revered C. P. Scott of the liberal *Manchester Guardian* admired in my youth long before it was transformed into the socialist-inclined *Guardian*. Scott delivered (in 1926) the immortal dictum once respected by all journalists: "Comment is free but facts are sacred." The liberal *Manchester Guardian* stood for the free market that respects the judgement of the consumer. Mr. Goodman's approach suggests disrespect for the values of the consumer.

The market does not suppose that the consumer is all-wise, but that only he or she knows where the shoe pinches, is anxious to make the best use of his/her money, will listen to advice and resents being told how to live by people who think they are his/her betters. That is how the consumer was developing a century ago until paternalistic government, favoured by well-meaning but shallow-thinking journalists with uncritical faith in the state, undermined the ability of the common people to learn from experience and from advice, and removed their power to decide how to live.

The "truth and democracy" that most journalists put "above the market" since the war led them, until recently, to welcome and propagate the power of the state in the lives of the ordinary people that has stunted their capacity to judge for themselves. Little wonder they often choose unwisely. If the people are to be treated like incompetents who waste their money and their substance on "tabloid mass circulation papers" that offer only "entertainment and trivia," the fault must lie at least in part with a system of education that did not teach them better. Yet socialist-inclined journalists on newspapers on the Right as well as on the Left were enthusiastic supporters not only of the principle of state education, which in practice means politicized education; they also campaigned for the principle of herding children of all abilities and potentials into a single kind of school. And the Education Correspondents, again with honourable rare exceptions like John Izbicki of *The Telegraph* and Tim Devlin of *The Times* who gave the idea of the school voucher a fair wind, also generally discredited the solution of emancipating the working-class family from the worst state schools by creating escapes (exits). The notion of a market in schooling, with choice by working-class as well as middle-class parents, shocked them when the idea was examined (but never tested in practice) by Sir Keith Joseph in the early 1980s and abandoned because of political and clerical obstruction that had little to do with the welfare of children. The unfounded faith of the general run of journalists in the benevolence of the state is a long time a'dying. They have little claim to the superior judgement that would make them mentors for the common man.

The occupational Achilles' heel of journalists in reporting and interpreting developments in education is that they depend for their information on the trade unions of teachers and other employees and government. Both are monopoly sources that cannot easily be checked or challenged.

The "profound social and political implications" of the mass circulation newspapers, continued Mr. Goodman, was that their "entertainment and trivia" reflected their role as "cash cows" for their owners rather than as "powerful political weapons" in "laying the groundwork for democracy." Editors were subject to commercial pressures from the owners which they would be able to resist better with "a basic state subvention to ensure a modest degree of independence." That solution would undermine another value of the market: independence from political influence. But the state that subsidizes the press from the people's taxes cannot ultimately refrain from intervention. It is answerable through parliament to the taxpayer. The rationale of the value of market capitalism is that independence lies best in a multiplicity of suppliers ensured by an open market. Technological change and the potentiality of new competition are better safeguards of independence than accepting money from politicians with ever-present anxieties about elections in the offing.

Some journalists have not yet discovered that democracy without free markets is a very precarious protection of the people from undisciplined power. Mr. Goodman thought that future newspapers would become more diversified: "But if we are to have a healthy democratic society, we need a better press."[6] There will be no better press without free markets.

It is not only the readers of newspapers who require guidance; the journalists who write them have too often departed from Scott's injunction to separate comment from facts. Low moral values are not the preserve of tabloid journalists who invade the citizen's privacy. Journalists with strong opinions in the heavy newspapers have the power to qualify fact with comment. Insinuation is a weapon of biased journalism. Their prejudices, likes and dislikes come through their reporting. The IEA was invariably prefixed by "right-wing" even when it was at its most radical. The venom, fury and hatred in the assessments of Mrs. Thatcher's character by some journalists, who lacked the wit to see she had prevailed over the old guard of High Toryism, provided the proletariat with real estate they would never otherwise have acquired, raised the incomes of most working people and done much more for the underdogs they favoured, must have dismayed the scholars of socialism.

With honourable exceptions, the values of some British journalists as reflected in their treatment of people they criticize are often less elevated than the values of their readers. Robert Harris savagely dismissed Lord Joseph, among the most scrupulous and upright politicians of the age, as displaying emotion in answering questions: "No doubt if you asked him the time his eyes would fill with tears."[7] The heavy newspapers have published material by serious journalists, especially in *The Observer, The Guardian* and *The Independent,* that have disfigured British journalism.

The Religious Critique and the Values of the Church

The market order that began gradually to be restored in the 1980s came under sustained attack from a new quarter—the archbishops, bishops and assorted prelates of the established Church of England.

6. Ibid.
7. Robert Harris, *Sunday Times,* May 1989.

Capitalism, thinly disguised as Thatcherism, was accused as immoral in argument that would fail a first-year undergraduate and possibly a sixth-former. Its flavour and quality were conveyed more temperately, though still begging the essential questions, in mid-1988 by a letter dated 27 May 1988 to the Prime Minister from a senior Bishop influential in the General Synod of the Church of England. Like other parliaments, the General Synod may not faithfully represent the diverse sentiments of the members of the Church, but it provides a platform for opinionated clerics who represent only themselves, though with influence far beyond the quality of their argument.

The Bishop adjured the Prime Minister to observe the moral teachings—values—of the Church on eight aspects of economic policy in terms that embraced almost all the economic errors of socialist thinking.[8]

On the distribution, or redistribution, of income: "Christians have always sought . . . an acceptance of the positive task of government in shaping society . . . [including] a particular commitment to the poor. . . ."

On the externalities: "Individuals are born into families and communities. The social dimension is fundamental and inescapable. Governments, therefore, have moral obligations to pursue policies which encourage community and mutuality . . . the hallmarks of a complete life."

On representative government and the welfare state: "government [should] accept on behalf of all in society a responsibility to play a crucial part in the fight against poverty, unemployment, victimisation, distress."

On the process of production: ". . . that people gain their wealth by legal means does not necessarily mean that they are morally acceptable."

On the market process as a zero-sum game in which some accumulate wealth at the expense of the rest: "wealth gained regardless of the rest of the community is difficult to justify."

On the morality of self-help: "Wealth acts as a barrier to the Kingdom of God if it encourages self-reliance and independence, tempting people to believe they are the masters of their own destiny."

On voluntary charity and coerced giving: "Is it not unrealistic to think that the needs of the poor can be met by individual charity?"

On the effect of government provision of free income: "Government has a duty to resist the myth that the poor are feckless people who might be tempted to greed or laziness if we give them too much."

The teaching of such clerics conveys an implied reprimand to the com-

8. Bishop of Gloucester, letter to the Prime Minister, 27 May 1988.

mon people who normally sense the urge to improve their condition and an implied acceptance of the post-war consensus that the state was the indispensable source of compassion but without recognition that it is also the source of much inequity, incompetence, deference to arbitrary influence and corruption. The teaching reveals a failure to understand the power of the market as the instrument of the ordinary people without political power or cultural influence. It fails to see the difference between the true charity and compassion of voluntary giving entailing conscious sacrifice and the false charity and impersonal compassion of coercive giving through the state which carries no voluntary act of sacrifice.

Seen through the pronouncements of such churchmen the Church seems to have abandoned its spiritual role as the teacher of moral precepts to join the queue of the political rent-seekers. In the nineteenth century the Church was a pillar of economic freedom, growing wealth and increasing private charity. In recent years it has joined the critics who denounce the morals and the values of capitalism. In the nineteenth century the Church was a main source of charity in establishing schools, building hospitals and providing almshouses for the old. Its churches were full. Since giving has been enforced by and through government, the Church has lost to the welfare state its role of compassion for the needy, the sick and the aged. Church attendances have fallen below one in ten. To keep its constituency, the Church has to replace its good works by urging the state to provide tax-financed alms. Its pleas for aid to the needy, the sick and the aged have become a political expedient. It has joined the landowners, the teachers, the university vice-chancellors, the surgeons, the railwaymen and other rent-seekers who bully complaisant politicians into larger subsidies at the expense of taxpayers who are not wealthy.

The Church has, in effect, conceded that capitalism has brought wealth and freedom of choice for many or most, but maintains that it has neglected the remaining poor of the "underclass." It discusses the symptoms of poverty, not its causes. Its solutions are the familiar supply of state income or services to all the poor, irrespective of the cause of their poverty, and on the assumption that none would accept "too much" aid supplied in part by taxes on people more deserving of help. It dwells on the income effect and ignores the price effects on incentives, self-respect and justice between the deserving and the undeserving poor.

It is politically profitable for churchmen to capitalize on their spiritual authority to urge compassion for the poor at no cost to themselves. The exceptional cleric has resisted the temptation. The Bishop of Peterborough, in an interview with the sharp-minded journalist Graham Turner,[9] said that the Church of England had become intellectually rather than spiritually driven: it had little to say to the millions who had a bit of money in their pockets other than that they should give it to the poor. "The Church of England . . . often seem[s] mean-minded to those struggling up the ladder . . . who have worked hard and made something out of their lives, both for themselves and [often] others." In his diocese, when the boot and shoe industry and the Corby steel works had closed, many small factories had been established by former employees who had discovered entrepreneurial qualities. The Church had not blessed them for their creative gifts but had seemed embarrassed by their success. By its "perpetual stress on caring for people in need, we seem to have little to say to those who by their efforts are helping to make provision for that caring." ". . . a lot feel there is no room for them in the Church."

It seems that the Church has uncritically accepted the well-worn criticisms of capitalism. The constant harping by socialist-minded academics and politicians on the exploitations of industry, the misdeeds of employers, the immorality of profits, the greed of private ownership and the rest, has undermined the very institutions and qualities, the mores and the values required to end the complacency and dependency of the post-war decades and to produce the resources required to succour the poor.

By its concentration on the symptoms of poverty rather than on its causes, the Church has retarded the process by which productivity and rising incomes trickled down from the rich to the middle-income groups and from them to the poor. Professor Plant, like the liberal academics, would wish for a faster rate of trickling down so that the trickle became a rushing stream of wealth to the poor. But the Church has been one influence among others that have slowed the trickle down until it almost dried up where the poor have looked to the state whose resources have been misdirected to the politically powerful.

The Bishop of Peterborough offered penetrating insights, based on knowledge of the economic standing of clerics, which explained their values and the failure of the Church. Many of its young men headed for the inner cities "where they find people waiting to be looked after." The task was less demanding than in the suburbs, where "half the congregation may have

9. Graham Turner, "Why no gospel for the better-off?," *Sunday Telegraph,* 26 March 1989, p. 15.

been to university, they ask a lot of questions and you've got to be on your toes." The synod at York had a motion on housing that produced a vote in favour of the abolition of the tax relief on mortgage interest. Most, said the Bishop, had no mortgage either because they had repaid it or lived in homes provided by the Church. Were they disinterested? Bishops educated at Eton, Sherborne, Marlborough and other "elitist" public schools had opposed the government's restoration of grammar schools for the able children of the working classes: "Shirley Williams did not destroy their schools; she destroyed *mine*" (italics in original).

"The Church," said the grammar school Bishop, "had become so trapped in the [post-war] consensus that there was now an automatic response to every issue." Many of the older church leaders had had their crucial religious experience in the 1950s and 1960s and "got stuck in the age of collectivist solutions." He was more hopeful of the younger Bishops.

The Bishop of Peterborough had sensed the public choice analysis of the pressures on government. The Church of England had to avoid becoming a church of vested interests rather than a church of the whole nation. It would be fatal if it courted interest groups and shirked offending them. The task of the Church was to embark on a decade of evangelism to the whole nation instead of dealing with the concerns of interest groups. (The role of a public philosophy that teaches categories of good and bad political behaviour is reviewed in the final chapters.)

Here was a prelate rejecting the temptations of church politics, seeing the danger of yielding to the vocal organized lobbies whatever their anxieties and faithfully serving the pastoral purpose of teaching the good life. Graham Turner's interview was published on Easter Sunday; the introduction said, echoing the non-consensus Bishop: "many Anglican churchmen seem to be more interested in sociology than in Easter." If true, it suggests that the Church of England has damned the values of capitalism without understanding them.

Its very misunderstanding of the genesis and the values of the economic system that produces wealth, its concentration on the symptoms of poverty and hardship to the neglect of their causes, has misled the Church of England into encouraging political irresponsibility in the indiscriminate dispersal of scarce resources to the rich as well as to the poor. A church-going peer, Lord (Ralph) Harris, whose stubborn Christian faith is affronted by the fallacious pleading from the Bishops' benches in the House of Lords, launched into a sad counter-condemnation of the spiritual leaders of the

Anglican Church for adopting the universal heresies of the age as witnessed in the assertions of the Bishops of Durham and Liverpool and the compromises of the Archbishop of Canterbury.[10] He contrasted the "aggressive, partisan, political-materialist manifesto of the Archbishop" (in the church report, *Faith in the City*) with a statement on unemployment and idleness by the Chief Rabbi and its unsentimental but refreshing precepts on private charity, family and (voluntary) community sharing, wealth creation (as distinct from distribution) and above all the work ethic:

"No work is too menial to compromise human dignity and self-respect";

". . . idleness is an even greater evil than unemployment, especially in a welfare state which maintains every citizen above subsistence level . . .";

"cheap labour is more dignified than a free dole";

"industriousness generates greater wealth than increased wages for decreasing hours of work."

This is evidently the Jewish work ethic[11] that parallels the Protestant work ethic that Tawney saw as the value that underlay capitalism.[12]

No church seems to be free of rent-seekers who would use the state and its coercive redistribution as a permanent crutch rather than emergency first aid for the poor. They see public ownership as more moral than private ownership, condemn self-concern as selfishness and confuse motive with consequence. Yet recent researches of the Argentine economist Alejandro Chafuen indicate that the human values of the harmonious society later developed by capitalism were seen clearly by the Catholic pre-capitalist late Scholastics of sixteenth- and seventeenth-century Spain, later transmitted in the writings of the Dutchman Hugo Grotius, the German Samuel von Pufendorf and other Protestant writers.[13]

They were especially penetrating on the rationale of private property and government finance. Their thinking on trade, the theory of money, value, price, wages, profits, interest and social justice anticipated some of the thinking of the classical economists. They were in no doubt about the distinction between private and public (common) ownership. The best known, St. Thomas Aquinas, said: "private property is necessary for human life . . . first, because each person takes more trouble to care for something that is his per-

10. Ralph Harris, *Beyond the Welfare State,* Institute of Economic Affairs, 1988.

11. Ibid.

12. R. H. Tawney, *Religion and the Rise of Capitalism,* 1926.

13. Alejandro A. Chafuen, *Christians for Freedom: Late Scholastic Economics,* Ignatius Press, 1986.

sonal responsibility . . . ; second, there would be chaos if everybody cared for everything; third, because men live together in greater peace where everyone is content with his own . . . quarrels often break out amongst men who hold things in common. . . ."[14]

The Russians who organized collective farms in the hope of higher output might have drawn a lesson from Domingo Bañez who warned in 1594: "We know that the fields are not going to be tilled efficiently in common ownership, and that there will not be peace in the republic, so we see that it is efficient to undertake the division of goods."[15] The enclosure of common land in England under Henry VIII discovered the evidence, unimagined by the British bishops of our day, who have yet to teach that the high productivity required to succour the poor requires a massive shift from the neglect of common (or socialist) ownership to the good husbandry of private (or capitalist) ownership.

Tomas de Mercado said similarly in 1571: "We can see that privately owned property flourishes, while city- and council-owned property suffers from inadequate care and worse management."[16] It is difficult to recall a contemporary cleric who has condemned the deterioration of council housing as a sin of government or comprehended the husbandry of personal ownership. De Mercado added: "If universal love will not induce people to take care of things, private interest will." Much socialist simplicity from Marx onwards might have been avoided if his followers had experienced these insights—or if the people they misled had applied the personal experience of their everyday lives.

Earlier, in 1567, Domingo de Soto wrote words that might have saved fruitless effort by the Yugoslav enthusiasts for self-management: "Each worker will try to appropriate as many goods as possible, and given the way human beings desire riches, everyone will behave in the same fashion. The peace, tranquillity and friendships sought by the philosophers will thus inevitably be subverted."[17]

To put their teachings into a proverb often cited by the late Scholastics: "A donkey owned by many wolves is soon eaten." There was not much respect for common public property among animals. The faith that the wolves will abstain and give the donkey long life is still intriguingly but mystifyingly

14. St. Thomas Aquinas, in ibid., p. 12.
15. Domingo Bañez, in ibid., p. 11.
16. Tomas de Mercado, in ibid., p. 11.
17. Domingo de Soto, in ibid., p. 11.

held by romantic politicians like Mr. Anthony Benn. The disagreeable truth, blurred by sentiment for 40 years, must be told, by liberal economists if not by clerics: common property turns humans into uncaring "wolves." No public respect is shown for publicly owned railways, hospitals, schools, telephones, tower blocks, parks etc. because the individual cannot identify the millionth part that belongs to him. Is it the chair in the hospital waiting room? the bandages cupboard? the radio in the ambulance? If he knew he might tend it as his own. He does not, and cannot know because *everything* is owned in common and *nothing* belongs to him. All that was another middle-class myth that misled the millions into voting for the politicians who deprived them of property that would have made them blossom.

More wisdom came from the clerics of sixteenth- to seventeenth-century Spain. Developments in public finance in later centuries were foreseen in 1619 by Pedro Fernando Navarrete: "The origin of poverty is high taxes. In continual fear of high taxes, [farmers] prefer to abandon their land, so they can avoid the vexations." On the limits of high tax rates to soak the rich, the Laffer curve that has shown higher yields at lower rates, and the ubiquity of tax evasion: "He who imposes high taxes receives from very few." On Gladstone's dictum that money fructifies in the pockets of the people and on the pre-Lawson public sector borrowing "requirement": "The king is not going to be poor if the vassals are rich, because riches are better kept in the hands of the subjects than in the thrice-locked coffers of the State Treasurers, who go bankrupt daily."[18] The spiritual leaders of the twentieth century have strayed far from the wisdom of the sixteenth because they have lived in a politicized society and have unconsciously absorbed its ethic of irresponsibility.

The Politicization of Values

The discussion of values has become politicized since compassion, sharing, charity and "caring" were transferred from personal judgement and private organization to the welfare state. These human instincts, which were developing under nineteenth-century capitalism, have been injected with political bias and opportunism. Debate is no longer between scholars searching for truth but between politicians searching for votes. In the scramble, the poor suffer.

18. Pedro Fernando Navarrete, in ibid., p. 12.

The instinctive values of the Church of England were seen in the instinctive condemnation by the Bishop of Stepney of a politician who produced a reasoned rebuttal of the notion of poverty as inequality. In May 1989 John Moore, the Secretary of State for Social Services, argued that poverty referred to absolute want, not relative possessions. People were poor who lacked food and the essentials of civilized living, not if they had less of them than their neighbours. In this absolute sense, poverty had virtually vanished from Britain. In the relative sense, poverty is with us forever, and the word is drained of meaning. The poverty that remained derived not from inadequacy but from misuse of income earned or provided by the state (primary and secondary poverty). The remaining poverty derived from defects of character that money support could not remove or was self-inflicted acceptance of mean conditions of living.

This is not a new revelation. The distinction between absolute and relative poverty was argued in the 1960s between the trio of sociologists, Titmuss, Abel-Smith and Townsend, and liberal academics at the IEA and elsewhere. The argument on the adequacy of income was won by the liberals in the 1960s with the general acceptance that the universal benefits of the welfare state had deprived the poor of higher incomes and should be replaced with selective benefits, more recently called "targeting."

The harmful effects of state assistance on personal character that weakened the will and capacity to self-help in escaping from poverty, dramatized in the influential writing of the American Charles Murray of the Manhattan Institute in Washington,[19] have emphasized the superiority of measures tailored to individual circumstances. The general principles of aid to the poor in capitalism argued for the continuing importance of money as the only ultimate teacher of discrimination and judgement in learning to choose the objects and services required in everyday living and in developing self-respect in the rebuilding of character. The main cause of the inability of many to contend with the opportunities and challenges of life, the inability to make choices, is the very structure of state services that have deprived many of the occasions for exercising judgement between alternatives in education, medical care, housing and pensions. If many are still incapable of making choices, the solution is not further increments of state-provided services that require no effort by parents, patients, home occupants or future pensioners, atrophy the faculties of discrimination and weaken the family by

19. Charles Murray, *Losing Ground: American Social Policy 1950–1980*, Basic Books, 1984; *In Pursuit of Happiness and Good Government*, Simon & Schuster, 1989.

usurping the role of parents, but distribution of the power to discriminate by the direct exercise of authority in the use, or withholding, of purchasing power.

Beyond the positive role of the state in arming all capable of learning choice with the power to exercise it lies its even more fundamental negative role of removing obstacles. Whatever good the state can do in its positive role is vulnerable to the arbitrariness and distortions of the political process. The negative role in removing obstacles is by definition less vulnerable. Here the main way to diminish the sense of poverty inculcated by low incomes remains in the destruction of the obstacles, mainly created by itself, to the movement from occupations, industries and regions where incomes are low to occupations, industries and regions where they are higher—regional aid, housing subsidies and trade union practices.

The Minister's statement was condemned by the politically minded in the press and the Church as insensitive to the remaining poverty. The expression of compassion for the poor is a cheap way to salve uneasy consciences; it produces proposals for yet more state assistance provided by other taxpayers. The contemporary Church is not on a higher moral plain than the laity. Instead of the hard thinking of the late Scholastics on ways to increase the production of wealth, in which the poor would share, its declarations are essentially for redistributing it from the fortunate to the unfortunate, with little thought for ways to strengthen the power of the poor to generate it by means that would also restore their self-respect.

The Bishop of Stepney acknowledged that some families in the most shabby tower blocks had several incomes and were "living very comfortably," some were "moonlighting" (earning in the black market) or were "professional welfare fiddlers," and that the organized poverty lobbies "can overstate their case," a candid confession that clerics have drawn their information from biased sources.[20] It is also a masterpiece of meosis for the natural tendency of professional lobbies to exaggerate their strong and minimize their weak arguments. Yet, said the Bishop, the Minister had shown an ignorance of the truth; he found "gravely insulting" the claim that the underclass of 1989 enjoyed "affluence beyond the wildest dreams" of the Victorian poor.

He acknowledged that poverty he saw in the East End of London was different from that portrayed by Dickens, but it was "just as real: it was the

20. Maurice Weaver, "East End bishop's world of want," *Daily Telegraph*, 15 May 1989, p. 5.

poverty of despair, of discouragement, of scraping. . . ." His main anxiety was that if the Minister succeeded in making the poor "invisible," "nothing will be done to help them."

The Bishop was offering the poor political first aid, not the means to help themselves out of poverty. He was advocating yet more redistribution of available resources, not methods of enlarging them. He was reflecting the errors of the age, not thinking for himself. He was offering the balm of socialism, not the hope of capitalism. He was applying the values of political dependency, not the values of individual dignity.

Saving Life by Capitalism and Socialism

The market system and the capitalist method of thinking are more humane than those of socialism because they would save more lives.

The non-market mind is instinctively shocked by the calculus of commerce. Doctors, artists and politicians accustomed to subventions from the public purse live in the unreal world in which they are insulated from the necessities of other mortals who must count the cost—every day, in everything they do.

Chance required me to have surgery in 1968. The surgeon dropped a stitch and provoked what was called post-operative haemorrhage. The rare blood group was out of stock. Search for a donor led in several hours to a bus conductor in Edgware. A crisis was averted with little time to spare. The episode was full of obvious questions for the economist.

Why the shortage? In a market, the offer of a high enough price produces supplies. But the voluntary donor system of the National Blood Transfusion Service does not tap all sources. Only those, it says, who give their blood can or shall be allowed to save life. This sounded like a national nose-cutting to save the national face.

So a Hobart Paper was arranged by two economists.[21] Their finding was that payment for blood might be desirable to supplement the evident inadequacy of the free blood. The Blood Transfusion Service has generally produced enough for normal requirements, but exceptionally, as with a rare blood group or a multiple accident on a motorway, a shortage was possible.

Outrage! The sociologists were precipitated into a state of acute shock. Professor Titmuss wrote *The Gift Relationship* to extol the high value of

21. Michael Cooper and A. J. Culyer, *The Price of Blood*, 1968.

giving over selling.[22] He was applauded by the sociologists (and by the surgeon who dropped the stitch). The economists criticized him for shallow thinking. But what of the values entailed in giving and selling blood? Giving was civilized and noble; selling was commercialized and offensive.

If this is the difference in the values of socialism over capitalism, the superior morals of capitalism are self-evident. If socialism puts the saving of life second to the payment for the blood that could save it, socialism is damned.

The debate has recurred in the sale of human organs. There is clearly a sense of revulsion against the use of the human body for monetary gain. The sale of hair seems acceptable; payment for blood is common in other countries. But the sale of kidneys or other human parts is distasteful. The story in early 1989 that a Turk had been persuaded by a British doctor to sell a kidney for £2,000 brought in a Conservative politician to head the supposed army of public revulsion. This is the routine reaction of party politics. Are Conservative politicians opposed to payment even if there are not enough voluntary offers to save all the lives that could be saved?

The moral dilemmas persist. Are the values of selling to rank before the values of saving life? Does the value of individual human decision—to pay or to die—count for nothing? Is the ultimate political value to be that the antipathy to commercialism shall prevail in order to buy votes on the cheap? Is nothing safe from the political process?

Are politicians protecting the dying who might survive with a bought kidney or the living who would survive with one? Are individuals to be prevented from risking their lives by other hazards—swimming, skiing, flying or crossing the road? And, if individuals defy political rules made with supposed majority approval, are minorities to be penalized? Does the political process know no bounds at all?

The reply must be that, since the political process rules more under socialism, it will put the principle preferred by the majority before the lives of minorities that would be saved under capitalism.

On Greed in Capitalism and Socialism

Politicians in search of power must be expected to use strong language, hyperbole, righteous indignation and verbal allusion. But the tendency to

22. R. M. Titmuss, *The Gift Relationship,* Allen & Unwin, 1970.

overgeneralize from particular circumstances must be resisted in the judgement between capitalism and socialism. An understandable temptation is to blame an economic system for the failure of governments that attempt to apply its principles.

No doubt critics of socialism have attributed blame for its failings to socialist politicians. The low productivity, industrial strife and other defects of the Wilson and Callaghan Governments were unavoidable results of their socialist corporatism. In contrast the inadequacies of Mrs. Thatcher's Governments as seen by her liberal critics are remediable and not the inevitable effects of capitalism.

Yet the socialist critics generally imply that the supposed undesirable results of what they call Thatcherism are the characteristic evils of capitalism. Among them greed is emphasized as the outstanding evil in a combative critique of Thatcherism by Gordon Brown, a Labour politician, in what the publisher calls an "informed and impassioned account of the true consequences for Britain of the Thatcher era."[23]

The alleged misdeeds of the ten years since 1979 will have been rebutted by Conservatives on political grounds. Liberal economists will question the underlying reasoning. The argument for replacing Thatcherism by the new socialism, as revised yet again in 1989 to include markets, raised the question of the trustworthiness of the political instrument, the Labour Party. Some observers took the political repentance at its face value; Robert Harris asserted that it was "a revolution in [the Labour leader's] entire political philosophy."[24] He reported the party leader as making a profoundly historic statement at a meeting of the Labour Party Executive Committee on 8 May 1989. The volte-face ran "Labour cannot inoculate itself from the capitalist system. It is the system we live in, and we have to make it work more effectively and more fairly." It is for the electorate to judge whether Labour will "make" capitalism work better than the Conservatives. It is the party political choice for the voter to decide whether Labour in 1991–2 is offering capitalism or socialism. Since the market under Labour will be directed by the state, the political process will decide how the market will be used, how far it will be regulated by the state, in which industries, and where it will be used at all. The fundamental choice for the elector will thus not be between

23. Gordon Brown, *Where There Is Greed: Margaret Thatcher and the Betrayal of Britain's Future,* Mainstream, 1989.

24. Robert Harris, *Sunday Times,* 14 May 1989, p. B3.

market socialism and the Conservative version of the market economy; it will remain between capitalism and socialism.

For the independent observer interested in the economic argument rather than the political prospects Mr. Brown's book was a most detailed rejection of the ten years of Mrs. Thatcher's policies. But as a rejection of the system of capitalism it had three shortcomings.

First, Mr. Brown did not show that the political deficiencies are the inevitable consequence of capitalism. "Greed" is a graphic epithet in party political debate. But "greed" is a doubtful word to describe the economic effects of Conservative policies. They have created or strengthened four main kinds of opportunities for individuals: to earn, to own, to save and therefore to give—to people, causes or principles. If these expressions of the urge to self-improvement and self-advancement are "greed," they are also what Adam Smith called the urge of every man "to better his condition." Mr. Brown used the strong word "greed" in a political sense to suggest not only selfishness, which describes the motive of mankind in all economic systems, socialist as well as capitalist, but also in the more offensive sense of avarice, rapacity or gluttony. There are two objections.

Self-improvement is the human motive that the socialist countries have discovered they must liberate if they are to obtain the increased productivity they have lacked. How much more reminding do socialists require? In early 1989 the outstanding socialist journalist John Lloyd, whose home truths are accepted by socialist journals which rejected the same home truths from liberal economists, wrote from Moscow, where he was the *Financial Times* correspondent, in the British monthly entitled *Samizdat* edited by Professor Ben Pimlott: "The discovery, now being made in slow stages, [is] that . . . the Soviet Union . . . cannot match advanced capitalist states even in social provision. . . ."[25] Socialism may have more elevated names for the urge of every man to better his condition. But the instrument is the same everywhere. Capitalism discovered long ago that the urge to ownership was both morally satisfying and economically efficient. The USSR will discover that leaseholds are not enough. The people want freeholds.

Second, if the urge to self-improvement under capitalism is best expressed by earning, owning and saving, it takes more questionable forms under socialism. The urge to own property under capitalism is benign con-

25. John Lloyd, "Where politics precedes law," *Samizdat,* January–February 1989, p. 24. The introduction ran: "Let us be hopeful about *glasnost.* But don't let's be naïve about the present or the past."

trasted with the urge to command power under socialism. The road to improvement under capitalism is property; under socialism, where there is no property to witness advancement, it is power. The urge to individual advancement is strong in both systems; its expression is more dangerous under socialism.

Socialists have neglected the wisdom of the English classical economists and writers who understood human nature better than Marx or Engels, Bryan Gould or Roy Hattersley, Neil Kinnock or Gordon Brown. "There are few ways," said Samuel Johnson in 1775, "in which a man can be more innocently employed than in getting money." ". . . money is the best friend a man can have," Anthony Trollope made Dr. Croft say in *The Small House at Allington* in 1864, "if it be honestly come by."

Here are two Victorian values: first, money in preference to power; second, honesty as the best long-term policy. The power structures of socialism inhibit both. It puts coercive power before relatively innocuous money. Political power in running monopoly industries creates more scope for dishonesty. Socialism, moreover, has gathered support by preaching envy of political power; the self-improvement of capitalism comes from economic emulation.

The second shortcoming of Gordon Brown's "greed" critique is that, even if all its criticisms of capitalism under Mrs. Thatcher were well founded, it did not establish a decisive case for socialism. That further stage in the socialist case would require a persuasive demonstration that the state control of the economy would be less objectionable than the market under capitalism. This was the task that Mr. Brown did not attempt.

The third shortcoming is that the criticisms of the market made little acknowledgement of the classical flaw in socialist thinking. Socialists have admitted that, after all, the market is indispensable. If they have been purblind for over a century until 1989, there can be little confidence that their belated confession is much more than a political tactic rather than, as Mr. Harris says, "a revolution in political philosophy." If there is no argument, there is also no evidence. Where can socialists show they have used the market to produce goods wanted by the people better than under capitalism? All we can see, in the USSR and China where the attempt is being made, is convulsion, torpor and incipient civil war.

In Britain the writings of the socialist politicians and academics are, so far, deficient in the machinery that will ensure consumer dominance over the producer in the market and over the politician in the political process. That requirement, satisfied by capitalism as it has been and even more as it could be, is what British socialists—in all parties, in the bureaucracy, among the regulators, in local government and elsewhere—have so far not accepted, nor generally understood.

The Values of the Market

The superior values of capitalism over those of socialism can be distilled from the foregoing discussion.

1. The values of the market are superior to the values of the political process because it allows people to express their judgements, preferences, feelings, prejudices, likes and dislikes as individuals without going through the political filter of majority (or largest minority) approval.
2. Respect for the unique individual is the basis of the moral life. An individual forced to do good by law is acting amorally.
3. Individuals learn only by living as they know best and making mistakes. Well-meaning political tutelage can destroy the learning process.
4. Even when the individual can learn nothing from mistakes where their effects for him are final and fatal, they can teach lessons for others. A man who dies in the attempt to climb Everest, test a new medicine or fly a new aircraft benefits others by the new knowledge.
5. Private property is the indispensable requirement for the individual to learn the lessons of responsibility by benefiting from success and suffering from failure.
6. The machinery of economic activity must put the interest of man as consumer over his interest as producer. Only the market under capitalism, not under socialism, can perform this task.
7. Competition is essential to enable consumers to compare and contrast alternatives. Under socialism a single supplier excludes comparison and cannot claim superiority. No-one can know if a monopoly, state or private, offers the best possible since it is the only source.
8. The decentralization and diffusion of political power are the necessary conditions for economic freedom in the use of scarce resources.
9. Since government is inherently inefficient in hitting targets, it gives itself the benefit of the doubt. It overshoots where it is politically easier than to undershoot, and undershoots where it is politically easier than to overshoot. It tends to over-regulate industry because

the risks of under-regulation (as in medicines or financial services) are more apparent, but the public interest is better served by under-regulation, which proliferates alternatives. It tends to overtax covertly where possible because it is more popular to reduce than to raise taxes, but the public interest prefers undertaxation. It tends to inflate its powers covertly because it is easier to relax than to expand them, but the public interest is served more by too little than by too much government. The market is superior to government because it tends to undergovernment and operates with least government.

10. The voluntary communal life that emerges in an otherwise market-dominated capitalist society is preferable to the enforced communal life of a market-suppressed socialist society.

CHAPTER 13

The Verdict

> In terms of the values held by the majority of people in the world today, a choice in favour of capitalism is more plausible in the light of the empirical evidence available.
>
> Professor Peter Berger, *The Capitalist Revolution*

> Political writers have established as a maxim, that, in contriving any system of government, and fixing the several checks and controuls of the constitution, every man ought to be supposed a *knave*, and to have no other end, in all his actions, than private interest. (Emphasis in the original)
>
> David Hume, "Of the independency of Parliament," *Essays Moral, Political and Literary*

> On reading my [news]paper I see the Government of East Germany has lost confidence in the people. I suggest they dissolve the people, and hold an election for a new people. (After the 1953 Berlin uprising)
>
> Bertolt Brecht, *Brecht on Brecht*

The verdict from economic argument and historical evidence is that the political process under all systems is denying the peoples of the world their true inheritance of peace, liberty and prosperity. Since capitalism is less dominated than socialism by politics because it rests essentially on the market, it is the superior politico-economic system.

The Responsible Market and Irresponsible Politics

The teaching of the socialist mind on the necessity or benevolence of politics has inverted the truth. Professor Crick wrote *In Defence of Politics*. Professor Marquand in *The Unprincipled Society* would make the political process dominate society. Shirley Williams entitled her book *Politics Is for People.* The argument and the evidence do not support them. But the veneration of politics continues unabated. Politics as it has developed acts on balance *against* the common people in favour of political people. The proponents of politics may one day build a system of government that faithfully reflects the public will, although the devices are more likely to come from students of government aware of its dangers than from the Crick-Marquand-Williams enthusiasts for politics as a way of life for every man. The forthcoming *Primer on Public Choice*[1] will indicate what might be done to limit, discipline and subjugate government by the general will to serve rather than dominate it. Even then, government would be limited to unavoidably collective functions because it is no match for the market as the defence of the common man.

The principle argued in this book is that, because the common man can exert himself better in the market as it could be than in the political process, the market must be superior to the political process. The market must, where possible, be independent of the political process, not its creature. The aim must be to take human action out of politics.

Capitalism gives the political process less scope than socialism in ruling private lives. But in all capitalist countries, even in Switzerland, the least politicized, the political process has been allowed too much scope by proceeding beyond the ambit of unavoidably collective functions to invade private lives.

The market process characteristically induces individual action at its best; the political process generally induces individual action at its worst. The market impels responsible spending decisions informed by knowledge of costs of alternatives to themselves and of the opportunity costs of resources as a whole. Political motivation incites irresponsible decisions: in the polling booth irresponsibility is fomented by ignorance of the costs (or benefits) of the policies to be supported by votes; in legislatures irresponsibility is generated by myopic calculation determined by the dates of elections.

The market is the locale of reflection, consideration and thought for others—family, friends, causes. The ballot box is the locale of hurried decision based on slogans that oversimplify rather than illuminate party policies, on imagined personal qualities of candidates and on passing events that may be forgotten before elected candidates legislate. The spending choices

1. Charles Rowley, Arthur Seldon and Gordon Tullock, *Primer on Public Choice*, Blackwell, forthcoming.

made in the market are models of informed reflective duty contrasted with the voting impulses in June 1989 for the Strasbourg Euro-Parliament candidates of the Greens whose opposition to economic progress (mis-called "growth") was not assessed in its cost to the poor, the halt, the lame and the blind.

The Green notion that the state restriction of economic progress to save the environment would not be coercive because public opinion would have changed is an assumption, like that of Marx, that evades rather than solves the human dilemma in conditions of continuing scarcity. Fundamentally, the Green philosophy is paternalistic at its best, elitist-authoritarian at worst and little different from the characteristic middle-class socialist approach of confronting scarcity with coercion.

The notion that the care of the environment is necessarily safer in the hands of government and its political imperatives is the characteristic *non sequitur* of the collectivist response to what seems a new problem. The realities of political practice—its subjection to pressures, its anxiety about voter reaction at by-elections, its bureaucratic indecision—are ignored. The notion that government would have a more responsible longer view in husbanding non-renewable natural resources than people who owned them is the opposite of the lessons of experience. The political process is riddled with short-termism. The socialist mind is clouded by market failure and oblivious to, or untroubled by, government failure. The scope for extending property rights—on the seabed and in the air, as well as the land and its natural and animal resources—to strengthen preservation and conservation and so anticipate deterioration or destruction of desirable features of nature, with its more dependable incentives than the precarious reactions of government to natural disaster or public protest, is still not understood. The extension of market inducements—the charging proposed in the early 1970s by Professor Wilfred Beckerman[2]—is overlooked. Raymond Plant urged these two solutions, rather than state ownership, on fellow socialists and voters attracted to the Green Party without thought for its results in very extensive state powers.[3] His third solution of state regulation is more debatable. Government regulation, no less here than elsewhere, is exposed to the abuses and corruptions of politics. Certainly not until the market solutions are exhausted should the politicized expedients be risked. Since property rights

2. Wilfred Beckerman, *Pricing for Pollution,* Institute of Economic Affairs, 1975, 2nd edn. 1990.

3. Raymond Plant, "Can the Greens ever appeal to the poor?," *The Times,* 26 June 1989.

and charging methods have barely been considered, there is a long way to go before the state should be entrusted with still more powers that it will be tempted to misuse.

The carelessness of government in the care of the environment has long been concealed, not least in the authoritarian socialist countries. The world knows, from the ample pamphleteering of The Friends of the Earth in capitalist societies, of commercial exploitation and the rain forests, air and water pollution, the risks of nuclear power and toxic wastes. It knows little of the degradation of the environment in the closed socialist economies. Like man-made disasters of air and land transport calamities in state economies, the callous neglect of the natural and animal kingdoms has been a closed book.

Since about 1985 Soviet *glasnost* has been lifting the political veil. The full evidence of disasters has yet to be uncovered. The few incidents cautiously disclosed in recent years form the visible part of the communist ecological iceberg. Zan Smiley of *The Daily Telegraph* reported on the degradation of the (inland) Aral Sea.[4] The disaster of pollution, with widespread ill-health in the surrounding population among five out of six children, said *Socialist Industry*, the economic daily of the Communist Party Central Committee, had been caused by "the greedy shortsightedness of bureaucrats and economic planners." "Lack of cohesion" between Gosplan (Ministry of Planning) and Gossnab (Ministry of Supplies) and "abuse" had produced "a zone of ecological disaster." Before Gorbachev the environmental degradation of socialist planning would have been denied, concealed or explained away, as was the disaster at Chernobyl. We do not know how much still is a closed book.

The cure for market failure in the environment is market improvement, not yet more political influence. Markets are improved largely by internalizing external damage, such as phasing out aerosol gases that destroy ozone, and by refining property rights to identify ownership, responsibility, rewards for good stewardship and penalties for negligence. The political process would display its characteristic and inevitable incompetence, erratic procrastination, place-seeking and corruption. The solution, in short, is more capitalism and less socialism. In capitalism the consumer and the investor can shun industries that damage the environment; under socialism their decisions are usurped by the political planners.

4. Zan Smiley, "Aral Sea threatens the world," *Daily Telegraph*, 21 June 1989, p. 10.

The political process knows no bounds. It is an unavoidable ingredient of civilized society, although it has become the master rather than the servant of the people. In its essentials it claims to be based on the principles of good government refined down the ages by the best minds from John Locke, David Hume and Adam Smith in Britain, Thomas Jefferson, Alexander Hamilton and James Madison in the United States, Alexis de Tocqueville in France and Wilhelm von Humboldt in Germany. Choice between the alternative principles—substantially, in the terms of this book, libertarian or authoritarian—that will govern the powers and conduct of government requires reflection by the citizen whom democracy has made potentially sovereign but not yet in practice.

Yet in our day the practice of politics brings it into disrepute even where it is unavoidable. Its failures degrade the noble vision of democracy created by Lincoln's memorable words that have inspired the downtrodden of the communist world (although the government of, by and for the people that he envisaged has not "perished"; it has never been created). He hoped that the sacrifice of the men who had fallen in 1863 in the Battle of Gettysburg would inspire the generations that followed. But the behaviour of millions in the political process mocks the dead of Gettysburg, and in our century of the dead who resisted the tyrannies of Stalin, Hitler and Mussolini. And it mocks the plaster cast of the Statue of Liberty that the students of Beijing erected in the communist Tiananmen Square before they were killed.

In the European elections the Hunting and Fishing Party of France received 2.5 per cent of the votes cast; in Britain the Raving Loony Party, the Humanist Party, the Protestant Reformation Party and the Corrective Party recorded thousands of votes. Fewer than half the voters in some of the twelve countries troubled to vote. The half that voted did not know what they were doing: for whom they voted, what he or she would do, the effects, the benefits or the costs. The political process is treated with disdain or wholly ignored by millions. Yet in the market *all* the voters spend *every* pound with infinitely more thought, knowledge and responsibility.

The political parties with the most votes from the uninformed, the misled and the trusting in the elections for the European Parliament will for years decide, so far to a small but a growing extent, the lives of everyone in the twelve countries of the European Economic Community (EEC)—large minorities or majorities varying with the vagaries of voting systems from "first past the post" to varieties of proportional representation.

The political process creates a Jekyll and Hyde dichotomy in human behaviour. It transforms the scrupulously conscientious individual as a shopper in the market into a cynical dilettante in the polling booth. The millions who do not vote presumably take no interest at all in principles, policies or politics, or, if they do, have pronounced a plague on all their houses. But the millions who vote take little or no trouble to discover and compare the alternative sets of principles they are offered.

Yet it is rational behaviour to reject the waste of money, effort and time in casting a vote that will have an infinitesimal effect on the outcome of candidate elected, and policies and principles for which the vast electoral machinery has been erected. This is the "rational voter" hypothesis of an early pioneer in the economics of politics, the American economist Anthony Downs.[5] But it is the very Achilles' heel of the political process. The citizen, says the socialist, is to be made sovereign by the participation and accountability claimed as the supreme virtue of politics. But if its inducement for the citizen to exercise the instrument of his sovereignty is negligible, it is almost ineffectual contrasted with the power to command, discipline and discard unsatisfactory suppliers in the market by withdrawing purchasing power. If the political process has to depend on the vague sense that individual voting influences the outcome of elections and the seminal questions of peace and war, prosperity or penury, liberty or slavery, it rests on shifting sands. Most of the activity of government could be performed better by the market, but government refuses to yield the functions in which it has failed.

If the European children of the British, the French, the West Germans, the Italians, the Belgians, the Dutch, the Irish, the Luxembourgians, the Danes, the Spaniards, the Portuguese and the Greeks are to be taught the arts of responsible living, the so-called active citizenship being mobilized by the politicians to make their profession acceptable, the exemplar is the market process, not the political process.

The claims of political scientists that politics deserves defence (Crick), should be made the master of the market (Marquand) or is for the people (Williams) are unsupported by argument and denied by experience.

The solution urged by politicians for everyone to become a politician—an active citizen or part-time politician—is political self-preservation: it is made with the subconscious sense that they are the experts who would prevail because not everyone would excel at politics, many would shirk it and most would be better employed—for themselves and the nation—at their non-political specialisms. It is the politicians' *post hoc* rationalization of their profitable and satisfying profession. It is no more elevating or realistic

5. Anthony Downs, *An Economic Theory of Democracy*, Harper & Row, 1957.

than the invitation of the linguist that everyone shall learn foreign languages, of the sportsman that everyone shall excel at the athletic arts or of the operatic prima donna that all should learn to sing. They all know that not everyone can: their supremacy is safe. Adam Smith, who lauded the division of labour, would have wondered at the failure of posterity to see that it is the source of the world's well-being.

The market is the centre in which suppliers of goods and services offer competing specimens that buyers can compare, sample, judge and reject every day, week, month or year. Politics is the cockpit of competing claims to be efficient, just, honest and faithful by politicians who cannot be brought to book because the results of their policies are unpredictable, unidentifiable or virtually immeasurable. Suppliers in the market show their prices; politicians have no prices to show. Shakespeare spoke of Caesar:

> The evil that men do lives after them
> The good is oft interred with their bones.

The evil done by business men is loudly declaimed in their lifetime; the good enriches the generations long after them. The good done by politicians is acclaimed in their lifetime; the bad is forgotten in their memoirs and often in the histories of their times.

Examples abound in recent decades. Few recall the innocent errors of men in power who wished to do good. Clement Attlee presided over the installation of the post-war welfare state 40 years ago that has outlived its day yet looks like lingering for another 40 years despite unimagined advance in incomes and technical change that make it anachronistic. Harold Macmillan confused counsel in British statecraft by continuing his muddled thinking on *The Middle Way*, a 1930s book re-issued in 1966 when it confirmed the confusion: in it he combined capitalism with socialism and produced the misbegotten child of corporatism.[6] Harold Wilson bolstered the power of the trade unions that recoiled against his hapless successor. Edward Heath risked the damaging inflation of 1974–5. They, and others before them, meant well but did harm from which we suffer today: Lloyd George introduced national insurance prematurely; Benjamin Disraeli strengthened the trade unions to win the workers' votes; Lord North, it was said, lost the American colonies. Among lesser ministers the numbers who may have in-

6. Harold Macmillan, *The Middle Way*, Macmillan, 1938.

tended good but left a legacy of harm are legion. They understandably took short views to deal with the urgencies of the hour, but have left us, 20, 50, 100 or 200 years later, suffering the consequences.

In the market the sellers supply knowledge explicitly or indirectly by experience of their wares. In politics the well-intentioned blind lead the innocent blind.

The verdict that, because it makes less use of the political process capitalism is superior to socialism, is that of the peoples of the world when they are able to act in the market and are not blinded by the arbitrary mechanisms and idiosyncratic appeals of politics. Instinctively they sense this distinction; they may be misled by the self-styled democratic political people to vote for socialism under various names, but in their day-to-day lives as shoppers, buyers and customers they show they prefer the superior economic democracy of capitalism. They misuse their uninformed uncaring vote (and their replies to opinion polls), but they save themselves and their families by the care they exercise in the market.

The Superiority of Capitalism

The verdict is threefold in favour of capitalism. First, capitalism is the most effective method of organizing human cooperation in production that the world has known, possibly three or four times more effective than socialism.

Second, capitalism is the only economic order known to man that combines high productivity with individual liberty in choice of occupation, family life, voluntary association in social, artistic or cultural activity and political order.

Third, a world of capitalist countries which minimized the domain of government and maximized the activities of men and women in the market at home and overseas would be more prone to keep the peace than a world of socialist states because it is more likely to create an international market in which individuals and private firms rather than governments, traders rather than politicians, buy from and sell to one another. The much maligned multinational companies are by definition vested interests in favour of world peace. International associations of all kinds would reduce the threat to humanity of nuclear war, prevent or minimize the pollution of the environment and agree on ways to deal with human calamities like famine the more they are linked by market relationships of mutual interest. The economic success of cooperating states based on minimal government would also encourage the liberalization of the communist blocs. The approach to formulating the conditions of world peace and harmony revealed by the analysis of the economics of politics has been impressively demonstrated by Professor Peter Bernholz.[7]

Capitalism yields its benefits to all who want them. Individuals, groups, sects, tribes, races, creeds and nations may prefer a style of life in a religion, a form of communal society or an equal sharing of joint products. They may be willing to pay the price in lower standards of life, restricted liberties, a larger risk of domestic tension, disease or international war.

That would be a rational choice if it were an informed decision based on knowledge of the alternative sacrificed, the high cost of rejecting capitalism. People who prefer other lifestyles to the higher productivity of capitalism cannot then complain that their food is inferior, their clothing coarser, their infant mortality rates higher, their housing poorer, their education more primitive and their understanding of the arts meaner. They cannot complain if they are not able to display their talents in new activities in the world of art or new businesses to produce goods or services that they have devised. They cannot complain if civic life is interrupted by frictions or if their leaders engage in periodic imperialist adventures. But nor can they morally expect others who choose capitalism to save them.

Whatever their cultural preferences, their material standards of living will be higher, their liberties more secure and military violence less likely the more they work with the institutions of capitalism—private property, an open welcome in a free market for new ideas and methods of production, low taxation and a minimal state with the smallest possible number of (and distraction from) politicians, bureaucrats and officials.

The common people would place a higher value on material possessions and amenities—the staples of food, clothing and shelter, education and medical care—and a lower value on the non-material artistic or cultural values of the mainly middle-class people who rule them with more ample material comforts. The High Tory Sir Ian Gilmour complained in a televised interview that people spent too much time talking about money. Norman Tebbit, whom I would call a populist Low Whig, retorted that was the view of people with ample.

7. Peter Bernholz, *The International Game of Power*, Mouton, 1985.

Capitalism and Religion

Capitalism can raise living standards under all religions. Whatever the faiths of individuals and peoples, they will lead more comfortable lives the more they make use of capitalism. They may prefer less materially comfortable lives for themselves and their children in favour of spiritual comforts, but their choice will not be known if it is made for them by others wielding majorities in political decisions.

Capitalism developed in Protestant Europe under the influence of the Christian-Judeo work ethic, but it is independent of religion. It has benefited people in the Far East where Christianity is rare and Judaism almost unknown. And it would benefit people on other continents who worship no god or many.

No moral obloquy attaches to people who work for material gain. The error is to suppose that to work for gain is to express selfishness or materialism. There was more voluntary charitable giving in the capitalism of the mid-nineteenth century than there is in the semi-socialism of Britain in the late twentieth century. And there is more charitable giving in the capitalism of the United States than in the semi-socialism of the post-war British welfare state.

The moral criticisms of capitalism have been accepted too lightly. The economist Professor Brian Griffiths, who wrote *Morality and the Market Place,* is sensitive to the criticism that capitalism is the system in which "literally everything should be bought and sold."[8] That criticism is, of course, not true: much is given without price in families, between friends, to causes. But if anything is not priced by the people buying and selling it, its value is set by politicians. They know less about value than the individuals who buy and sell, and who gain by care or lose by carelessness. Political people who enjoy using other people's money (mostly taxes) are by definition less informed and less responsible. The pricing of human organs that seems distasteful and above commercial calculation is the method of evoking supplies from volunteers. The alternatives are to coerce giving or to lose lives, both more questionable motives for deciding value.

Nor is it wise to couple libertarian capitalism with socialism in the supposed neglect or rejection of the religious basis for life. There is nothing in

8. Brian Griffiths, *Morality and the Market Place,* Hodder & Stoughton, 1982, 2nd edn. 1989.

capitalism that tells the individual what to do with his pay or wealth, to act selfishly or unselfishly. Professor Griffiths is right to look to "a moral standard" to guide conduct; many find it in religion, most in Britain in Christianity, some in other faiths, and some in secular or humanist beliefs. But the alternative moral standard, a public philosophy that teaches the immorality of the use of transient power, by business, the professions or trade unions, to extract favours from government at the expense of the unsuspecting taxpayer or consumer, can come from understanding the rules of ethical behaviour in all religions or none. We cannot look to the secular power of people temporarily in government to observe higher moral standards than the rest of mankind.

Professor Griffiths, like some Conservative academics and others who follow Edmund Burke, puts the church and other "mediating structures" such as trade unions and professional associations as necessary buffers between the private life of individuals and the megastructures of society. The assumption that all individuals can participate with more or less similar effect in the mediating structures lies at the root of the Crick-Marquand-Williams socialist view that the state is safe if it is accountable to all citizens. The notion that citizenship will save the state has spread to Conservatives as well as socialists. The hope of making the vast machinery of the state accountable to participating citizens is the last refuge of the opponents of individual sovereignty in the market. The solution is the opposite: to make the state as small as possible.

The Unreliable Verdict of the People by Opinion Polling

Apart from the market there is no comparable mechanism for discovering either individual preferences in private goods or the general state of public opinion on the unavoidably collective functions of government.

All notions of discovering "the general will" lend themselves to abuse by dictators or democratic politicians who look for a plausible validation for an otherwise implausible national policy. The British Labour Party in the early 1970s evolved the "social contract" for the arrangement by which its Government yielded social legislation and trade union privileges in return for promises of support for an incomes policy of agreed wage increases. The term echoed the "social contract" of Thomas Hobbes in the mid-seventeenth century, John Locke in the late seventeenth century and Jean-Jacques Rousseau in the eighteenth century to acquire spurious authenticity. But it was a capitulation to a vested interest in the effort to run a corporatist economy. It was in no sense a measure of the public interest but one more instance of the harm done by the opportunistic political process.

A second, more sophisticated but no less flawed, attempt to arrive at a measure of the general will was Arrow's social welfare function, finally admitted by its author to be "impossible" and best remembered as a social welfare fiction.

The third attempt, also flawed, is having strong influence on British political opinion, government policy and especially the welfare and taxation policies of the political parties. The inability of government to ascertain the wishes of the people, both at General Elections because citizens cannot indicate opinions on single policies, and between General Elections because their resort to their elected representatives is desultory and fragmentary, has produced the substitute of frequent detailed opinion polls based on samples of the populace.

Where they are limited to ascertain general sentiment on public policy issues, like the death sentence for murderers, or on constitutional questions, like Home Rule for Scotland, they may be of interest as a substitute for a full national referendum or plebiscite in which every eligible voter, citizen or taxpayer may state a personal opinion. More sophisticated techniques, such as electronic devices by which voters can instruct their political representatives on Bills being passed into law, are being studied by public choice economists as means of obtaining voter opinion on the unavoidably collective functions of government.

But it is another political delusion, reflected in the Labour Party rethinking urged in *Meet the Challenge, Make the Change,* to suppose that electronics will, at last, validate the socialist claim that government can be made responsive and responsible to the people. Television screens, phone-ins or push-button voting will not enable the people to exert their will with their representative in legislatures and to prevail over them by "participating" in political decision-making. It may make politicians more aware of vague uninformed public *opinion* on public goods like unilateral versus multilateral disarmament or the degree of adhesion to the EEC, but it is ineffective in expressing specific informed public *preferences* in private goods, which government also extensively supplies.

There is no such notion as public "opinion" in private goods without knowledge of price (chapter 5). Electronic voting cannot transmit the prices of services to individual citizens. That can be done only by markets. Even in the supply of public goods electronic voting would remain at the mercy of the representatives' interests, which often conflict with that of their constituents, legislative horse-trading, pressure from organized interests and the rest of the catalogue of imperfections of the democratic political process.

There is no escaping the solutions: constitutional or other disciplines on government in the supply of unavoidable public goods and return to the market for the supply of private goods.

Individuals may have broad opinions on macro-economic subjects like public goods that can be indicated by absolute answers of "yes" or "no." But opinion polling has been extended into micro-economic questions in which individuals will have specific preferences that must be indicated more specifically: not only by answers of "more" or "less," but still more specifically by "how much more" or "how much less." These are questions that enquire into intimate personal preferences between more or less government expenditure on services that are private goods and the alternatives of higher or lower taxation.

To indicate opinion on such micro-economic preferences individuals have to be told both the individual increase in welfare benefits and the individual increase in tax payments that they may require. Their replies will clearly vary with the tax cost. If the cost of better welfare services is low in added taxes, more people will be in favour than if the tax cost is high. But the extent of "better" must also be indicated: *how much* more taxes for *how much* better services? If the improvement is small for a given tax cost, fewer people will favour the proposal than if the improvement is large.

Opinion polling that does not quantify the individual cost or benefit claims to have found a growing willingness in the 1980s to pay higher taxes for more or better state welfare. The efforts to check such results by indicating the extent of the improvement or the tax cost have been rare. Such priced surveys on state education and medical care periodically commissioned by the IEA since 1963, necessarily based on national samples, found a generally growing though fluctuating preference for tax refunds in varying forms such as vouchers with which to pay for welfare services in the market.[9] Larger priced surveys, possibly annually, perhaps sponsored by the Treasury, could yield more systematic information on the underlying trend in British personal preferences between higher or lower taxation for state or private welfare. The opinion polling organizations could also incorporate the pricing

9. Ralph Harris and Arthur Seldon, *Welfare without the State,* Institute of Economic Affairs, 1987.

principle into their surveys to replace price-less polling that could mislead government about public opinion on the welfare state. My expectation is that, as incomes rise in the 1990s, more people down the income scale will want refunds of taxes to pay for education by fees and medical care by insurance in an increasingly responsive market.

The Impairment and Triumph of Capitalism

I set out to salute capitalism as the potentially most productive and least coercive politico-economic system that the world has known. It is not as productive as it could be because it is persistently undermined by the lingering socialist superstition that the political process is benevolent and should be enlarged as the ultimate protector of the people. The result is that capitalism as we know it is more coercive than it must be because it has not yet learned to discipline the political process, which may be necessary but is inherently imperialist and chronically vulnerable to pressure from sectional producer interests.

The verdict is based on the reasoning and evidence set out in the preceding pages. Two episodes help to crystallize the evidence. It is unlikely that they are isolated or untypical; rather, they illustrate developments in the rest of the economy, the polity and society.

The first, in local government in the north of England, began in 1971 with an intention by the District Council of Harrogate in the West Riding of Yorkshire to investigate the potential of the town as a venue for conferences and exhibitions. This record of events appeared in the town newspaper.[10]

Management consultants recommended the creation of a conference centre (and other facilities). In 1974 an estimate put the cost at £7.4 million. Building began in 1974, with expectation of completion in time for the annual Confederation of British Industry (CBI) conference in 1979. In that year the estimate for the uncompleted Conference Complex was raised to £11 million and later to £14 million. By 1981 it had risen to £27 million and by 1989 to £34 million. The Conference Complex was finally opened for its first commercial event at the end of 1981. The estimated cost had risen fourfold over the years. A Harrogate Councillor, Cecil Margolis, labelled "Whig," who had long foretold the increases in cost and questioned the successive explanations by officials, had been discounted by the Conservative Council but was

10. *Harrogate Advertiser*, March 1989.

substantially vindicated by events. The political process abhors the lone voice that speaks unwelcome truths.

Professor Keith Hartley of the nearby University of York used the Harrogate Conference Complex as "a case-study in local government spending" and raised questions about the role of local government in the country as a whole still too rarely asked.[11] What is the "proper" business of local government? Why do its costs seem out of control? What solutions has it failed to adopt?

Since 1980 some competition has been introduced into the supply of local government services. But local politicians, bureaucrats and trade unions resist further measures. The attempt to undermine the obstruction of local government by transferring some of its powers to central government is another half-way house in political tactics that may secure early results but builds resistances in central government to handing the control to the individual people who pay the taxes and have to accept the services. The Department of Education bureaucrats have sought for 20 years or more to control school teaching, to which the Conservatives in 1989 finally yielded in the National Curriculum. The ultimate remedy is the political solution of de-socializing local services that are not public goods requiring collective creation or the economic solution of charging individually for each service rather than collectively, as the Government has enacted, by a community charge for all local services which is in effect a tax that obscures the cost of individual services.

More generally, while de-socialization is a politically appealing method because it is more spectacular and raises funds more quickly, it remains a politicized solution subject, not least, to the weakness that it conceals individual preference as expressed no better than in the market that individual charging would create.[12]

With the best of intentions from the local government in office, the Harrogate episode illustrates the familiar reliance of politicians on large unquantifiable claims to create beneficial externalities that are incapable of proof or disproof until after the event, when the taxpayers' money has been spent on a project to which they could not assent because government offers no opportunity for the expression of opinion on individual projects.

The second illustration is of a developing public demand ("need") for a

11. Keith Hartley, "The economics of bureaucracy and local government," in *Town Hall Power or Whitehall Pawn?,* Institute of Economic Affairs, 1980.

12. Arthur Seldon, *Charge,* Temple Smith, 1977.

service that would have taken much longer to supply by the bureaucratic method of government, through its machinery of consultation with all the bureaucratic and trade union interests that claim a prior opinion (a euphemism for virtual veto), than by an initially small-scale private venture in which knowledge of personal circumstances can produce sensitive results and enlarge the sum total of human happiness.

The government labour exchanges, conceived by Beveridge 80 years ago to match supply and demand when unemployment was thought to be a problem of industry rather than of government, have failed in their task, as amply evidenced in the growth of private staff agencies, to match the supply of diverse staff skills and talents with the variegated demand for them. The change of name to "job centres" has evidently not sufficed. Government has had to embark on costly advertising to commend industrial training in the effort to match "the workers without jobs to the jobs without workers." The central question of the division of the cost of retraining between government, employer and employee would have been solved decades ago if the labour market had been allowed to develop without trade union restrictions and government over-regulation.

Matching supply and demand in the labour market can evidently be done better, certainly for some kinds of work in offices, homes and hospitals, especially in emergency, by flexible agencies that suit individual employees to individual employers by personal knowledge of both, than by centralized bureaucratic organizations hindered by standardized procedures, the dictates and the delays of documentation and the rigidities of hierarchy. Professor Christina Fulop argued in 1971 for charging by the state employment agencies as a means to make them more efficient, another good idea from the IEA stable ignored by government.[13]

The continuing gaps in government employment machinery are being filled by private agencies. The enterprise originating in the Kentish town of Tonbridge has grown to match the requirements of hospitals and individuals at home for nurses or domestic staff and of firms for office staff.

In 1979 I ventured the view that the Labour Party, as we had known it, would not rule again, and suggested, as one reason, that the emergence in almost all activities of women was a good augury for the prospects of a market economy.[14] They were more inclined to the micro-economic activity of meeting individual requirements than men who tended to lend themselves

13. Christina Fulop, *Markets for Employment*, Institute of Economic Affairs, 1971.

14. Arthur Seldon, *Crossbow*, October 1979.

to the macro-economic, collective machinery of votes in factory or trade union meetings. The importance for the choice between capitalism and socialism of the increasing prominence of women is argued in chapter 14.

Women have since appeared increasingly in industry, in the professions and as innovators in personal services. The staff agency in Kent was the creation of a woman entrepreneur with a special genius for matching individual supply and individual demand in crisis. Consultus Services was founded by Anne Palmer Stevens, described as "one of the sub-species of English women who might have built the Empire, controlled dynasties, and beaten all-comers at bridge, all without a thought for feminism."[15] As the largest part of its work, the agency provides increasing numbers of older people with living-in help. With others it anticipated the efforts of government in 1990 to enable ageing people to be tended in their homes rather than in often forbidding local authority institutions. The additional financing for this purpose announced by central government in July 1989 would have been better allocated to individuals, again perhaps as earmarked vouchers, than to local government as public expenditure susceptible to political influence.

Domestic agencies sometimes have short lives partly because of the wearing task of pairing the intensely personal requirements of ageing and other people as employers with the individual talents and temperaments of nursing or domestic employees. The Consultus agency has developed by progressive expansion from a bicycle-shed to a tightly integrated office, computerized to ease and expedite the matching of supply and demand nationwide, and drawing on worldwide staff serving clients from commoner to peer of the realm and from anonymous citizens to former Prime Ministers.

It may be predictable to add that the collectivist-minded politician who runs inefficient and spuriously named public services instinctively dislikes the competition from private suppliers of labour that authentically serve the public to its evident satisfaction. Mrs. Barbara Castle thought in the 1970s to outlaw private staff agencies or to regulate them out of independent existence.

The local authority in Harrogate and the personal enterprise in Tonbridge graphically illustrate, much more than hypothetical reasoning on general trends or detailed statistics that conceal variations in quality, the contrast between the impairment of capitalism by even well-intentioned government and its triumph by the spirit of individual endeavour. The Con-

15. Patience Wheatcroft, "In charge of the old brigade," *Daily Telegraph*, 17 April 1989.

ference Complex would have been accomplished more economically by a private venture, to its profit and the advantage of the town and its taxpayers. The staff agency accomplishes its task more expeditiously and more sensitively than if performed by a public agency planned from Whitehall or from town hall, with rules to obey, trade union restrictive practices to observe and short-term political motivations to satisfy.

The Instinctive Judgement of the People

The verdict of the common people on capitalism round the world, wherever they have been free to choose, has been the opposite of the judgement of the intellectuals, the politicians, the bureaucrats, the literati and lately the Church that the people must be tutored by their betters. The people have chosen well, even if by instinct and common experience rather than by the cerebration of socialist academics or by the revulsion of the socialist-minded literati against commercialism. The flight in late 1989 of East Germans to West Germany is not only a flight from socialism to capitalism: it will accelerate the replacement of socialism in East Germany by capitalism. The East Germans who return will find that socialism must be replaced not only by democracy but by capitalist markets to reach West German living standards.

The notion that the people want government to grow, and grow and grow is a simplistic heresy of the age. Its alleged support by opinion polling, the flawed substitute for the markets in education, medical care and other welfare services suppressed by government, has been accepted by credulous newspaper editors who presumably pay large sums to tell the people what they are supposed to know.

The instinct of the common people in deciding between the two politico-economic systems has reflected the scepticism of politicians recorded by David Hume of his contemporary eighteenth-century "political writers" rather than the judgement of twentieth-century "political writers" that politicians can be accepted as benevolent public servants yearning to do good without thought for their personal or political fortunes.

The people have judged economic systems by the micro-economic results for them in their daily lives: their food, clothing, shelter, comforts, amenities and range of choices. Students of politics have judged politico-economic systems by their macro-economic and macro-political results in government policies. The people think of the quantity and quality of goods and services. The political observers are primarily interested in the character and motives of the political actors. Professor Mitchell put the contrast pointedly:

the politician asks not how much the people value government services sufficiently to pay for them, but how many people value them enough to vote for him.[16]

The newspapers, television screens and radio are dominated by the doings and sayings of public men and women who are occasionally superior or inferior but mostly more or less like the rest of us. It was left to Shakespeare to personify the type in the evocative words about Julius Caesar not sufficiently or indelibly learned at school and applied in the ballot box:

> he doth bestride the narrow world like a Colossus; and we petty men walk under his huge legs. . . .

And for the rest of us:

> The fault . . . is not in our stars, but in ourselves, that we are underlings.

That is where the people have been shrewder than the observers. David Hume's judgement of people in politics now seems harsh. We cannot assume that every politician is "a knave." Those who know politicians know many to be upright, public spirited, anxious to use whatever influence they acquire to right wrongs and do good, moved by principle rather than predominantly by personal interest. Clement Attlee, the middle-class major who thought he could do good through socialism, Jo Grimond, the rare Whig in British Liberal politics who might have done better than Asquith, whose granddaughter he married, and Margaret Thatcher, the radical Conservative who championed economic liberalization, would be British exemplars from each party. Abroad, Ludwig Erhard, Ronald Reagan and Lee Kwan Yew would qualify. The judgement of Bertrand Russell on the decisive influence of personality in politics, so that their countries would have developed differently in their absence, for good or ill, could be generalized, among heads of governments, from Bismarck to Churchill, from Roosevelt to Stalin.

Yet if David Hume's political writers of the eighteenth century were too harsh about people in politics, political writers of the twentieth have been disingenuously and uncritically too lenient and charitable. Despite 40 years of the failure of government to do what it held itself able to do—to master inflation, prevent unemployment, ensure efficiency in industry, safeguard the sick, the old and the poor—the impression created by many political writers of our day, from close study of people in public life and politics, is of

16. W. Mitchell, *Government As It Is*, Institute of Economic Affairs, 1988.

a race apart, wise and benevolent, well informed about the world and his wife, who put the interests of others before themselves.

The last of these supposed virtues lies behind the daily discussion of the doings of politicians as exceptional individuals, selfless public servants, who seek the truth and yearn to apply it whatever the effects on their personal power, prestige or incomes. This is the fable that has lowered the guard and misled the people of the twentieth century into giving much larger powers to politicians than if Hume's realistic scepticism of the eighteenth century had remained with the political writers of today. And it is a reason why socialism has invaded everyday life, and capitalism has retreated much further, than their performance round the world has justified.

Politically Created Friction and Conflict

If the rule of majorities in the political process, or of minorities in systems with more than two political parties, has to be accepted for unavoidably collective functions, its disadvantages do not have to be accepted anywhere else.

The tyranny of the political process is the unnecessary subjection of the individual to the decisions of other individuals as voters, with whom he must conform not because their collective judgement is better than his, or because they know more, or are more concerned with his well-being, but solely—solely—because there are more of them. Majorities rule even where they are irrelevant. And they provoke avoidable discord between people among the many and people among the few.

These conflicts or frictions are the outcome of the political process wherever it is used, in capitalism as well as in "democratic" socialism; but since it is used to decide the use of resources in a larger part of "democratic" socialist than in capitalist systems, socialism causes more friction or conflict than capitalism. "Democratic" is quoted because society does not reflect individual sovereignty unless it is based as far as possible on free markets; even where socialist society maintains a semblance of markets it is based ultimately on collective sovereignty through the political process.

From political rule by majority (or minority) follows avoidable friction or conflict in almost all the main forms of human behaviour and organization. Since writing about these unnecessary forms of social tension in 1978,[17] I have been lengthening the list.

17. Arthur Seldon, in *The Coming Confrontation,* Institute of Economic Affairs, 1978.

The general cause of friction is the continually extended use of the political process of majority decisions in representative assemblies from public goods where it is, or has been thought, unavoidable to personal goods with separable benefits. This is the unnecessary use of socialism in the invasion of private activities that individuals or groups can voluntarily decide for themselves without the intermediation of government.

1. Regional or national friction: the most evident is the regional or national friction created by the majorities who decide how minorities—the groups and individuals who have values different from the herd—shall live. The Scots may sense that the more numerous English and Welsh in the British Parliament at Westminster decide, or strongly influence, their arrangements in education, medical care, housing and other personal services which are not the necessary business of government. They have to accept majority decisions in the public goods of defence and others, although even in law and order they may want to vary the rules to reflect their circumstances. But to require them to accept majority decisions of "outsiders," even those who subsidize them, in activities they can arrange themselves may rightly be seen as objectionable. The Welsh may say much the same about the more numerous English and Scots.
2. Sectarian or religious tension: the grievous troubles in Northern Ireland since 1969 have antecedents going back far into Irish history. No single solution is likely. But I have yet to see a discussion of the effects of "majoritarian" government in which the minority of Catholics have decisions on activities that could be run individually or collectively by Catholics decided by the more numerous Protestants. In the market individuals or groups take what they want and pay for it. If education, housing and other services were decided by Catholics as individual consumers in the market rather than by voting to elect representatives in Northern Ireland or in the Westminster Parliament to speak for them, the occasions of possible tension would be reduced. The unnecessary collectivization of life in Northern Ireland could be at least one removable cause of dissension between Catholics and Protestants who could live peaceably as producers and consumers of goods and services that people of both faiths have decided individually as consumers in free markets rather than collectively as voters for political parties.

3. Racial or religious suppression: native minorities and immigrants practising minority faiths in Britain live in homes, have their children educated in schools, are tended by doctors and nurses and use many local services decided by majorities of mostly white Anglo-Saxon Protestants. Those who may desire single-sex schools for their daughters or schools that teach the ethics of their faith pay taxes for schools decided by the representative machinery of politics in which they are outvoted. The solution is not to create "free" state schools for separate groups but to return taxes to individuals to pay for the schools they prefer.
4. Innovators inhibited: the minorities of exceptionally original, talented or adventurous people in industry, the arts, sport and other activities which require a readiness to take risks are coerced by the progressive taxes on their precarious rewards voted by majorities of their security-minded, worthy but unexceptional fellow citizens.
5. Independent employment burdens: minorities of the self-employed and small-scale service specialists in manufacturing and trading are, despite recent aid to small or new business, burdened by legislation (as on the chimera of job security) passed into law to appease majorities of employees with many more votes.
6. Occupational coercion: majorities of established doctors, actuaries, lawyers, architects, printers, engineers, dockers and others coerce minorities of would-be entrants to "their" professions and occupations by acting as judges and juries in unnecessarily high standards, unnecessarily costly training, unnecessarily testing examinations or unnecessarily long apprenticeships.
7. Familial debility: minorities of parents and children, poor as well as rich, are legally coerced by political majorities into paying for a wide range of government services, from schools to swimming pools and medical care to libraries, that are not public goods, that they may not want and that they have had no political opportunity to reject, but are induced by financial pressure to use. Family bonds are weakened and family life strained by the embarrassed confession of parents that they have no power to help their children, and the knowledge of children that they have to look to outsiders to help them in the setbacks and crises of everyday life.
8. *Urbs in rure:* town is set against country by the opposition of urban activists to the pastimes of minorities of countrymen. From fly-fishing to fox-hunting, whatever the arguments for or against, rural

pursuits can be prohibited by laws urged by the political representatives of town-dwelling majorities.

9. Bureaucratic privilege: the temporary majority (or minority) of politicians in power is influenced by the swollen minority (once around 30 per cent, reduced by de-socialization but still numerous) of the labour force in government employment to grant security of tenure, overstaffing, inflation-proofed pensions, subsidized housing, official cars, "eating for the Queen" on official occasions and excessive holidays in high-cost "public" employment at the expense of the majority of often lower-paid taxpayers.
10. Committee power: minorities of politically talented people coerce majorities of domestically oriented people into accepting committee-controlled public services from which they mostly cannot escape.
11. Gender dominance: majorities of activist political men pass laws binding on politically inactivist, because better engaged, women. The argument of feminists for at least equal numbers of MPs because women outnumber men is no stronger than the argument for proportional representation by colour of hair or dependence on false teeth. MPs are elected presumably because voters believe them competent or faithful representatives of their opinions, in which their sex, race or colour is irrelevant. The herding of people by irrelevant characteristics is yet one more mischief of the political process. The solution is again to confine the mischief to the minimum collective functions of government.
12. Reverse discrimination: embattled minorities of elitists coerce dispersed majorities by preferment for individuals on arbitrary grounds of immigration, race, colour or income.
13. Cultural discrimination: minorities in the world of art persuade politicians to coerce "uncultured" majorities into financing minority preferences. Working-class spectators of unsubsidized football subsidize middle-class patrons of the opera.
14. Patrician exploitation: majorities of radio listeners and television viewers are denied wider choice of broadcast programmes by the artificial government restriction of broadcast channels urged by arbitrary arbiters of taste.
15. Labour discrimination: minorities in organized trade unions have persuaded politicians to exclude the unorganized or lower-paid women, coloured or young workers, from higher-paid work by de-

vices varying from spurious claims to superior competence to minimum wage legislation.

In all these activities, and more, individuals are smothered by collective decisions in the political process. They do not decide for themselves, or for families or small voluntary private groups, as individuals; decisions are made for them by others in a majority of a region or country. The political process has been enlarged to invade the personal liberties that would have developed under capitalism where government was limited to the irreducible minimum of public goods.

Power in Public and Private Life

The character and qualities of people in public life, contrasted with their behaviour in private life, are an essential reason why capitalism is superior to socialism. Public life gives individuals very much more power than they would acquire in private life. People in politics who would not be entrusted by pensioners with a few hundred pounds or by building societies or unit trusts with thousands can aspire to control millions and billions of pounds. The prize of power in the political process attracts armies of saints and sinners. Capitalism scores heavily over socialism because, whether men or women are saints or sinners, it confines their powers much more to the unavoidable activities of politics.

Capitalism could minimize the use of the political process and maximize the use of the market. It could make politics relatively unimportant. Moreover it could make for a more harmonious society than socialism because it could more easily correct for the differences in financial power that influence access to the market than socialism could correct for the differences in cultural power that influence access to the state.

These differences also point to the superiority of capitalism over socialism in passing four less obvious but essential tests of the good society.

1. How firmly does capitalism or socialism put the interest of man as consumer before his interest as producer?
2. How strongly does it strengthen the power of the individual to escape from the tyrannical state or monopolistic supplier by exits to alternatives?
3. How effectively does public policy in capitalism or socialism put the price (incentive) effects of government measures before their income effects?

4. How far does government in capitalism or socialism assess and allow for the ultimate incidence as well as the immediate impact of its measures?

Essentially the verdict on capitalism for the eternal debate on the most desirable economic system for mankind cannot be absolute—a formal judgement of its strengths and defects. It must be relative or comparative—a judgement of the strengths and defects of capitalism compared and contrasted with the strengths and defects of socialism.

The judgement and the choice between the two turn on the capacity to achieve desired goals: material prosperity; personal, family, civil, cultural and artistic liberty; a sense of social harmony and community, with equity and generosity for the unfortunate; stability with low or zero inflation and full or high employment; not least, friendship with other countries based as far as possible on individual rather than political relationships as the basis of peace.

The verdict on capitalism must turn on the relative judgement of socialism. It must be based on a balance sheet of assets (strengths) and liabilities (defects). Proponents of both must be prepared to accept that the system judged, on balance, superior may be relatively inferior in some qualities. Socialism may be capable of acting more quickly than capitalism in creating equality, developing industrialization and safeguarding the environment. That is what we should expect from a system that works more by initiatives or commands from the top of the pyramid, the centre of the economic mechanism, than from another that waits for opinions and preferences from the base of the pyramid, the circumference of the mechanism.

Capitalism may be slower than socialism. In the past it has often been slower. Whether it is necessarily slower than socialism in reaching its goals, whether a capitalism that made the most use of markets by confining government to its minimum role would be slower, is a fundamental subject of the debate between socialists who continue to espouse the vision of socialism and liberals who assert the superiority of capitalism as it could be.

The socialist vision is an unrealizable mirage because it lacks the knowledge, incentives and freedom of capitalism. And the peoples of the world show no signs of wanting to move towards it. But are there immovable obstacles in the way of realizing capitalism as it could be? In the final chapter I argue, on the contrary, that there are more forces for than against the world moving towards capitalism.

The question remains whether socialist equality is created at a higher cost in personal liberty than capitalist equality. Socialist industrialization can be developed more quickly than capitalist industrialization, but the price may again be higher. In the end the economist must insist that the choice between the two cannot ignore the price of achieving their varied—and diverse—objectives.

If the proponents of each cannot claim that it is necessarily superior to the other in all qualities, the choice is between two imperfect systems, and the preference between them must be for the one with the relatively fewer evils. The verdict can be made only by a judgement of comparative achievements or failings.

The Final Choice

The capitalist system as it could be would make the maximum use of the market. It once seemed that socialism would make the maximum use of the state. Socialism as it could be is now less identifiable. In addition to all the historic varieties of socialism there is now the debate between socialists on how far it should, or can, use markets.

The book entitled *Socialisms* has come into its own.[18] Marxists like Hobsbawm and Left Labour politicians like Ken Livingstone[19] see a continuing role for a dominant state; former Marxists like Gorbachev by necessity want an expanding use of the market; British Marxists like Stuart Hall reluctantly see growing scope for the market; British Labour-Fabians like Raymond Plant would incorporate markets into a new individualist socialism, and imply a diminishing role for the state. There is still a hankering after the state for its supposed benevolence. A left-inclined academic at the LSE sees socialism as exalted: "the existence of public services is equated with a nation's degree of civilisation."[20]

Yet the essential difference between capitalism and socialism remains. Capitalism rests on the market process to generate the resources that underlie its economic, political and social fabric. Socialism, whether or not it uses the market, rests ultimately on the political process, centralized through the state or decentralized through local organization, to generate its resources.

18. Anthony Wright, *Socialisms,* Oxford University Press, 1986.
19. Ken Livingstone, *Livingstone's Labour: A Programme for the Nineties,* 1989.
20. Tony Travers, *Accountancy Age,* November 1988.

The critics of capitalism condemn its commercialization of human activities. This is their description of the market process: it induces people to be concerned solely with making a profit, with self-interest, with their immediate concerns and with the short run; to ignore or neglect the effects of their activities on other people, and to show no compassion for the unfortunate, no interest in sharing with others and no care for the environment. From this catalogue of condemnation emerges the *non sequitur* that capitalism must give way to socialism. The implication and the claim are that the abuses and excesses of capitalism will be avoided in socialism. That million-mile leap in logic once misled the world. It can no longer be accepted without challenge.

The alternative to capitalism (as it has been) and its market process described as "commercialization" is not a socialism cleansed of its evils or a political process that creates government of the people, by the people and for the people. The alternative to commercialization is politicization. If capitalism is replaced by socialism, the market process and its commercialization, with its strengths and weaknesses, will be replaced by the political process and by politicization, with its more doubtful strengths and less removable weaknesses.

If we reject commercialization of human life in work, the daily round, social activities, culture, academic learning, leisure and sport, we should have to live with the politicization of work, the daily round, social activities, culture, academic learning, leisure and sport.

That is the alternative. There can be no doubt which is preferable. The market process allows decisions to be made by individuals for themselves; the political process requires them to be made by collectives and imposed on individuals and minorities. The market process aggrandizes the individual; he may be wrong, but his decision decides. The political process suppresses the individual in collective decisions.

Capitalism is debilitated if overgovernment exposes it to the demands of the rent-seekers. The argument on externalities is too easy. We can all claim that our work does untold good to many of our citizens and generations to come. The author of every book is sure that it should be read by the world and his wife, all of whom would gain from its barely appreciated information, its invigorating reasoning, its fine writing and its inspiration. The world and his wife comprise an endless line of people who are sure that they could do untold good with more of other people's money. No wonder British broadcasting sometimes seems to act like components of a National Importuning Service.

Individuals and Groups under Capitalism

The market of capitalism treats people as individuals; the political process of socialism herds them into categories. Capitalism makes for harmony, socialism for friction. The most urgent case is that of race.

"The market is colour blind." To the liberal this is a statement of the obvious. To the socialist it is a disagreeable assertion he does not wish to examine for fear that it might be true.

That it is true everywhere, in every continent, is common knowledge. A shopkeeper in Singapore does not examine the colour of his customers—whether dark brown, light brown or pink. But the people who have gained most from repressing the black workers in South Africa are the less-skilled or unskilled white workers. In the 1920s the white trade unions supported the mainly white Dutch policy of apartheid. The white capitalists had, and have, most to gain from a free market in labour for blacks as well as whites.[21] I have yet to read a socialist analysis of apartheid that acknowledges this truth. The work of the white British Professor W. H. Hutt and more recently of the two leading black American economists, Professors Thomas Sowell and Walter Williams, and of the white South Africans Leon Louw and Frances Kendall leaves no doubt of the general principles.[22]

The essence was explained by a slightly built, much-loved, fearless, cockney Professor of Economics who spent most of his working life in South Africa. W. H. Hutt was a classical liberal economist who taught and wrote the truth, the whole truth and nothing but the truth throughout his 89 years until 1988. He cared not a fig for the vested interests he offended (although he defended the system by which they lived), nor the academics, not least J. M. Keynes, whom he attacked when he thought they taught dangerous untruths, nor the politicians whom he accused of sacrificing principle for expediency and disguising it as "politically impossible."

In a short book in 1964 he argued that the origins of apartheid lay not in the competitive economy of South African capitalism but in early twentieth-century government regulation of the labour market introduced mainly by

21. The most recent, and most powerful, study on this weakness in socialist writing is by the black American economist Professor Walter Williams in *South Africa's War against Capitalism,* Praeger with the Cato Institute, 1989.

22. Thomas Sowell, *Race and Economics,* Longman, 1979, and other writings; Louw and Kendall, *South Africa: The Solution,* Amgia Publishers, 1986; Russell Lewis and others, *Apartheid, Capitalism or Socialism,* Institute of Economic Affairs, 1986; and many more writings.

pressure from what socialists still call the "progressive" forces of the white trade unions, partly stimulated by the American International Workers of the World, and their allies among the socialist intellectuals, and from "Jim Crow" laws which enforced racial segregation.[23]

The blacks in South Africa have fared, and prospered, better under capitalism than they would have done under socialism. A former Left Book Club author, Dr. George Sacks, who taught and practised surgery at the Groote Schurr Hospital in Capetown, testified that black South Africans in his wards (where they did not pay) received better treatment than many white patients in the NHS hospitals he saw when he came to England to help edit *The Lancet* in 1955, where his opinion offended colleagues who were long-standing devotees of the NHS.

The black and other emerging workers of today throughout Africa and around the world would gain more from capitalism, which would treat them as individuals, than from socialism, which would treat them as members of a race. The Chinese in Singapore do well because the market rewards them for their personal skills. Workers of the world of all races and colours would not gain from the chains of socialism. That is the ultimate verdict in favour of capitalism.

23. W. H. Hutt, *The Economics of the Colour Bar,* Institute of Economic Affairs, 1964.

CHAPTER **14**

Prospects

. . . history forces on us a salutary agnosticism with regard to the long-term prospects for capitalism.

Robert Heilbroner, *The New Palgrave Dictionary of Economics,* 1987

The strength of Hong Kong's capitalist system is a better guarantee of its survival than the 1984 Sino-British Joint Declaration [which agreed to maintain the free market for 50 years after the British departure in 1997].

Zhou Nan, Deputy Foreign Minister of China, *The Times,* 6 March 1989

. . . if the politicians do not ruin the world in the next 15 years there is hope for liberty.

F. A. Hayek, in A. Seldon (ed.), *The New Right Enlightenment*

Less than 75 years after it officially began, the contest between capitalism and socialism is over: capitalism has won. The Soviet Union, China and Eastern Europe have given us the clearest possible proof that capitalism organizes the material affairs of humankind more satisfactorily than socialism . . . the great question now seems how rapid will be the transformation of socialism into capitalism, and not the other way around, as things looked only a half century ago.

Robert Heilbroner, *The New Yorker,* 23 January 1989[1]

In the final years of the twentieth century and the early decades of the twenty-first century the forces making for the advance of capitalism and the demise of socialism will be stronger than the forces making for the advance of socialism and the demise of capitalism.

1. Cited in *Pathfinder,* Centre for Education and Research in Free Enterprise, Texas A&M University, November 1989.

So far Professor Heilbroner's unexpected but candid volte-face from the scholarly scepticism about the future of capitalism in late 1987 to the resigned acceptance of the ultimate demise of socialism in early 1989 is the rare, if not the first, confession from a leading socialist economist that the days of socialism are numbered. In his *New Palgrave Dictionary of Economics* entry on "Capitalism" in 1987,[2] Professor Heilbroner reprimanded academics "professionally charged" with clarifying "the fate of capitalism" for "historical indifference . . ." to judgements of historic projection, such as those of Adam Smith through Marx to Schumpeter. He may now have exchanged unwarranted scepticism for premature certitude. His socialist confrères will not lightly admit error. They will be a main bar to the pace of the change he now concedes.

The resistances to the replacement of socialist politics, except where unavoidable, by the capitalist market, wherever it is superior, will be formidable. But they will meet counter-influences making for the subjection of life political to the life domestic, familial, artistic and cultural, which are threatened by the dominance of politics.

The Waning Influence of Socialist Ideas

The four kinds of forces in the burgeoning of capitalism lie in the influence of ideas, the role of vested interests, the emergence of chance circumstances and the advent of commanding individuals opposed to or championing the liberating power of capitalism.

The emphasis on each kind of influence has had its philosophically diverse champions. Their interrelationships are a subject of continuing debate among political economists. J. M. Keynes, who remained a liberal despite the efforts of his acolytes to make his criticism of classical liberal economic teaching serve socialist purposes, claimed that "the world was ruled by little else" than ideas. They took time to influence minds, but politicians were *always* influenced by ideas; the danger was that they regurgitated the ideas of their early years that had become outdated by the time that they acquired power. The emphasis on vested interests has survived since Marx, but has been interpreted differently by the economists and political scientists of the public choice school. The importance of "conspiring" circumstance, without which ideas might be ignored, was injected into the discussion by John Stuart Mill. And the influence of exceptional individuals has been amply dis-

2. Robert Heilbroner, "Capitalism," in John Eastwell, Murray Milgate and Peter Newman (eds.), *The New Palgrave Dictionary of Economics*, Macmillan, 1987, p. 353.

cussed by historians and philosophers; Bertrand Russell said that their importance was "unduly minimised" by people (he must have meant Marxists) who believed they had discovered "the laws of sociological change" and instanced Bismarck as making Europe different from what it would otherwise have been.[3]

The idea that has most undermined the repute of capitalism has for a century been Marxism. It is ironic that a thinker who emphasized interests as the dominant influence on human affairs produced the idea that has overcome the vested interests of capitalists and inspired the creation of communist states which for a time ruled over most of mankind. Socialism with a Marxist origin has been the dominant idea among all the ideas that have influenced political government and economic order in all the continents. Measured by population and area it still, by the early 1990s, held sway, by coercion rather than by conviction, over most of Europe until 1989 and still in Asia, large tracts of Africa and parts of South America. But measured in production of goods and services and living standards it has become a transparent failure embarrassing to its former adherents. It no longer constitutes a formidable intellectual assault on the case for capitalism.

The idea of social democracy retains the hope of many, especially in Europe, who wish to combine the productivity of capitalism with the just distribution of socialism. But they have not yet shown how to combine the two. Their dilemma is that socialist distribution would enfeeble capitalism and destroy the wealth that it produces for redistribution.

The latest social democratic emphasis on making the state acceptable by basing it on general political participation in its machinery is more significant for its evidence that the socialist mind is reluctant to lose the state as the final arbiter in ordering society than for its political realism. "Everyman a capitalist" is a realistic aim, and it is being realized by contemporary social change and technical advance. "Everyman a politician" is unrealistic or wishful thinking that distracts attention from the task of building civilized society based on cooperation between men and women with diverse but complementary scientific, artistic, political and domestic faculties, and it is being realized nowhere in the world except in small, usually backward, tribal societies. The object is not as many people as possible in politics but as few as necessary, so that we can get on with the business of improving life instead of perpetually contending about who shall control it.

Politics must be reduced to a necessary but specialized and minor service

3. Bertrand Russell, 1954, quoted in Andrew Gamble, *The Free Economy and the Strong State: The Politics of Thatcherism,* Macmillan, 1988, p. v.

in numbers and resources, like tree-felling or dentistry. The few politicians required for the few unavoidably collective functions can be hired and fired like the rest of us, and not allowed to stay too long and forget their place. We should regard them with scepticism, not with reverence. The British Parliament should revert to its nineteenth-century attendance of a few months a year. Politics has come to dominate our lives largely because of socialist teaching. A socialist reviewer of *Market Socialism,* Charles Seaford, who disapproved of the market even under socialism and preferred Professor Marquand's universal public debate, proposed adult education as the means to equip everyman to join as fully paid-up debaters.[4] Such escape into mysticism is the ultimate end of the road to social democracy.

The market socialist idea is an improvement on previous variants of state socialism but has not escaped from the socialist faith that the political process could and would operate the market to serve man as consumer. It still envisages a large and active but therefore bureaucratic, unjust and potentially corrupt political prime mover in human society.

The conservative critique of liberal capitalism, that the market disturbs continuity and is indifferent to cultural values, is similarly dependent on the creation of a benevolent state machine run by saints and seers.

None of the main ideas critical of capitalism (chapter 9) removes its superiority over the alternatives they offer. The world has had to endure a century of autocratic communism, enervating and debilitating socialism and hierarchical conservatism to accept, at last, that the disadvantages of liberal capitalism are a price worth paying for its unique power to produce high living standards without suppressing personal liberties or fomenting periodic international strife.

The literati add nothing to the academic criticisms, and seem unaware of their intellectual impotence and defeat.

In the realm of economic and political theories, the purpose of which is to explain reality, ten main advances in economic and political thinking, historical re-interpretation and legal reformulation have been to the advantage of the case for capitalism (chapters 7 and 8). The prospect for capitalism in the decades ahead has been strengthened in so far as the affairs of men and women are influenced by the ideas that best survive criticism and the test of experience. Ideas may be not only obstructed by vested interests but also reinforced. The truth is that individuals can be on both sides at once. The in-

4. *New Statesman and Society,* 9 June 1989, p. 37.

terests that could strengthen the liberal idea are discussed below as "conspiring circumstances." But the obstructive interests are formidable.

The Obstructive Interests

Marx spoke of the dominance of interests over ideas in deciding the structure of society, and the modern analysis of the economics of politics has dissected "the rent-seeking society." But Marx was imprisoned by the notion of class interests, in particular the conflict between the capitalist class and the working class. Because his approach to the analysis of the conflicts of interests was sociological, which analyses the joint interests of groups, rather than economic, which analyses the more relevant motivations of individuals, Marx arrived at classes defined by industrial functions rather than at individuals in the market.

In the real world the interests of both capitalists and workers differ in each group. The interests of capitalists differ fundamentally according to whether they see themselves as buyers or sellers. Their interest as sellers makes them prefer monopoly; as buyers they prefer competition. The interests of workers similarly differ: as sellers of labour they overtly prefer to be organized in monopoly selling organizations like trade unions; as buyers of the products or services of other workers they instinctively prefer competition between firms, wholesalers and retailers.

The fundamental division of interests is not between the social classes of capitalists or workers but between market status as producers or consumers, sellers or buyers. It is not between *different groups* of people but *within the same groups* and *the same people as individuals.* It is this dichotomy of interests within each of us that creates the difficulty of evolving institutions that would induce individuals to serve the primary aim of these two conflicting interests.

The primary aim must be to serve our interests as buyers or consumers. If we put our interests as producers or sellers first we shall want to safeguard our jobs, occupations or industries against invaders or technical change, put up barriers against them and end in beggaring ourselves by defensive protectionism, stagnation and decay.

That was the fate of the mercantilist system and is the fate of every politico-economic system that encourages us to put our interests as producers before our interests as consumers. Not the least is socialism. The only system that enables and induces us to put our interests as consumers before our own interests as producers is the free market.

This is the unique prize of the market economy of capitalism. Unfortunately it is also the most stubborn difficulty in the way of maintaining a liberal capitalism. People tend to see clearly their interests as entrepreneurs, managers, farmers, shopkeepers, accountants, engineers, technicians, doctors, lawyers, teachers, train-drivers, miners, carpenters or cooks. But they tend to see their interests as consumers only very dimly. Work is the source of income and of standing in society; how it is spent, and the prices or qualities of the goods and services it buys, seem secondary. Therefore people as producers organize with other like producers to defend and raise income much more than they organize with others as consumers to keep prices down and quality up.

Often the most effective method is organization as producers to extract favours from government—subsidies, tax concessions, restrictions on competition, barriers against imports and much else—because the benefit is concentrated on a relative few but the cost is spread over many taxpayers or consumers who do not observe their loss and rarely resist the action of government in yielding to the organized few at the expense of the innocent many. The industrial, professional and trade union producer interests have become well entrenched down the years and would strenuously oppose the removal of their subventions and privileges. They have obstructed government in the last ten years when it attempted to serve the general consumer interest best by promoting choice between competing suppliers.

This is the temptation to which we would all succumb if we could. We are engaged in a war against ourselves. And if we do not create the mechanism that will discipline our self-destructive instinct, we shall impoverish ourselves and destroy the hopes of better standards, of generous compassion for the remaining poor in the West, of more assistance to the peoples (not the governments) of the Third World, of building the world that science is making possible and of safeguarding the natural world we have inherited.

These are the rent-seekers. They reside in all of us. No government so far has been able to neutralize them. The British governments since 1979 have been more successful than all earlier post-war governments, but they have met strong opposition from, and have made concessions to, the interests in their projected reforms of the nationalized or regulated industries and services from coal mining and transport through education and medical care to financing local government.

The interests of producer rent-seekers are the challenge that government has failed to meet in the development of the liberal capitalism the people as consumers would welcome. Two Nobel Laureates, Milton Friedman and

J. M. Buchanan, have warned liberals against complacency. Professor Friedman's caution was considered in chapter 3. Professor Buchanan has concluded: "we are doomed to continued frustration if we expect advance towards the libertarian ideal of a minimal protective state in which the massive government economy of our present is dramatically reduced in size, scope and power, and in which the generative forces of the market are allowed much more room. . . ."[5]

Cautionary admonitions from such sources must sober liberal expectations. Yet it is possible to take a more hopeful view of likely developments in the coming decades. Professor Friedman's warning considered in chapter 3 is reconsidered below. Professor Buchanan's doubt about a liberal future lay partly in the self-inflating welfare state that required increasing expenditure independently of political decisions. His examples were American, but the principles apply to Britain and elsewhere: social benefits could be claimed by decisions of the claimants (in Britain women who bear children outside marriage have a "right" to a subsidized council home—the equivalent of the "moral hazard" in private health or other insurance if the person insured can influence a claim by his conduct); scientific invention, as in keeping dying people chemically alive, created an open-ended demand for the latest advances for everyone; the NHS has encouraged the cruel deception and impossible expectation of "the best medical care for everyone," the increasing number and life expectancy of the aged will raise the cost of pensions endlessly; more government expenditure is being financed by debt which is politically convenient because postponable rather than by current taxes.

A further mischievous reason for pressure to increase government expenditure, in Britain if not in the United States and possibly in Europe under the social charter of the EEC, is the elementary error of socialist thinking that, as national wealth grows, the politicians should spend more on state welfare services. The commonsense truth is the opposite: since personal incomes also rise the state could spend (and tax) less. But the expectation has been created by vote-hunting politicians and will not easily be countered.

All these sources of increasing resistance to reform of the welfare state seem to be the most powerful reason to expect continuing socialization of a very large part of the British economy—in the early 1990s about a half of economic activity.

Yet developments in British institutions and attitudes could make the

5. J. M. Buchanan, "Our Times: Past, Present and Future," *The Unfinished Agenda*, Institute of Economic Affairs, 1986, p. 34.

transition from the state to the market in welfare as well as in industry, the universities, art and culture less traumatic and more likely than it has appeared. Professor Buchanan offered a fundamental reason for caution in the economics of politics. The burgeoning welfare state, and the massive transfers of wealth it seemed to make possible, created large constituencies and irresistible compunction for politicians to win political power. The statesman-politician, who took the long view for the good of his country, was replaced by the career-politician, who was responsive to the immediacies of organized pressure groups but with no interests in the eventual consequences. Professor Buchanan has long argued that the solutions no longer lie in improvements to policies within the existing political structures but in reform of the structures to prevent government from continuing its myopic suicidal tendencies. Hence a new "constitutional economics" has developed in the United States.

The disciplining of government, whether by constitutional or other means, is also the task in Britain. It may be more difficult, without a written constitution that can be changed by amendment, to limit the powers of government to overtax, overcentralize, over-inflate and overcapitulate to pressure. There is a vicious circle in expecting the political process to be of advantage to all without apparent cost, huge but hidden in the labyrinths of a political process that has degraded democracy. Yet there are institutional and cultural changes (below) that seem likely to weaken the power of government.

The Conservatives have produced a Prime Minister who has assembled three governments manned in part by conviction politicians, the equivalent of Professor Buchanan's statesmen-politicians. The main adversary, the Labour Party, has had to announce its historic abandonment of state socialism and acceptance of the market, on paper if not in principle. Yet it retains its historic faith in the state, extended in 1989 to the new and paradoxical task of shaping the market that, to produce its desired results, must invade much of its functions and powers. The renewed Labour Party clearly continues to see the political process as superior to the market process. It does not yet see the market as the focus and the instrument of the people's decisions and sovereignty, with government as their servant in the market, not its master. If the Labour Party is to do as it claims, it must abandon the teachings of a century. But it shows no awareness of government failure, or of the superiority of the market as a daily referendum in economic democracy that reflects individual preferences more faithfully than does the political process.

This political approach continues to attach more respect to the decisions of the people as voters in the ballot box than to their decisions in the market. Under its rule the failed and flawed political process would continue to dominate society, where it has been over-extended beyond the province of unavoidably collective functions. It might produce conviction politicians, but their convictions would continue to favour the state over the market. The market, with its decisions of the people as consumers, would be tolerated on sufferance and under strict supervision and control by politicians. The political and the market processes would not be equals; even if they were presented as such, there can be little doubt which would be *primus inter pares.*

Milton and Rose Friedman's detailed solution for overcoming *The Tyranny of the Status Quo,*[6] erected and defended by "the iron triangle" of politicians, bureaucrats and beneficiaries, would require a British version. Their American package deal to make the general interest prevail over sectional interests is the election of a president committed to disciplining government or a Constitutional Amendment passed by a Constitutional Convention required by two-thirds of the states with its amendments ratified by three-quarters of them. In 1982 the US Senate, prodded by 31 of the 34 states required for the two-thirds majority of the 50 states, supported an amendment requiring Federal Budgets to be balanced each year. This was the monetarists' and public choice economists' triumph over the Keynesianism which urged political use of budget deficits. The Friedmans proposed further amendments, *inter alia* to give the President an item veto (on individual taxes), to replace the progressive income tax by a single rate on all taxed incomes and to limit the rate of increase in the supply of money by the Federal Government.

In Britain, where unnecessary socialization has proceeded much further than in the United States, disciplines on government would have to require it above all to purge itself of avoidably collective functions. That fundamental reform would substantially help it to balance annual budgets, veto taxes, replace the progressive income tax by a single-rate tax and limit the annual increase in the supply of money.

The second most urgent requirement would be to enact a new inalienable right of every man, beyond the power of political majorities, to compete with existing producers, suppliers and other vested interests. We must return from the worship of monopoly, whether "public," professional, trade union, autonomous, charitable or any other, to the suspicion of monopoly

6. Milton Friedman and Rose Friedman, *The Tyranny of the Status Quo,* Harcourt Brace Jovanovich, 1984.

of the early Stuarts. No man shall have the power of sole supply. The presumption is that every service can be supplied competitively unless proved to the contrary. To echo the language of the Marxists, the socialist idolatry of monopoly must be consigned to the dust-bin of history. The aim should be to remove the political filter through which man's ingenuity in devising new techniques, methods, products, services must pass to satisfy politicians before it can be adopted and applied for the good of mankind.

Ancillary reforms would further ease the task. Reduced government expenditure, by a combination of de-socialization or charges for all chargeable services, from education to medical care and libraries to national parks, would ease the balancing of budgets. De-socialization of the Bank of England would help to remove the control of the supply of money from short-run political influence, as in West Germany. The central object would be to remove as much as possible of economic life from the realm of politics.

Whether politicians will thus deprive themselves of their powers is the unanswered question. Their instincts are to extend rather than curtail their empires. Yet social and economic change may take power from them. For their powers are circumscribed by the stronger power of the people in the market. The people's economic power to bypass or defy government sets the limit to the political power of government. There is little purpose in passing laws that will be ignored or broken. "I do not know," said Edmund Burke, "the method of drawing up an indictment against an whole people."[7] There is no way that modern government can fine or imprison a whole people. The otherwise honest and law-abiding tax-evaders would alone flood the penal system. The contemporary trends in social advance and technological change reviewed below are the "conspiring circumstances" that could make the bypassing and defiance of government, with its high taxes and burgeoning bureaucracies, easier and more profitable. They could thus dissuade government from policies that it learns are becoming politically impracticable and therefore "politically impossible."

The Exceptional Statesmen-Politicians

No government will lightly initiate the act of self-abnegation in reducing its powers. But it may develop politicians who sense the changing mood of public disapproval of excessive government. Both will require exceptional politicians—the fourth of the influences on events.

7. Edmund Burke, Speech on conciliation with America, 23 March 1775.

The determined resistance to the interests that will impenitently oppose the liberalization of the economy and society will require exceptional politicians, who have been rare since the emergence in the late nineteenth century of the active state and its capacity to favour the influential. Britain produced them in its liberal phase, and by definition could produce them again when the century of socialist interlude and cul-de-sac has ended. The urgent requirement for them is in the present interregnum between socialism and capitalism, when the long onward march of the common people from stringency to plenty, serfdom to liberty, socialism to capitalism has been resumed.

It requires a William Pitt, who knew Adam Smith and his writings, a Robert Peel, who repealed the Corn Laws in defiance of the landed interest, a Gladstone, who wanted money to fructify in the pockets of the people, a Churchill, who read *The Wealth of Nations* and was a Whig in his hostility to socialism rather than a High Tory who absorbed it. History may judge that Mrs. Margaret Thatcher is of their breed. The political scientist Professor Maurice Cranston has put her in the class of Churchill, Charles de Gaulle of France and Ronald Reagan of the United States, the only British Prime Minister whose name has been dignified as the description of a philosophy (Thatcherism), who "has done more than anyone to change the country politically, economically, and socially," and who changed the leadership of the Conservative Party "from the traditional upper-class Tory amateurs and paternalists to diligent middle-class petit-bourgeois 'outsiders.'"[8]

Whatever the verdict of history on leaders who have shaped history in the past, the requirement in the future, in so far as it remains to be shaped by human beings in addition to favourable conspiring institutions, is for statesmen-politicians who see the damage done to economy and society by over-expansion of the political process. They will have the task of presiding over the liquidation of the empire of redundant impertinent parasitic politics, which might be described disrespectfully as RIP. Their main philosophical principles will be the precedence of liberty over equality and the creation of the minimal state.

Such statesmen-politicians will have the task of defeating the modern replicas of the medieval barons who defied the king and laid the land waste in their battles for supremacy. They now defy the economic sovereignty, the general interest, of the people. The exceptional statesmen-politicians may be found in the Conservative Party if it can subdue its powerful remaining

8. Maurice Cranston, "Margaret the magnificent," *The American Spectator,* April 1988.

corporatists who believe that they can divine and pursue the general interest against the importunities of the sectional interests. Or, if the Conservative corporatists prevail, the required men or women may emerge in a new political alignment which the Social Democratic Party under Dr. David Owen could still forge. They are least likely to come from the Labour Party which is still too socialist in inspiration and aspiration to legislate disciplines on itself if it acquired power by its newly professed understanding of the market.

Conspiring Circumstances

The task of the statesmen-politicians will be the lighter the more what John Stuart Mill called "conspiring circumstances" develop spontaneously to ease the transition from the state to the market, from the socialism that has failed but refuses to depart to the capitalism that is struggling to resume after a century but is resisted by intellectual error and the interests it allowed to develop by stifling competition. There are eight of these conspiring circumstances.

Defiance by Escape to the Underground

Observers of the struggle between capitalism and socialism continue to ignore the evidence around them that, however they vote, even for socialism, the people instinctively practise capitalism. From the industrialized West through the socialist countries to the Third World the pretensions of the politicians to serve the people are belied by the people's rejection of the politicians through escape to the market—white, black or grey.

From Britain through Hungary to Peru the people cock a snook at politics wherever they can. Official government statistics persistently understate what Ortega y Gasset could have called the increasing fiscal "revolt of the masses."[9] The understatement reveals the cultural dilemma of the established bureaucracy. Understatement by the bureaucracy of the true extent of tax avoidance and evasion is intended to indicate that the Treasuries of the world are in control of the haemorrhage of government revenue. Avoidance is legal but could be as much of a drain on revenue as illegal evasion. Yet understatement of tax rejection weakens the case for a larger army of tax inspectors.

9. José Ortega y Gasset, *The Revolt of the Masses,* Allen & Unwin, 1932; renamed *Rebellion of the Masses* (in English), Notre Dame University Press, 1982.

Mr. Anthony Christopher, the General Secretary of the Inland Revenue Staff Federation (the tax inspectors and collectors), who has contributed authoritative observations to IEA events and Papers, and inspired the Labour Party's think-tank to perform for socialism what he judged the IEA to have performed for economic liberalism, has made the plausible economic case for additional tax-gatherers that their additional cost would be far exceeded by the additional revenue recouped in taxes. (Economists would say he was right to argue that the marginal revenue could exceed the marginal cost.) This could be the income effect of increased input into tax-gathering. What remains unknown is the price effect on the tax avoiders and evaders, for the argument hints at the probably sizeable undetected tax rejection, which makes official estimates even more undependable than independent estimates, such as those of Professor Edgar Feige,[10] have indicated. He arrived at 15 per cent for Britain, around twice the official estimate. Even this calculation could not have included the ultimate form of tax rejection in the informal deals made to exchange goods for goods, or services for services, or goods for services not only between acquaintances but between trading opposites which entail no payment and little risk of detection. There is an indefinable boundary in the gradations of transactions between friends and between companies. The taxation of the modern activist state has restored barter as an extensive, unrecorded and untaxed form of friendly exchange and business enterprise.

More fundamentally, the modern state has brought a cultural change in the historically law-abiding British. Tax rejection, in which legal avoidance teaches the high rewards of illegal evasion and merges into tax "avoision," has become so generalized that it is discussed in private and in public without a sense of moral turpitude. It also induces the insincerity apparent in the opinion polling that claims to have discovered widespread public willingness to pay higher taxes (unspecified) for more/better welfare (unquantified).

The economic underground in the West has expanded for a further reason unexamined by the advocates of larger government and higher taxes. The expanding political process has excluded from influence the bulk of people without the political talents required to succeed in life under an active state that regulates, controls and dispenses subventions. They cannot compete on what seems to them acceptable fair terms with the political

10. Edgar Feige, "The UK's unobserved economy," *Economic Affairs,* July 1981.

people. Their mainly technical, artistic, commercial or other skills are at the mercy of the political people who run the industries or services in which they work. They are impelled to escape not only from what they see as oppressive or confiscatory taxation; they flee from subjection to the culture of the people, whom they also see as not making a better contribution than themselves to the well-being of the nation.

The ability of the citizen to escape from the burgeoning political process makes abortive the proposals of Labour and some Conservative politicians to confirm or extend the power of government. The protection of the natural environment may, in some elements, become a new and growing unavoidably collective function (public good) of government. But the citizen confronted by extensive functions of government in total, which cause resentment by taking on average half of his earnings, cannot distinguish between the avoidable because potentially private and the unavoidable collective functions, the public goods and the public "bads." Unless the total tax take from the citizen is reduced, increasing escape from taxes will prejudice the prospect of attention to the environment or other new acceptable government functions. Tax rejection is no respecter of purpose; the good suffer with the bad.

Tax rejection in the socialist countries is, by definition, unknown; since all socialist statistics are suspect and politically tainted, it is certainly even larger than in the capitalist West. If the unrecorded economy in Britain including barter is 20–25 per cent, it is probably nearer 40 per cent in communist Europe. The capitalist underground may be condemned by communist politicians and socialist academics alike as immoral, but the socialist fiscal underground is the lifeblood of the people under communism. Socialist man will work for bread or vegetables; he will not exert himself to vote for socialist policies that bring no bread or vegetables to the shops.

The most spectacular evidence that the market, legal or illegal, evokes the suppressed productive faculties of the individual comes from the Third World. The planned economies of the underdeveloped or developing countries have failed to mobilize the self-preservation instincts of their peoples (chapter 4). It required the prospect of visible immediate personal advantage to galvanize the peasants of Peru into activity in which they could use whatever skills they inherited or acquired. The Western press has again conveyed a misleading impression of their plight and hopes; the superficial broadcast programmes have missed the underlying political causes and ignored the latent individual potential for self-emancipation. Even the World Bank has been misled by the development economists.

The peoples of the Third World have been so long oppressed by the political process that they are escaping to the refuge of the underground market of private production and exchange. They have suffered so much from socialist failure that they are saving themselves by capitalist success, even if illegal. Ultimately the peoples of all the continents, not least the poor, demonstrate the insight of Adam Smith that men and women want above all to "better their condition."

What is happening all over the socialist Third World, varying with the ferocity of Marxist- or Maoist-inspired government penalty and the sense of deprivation, is an outbreak of capitalism—but outside the official economy since it is suppressed within it. The innate capitalism of the peasant is most vividly exemplified by the developments in Peru documented by the economist Hernando de Soto in *The Other Path,*[11] so entitled to point the contrast with the grandiosely named Marxist or Maoist Shining Path of centralized state planning and the paternalist liberation theology of the church.

The people in and around Lima wanted not political planning but individual freedom to use their latent entrepreneurial talents. Since their governments have denied them liberty they took it into the underground and made it a paradise so quickly that it is overwhelming the official politically failed planned economy, and has been producing some two-thirds of the country's output.

These developments are emerging elsewhere in the Third World and will emerge more strongly as its results are learned. *The Other Path* is subtitled *The Invisible Revolution in the Third World.* But just as the New World of America came to the rescue of the Old World in the war against Hitler, the Third World could come to the aid of the First World of the industrial West, where the lessons of informal capitalism, outlawed but irrepressible, will echo wherever the official economy is prevented from being liberalized by the iron triangle of politicians, bureaucrats and beneficiaries of government.

Capitalism will find a way, officially or unofficially, to liberate itself from the vested interests it has tolerated. In this and other ways it corrects itself; it is corrigible. If the Third World can find the way, the communist world cannot be far behind. The difference is that capitalism could do it by peaceful if illegal means; socialism may have to risk or suffer civil strife or armed violence. Rather the black or grey market than Tiananmen Square, the Georgian gassing, the East German water cannon or the Polish murders.

11. Hernando de Soto, *The Other Path: The Invisible Revolution in the Third World,* Harper & Row, 1989.

The Market Regiment of Women

A second reason for the view, confident but not complacent, that liberal capitalism will prevail before long in the decades ahead is the again too little understood consequences of the emergent influence of women in economic affairs. They are becoming more active in all walks of life, political as well as economic. In the political process their influence may not be different from that of men; its inducements and motivations are strong enough to affect all humans. Yet women are less accustomed to the herd instinct of political life; they are more likely to rebel as individuals than acquiesce in the *Gleichschaltung* of the political process which suppresses individuality in its majoritarian procedures.

But in the economic world the influence of women will be very different from that of men. Broadly, men in industry organize themselves as producers in macro-economic organizations. The division of labour so far has allotted the function of purchasing consumer for household supplies mainly to married or unmarried women. The archetypal family has been headed by the earning male and the spending female. Even where women work and earn, they retain the main function of shopper and consumer, even when shopping with males. Men are more characteristically political animals and women domestic. The more women that work and earn, the stronger will be their influence in household budgeting.

Men are still inclined to delegate their political opinions and market bargaining to industrial, professional and trade union organizations that produce collective decisions by majorities of the activists. Women are more characteristically makers of individual decisions in the market. The increasing influence of women as shoppers and consumers relative to that of men will induce and fortify government to withstand the importunities of organized producers.

The Decline in Unavoidably Collective Functions

The extent of capitalist economic activity will in part turn on the volume of government expenditure required for unavoidably collective functions. The outcome will be decided mainly by two trends: the political ability of government to remove hitherto collective but potentially private functions to the market, and the net balance between the almost certain reduction in resources and expenditure required for military defence and the possible but problematic increase required for environmental conservation.

The avoidably collective functions, including many welfare services, will have to be increasingly transferred to the market if the taxes to finance them are increasingly rejected and more individuals with rising incomes resort to the market to find higher quality (below).

Government expenditure on defence will fall as the communist countries find that they have to transfer scarce resources to consumer goods to keep pace with the West and the USSR accepts the inevitability of political democracy and the market in its former satellites. Government expenditure on environmental damage will not necessarily rise and may fall as means are devised to provide safeguards by market inducements (chapter 13). This view is beginning to receive more general acceptance outside the school of market economists, on the Left again led by Professor Plant.[12]

The Rise of the Workers

As incomes rise more people down the income scale will want and be able to pay for better services than the state claims (but fails yet again) to supply equally to all. *Embourgeoisement* is yet another cultural trend conveniently misunderstood and underestimated on the Left and still often on the political Right.

It is hardly necessary to emphasize or illustrate this further political inducement on governments, however reluctant, to de-socialize their services, distribute money and let the citizen shop for the higher quality to be found in the market.

In 1983 the Conservative Government withdrew from its attempt to emancipate individual parents in choice of school by the education voucher because of divisions within its ranks and opposition from the organized teachers, who hinted at strikes, and from the Church. In 1993, when real incomes will have risen by a quarter or a third, more parents will have withdrawn from unsatisfactory state schools and will demand a return of taxes to help pay school fees. In 2003, when incomes may have doubled, no politician will condemn the education voucher and hope for re-election. But the market would have generated parental choice much faster than the slow painful oppressive political process. So far parents have waited for the politicians to open the market. By the turn of the century they will flee from the paternalist state faster than the East Germans fled in the late 1980s.

12. Raymond Plant, "Can the Greens ever appeal to the poor?," *The Times*, 26 June 1989.

The rejection of the state in education will be followed in other politicized services as rising incomes enable more of the common people to use the market.

From Non-profit to Profit

A glory of British life has been its energies in organizing good causes without thought for private gain. There may be psychic rather than monetary benefit, but the result in helping people who cannot help themselves is the same. Yet there has also been the related prejudice that activities run for profit are objectionable.

The criterion must lie in the results for the people that it is intended to aid. If non-profit ventures produce less goods and services than for-profit, or less quickly, or so slowly that the socialist-inclined critics conclude that only government can produce them in larger quantities or more quickly, thinking must change: the prejudice must be abandoned as a cultural indulgence that satisfies the culture at the expense of the helpless.

For-profit ventures have the faults of other private ventures, but also the strength of the risk of failure. Non-profit ventures have the strength of a sense of mission, but the fault of an absence of a sense of urgency, especially if there is little or no competition from profit-making and loss-fearing organizations.

Sanity lies in allowing both kinds of initiative to show their advantages in more vigorous competition. The American educationist Professor Myron Lieberman[13] has argued that the American private schools, for which there is increasing demand, have not responded promptly to it because they are mostly non-profit ventures. The appearance of a stronger element of with-profit enterprises in the supply of welfare and other services, in Britain and Europe as well as in the United States, would be a substantial influence in offsetting the vested interests in favour of state institutions.

The for-profit enterprises have begun to appear in Britain in American hospital companies whose costings are far advanced contrasted with those of NHS hospitals. As the EEC develops there will be scope for European health insurance companies and other capitalist ventures.

13. Myron Lieberman, *Privatization and Educational Choice*, St. Martin's Press, 1989.

Technology Fortifies the Market

The discovery by the Marxists that new technology is replacing mass production heavy industry by medium-sized and small units in these "New Times" is a characteristic episode in Marxist historicism. Changing technology is a continuing process of undermining concentrations of private industry in monopolies, cartels and restrictive agreements. It is precisely in the socialized industries and services that new technology has been decelerated and prevented from having its prompt salutary effect. It is precisely here that it will break down the socialized sector of capitalism.

Teaching does not have to be conducted in large buildings called schools or universities if learning can be absorbed at home or in small local groups by computer technology. Hospitals will have to be smaller to accommodate the convenience of visiting families as well as, if not rather than, the ordinances of doctors. Housing will no longer be built by government. Pensions are not the business of the state. Coal is better mined in pits run by private firms much smaller than the country-wide coal mines. Transport is better supplied by flexible local coach and bus companies.

The twenty-first century will have to pay more attention to the elector as a consumer with a widening range of goods and services among which to choose than as a producer huddled in large "works" and voting "aye" in obedience to trade union officials. Technology will make production more suited to the opportunities and devices of capitalism than to the standardized procedures of socialism.

Democracy Is Not Enough

The contrast of recent years in the socialist world has been of increasingly full ballot booths but often meagrely stocked or nearly empty shops. The socialist teaching has been that the supreme aim is political, every man and woman to have a "say," the sanctity of the decisions of "democracy." The Russians are said to be liberated by democracy and its historic votes after 70 years for the Deputies in the People's Congress. The Chinese students have shown that they were ready to die for democracy. The Africans in South Africa are demanding democracy. The Poles achieved "democracy" in August 1989, the Hungarians, East Germans, Czechs and others in the early 1990s.

But if democracy does not produce the food and drink, the clothing and homes, the motor cars and holidays that technology makes possible, and capitalism produces in abundance, it is not sufficient to teach or demand democracy. The power to vote is to little purpose if it does not bring the power to eat. Democracy is not an end; it is the means to bread and liberty. And if it does not bring the market and its abundance, the people may have to choose between democracy and the market.

That is the tragic choice not discussed in Britain. In the West, the market has brought democracy, in the East not yet everywhere. But in the West and the communist/socialist world democracy has not, yet, brought the market. It remains to see how long the new democracies of Hungary and Poland and the rest will take to create free markets, and how the people will react if they have to wait year after year. If the political democracies do not give them official markets, they will create unofficial markets.

Which of the two do the people put first? There can be little doubt that political democracy will not be accepted at its face value unless it brings economic democracy—the liberties, choices, high quality and rising standards of the market. Gorbachev has belatedly accepted this inconvenient conclusion. Deng Xiaoping saw it earlier but, in the alternating battle for power between the state and the market designed to ensure a soft landing to capitalism, he had to reverse the engine of the market in June 1989, for an unknown interval, to avoid losing control of the rate at which it was introduced. The democratic Solidarity coalition in Poland will fail if it shirks the market. The African leaders will have to follow the West and the new capitalisms of the Third World in introducing capitalism. They will want to control it at a rate that enables them to cling to political power. But the people will be less inclined to wait the more they learn of the living standards of Western capitalism.

The Lessons of Experience: Murder Will Out

Yet the eighth in this list of conspiring circumstances could be the most powerful in working for the restoration of capitalism, both in the East where it has been suppressed and in the West where it has been emasculated.

In the 1930s when I was an undergraduate at the LSE socialists of integrity could advocate socialism without the handicap of knowing much about how well or ill it would work in practice. Their consciences were clear. The USSR was hidden from Western visitors. When the social democrats or democratic socialists met in the spacious rooms of the LSE or the dingy offices of the New Fabian Bureau they had no evidence of socialism in practice to guide or warn them.

Today the socialists who urge socialism, or more socialism, have no such defence. The people know from their daily experience over the decades.

Until recent years it was possible for socialists to argue that socialism could not be judged as bad because it had nowhere been tried. Some continue to argue that no-one has had the good fortune to live under "real" socialism. But the people who have lived under socialism as it has been have waited long enough and are not prepared to wait for "real" socialism as it could be. They have been risking communist bullets to show they will wait no longer—not only for the right to vote in polling booths but for the right to buy what they want in the market.

Socialist intellectuals can no longer present socialism as a vision. For millions it has become a reality—from the communist extreme in the USSR through the milder forms in Sweden and Austria to the socialized sectors of the capitalist West. It no longer rings true for Roy Hattersley to maintain that "It is possible, by collective action, to . . . [increase] equality and, in consequence, [give] reality to the notion of liberty by providing the power which makes the generality of men and women capable of exercising the rights of free citizens."[14] It was plausible to make that claim in the 1930s; in the 1980s and 1990s, after 50 or 60 years of "collective" action of all kinds, in all sorts of conditions, under saints and sinners, it is no more than an empty promise. There is nowhere it has been done and no reason to suppose it can or would be done.

It is too late now to argue that communism has a human face, social democracy will become less repressive and nationalized industry and welfare will become more accountable. The intellectuals may believe what they say. The people can reject socialism, even state welfare, and flee to the market.

The experience of socialism by the millions has destroyed the ability of the socialist intellectuals to continue advocating a socialism they once claimed had not existed. That is the most powerful "circumstance" that is "conspiring" with all the others to make capitalism more probable than socialism in the future.

Socialist Teaching and Capitalist Performance

This book has had to refute the mistaken judgments of capitalism by its socialist-minded critics as a prelude to a review of its economic and political strengths and weakness. The general public has been misled for a century or more by academic, political and literary interpreters of capitalism who did not, and still do not, understand its strengths (or its weaknesses).

14. Roy Hattersley, Foreword to Elizabeth Durbin, *New Jerusalems: The Economics of Democratic Socialism*, Routledge, 1985, p. xi.

"A study of the history of opinion," said J. M. Keynes "is a necessary preliminary to the emancipation of the mind."[15] The best socialist minds are turning to a better understanding of the capitalist system, once the object of venom and derision. Yet the case for capitalism is stronger than they allow even now.

Capitalism must be judged not only by what it has achieved, despite its shortcomings, but even more by what it could achieve if the political process were corralled to its essentials and refined much more than it has been so far to reflect the micro-economic preferences as well as the macro-economic opinions of the citizenry.

The critics of capitalism have been predicting its final collapse since its infancy. For 150 years Marxist and other socialists, from Friedrich Engels in 1844 through John Strachey in 1936 to Professor Eric Hobsbawm in 1988, have identified "capitalist crises" that marked the end of capitalism. Engels cited the "crisis" of the 1840s, Strachey had ample "evidence" in the Great Depression of 1929–31 (analysed with conviction and relish in *The Nature of Capitalist Crises*[16]), and Professor Hobsbawm was up to date with the latest stock exchange "crisis" of October 1987.

Socialists saw the downward curves of capitalism as precipitous straight lines that went through the horizontal axis—at which point the capitalist exploiters of the proletariat would be expropriated.

The opposite process of expropriation of the communist exploiters by the exploited workers, now emerging in the communist world, was not discussed by Marx and is not yet discussed by his successors. The revolt of the masses against political pretension and bureaucratic insensitivity was not foreseen by the Fabians, and is now not followed to its ultimate conclusion by their successors. The upward curves of capitalist progress were dismissed by the Marxists and the Fabians as the short-lived silver linings round the black clouds of capitalist poverty and injustice, immiseration and alienation, unemployment and inflation.

The Marxists and other socialists were not the only prophets of doom. They were certain of the final demise of capitalism, and were glad of it. But others were sceptics of its future, and not always glad. ". . . all the great economists," said Professor Heilbroner with no apparent regret, "have envisaged an eventual end to the capitalist period of history."[17] David Ricardo, al-

15. J. M. Keynes, *The End of Laissez Faire,* 1926; in *Essays in Persuasion,* W. W. Norton, 1963.
16. John Strachey, *The Nature of Capitalist Crises,* Gollancz, 1936.
17. R. Heilbroner, "Capitalism," p. 353.

though Lionel Robbins included him among the great English classical economists,[18] and John Stuart Mill, who wrote a paean of praise to liberty but saw good in socialism in the 1850s (he would have more difficulty in the 1990s), anticipated capitalist growth fading into a stationary state. And Marx (whom Heilbroner classifies as a great economist) thought he saw a succession of worsening capitalist crises until the system could no longer resolve its elusive but evidently postponable internal contradictions. These critics were not saddened by their predictions.

Yet others who doubted the future of capitalism also saw its virtues and did not welcome its supercession by socialism. J. M. Keynes argued in 1936 for the "socialization" of investment,[19] although he would not have followed the path that his Cambridge followers took into Marxism if he had lived after 1946. Joseph Schumpeter saw the very success of capitalism as producing criticism of its faults that leaned towards bureaucratic socialism.[20]

Professor Heilbroner's conclusion in 1987 that "history forces on us a salutary scepticism" on the prospects of capitalism was generous recognition of the conflicting arguments of the economists as well as of the conflicting evidence of history. In early 1989 he saw the conflict resolved in favour of capitalism. There is now less certainty about the future of socialism among other socialist critics and sceptics. Capitalism, after all the prophecies, is not doomed to collapse. On the contrary, concludes the pragmatic vote-hungry British Labour leader, it has to be accepted and, if not welcomed, reluctantly recognized.

The change in mood has not come too soon. It would be difficult to sustain the certitudes of impending or eventual collapse when the socialist countries are moving towards, or back to, capitalism. Their politicians have decided that, whatever the opposition from the socialist military and industrial establishment and the socialist ideologists, the mechanism of capitalism, the market, is necessary to raise their living standards, because they can no longer conceal the vivid and obtrusive contrast with the capitalist West. Their economists at home, whose predecessors had anticipated them and the new politicians by two or three decades in seeing the necessity of the market in the 1950s, no longer have to maintain the pretence that central planning is a superior method of using scarce resources. Their spokesmen

18. Lionel Robbins, *The Theory of Economic Policy in English Classical Political Economy*, Macmillan, 1952.

19. J. M. Keynes, *The General Theory of Employment, Interest and Money*, Macmillan, 1936.

20. Joseph Schumpeter, *Capitalism, Socialism and Democracy*, Allen & Unwin, 1943.

no longer have to engage in ritual denunciation of the inefficiency and degeneration of capitalism. And socialist economists in the West, like Professor Alec Nove, can now urge the adoption of markets without risking the displeasure of communist leaders or the loss of visas.

Politicians in the West, who were once guarded in using the names of economic systems long in bad odour and likely to lose votes, are more ready to declare open and unembarrassed support for capitalism and the market. The change from the interwar years is almost apocalyptic. I cannot recall a Conservative or Liberal politician of the 1930s who said a good word for capitalism. "Private enterprise" was generally as far as they would venture as the name of the system they preferred. There would be condemnation of socialism but no championship of capitalism.

The change in the intellectual debate, and the recognition by the more sophisticated socialist academics that the market was indispensable and that the economic liberals were not, after all, Marx's "lackeys of the capitalists," have emboldened the non-socialist or anti-socialist politician. Mrs. Thatcher is the first British Prime Minister who openly espouses capitalism. The prefix "popular" may be added by cautious public relations advice, but it is justified by the efforts of her three Governments to spread private ownership, not least through de-socialization.

If the communist leaders do not yet explicitly welcome capitalism, they no longer condemn it—except in the satrap dependencies like Cuba or the last redoubt of Romania. But they increasingly practise it. If the Labour or Social Democratic socialist leaders in the West dare not yet openly welcome capitalism by name, they practise it in office, as in Australia, New Zealand, Spain, Greece and West Germany. In opposition they incorporate it into their thinking and revisions of policy, not least because it can win rather than lose votes, as in Britain and Italy.

If socialist politicians in the West, like John Smith, Bryan Gould and Roy Hattersley in Britain, do not yet openly welcome capitalism by name, it is largely because their doctrinaire-minded activists retain a deep lingering distaste for the system, and their middle-class socialist literati continue to inveigh against it. The socialist leaders may have to suffer, for many more years until their unregenerate intellectuals pass away, the disadvantage of appearing to espouse a socialist system that their working-class supporters reject in their daily lives and condemn a capitalist system from which their supporters benefit. Until the day when they can openly say what they know, that they are no longer socialist, which may come too late to win office, they compromise between the dawning conviction that they have accepted the irrelevance of socialism and the avoidance of condemnation by their socialist supporters, by describing themselves as Labour, democratic socialists or social democrats.

The most sophisticated form of this art, displayed by David Marquand among academics and Dr. David Owen among politicians, is a combination of an acceptance and a condemnation of capitalism. The Marquand and Owen combinations differ. The academic accepts capitalism for its decentralization but rejects it for its neglect of the life cultural. The politician accepts it for its productivity but rejects it for its harshness in distribution; in the IEA journal *Economic Affairs,* Dr. Owen combined the necessity of market competition with the desirability of state redistribution—in the fashionable language of the day, competition with compassion.[21]

Both combinations are at fault because they want the indispensable strengths of capitalism without its incidental weaknesses. They would risk losing the baby with the bathwater. They want to have their cake and eat it. This is the misunderstanding of capitalism that has prevented the critics from accepting it and has sent them searching for the false god of socialism. Both combinations are unrealistic ideals which would remove the weaknesses of capitalism by means that destroyed its strengths. The weaknesses they identify can be removed, or minimized, but it must be done by means that preserve its strengths. If they had applied their talents to this task they might have refined a capitalism that yields most of its advantages with the least of its disadvantages. Instead both would emasculate capitalism by the injection of socialism.

The opposite approach is to attempt to save socialism by grafting on to it the capitalist mechanism of the market. Again, this is the approach of socialists who have come to understand the necessity of the capitalist market but who remain socialists on historical or emotional grounds—that only socialism can safeguard the so-called socialist values of community, compassion, sharing.

The most impressive of these attempts to save socialism by importing capitalism is that of Raymond Plant.[22] His attempt (with Kenneth Hoover) is the best so far to save socialism because he is one of the few critics of capitalism who shows knowledge of the literature of the liberal economists.

21. David Owen, "Agenda for competition with compassion," *Economic Affairs,* October 1983.

22. Kenneth Hoover and Raymond Plant, *Conservative Capitalism in Britain and the United States,* Routledge, 1989.

The Plant approach displays the recent historic change in the attitude on the British Left to capitalism from contemptuous dismissal to respectful study and the desire to learn in order to assess. The publisher's "puff" on the back cover is not only a compliment to the authors but a condemnation and rejection of (most) other authors, socialist and formerly socialist: "it is one of the few critical appraisals of the New Right based on a clear understanding of what the arguments for the free market really are." The significant aspect of the book is that it sets out as a critique of capitalism but ends as an admonition to socialists to learn from it and to modify their conception of socialism to embody elements of capitalism.

Both critique and admonition are original. The critique of capitalism is more sophisticated than in other socialist writing, although it still judges capitalism as it has been, rather than as it could be. But even more unprecedented is the scholarly candour with which socialists are advised both to learn the capitalist case and to adjust socialism accordingly.

The lessons that Professor Plant urges socialists to learn are of special interest. It is "now a matter of urgency . . . to update and rethink the tradition of R. H. Tawney and others . . . as the free-market conservatives [he meant liberals] have rethought and updated the tradition of classical liberalism." Not least, he shows some scepticism of the new notion of "citizenship" to save the socialist argument (subjecting the state to popular control) until it is clear what it implies in "values and policy."

A Call to the Intelligentsia

Of the four influences on policy—ideas, interests, conspiring circumstances and personality—ideas remain the dominant influence in shaping the institutions that determine how the common people will live. Capitalism would not yield to the critics even if their argument were stronger. Capitalism is too deeply ingrained in human aspirations. Whatever the intelligentsia may think, people will trade with one another, inside or outside the law, to improve their condition.

But the critics are seeing their errors. Robert Heilbroner changed quickly from confident scepticism about the future of capitalism in 1987 to resigned recognition that it was indestructible in 1989. Capitalism has never been, is not and never will be faultless. But it can remove much of its imperfections. The socialist alternative of incorporating the market as a subordinate instrument of the state is little more than one more attempt to salvage the socialist vision.

Yet if the fate of the common people is their concern, socialist thinkers can help them most by joining the task of fashioning a less imperfect capitalism.

Prospects—the Contrast between the East and the West

This book has dealt with economic ideas and principles rather than with political policies and action. Yet during the time when it was written, from October 1988 to July 1989, with updating in October 1989, the world has moved faster than the theories (possible explanations) about why it changes. Ideas are continually refined and there is more to say about the working and merits of capitalism and socialism in October 1989 than there was in October 1988. But the world of events has moved faster in that one year, much faster than could have been expected in 1988; and it will no doubt have moved much more by 1990 when the book is published. The resignation of the East German Communist "Government" on 7 November and of the Politburo on 8 November came in what was regarded as the most "hard-line" of the communist countries. The communist world is crumbling. But the teaching of socialism remains undaunted in the West.

Nor is there much doubt about the direction of change in events and action. It has been wholly one way from socialism to capitalism. The resignation of the East German Communist Government on 7 November and of the Politburo on 8 November will reverberate in the less rigid communist countries, not least in the USSR, which began the retreat from Moscow communism with Gorbachev's openness (*glasnost*) and reconstruction (*perestroika*) in 1985. Both meant less socialism without calling it capitalism. Three aspects call for attention.

First, it is more dramatic in the USSR and Eastern Europe, but no less fundamentally if more quietly in the smaller countries—in Asia even Cambodia, in South America even Nicaragua—which attract less attention in the media.

Second, there is still the superficial emphasis on the political process of representative democracy rather than on the more fundamental market process and its property rights, freedom of individual entry in economic activity, freedom of contract and minimal government.

Third, while the socialist world has moved on to embrace the markets and private property of capitalism, the socialists of the West continue to preach socialism. The last is the most revealing.

The spectacular developments in communist Europe are more immediately significant for the concessions the USSR may be ready to make to the West, not least in nuclear disarmament, because it urgently requires the financial aid and capitalist expertise without which the escape from economic backwardness will be too slow to save the political power of the socialist leaders. But in the lives of the individuals who comprise the common peoples, the change from socialism to capitalism in the smaller countries is no less dramatic.

The euphoric emphasis on the emergence, or rather re-emergence, of democracy in the socialist countries reflects the unreflecting dominance in Western thinking on the nominal political freedoms of the ballot box to the neglect of the economic freedoms in the market. Political democracy may seem the necessary means by which the peoples of the belatedly liberated socialist countries can use their new powers of the ballot box to vote into reality the next stage of the substantive freedoms of the market. But the experience of the past century in the West teaches that political democracy is not enough. It has still not created government of the people, by the people, for the people. Mikhail Gorbachev will have to go a long way in economic reality to reach the political vision of Abraham Lincoln.

The contrast between the reluctant abandonment of socialism by the socialists of the East and the continuing advocacy of socialism by the socialists of the West remains for perplexed philosophers to unravel. The affliction debilitates the full range of thinking on the Left, from the intellectual revisionists of *Marxism Today* to the political revisionists of the British Labour Party. The Marxists of Eastern Europe and other continents who know Marxism in theory and practice are abandoning it. The Marxist and Labour socialists who still dream of a socialism shorn of its defects continue to dream.

The most tenacious adherents of socialism are not the common people concerned about their daily lives but the intellectuals concerned about the thinking that provides their psychological sustenance. The politicians concerned about their professional interest in power, perhaps to do good though often in practice harm, appear midway in the range.

The people want to change from socialism to capitalism as soon as they see their families will lead more comfortable lives, with food in more dependable supply, clothes that elevate their spirits, homes that provide privacy. They have waited for socialism long enough. The promises remain promises. They will now change to capitalism as soon as they are allowed by their socialist leaders, as the East Germans began to show in the late summer of 1989, bypassing Erich Honecker's Wall through Hungary and Czechoslovakia.

The politicians will change from socialism to capitalism when they see coercion has run its course and there are more votes in higher living standards. Honecker's successor, Ogen Krenz, attempted within 14 days of his succession to liberate East Germany not from socialist conviction but with the vain hope of retaining power. Yet the idea of socialism will live long after it has been rejected by the people and jettisoned by the politicians because it will be sustained by the intellectuals in their minds, their writings, their teachings.

This is the decisive influence for the future of the West, especially of Britain. The intellectuals of Eastern Europe began to see in the 1950s that socialism had failed. They spoke of pricing, profits and markets, but the politicians thought their instrument of coercion might yet produce the higher productivity of which they prematurely boasted. The intellectuals of the 1980s–1990s have won the argument because coercion has failed after 70 years. They are at one with their politicians. What can they think of their opposite numbers in the West?

The intellectuals of the West, especially in Britain, where socialist government has had to alternate with capitalist government, persist in their faith, their profession and their advocacy. They not only have the ears of the Labour-socialist politicians; they are themselves often politicians. For them nothing has changed: the argument against socialism falls mostly on deaf ears; the evidence against socialism is denied. They will continue undaunted their "struggle" for socialism. The Marxists speak of renewal, of discovering a new political strategy (alliances with non-socialist groups) "along the road to socialism."[23] The Labour revisionists talk markets but plan socialism. There is agonizing re-appraisal, but always there is socialism.

The intellectuals of the USSR, Poland, Hungary, Yugoslavia and even East Germany may wonder at the unreasoning loyalty of socialists in the West to the long line from Marx and Engels, through Lenin and Trotsky, Laski and Strachey, to Crosland and Crossman. But the socialists of Britain (and the world) will fight capitalism in the footnotes, the meetings, the lecture rooms, the journals, the theatre. They will never surrender, because they cannot, like true social scientists, recognize and concede error. The exceptions remain exceptions.

Some socialist thinkers have abandoned socialism to the extent of understanding and accepting markets. Most remain faithful to the socialist dream

23. Martin Jacques et al., "Facing up to the future," *Marxism Today*, September 1988, p. 11.

in the beneficence of the saints and seers they see as forming governments. The rest of the world must leave them to their dreams while it refines the imperfect instruments developed in capitalism for providing mankind with an increasingly tolerable and civilized world.

The prospects for capitalism in general are bright. The hope that the market will soon be allowed to emancipate the common people remains unclear. The USSR produced a Gorbachev because market forces, technological advance and social aspirations have made the Russian and subject peoples impatient for the living standards of the West. But the living standards of the West are still restrained and unnecessarily unequal because the political process has too many beneficiaries in all political parties. The Labour Party has not yet learned the lessons. The middle parties have lost their way but may yet produce a market-based competitor to the Conservatives. The market-oriented Whigs in the new Conservative Party will have to jettison the remaining High Tories and recruit the millions of aspiring skilled and semi-skilled men and women who want a market economy in which they can realize their potential. Since their incomes are rising by some 2.5 per cent a year and will rise by 50 per cent in 20 years, more will be able to scorn the state and turn to the market. The common people will not be denied much longer.

Envoi: A Promise Kept

The people among whom I lived in the East End of London for the first 15 years of my life, who live on into their seventies and eighties, were mostly the children of working-class parents. Some were beginning to emerge from poverty by 1931 when I was moved away from our gas-lit house, with its single cold-water tap and lavatory in the yard and its single lilac tree in the 50 square feet of garden, to the house lit with electricity, grandly called Belmont Lodge, with its bathroom, carpeted floors and garage in Stroud Green.

Around the age of 11 I made a silent promise: when I grew up and had acquired a motor car, I would return to my friends, the children in Oxford Street, E1 (now Stepney Way) who had never tasted what we now call affluence, and take them all on free rides round the block.

In my childish mind, my friends would remain children. (I had not then heard of Peter Pan.) I acquired a motor car, at the late age of 32 in 1948, a prewar Morris 8 used in the wartime Auxiliary Fire Service and sold cheap to war pensioners. But by then many of my friends had also moved away to outer London suburbs, and probably acquired motor cars before I did.

The system that gave them motor cars, and much else, was capitalism. If socialism had replaced capitalism in Britain, or if they had lived in socialist Eastern Europe, from which the parents of some had come, few would have had cars, or much of anything else. The system we as children hardly understood, but were taught to revile, had emancipated them from the slavery of poverty. Many have done well under capitalism: one is a captain of industry, another a Professor of Town Planning, a third a Professor of Political Science in Australia; some have become middle-class professionals; several prospered in private enterprise. (One has subscribed a commendation on the cover; another I did not then know, who had lived in nearby Hoxton, has provided the Foreword.)

They had to escape from the legacy of teaching that capitalism was wicked and only socialism could save them. Yet that is what their children in turn were taught, and their grandchildren are now being taught. They are still asked to believe in the power of government and the benevolence of politicians rather than in themselves and their potential power in the market. That socialism keeps the working people round the world poor is still denied or obscured.

The children of my childhood who have lived with the liberties of capitalism have mostly seen through socialism. Their daily experience of the opportunities given them by capitalism has taught them more in daily practice than the continuing teaching of impenitent socialists in schools, the newspapers, fiction, broadcasting and the theatre. A gulf has been created between the lives experienced by my generation and the tainted history our children are taught by professional and political teachers who have learned little or nothing from history.

I hope this book will remind my childhood friends, and perhaps some like them elsewhere in England and overseas, of their early lives, the lifelines of the capitalist market with which they finally threw off the poverty of their childhood, and the promises of socialist-minded politicians of all parties that ended in endangering and almost suffocating the liberties that enabled them to save themselves in the market.

They were not emancipated by socialism, but despite the industrial and welfare socialism that has wasted much of the nation's substance. The socialist academics have had to confess that they were wrong. But the retailers of socialism remain in the schools and the media. The socialist politicians still want power. What remains of socialism would be safe in their hands, and they would extend it under new names.

I could not return with a motor car to give the children of my childhood the free rides as I dreamed. The system they were taught to deride has given them their own motor cars, and much else they would not have had under socialism. In helping over the years to restore the intellectual repute of capitalism, and in this book, my vindication of capitalism, I have kept my childish promise.

DESCRIPTIVE GUIDE TO READINGS

A bibliography of capitalism, ranging from classical liberal to free-market libertarian writings, would form the ideal background to a book that argues the case for capitalism as it could be against socialism as it has been and must be. This Guide indicates briefly the contents of books cited or consulted.

The titles listed below are those the contents of which are not sufficiently or not at all indicated in the text. Additional works are indicated in the footnotes or sources in the books listed.

The focus here is mainly economic, though there are economic aspects of all human activities. Capitalism has also been re-assessed more favourably in recent years by specialists in politics, philosophy, sociology, psychology, law and history, as well as in aesthetics and the arts. Books on these aspects are described by Chris Tame in *The "New Right" Enlightenment,* listed below.

I am sensitive that I have done more justice to the scholars whose works I consulted most while writing the book than to others from whom I have drawn inspiration since my student days. I hope the names of the authors will guide readers to other of their writings.

For ease of reference I have grouped separately in order of date of first publication the Hobart Papers and other papers from the Institute of Economic Affairs that presented specific solutions to problems. Many other IEA papers made more general proposals for economic reforms.

To supplement full-length studies the journals listed carry papers on current developments that will keep students informed of the continuing debate in the theory and practice of market systems and the defects of government services and regulation.

For readers overseas I have added a list of "think-tanks" of which I have some knowledge that specialize in the study of economic and other aspects of markets and capitalism, as a guide to books and reports published by them or others in their countries in addition to titles listed below.

Acton, Lord, *Essays in the History of Liberty*, Liberty Fund, 1985.
Volume 1 of three volumes of the nineteenth-century liberal historian and political thinker, a confidant of Gladstone, provides a rare insight into the politics of liberalism for students and the citizen. Acton is remembered for his aphorism which goes to the root of the libertarian argument for minimal government: "Power tends to corrupt, and absolute power corrupts absolutely."

Acton, H. B., *The Morals of Markets*, Longman and Institute of Economic Affairs, 1971.
The philosopher who was Professor of Moral Philosophy at the University of Edinburgh was asked by the IEA to judge the morality of buying and selling, which has long troubled man's conscience as based on selfishness contrasted with the high-mindedness in politics and the professions.

Anderson, Annelise, and Bark, Dennis L. (eds.), *Thinking about America: The United States in the 1990s*, Hoover Institution, 1988.
A compendium of 47 essays by 51 eminent (mostly) American academics, including four Nobel Laureates, politicians, four living Presidents, and others on the outlook for capitalism; from the influential Hoover Institution at Stanford University.

Anderson, Martin, *Revolution*, Harcourt Brace Jovanovich, 1988.
A former Professor of Economics at Columbia University, President Reagan's chief adviser on domestic and economic policy in the early 1980s, assesses the efforts to restore and strengthen capitalism in the United States.

Anderson, Martin, *The Unfinished Agenda*, Institute of Economic Affairs, 1986.
Essays by Professors J. M. Buchanan, R. H. Coase, Milton Friedman, F. A. Hayek, W. H. Hutt, Israel Kirzner, Patrick Minford, Gordon Tullock, Sir Alan Walters and B. S. Yamey on the political economy of government policy; quoted in the text.

Ball, Alan M., *Russia's Last Capitalists*, University of California Press, 1987.
Professor Ball of Marquette University re-examines the significance of the forgotten capitalists licensed by Lenin to rescue collapsing socialism in the 1920s but suppressed by Stalin in 1928.

Barry, Norman, *On Classical Liberalism and Libertarianism*, Macmillan, 1987.
A main work from the independent-minded British political scientist who is generally of the classical liberal and libertarian schools but differs on some aspects from other members.

Bauer, P. T., *Reality and Rhetoric*, Weidenfeld & Nicolson, 1984.
An incisive analysis of the confusions in (mainly) socialist writing on the developing countries by Professor Lord Bauer, a foremost exponent of liberal economics.

Becker, Gary, *A Treatise on the Family*, Harvard University Press, 1981.
The pioneering work on the analysis of the economic aspects of the family, with costs and benefits like other institutions, following Becker's more general *Human Capital* and *The Approach to Human Behaviour*, both Columbia in the 1970s.

Beenstock, Michael, *Work, Welfare and Taxation*, Allen & Unwin, 1987.
Professor Beenstock, formerly of the City University, now in an Israeli university, analyses the market approach to the taxation on earnings and the effect of the supply of labour.

Bell, Daniel, and Kristol, Irving (eds.), *Capitalism Today,* Mentor, 1970.
Two notable American sociologists who came to accept the strengths of capitalism present 12 essays by (mostly) American academics and observers on the contrast between the achievements of capitalism round the world and the then continuing reservations of its critics.

Berger, Peter L., *The Capitalist Revolution,* Gower, 1987.
A former "bourgeois socialist" sociologist explains his conversion to capitalism based on his examination of the evidence on the performance of capitalism and socialism round the world. Discussed in the text.

Berki, R. N., *Socialism,* Dent, 1975.
A political scientist on the Left explains the varying historical forms of socialism. A book with comparable purpose is noted under Wright.

Bernholz, Peter, *The International Game of Power,* Mouton, 1985.
An original application by the Professor of Economics at Zurich University of public choice analysis to the explanation of the relationships between nations.

Binyon, Michael, *Life in Russia,* Hamish Hamilton, 1983.
An enlightening insight by *The Times* man in Moscow, 1978–82, into everyday human activities in contrast with the (pre-Gorbachev) official presentation of harmony and contentment.

Black, Duncan, *The Theory of Committees and Elections,* Cambridge University Press and Kluwer, 1958, 1987.
A (largely arithmetical-geometrical) pioneering text by a British (Scottish) economist on the difficulties of non-market, political decision-making. Committees choose between motions; elections choose between candidates: such political machinery can misread the preferences of the people it claims to represent.

Blake, Robert, *Conservatism in an Age of Revolution,* Churchill, 1976.

Blake, Robert, *The Conservative Party from Peel to Thatcher,* Fontana, 1985.
The Oxford historian records the changing attitude to capitalism of the Conservative Party, ending with the latest phase of the adoption of market liberalism by the reformist Conservatives under Margaret Thatcher, in which he attributes the influence of the IEA after its "near exile in an intellectual Siberia."

Blaug, Mark, *Economic History and the History of Economics,* Wheatsheaf, 1986.
A historian of economic thought traces the thinking of liberal and Marxist economists on capitalism and socialism.

Blaug, Mark, *Economic Theory in Retrospect,* Cambridge University Press, 1962.
A more advanced but enlightening text for the student of the history of economic thought which shows the early ideas and their gradual refinement.

Block, Walter, Brennan, Geoffrey, and Elzinga, Kenneth, *Morality of the Market,* Fraser Institute, 1986.
Papers and commentaries by economists and others from a seminar of the Canadian market-oriented think-tank that dispel the fallacies periodically repeated by the clerical critics of capitalism.

Bloomfield, Jon (ed.), *The Soviet Revolution,* Lawrence & Wishart, 1989.
The tenacious publishers of Marxist/socialist books assemble 16 articles by 14 authors from *Marxism Today* (two summarized from the left-wing *Political Quarterly* and the Soviet *Literaturnaya Gazeta*), with some newly written, on the "remaking" of socialism in the USSR in the faith that the USSR can "transform" itself.

Bosanquet, Nicholas, *After the New Right,* Heinemann, 1983.
Optimistic title by a temperate critic of economic liberalism, written before market socialism came to be the alternative of British socialists to the market liberalism of the "New Right" and the acceptance of the market in the communist countries.

Brittan, Samuel, *A Restatement of Economic Liberalism,* Macmillan, 1988.
The doyen of British academically inclined economic journalists refines the arguments of his 1973 book *Capitalism and the Permissive Society.*

Brown, Gordon, *Where There Is Greed,* Mainstream, 1989.
Assertive condemnation of the Thatcher Governments and their pro-capitalism policies in the 1980s by a promising Labour politician.

Buchanan, J. M., *What Should Economists Do?* Liberty Fund, 1979.
Two groups of the many writings of Buchanan, sometimes in collaboration with others in the public choice school. (1) A collection of 23 essays on the application of economics to the world of politics by extending micro-economic individual decision-making to macro-economic collective government decision-making: medical care in the British NHS and the United States, national budgeting, earmarked taxes, the financing of education and other political activities. (2) Sixteen articles by Buchanan on the nature of economics and the role of economists with special reference to the economics of politics.

Buchanan, J. M., and Tollison, R. D. (eds.), *Theory of Public Choice,* University of Michigan Press, 1972.
A collection of 21 essays by 13 authors on the application of economics to political theory and practice.

Buchanan, J. M., and Tullock, G., *The Calculus of Consent,* University of Michigan Press, 1962.
Generally regarded as the seminal text of the Founding Fathers of public choice from which most of the writings on the economics of politics followed.

Buchanan, J. M., and others (eds.), *Towards a Theory of Rent-Seeking Society,* Texas A&M University Press, 1980.
Essays by public choice economists and other academics on the development of organized groups that induce government to grant political privileges not available in the market.

Buck, Trevor, and Cole, John, *Modern Soviet Economic Performance,* Blackwell, 1987.
Professor Cole (geography) and Trevor Buck (industrial economics) of the University of Nottingham analyse evidence on USSR economic performance with the approach of the Czech market socialist economist, Janos Kornai, which judges the efficiency of enterprises by their market rewards.

Bullock, Alan, and Stallybrass, Oliver (eds.), *Dictionary of Modern Thought,* Fontana, 1977.

Reference book based mainly on conventional political theory with little attention to the economics of politics.

Butler, Eamonn, *Hayek,* Temple Smith, 1983.

Simply written introduction suitable for the general reader and the student.

Caute, David, *The Fellow-Travellers,* Yale University Press, 1988.

Revised and updated edition of a 1973 book that divulged the gullibility of socialist idealists who over 50 years accepted the myths of the achievements of Soviet and other national forms of socialism.

Chafuen, Alejandro, *Christians for Freedom,* Ignatius Press, 1986.

The author traces classical liberal economic thought to the Spanish "Late Scholastics" of the seventeenth century. Discussed in chapter 12.

Cheung, S. N., *Will China Go Capitalist?* Institute of Economic Affairs, 1982.

An early forecast by a Chinese-American economist that China would have to adopt capitalist institutions.

Collard, David, *Prices, Markets and Welfare,* Faber, 1972.

A scholarly study by a socialist-inclined economist of "market failure"—the technical and ethical objections to the market, especially in housing, redundancy, "big business," the social services and international trade. A book to read with parallel studies of "government failure."

Cowen, Tyler, *The Theory of Market Failure,* George Mason, 1988.

Eighteen critiques of the conventional view of the inability of the market to respond to individual demands.

Crick, Bernard, *George Orwell: A Life,* Secker & Warburg, 1980; Penguin, 1982.

Quoted in the text.

Crick, Bernard, *In Defence of Politics,* Penguin, 2nd edn., 1982.

Described by the author as "an attempt to justify politics" though without explanation of the economics of politics (public choice). The original version, Weidenfeld & Nicolson, 1962, revised for Pelican in 1964 and much reprinted, was a presentation of political democracy in conventional political science; the second edition, in 1982, added an explicit appendix, "A Footnote to Rally Fellow Socialists," which helps to explain the author's defence of politics as the characteristic instrument of socialism.

Crozier, Brian, and Seldon, Arthur, *Socialism: The Grand Delusion,* Universe Books, 1986.

A guide in plain English to the false theories and objectionable practice of socialism round the world.

Deacon, Alan, and Bradshaw, J., *Reserved for the Poor,* Blackwell and Martin Robertson, 1983.

A temperately argued review, subtitled "The Means Test in British Social Policy," by two left-wing academics of the debate on universal and selective benefits in the British welfare state.

Derry, John W., *The Radical Tradition,* Macmillan, 1967.
A study of British radicals from Tom Paine to Lloyd George, some (Cobden and Bright) clear-sighted defenders of liberty, others (Robert Owen, Joseph Chamberlain, etc.) confused, several brilliant but mercurial (Jeremy Bentham, J. S. Mill etc.).

Dicey, A. V., *The Relation between Law and Public Opinion in England,* Macmillan, 1905.
The classic study of the impact of ideas on the development of the law in the nineteenth century.

Dolan, E. G. (ed.), *The Foundations of Modern Austrian Economics,* Sheed & Ward, 1976.
A rare collection of 14 essays by the chief exponents, mostly in the United States, of the Austrian School of liberal economics from Menger and Wieser to Mises and Hayek still too little known in Britain. E. D. Dolan, Israel Kirzner, L. M. Lachmann, Gerald O'Driscoll, Murray Rothbard and Sudha Shenoy present a clearly written introduction for the general reader as well as the student. The Austrian School of economists explains many of the fallacies of socialism.

Dorn, James, and Manne, Henry, *Economic Liberties and the Judiciary,* George Mason, 1987.
A collection of 16 essays, with commentaries, on the role of the US courts in countering the invasion of individual economic freedom by temporary political majorities. Its interest for readers in Britain is as a stimulus to evolving means of protecting property rights and freedom of contract to discipline the political process in a country without a formally written constitution. The book provokes the question for Britain whether and when the legislature in Parliament must necessarily prevail over the judiciary in the courts.

Dowd, Kevin, *The State and the Monetary System,* Philip Allan, 1990.
A British study of the case for putting money into the competitive market to put with the American study by George Selgin.

Downs, Anthony, *An Economic Theory of Democracy,* Harper & Row, 1957.
A pioneer in public choice argued that the most realistic assumption for the motivation of people in government, and the most capable of explaining politics in practice, is self-interest, tempered in politics as in other professions by the tests of honesty and morality, and especially in politics by the urgencies of national crisis. Politicians exchange policies for the public's support. They supply what the people want at the price of their votes. The traditional conventional assumption was that politicians were motivated primarily by the intention to serve the public without regard for their own interests.

Durbin, Elizabeth, *New Jerusalems: The Economics of Democratic Socialism,* Routledge, 1985.
Scholarly study by Professor Durbin, daughter of Evan Durbin, of the interwar British pioneers of market socialism.

Eatwell, John, Milgate, Murray, and Newman, Peter (eds.), *New Palgrave Dictionary of Economics,* MacmMillan, 1987.
The 4-million-word mixture of liberal scholarship and grotesquely overnumerous

and overlong, and often tendentious, Marxist entries. Not suitable for most students, for whom it was nominally intended, and often too mathematical for the general reader. The Dictionary reflects the contrast between the continuing interest in Marxism by academics in the West and the increasing interest of socialist economists in market capitalism accompanying the fading practice of Marxism in the formerly Marxist-inspired countries.

Erhard, Ludwig, *Prosperity through Competition,* Thames & Hudson, 1958.
The architect of the German economic miracle explained why the German economy flourished by mobilizing its diverse elements in the market.

Eucken, Walter, *The Foundations,* Hodge, 1950.
The intellectual father of the German economic miracle outlined the general principles that underlay its policies.

Fitzgerald, Randall, *When Government Goes Private,* Universe Books, 1988.
A survey, subtitled "Successful Alternatives to Public Services," from a US think-tank, the Pacific Research Institute for Public Policy, of the replacement of US local, state and federal government services by contracting out, voluntary agencies, commercial enterprise and other private initiatives.

Flew, Anthony, *The Politics of Procrustes,* Temple Smith, 1981.
The undaunted Professor of Philosophy vigorously exposes the contradictions in the conventional socialist argument for enforced equality.

Forgacs, David, *A Gramsci Reader,* Lawrence & Wishart, 1988.
A selection of the writings from 1916 to 1935 of the Italian Marxist Antonio Gramsci, 1891–1937. Written mostly in technical Marxist language. Discussed in chapter 3.

Friedman, David, *The Machinery of Freedom,* Harper, 1973.
Short and incisive demonstration by a leader of the American school of "anarcho-capitalism" that most so-called "public" services provided by government can be better supplied in the market. Subtitled "Guide to a Radical Capitalism."

Friedman, Milton, and Friedman, Rose, *Tyranny of the Status Quo,* Harcourt Brace, 1983.
The latest in the joint works of the Friedman partnership examines the three sectional interests in the "iron triangle" of politicians, bureaucrats and their beneficiaries that obstructs government in the United States and the United Kingdom where it tries to serve the general interest.

Gamble, Andrew, *The Free Economy and the Strong State,* Macmillan, 1988.
A Marxist-inclined assessment by the Professor of Politics at the University of Sheffield of "the politics of Thatcherism," described as the apparent contradiction between economic liberalism and political authoritarianism in the task of tackling Britain's "decline."

Goldman, Marshall, *USSR in Crisis,* Norton, 1983.
This well-written examination of the pre-Gorbachev Soviet economy by an economist at Harvard presaged the inevitability of the later attempts to escape from the stagnation of communism.

Goodin, Robert E., and Le Grand, Julian, *Not Only the Poor: The Middle Classes and the Welfare State,* Allen & Unwin, 1987.

The latest of Le Grand's research-based assessments (with a co-author) of the failure of the welfare state in Britain, the United States and Australia to fulfil its promise of redistributing income from rich to poor because of the cultural power of the middle classes.

Gorbachev, Mikhail, *Perestroika,* Collins, 1987.

The new "liberal" leader of the USSR explains the "reconstruction" revolution he hopes will save communism in the image of Lenin. Written before the introduction of Soviet political "democracy" in 1989 and the emergence of the new "parties" of pro-*perestroika* liberals (or radicals) and anti-*perestroika* conservatives and before the unresolved conflict between politically desirable communism and the economically indispensable market was faced in the 1990s.

Gould, Bryan, *Socialism and Freedom,* Macmillan, 1985.

The intellectually most sophisticated attempt at "a new theory" of "democratic" socialism by a former socialist academic turned politician to reconcile the irreconcilable conflict between freedom and socialism.

Grassl, Wolfgang, and Smith, Barry, *Austrian Economics,* Croom Helm, 1986.

An exposition of Austrian thinking for students.

Gray, John, *Hayek on Liberty,* Blackwell, 1984.

Elegantly written study, especially valuable for its 35-page bibliography of Hayek's writings until the early 1980s. A companion volume to Gray's *Mill on Liberty,* Routledge, 1983.

Gray, John, *Liberalisms,* Routledge, 1989.

Collection of 12 published essays on aspects of liberalism in the works of John Stuart Mill, Karl Popper, Robert Nozick, Hayek, Herbert Spencer, J. M. Buchanan, John Rawls and Michael Oakeshott, with a new pessimistic Postscript arguing the debatable outlook, "After Liberalism."

Green, David, *The New Right,* Wheatsheaf, 1987.

A non-technical account, especially informative for newcomers, of the main strands of thought in "The Counter-revolution in Political, Economic and Social Thought" of economic liberalism and their applications to public policy.

Green, David, *Working-Class Patients and the Medical Establishment,* Gower/Temple Smith, 1985.

The evidence by the most enlightening British political scientist/historian writing on the welfare state that the British working classes were capable of using the market to develop medical services in which they asserted their consumer sovereignty over doctors before the alliance of politicians and organized doctors destroyed their bargaining power.

Greenaway, David, and Shaw, G. K., *Public Choice, Public Finance and Public Policy,* Blackwell, 1985.

Described in the text.

Griffiths, Brian, *Morality and the Market Place,* Hodder & Stoughton, 1982.

A practising Christian economist presents the argument that, contrary to the claims of leading church prelates, Christianity indicates a moral alternative to both capitalism and Marxism; does not clarify the implied moral conflict between Christianity and capitalism.

Gwartney, J. D., and Stroup, Richard, *Economics: Private and Public Choice,* Harcourt Brace, 1982.

One of the best American textbooks for students because it analyses imperfections in public (collective, political) as well as private (market) choice-making in the use of scarce economic resources. Its easy exposition also makes it suitable for the general reader who wants to understand the elements of economic reasoning often lacking in British public discussion.

Haag, Ernest van den (ed.), *Capitalism: Sources of Hostility,* Epoch Books, 1979.

A collection from the US think-tank, the Heritage Foundation, before the Reagan and Thatcher years, of seven explanatory, slightly defensive essays on economic, political and psychological elements in the irrational causes of hostility to capitalism.

Hadley, Roger, and Hatch, Stephen, *Social Welfare and the Failure of the State,* Allen & Unwin, 1981.

An attempt to propose new collective methods of providing welfare services based essentially on the familiar notion of citizen-participation in place of the failed bureaucratic collective methods.

Hall, Stuart, *The Politics of Thatcherism,* Lawrence & Wishart, 1983.

Essays, revised from *Marxism Today,* by 17 authors on the impact of the early years of "Thatcherism" on a range of issues from "the world crisis of capitalism" to "the labour movement." Written before the general socialist admission that capitalist markets were indispensable.

Hall, Stuart, and Jacques, Martin (eds.), *New Times,* Lawrence & Wishart and *Marxism Today,* 1990.

A collection of 32 articles, mostly from *Marxism Today,* edited by Professor Hall and the Editor of *Marxism Today,* on aspects of "New Times," the name given to the new trends in society, the change in capitalism from standardization to diversity, the transition from Fordism to post-Fordism, "the rise of 'flexible specialization' in place of the old assembly-line world of mass production" (p. 12) discussed in chapter 4 above and the future of "the Left." The discussion was initiated by the editorial board of *Marxism Today* at a seminar in May 1988 and reported in the October 1988 number as "Facing up to the future." The authors of the articles include non-Marxist David Marquand and others.

Harris, David, *Justifying the Welfare State,* Blackwell, 1987.

A scholarly analysis of the conflicting critique of the welfare state by the market-oriented "new right" and the social democratic defence by the "new left" which recognizes the necessity of markets if "kept firmly in place" by a "socially just community determined to treat all its members as equals" in citizenship; the imperfect working in practice of representative government is not discussed.

Harris, Ralph, and Seldon, Arthur, *Not from Benevolence . . .*, Institute of Economic Affairs, 1977.

A survey, with a title drawn from Adam Smith, of the increasing study of the market by economists as seen in the first 20 years of the IEA, written by its two economist founders.

Harris, Ralph, and Seldon, Arthur, *Welfare without the State,* Institute of Economic Affairs, 1987.

Final report on five field surveys, in 1963, 1965, 1970, 1978 and 1987, of macro-economic opinion and micro-economic preferences in state and private welfare, especially education and medical care. The distinguishing method in the micro-economic enquiry was the use of pricing, not normally used in opinion polling. The conclusion was that the choices—opinions and preferences—of the British public had been suppressed in the post-war welfare state.

Haseler, Stephen, *The Battle for Britain: Thatcher and the New Liberals,* I. B. Tauris, 1989.

A political scientist who teaches at a London polytechnic and an American university argues that the radical enterprise revolution based on the re-assertion of a new bourgeois middle class in the market, called "Thatcherism," will replace paternalism of the Left and the Right in the twenty-first century.

Hattersley, Roy, *Choose Freedom,* Michael Joseph, 1987.

A Labour politician argues for "minimum" but "positive" state action to protect and extend individual liberty by ensuring equality. Discussed in chapter 5 and elsewhere.

Hayek, F. A., *The Counter-revolution of Science,* Liberty Fund, 1972.

Essays in the abuse and decline of reason, the harmful effects on the social sciences of the method of reasoning in the natural sciences, and the confused thinking of the early and recent socialist-inclined social engineers.

Hayek, F. A., *The Fatal Conceit,* Routledge, 1988.

Hayek's most recent book: discussed in the text.

Hayek, F. A., *Studies in Philosophy, Politics and Economics,* Routledge, 1967.

A collection of 23 articles on philosophy and politics in which Hayek says he had to "qualify" himself in order to discuss the problems he analysed as an economist. Includes *The Intellectuals and Socialism,* on the power of the "second-hand dealers" in ideas to influence "thinking people" who unthinkingly accept their interpretations of scholarship.

Hayek, F. A. (ed.), *Collectivist Economic Planning,* Routledge, 1935.

Discussed in the text.

Heertje, Arnold, *Schumpeter's Vision,* Praeger, 1981.

Essays by academics—Paul Samuelson, Tom Bottomore, William Fellner, Gottfried Haberler and Robert Heilbroner—assessing Schumpeter's *Capitalism, Socialism and Democracy* after 40 years, several (predictably Bottomore, Heilbroner) emphasizing but others, perhaps sensing the developments of the 1980s, rejecting his pessimism.

Heilbroner, Robert L., *The Nature and Logic of Capitalism,* Norton, 1985.

An interpretation, ambiguous in its dependence on Marxism, but ultimately hostile.

Heritage Foundation, *Guide to Public Policy Experts,* Heritage, 1989.
Latest in the annual series on worldwide academic and other market-oriented authorities on economic and political policies. Invaluable for the student of liberalism (European sense).

Hirschman, A. O., *Exit, Voice and Loyalty,* Harvard University Press, 1970.
The original discussion of the distinction between the market power of exit for the consumer and the much more proscribed political power of voice for the voter.

Hoover, Kenneth, and Plant, Raymond (eds.), *Conservative Capitalism in Britain and the United States,* Routledge, 1989.
The most recent critique of capitalism by Raymond Plant; discussed in the text.

Hume, David, *Essays Moral, Political and Literary,* Liberty Fund, 1985.
Essays of the eighteenth century classical liberal thinker written in the mid-1700s provide students and the citizen with an insight into the philosophy, more profound than that of socialism, that informed the teaching of the classical economists. "The independency of Parliament" is quoted in the text.

Huntford, Roland, *The New Totalitarians,* Allen Lane, 1971.
A fundamental re-assessment of the claims for Swedish socialism by a sympathetic critic: the high price in personal integrity and autonomy paid for the security of the social democratic welfare state increasingly questioned in the 1980s.

Hutchison, T. W., *The Politics and Philosophy of Economics,* Blackwell, 1981.
A collection of six published and three new essays on Marxist, Keynesian and Austrian thinking. Scholarly but clearly written; enlightening for laymen as well as students.

Hutton, Graham, *We Too Can Prosper,* Allen & Unwin, 1953.
An early post-war study of the way Britain could emulate the market economy of the United States.

James, Michael (ed.), *Restraining Leviathan,* Centre for Independent Studies, 1987.
An incisive review from the market-oriented Australian think-tank of the scope for reducing the writ of government by deregulation, de-socialization (privatization) and other means in spite of the bureaucratic and other obstacles.

Jasay, Anthony de, *Social Contract, Free Ride,* Oxford University Press, 1989.
An original re-examination of the content and extent of public goods, which argues that, although they have a tendency to expand, many could be supplied in the market.

Jasay, Anthony de, *The State,* Blackwell, 1985.
A powerful assault on the potentially tyrannical state as an entity with a will, powers and interests of its own that it will not lightly forgo.

Jewkes, John, *Ordeal by Planning,* Macmillan, 1947.
Early post-war revelation of the reality of state "planning"—its wastes, abuses and arbitrariness—by a war-time Head of the Economic Secretariat of the Cabinet. A revised version, *The New Ordeal by Planning,* was published in 1968.

Jewkes, John, *A Return to Free Market Economics?* Macmillan, 1978.
A scholarly critique of the baleful effects of government controls from an Oxford

economist who saw them from the inside during the 1939–45 war and an account of his warnings that were ignored until the 1980s.

Johnson, Nevil, *In Search of the Constitution,* Pergamon, 1977.

The Oxford political scientist considers the implications of the post-war growth of government and the constitutional reforms they make necessary.

Johnson, Paul, *The Recovery of Freedom,* Blackwell, 1980.

Essays and addresses by a formidable dialectician, once socialist, on the failure of socialism and the future of the libertarian alternative of capitalism.

Jowell, Roger, et al., *British Social Attitudes: The 1987 Report,* Social and Community Planning Research, 1987.

An influential research report in a series since 1884 that has claimed to find increasing public readiness to pay more taxes for socialized welfare services, findings rendered doubtful by the absence of information on individual pricing of benefits and individual tax costs.

Kavanagh, Dennis, and Seldon, Anthony, *The Thatcher Effect,* Oxford University Press, 1989.

Assessment of "A decade of change" by 25 academics and others, sympathetic, hostile and neutral.

Kenedi, Janos, *Do It Yourself: Hungary's Hidden Economy,* Pluto Press, 1981.

An account from the inside of the indestructibility of markets under socialism.

King, D. S., *The New Right,* Macmillan, 1987.

A discussion of the return of classical liberal thinking by a political scientist at the University of Edinburgh: left-wing in flavour but scholarly; concludes that the market must be incorporated in left-wing political policies.

Kirzner, Israel, *Discovery, Capitalism and Distributive Justice,* Blackwell, 1989.

The latest work from one of the most profound liberal economists argues that, since new resources and products are discovered, created and added to the existing supply, the familiar aphorism "finders keepers" provides the principle of justice for the ethics of capitalism: a new approach that circumvents the Rawls argument on a larger role for government in redistributing resources in favour of the Nozick argument for a smaller role.

Kristol, Irving, *Two Cheers for Capitalism,* Basic Books, 1978.

Modified rapture from an acute observer and convert from socialism.

Lekachman, Robert, and Loon, Borin van, *Capitalism for Beginners,* Writers & Readers Coop., 1981.

A simply written graphically illustrated book directed at the unsophisticated younger reader on the evils of capitalism, presented in scholarly manner with unconcealed bias. The last paragraph offers the first mention of the proposed alternative, "democratic socialism," without definition, explanation, argument or evidence.

Lepage, Henri, *Demain le Libéralisme,* Librairie Générale Française, 1980.

An exposition of "the new economics" by former journalist who discovered it in the late 1970s and has brilliantly explained it for French-speaking general readers. It followed his widely read *Demain le Capitalisme,* Open Court, 1978.

Letwin, Oliver, *Privatising the World,* Cassell, 1988.
A study of de-socialization in economic theory and in growing practice round the world, with a discussion of political, financial and administrative methods, by a political economist with experience in government and finance.

Letwin, William, *Against Equality,* Macmillan, 1984.
Essays by economists and others on the weaknesses of the arguments for equality.

Levacic, Rosalind, *Economic Policy-making,* Wheatsheaf, 1987.
An outstanding, because realistic, scholarly explanation of the formation of economic policy by the political process of present-day representative democracy, with illustrations of the effects of the voting machinery, the behaviour of politicians, the activities of bureaucrats, the interactions between politics and pressure groups.

Lieberman, Myron, *Privatization and Educational Choice,* St. Martin's Press, 1989.
A well documented analysis by an American academic and practical educationist of the failure of "public" (state) education, based on the public choice approach. Two central themes are the following: the movement to widen choice in the state sector disguises the intention to avoid choice between state and private schools; it is unrealistic to expect the benefits of competition to emerge from non-profit private schools. Methods of invigorating competition are proposed: contracting out by state schools to private education, home schooling, vouchers, franchised learning centres and other methods of privatization. The author discusses the ethical issues in private education for profit.

Luard, Evan, *Socialism without the State,* Macmillan, 1979.
A pioneering attempt to reject the state as the necessary basis of socialism in favour of "socialism at the grass-roots" before the later explicit incorporation of the market into socialist formulations.

Macfarlane, Alan, *The Culture of Capitalism,* Blackwell, 1987.
A study by the Cambridge historian and anthropologist of capitalism as a culture that shapes the social and spiritual as well as the material conditions of human life and of its origins in human instincts over the centuries in Western and other societies.

Machlup, Fritz (ed.), *Essays on Hayek,* New York University Press, 1976.
Assessment of Hayek in his seventies, assembled by an Austrian-American associate in eight essays by Milton Friedman, Max Hartwell, Shirley Letwin and others.

Marquand, David, *The Unprincipled Society,* Cape, 1988.
Former Labour politician and *Guardian* journalist turned academic argues for the "persuasion" of the "preceptoral" society as the alternative to the command economy of socialism and the exchange economy of capitalism; contested in this book.

Marsland, David, *Seeds of Bankruptcy,* Claridge, 1988.
A sociologist formerly on the Left analyses the bias against business enterprise in the writings and teaching of sociologists to conform to socialist presuppositions, with illustrations from textbooks and school examinations. Professor Marsland questions the state subsidization of a subject misused to undermine student understanding of the conditions of freedom.

Matthews, Mervyn, *Privilege in the Soviet Union,* Allen & Unwin, 1978.
A University of Surrey observer of the USSR, where he lived for some years, wrote a study of everyday elitism in lifestyles which contrasts sharply with the continuing claims from socialist academics (Bernard Crick and others) and literati (Margaret Drabble and others) that socialism creates, or is capable of creating, equality. "The very existence of the privileges removes much of the justification for the Bolshevik Revolution."

Matthews, R. C. O. (ed.), *Economy and Democracy,* Macmillan, 1985.
Papers on markets in commodities and in votes, the characteristic province of the economics of politics, delivered at the 1984 British Association for the Advancement of Science. Professor C. K. Rowley explains the relationship between economics, politics and the law in the formation of public policy. The Editor, R. C. O. Matthews, Master of Clare College, Cambridge, argues that Anthony Downs's proposition (above, Downs's book) goes too far but concedes it is superior to the opposite assumption that politicians are philosopher-kings motivated solely by concern for the public interest.

McKenzie, Richard, *The Fairness of Markets,* Lexington Books, 1987.
An American economist argues that the market is superior to government not only in efficiency but more importantly in ethics ("fairness") because the evidence from a wide range of public policy is that government is distorted by special interest groups and cannot know the effects of its policies on the people so that they are often the opposite of those intended and therefore cannot be moral.

McKenzie, Richard (ed.), *Constitutional Economics,* Lexington Books, 1984.
A collection of essays by 14 authors based on a Heritage Foundation seminar on the theme, clearly put by its President, Edwin Feulner, "If we give government powers to further the general welfare, how do we restrain it from using its powers, economic and political, to harm the general public for the benefit of the few?" The authors are mostly American but the general principles they discuss apply everywhere.

McLean, Iain, *Public Choice,* Blackwell, 1987.
An introduction by an Oxford political scientist to the economics of politics, more suitable for the student than for the layman, that draws implications for government policy different from those of most public choice economists and political scientists.

Mill, John Stuart, *Representative Government,* Dent, 1861.
The classic on the evolving nature, benefits and working of indirect government in Mill's collection, *Utilitarianism, Liberty, Representative Government.* Published by Dent, 1972. The 20-page introduction by H. B. Acton and a chronology set the scene for newcomers.

Miller, Margaret, *The Rise of the Russian Consumer,* Institute of Economic Affairs, 1965.
An early IEA study by a British economist who knew the USSR scene well discussed the stirrings among its economists on the necessity for markets and pricing in the 1950s. Action had to wait 30 years until Gorbachev.

Mises, Ludwig von, *The Anti-capitalist Mentality,* Van Nostrand, 1956.
A study of the persistent unreasoning hostility to capitalism.

Mises, Ludwig von, *Human Action,* Henry Regnery, 1948.
Mises's *magnum opus* on the universality of the explanation by Austrian economics of human activity.

Mises, Ludwig von, *Socialism,* Liberty Fund, 1979.
One of Mises's most influential works, originally published in 1922, re-published in the low-price series of Liberty Classics. Long known to liberal scholars, could now be read by socialist academics and politicians for its enlightenment on the impossibility of market socialism.

Mitchell, William, *Government As It Is,* Institute of Economic Affairs, 1988.
Used in the text.

Mueller, D. C., *Public Choice,* Cambridge University Press, 1979.
A good technical introduction to the economics of politics for the student. Requires to be supplemented by more recent writing.

Murray, Charles, *In Pursuit of Happiness and Good Government,* Simon & Schuster, 1988.

Murray, Charles, *Losing Ground: American Social Policy, 1950–1980,* Basic Books, 1984.
These two books have established the repute of the author, from the market-oriented Manhattan Institute think-tank, as a critic of post-war American government welfare policies which led him to conclude that the solutions to poverty, ignorance, crime lie in individual, voluntary, local initiatives.

Nishiyama, Chiaki, and Leube, Kurt R. (eds.), *The Essence of Hayek,* Hoover Institution, 1984.
A collection of 21 Hayekian seminal pieces from the Hoover Institution at Stanford University on his 85th birthday; includes the refutation in the 1982 IEA journal *Economic Affairs* of the socialist argument that markets under socialism can produce the same information on supply costs and demand as markets under capitalism.

Niskanen, W. A., *Reaganomics,* Oxford University Press, 1988.
Professor Niskanen, a specialist in the economics of bureaucracy and formerly on the US Council of Economic Advisers, assesses the successes and failures of the two Reagan Governments in their most ambitious attempt since the 1930s New Deal to change the direction of US economic policy. A rare insight into the political obstacles that prevented the attempted revolution to liberalize an overtaxed and over-regulated economy.

Novak, Michael, *The Spirit of Democratic Capitalism,* AEI and Simon & Schuster, 1982.
A former theologian at the US think-tank, the American Enterprise Institute, asserts the moral case for "democratic" capitalism.

Nove, Alec, *The Economics of Feasible Socialism,* Allen & Unwin, 1983.
A book by the authority on Soviet economy directed at fellow socialists to convince them that socialism is not feasible without markets rather than at non-socialists to persuade them that feasible (market) socialism is preferable to capitalism.

Nozick, Robert, *Anarchy, State and Utopia,* Blackwell, 1974.
A major philosophical work by the Professor of Philosophy at Harvard, a convert from socialism, on the new libertarian view of the minimal functions of the state,

including a rejection of the socialist view that inequality is necessarily unjust and an assessment of anarcho-capitalism.

O'Driscoll, G. P., and Rizzo, M. J., *The Economics of Time and Ignorance,* Blackwell, 1985.
The foundations of Austrian "subjective" economics which questions the claims for government control or regulation of economic activity and restores the supremacy of individual choice in markets as the essential centre of economic life.

Olson, Mancur, *The Logic of Collective Action,* Harvard University Press, 1965.

Olson, Mancur, *The Rise and Decline of Nations,* Yale University Press, 1986.
The two main works of a leading public choice economist at Maryland University present new, though not yet generally accepted, theories (explanations) of economic activity illustrated by evidence from history and contemporary world events. The first discusses the public goods produced by (large but not necessarily by small) private organization in pressure groups such as trade unions and corporations; the second develops the argument to explain the varying post-war growth, stagnation or decline of countries and regions by the debilitating effect of collusive cartels that induce government to slow down economic advance. Societies in which these lobbies have been weakened or destroyed by war or revolution have become the most dynamic.

Pimlott, Ben (ed.), *Fabian Essays in Socialist Thought,* Heinemann, 1984.
Nineteen essays by socialist academics and writers, including the most sophisticated—Elizabeth Durbin, Alan Ryan, John Eatwell and Steven Lukes—on the changing nature and future of socialism. Most were optimistic.

Pirie, Madsen, *Privatization,* Wildwood House, 1988.
Content indicated in the text, chapter 4.

Popper, Karl, *The Open Society and Its Enemies,* Routledge, 1962.
A philosophical work on the conditions of the free society, influenced by Hayek, by a former Social Democrat.

Preobrazhensky, E., *The New Economics,* Oxford University Press, 1965.
The author, a foundation member of the Bolshevik Party, wrote this book in 1926 on the economics of socialist industrialization in a largely peasant country. It was suppressed by Stalin, who was bent on rapid industrialization at any human price, and the author was branded a "Trotskyist" and shot in 1937. He was an embryo market socialist before his time who urged that the peasants be encouraged by incentives. Stalin wanted them coerced by collectivization. An explanatory introduction to the 1965 edition by Professor Nove reveals why Stalin suppressed the book.

Priestley, J. B., *Out of the People,* Collins, 1941.
An influential pre-war and wartime literary figure with socialist sympathies voiced doubts in wartime broadcasts and writings about socialism that were ignored in the post-war policies on state industry and welfare.

Rabushka, Alvin, *From Adam Smith to the Wealth of America,* Transaction Books, 1985.
An American economist argues that the state economy—over-regulation, high taxes, bureaucracy, debt—can be reversed, as it was in a wide range of circumstances from mid-nineteenth-century Britain through late nineteenth-century

America to late twentieth-century Asia. He maintains the reversal can be repeated in the future.

Radice, Giles, *Labour's Path to Power,* Macmillan, 1989.

A politician's argument for his party to accept "The New Revisionism," following the historic revisionists, Eduard Bernstein in 1899 and Anthony Crosland in 1956 and the 1959 Bad Godesberg abandonment of socialism by the German Social Democratic Party and its acceptance of the market. Radice adds the familiar reservation that the market shall be subject to political control.

Radnitzky, Gerard, and Bernholz, Peter (eds.), *Economic Imperialism,* Paragon, 1987.

Unusual assembly of 14 essays applying economics to subjects still considered "non-economic" by John Gray, James Coleman, Henry Manne (on corporation law), Jack Hirschleifer (conflict), Gordon Tullock (autocracy), the Editors and others.

Rand, Ayn, *Capitalism: The Unknown Ideal,* New American Library, 1964.

A classic of the radical libertarian school in the United States, much reprinted, by the American libertarian novelist whose writings stimulated the revival of classical liberalism and influenced American philosophers; with chapters by Alan Greenspan, later chairman of the US central (but private) bank, the Federal Reserve, Nathaniel Brandon, a psychologist, and Robert Hessen, an economic historian. Two other influential Rand books are *Atlas Shrugged* and *The Fountainhead.*

Redwood, John, *Popular Capitalism,* Routledge, 1988.

The former Oxford economist, political adviser, practical banker and most recently politician writes on the worldwide rejection of government economy in favour of de-socialization (privatization), deregulation and private ownership of industry.

Rentoul, John, *Me and Mine,* Unwin, 1989.

A brightly but bitterly written condemnation of "the new individualism" by a former Deputy Editor of *The New Statesman,* later a reporter on a BBC political programme. Contests the view that the 1980s liberal policies changed British values to self-reliance but remain collectivist. Concludes from academic surveys and opinion polls that government provision of services will follow "Thatcherite Conservatism."

Robbins, Lionel, *Economic Planning and International Order,* Macmillan, 1937.

An early Robbins book that asserted the superiority of economic liberalism over socialism when the economists were distracted by the 1936 Keynes *General Theory* whose short-term attractions for the cure of unemployment concealed its lasting damage to economic thinking and practice.

Robbins, Lionel, *The Economic Problem in Peace and War,* Macmillan, 1947.

The use of markets in the use of scarce resources in war and peace; discussed in the text.

Robbins, Lionel, *The Theory of Economic Policy,* Macmillan, 1952.

An early post-war review of classical economic liberalism in the writings of David Hume, Adam Smith, Jeremy Bentham, Thomas Malthus, David Ricardo, Nassau Senior, J. R. McCulloch, James and John Stuart Mill.

Rogge, Benjamin, *Can Capitalism Survive?* Liberty Fund, 1979.

A thoughtful reply by an American economist to the doubt about the future of capitalism expressed by Joseph Schumpeter in his 1942 *Capitalism, Socialism and Democracy.*

Roth, Gabriel, *The Private Provision of Public Services,* Oxford University Press, 1987.
The author, a civil engineer turned economist, studied the developing countries for the World Bank and concluded that the private supply of many services thought to be in "the public sector"—education, health, electricity, telecommunications, urban transport and water—was often superior to government supply.

Rothbard, Murray, *Man, Economy and State,* Nash, 1976.
The author's main work in Austrian economics. His *Power and Market,* Sheed Andrews, 1970, argued for a minimal state; *For a New Liberty,* Macmillan, 1973, stated the economic argument for "anarcho-capitalism."

Rowley, Charles (ed.), *Democracy and Public Choice,* Blackwell, 1987.
Papers by J. M. Buchanan, W. A. Niskanen, Mancur Olson, Richard Wagner, Dennis Mueller, Robert Tollison, Douglass North, Arthur Seldon and others at a Liberty Fund seminar in honour of Gordon Tullock, a Founding Father of public choice.

Sampson, Geoffrey, *An End to Allegiance,* Temple Smith, 1984.
A rare book by a Professor of Linguistics on the growing work of scholars who have searched for methods of maintaining freedom in human activity, economic and otherwise, the functions of government, including the minimal state of "anarchy" under capitalism, the role of the entrepreneur, the power of the professions over the individual. He ends with a caution against overdependence on the state.

Schumpeter, J., *Capitalism, Socialism and Democracy,* Allen & Unwin, 1942.
The classic pessimistic work on the future of capitalism by an Austrian-American economist who favoured it over socialism. Since then much disputed by scholars and refuted by world developments.

Schwartz, Eli, *Trouble in Eden,* Praeger, 1980.
A comparison between the British and the Swedish social democratic economies: Sweden, the exemplar of British socialists, seemed until recently to avoid the debility of British socialism because its egalitarian policies were less drastic, the people more homogeneous and less prone to friction and the economy more disciplined by international competition.

Scruton, Roger, *The Meaning of Conservatism,* Macmillan, 1984.
The Conservative philosopher discusses the doctrines of conservatism in senses sceptical of or hostile to the liberalism of the free market.

Scruton, Roger, *Thinkers of the New Left,* Longman, 1986.
The philosopher who has generally written in the school of conventional conservatism turns to a demolition of socialist thinking that is more favourable to market liberalism.

Seldon, Arthur, *Charge,* Temple Smith, 1977.
A systematic argument in favour of charging for individual national and local government services as the means to increase efficiency and fiscal equity, with rejection of the objections of political impossibility, administrative impracticability and social undesirability.

Seldon, Arthur, *Corrigible Capitalism, Incorrigible Socialism*, Institute of Economic Affairs, 1980.

Concise statement of the argument that the faults of capitalism are relatively incidental, identifiable and easier to correct than the more organic and less identifiable faults of socialism.

Seldon, Arthur, *Wither the Welfare State*, Institute of Economic Affairs, 1981.

Argued that the gradual rise in incomes and technological change would erode state welfare by moving demand to the private competitive market.

Seldon, Arthur (ed.), *The Litmus Papers: The National Health Disservice*, Centre for Policy Studies, 1980.

Essays by economists, doctors and others on the continuing failures of the NHS as a tax-financed state system; internal financial disciplines and markets were attempted in the late 1980s but with tax financing.

Seldon, Arthur (ed.), *The "New Right" Enlightenment*, E & L Books, 1985.

Essays by 20 younger academics, John Burton, David Green, Andrew Melnyk, Peter Saunders, Nigel Ashford, Chris Tame, Chandran Kukathas and other exponents of economic liberalism, heralded by F. A. Hayek.

Selgin, George, *A Theory of Free Banking*, Cato Institute, 1988.

An American study of the case for supplying money by private competitors instead of by a state monopoly.

Shand, Alexander, *The Capitalist Alternative*, Wheatsheaf, 1984.

The subtitle, "An Introduction to Neo-Austrian Economics," describes the contents, a rare guide for the student to the writings of the school of economics that provides much of the intellectual reinforcement for capitalism.

Short, Philip, *The Dragon and the Bear*, Hodder & Stoughton, 1982.

An enlightening insight into life in China and the USSR by the BBC's correspondent based on close observation in the 1970s which anticipated subsequent economic and political developments.

Skidelsky, Robert (ed.), *Thatcherism*, Chatto & Windus, 1988.

Papers for and against the version of economic liberalism as practised by the British governments of the 1980s. Some do not clarify the distinction between economic liberalism and the expediencies of political conservatism. Contains Professor Hahn's paper "On Market Economies" discussed in chapter 6.

Smiles, Samuel, *Self-help*, John Murray, 1958.

Centenary edition of the 1859 classic on the potential for individual initiative. The concluding chapter on character could be re-read in every generation as a reminder of the effects on character of the welfare state and socialism.

Smith, Hedrick, *The Russians*, Ballantine, 1976.

A mostly brilliant account, frequently reprinted, by an American journalist of life in the USSR in the early 1970s, based largely on personal contact with the people; with some contestable judgements; identifies the concentration of industrial effort on measurable quantity (plan fulfilment) to the relative neglect of immeasurable quality.

Soto, Hernando de, *The Other Path: The Invisible Revolution in the Third World,* Harper & Row, 1989.

A rare account of how the market can go underground to salvage an economy in which spontaneous human exchange has been politically outlawed.

Sowell, Thomas, *Marxism: Philosophy and Economics,* William Morrow, 1985.

A closely reasoned rejection of Marxist thought by the redoubtable black American economist, enlightening for the newcomer and disturbing to the true believer.

Stigler, George, *The Citizen and the State,* Chicago University Press, 1975.

Elegant and witty essays by the Chicago Nobel Laureate on arguments and errors in the debate on the role and competence of the state in regulating economic activity.

Stiglitz, Joseph, *The Economic Role of the State,* Blackwell, 1989.

A recent sophisticated restatement of the arguments for and against the necessity of the state in economic life.

Sugden, Robert, *Economics of Rights, Co-operation and Welfare,* Oxford University Press, 1986.

Essentially the argument that individuals will often voluntarily evolve rules that improve beneficial cooperation between them without intervention by the state to devise laws and enforce them.

Sweezy, Paul M., *Socialism,* McGraw-Hill, 1949.

A post-war statement of the case for socialism by a leading Marxist exponent at Harvard that would have to be revised in the light of later developments.

Tame, Chris, *The Moral Case for Private Enterprise,* Bachman & Turner, 1979.

A chapter in a book (*The Case for Private Enterprise,* Cecil Turner, ed.) by a foremost exponent in Britain of the libertarian argument on a wide range of issues, published by the Libertarian Alliance, overseas journals, in conference papers; on the classical liberal analysis of class, the New Mercantilism, the case against a Bill of Rights and others.

Thompson, E. P., *The Making of the English Working Class,* Gollancz, 1963; Pelican, 1968.

The much reprinted and controversial reinterpretation of history with a Marxist flavour in the early years of capitalism, 1780 to the first Reform Act of 1832.

Tollison, D. R., and Vanberg, V. J. (eds.), *Explorations into Constitutional Economics,* Texas A&M University Press, 1989.

A collection of 31 pieces of writing by J. M. Buchanan, some with co-authors, several new, on the nature and effects of the political rules governing economic activity.

Tullock, Gordon, *Private Wants, Public Means,* Basic Books, 1970.

The subtitle, "An Economic Analysis of the Desirable Scope of Government," indicates the content: a concise statement by a Founding Father of public choice of its new method of thinking about government and its revelation of the advantages and disadvantages of internalizing externalities by individual choice or by group choice in local voluntary associations, by a country or by world government.

Tullock, Gordon, *The Social Dilemma,* Public Choice Society, 1974.

The subtitle, "Economics of War and Revolution," indicates the contents.

Urban, G. R., *Can the Soviet System Survive Reform?* Pinter/Spiers, 1989.
Penetrating insights based on interviews with seven Soviet and other observers of the USSR. Discussed in chapter 4.

Vaizey, John, *Capitalism and Socialism,* Weidenfeld & Nicolson, 1980.
A résumé of the arguments for and against both systems.

Veljanovski, Cento, *Selling the State,*Weidenfeld & Nicolson, 1987.
Reviews the methods and extent of de-socialization (privatization) of the 1980s, assesses the arguments for and against and considers the issues in the government regulation of formerly socialized industry.

Waldron, Jeremy, *The Right to Private Property,* Oxford University Press, 1988.
Essentially the argument that as there is a right to free speech on the ground that all benefit there is also a right to private property. This is the socialist argument on equality: the advantages of access to private property are not an argument for equality of ownership, or even equality in access.

Watson, George, *The English Ideology,* Allen Lane, 1973.
Elegantly written study of "the language of Victorian politics" by the Fellow of St. John's College, Cambridge. A corrective to the 1980s' misrepresentation of "Victorian values."

West, E. G., *Education and the State,* Institute of Economic Affairs, 1965, 1970.
The book that initiated the post-war argument on the necessity of the state in the provision of education. Professor West maintained that education was emerging before the origins of state education in 1870 and that it would have developed better without it.

West, E. G., *Education and the Industrial Revolution,* Batsford, 1975.
In this sequel Professor West examined the evidence further and reinforced his conclusions by refuting the arguments of the academics and the novelists in falsifying Victorian history.

Whitney, Ray, *National Health Crisis,* Shepheard-Walwyn, 1988.
A former Health Minister re-examines the failures of the NHS and concludes in favour of financing by insurance still resisted by the governments of the 1980s.

Whynes, David K., and Bowles, Roger, *The Economic Theory of the State,* Martin Robertson, 1981.
An economic analysis of the rationale, nature and role of the state in the light of public choice, Marxist and other approaches, with implications for practical policy.

Williams, S., *Politics Is for People,* Penguin, 1981.
Shirley Williams argued that "politics" is or could be for "the people." Contested in the text.

Williams, Walter E., *South Africa's War against Capitalism,* Praeger and the Cato Institute, 1989.
A study by one of America's two leading black economists (the other is Professor Thomas Sowell, above) on the conflict between the national socialism of racial discrimination in apartheid and free-market capitalism. The argument is that apartheid is better dissolved micro-economically by free markets for individual

black people than macro-economically by statist laws and regulations on land ownership, entry into enterprise, and the labour market for people denominated in categories by colour.

Wilson, Thomas, and Skinner, Andrew (eds.), *The Market and the State,* Oxford University Press, 1976.

Essays by 11 leading economists in honour of Adam Smith on the bicentenary of *The Wealth of Nations* weighing the present-day validity and relevance of its teachings in 1776. The close analysis of technical aspects by some contributors obscured the surviving significance of the general principles of 1776 as vindicated by developments since 1976.

Winiecki, Jan, *Economic Prospects—East and West,* Centre for Research into Communist Economies, 1987.

Winiecki, Jan, *Gorbachev's Way Out?* Centre for Research into Communist Economies, 1988.

Two papers by a Polish economist on the essentially capitalist economic reforms that confront the communist economies and how they can be introduced.

Wiseman, Jack, *Cost, Choice and Political Economy,* Edward Elgar, 1989.

A collection of Professor Wiseman's selected writings which indicate the importance he attaches to Austrian "subjective" micro-economics, the analysis of public choice and a libertarian approach. Twelve essays are prefaced by an engaging autobiographical introduction and followed by a concluding essay, "The Way Ahead: A New Political Economy," the theme of a forthcoming book.

Woolton, Barbara, *Freedom under Planning,* Allen & Unwin, 1945.

The effort of the veteran socialist economist to meet the argument of Hayek's *Road to Serfdom* that "the worst" would rise to the top under socialism by supposing that it could create conditions in which "the wise and public-spirited" could rise to power, the familiar assumption of government benevolence.

Wright, Anthony, *Socialism: Theories and Practices,* Oxford University Press, 1986.

Exposition by a sympathetic author of the forms of socialism.

Hobart and Other Papers and Books from the Institute of Economic Affairs with Specific Proposals for Reform (in Date Order)

Seldon, Arthur, *Pensions in a Free Society,* 1957.

Proposed the gradual but complete de-socialization of all state pensions. Tax encouragement of private pensions was introduced in the 1980s. The "basic" state pensions continued, indexed by average prices.

Harris, R., Naylor, Margot, and Seldon, A., *Hire Purchase in a Free Society,* 1958.

Argument for the removal of restrictions on hire purchase financing of consumer and capital goods as discriminatory devices distorting market preferences and prone to political misuse and avoidance. These restrictions were not used in the 1980s use of interest rates to discipline inflationary pressures.

Roberts, Ben, *Trade Unions in a Free Society,* 1959.

An early argument that the powers of trade were excessive, damaged productivity and exacerbated inflation and should be curtailed. Government action was taken in the early 1970s and more effectively in the 1980s.

Yamey, Basil S., *Resale Price Maintenance and Shoppers' Choice,* 1960.

Proposed abolition of uniform resale pricing. Enacted 1963.

Macrae, Norman, *To Let?* 1960.

Proposed radical removal of rent restriction. Rents were gradually "loosened" but restrictions remained into the 1990s.

Lees, D. S., *Health through Choice,* 1961.

Proposed gradual de-socialization of the NHS. Internal reforms in the 1980s but no general transfer to the market by 1990.

Herbert, A. P., and Harris, Ralph, *Libraries: Free for All?* 1962.

Proposed annual fee (Herbert) or charges per borrowing (Harris). No action by 1990.

Peacock, A. T., and Wiseman, J., *Education for Democrats,* 1964.

Proposed, *inter alia,* school vouchers. Investigated 1981–3 but abandoned because of political, trade union and church opposition.

Carmichael, John, *Vacant Possession,* 1964.

Argued for transfer from council to private housing. Council sales introduced in 1980s; one in six sold by 1990.

Thomas, Denis, *Competition in Radio,* 1965.

Proposal for licensing the private (pirate) radio stations as a first step to a competitive market in British radio.

Burn, Duncan, *The Future of Steel,* 1965.

Early proposal for the de-socialization of the steel industry. De-socialized in the 1950s, re-socialized in the 1960s, re-de-socialized in the 1980s.

Roth, Gabriel, *A Self-financing Road System,* 1966.

Proposal for charges proportionate to use of roads by individual vehicles. Adapted by the Labour Party Institute of Public Policy Research in 1989. No action by 1990.

Hicks, John, *After the Boom . . . ,* 1966.

Proposal for Treasury limits on local government borrowing as a means to reduce government expenditure and ease the deficits in external payments. Limits in varying forms attempted in 1970s and 1980s.

Lees, D. S., *Economic Consequences of the Professions,* 1966.

Proposal for the removal of restrictive practices by which the professions limit entry (supply) and maintain their price (remuneration) above the competitive rates. Professions included in control of restrictive practices in 1980s: opticians' cartel in sale of spectacles ended in 1987; lawyers' cartel partially liberalized in 1990.

Bauer, P. T., and Ward, Barbara, *Two Views on Aid to Developing Countries,* 1966.

Early intellectual debate: Bauer generally critical and opposed, Ward generally sympathetic and in favour. The issue is whether easy aid strengthens or weakens the recipients. Since repudiation of debts by Third World countries in the 1980s, the capitalist lenders are more selective and require better evidence of effective use of funds to stimulate economic improvement rather than bolster political autocracies.

Pennance, F. G., *Housing, Town Planning and the Land Commission,* 1967.
Proposed the auctioning (pricing) of planning permissions. No action by 1990.

Seldon, A., and Gray, H., *Universal or Selective Benefits?* 1967.
Proposal for systematic replacement of undiscriminating by "targeted" state welfare benefits in cash and kind. The argument was increasingly accepted in the 1970s and applied tentatively in the 1980s.

Houghton, Douglas, *Paying for the Social Services,* 1967.
Argument by former Labour Minister of Social Services for charges for some social services. Dental and opticians' charges raised in the 1980s.

Seldon, A. (ed.), *The Theory and Practice of Pricing,* 1967.
Fourteen essays by young university and other economists outlining original proposals for competitive market pricing in government or regulated industries—water, fire services, refuse collection, agricultural products, electricity and others.

Burn, Duncan, *The Political Economy of Nuclear Energy,* 1967.
The first British economist to raise doubts about the scientists' claim that nuclear power was generally cheaper than coal or gas.

Thomas, Denis, and Peacock, A. T., *Copyright and the Creative Artist,* 1967.
Proposal that (music) copyright should not restrict public access.

Curtin, Timothy, and Murray, David, *Economic Sanctions and Rhodesia,* 1967.
Argument against sanctions. Reflected, for various reasons, in 1980s' British Government opposition to sanctions on South Africa.

Cooper, M., and Culyer, A. J., *The Price of Blood,* 1968.
Proposed payment for blood if voluntary supplies proved inadequate to save life. No action by 1990.

Caine, Sir Sydney, *Paying for TV?* 1968.
Proposed payment by meter for individual programmes. Independent (private market) channels began payment by periodic fees for channels in 1990s.

Ferns, Harry, *Towards an Independent University,* 1969.
Argument, originating in the IEA, for the establishment of a private centre of higher education to escape the political influence in the state universities. Buckingham University began to accept students in 1976.

Robinson, Colin, *A Policy for Fuel?* 1969.
The first of four IEA papers by Professor Robinson, sole or with Eileen Marshall, arguing for the introduction of market influences into the coal industry, including, in *Can Coal be Saved?* 1985, the proposal that groups of pits be combined with the power stations they serve for sale to private industry. Measures to de-socialize power appeared in the late 1980s.

Whetstone, Linda, *The Marketing of Milk,* 1970.
Proposal for abolition of the Milk Marketing Board. No action by 1990.

Griffiths, Brian, *Competition in Banking*, 1970.
Proposed replacement of bank "cartel" by competition in bank charges, interest on lending and services. Competition developed in the 1970s and especially in the 1980s with liberalization of the market in financial services, but with risk of over-regulation.

Lewis, W. R., *Rome or Brussels?* 1971.
An early prescient warning, on public choice grounds, against the frustration of the liberal aims of the Treaty of Rome by the bureaucratic machinery of Brussels. Government reaction against Brussels intensified in the late 1980s.

Fulop, Christina, *Markets for Employment*, 1971.
Proposal that employment exchanges (later job centres) charge fees to improve their efficiency and encourage competition. Opposed by Labour in the 1970s. No government action by the Conservatives in the 1980s.

Whetstone, Linda, *A Market for Animal Semen?* 1972.
Proposal for a market to be developed with market pricing to encourage the production of required supplies of requisite quality.

Jacoby, Neil, and Pennance, F. G., *The Polluters: Industry or Government?* 1972.
An early general argument that government as well as private industry generates pollution of the environment and that the solutions lie in charges or taxation as economic restraints.

Wood, J. B., *How Much Unemployment?* 1972.
Argument that the (then) official unemployment statistics were defective and should be revised. Revisions were made in the 1980s.

Beckerman, W., *Pricing for Pollution*, 1975.
Detailed argument with specific proposals for charges or taxes to discipline pollution by polluters presented by Oxford economist after signing Minority Report (with scientist Lord Zuckerman) to the 1972 Report of the Royal Commission on Environmental Pollution. Argument repeated by economists in 1989. Prospective government action indicated in 1989. IEA paper republished in 1990 with postscript by the author.

Hayek, F. A., *Choice in Currency*, 1976.
Proposal for repeal of the laws on legal tender so that nationals are free to use other monies. Regarded as far-fetched, but echoed in 1989 (next item).

Hayek, F. A., *Denationalisation of Money*, 1976.
The refined argument for the supply of money by private bankers to prevent debasement and inflation. A half-way approach by competition between national currencies proposed by the British Chancellor of the Exchequer for the EEC in 1989.

Harris, R., and Seldon, A., *Pricing or Taxing*, 1976.
Argument, made to the Layfield Committee on Local Government, for the replacement of local taxes by charging for individual services. The half-way house of charging for groups of services ("community charge") was introduced in 1990.

Colin, Clark, *Poverty before Politics,* 1977.
Proposal for a reverse ("negative") income tax. Modified versions (Family Income Supplement etc.) introduced in 1980s.
Crew, Michael, and Young, Alistair, *Paying by Degrees,* 1977.
Proposals for financing university and other higher education by private loans and government vouchers. Government loans for tuition indicated in 1989 for early 1990s.
Gough, T. J., and Taylor, T. W., *The Building Society Price Cartel,* 1979.
Proposal for competition in the financing of home purchase by mortgages. Developed in the 1980s with the deregulation of financial services.
Miller, Robert, and Wood, John, *Exchange Control for Ever?* 1979.
Proposal for abolition of the machinery and the practice of exchange control. Practice abandoned in 1979; machinery abolished in 1987.
Sloane, Peter, *Sport in the Market,* 1980.
Professor Sloane's analysis was thought in questionable taste, the characteristic view that cultural activities rise above economic calculation. The view that sport would be strengthened if it looked to its efficiency has gained ground in recent practice in financing, marketing, facilities for spectators etc., emphasizing that all human activity has economic aspects if resources are scarce.
Senior, Ian, *Liberating the Letter,* 1983.
Proposal for the de-socialization of the postal services of the socialized Post Office. Private delivery permitted in 1980s subject to £1 minimum charge, which effectively retained much of Post Office monopoly.
Harris, Ralph, and Seldon, Arthur, *Shoppers' Choice,* 1984.
An economic argument for the liberalization of the Shops Acts. Government Bill failed in 1986.
Denman, D. R., and Wiseman, J., *Markets under the Sea,* 1984.
Proposal for private property rights to improve the use of the seabed. Opposed by UN Law of the Sea, not signed by the British Government.
Reekie, Duncan, *Competition and Home Medicines,* 1985.
Argument for decreased reliance on prescription of medicines by doctors and increased freedom for self-prescribing by consumers. No action by 1990.
Dowd, Kevin, *Private Money,* 1988.
Developed the argument for the de-socialization of money and the Bank of England.

Journals (with Publishers)

American Spectator (Arlington, Virginia).
The Cato Journal, Cato Institute (Washington, DC).
Economic Affairs, Institute of Economic Affairs.
Encounter (London).

Free Life, The Libertarian Alliance (London).
The Journal of Law and Economics, University of Chicago.
The Journal of Libertarian Studies, Center for Libertarian Studies (Burlingame, California).
Ordo, Gustav Fischer Verlag (Stuttgart, New York).
Policy Review, Heritage Foundation (Washington, DC).
Reason, The Reason Foundation (Santa Monica, California).

"Think-tanks" as Sources of Information on Books and Papers on the Market in Capitalism

Great Britain (with dates of foundation)

The Adam Smith Institute, London, 1977.
Atlas Economic Research Foundation (UK), Hartfield, Sussex, 1983.
The Centre for Policy Studies, London, 1975.
Centre for Research into Communist Economies, London, 1983.
The David Hume Institute, Edinburgh, 1985.
The Institute of Economic Affairs, London, 1955.
The Libertarian Alliance, London, 1966.
The Social Affairs Unit, London, 1980.
The Social Market Foundation, London, 1988.

Overseas (with locations)

AFRICA
The Free Market Foundation, Johannesburg.
Institute of Economic Affairs, Ghana.

ASIA
Chung Hua Institution for Economic Research, Taipei, Taiwan.
Hong Kong Center for Economic Research, Hong Kong.
Indian Institute for Public Policy Research, Bombay.

AUSTRALIA
Australian Institute for Public Policy, Perth.
Centre for Independent Studies, Sydney.

CANADA
The Fraser Institute, Vancouver.
The St. Lawrence Institute, Montreal.

EUROPE

Austria
Carl Menger Institute, Vienna.

Germany (West)
Aktionsgemeinschaft Soziale Marktwirtschaft, Heidelberg.
Institute for Economic and Policy Research (Kronberger Kreis), Frankfurt.
Walter Eucken Institut, Freiburg.

Iceland
The Jon Thorlaksson Institute, Reykjavik.

Ireland
The Edmund Burke Institute, Co. Wexford.

Northern Ireland
Ulster Institute for Economic Research, Coleraine.

Norway
Fremskrittspartiets Utrednings Institutt, Oslo.

Spain
Fomento del Trabajo Nacional, Barcelona.

NEW ZEALAND

New Zealand Centre for Independent Studies, Auckland.

SOUTH AMERICA

Argentina
Centro de Estudios Sobre la Libertad, Buenos Aires.

Brazil
Instituto Liberal, Rio de Janeiro.

Guatemala
Universidad Francisco Marroquín, Guatemala City.

Mexico
Centro de Investigaciones Sobre la Libre Empresa, Mexico City.

Peru
Instituto Libertad y Democracia, Lima.

USA

Atlas Economic Research Foundation (USA), Fairfax, Virginia.
Cato Institute, Washington, DC.
Center for Research in Free Enterprise (Texas A&M University), Texas.
Competitive Enterprise Institute, Washington, DC.
Foundation for Research on Economics and the Environment, Dallas, Texas.
The Heritage Foundation, Washington, DC.
The Hoover Institution, Stanford, California.
The Independent Institute, San Francisco, California.
The Institute for Energy Research, Houston, Texas.

The Institute for Humane Studies, Arlington, Virginia.
James Madison Institute, Tallahassee, Florida.
The Manhattan Institute, New York.
National Center for Policy Analysis, Dallas, Texas.
Pacific Research Institute, San Francisco, California.
Political Economy Research Center, Bozeman, Montana.
The Reason Foundation, Santa Monica, California.

APPENDIX

CONTENTS OF THE COLLECTED WORKS OF ARTHUR SELDON

VOLUME 1 **The Virtues of Capitalism**

Corrigible Capitalism, Incorrigible Socialism, 1980
Capitalism, 1990

VOLUME 2 **The State Is Rolling Back**

The State Is Rolling Back, 1994

VOLUME 3 **Everyman's Dictionary of Economics**

Everyman's Dictionary of Economics (with F. G. Pennance), 1965, 1975

VOLUME 4 **Introducing Market Forces into "Public" Services**

Which Way to Welfare? 1966
Taxation and Welfare, 1967
Remove the Financing Flaw in "Public" Services (from *Catch '76*), 1976
Charge, 1977
Micro-economic Controls (from *The Taming of Government*), 1979
The Riddle of the Voucher, 1986

VOLUME 5 **Government Failure and Over-Government**

Change by Degree or by Convulsion (from *The Coming Confrontation*), 1978
Individual Liberty, Public Goods and Representative Democracy (from *Ordo*), 1979
Avoision: The Moral Blurring of a Legal Distinction (from *Tax Avoision*), 1979
The Dilemma of Democracy, 1998
Public Choice in Britain (from *Government: Whose Obedient Servant?*), 2000
On the Liberal Emancipation of Mankind (from *Vordenker einer neuen Wirtschaftspolitik: Festschrift für Christian Watrin*), 2000

VOLUME 6 The Welfare State: Pensions, Health, and Education

The Reluctant Crutch: Replace the Repressive State by the Liberating Market (from *Time and Tide*), 1959

Pensions for Prosperity, 1960

The Future of the Welfare State (from *Encounter*), 1967

After the NHS, 1968

The Great Pensions "Swindle," 1970

Wither the Welfare State, 1981

Pensions without the State and The Verdict of History (from *Re-privatising Welfare: After the Lost Century*), 1996

The Retreat of the State in Social Welfare (from *The Retreat of the State*), 1998

VOLUME 7 The IEA, the LSE, and the Influence of Ideas

The Essence of the IEA (from *The Emerging Consensus*), 1981

New Hope for Economic Policy in a Changing Polity (from *Agenda for Social Democracy*), 1983

Recollections: Before and after *The Road to Serfdom* (from *Hayek's Serfdom Revisited*), 1984

Economic Scholarship and Political Interest (from *Ideas, Interests and Consequences*), 1989

From the LSE to the IEA (from *Economic Affairs*), 1998

The Making of the Institute, 2002

Cumulative Index

INDEX

The text for this book is set in Minion; the display type is Meta Plus Book. Both are relatively new faces, chosen to reflect Seldon's influence on and activity in contemporary social and economic thought. Minion was designed by Robert Slimbach for Adobe in 1990. In spirit and intent it derives from the Garamond tradition. Meta, designed by Erik Spiekermann in 1993, with open spacing for legibility at small sizes, has grown into an extended family and is now widely used.

Printed on paper that is acid-free and meets the requirements of the American National Standard for Permanence of Paper for Printed Library Materials, z39.48-1992. ♾

Book design by Barbara Williams, BW&A Books, Inc., Durham, North Carolina
Typography by Graphic Composition, Inc., Athens, Georgia
Printed and bound by Edwards Brothers, Inc., Ann Arbor, Michigan